WITHDRAWN FROM
TSC LIBRARY

D1564173

Second Edition

COMPARATIVE AND INTERNATIONAL CRIMINAL JUSTICE

Traditional and Nontraditional Systems
of Law and Control

Charles B. Fields
Eastern Kentucky University

Richter H. Moore, Jr.
Late of Appalachian State University

WAVELAND
PRESS, INC.
Long Grove, Illinois

For information about this book, contact:
 Waveland Press, Inc.
 4180 IL Route 83, Suite 101
 Long Grove, IL 60047-9580
 (847) 634-0081
 info@waveland.com
 www.waveland.com

Copyright © 2005 by Waveland Press, Inc.

ISBN 1-57766-350-0

All rights reserved. No part of this book may be reproduced, stored in a retrieval system, or transmitted in any form or by any means without permission in writing from the publisher.

Printed in the United States of America

7 6 5 4 3 2 1

Contents

PART I
Crime and Criminality: An International View

PART II
Policing and Social Control

PART III
Law and Justice: Judicial Systems—Formal and Informal

Part IV
Corrections, Punishment, and Juvenile Justice

Preface

Since the first edition of this text was published in 1996, much has happened. On a global scale, the events of September 11, 2001, and reactions to them have changed our world forever. On a more personal level, Richter Moore, the co-editor of this text and valued member of the academic community of criminal justice and criminological scholars, passed on. As a teacher, scholar, mentor, and friend, he is certainly missed by us all.

When I first began my post–military studies, I transferred to Appalachian State University in the late 1970s and first became a student of Richter Moore. He was then department chair of political science/criminal justice and soon to be president of the Academy of Criminal Justice Sciences. After accompanying him to a few professional meetings and with his guidance, I knew that I wanted to pursue an academic career. I was only one of many who were inspired and influenced by his love of teaching and his strive for excellence.

When we first decided to compile this collection, Richter and I were unsure about what exactly to consider and include. Between us, we have taught several thousand students in various comparative criminology and criminal justice systems, comparative legal systems and related classes, constantly having to scrounge and assemble new and updated materials. Only recently have texts become available which attempt a comprehensive and diverse approach useful to both students and instructors. The collection in this edition seeks to provide the reader with an extensive overview of comparative and international criminal justice complementing, and supplementing, these existing texts; it is not, nor is it intended, to be exhaustive.

As was the case with the first edition of this text, the chapter selection was very subjective. While deciding to retain many of the original chapters with little or no changes, the new offerings reflect a diversity of topics as well as ideology. The majority of chapters were specifically written (or revised) for this reader with very few published elsewhere. Almost two hundred articles, abstracts, conference papers, and ideas were examined, resulting in this final selection.

Geographic diversity and variation was sought as well. As the title indicates, traditional systems of justice are included, as well as some examples of very nonconventional methods of dispute resolution and punishment from around the globe. They range from participant observation in a residential juvenile facility in Japan to an insightful examination of hand amputation for theft in Islam. Many contemporary texts deal with comparative and international criminal justice by focusing mainly on well established institutions in modern Western democracies. While the study of these systems is important and they more easily parallel ours, limiting ourselves to such comparisons does little to increase or enhance our appreciation and understanding of systems that differ greatly from our own.

The twenty-nine chapters of the text are organized into four sections. Part I deals with an overview of crime and criminality from comparative and international perspectives. Policing and social control are covered in Part II. Formal and informal judicial systems comprise Part III, and Part IV includes chapters that deal with corrections and juvenile justice. The appendices contain four recent UN resolutions/treaties on combating international drug trafficking, protection of prisoners, crime prevention, and guidelines on the use of the death penalty.

This book could not have been possible without the patience and cooperation of the many chapter authors. Gayle Zawilla and Neil and Carol Rowe encouraged me throughout the project and helped me through some difficult times along the way. In fact, Gayle should take most of the credit for keeping me motivated and for my finally finishing the text.

Finally, to those who recognized early the necessity for the comparative approach, and to the late Richter Herman Moore, Jr., this book is dedicated. I hope you find it both engaging and worthwhile.

Globalization and Criminal Justice
A Prologue

Foreword to the Second Edition

This book on comparative criminal justice, encompassing traditional and nontraditional systems of law and control, is so comprehensive and thorough as to merit the connotation encyclopedic. All those engaged in the sphere of comparative and international justice will find that access to this work will save them much time and labor. The 29 chapters embody an academic exercise aimed at a comparative study and evaluation of the criminal justice systems of various nations, identifying similarities and dis-similarities in these systems, particularly in their structure and operation.

The collection consists of five parts with contributions from academics and experts in various fields of international law. The main thrust of the work lies in its inherent realization that in the field of crime and criminal-ity and in the dispensation of criminal justice, the world has become increasingly globalized. Values and norms are evolving in a global context, and international institutions are playing a more central and decisive role in upholding them.

However, globalization has its stumbling blocks. Take, for example, the case of the International Criminal Court. The United States, the most powerful nation state in the world at the present time, is one of only seven nations to vote against the Rome Statute of the ICC in 1998. The reason? The United States is apprehensive that the ICC may exercise its jurisdiction to conduct what it refers to as politically motivated investigations and prosecutions of U.S. military, political, and other personnel.

Although the recent U.N. Commission on the Darfur situation in the Sudan did not say that genocide has been committed against the Africans in Darfur, it did come to the conclusion that there was evidence that crimes against humanity have been committed. Where should the culprits be tried? In the ICC or in Arusha? The latter's tribunal is favored by the United States, while the former is not. If, as seems likely, accused persons in the Democratic Republic of the Congo are indicted in the future for Crimes against Humanity perpetrated in that country, should they be tried in the ICC, without the backing of the United States, or in the Special Court for Sierra Leone, which has U.S. support?

This articles in this book draw the reader to the conclusion that international criminal justice and the *jus cogens* in international law must be the anchor in international relations and must be applied, whether or not it restricts or limits the sovereignty of nations. It is indeed clear that crime is no longer a local, provincial or national problem. In the twenty-first century, more than ever before, It is very much an international phenomenon.

Justice George Gelaga King,
United Nations Special Court for Sierra Leone, Appeals Chamber
February 2005

Foreword to the First Edition

Globalization has occurred. Some people are as yet unfamiliar with the term, and some may need elucidation; yet every American needs to be sensitized to an enormous development that is changing our lives in every respect. That development is globalization, or the sudden interdependency of events and of the actions of people and governments around the world.

Consider that as recently as 1950, the United States of America was virtually self-sufficient, with too few imports to speak of, and with a mere $10 billion in exports. By 1992, foreign countries were selling $763 billion worth of their goods in America, and we were exporting $730 billion in goods. Consider also how the world has shrunk in time and distance. Jumbo jets transport traders and tourists, politicians, and students, from one continent to another in a matter of a few hours. Forty million tourists come to our country from abroad annually, and a comparable number of Americans travel abroad.

The worldwide communications network has miraculously expanded. We thought that touch telephones were a great invention, some years back. Today we communicate via satellites, through cellular phones, computer networks, faxes and E-mail. Even the most complex information can be transmitted from home to home, office to office, instantaneously. Television has revolutionized our lives. We can actually see and hear an event as it occurs halfway around the world (or on the moon, for that matter). Information, culture and knowledge have become an instantly exchangeable commodity. Lastly, consider the political globalization that has taken place through establishment of supergoverning bodies (like the United Nations and its organs, the European Community and other regional groupings of countries), fostered by regional (like NAFTA) or worldwide (like GATT) agreements. It involves us in peacekeeping missions in all parts of the world. American judges, together with judges from all over the world, are presiding over cases involving the entire world.

The wonders and benefits of commercial, transportational, communicational, cultural and political globalization also have entailed considerable side effects: in commerce, fraudulent and unfair trade practices—once confined to a town or country—now have worldwide dimensions. Communications systems and networks are being equally exploited by terrorists and drug smugglers, who, moreover, travel on the same jumbo jets that transport tourists. Cultural globalization has led to the import of foreign value systems in many countries around the world—often with destructive consequences.

In the past, the field of criminal justice has been impervious to globalization. Prior to 1991 American textbooks on criminal justice and criminology had virtually no references to events or experiences abroad. Crime seemed to be a local matter, or perhaps a national problem, but not an international one. The literature of our profession was provincial—with a few notable and prophetic exceptions. There was both a fear (because of lack of understanding) of things foreign, and the vestige of the old American (isolationist) credo that we get along best by ourselves.

Recent events make fear and isolationism obsolete. Three events, above all, have dramatically demonstrated that we, too, are affected by foreign events, by ideological exponents and their use of explosives, and by foreign machinations that result in domestic dollars lost:

> On December 21, 1988, PAN AM flight 103 was downed by a terrorist bomb over Lockerby, Scotland, with the loss of 270 lives—mostly Americans on their way home for the holidays. The local constable of Lockerby was hardly capable of handling the investigation. The United States had no jurisdiction—but took the lead in an investigation extending to fifty countries. Indictments have been handed down against two Libyans, but we are not even sure that they are the principal suspects. Nor do we have them in custody.

> On February 26, 1993, an enormous blast rocked New York's World Trade Center. Six lives were lost, over 1,000 were injured, and world trade was dealt a serious blow. The bombing was executed by near-Eastern perpetrators, operating out of Jersey City, New Jersey. Yet this was meant to be only the beginning! Other bombing targets included the United Nations Headquarters, the New York City FBI Headquarters, the Holland and Lincoln Tunnels and the George Washington Bridge. (Twelve defendants are on trial at the time of this writing.)

> There is (or was) a Bank of Credit and Commerce, with sixty-eight locations in sixteen countries, founded in a Gulf sheikdom. The bank, it turned out, was engaged in few, if any, legitimate transactions. It largely existed to finance international criminal activities and to benefit its officers. It is estimated that by the year 2010 this scam will have cost American taxpayers $100 billion, yet few persons have been

indicted in the United States so far. (One was acquitted, one found unfit to stand trial, and one is expected in the United States on an extradition request.)

These events demonstrate that in a globalized world, local police and county prosecutors can no longer protect us from criminals operating worldwide.

International dependency comes even closer to home when we look at our current gang problem. The old-style Mafia organizations of Sicilian origin seem to have lost much of their control, thanks to good law enforcement with an ability to understand and infiltrate such organizations. However, new ethnic groupings have emerged that present new challenges that we are not yet prepared to meet:

- Chinese gangs import more than 100,000 slave labor immigrants annually.
- Russian gangs trade in anything profitable from bootleg gasoline to nuclear material.
- Jamaican gangs ruthlessly engage in the arms and drug trade.
- Albanian gangs excel in burglary.

There are also Japanese, Cambodian, Filipino, Samoan, and other ethnic gangs. American criminal justice is only beginning to search for solutions to problems generated by such groups.

Globalization has hit us hardest in the drug trade. The world is covered with a spider's web of connections, touching every part of the globe: The Golden Triangle and Golden Crescent Networks and the Medellin and Cali cartels (controlling drug production and distribution from the Andean countries of South America) all impact America's and Europe's crime scene. Globalization is about to threaten our very existence through vast ecological criminality which, unless checked, would severely damage the food, water and clean air supply for all of us.

Globalization, in sum, has confronted criminologists and criminal justice specialists with three new tracks in research, policy making, and education—namely, those focusing on (1) the increasing prevalence of international crimes, many of them spawned by reemerging ethnic conflicts; (2) the rapid growth of transnational criminality; and (3) the recognition that much of crime that previously had been regarded as local is the product of globalization.

In response to the new challenges, scholars are increasingly engaged in international-comparative studies. A new subscience, *Comparative Criminology*, has emerged, which is largely composed of the application of the comparative (in legally/culturally diverse settings) method to the science of criminology. Agreement is in the making about how comparative criminologists proceed.

1. They start with an identification of countries/cultures to be studied.
2. They analyze the legal systems represented by those countries/cultures.

3. They study the history, culture, and political and socioeconomic conditions of these countries/cultures.

4. They identify and analyze the crime and criminal justice actualities.

5. They identify and analyze the specific issues to be compared.

6. They select existing or create new data bases.

Only then does the real work of scientific comparison begin. Comparatists have identified at least three principal purposes of comparative criminological studies:

1. The theoretical goal: to test criminological theories or constructs that heretofore had been developed (and tested) on the basis of a single culture (usually American);

2. The utilitarian goal: to learn from each other's experience with a view toward identifying culturally transplantable responses to crime and to criminal justice problems; and

3. The strategic goal: to develop international global strategies for dealing with crime problems effecting all humankind.

As yet, the academic community in criminology and criminal justice is ill prepared to assume responsibilities of such immense dimensions. A beginning was made as early as 1978: Dr. Richter H. Moore, Jr., then president of the Academy of Criminal Justice Sciences, had more than local justice in mind when he invited the chief of the United National Crime Prevention and Criminal Justice Branch to be the keynote speaker at the convention of the Academy of Criminal Justice Sciences in Philadelphia. Dr. Moore was one of the first to recognize the process of globalization of life, of crime and of needed criminal justice responses, and his initiative has borne fruit.

Today he and his collaborator, Dr. Charles B. Fields of California State University–San Bernardino, are presenting this globe-spanning volume to the students and researchers of criminal justice in America. It is a far-reaching and vitally necessary introduction for American students of criminal justice into the complexities of crime and justice far afield—yet so near, because we have become globalized. Comparative and international criminal justice, once regarded as an esoteric subject, now is central to American criminal justice because we are part of the world—maybe the center of the world—as receivers of and contributors to crime and justice worldwide. This volume eminently proves our point.

G. O. W. Mueller, J.D., LL.M., Dr.Jur. (h.c.)
Distinguished Professor of Criminal Justice, Rutgers University
Chief (Ret.), United Nations Crime Prevention and
Criminal Justice Branch

Freda Adler, Ph.D.
Distinguished Professor of Criminal Justice, Rutgers University
President, American Society of Criminology

Introduction

Comparative Criminal Justice
Why Study?

Richter H. Moore, Jr. & Charles B. Fields

Today there is a greater complexity and interdependence in the world than ever before. No longer can we solve international problems on our own, nor can we declare ourselves immune to them. Consequently, the United States must have a higher level of international expertise than at any time in its history.

The rapidity of societal, political, and technological changes of the world in which we live is almost beyond comprehension. These changes and advances have created growing demands for goods and services, some of which are supplied only by a criminal economy. A new mobility has increased trade and tourism. Scientific and cultural cooperation are expanding at an undreamed-of rate. At the same time these changes have brought war, peace, and crime of unprecedented proportion.

The end of the twentieth century, as that of the nineteenth, saw a world dramatically changing; the parallel is startling. Old boundaries and political systems are crumbling. Nationalism and provincialism are running rampant. Nation states are disintegrating, leaving old hatreds long suppressed by their governments to resurface. At the same time political and social tribalism are reemerging, the world's economy is globalizing.

For some, this global reorganization has been termed the "new world order." However, as one writer says, it has "given rise to a volatile dangerous, often ugly and traumatic new world in which regimes, boundaries, identities, and resources will be intensely and violently contested" (Galley, 1994). This global reorganization touches every part of the world and every society. Its ramifications are so widespread that it might more accurately be called the "new world disorder." It is a disorder marked by changes in actual circumstances which involve the transformation or disintegration of communities and system of categorization. This is a disorder marked by upheavals in thinking about identity. Numerous underlying beliefs and standards that have long regulated individuals and groups and have quite directly determined identity designations are being uprooted, if not abandoned. In part this disorder is due to the globalization of information. The universalization of information often has led to the globalization of incorrect perceptions, unreachable expectations, and a worship of technology. Information and technology penetrate all facets of human life. Satellites, video, microprocessors, and computers open the world of information to all. A global network that will allow instant communications among virtually all people on this planet will be with us before the end of this decade. Information through interactive television and computer services will be available in the remotest parts of the world. This global internet will link businesses, governments, researchers, academics, and individuals (Manney, 1994).

Information and technology have created a world in which the bases of power are shifting. New power centers are being created. The world has moved into a new society, the information society, in which the ability to use information and turn it into knowledge is the source of power. Alvin Toffler, in *Powershift*, makes the following assumptions about power:

> Violence, which is chiefly used to punish, is the least versatile source of power. Wealth which can be used both to reward and punish, and which can be converted into many other resources, is a far more flexible tool of power. Knowledge, however, is the most versatile and basic, since it can help one avert challenges that might require the use of violence or wealth, and often be used to persuade others to perform in desired ways out of perceived self-interest. Knowledge yields the highest quality power. (1990:474)

This assumption of Toffler, along with the globalization of the economy and the universalization of information, requires that we look at crime, criminal activities, criminal organizations, and criminal justice systems from a global perspective—not a parochial, self-centered, myopic one.

Communications and information technology not only are forces for progress but also open new frontiers of criminal activity. Just as the telegraph at the beginning of the twentieth century opened the realm of off-track betting and led to the creation of criminal organizations based on gambling, and as the automobile and the machine gun in the 1920s created a whole new world of crime and criminal businesses, so too today's technology is leading to innovative, global criminals and criminal enterprises. Communications technology is forging closer ties between criminals and their organizations worldwide.

Society in today's world is dramatically changing. Technology is accelerating these changes. New ways to provide for the security of persons and property must be planned for and developed, not just in one country but worldwide. Consequently, we must be aware of the changes in the patterns of crime, the types of criminals, and the changing makeup and power of criminal organizations. Those meeting the challenge of crime today must of necessity be educated, sophisticated individuals who not only must be thoroughly familiar with the latest technology—be it computers, robotics, cybermotion, bionics, biogenetics, electronics, or communications—but also must be aware that crime is now international as well as local in many of its aspects.

Criminals and criminal organizations, like their counterparts in business, are globalized (Drozdiak, 1992; Martens, 1991). They have taken advantage of the information and technological revolution to as great or a greater degree than has government and business, and to a far greater degree than has the criminal justice community. The information and intelligence networks of some crime groups are superior to those of law enforcement agencies (Molloy, 1990). Criminal confederations are operating intelligence systems, developing technology, and honing criminal techniques on an international scale. This does not bode well for the criminal justice organizations of the nations of the world.

Leaders of worldwide criminal communities are well aware of what is happening in the world around them. They have taken advantage of the universalization of information, the globalization of technology, and the "new world disorder" to move to new frontiers of criminal activity.

The fragmentation of old colonial empires and the breakup of mid-twentieth-century nation states have created new states that are frequently unstable, economically insecure and governed by inept, corrupt officials. Often these officials are members of or are tied to criminal groups within their country. The criminal justice officials of such countries cannot be expected to enforce criminal laws against criminal enterprises that operate not only within their boundaries, but with the permission or at least acquiescence of the government.

In today's society it is essential that criminal justice students be aware of the existence of crime and corruption in criminal justice systems, for they may be called upon to operate in such an environment. In recent years, American military personnel have been called upon to go into such environments for policy or humanitarian purposes. They must be made fully aware of not only the military dangers but also the criminal temptations. The study of comparative criminal justice can aid in understanding the problems faced in other countries, whether one goes there as a military member, a business person, or a tourist. Businesses operating in a corrupt environment cannot expect the local law enforcement authorities to protect their interests. Consequently, a company may need a private security force capable of protecting its property and personnel, staffed with individuals who possess an understanding of the criminal justice system with which they are dealing. The study of comparative criminal justice can help develop the expertise to deal with corrupt law enforcement and government officials.

The new world disorder often does not follow or meet the traditional standards of value, civility, right and wrong, and law and order. This applies whether in a foreign country, a riot-torn American city, or a crime-ravaged neighborhood. A look at what others are doing in similar situations may assist in understanding why particular criminal actions take place and in suggesting some responses to them.

Criminal enterprises have developed as a major international financial force. Organized crime leaders appear in the *Forbes* and *Fortune* list of the world's wealthiest individuals (Gladstone, 1992). Each year new individuals from the world's criminal organizations are added to the list. Profits, particularly from drug trafficking, have led to the establishment of major crime cartels and international conglomerates that financially rival many of the world's major corporations. Their enormous illegal profits have allowed criminal syndicates to establish giant worldwide financial empires with major investments in legitimate businesses.

The leaders of major transnational criminal enterprises are aware of the weaknesses and strengths of criminal justice systems around the world and use this knowledge to their advantage and profit. For example, the Colombian drug cartels are known to have major portfolios which include substantial holdings of stock in many of the Fortune 500 companies. The Yakuza is known to have major stock and real-estate holdings around the world, including substantial investments in the United States (*Organized Crime Digest*, 1990:1; 1994). The Mafia had long invested in legitimate business enterprises (Kwitny, 1979).

International groups are not only involved in owning shares of multinational corporations but are becoming involved in their management. Already drug cartel leaders are sending some of their offspring to major universities in the United States, including Harvard Business School (Farah, 1993:A16). Members of emerging Russian organized crime groups are already well educated; some hold doctorates in mathematics, economics, electrical engineering, and other specialties (Friedman, 1993). Members of Chinese, Japanese, Nigerian, and other criminal organizations are equally preparing themselves. Comparable background and training for criminal justice personnel is an absolute necessity.

Crime groups or criminal organizations control the governments of some countries either directly or indirectly (*Organized Crime Digest*, 1989:2A). In most of the new states evolving from the former Soviet Union, organized crime groups are tied closely to the government and essentially control the country's economic system (Dobbs, 1992; Solomon, 1993:39). In countries such as Nigeria and Colombia, criminal organizations have virtually paralyzed government. If organized crime members are arrested and tried, they receive special treatment. In Japan, the Yakuza has been tied very closely to major government figures and has had a considerable role in some aspects of government policy. The Mafia has long influenced government policy in Italy and been tied closely to politicians in the United States. As members of criminal organizations become more educated, they will become more attuned to the ways of politics. They will become more actively involved to assure that their interests are protected.

They will use the politicians and the politicians will use them to a far greater degree than in the past, for their stakes are globalized.

Alvin Toffler, in *Powershift*, declares:

> Because people have needs and desires, those who can fulfill them hold potential power. Social power is exercised by supplying or withholding the desired or needed items and experiences. Because needs and desires are highly varied, the ways of meeting or denying them are also extremely varied. There are, therefore, many different "tools" or "levers" of power. Among them however violence, wealth, and knowledge are primary. Most other power sources derive from them. (1990:473–74)

Criminal organizations worldwide are meeting the needs and desires of the people that are not easily met legitimately, thereby acquiring great power and becoming a force in world society that must be recognized and dealt with if law and justice are to continue to be a viable part of life. Therefore, it becomes imperative for students of criminal justice to be aware of criminal justice systems other than their own in order to be able to meet the challenges of crime in the contemporary world.

Comparisons of governments and legal systems have been made for almost as long as governments and law have existed. The Old Testament contains not only an exposition of Jewish law and punishments but discussions of other governments, their laws, and punishments. Aristotle, for his *Politics*, sought to discover which political system would be the best and studied the constitutions of 153 city states and nations from the known world of his day. Solon, in drafting the laws of Athens, followed Aristotle's lead. The Romans, in developing their law, borrowed from throughout their empire.

The utility of comparative study has long been recognized but becomes more and more important as the world grows smaller. Comparativists generally agree there are several basic reasons to use the comparative approach, whether studying governments, legal systems, or criminal justice systems. While approaches to comparative study may have changed, Hicks (1983) notes:

> The focus in comparative law has changed from a narrow technical emphasis with general classifications of families or styles of law into a more unified historical, cultural, and practical perspective. A study of comparative law has evolved into a study of legal systems. . . .
>
> The change in focus of comparative law is part of a reorientation of legal theory from the study of rules and concepts of law to the study of the experiences of legal systems as social orders. History, anthropology, and philosophy contribute to this reorientation. Hence, the goal of comparative law as a universal system of law and order has been and hopefully, always will be a source of inspiration to all concerned. . . .
>
> The idea of systems of law involves more than the substance and procedure of law, its rules, techniques, and styles; it involves the relationship of the whole to itself, as an internally consistent form of ratio-

nal expression of ideals of order or justice, and also an external perspective of how the whole of law, as defined internally, relates to the whole of society. . . .

A complete study of comparative law, therefore, would include a consideration of the interplay between law, society, and politics, with some overview of the theories and possibilities of social change and evolution. (pp. 83–34, 92–93)

The reasons for comparative study have become even more important. The comparative method studies the similarities and differences not only in institutions but in the societies and cultures in which these institutions exist. In studying comparative criminal justice, the student must have some awareness of the society and the culture in which an institution exists. This leads us to the reasons for using the comparative method to study criminal justice.

First, comparative study leads to greater international understanding. The more one knows about another people, society, or culture, the greater the potential for understanding their actions and their responses to problems and situations. As noted earlier, crime has become a matter of international concern. Crime is carried out today on a transnational basis, and to meet it international understanding and cooperation are required.

Cooperation requires knowledge. There must be some basic knowledge of whether the requested help can be or will be provided. Do the laws preclude the extradition of citizens? Is the act for which an individual is sought a crime in the country where he or she has found sanctuary? Comparative study can help to answer these types of questions. Knowledge of another system may prevent making embarrassing requests and there by promote better understanding.

Knowledge of other systems may also lead to cooperation and understanding in the adoption of uniform laws through treaties in subjects such as human exploitation, aircraft hijacking and terrorism. Joint efforts such as multinational police investigations and task forces to stop such activities as drug and nuclear smuggling have become a reality in recent years. Regional unification of laws in some areas of criminal justice have come about in organizations like the European Union.

Second, comparative study helps to understand one's own system and improve it. We cannot examine or study another political, economic, legal or criminal justice system without at the same time, at least in our mind, making comparisons with our own. As we view a foreign government and compare its parliamentary government with our presidential one, we look at the weaknesses and strengths of our system. Viewing the legal system of another country, especially one like England from whence ours came, we can see changes they have made that we have not—changes which in today's world may well speed up the judicial process and eliminate antiquated institutions which are not now needed.

Our examination of another system can lead to improvements or reenforce our determination to maintain unchanged aspects of our system. As we view the inquisitorial system of France or Germany, we may look more closely at our use of the jury in our adversarial system and raise questions as to whether in today's world it is the best way of arriving at the truth and doing justice in a criminal trial while at the same time protecting society, considering the victim and guarding the rights of the accused.

Only the most gullible would attempt to insinuate a foreign institution into a criminal justice system of different social mores, cultural values and political customs without modification of the idea underlying the institution to be transplanted. Ideas for the police system in the cities of the United States in the nineteenth century were borrowed from England. A number of ideas concerning community policing in today's United States have come from an examination of policing in Japan. France, in its prison reform movement in the nineteenth century, borrowed from the United States, using the Pennsylvania and Auburn systems as examples.

Comparative study of criminal justice enables-even requires-us to know, recognize, distinguish, define and explain the differences and similarities between our system and that of others. Hamson and Pucket (1955), in discussing comparative law, put it thus:

> It is a good deal easier to have a dispassionate and clear view of our own system of law, of its advantages as much as of its disadvantages, if we begin to see it in the contrasts which it presents to another system; if we look at it in the tell-tale mirror of that other system which may reject as strange or even barbarous our most established and unquestioned principles. (p. 6)

Third, comparative study contributes to the development of criminal justice theory and can lead to legal reform. Observations in one society of a particular criminal phenomenon can be observed in other countries to determine if this is a universal phenomenon or one limited to a single society. David and Brierley (1981) noted how legal theory can benefit from comparative study:

> Jurisprudence or general legal theory can also benefit from comparative studies. The historical origins of the classifications known to any system, the relative character of its concepts, the political and social conditioning of its institutions, all these are really understood only when the observer places himself outside his own legal system, that is to say when he adopts the perspective of comparative law. (p. 5)

Hans Jescheck (1981) recognizes that criminal law affords only one possible method of social control. Comparative law has led to internationally recognized principles of criminal law reform:

> Comparative criminal law is a branch of criminal law science and is thus a normative science. It can present a picture of foreign legislation and judicial practice for the purpose of criminal law reform . . . a comprehensive grasp of the full significance of foreign criminal law requires constant co-operation between comparative criminal law and

comparative criminology. Comparative criminal law has already been
in existence a long time, whereas comparative criminology is still a
young, although fully developing, science. Their integration lies in the
future. (pp. 24–25)

Hicks, in his essay "The Jurisprudence of Comparative Legal Systems"
(1983), says of comparative law:

> Comparative law must open up the possibility of a discourse concern-
> ing law and society that overcomes the alienating effects of thinking in
> terms of norms, rules, or rights. . . . The conceptual framework of law
> for the study of comparative legal systems must include the aspects of
> law's appearance in social order in relation to religion, politics, and
> ethics; the qualities of law's maintenance, whether original, reflective,
> or actual; and the realities of law's processes, substance, and ideals.
> (pp. 97–98)

Comparative law provides many aids as we move toward developing theories and reforms for criminal justice through its comparative study. Comparative study becomes more and more imperative. Increasingly, educators
must be concerned with education for the global age. We are obliged to
recognize we are participants in an ever-shrinking world and have responsibilities, influence, rights and privileges as participants in the global system. Our growing interdependence on the rest of the world and the ever-
increasing impact of transnational interactions on human affairs demand
our attention. As interdependence grows, the need for substantial knowledge about global processes and issues; the unity and diversity of cultures,
nations and people; and the threats to human survival become more acute.
In the midst of the cold war, Shirley Hufstedler, then Secretary of Education under President Carter, put it thus:

> The world has changed profoundly since 1945. Today the effects of the
> events on one side of the world are likely to ripple all the way around
> the globe. Calculations of national sovereignty are routinely affected
> by the interest and needs of over 160 other nations. There is no longer
> a country on the face of this shrunken planet that can go it alone. Ken-
> neth Boulding said it well when he conjectured that "if the human race
> is to survive, it will have to change its way of thinking more in the next
> 25 years than it has in the last 25,000."
>
> In an age of . . . massive population movements, and fluctuating
> currencies, it is increasingly difficult to separate domestic from global
> issues. Our civic concerns can now be rarely seen in purely local or
> national terms, and few non-American events are any longer in fact,
> extraneous to our lives. Our mass media reflect these new complexities
> fairly well; but the interrelatedness of global and national events is
> still only marginally reflected in what young Americans are learning in
> their schools and colleges. (1980:8)

What Secretary Hufstedler said a decade and a half ago is just as applicable today. Not only is there an interdependence in terms of goods and

services, but there is an interdependence in terms of discovery and knowledge. Intellectual and scientific interests are not confined to a single state but are international in nature (Groennings, 1980). Mobility of people seems to have been an inherent and persistent human trait since the dawn of history, searching, seeking new discoveries and new knowledge. Alexander the Great took scholars with him on his conquest who collected materials and knowledge to send back to Greece, and especially to his professor, Plato. Marco Polo was not only interested in a trade route to China but in gathering knowledge that could be used in Europe, and much of what he brought back was such knowledge rather than trade.

From the nomad to the soldier/adventurer, to the immigrant, to the trader entrepreneur, to the rover, to the tourist, to the student, the desire to wander has been a consistent one. Throughout the ages and with a multitude of motivations, people have been seeking new lands, new opportunities and new knowledge. Seeking knowledge of other criminal justice systems in the interdependent world of today is no different.

We in the United States have had an unfortunate tendency to be very provincial, to think we have all the knowledge and do not need to go beyond our borders to learn. Regrettably, our communications have been mainly one way—outward. We do not hear the rest of the world very much—until very recently, not even our closest neighbors, Canada and Mexico-primarily because we do not listen. In part, this has been a result of our looking inward and ignoring the problems of the rest of the world until they come upon us, and our national ego would not let us accept answers to problems we did not solve. No longer can we ignore the problems of the rest of the world, nor the workable solutions they have found to problems we have: "The artificial isolation and intellectual compartmentalization hardly fits today's world, we must somehow try to equip our students with sufficient empathy to understand and deal realistically with other cultures" (Hufstedler, 1980).

If we do not, as Clark Kerr pointed out:

> We will never overcome the typically American feeling that if we can only make clear where we sit, all reasonable people everywhere will agree with the correctness of our policy stands instead of "stubbornly" holding to their own. Only by sitting in another's place can we learn that there are real and legitimate conflicts of values and interests among the peoples of the world, as well as a common core of humanity and concern about our mutual planetary home. (quoted in Hufstedler, 1980:8)

Exchange of knowledge is by no means a one-way street. A decade and a half ago Ezra Vogel, in his book *Japan As Number One* (1979), set forth a series of lessons that the United States could learn from Japan in dealing with everything from management to crime control.

The criminal justice community around the world faces unstructured violence, a fact of international life. Riots as a result of joblessness, racism, ethnic hatreds, and starvation; religious violence in places like Northern Ireland, Israel, Palestine, Egypt, and Algeria; and violence in sports and entertainment events in Europe, Latin America and the United States require some comprehension as to why the problems exist and how others meet them. Shared results provide an understanding of those things in a foreign society which have triggered violence and may well provide an understanding of what may trigger it in the United States.

There is a growing interdependence in crime control. Without the help of other states, havens for international criminals can and will be established. International criminal conspiracies have become the chief source of supply of illegal goods not only in the United States, but in countries around the world. Terrorism is not confined to the borders of a single country. To attempt its control, whether for isolated or indiscriminate bombings, airplane or ship hijackings, kidnappings, or murder, the concerted moves by the criminal justice agencies of many nations are called for more and more frequently. Interdependence in law enforcement is essential today, yet we know almost nothing about the policing in countries other than our own.

Criminologists and criminal justice educators have been extremely slow in providing an international dimension to the study of criminal justice and adding an international perspective to criminal justice and criminology programs. We remain extremely parochial in our views, apparently believing we have all of the answers, and are unwilling to examine foreign views in order to learn from others.

We consider it important that we are privileged to exist and operate as a democracy. For us the view of the citizen counts, but the basis of an advanced democratic society is an informed, enlightened and rational citizenry. From a perspective of national interest we have a responsibility as criminal justice educators in a democratic system to provide a broader awareness of problems and potential solutions to our students than that of parochial, "cowboy" justice. We must expose them to the problems and solutions from an international perspective, especially when viewed from America's changing place in the world today.

Change affects us all, and as a consequence we need an awareness of other people's attitudes as well as some understanding of what the impact of our attitudes and actions, whether in the field of politics, economics or criminal justice, has on the rest of the world. Over two decades ago Professor Edwin Reischauer, a former ambassador to Japan, set forth the long range view of our educational needs:

> We need a profound reshaping of education if mankind is to survive in the sort of world that is fast evolving. . . . Before long humanity will face grave difficulties that can only be solved on a global scale. Education . . . is not moving rapidly enough to provide knowledge about the outside world and the attitudes toward other people that may be essential for human survival within a generation or two. (Reischauer, 1973:4)

In 1979, the President's Commission on Foreign Language and International Studies declared that we need a capability in specialized knowledge of foreign societies; foreign cultures; and the major issues in international relations, political, economic, military, social, and demographic factors. Not only must this capability exist in the federal government, especially in the agencies dealing in foreign affairs, but it is required outside government-especially in the universities, so they can train new specialists, maintain and extend our international expertise through research, and serve as a reservoir of knowledge accessible to government, business and labor, the media, and other users (President's Commission, 1979).

The Commission found that our nation's international expertise was then inadequate. Certainly we in criminal justice would have to agree that our expertise in other criminal justice systems is inadequate. Criminal justice educators must expand their commitment to international and comparative education. The 1979 President's Commission on Foreign Language and International studies made this clear when it warned:

> On a planet shrunken by the technology of instant communications, there is little safety behind a Maginot line of scientific and scholarly isolationism. In our schools and colleges as well as in our public media of communications, and in the everyday dialogue within our communities, the situation cries out for a better comprehension of our place and our potential in a world that, though it still expects much from America, no longer takes American supremacy for granted. (1979:2)

Bibliography

Bonham, G. W. (1980). "Education and the World View." *Change* (May/June): 2–7.

David, Rene, and John E. C. Brierley (1981). "The Significance of Comparative Law for Criminal Law Reform." *Hastings International and Comparative Law Review* (Fall): 1–25.

Dobbs, Michael (1992). "In Caucasus, a Caldron of Strife." *Washington Post* (October 25): A1.

Drozdiak, William (1992). "World Crime Groups Expand Cooperation, Spheres of Influence." *Washington Post* (October 5): A12.

Farah, Douglas (1993). "Colombian Drug Flows Unabated." *Washington Post* (March 9): A14.

Friedman, Robert L. (1993). "Brighton Beach Goodfellas." *Vanity Fair* (January): 27–41.

Galley, Phillip (1994). "Time Bombs." *Winston-Salem Journal* (March 30): 11.

Gladstone, Rick (1992). "Latin America Growing Rich in Billionaires." *Johnson City Press* (July 7): 12.

Groennings, S. (1980). "Why Global Perspectives?" *National Association of Secondary School Principals Bulletin* (November): 35–42.

Hamson, Charles J., and Theodore Pucket (1955). *The English Trial and Comparative Law.* Cambridge: W. Heffer.

Hicks, Stephen C. (1983). "The Jurisprudence of Comparative Legal Systems." *Loyola of Los Angeles International and Comparative Law Journal* 16 (1): 83–102.

Hufstedler, Shirley M. (1980). "World In Transition." *Change* (May/June): 8–9.

"Japanese Mobsters Invest Heavily in Textile Firm" (1990). *Organized Crime Digest* (December 26): 3-4.

Jescheck, Hans-Heinrich (1981). "The Significance of Comparative Law for Criminal Law Reform." *Hastings International and Comparative Law Review* (Fall): 1–25.

Kamba, W. J. (1974). "Comparative Law: A Theoretical Framework." *International and Comparative Law Quarterly* (July): 485–519.

Kwitny, Jonathan (1979). *Vicious Circles: The Mafia in the Market Place.* New York: W. W. Norton & Company.

"Mafia Owns Southern Italy" (1989). *Organized Crime Digest* (September 27): 6.

Manney, Kevin, and Paul Wiseman (1994). "New Venture Seeks to Cover Earth." *USA Today* (March 22): Al.

Martens, Frederick T. (1991). "Transnational Enterprise Crime and The Elimination of Frontiers." *International Journal of Comparative and Applied Criminal Justice* (Spring): 99–107.

Molloy, Maureen (1990). "Security Lagging Behind Technology, Report Finds." *Network World* (December 10): 23, 25.

President's Commission on Foreign Language and International Studies, Report to the President (1979). *Strength Through Wisdom, A Critique of U.S. Capability.* Washington, DC: U.S. Government Printing Office.

Reischauer, Edwin (1973). *Toward the 21st Century: Education for a Changing World.* New York: Knopf.

Solomon, Andres (1993). "Young Russia's Defiant Decadence." *New York Times Magazine* (July 18).

Toffler, Alvin (1990). *Powershift.* New York: Bantam Books.

Vogel, E. F. (1979). *Japan As Number One.* Cambridge: Harvard University Press.

"Yakuza: Quietly Investing in the U.S." (1994). *Organized Crime Digest* (February 9): 102.

PART I

Crime and Criminality
An International View

1

Measuring Cross-National Crime and Criminality
Methodological Considerations and Concerns

Charles B. Fields, Jeffrey E. Arrigo, & Kelly R. Webb

> If we limit ourselves to one national unit of one contemporary (usually Western) society, we cannot possibly hope to catch many really fundamental differences among human types and social institutions.
>
> —C. Wright Mills, *The Sociological Imagination* (1959)
> (quoted in Newman, 1980:11)

The study of crime and criminality, in the comparative sense, represents considerable challenges to those who teach and research in the area, for several reasons. First, the scope of international problems is exceedingly more vast than the varied national or local problems we have traditionally addressed in criminology and criminal justice. Additionally, these problems tend to be highly complex (at least in relation to those with whom we are used to dealing). Second, while these social problems are escalating at a rapid pace (e.g., Eastern Europe, the former Yugoslav Republic), as is the necessity to find immediate viable solutions, we are not often oriented to quick and concerted efforts. This is perhaps due to many factors inherent in contemporary American society, our academic preparation, the emphasis on theoretical rather than applied research, and so forth. A third and related complicating factor is that our typical parochial approach to the study of social problems, especially crime and criminal behavior, is largely inadequate for the study of "world order" problems. One thing we have (or should have) learned is that criminality and criminal justice systems cannot be studied apart from the other "systems" (cultural, political, economic, etc.), nor can they be examined using our typical *reductionist* approaches.

Prepared especially for *Comparative and International Criminal Justice, 2/E.*

In 1980, at the annual meeting of the Academy of Criminal Justice Sciences, the late Leonard Hippchen of Virginia Commonwealth University led a discussion and presentation entitled "Problems in World Criminology/Criminal Justice" (1980). He suggested six areas of research, policy development, and education in "world criminology" that he felt must be explored in order for the successful development and use of new approaches and methodologies. The first and most important was his call for more studies of international crime trends, the improvement of record-keeping methods, and the production of valid crime statistics.

This article addresses cross-national crime and criminality, focusing on the few systematic efforts at collection of reliable and credible crime statistics and the various potential methodological problems encountered when using these datasets.

International Crime Statistics: Sources and Availability

According to available statistics, crime rates have increased dramatically since the 1960s in almost every developed nation, Japan being the exception (van Dijk and Mayhew, 1992). While crime is perhaps the one problem that affects all nations, it is only during the last few years that there have been any systematic efforts to collect and analyze crime cross-nationally, ostensibly for comparative purposes. In fact, there has been some reluctance to proceed in this area. Some feel, for example, that: ". . . the technical and theoretical problems of international cross-cultural comparisons are, at present, so large and the utility of any results which might be obtained in such doubt that priority should not be given to studies of this kind" (Report, 1966:26). Wikstrom (1991) sees cross-national studies of crime and criminality traditionally focusing on three main purposes: (1) identifying common and unique features of crime and its correlates, (2) evaluating existing theories or generating theory to account for commonalities and unique aspects of crime (see, e.g., Bennett, 1980), and (3) providing perspective on our own criminality (p. 73).

Over the past few years, there have been several attempts to gather reliable measures of cross-national crime and criminality, focusing on one or more of Wikstrom's purposes. While each of the following data collections has its own particular set of strengths and weaknesses, one must exercise caution when utilizing their results.

United Nations World Crime Surveys[1]

It has long been recognized by the United Nations (as early as 1950) that a "world crime" database was needed if member states were ever to cope with increasing crime and criminality. The UN also realized the problems inherent in such an endeavor. Early documents indicate the willingness of the organization to "prepare a standard classification of offenses and the collection of and publication of criminal statistics . . . a manual or handbook which would suggest minimum standards for the collection, analysis and presentation of criminal statistics" (quoted in Vetere and Newman, 1977:253).

As new categories of crime (e.g., computer related, environmental) appeared and traditional methods of confronting crime were unsuccessful, the UN decided to initiate a crime data-collection effort among the member states. From 1972 through 1977, several resolutions were introduced in the General Assembly requesting member states to provide information on crime prevention and control in their respective countries. At the Sixth (Caracas, 1980) and Seventh (Milan, 1983) United Nations Congresses on the Prevention of Crime and the Treatment of Offenders, widespread support for regular crime surveys and recommendations concerning how best to collect and analyze the information provided the impetus for the continuation of the World Crime Surveys.

The first survey collected data on a small number of offenses and on the criminal justice process for the years 1970–1975. Sixty-four countries responded, but 14 provided no statistical information. The second survey collected information on a wide range of offenses, offenders, and criminal justice process data for the years 1975–1980. Seventy-eight countries responded to the second survey.

There are several factors that make comparisons of the two surveys difficult. For example, 25% of those responding to the first survey did not respond to the second, and 30% responding to the second did not respond to the first. Furthermore, many questions that were asked on the second survey were not included on the first; the questionnaires used were very different. While the first survey was only 17 pages in length, the second contained 161 pages.

In 1990 and 1991, the World Crime Survey Validation Project, conducted by the School of Criminal Justice at the University at Albany (NY) for the Bureau of Justice Statistics, attempted to reconcile the differences between the first two surveys. Results from an additional validation survey (covering the same time period) and yearbooks, annual reports, statistical abstracts, and other publications from member states were examined to supplement information contained in the surveys. A third-world crime survey covering the period 1980–1985/6 was conducted. Results from this survey were presented to the Ninth United Nations Congress on the Prevention of Crime and the Treatment of Offenders in Tunis.

The Fourth United Nations Survey on Crime Trends and Operations of Criminal Justice Systems covered the period 1986–1990. The results were compiled and reported at the United Nations Congress in Cairo, April/May, 1995, and were published in late 1996 or early 1997. The fifth survey covered the time period 1990–1994; the sixth survey covered the time period 1995–1997; and the seventh survey covered the time period 1998–2000. Of the 203 countries that were furnished questionnaires, 82 of them responded.

The eighth survey covered the time period 2001–2002 and was sent to 191 different countries in August of 2003. Raw data is available for all the surveys with the exception of the eighth survey.

Comparative Crime Data File (CCDF)

In 1972, Dane Archer and Rosemary Gartner began assembling a massive cross-national file of longitudinal offense data.[2] Covering the years 1900–1972, the project took more than five years to complete and eventually expanded to include 110 nations and 44 urban areas.[3] Data were collected from three primary sources: First, information was requested from various national and metropolitan government sources. Initially, these sources were obtained from correspondence with consulates and embassies maintained in the United States requesting referrals to specific agencies or authorities in their home countries. Although all three methods generated data for the CCDF, this was the most productive (and most interesting) method. Second, annual statistical reports and other official documents of those countries that publish (or published) annual crime data were collected. Hundreds of national statistical annuals were examined that yielded little that the authors were able to use, primarily because many nations surprisingly do not provide crime information in their statistical publications. Since the vast majority of the reports were written in the nation's primary language (providing data with much explanation), there was also the problem of interpretation and classification of some specific crimes. Third, records kept by various national or international agencies were examined; this was the least satisfactory method. Crime records from the International Criminal Police Organization (INTERPOL) were assembled but provided little useable information. The major problem was that INTERPOL only began assembling and publishing crime data in 1953 and then only for 40 nations (with no separate data for cities) (Archer and Gartner, 1984:18–19).

While the authors attempted to get additional information from various United Nations sources, they were ultimately unsuccessful. The United Nations did not, at the time the CCDF was compiled, furnish much longitudinal data on crime; what was available was limited and quite dated. For example, an index of the number of offenses known to police was reported in the late 1940s, but only for a small number of member nations. Intermittently from 1946 through 1956, juvenile court conviction information was included in various publications (Archer and Gartner, 1984:20–21). There also seemed to be a reluctance on the part of the many individuals contacted not only to provide the information requested but even to admit the data existed.

INTERPOL

The International Criminal Police Commission (ICPC) was established, after much difficulty, in 1923 in Vienna. Renamed the International Criminal Police Organization (INTERPOL) in 1955, the organization's headquarters moved to France and has since become one of the more respected international agencies devoted to law enforcement and crime data gathering. Since the early 1950s, INTERPOL has collected annual crime and criminal justice statistics in several countries and publishes *International Crime Statistics* on a regular basis (Reichel, 1994).

Statistics are gathered on number and types of crime, offenders, and cases cleared (solved) for each member nation. Murder, sex offenses, fraud, larceny, counterfeiting, and drug offenses are among the crimes included, and the reporting policy is as follows:

1. Because of the variations in definitions of crimes in different countries, the forms only refer to several wide categories which are more or less universally recognized as indictable offenses in ordinary law.

2. The definitions of these categories are very wide in order to allow the use of national crime statistics without too many modifications.

3. Each State is allowed a certain amount of latitude in the interpretation of these definitions, and the nature of crime is determined according to the legislation of each State.

4. The forms are intended to show the trends in crime rather than its actual extent (INTERPOL, 1953/54 and 1981; Vetere and Newman, 1977:255).

Bennett (1990) discusses three potential problems and concerns with using the INTERPOL data. First, data may contain "systematic bias due to the reporting countries' failure to employ consistent operational definitions of crime and offender types" (p. 2). Second, there may also be bias related to national reporting practices, ranging from apparent political manipulation of the data to differences in collection methods. Third, concerns that differential operations of national justice systems make arrest statistics potentially problematic as well (p. 4). These and other methodological concerns are addressed in subsequent sections of this article.

World Health Organization (WHO)

The World Health Organization collects and annually distributes detailed statistical information providing an overview of national and global trends regarding health and mortality. Homicide is the only offense detailed by WHO, but their data are mentioned in this discussion because they are compiled based on death certificates issued by medical examiners (Huang, 1993) and not just on police reports. Several researchers (e.g., Vigderhous, 1978) have found WHO homicide data to be highly reliable across nations.

Crime in Western Societies, 1945–1974 (GURRS)

This data collection includes summary information on crime in sixteen Western societies (plus Israel and Japan) from 1945 to 1974. Both offenses known to police and convictions were included; the primary focus was to gather data "from both ends of the justice 'funnel'" (Gurr, 1977:43). In addition, demographic statistics (including national population and population age 15–24) were compiled for use in constructing certain indicators. The data collected by Gurr were obtained from several official publications of each country, including general and specialized yearbooks.

The eighteen "economically developed" nations were grouped into five categories: (1) English-speaking, (2) Scandinavian, (3) Germanic groups, (4) residual category (other European, included France, Ireland, Italy, and the Netherlands), and (5) Israel and Japan, included because their cultures differed dramatically from the others'. The only "developed" nations not included in the survey were Iceland, Belgium, and Greece; the data related to crime for these countries appeared to be too inconsistent or sparse to be useful (p. 43).

Indicators and composite measures of crime[4] were constructed, and it should be noted that the author did not attempt to compare countries relative to which had the greatest levels of crime. Furthermore, Gurr's purpose was to document crime trends, not to explain them. He argued:

> . . . that the idiosyncratic features of each country's legal, police, and crime reporting systems tend to remain the same over time. When significant legal or reporting changes *are* introduced, they usually are easy to detect and take into account—as we have done when adjusting for artifactual changes . . . (p. 48)

Correlates of Crime, 1960–1984 (COC)

This collection, compiled by Richard R. Bennett (1990) in 1987, contains data on crime and relevant social, economic, and political information deemed related to crime for 52 nations over a 25-year period. While not a random sample, the nations included are drawn from the seven major regions of the world representing diverse levels of development, economies, political environments, and criminal justice systems. Three criteria for selecting the sample were employed: (1) membership in INTERPOL, (2) available crime data reported to INTERPOL between 1960 and 1984, and (3) only three of INTERPOL's two-year crime data reporting periods could be missing. Applying these criteria to all 117 nations reporting data to INTERPOL since 1960, 52 were included in the final sample.

Six categories of crime (murder, major larceny, minor larceny, fraud, counterfeiting and total offenses) are included in the crime section of the data,[5] and offender data were reported for the five INTERPOL (total offenses excluded) categories listed above. Missing data were approximated based on examination of both prior year information and data after the missing year(s).[6]

The author sees the Correlates of Crime data as perhaps the most useful of those available: "(1) it contains a very diverse sample of the world's nations, (2) the data are longitudinal and the reporting time span is consistent and comparable across nations, and (3) the dataset not only contains crime data, but also offender, and national social, economic, and political indicators" (Bennett, 1990:7).

Dutch Ministry of Justice International Crime Surveys, 1989, 1992, 1996, and 2000

In 1989, the Dutch Ministry of Justice instituted the first sweep of the International Crime Survey (ICS). Two thousand respondents in fourteen counties were interviewed by telephone as to their victimization experiences; additional sociodemographic and social life information was also collected (van Dijk and Mayhew, 1992:1–2). Japan conducted an ICS-based survey, with minor differences in questions and sampling. Smaller surveys using the ICS questionnaire were conducted in Warsaw and Surabaja (Indonesia). The average response rate (completed interviews out of eligible households selected) was 41% (p. 5).

In cooperation with the United Nations Interregional Crime and Justice Research Institute (UNICRI), the Ministry of Justice again in 1992 surveyed seventeen countries and nine cities (in nine different developing countries). The participants in the first survey and a number of other countries were asked to participate specifically to: (1) enlarge the scope for comparison by increasing the number of industrialized countries covered, (2) provide East European Countries in particular with the opportunity of improving their understanding of crime and law enforcement, and (3) implement some improvements in the methodology of the survey (van Dijk and Mayhew, 1992:1–2). Twelve major types of victimization are covered by the surveys. Response rates for the 1992 ICS were generally higher than in 1989. For most of the countries surveyed, computer-assisted telephone interviewing (CATI) along with face-to-face interviewing was used. The essence of the ICS (currently ICVS—International Crime Victim Survey) is standardization; not only are the same questions asked in each nation, but descriptions of crimes are used rather than labels such as "robbery." Thus, the ICVS is able to avoid national variations in reporting, defining, or recording crimes (Neapolitan 2003).

The 1996 and 2000 surveys were built on the 1989 and 1992 surveys. A few changes were made adding more detailed questions on the topics of completed burglary, robbery, sexual incidents, assaults/threats and burglar alarm ownership to maximize the amount of data to be analyzed. More countries were also added, expanding the coverage to twelve industrialized countries with all but one of the countries in central and east Europe and fifteen developing countries.

British Crime Survey Series, 1982–2004

Beginning in 1982, the Home Office Research and Planning Unit began carrying out the British Crime Survey (BCS), with subsequent surveys in 1984, 1988, 1992, 1994, 1996, 1998, 2000 and 2001. In 2001, the BCS moved to an annual cycle. Each wave measured victimization in the previous year. The samples consisted of about 10,000 (now 40,000) individuals aged sixteen and older living in England and Wales. Prior to 1992, the samples were taken from the Electoral Register. The Postcode Address File (listing all postal delivery points) provided the sampling frame for the 1992 and subsequent surveys. In 1982 and 1984, separate but parallel surveys began in Scotland (sample of 5,000) as is the case in Northern Ireland (Hales, 1993; Mayhew and Hough, 1992; Mayhew, Mirrlees-Black and Maung, 1994).

While the British Crime Surveys are not comparative in nature, they nevertheless should be examined (along with the National Crime Survey from the United States) as excellent examples of national attempts to measure criminal victimization accurately and comprehensively.

Methodological Considerations

Since the first systematic efforts to collect and compare cross-national crime and related statistics, important questions have been raised concerning various methodological problems encountered when using these sources of data. The following brief discussion delineates these problems very generally; when using these data, one should be aware that these are only a few of the many potential concerns that may arise.

Comparability of Indicators and Definitions

Problems in comparative research on crime and criminality have been widely recognized (see, e.g., Archer and Gartner, 1984; Kalish, 1988; Shichor, 1985, 1990; Bennett and Lynch, 1990; Stack, 1984; Huang and Welford, 1989). Most researchers agree that differences in definitions of crime and various indicators used pose several problems in researching and comparing cross-nationally. Archer and Gartner (1984:45) see several potential indicators of various offenses inherent in any criminal justice system:

1. Offenses known—the number of criminal acts known to police
2. Arrests—the number of suspected offenders detained
3. Indictments—the number of persons brought to trial
4. Convictions—the number of persons found guilty of an offense
5. Incarcerations—the number of persons sent to prison (or other institution)
6. Prison population—the total number of persons incarcerated at any one time

Determining and comparing these indicators, however, may not be an easy task, even within one particular country. Laws in the United States can vary substantially between states. For example, while "offenses known to police" was once considered highly accurate, most researchers feel that no *official* measure[7] comes close to the actual amount of criminality existing in society (p. 45).

The primary definitional problem concerns whether crimes have equivalent meanings between nations. Countries may (and most often do) differ in behaviors identified as coming within the scope of the criminal law. For cross-national comparisons of crime rates and criminality to have any validity at all, it is essential that the definitions be somewhat similar.

Obviously, a cross-cultural/national approach will have to deal with the problem of finding common denominators for the categories of behaviors observed. For example, INTERPOL defines murder as "any act performed with the purpose of taking human life . . . excludes abortion but includes infanticide" (including attempts) while the WHO makes no distinction between intentional and unintentional homicides (excluding attempts—in this case a separate, legal distinction) (Kalish, 1988:4). The UN definition of homicide includes only "death purposely inflicted by another person, including infanticide." It is interesting to note that Japan defines assault that results in death as assault, not homicide, and the former Czechoslovakia classified rape that resulted in death as rape, not homicide (Kalish, 1988:4).

In another case, the rates of robbery and theft in the former Czechoslovakia included only crimes involving individuals and individual property; the same offenses against public or state property fell under a different category. Not surprisingly, robbery and theft rates appeared significantly underestimated (Kalish, 1988:4). It should be noted that Kalish, who used data from the United Nations, INTERPOL, and WHO, points out that differences *between* countries are still more substantial than those she found *across* the countries studied (p. 4)

Differences in indicators and definitions are of special concern for descriptive studies comparing levels of crime between countries. For example, comparing homicide rates of two (or several) countries would be impossible if only "convictions" are available for one and only "offenses known to the police" for the other. Thus, indicators of both measures for at least one sample jurisdiction would be helpful. It would then be possible to compute the ratio of these two indicators and make an estimation for the one that is missing (Archer and Gartner, 1983:46–47).

Unlike descriptive studies, analytic research, focusing on crime trends or the correlations between crime and other factors, is less affected by these differences. Even significantly erroneous measures of crime may still pose no threat to analytic generalizations (Bennett and Lynch, 1990:157). Wolfgang (1967) has also suggested, among other things, that the legal definitions of crime should be eliminated when comparing across nations, replacing these with information regarding the type and extent of physical injury or the monetary value of property stolen or damaged.

Collection Practices

Each of the aforementioned datasets were compiled using information collected from various nations that might (and most often do) utilize very diverse crime collection strategies and procedures. Adler (1983), in her seminal comparative study of several nations, notes that figures reflecting the actual level of crime may be distorted at local, provincial, and national levels, thus weakening the possibility of reliable cross-national comparisons (p. 3).

The quality of crime reporting is likely to be influenced by a variety of practices and techniques in different societies (Shichor, 1990; Huang and Welford, 1989), honesty or dishonesty of the police administrators involved in the collection and compilation process (Adler, 1983), and manipulation of the data for political reasons (Shichor, 1985).

For example, in every case involving multiple offenses by the same person, the Uniform Crime Reports in the United States includes only the most serious (Reichel, 1994:32), whereas some countries would count them all in the crime statistics. Interestingly, INTERPOL guidelines for reporting such cases are very similar to those in the United States (Bennett and Lynch, 1990:158).

Those conducting the research for the International Crime Victim Survey found problems in developing countries when interviewing women. Often the researchers had to obtain permission from the head of the household and allow them to be present during the interview, which would have a direct effect on how individuals would respond to questions on sexual victimization (Zvekic, 1996).

In the early 1980s, the Chicago police fell under scrutiny for allegedly discarding massive numbers of crime incident reports. As a result of the subsequent investigation and improved reporting, a 25 percent increase in crime was registered in the city (Reichel, 1994:32). The former Soviet Union, where various crime statistics were regularly collected and processed by a number of governmental agencies, represented one of the most blatant examples of political control in crime reporting. Until the 1980s, crime data in the Soviet Union had never been released, but with *perestroika* (restructuring) and openness, the state began to declassify its archives.

Some scholars claim that developing nations tend to have lower crime rates since their collection and recording systems are less advanced (Huang and Welford, 1989:31). Others, however, downplay the significance of development and argue that the difference in crime reporting between less and more developed countries is not significant (Krohn, 1978:660).

To deal with this particular methodological concern, Adler (1983) suggests:

> . . . to validate the statistics by other quantified or unqualified information, such as rates of offenses reported to the police where available, or previous statistics, but, above all, by a process of informal peer-group evaluations with regions . . . (p. 3)

Problems can also be found in the collection practices of those conducting the research through different methods of sampling. Examples of this can be seen in the research of the International Crime Victim Survey. When sampling industrialized countries, respondents were contacted through random-digit dialing. This was not possible in many of the developing countries due to a lack of technology; therefore, surveys were carried out on a city-by-city basis, sampling only areas with populations greater than 100,000. Not being able to sample the entire country automatically creates a distorted representation of criminal activity within that country. Regarding physical access to the communities, researchers found difficulty accessing wealthier communities due to very tight security controls. Similar instances occurred in poor communities, as researchers often had to negotiate with the local leaders before anyone could be interviewed (Zvekic 1996).

Underreporting

A problem related to and an extension of collection practices is the widely debated issue of underreporting. Underreporting, the underestimation of actual crime rates, affects virtually any data extracted from official police reports of a given country. Most of the collections described in this article, including those by INTERPOL and the United Nations, rely at least partially on cross-national statistics collected by official police sources. The United States, for example, provides the various international data banks for the Uniform Crime Reports—police records gathered nationwide and published annually by the FBI. The weaknesses of the UCR and other official sources alike stem from the fact that the police cannot possibly be aware of all incidences of crime. Although it is beyond the scope of the present discussion to go into much detail, the following examples illustrate the problems.

On many occasions and for different reasons, people are reluctant to report the offenses they witness or experience. For instance, petty thefts involving small amounts of money are likely to remain unreported, as are simple assaults by an acquaintance. Some also support the idea that victims tend to report crimes more often if their stolen or damaged property is insured (Skogan, 1984; Fairchild, 1993).

In his cross-national study, Skogan (1984) made an interesting observation:

> In every jurisdiction there is a great deal of underreported crime—even in the most "civil" places, where cooperation with the police was presumed to be high—and everywhere the decision to report seems to be dominated by a rational calculus regarding the costs and benefits of such action. (p. 114)

In general, the more serious the crime, the more likely it is to be relayed to the authorities. Thus, as Archer and Gartner (1984) point out, both United

States and cross-national data on homicide should be less suspect than data on lesser crimes. It should also be noted that underreporting primarily tends to affect the absolute level of offenses. For example, cross-national comparisons of the levels of burglary in two countries may be invalidated if there is a difference in underreporting proportions between them, if the *ratio* of reported crime to the total crime rate varies (p. 36).

It is generally accepted that official crime statistics are an underrepresentation of crimes being committed. This is much more of a problem in China than in Western countries. The sources of methodological problems are not always found in the definitions of crime; they can also be found in the composition of societies and their cultures. In China, cultural philosophy and religion can play a role in how people of a society report what some would call criminal incidents to the police. One of the central aspects of Confucian tradition is a hierarchical relationship that specifies each individual's status in their family society. As a result, those being victimized by someone of a higher status are less likely to report certain forms of criminal activity. This has a direct effect on how individuals report crime as well as affecting the underdevelopment of certain laws (He and Marshall, 1997).

In a series of attempts to determine the "hidden" or "dark" figure of crime, victimization surveys have been conducted in several countries. The United States Census Bureau has conducted the National Crime Survey since 1973. On an international scale, the Dutch Ministry of Justice (1990) began the previously mentioned International Crime Surveys in 1989. Another national attempt is the British Crime Survey discussed earlier in this article. Victimization surveys have been used to point out that approximately one-third to one-half of all crime goes unreported (Fairchild, 1993:9).

Most criminologists agree that victimization surveys still do not account for all crime committed. For one reason or another, these surveys may not accurately measure offenses such as sexual assault, since victims are still less likely to report these crimes. Respondents may also inflate the statistics by compressing the period of time in which the crimes actually occurred (Archer and Gartner, 1983:33) or by misinterpreting some past incidents as criminal (Reichel, 1994:33)

Research conducted by the Council of Europe shows extreme irregularities in Sweden's rape statistics from 1990 through 1996. During these years the average number of rapes from 35 different countries ranged from a low of 6.0 per 100,000 to a high of 6.8 per 100,000. Included in these figures were Sweden's statistics, which were disproportionately higher than any other country. The Swedish numbers ranged from 16.5 per 100,000 to 24.7 per 100,000. These statistics suggest that a Swedish woman is three times more likely to be raped than other European women; this, however, is probably not the case. The source of these irregularities is probably due to the method of collecting data on these offenses in Sweden. Rape laws in Sweden are more loosely defined than in other countries and are applicable in many different ways, which generates a higher number of cases. In addition, the number of incidents reported, not the number of cases or victims, are counted for statistical purposes. An example of this can be seen in a 1993 case of a young man who reported being the victim of sexual abuse over 100 times by his stepfather over a 10-year period. All of these 100 incidents were added to the statistics of 1993 data (Von Hofer 2000:77–89).

Conclusion

Vetere and Newman (1977:261–63) suggested several years ago that future cross-national crime research should focus on enhancing the comparability of data. Based on information obtained from the Third United Nations Survey, the following issues were identified that need to be addressed when determining the methods and procedures for the collection of cross-national crime and related data in the future (Pease and Hukkila, 1990):

1. The amount of reported crime has continued to increase.
2. The control of crime is increasingly shifting to agencies and mechanisms outside the criminal justice system proper.
3. The taking of a final decision on criminal cases is shifting from the courts . . . to the prosecutor and the police.
4. Alternative means must be sought for collecting data.
5. There is no clear relationship between criminal justice resources and the problem of crime.
6. There is a need for a clearer analysis of where the actual "problem" of crime lies.
7. There is a need for a more realistic appraisal of the potential of the various crime control options.
8. The criminal justice system should be submitted to regular review.
9. The extent of the use of imprisonment should be limited.
10. Special attention should be paid to limiting the length of pretrial detention (pp. 1–8).

If we keep the above trends and recommendations in mind, as well as the cultural and national differences in crime definitions and comparability, future research should proliferate. With the increasing importance of cross-national research and data on crime and criminality, these efforts should dramatically increase (Cole, Stanislaw, and Gertz, 1987).

Notes

[1] Information in this section was contained in documentation accompanying the First through Eighth World Crime Surveys provided by the Inter-University Consortium for Polit-

ical and Social Research (ICPSR) and through the United Nations Criminal Justice Information Network (UNCJIN). Special thanks to Graeme Newman (University at Albany) and
Adam Boulekous (System Operator for UNCJIN) for providing earlier surveys electronically.
[2] Offenses included in the dataset are: murder, manslaughter, homicide, rape, assault, robbery, and theft.
[3] For a list of countries and international cities surveyed in the study, see Archer and Gartner
(1984:171–328).
[4] Specific categories of crime include: (1) murder, manslaughter; (2) assault; (3) robbery;
(4) burglary; (5) larceny, petty theft; (6) white-collar crime; (7) sexual and moral
offenses; and (8) public order offenses. Composite measures were constructed as follows:

Crimes of Aggression Murder + Assault
Serious Theft   Robbery (+ Burglary, if separately given)
All Theft   Robbery + Burglary (if separately given) + other theft

[5] According to the authors, sexual and drug-related offenses were not included due to the
consensus among most of those doing cross-national research that data for these offenses
are the least reliable.
[6] For an in-depth discussion of data-collection procedures and extrapolation of missing data,
see Bennett, 1990:4–6, 10–29.
[7] Victimization surveys are perceived by many to be a more accurate measure of actual criminality within a society. But there are few which are comparable over time (except for the
National Crime Victim Survey conducted by the Bureau of the Census) and cross-national
in nature.

Bibliography

Adler, Freda (1983). *Nations Not Obsessed with Crime*. Littleton, CO: Fred B. Roth-
man & Co.
Archer, Dane, and Rosemary Gartner (1984). *Violence And Crime in Cross-National
Perspective*. New Haven: Yale University Press.
Bennett, Richard R. (1980). "Constructing Cross-Cultural Theories in Criminology."
Criminology 18: 252–68.
———— (1990). *Correlates of Crime: A Study of 52 Nations, 1960–1984* (Codebook).
Ann Arbor, MI: ICPSR (distributor).
Bennett, Richard R., and James P. Lynch (1990). "Does a Difference Make a Differ-
ence? Comparing Cross-National Crime Indicators." *Criminology* 28 (1): 153–81.
Bureau of Justice Statistics (1987). *Imprisonment in Four Countries. Special Report*.
Washington, DC: U.S. Department of Justice.
Clifford, W. (1978). "Culture and Crime-In Global Perspective." *International Jour-
nal of Criminology and Penology* 6: 61–80.
Clinard, Marshall B. (1978). "Comparative Crime Victimization Surveys: Some
Problems and Results." *International Journal of Criminology and Penology* 6:
221–31.
Cole, George F., Stanislaw J. Frankowski, and Marc G. Gertz (eds.) (1987). *Major
Criminal Justice Systems*, 2d ed. Beverly Hills: Sage Publications.
Dutch Ministry of Justice (1990). *International Victimization Survey, 1988* (Code-
book). Ann Arbor, MI: ICPSR (distributor).
Fairchild, Erika (1993). *Comparative Criminal Justice Systems*. Belmont, CA: Wads-
worth.
Friday, Paul C. (1973). "Problems in Comparative Criminology: Comments on the
Feasibility and Implications of Research." *International Journal of Criminology
and Penology* 1: 151–60.

Gurr, Ted R. (1977). "Crime Trends in Modern Democracies Since 1945." *International Annals of Criminology* 16: 41–85.

Hales, Jon (1993). *1992 British Crime Survey (England and Wales): Technical Report.* London: Social and Community Planning Research (SCPR P.1193).

He, Ni, and Marshall H. Ineke (1997). "Social Production of Crime Data: A Critical Examination of Chinese Crime Statistics." *International Criminal Justice Review* 7: 46–64.

Hippchen, Leonard J. (1980). *Problems in World Criminology/Criminal Justice.* Presentation at the annual meeting of the Academy of Criminal Justice Sciences, Oklahoma City (March 12–15).

Home Office (2005). *British Crime Survey, Research Development Statistics.* Available: http://www.homeoffice.gov.uk/rds/bcs1.html (accessed January 24, 2005).

Huang, W. S. Wilson (1993). "Are International Murder Data Valid and Reliable? Some Evidence to Support the Use of Interpol Data." *International Journal of Comparative and Applied Criminal Justice* 17(1): 77–89.

Huang, W. S. Wilson, and Charles F. Welford (1989). "Assessing Indicators of Crime among International Crime Data Series." *Criminal Justice Policy Review* 3(1): 28–48.

INTERPOL (1953/54). *International Crime Statistics for 1953–54.* Paris: Saint-Cloud. (1981).

——— (1981). *International Crime Statistics for 1979–1980.* Paris: Saint-Cloud.

Kalish, Carol B. (1988). *International Crime Rates. Bureau of Justice Statistics, Special Report.* Washington, DC: U.S. Department of Justice.

Krohn, M. (1978). "A Durkheimian Analysis of International Crime Rates." *Social Forces* 57 (December): 654–70.

LaFree, Gary, and Christopher Birkbeck (1991). "The Neglected Situation: A Cross-National Study of the Situational Characteristics of Crime." *Criminology* 29(91): 73–98.

Mayhew, Pat, Catriona Mirrlees-Black, and Natalie Aye Maung (1994). *Research Findings* (No. 14), "Trends in Crime: Findings From the 1994 British Crime Survey." London: Research and Planning Unit, Home Office (September).

Mayhew, Pat, and Mike Hough (1992). "The British Crime Survey: The First Ten Years." *Journal of the Market Research Society* 34(1): 23–38.

Neapolitan, L. Jerome, (2003). "Explaining Variation in Crime Victimization Across Nations and Within Nations." *International Criminal Justice Review* 13: 76–87.

Newman, Graeme R., and Franco Ferracuti (1980). "Introduction: The Limits and Possibilities of Comparative Criminology." In Graeme R. Newman (ed.), *Crime and Deviance: A Comparative Perspective* (pp. 7–16). Beverly Hills: Sage Publications.

Pease, Ken, and Kristiina Hukkila (eds.) (1990). *Criminal Justice Systems in Europe and North America.* Helsinki: Helsinki Institute for Crime Prevention and Control.

Reichel, Philip L. (1994). *Comparative Criminal Justice Systems.* Englewood Cliffs, NJ: Prentice Hall Career & Technology.

Report on the Inter-Regional Meeting on Research in Criminology: Denmark-Norway-Sweden. 18 July–7 August, 1966.

Shichor, David (1985). "Effects of Development on Official Crime Rates, 1967–1978: Homicide and Larceny Patterns Differ Greatly." *Sociology and Social Research* 70: 96–97.

——— (1990). "Crime Patterns and Socioeconomic Development: A Cross-National Analysis." *Criminal Justice Review* 15(1): 64–77.

Skogan, Wesley G. (1984). "Reporting Crimes to the Police: The Status of World Research." *Journal of Research in Crime and Delinquency* 21(2): 113–37.

Stack, Steve (1984). "Income Inequality and Property Crime: A Cross-National Analysis of Relative Deprivation Theory." *Criminology* 22(2): 229–57.

Szabo, Dennis (1975). "Comparative Criminology." *Journal of Criminal Law and Criminology* 66(3): 366–79.

United Nations (1993). *Crime Trends and Criminal Justice Operations at the Regional and Interregional Levels: Results of the Third United Nations Survey of Crime Trends, Operations of Criminal Justice Systems and Crime Prevention Strategies.* New York: United Nations. Accessed October 19, 2004, from http://www.unodc.org/unodc/en/crime_cicp_surveys.html

van Dijk, Jan J. M., and Pat Mayhew (1992). *Criminal Victimization in the Industrialised World: Key Findings of the 1989 and 1992 International Crime Surveys.* The Netherlands: Dictorate for Crime Prevention, Ministry of Justice.

Vetere, Eduardo, and Graeme Newman (1977). "International Crime Statistics: An Overview from a Comparative Perspective." *Abstracts in Criminology and Penology* 17(3): 251–73.

Vigderhous, Gideon (1978). "Methodological Problems Confronting Cross-Cultural Criminological Research Using Official Data." *Human Relations* 3: 229–47.

Von Hofer, Hanns (2000). "Crime Statistics as Constructs: The Case of Swedish Rape Statistics." *European Journal on Criminal Police and Research* 8(1): 77–89.

Wikstrom, Per-Olof H. (1991). "Cross-National Comparisons and Context-Specific Trends in Criminal Homicide." *Journal of Crime and Justice* XIV (2): 71–95.

Wilkins, Leslie T. (1980). "World Crime: To Measure or Not to Measure." In Graeme R. Newman (ed.), *Crime and Deviance: A Comparative Perspective* (pp. 17–41). Beverly Hills: Sage Publications.

Wolfgang, Marvin E. (1967). "International Crime Statistics: A Proposal." *Journal of Criminal Law, Criminology and Police Science* 58: 65–69.

Wood, Martin (2003). *Offending in England and Wales: First Results from the 2003 Crime and Justice Survey.* London: Home Office, Research, Development & Statistics Directorate.

Zawitz, M. W. (ed.). (1988). *Report to the Nation on Crime and Justice.* Washington, DC: Department of Justice.

Zvekic, Ugljesa (1996). "The International Crime (Victim) Survey: Issues of Comparative Advantages and Disadvantages." *International Criminal Justice Review* 6: 1–21.

2

Exporting U.S. Organized Crime
Outlaw Motorcycle Gangs

Thomas Barker

The popular image or myth surrounding outlaw bikers has been that of social misfits driven by freedom of the road on the seat of a Harley, wind whipping their long hair—outsiders showing their contempt for society through drinking, drug taking, and deviant sexual acts. Just "Good Ole Boys" living up to the patch some of them wear—FTW (Fuck the World). One researcher, who was a member of the Pagans—an outlaw motorcycle gang (OMG)—for two years (1973–1974), describes OMGs as a subculture whose members operate within the "saloon society" milieu of lower-class taverns and either cannot or will not "fit in" conventional social life (Quinn, 1987:47).

According to Quinn (1987), these bikers refer to themselves as "one-percenters." The term originated from a statement made in the 1940s by the president of the American Motorcycle Association (AMA) that one percent of the bikers were the ones causing trouble and bad publicity for all those who ride motorcycles.

George Wethern (1978), former Oakland Hell's Angels vice president and one of the first of many Hell's Angels informers, recalls a 1960 state-wide meeting of all California Hell's Angels leaders and leaders of other rival clubs such as the Gypsy Jokers, Road Rats, Galloping Gooses, Satan's Slaves, the Presidents, and the Mofos. The purpose of the meeting was to form a united front against police harassment. The leaders decided to unite themselves under a "one percenter patch" in order to distinguish themselves from pretenders and weekenders like the members of the AMA. Wethern says he and Sonny Barger were the first to get one percent tattoos. Since that 1960 meeting, all outlaw motorcycle members refer to themselves as one-percenters and wear the "1%" patch. Back then, outlaw bikers were more likely to come to agreement over common interests than they are today. Their movement into criminal activities changed that spirit.

Prepared especially for *Comparative and International Criminal Justice, 2/E.*

From Clubs to Criminal Gangs

In the formative years of the 1960s, the Hell's Angels and other outlaw clubs developed cultural traditions that would define them forever. The early outlaw club members were white supremacists with a definite anti-black attitude (the typical motto for membership being: no niggers, no cops, no snitches) and male chauvinists who treated women (except their "old ladies"—wives or "steady squeezes") as sexual objects. They governed their meetings by rules, including parliamentary procedures (Wethern [1978] reports that even the charismatic Sonny Barger occasionally lost the vote on some issues of club business). They also claim to espouse a cultural tradition of brotherhood—embodied by such slogans as Angels Forever, Forever Angels, Angels Come First, No Snitching, and other expressions of mutual support, camaraderie, and love between equals. However, contrary to their stated hatred for snitches/informants and allusions to brotherhood, members have turned on one another when things got tough and long prison sentences were threatened, especially with the advent of RICO prosecutions (discussed later in this article).

American-based OMGs share characteristics with AMA-recognized clubs. They have written constitutions, bylaws, and a hierarchical leadership structure, and the members pay dues and attend regular meetings. Lavigne (1999) remarks that the Hell's Angels spend as much time at meetings as corporate executives do. Admittedly, this is an exaggeration, but Hells' Angels hold meetings at all levels of their organization: chapter, regional, West Coast, East Coast, and worldwide. Lavigne includes examples of constitutions, bylaws, and meeting minutes of the Hell's Angels and Bandidos in his books. Veno (2002), in his study of Australian outlaw clubs, reports that club meetings, mandatory runs, and other club obligations cause many Australian "bikies" (bikers) to leave the clubs because the myriad club-related responsibilities leave them with little time for a life of their own. In addition, OMGs have incorporated and trademarked their logos. However, the similarity with other motorcycle clubs stops there. According to the Los Angeles Police Department, OMGs are organizations whose members use their motorcycle clubs as a basis for criminal activities (Haut, 1999).

Since their origins in the early 1940s, some U.S. OMGs have become highly organized criminal networks motivated more by criminal interests than by hedonistic pursuits. Experts on OMGs say that outlaw motorcycle gangs are the only sophisticated, organized crime groups that we export from the United States on a worldwide basis (Trethewy and Katz, 1998; Smith, 1998). Some have established ties and working relationships with traditional organized crime (OC) groups such as La Cosa Nostra, Colombian cartels, and even the Chinese Triads (Haut, 1999; Trethewy & Katz, 1998). OMG members have acted as hit men for traditional OC groups

(Smith, 2002). Interpol classifies OMGs with Mafia-type organized crime groups, based on the following criteria: highly structured hierarchies, internal rules of discipline, codes of ethics [sic], and diversity in illegal and legitimate affairs (Kendall, 1998).

Outlaw Motorcycle Gangs as Organized Crime

Broadly speaking, the FBI has defined organized crime as:

> Any group having some manner of formalized structure [which is true for all OMGs] and whose primary objective is to obtain money through illegal activities [which fits many chapters of the groups discussed in this article]. Such groups maintain their position through the use of violence or threats of violence [a defining characteristic of OMGs], corrupt public officials, graft, or extortion, and generally have a significant impact on the people in their locales or regions of the country. (Federal Bureau of Investigation, n.d.)

There have been some published accounts (academic sources, court cases at the state and federal level, law enforcement/government reports, popular literature, and several "crooks" books written by former OMG members) that corroborate such OMG exploits and actions. In one of the first scholarly works on OMGs as organized crime, the author utilizes Donald R. Cressey's (1969) seminal definition of organized crime, stating:

> . . . one percenters reject the standard of the other ninety-nine percent by the adoption of outlandish uniforms with Nazi-Germany trappings to instill fear; performing of weird initiation rites [including the performance of deviant sexual acts witnessed by other members and the commission of criminal acts]; gaining the respect of law-abiding groups through fear and intimidation. (Hill, 1980: 27)

While Hill accurately details some characteristics (i.e., rejection of society's norms, initiation rites, use of fear and intimidation) of current OMG members and groups, the rest of his description is far off the mark and is as outdated as Cressey's definition of organized crime. Biker gangs, including the Hell's Angels, have been penetrated on numerous occasions by undercover police officers—some of whom became club "officers." These undercover operations found that alleged OMG initiation rites such as deviant sexual acts and commission of crimes are not required for membership. Furthermore, OMG recognition of public deviant sexual activities has died out, as has their penchant for Nazi memorabilia and attire (Wethern, 1978).

Documenting the evolution of OMGs into organized crime gangs is a difficult endeavor, because as criminal groups they are dangerous and secretive, prohibiting access to outsiders, and they do not publish membership lists or histories. (Some OMGs have published "histories" on their

Internet Web sites, but these accounts appear to be self-serving narratives of dubious accuracy. However, these Web sites, maintained by a majority of the groups, are an excellent source of information for pinpointing locations of chapters and affiliates.)

It appears from Wethern's accounts (1978) that the first movement into organized crime activities for the Hell's Angels began with the control of psychedelic drugs in the San Francisco Haight Street district in the 1960s. At the end of that decade, the Hell's Angels had evolved from a club whose members held unskilled labor jobs to an organization whose members were "employed" as drug pushers. Wethern and his crew handled the psychedelic drugs, another Angel ran the mescaline traffic, and Ralph "Sonny" Barger controlled the heroin and cocaine.

Although "prospects" (prospective members) still had to have a reputation as outlaws, new members were no longer chosen solely on traditional biker values. A more important job qualification for prospects was what they could contribute to the drug trade—provide a drug route link, manufacture a drug, supply chemicals, or distribute drugs to an untapped area (Wethern, 1978: 102). Newly prosperous drug-dealing Angels were buying new Harleys; luxury cars like Cadillacs, Corvettes, and Jaguars; numerous automatic pistols and machine guns; and even exotic animals such as lions. Membership climbed to 500 in 21 chapters (10 in California, 8 out of state and 4 international—Australia, England, Switzerland, and West Germany). It was also during this period (in 1968) that the Oakland Hell's Angels chapter performed its first execution, of a member who had stolen Sonny Barger's coin collection. During this same decade, other biker gangs followed the Hell's Angels' lead into the drug-trafficking market in their own respective areas.

The bikers, particularly the Hell's Angels, were still being lionized in the media. However, the much-publicized murder committed by a Hell's Angel during the 1968 Rolling Stones concert at Altamont Park in California resulted in a change in tactics and in the public facade of Outlaw Motorcycle Clubs. In the 1970s, the already established biker gangs began to clean up their images and, through expansion and growing sophistication, escalated their involvement in diverse criminal operations (Reid, 1981; Haut, 1999). Their lower profile succeeded in attracting less attention from the media. However, some law enforcement agencies woke up to the realization that the clubs had become organized crime groups—hence the label "outlaw motorcycle gangs."

The FBI began investigating OMGs, particularly the Hell's Angels, in 1981 under its Organized Crime Program. Sensing the law enforcement push to eliminate them, Sonny Barger proposed the following reason for such efforts:

> First of all, we're a virtual army. We're all across the country, and now we're in foreign countries also. We have money, many allies that are outlaw bikers that are not Hell's Angels, that would probably do any-

thing we asked them to, if something happened. Like a revolution. Or anything like that. (quoted in Lavigne, 1987: 27)

A two-year undercover investigation by an FBI agent begun in 1982 and known as "Operation ROUGHRIDER" involved 11 Hell's Angels chapters in seven states (Operation ROUGHRIDER, 1985). At that time, the Hell's Angels had 64 chapters in 13 countries. Drugs confiscated during this operation included: methamphetamine, cocaine, marijuana, hashish, PCP, and LSD. Also, a 1982 RICO (Racketeer Influenced Corrupt Organization) prosecution against Outlaw Motorcycle Club members from Florida, Georgia, North Carolina, and Tennessee involved allegations of white slavery and transporting women across state lines for immoral purposes (Smith, 2002).

The federal government's first attempt to prosecute the Hell's Angels as a criminal organization under RICO was a dismal failure. In a trial where the government paid a former Hell's Angel $54,000 to testify and gave him immunity for six murders, the defense was that members' acts were individual acts and not organization acts. The jury could not reach a verdict, and the judge declared a mistrial. A second trial also ended in a hung jury, and all charges were dropped against Barger and 17 other Hell's Angels (Lavigne, 1987; Barger, 2000).

In 1986, a nationwide raid targeting OMGs by the Bureau of Alcohol, Tobacco and Firearms (BATF) resulted in the arrest of four chapter presidents of the Big 4 (Hell's Angels, Outlaws, Bandidos, and Pagans) and presidents of some of the affiliated biker gangs such as the Devil's Disciples, Diablos, and Trampers. This crackdown, the largest operation by the BATF up to that time, resulted in the seizure of sawed-off shotguns, handheld machine guns, silencers, rifles, handguns, ammunition, hand grenades, and dynamite, as well as drugs—cocaine, marijuana, and PCP (Anon, 1986). Efforts against OMGs were also being conducted at the local level. An investigation by the Fayetteville, North Carolina, police department into thefts of Harley-Davidson motorcycles and insurance fraud led to a local Hell's Angel chapter (Johnson, 1981). The investigation resulted in arrests in twenty states. A 1982 law enforcement report listed the criminal activities of major motorcycle gangs as: manufacturing and distribution of narcotics, prostitution, weapons-related violations, extortion, murder, arson-for-hire, pornography, protection rackets, loan sharking, interstate transportation of stolen property and stolen vehicles, and insurance fraud (Davis, 1982). The profits from these illegal activities were being invested, not only in legitimate businesses but also in international expansion.

International Expansion

The movement during the 1960s of outlaw motorcycle gangs into drug trafficking, an inherently international criminal market, increased the expansion of American-based OMGs beyond the boundaries of the United

States. The already established interlocking networks with biker clubs/ gangs in other countries allowed American-based bikers to link common criminal enterprises and the benefits derived therefrom. These U.S. gangs had now entered the global marketplace of crime. The international implications were recognized by the law enforcement community in the early 1980s (Doughtie, 1986). In a 1984 report from the General Secretariat of Interpol the Hell's Angels and Outlaws were reported to have chapters in Canada (Interpol, 1984). The Hell's Angels were said to be the only motorcycle gang with chapters in twelve countries (seven Western European countries—Great Britain, West Germany, Netherlands, Denmark, Switzerland, France, and Austria—as well as in Australia, New Zealand, Japan, Canada, and the United States). Since that report was issued, the Hell's Angels have expanded even further, and other U.S. biker gangs have established chapters outside the United States.

In 1991, Interpol created Operation Rockers to deal with the rapid expansion of OMGs throughout the world (Smith, 1998). Named after the banners on top and bottom of the gang's colors, Project Rockers (still in operation) has the following objectives:

- to identify motorcycle gangs that are engaged in continuous criminal activities;
- to identify each gang's membership, hierarchy, modus operandi and specific criminal activity;
- to correlate the information for analysis and dissemination;
- to assist member countries in the exchange of criminal intelligence information; and
- to identify specific contact officers within the NCBs [Interpol's National Central Bureau in member countries] and law enforcement agencies having expertise with outlaw motorcycle gangs.

As of 2000, in addition to the United States there are 28 countries participating in Operation Rocker, including all those containing current chapters of the Hell's Angels. The organization now has annual meetings, and a Project Rocker Newsletter was initiated in 1998 (McClure, 2000). This newsletter contains information on international OMG activities obtained from reports from NCBs and other intelligence sources. Although Operation Rocker has had some success in dealing with OMGs, it has not stopped their expansion.

In 2002, the vice president of the Arizona Nomads chapter of the Hell's Angels was sentenced to 180 months in prison and the chapter president was sentenced to 60 months, for conspiracy to possess with intent to distribute methamphetamine (U.S. Attorney General District of Arizona, 2002). The case involved procuring methamphetamines from club members in South Africa and distribution in Massachusetts and New Mexico— an operation that was truly international in scope.

American-Based OMGs with International Chapters

Hell's Angels

The Hell's Angels are the largest and most prominent international motorcycle gang. They are also known as the Local 81, after the placement of the letters H (8th) and A (1st) in the alphabet, and as The Big Red Machine and the Red and White (their colors). Supporters and known associates are allowed to wear Local 81 and Big Red Machine patches, but not the Hells Angels (without the apostrophe), which is a registered logo worn only by patched members.

The first chapter of the Hell's Angels was formed in San Bernardino, California, on March 17, 1948. However, this chapter (formed by a group of disaffected World War II veterans known as the Pissed Off Bastards of Bloomington) bore little resemblance, other than its name, to the Hell's Angels of today. According to Sonny Barger (the first president of the Oakland Hell's Angels, the former national president, and some say the de-facto leader of today), he and his fellow bikers formed the modern Hell's Angels in April of 1957 without knowing that other Hell's Angels chapters existed in California (Barger, 2000: 30).

The official Web site of the Hell's Angels lists 30 chapters in the United States. However, the author has reason to believe that only those chapters with Web sites are listed, and many other U.S. chapters may exist. The Angels' first expansion outside the United States occurred in 1961 (Auckland, New Zealand). The first European chapter was established in London in 1969, followed by Zurich in 1970, Hamburg in 1973, and a Paris chapter in 1981 (Haut, 1999). At the present time, the Hell's Angels list chapters in 23 countries (USA, Canada, Brazil, Argentina, South Africa, Australia, New Zealand, Spain, France, Belgium, Holland, Germany, Switzerland, Liechtenstein, Austria, Italy, England/Wales, Finland, Norway, Denmark, Greece, Bohemia/Czech Republic, and Portugal) and two hangaround chapters in Russia and Chile (http://www.hells-angels.com/charters.htm).

The Hell's Angels are a crime problem in Canada as well as in the United States. Organized biker clubs/gangs have existed in Quebec since the early 1930s; however, Canadian experts say that biker gangs were not a problem until the Hell's Angels arrived (Alain, 1995). The Hell's Angels–Quebec were established in 1977. Canadian authorities now consider the Hell's Angels to be one of the most powerful and well structured criminal organizations in Canada (CICS, 2000), consisting of at least 18 chapters. These chapters and associates with puppet clubs and alliances with other organized crime groups make the Hell's Angels (HA) a national priority for Canadian law enforcement.

The Canadian Hell's Angels seem to be a particularly vicious and brazen criminal organization. In 2002, Quebec Hell's Angels president Maurice "Mom" Boucher was convicted of two counts of first-degree murder for ordering the deaths of two prison guards in an attempt to intimidate the Canadian criminal justice system (Macafee, 2002). This was the second trial for Boucher on these charges. The first trial ended in an acquittal, but a new trial was ordered after the Supreme Court heard an appeal from the prosecution.

Canada uses the Hell's Angels as the touchstone in defining outlaw motorcycle gangs. According to the Provincial Court in Alberta, an outlaw motorcycle gang has the following features (quoted in Haut, 1999, p. 28):

- a structure based on that of the Hell's Angels;
- rules and principles which allow for the use of extreme violence in the best interests of the gang and its members;
- very strict membership conditions that require applicants to prove their "worth";
- associates who provide services to the gang or connect it to other gangs;
- the "colors" (sleeveless vest with club patch on the back), which are the most important aspect for the members;
- use of fortified clubhouses;
- the gathering of information about enemies (i.e., other gangs and the police);
- involvement in criminal activities, which is the gangs' *raison d'être*.

The Quebec Hell's Angels were involved with La Cosa Nostra and the Colombian drug cartels in an attempt to smuggle tons of cocaine into Europe (Smith, 1998). The Canadian Angels are involved in the following criminal activities: importation and distribution of cocaine, production and distribution of methamphetamines, cultivation and exportation of high-grade marijuana, illegal trafficking of firearms and explosives, collection of protection money from both legitimate and illegitimate businesses, fraud, money laundering, and prostitution. In 2001, their nine-year war with the Quebec Rock Machine OMG had led to 160 deaths, including innocent bystanders. The Rock Machine members have recently become patched Outlaws (another American-based, worldwide OMG and a bitter enemy of the Hell's Angels, discussed more thoroughly in the following section), who have had a presence in Canada since the late 1970s (Reid, 1981).

The Nordic chapters of the Hell's Angels and the Bandidos (American-based) were involved in violent warfare in the late 1990s (Brown, 1999, Lavigne, 1999). The battles waged with weapons, such as explosives and shoulder-fired anti-tank missiles, led to 11 deaths and numerous injuries to innocent bystanders. They were fighting over the sharing of the lucrative criminal market in Scandinavian countries (Brown [1999] states that the open seas of the Nordic countries are ideal for drug activities).

The Hell's Angels–Germany were established in 1973 and quickly became the target of investigation by the Hamburg police. They were suspected of being involved in narcotics trafficking, extortion, illegal possession of firearms, and assault. After an 18-month investigation, simultaneous raids in August 1983 in West Germany, the United States, and Switzerland led to the arrest of 15 members and 13 associates (Sielaff, 1988). Thirteen Angels were convicted.

The Hell's Angels have been a problem in Australia for over twenty years. In the 1980s both chapters and puppet gangs have been involved in narcotics, prostitution, major armed robbery, movement of arms and explosives, fencing, assault, and murder (Reid, 1981). The Melbourne chapter of the H.A.M.C. (Hells Angel's Motorcycle Club) had strong connections with the Oakland, California, H.A.M.C. as early as the late 1970s.

The latest raid on the Hell's Angels in Los Angeles, San Francisco, Arizona, Alaska, Washington State, and Nevada took place on December 3, 2003, as a result of a two-year undercover operation by two federal officers (AP National, 12/3/2003). The raid resulted in the arrests of 57 Hell's Angels members and associates.

The Outlaws Motorcycle Club

According to their national Web site (http://www.outlawsmc.com/history.html), the Outlaws is the oldest and first "1%" motorcycle club, despite that same claim by their bitter rival, the Hell's Angels. They claim to have been established in 1935 as the McCook Outlaws Motorcycle Club out of Matilda's Bar on old Route 66 in McCook, Illinois, outside Chicago. In 1950, the club's name was changed to the Chicago Outlaws. In 1963, the Outlaws MC became an official member of the One Percenter Brotherhood of Clubs, the first true one-percenter club east of the Mississippi. The Web site states that in 1965 the club became the "Outlaws Motorcycle Club Nation."

Since 1935, the Outlaws have grown into one of the largest motorcycle clubs worldwide and one of the largest (maybe second behind the Hell's Angels) outlaw motorcycle gangs in the world. The Outlaws Web site lists 66 chapters in U.S. states and 90 chapters in countries outside the United States (including 7 chapters in Canada).

Illinois	10	Oklahoma	1	England	14
Georgia	4	Wisconsin	5	Wales	2
Maine	1	Florida	9	Belgium	6
New Hampshire	2	Kentucky	1	Germany	33
Ohio	6	Michigan	6	Ireland	3
Tennessee	4	North Carolina	4	Norway	3
Connecticut	1	Pennsylvania	2	Sweden	1
Indiana	3			Italy	1
Massachusetts	5	Canada	7	Poland	5
New York	2	Australia	14	Thailand	1

However, the Outlaws News and Events newsletter of November 2003 (www.outlawsmc.com/events [accessed 12/6/2003]) lists new chapters in Fayetteville, AR; Charlotte County and West Volusia County, FL; Southern Indiana; Grand Junction, CO; and a prospective chapter in Lexington, KY. The same newsletter lists new chapters in Shelby County, KY (August 2003); Johnstown, PA (August, 2003); Kalamazoo, MI (May 2003); Knox County, IL (May 2003); Madison, WI (April 2003); Enfield, CT (March 2003); Boston North Shore and Columbus, OH (February 2003); Portland, ME (January 2003); and new chapters in Wilkes-Barre, PA, and North Atlanta, GA, in November and December of 2002. Internationally, the Outlaws list a new chapter in Brescia, Italy.

In cities and countries where both the Outlaws and Hell's Angels have chapters, there is continual warfare between the gangs. This will surely continue with the addition of new chapters in "Angel Country." Particularly ominous is a statement in the Outlaws newsletter thanking the Mongols, the Bandidos, and the Sons of Silence for their "support and display of Brotherhood in welcoming the AOA [American Outlaw Association] to Colorado."

The Outlaws are affiliated with the Bandidos but consider themselves sworn enemies of the Hell's Angels. Outlaws proudly wear patches signaling their hatred for the Angels—AHAMD (All Hell's Angels Must Die) and ADIOS (Angels Die in Outlaw States). The animosity between the two biker gangs apparently started on July 4, 1979, in Charlotte, North Carolina, where the two OMGs were involved in a violent struggle for control over the drug and prostitution markets in that city. Each gang was absorbing and "patching over" the existing gangs when on July 4, 1979, five members of the Outlaws were murdered in their clubhouse. This was the worst mass murder in Charlotte's history. The murders are still unsolved, but both the Outlaws and law enforcement authorities believe the Hell's Angels are responsible. Many Outlaws wear a 7-4-79 patch to remember the date and to fuel their hatred for the Hell's Angels.

Law enforcement sources say that drug trafficking is the Outlaws' main source of income (National Alliance of Gang Investigators Association, nd.). The NAGIA reports that "Canadian Blue" diazepam (an addictive drug similar to Valium) is manufactured in Ontario, Canada, and smuggled into the United States for distribution. The same source says that Florida Outlaw chapters buy cocaine from Colombian and Cuban sources for distribution in the United States. Florida and Georgia chapters also manufacture their own methamphetamine.

The international president of the Outlaws, Harry Joseph "Taco" Bowman, was recently convicted of racketeering, conspiracy to murder, and various drug and firearms offenses (*U.S. v. Bowman*, 2002). He was tried and sentenced to life in prison after two years on the run, during which he was on the FBI's Ten Most Wanted List. Court testimony revealed that Bowman had been living in an affluent Detroit suburb, sent his children to private schools, and drove an armor-plated Cadillac. The Ottawa Outlaws (with 14 patched members) are said to be involved in drug trafficking, prostitution, and nude dancing agencies (RCMP, 1999). They have an uneasy truce with the dominant Hell's Angels groups.

The Bandidos

The Bandidos were formed in Houston, Texas, in 1966 by the late Donald Eugene Chambers to control drug trafficking and prostitution in Texas. Since that time, The Bandido Nation has been called by the National Alliance of Gang Investigators (NAIGA) the fastest growing OMG in the United States, with 30 U.S. chapters and one in Australia. There is no date on the NAIGA report, but it must have been published several years ago, because the Bandidos have certainly lived up to their growth potential. According to their national Web site (http://www.bandidosmc.com), the Bandido Nation has 85 U.S. chapters in 13 states:

New Mexico	13	Texas	27	Louisiana	4
Washington	13	Alabama	2	Mississippi	2
Colorado	3	South Dakota	3	Nevada	2
Wyoming	1	Arkansas	1	Montana	1
Oklahoma	1				

There is also a national U.S. chapter and a Nomads chapter, reportedly made up of longtime members who act as a security element, taking care of counterintelligence and internal discipline. The Web site states that "More [chapters] Are Coming."

The Bandido Nation lists 73 chapters in 13 countries outside the United States: Canada–4, Australia–12, Belgium–1, Denmark–12, Finland–2, France–5, Germany–26, Italy–2 (probationary), Luxembourg–1, Norway–5, Sweden–3, Thailand–2 (probationary), and the United Kingdom–2. In Finland, where the authorities consider biker gangs to be the largest organized crime group, a 2000 massacre in a local pizzeria left three Bandidos dead, including the Bandidos' Finnish president, and several bystanders were injured. The revenge-motivated shooting incident was carried out by members of the Cannonball Motor Cycle Club Lahit, Finland, chapter in its fight for dominance in Finland.

As stated earlier, the Bandidos and the Outlaws are affiliated. They list each other as links on their Web sites, and they socialize together. There are reports that the Outlaws provide the Bandidos with drugs for resale, participate in joint criminal ventures, and own property and legitimate businesses together. They are also united in their hatred for the Hell's Angels.

In 1996, an explosion occurred at the Copenhagen, Denmark, headquarters of the Hell's Angels, killing one and injuring 20. Reportedly, the bombing was part of the two-year struggle between the Angels and the Bandidos over the drug markets in Denmark, Finland, Norway, and Sweden. The Hell's Angels established a chapter in Denmark in 1977. They were the only American-based OMG until 1993, when the Bandidos established a chapter, setting off the so-called Nordic Wars.

Other Outlaw Motorcycle Gangs

Reportedly, the Gypsy Jokers are the largest Australian OMG. Although the Gypsy Jokers are Australian based, there has been a Gypsy Jokers OMG in America with chapters in Washington and California since the early 1960s. Veno (2002) reports that when the American Gypsy Jokers learned of the Australian Gypsy Jokers, they invited them to the United States and, after a night of partying, the two gangs affiliated with one another.

There are other American-based OMGs that represent organized crime threats, particularly the Pagans. Although they have no international chapters as of this writing, the Pagans have had ties with other international organized crime groups, such as the Mafia and the Colombian cartels. The Pagans have waged their own forty-year war with the Hell's Angels. The latest battle occurred in Plainview, New York, in February 2001. The knife and gunfight resulted in one death, twelve persons injured, and seventy-three Pagans arrested. As a result of this battle, the Hell's Angels are now moving into Philadelphia—formerly Pagan territory—and "patching over" Pagans and other biker gangs. No doubt this will lead to further conflict between the two gangs.

Other American-based OMGs, such as the Sons of Silence, the Mongols, the Avengers, and the Vagos, have chapters in one or more countries outside the continental United States. The Sons of Silence list a chapter in Germany. The approximately 200-member Mongols MC has 21 chapters in this country and several chapters in Mexico. They were recently involved in a violent shoot-out with the Hell's Angels in Harrah's Casino in Laughlin, Nevada, that left three dead. The Black Pistons Motorcycle Club—official supporters of the Outlaws, according to their Web site—has 21 U.S. chapters, seven in Canada, and one in Germany. The 200-member Vagos MC has chapters in California, Nevada, Hawaii, and Mexico. The Avengers MC claims to have chapters in Michigan, Ohio, Florida, Indiana, West Virginia, and Malta. (The author is currently attempting to identify all American-based motorcycle gangs with chapters overseas. This is an area of organized crime that has been "under-researched" by most scholars.)

Conclusion

There is ample evidence to document that The Big Three—the Hell's Angels, the Outlaws, and the Bandidos—have made major expansion efforts into countries throughout the world. They have "patched over" existing biker gangs in these countries, engaging in violence and increasing in influence and wealth. There is every reason to believe that their expansion efforts will continue as long as the profits are there.

References

Alain, Marc. (June, 1995). The rise and fall of motorcycle gangs in Quebec. *Federal Probation,* 59(2).

Anon. (1986). U.S. takes action against motorcycle gangs, leaders. *Organized Crime Digest* (May).

Barger, R. (2000). *Hell's Angels: The life and times of Sonny Barger and the Hell's Angels Motorcycle Club.* New York: William Morrow.

Brown, Peggy. (1999). Nordic motorcycle gangs. *International Criminal Police Review,* 474–475.

CISC. (2000). Outlaw motorcycle gangs. *Criminal Intelligence Service Canada–2000.*

Cressey, Donald R. (1969). *Theft of the nation: The structure and operations of organized crime in America.* New York: Harper & Row.

Davis, Roger H. (1982). Outlaw motorcyclists: A problem for law enforcement. *FBI Law Enforcement Bulletin,* 13–22.

Doughtie, John A. (August, 1986). Motorcycle gang investigations: A team effort. *FBI Law Enforcement Bulletin,* 19–22.

Federal Bureau of Investigation. (n.d.). Available: http://www.fbi.gov/hq/cid/orgcrime/glossary.htm (accessed February 7, 2005).

Haut, François. (1999). Organized crime on two wheels: Motorcycle gangs. *International Criminal Police Review,* 474–475.

Hill, T. (1980). Outlaw motorcycle gangs: A look at a new form of organized crime. *Canadian Criminology Forum, 3*(Fall), 26–36.

Interpol. (1984). Motorcycle gangs. *ICPO-Interpol General Secretariat.*

Johnson, W. C. (1981). Motorcycle gangs and organized crime. *Police Chief,* 32–33, 78.

Kendall, Raymond E. (1998). The international problem of criminal gangs. *International Criminal Police Review,* 469–471.

Lavigne, Yves. (1987). *Hell's Angels: Taking care of business.* Toronto, Canada: Random House.

Lavigne, Yves. (1999). *Hells Angels at war.* Toronto, Canada: Harper Collins.

Macafee, M. (2002). Biker trials, not turf wars, will dominate scene in 2003, experts say. Available: http://canoe.ca/CNEWS/LAW/bikers/2002/12/19/8224-cp.html (accessed February 7, 2005).

Mandelkau, Jamie. (1971). *Buttons: The making of a president.* London: Sphere Books Limited.

McClure, Gwen. (2000). The role of Interpol in fighting organized crime. *International Criminal Police Review,* No. 481.

National Alliance of Gang Investigators Association. (n.d.). Motorcycle gangs. *NAGIA.*

Operation ROUGHRIDER. (May 15, 1985). After three years on the road, FBI arrests "Angels" in nationwide raid. *Narcotics Control Digest,* 4–5.

Quinn, James F. (1987). Sex role and hedonism among members of "outlaw" motorcycle clubs. *Deviant Behavior, 8,* 47–63.

Reid, Kenneth E. (1981). Expansionism—Hell's Angels style. *Police Chief, 48*(5), 38–40, 69, 78.

Sielaff, Wolfgang. (1988). Organized criminal activity in the Federal Republic of Germany. *Police Chief,* November, 76–79.

Smith, B. W. (1998). Interpol's "Project Rocker" helps disrupt outlaw motorcycle gangs. *Police Chief,* September, 54–66.

Smith, Richard C. (2002). Dangerous motorcycle gangs: A facet of organized crime in the mid Atlantic region. *Journal of Gang Research, 9*(4), 33–44.

Trethewy, Steve & Katz, Terry. (1998). Motorcycle gangs or motorcycle Mafia? *Police Chief, 66*(4), 53–60.

U.S. v. Bowman (2002). U.S. 11th Circuit Court of Appeals—*U.S. v. Bowman* No. 01-14305.

U.S. Attorney General, District of Arizona. (June 18, 2002). Press release number 2002–109.

Veno, A. (2002). *The brotherhoods: Inside the outlaw motorcycle clubs.* Crows Nest, NSW, Australia: Allen & Unwin.

Wethern, George. (1978). *Wayward angel.* New York: Richard Marek.

3

Victimization of Women in African Society
Conflict between the Sexes and Conflict of Laws

Edna Erez & R. Bankole Thompson

Victimization of women in Western societies continues to be a prominent topic of criminological research and social activism (e.g., Dobash and Dobash, 1992; Palmer, 1989). In African societies, with few recent exceptions, no such trend exists. This is due primarily to the existence of a bedrock of beliefs and traditions in African society about the inferior, dependent, and subordinate status of women. Forms of victimization such as clitoridectomy (female circumcision), sexual abuse of female children,[1] wife battering, and marital rape are rooted in African culture and are perceived as male normative prerogative.

By contrast, the inherited Western legal systems in most former colonial African states proscribe such acts. The practices and customs emanating from, or expressing, the subordinate status of women are in constant tension with conceptions of women's autonomy and independence prevailing in Western laws.

In Sierra Leone tribal society, the status of men and women is clearly defined as dominant and submissive, respectively; masculine and feminine traits are traditional and inflexible (Hazou, 1990). In the tribal culture, men have the power, prestige, and privileges by virtue of being men; women are treated as social inferiors. Describing the status of women in the tribal population, Taylor (1975:130) suggests that their position is similar to that of a minor. A single woman is under the guardianship of her father, or, in his absence, the head of the family. If her father still lives with his own father, she is under the guardianship of the grandfather. A married woman is under the guardianship of her husband. Upon his death, as a widow, her guardianship passes on to the new head of the family until she

Prepared especially for *Comparative Criminal Justice, 1/E.*

remarries. The fact that the "native" woman in Sierra Leone is deemed to be the property of some man (father, husband, or some other head of the family) has far-reaching implications for a woman's interpersonal and sexual relations and rights, especially if she is married. If she is married, her husband cannot be held criminally culpable for any form of victimization to which he may subject her, physically or sexually, except for homicide. Under certain conditions and for some types of physical abuse or sexual misconduct, a husband may be civilly liable to pay compensation to the woman's family and fees to the tribal elders. Customary-law marriages are marriages (contracts) between families, not merely between individuals, so the woman's family continues to maintain interest in her well-being throughout her marital relationship. Women are also economic assets to their families—a source of income, either as workers in this agrarian society or as property with which transactions are made (i.e., dowry), paid by the prospective husband to the woman's family.

The smaller segment of Western-cultured Sierra Leonean females (Krio women) enjoy some autonomy and are not viewed legally as the property of males, but even in this Westernized segment of the population, male attitudes have been very slow to change. Most of these men still perceive themselves as the dominant sex, a perception which colors their interactions with women in that society, whether "native" or "non-native." Sierra Leone society, therefore, practices a clear and all-pervasive gender inequality that shapes the legal and social definitions of intersexual interaction or behavior.

This article delineates the forms of women's victimization and the normative structures that facilitate them in one country in Africa. Sierra Leone is used here as a case study because, like many other countries in Africa, it is characterized by legal pluralism and some degree of cultural heterogeneity. The disparities between the customary law and the general (English) law in Sierra Leone, the various forms of women's victimization in that country, and the solutions applied for maintaining the coexistence of its disparate and contradictory legal systems are explained.

Illicit Sexual Behavior and Rape: Customary vs. General Law

Generally, tribal society views the purpose of sexual relationships as procreation. Marriage is considered important and is the only appropriate framework for accomplishing this aim. The age of marriage is set by reaching puberty. Parents often give away their daughters to suitable men, those able and willing to pay the dowry, at an age as early as nine or ten. Girls in tribal society are therefore viewed as ready and suitable partners for sexual relations at a very young age. Prior to marriage, girls have to be initiated into the "women's secret society." The purpose of initiation is to prepare the young girl for marriage. In the course of this ritual, clitoridectomy (female circumcision) is performed to assure that the girl will be faithful to her future husband.

Illicit or wrongful sexual behavior in customary law includes all sexual relationships that are not within the framework of marriage. In addition, some sexual taboos apply to marital sexual relationships. Thus, in this tribal society any sexual intercourse between a man and a woman outside marriage is a wrongful act, regardless of whether the woman consented to the sexual encounter or whether she was a virgin. In these cases, the violator has to pay compensation to the woman's family. If the woman was a virgin, the quantum of compensation is higher, as it includes what is known as "virgin-money."

For the purpose of resolving issues of illicit sex it is irrelevant that the male offender is the prospective spouse of the victim (which sometimes is the case). Where sexual intercourse takes place between the prospective male spouse and the woman to whom he is engaged to be married before the latter's initiation into membership of the women's secret society, the prospective husband commits a wrong under customary law. In this case, the compensation recoverable will include initiation expenses. Under the customary laws of the Mendes and Temnes, the main tribes of Sierra Leone, members of the victim's family may withhold consent to the marriage. Even in such circumstances, the initiation expenses are not refundable.

A man who has sexual intercourse with a woman to whom he is not married, regardless of whether there was consent on her part, commits a wrong under customary law. Tribe members refer to this violation as "woman-palaver"; in the court terminology the suit is called "woman-damage." If proven, the offender is liable to compensate the husband, or the father if the woman is unmarried, in monetary terms. The phrase "woman-palaver" has a substantive legal meaning analogous to the English-law concept of trespass in that the sexual act itself, which is the basis for the action, constitutes a trespass on, as it were, property not belonging to the offender (Erez and Thompson, 1991). This interpretation is in accord with the customary perception in African societies of a woman being the property of her father or husband (if married) and thereby inheritable in much the same manner as any tangible or personal property (Smart, 1983; Taylor, 1975), hence the notion of "damage" to property.

Certain kinds of marital sexual acts are also wrongful under customary law in Sierra Leone. In customary law, the principle governing marital sex is that a husband has extensive sexual rights over his wife or wives. A customary-law wife may not, therefore, ordinarily refuse to have sex with her husband unless she has a "reasonable cause." The situations that may amount to "reasonable cause" under customary law include the following: (a) serious illness that renders the wife physically incapable of having sexual intercourse; (b) menstruation; (c) suckling a very young child within the prescribed weaning period; (d) having sexual intercourse during the daytime;[2] (e) "having sexual intercourse in the bush" (The land is viewed in the customary tradition as a form of subsistence for the livelihood of the family. It also belongs to the ancestors, the living, and future generations and, as a result, is sacred. Sexual intercourse on farmland is therefore taboo, as it desecrates the value of the land); and (f) having sexual intercourse on a feast day (i.e., the festival of Rahmadan for tribal Muslims) (Smart, 1983:101). However, these categories are not exhaustive.

In such circumstances of "reasonable cause," the question arises whether a husband who forces his wife to submit to sexual intercourse with him commits marital rape. The question is *prima facie* complicated. However, in the context of Sierra Leone customary law, the notion of marital rape is anomalous for two main reasons: the first is that the object of customary-law marriages is the legitimization of sexual intercourse between the parties and the procreation of children; the second is that in the eyes of customary law, a married woman remains the property of her husband for the duration of the marriage. Therefore, in those circumstances a husband cannot properly be held to have violated his own property.

An important legal consequence of guardianship (by husband or any other head of family) is the procedural incapacity of the person under guardianship to sue his or her legal guardian as long as the relationship exists. It is inconceivable, from the perspective of the existing law, that a customary-law wife in Sierra Leone can successfully maintain an action for marital rape against her husband. Apart from certain sociocultural sanctions attached to violations of taboos defined as "reasonable cause," it is unlikely that a customary-law wife will have any legal remedy against a husband who forces her to have sexual intercourse with him in any of the foregoing situations.

Other sexual wrongs under customary law include (a) sexual intercourse between a man and a widow during the period of observance of funeral obsequies of her deceased husband; (b) sexual intercourse between a man and a girl whose initiation into the women's secret society has not been completed; and (c) incestuous sexual relations. With respect to (c) under customary law, the incestuous act constitutes a wrong against the ancestors and is perceived as disturbing the rhythm of social cohesion that binds the family together. The remedy for incestuous behavior takes the form of expiation and ritual sacrifice, which results in the purification of the parties involved. The practice varies from one ethnic group to another. The traditional ceremony involves bathing both the offender and the victim in public and performing a purification ritual. Its purpose is to pacify the ancestral spirits for what is seen as an ignominy or curse on the family. The modern trend, especially in urban areas, is either to bathe the offender and the victim in private or to impose pecuniary or in-kind fines and utilize the money, or whatever is given, to appease the ancestors by way of sacrificial offerings (Smart, 1983:134).

It is significant that in all the cases of wrongful sexual activities under customary law in Sierra Leone, the consent of a female victim to the act does not operate legally or otherwise to exculpate the offender from liability or to mitigate its wrongfulness. For a single woman as property of her parents, and for a married woman as property of her husband, her consent is immaterial and is deemed to be nonexistent since, notionally, women have no such privilege in the customary law.

Under customary law, when it is alleged that illicit sexual intercourse has taken place between a man and a woman, for the purpose of proving the allegation there is always a strong presumption that the victim's complaint is true. In such a tradition there is a belief that a woman should confess a wrongful sexual act or else she will suffer ill fate and misfortune, divinely inflicted. Thus, women feel a compulsion to confess illicit sex and are invariably believed.

Though the presumption about the veracity of women's reporting illicit sex is strong, it is rebuttable, but the burden of rebutting it is on the offender. Where he admits the wrongdoing, his admission operates as a corroboration of the victim's story.

This presumption of guilt of the offender following a confession by a woman contrasts sharply with the approach and procedures for proving the allegation in the prosecution of forcible or statutory rape under the general law in Sierra Leone. In the general law, the burden is on the prosecution to prove every material element of the offense beyond a reasonable doubt. Further, the testimony must be corroborated before the defendant can properly be convicted. Where a defendant is convicted on the uncorroborated testimony of the victim, his conviction will, as a matter of law, be overturned on appeal.

In contrast to the customary law, the general law of Sierra Leone, which embodies the inherited English law, criminalizes forceful sexual intercourse, defines it as rape, and classifies it as a felony. Rape is defined as "having unlawful intercourse with a woman without her consent by force, fear or fraud." The maximum penalty for forcible rape is life imprisonment at the discretion of the court. To constitute rape, there must be a penetration, however slight, but not necessarily ejaculation.

The gist of the common-law offense of rape (forcible rape) is the lack of consent. Situations in which a woman with whom the offender had sex may be viewed as not having consented to the act, such as when sleeping, purposely intoxicated by the offender, unconscious, or mistakenly taking the man as her husband, are also defined as rape. It is no excuse that the woman has first consented, if the act was afterwards done by force or against her will; nor is it a defense that she consented after the fact. It is immaterial that the victim was a common prostitute or the concubine of the defendant, although such facts will weigh with the jury as to the probability of the fact that the act took place with the victim's consent.

The second type of rape under the general law in Sierra Leone is statutory rape. There are two categories of this offense. The first is defined as "unlawfully and carnally knowing and abusing any girl under the age of thirteen, whether with or without her consent." It is a felony punishable with a maximum of fifteen years imprisonment at the discretion of the court. The second is defined as "unlawfully and carnally knowing and abusing any girl under the age of fourteen years, whether with or without her consent." It is a misdemeanor punishable with a term of imprisonment not exceeding two years at the discretion of the court. To constitute statutory rape it is not, as with forcible rape, "necessary to prove the actual emission of seed . . . but the carnal knowledge shall be deemed complete upon proof of penetration only." However, consent of the victim is immaterial, nor is the gist of the offense having sexual intercourse with a virgin, a commonly held misperception among most male offenders charged with statutory rape in Sierra Leone.

Reporting Rape, or Other Sexual Violations, and the Courts

The inferior social position of women in Sierra Leone is generally not challenged by rural tribal women. Most of them acquiesce to their position of inferiority relative to men, and often perceive themselves the same way their male counterparts do, as predominantly objects of sexual gratification.

Because women in the tribal society are viewed as property belonging to the head of the family, coupled with the tendency to believe women who allege that they have had sexual relations with a man, whether willingly or forcibly, the vast majority of cases of illicit sex (with or without consent) are resolved informally (*en famille*). The most common approach to resolving the issue when the victim is a young girl is for the representative of the girl's family to complain to the man involved and to negotiate the appropriate pecuniary compensation for the act. If the girl was a virgin, her family will often demand that the man marry her to legitimize the sexual act, and to spare them the shame and burden of marrying off a woman who is not a virgin. In cases where an informal agreement cannot be reached, the family invokes jurisdiction of the customary law court, a body well-versed in the customs and beliefs of the indigenous group and therefore preferred, particularly when lack of consent on the part of the victim is not an issue. When this court (which does not recognize the notion of rape) does not succeed in settling the case satisfactorily (i.e., set the appropriate compensation or convince the man to marry the woman), and when lack of consent is an issue or the victim is under age, the family may report the case to the police and initiate the criminal process in a general law court. Because in the general law forcible rape is punished by a life sentence and statutory rape by fifteen years in prison for felony and two years imprisonment for misdemeanor, a threat of complaint to the general law court is an incentive to settle a case of forcible sexual encounter out of court *en famille*. The general law thus operates as a deterrent and forces conformity to the customary law.

The occurrence of sexual encounters depends on the offender defining a situation as appropriate and in a suitable location, away from public view. For instance, in one case tried before the general court, the victim had gone to fetch water from a stream in a nearby bush. The defendant was there at the time, felling trees and cutting them into pieces of wood. When he saw the victim, he asked her to assist him in carrying some of the wood into the town, and when she got close to him, the offender grabbed her and threw her onto the ground. He then forcibly had sexual intercourse with her. There was evidence that at the time of the incident the victim was not a virgin. The court was also told that efforts to resolve the dispute *en famille* failed and that these efforts were at the offender's initiative. The defendant was eventually convicted of statutory rape.

Often, the fact that the offender initiated efforts to settle the matter amicably, out of court, is interpreted as admission of guilt and influences the jury's guilty verdict. This is precisely the object of using such evidence in a rape trial.

The behavior of the woman, or its interpretation by the male who interacts with her, is often not a factor in the decision to rape a woman (particularly when the victim is a young girl). Normal heterosexual intercourse between a man and a woman in the traditional society of Sierra Leone is understood to be an act in which the man overcomes the resistance of a woman. As the standard pose of the traditional woman is reluctance, it is difficult for the man to interpret the woman's behavior as willing or unwilling (see also Sanday, 1981). Due to the perceived superiority of males in this society, women often submit to sexual demands after initial resistance. Consequently, the majority of men believe that overcoming a woman's initial resistance to the act is tantamount to consent. Most men also take the view that if a woman, by words or deeds, invites a man to interact with her or accepts a request for social interaction, she cannot complain of rape.

In one trial before the High Court in Sierra Leone, the offender, a non-native male aged about 43 years, was charged with forcible rape of a young unmarried native female, aged about 19 years. At his trial the offender raised the defense of consent, which the victim denied. The facts were that the victim frequently visited her friend who lived in the same compound as the offender. On one morning, when the victim visited her friend, the defendant asked the friend to make a match between him and the victim. The friend replied that she would if the victim was interested. The victim then conveyed the message that she would prefer being approached on the subject directly. The defendant thereupon invited the victim into his room and she accepted the invitation. After a short conversation, the defendant grabbed her, threw her onto his bed and forcibly raped her. The court was told that the victim not only resisted but also called out to her friend for help and complained to her that the man was raping her. The court was also told that when the friend intervened the defendant quickly released the victim. It was further stated in evidence that the friend questioned the offender about his conduct and that he replied that he was in love with the woman and wanted to marry her. He also implored the woman not to report the rape.

In support of his defense that the woman consented to the act, the defendant argued that the fact that the victim preferred to discuss the subject of becoming lovers directly with him, coupled with her acceptance of the invitation to go into his bedroom, led to only one reasonable inference—that she was not opposed to having sex with him. This argument, however, did not carry any weight under the general law. Nevertheless, this kind of reasoning prevails among the majority of males in the tribal society who view a woman who is interested in interaction as both morally culpable and legally estopped from protesting.

Statutory rape is more common than forcible rape in Sierra Leone. The relatively easy access to girls in an extended family setting results in many statutory rapes. In addition, some customary beliefs provide motives for men to have sexual intercourse with young girls. For instance, one prevailing belief is that an older man's sexuality may be bolstered as a result of sexual intercourse with a young girl. It is also strongly believed that a man who suffers from a venereal disease may be instantaneously cured if he has sexual intercourse with a young virgin.

In a case tried before the High Court of Sierra Leone, a native male aged about 41 years was charged with unlawful carnal knowledge and abuse of a native girl aged about seven years, contrary to Section 6 of Cap. 31 of the Laws of Sierra Leone. The defendant was the boyfriend of the girl's mother, and he visited them regularly at their home. On a certain night when the defendant knew that the girl's mother was away from home on some errand, he came to the house, crawled stealthily into the girl's bed, and forcibly had sex with her. At the time of the incident, the girl was a virgin and the offender was suffering from a venereal disease. He admitted in court that the purpose of the intercourse was to cure his disease. He was found guilty and sentenced to seven years' imprisonment.

Another common perception among native men in Sierra Leone is that if the man is not responsible for the girl's loss of virginity, he has not committed any wrong. In statutory rape cases, raising a defense that the offender was not the girl's first man implies that a girl who is not a virgin, as it is customarily put, already knows "man-palaver," thereby forfeiting any right to complain subsequently of being sexually violated. In effect, the right to complain is believed to be lost with the loss of sexual chastity. The girl's virginity, however, is of no relevance to the general law of statutory rape, which places a premium only on the girl's age.

Being aware of these prevailing beliefs, tribal mothers take special care in monitoring their young daughters' sexual development. Any sign of abnormal behavior is quickly spotted and checked for possible violation. Complaints to the offender soon follow, and negotiations about the remedies begin. Only if the offender refuses to pay the sum requested or rejects demands to marry the girl, who is no longer a virgin, does the case go to the general court. Invoking the law is rare, however, and most cases are resolved informally *en famille*.

The lack of punitive sanctions under customary law for illicit sex, and the deeply entrenched notion that financial compensation undoes these violations, sometimes leads tribal women to use sexual encounters for their own gain. The conception of prostitution or sex for hire, however, is nonexistent in tribal society (although in the western urban part of Sierra Leone, prostitution exists and is prohibited by law). In some cases tried before the general court, the women in question consented to have sexual intercourse with a man but, following the act, insisted that they be paid for it. The cases reached the general court because the parties could not agree on the price. In one case the defendant, a native male, aged about 60 years, was charged with both forcible rape and assault with the intent to ravish a native woman, aged about 22 years. At his trial, he raised the defense of consent to the act. The defendant was a pensioner. During the morning hours he would sit in the veranda of his house and invite female hawkers to sell their goods to him. On a certain day as the complainant, a hawker, was passing along the defendant's house selling peanuts, he hailed her and told her he wanted to buy peanuts. She responded and took her wares to the veranda where he was sitting. The man invited her to the living room and told her he wanted to have sex with her, and she agreed. After the act, the man bought peanuts from her. When she was about to depart, she demanded to be paid for the sex. An argument ensued as to the exact price. No agreement was reached. The woman tried to create an uproar but eventually left and later reported the matter to the police. The jury for various reasons convicted the defendant of assault with intent to ravish rather than rape, finding that the request to the hawker to sell him the peanuts was a pretext for an ulterior purpose.

Wife Sexual Abuse and Rape in Customary and General Law

Marital rape is another recognized form of victimization of women in Western society, (e.g., Walker, 1979). The recent developments in Western countries towards legal recognition of equality within marriage and the resultant reevaluation of the marital rape exemption have led to its abolition in many jurisdictions. Sierra Leone has not followed this trend, even though the country has a permanent machinery for law reform patterned after those found in common-law jurisdictions. The general law courts apply the marital rape exception, thus rendering rape in marriage a non-prosecutable offense. In customary law, the concept of marital rape is a contradiction in terms.

Because a married woman remains the property of her husband for the duration of the marriage under customary law, coupled with the rule that he cannot be held to have violated his own property and that a customary-law marriage is the legitimization of sexual relations, it is inconceivable for a wife to sustain an action for marital rape against her husband in the customary law courts. This is reinforced by the procedural rule that a customary-law wife cannot sue her husband (her legal guardian) as long as the marriage subsists.

Marital rape per se is not one of those sexual wrongs which customary law proscribes (Erez and Thompson, 1991). Customary law grants a husband extensive sexual rights over his wife or wives; the wife's lack of consent to the sexual act is immaterial. The operative principle is that a customary-law wife may not ordinarily refuse to have sex with her husband unless she has a "reasonable cause." The notion of "reasonable cause" imports some restrictions into the doctrine of absolute marital sexual rights of a husband. Violations of these restrictions on sex, however, do not amount to marital rape, as they do not address the issue of a wife's consent. In customary law, the woman's consent (whether she is single or married) is never required for sexual relationships (Erez and Thompson, 1991). Possible sanctions for such wrongful sexual acts may be in the form of pecuniary reparation to the wife's family.

In contrast, the general law recognizes rape as a crime. The gist of the common-law offense of forcible rape (as contrasted with statutory rape, which is sexual intercourse with a minor) is the lack of consent. However, where the victim is the wife of the offender, no offense is committed because the general law in Sierra Leone applies the marital rape exception.

The entrenched beliefs in the inherent right of a husband to his wife's sexual relations among members of the Sierra Leone tribal society, and the marital rape exception applied in the general law, have resulted in the reality whereby forced sexual conduct by a husband against his wife or wives is neither defined as an offense nor redressed in either court system. Statistics about the extent of the phenomenon are not available, but as sexual relations with one's wife are perceived as an absolute right of the husband, we surmise that forced sexual relations by husbands are quite common.

Another form of wife abuse which is sex related is the converse situation of the forced sexual conduct, namely sexual neglect. On occasion, a particular wife may become jealous, thinking that the husband pays much more attention to another wife or wives than to herself. The amount of relative sexual attention then becomes a source of perceived abuse. A neglected wife may ask the husband to provide her fair share of his sexual attention, and if he persists in his avoidance she will ask whether he no longer wants her as a wife. Because a customary-law marriage is viewed as the legitimization of sexual intercourse whose main purpose is the procreation of children, a married tribal woman who does not bear children will feel ashamed, unwanted, and unfulfilled—all of which are perceived as abuse. The community also frowns upon infertility (male and female). Avoidance of sex may thus result in embarrassment and accusation of infertility. A wife who is sexually neglected may become an object of scorn by the other wives and the family. Persistence in avoiding sexual contact with a particular wife may become a ground for the wife requesting a divorce.

Wife Physical Maltreatment in Customary Law: Discipline or Wife Abuse?

Consistent with the tribal perception in Sierra Leone of women as property belonging to the head of the family and, in the case of married women, to their husbands, the notion of spouse abuse is alien to tribal culture. As a rule, neither physical nor sexual abuse of wives by their husbands is viewed negatively by tribal members. Apart from homicide, the physical handling of wives in tribal communities is viewed as the prerogative of the husband. Under customary law, a husband has the right to administer "reasonable chastisement" to his wife for her misconduct. Justifications for exercising this right include a wife's disrespect for her husband, dereliction of domestic duties, flirting with other men, and adultery (Smart, 1983:108).

Tribal wives are expected to obey their husbands. A wife may not question a husband's command, nor talk back or be disrespectful to him or his family. In the tribal community respect is visually signified—wives always stoop down when they serve their husbands meals and are expected to leave the room if they are ordered to do so. Respect and obedience are expected in public as well as in the privacy of the home.

In a polygamous society, respect due to the husband is also extended to a senior wife. As husbands are not always present to supervise their household, seniority is highly important in the hierarchical structure of the polygamous marriage. Although husbands maintain complete control of the family at all times, they may delegate certain responsibilities to the senior wife. Junior wives are expected to obey her in the same way as they obey their husbands.

Dereliction of domestic duties, including those toward the husband's offspring, is one ground for chastisement. Thus, not serving meals on time, not having the food ready when the husband returns home, keeping the home untidy or unclean, and serving meals or drinks in unwashed utensils may result in physical chastisement. If a wife is believed to handle or discipline the children in an unreasonable way, or if she has taken the liberty to perform duties or exercise rights without prior approval, she may be verbally reprimanded or physically disciplined. If she neglects the children, fails to provide food or clothing for them, is suspected of not taking proper care of a sick child, or is blamed for the death of a child (as an agent of witchcraft) she can be chastised. In this last case, she may be severely punished or even ostracized. Likewise, if she comes home late, has unaccounted time in her absence, is dressed improperly, or has behaved otherwise in a manner that causes disgrace to the family (such as drinking in public), she can be physically disciplined.

Flirting with other men and adultery are major grounds for physical chastisement. If a wife is not at home when her husband expects her, or if he suspects unfaithfulness, she may receive a severe beating. The husband may also force her by physical means "to call name"—to divulge the name of the partner to the adultery. With the identity of the partner disclosed, the husband or other family members may request him to make reparation for the violation (Erez and Thompson, 1991). Interestingly, a polygamous husband also physically may abuse a wife who is jealous because he shows more affection for another wife or because he is believed to be having an extramarital affair and the wife confronts him with such an allegation.

"Reasonable chastisement" under customary law includes ostracizing a wife until she begs her husband to accept her, and beating her, though not to the extent of wounding her (Smart, 1983:108). "Reasonable chastise-ment" does not include beating a wife in public, although customary rules vary from tribe to tribe. The predominant customary-law view is that when a husband beats his wife in a public place he may be liable to pay a fine to the elders, as such conduct is treated as constituting a breach of the peace. Customary law also frowns upon beating one's wife in the home with the doors locked. The reason is that if the wife screams, no one could enter the house to rescue her. Such behavior is perceived as evidence of an intent to endanger her life (Smart, 1983:109). Such violations also may result in the imposition of a fine on the husband by the elders. Apart from these exceptions, the physical handling of a wife in customary law does not war-rant any sanctioning of the husband. Customary law does not prohibit physical abuse as long as it is administered within certain parameters.

As a general rule, tribal husbands will not apologize to their wives for their violent behavior. Native men view it as condescending to apologize to a wife. If the husband feels he needs to diffuse the tension that may have resulted from the beating or to placate a wife whom he has disciplined, he may pay her sexual attention. The sexual act is supposed to wipe out any insult inflicted by the beating.

In polygamous societies, physical maltreatment may take forms other than beating. In fact, polygamy has a high potential of generating various types of abuse. In a tribal agrarian community the wife shares the agricul-tural labor; she often works in farms. A wife who has fallen out of favor may be required to work harder and more often than other wives. She may also be required to perform certain manual tasks by a senior wife who may be jealous of her as a new and younger wife. Disparity in ages of wives, which may be one reason for jealousy, is often large: a senior wife may be 60 years old and a junior wife only 15. A husband who ignores such abuse may be vicariously responsible. If affection on the part of the husband for the junior wife has waned, he may turn a blind eye to it.

Generally, the tribal polygamous setting is one of rivalry and competition among the wives for the husband's affection and attention. When a husband shows more affection to a junior wife, who is then subjected to abuse by a senior wife, sympathy from other wives for a mistreated wife is rare. In some circumstances, however, a young wife may empathize with another young wife who is abused, particularly when the husband is much older than both of them and they were not willing parties to their marriages. Most tribal marriages are arranged by the families, and the women have no say in them.

Abuse in the form of neglect, or denial of protection from other wives, may also extend to the wife's children and their welfare. When means are sparse, favoritism may be one mode of coping with meager resources and may be unintentionally abusive. It can also be purposeful but, whether intentional or not, it is perceived as abuse by the wife who feels left out. The control over resources further highlights the husband's power within the polygamous setting and the wife's powerlessness and vulnerability to male control.

An extreme form of spouse abuse in tribal culture is the killing of a woman for ritualistic sacrifice. Being killed for sacrificial purposes, however, is not restricted to women—single or married. Minors, too, can be killed for sacrifice. Generally, such killings do not involve men as victims. The victimization of women in sacrificial killings is another manifestation of their inferior status and their being considered property of the head of the household, or, in the case of married women, their husbands.

In one famous case tried before the High Court (general law court), a leading politician contracted with an illiterate farmer to purchase the farmer's six-months-pregnant wife for the purpose of ritualistic sacrifice. On the scheduled date and place, the farmer handed over his wife to the politician in the presence of her brother. They all pinned the woman down to the ground, bound her hands and feet, and stuffed her mouth with clothing. The politician then took out a knife and ripped open the woman's abdomen and removed the baby and vital organs from her body, while the others held her firmly to the ground. A palm-wine tapper who was watching them from the top of a palm tree informed the police about the killing. The husband and the woman's brother were arrested and charged with murder and conspiracy to murder. The initial assumption of the police was that it was a case of an unfaithful wife having been killed by her enraged husband out of passion. Once the circumstances of the murder and the involvement of the politician were disclosed in the trial, the husband and the brother were convicted by the High Court and were sentenced to death. The politician was then arrested and charged with murder, and the condemned husband was the key prosecution witness at his trial. The husband stated in court that the politician told him he needed certain vital human parts to perform a ritualistic sacrifice as he was aspiring to become prime minister of Sierra Leone. The politician was also convicted and sentenced to death. All three participants were executed.

Wife Physical Maltreatment in the General (English) Law

In contrast to customary law, the general (English) law criminalizes beating and physical maltreatment of one's wife. Physical abuse of a wife comes under the general category of offenses against the person; specifically, common assault, assault and battery, assault occasioning actual bodily harm or causing grievous bodily harm, attempted murder, and murder, depending on the nature and extent of the injuries inflicted. The penalties for these forms of assault vary from one year imprisonment to a life sentence. Murder carries the penalty of death.

In the general law courts, a problem of proof in the prosecution of spouse-abuse cases stems from the evidentiary rule that the spouse (male or female) of a person charged with a criminal offense is neither a competent nor a compellable witness in the prosecution of the accused spouse (Thompson, 1989). This rule, originally applicable only to monogamous marriages in the common law, has been extended in statutory form to both monogamous and Muslim (polygamous) marriages in Sierra Leone.

Another legal technicality that has hindered meaningful intervention by the general courts in domestic-violence disputes is the interpretation of "grievous bodily harm." The prevailing judicial view is that the phrase means serious bodily injury. This phrase excludes kindred notions of harm to mental health or emotional and psychological trauma—conditions which usually accompany physical spouse abuse. Such a narrow interpretation of the phrase "grievous bodily harm" has resulted in police and prosecution screening out domestic-violence cases in which the female spouse has suffered serious mental, emotional, and psychological harm from repeated physical abuse of a nongrievous nature.

Another illustration of the judicial restrictive application of the assault laws to domestic violence cases is the legal interpretation of the meaning of "wound." Here, too, the general law courts have limited the meaning of the word to "incised wounds," "contused wounds," "punctured wounds," "lacerated wounds," or "gunshot wounds" which cause a break in the continuity of the skin. Taking into account the various ways in which bodily harm can be inflicted, this categorization is underinclusive. In the context of domestic violence in particular, such interpretation may exclude many injuries which are not marked by any break in the continuity of the skin.

Reporting and Responding to Wife Abuse

Perusal of court cases of the general-law jurisdiction reported between 1920 and 1973 (the last time judicial decisions were published in report form in Sierra Leone) reveals no record of any case involving domestic violence, short of homicide. Homicide is a common reaction to allegations of infidelity, particularly when the wife is suspected to be pregnant as a result of the adultery. As one defendant in a spousal murder case explained, if the child of the adulterous relationship was born, the offspring would be a constant reminder to the husband of his wife's sexual infidelity.

Reported court cases, however, are no indication of the extent and pervasiveness of the problem. The technical difficulties occasioned by the general law in relation to the criminalization of domestic-violence offenders and the inability to compel the abused spouse to testify obviously have led to a negligible rate of reporting and prosecuting spouse-abuse cases. Yet, we submit that wife battering, short of homicide, is pervasive and widespread in Sierra Leone, and that it often involves the infliction of grievous bodily harm by husbands on their wives. Several divorce cases adjudicated by the second author in the High Court of Sierra Leone disclosed extensive physical abuse and cruelty which became the ground for dissolution of the marriage.

Given the strongly held beliefs about the inferior status of women among both tribal and Krio communities, women rarely perceive physical maltreatment as a prosecutable offense, nor would they seek redress for abuse by reporting it to the police. In tribal culture, physical chastisement is often perceived as a measure of affection; external manifestation of affection (such as holding hands, kissing, or hugging) is perceived as licentiousness or sexual permissiveness. A husband who spares the rod is viewed as someone who does not care for his wife. This is true particularly in cases of adultery—if a husband who discovers adultery does not react violently to it, he is assumed not to love or value his wife.

The perception of women as property, who may be subjected to chastisement if need be, is also deeply entrenched among members of the police force in Sierra Leone, most of whom come from the tribal communities. The overwhelming majority of police officers subscribe to the customary-law view about the inferior status of women and will therefore not view the maltreatment of women as socially intolerable, criminal, or as warranting the intervention of the criminal justice system.

The effective remedy for abuse under the general (English) law for non-natives in Sierra Leone is a divorce. Under civil law, a spouse of a monogamous marriage can obtain a divorce on certain statutory grounds, including cruelty and constructive desertion. Physical cruelty is synonymous with physical maltreatment. In Sierra Leone law, cruelty is defined as "conduct of such a character as to have caused danger to life, limb or health, bodily or mental, or a reasonable apprehension of it." Constructive desertion occurs where one spouse, due to a grave abusive conduct on the part of the other, is compelled to withdraw from cohabitation. Yet, these are much broader concepts than the "grievous bodily harm" notion under the criminal law. The general law recognizes that grave marital misconduct undermines the marriage and should therefore entitle the innocent spouse to petition for its dissolution. As a ground for divorce, cruelty may involve one act which by itself is so grievous as to constitute cruelty or the accumulation of continued acts of ill-usage, none of which alone is sufficient to support a charge but which when taken together may constitute cruelty. Several cases adjudicated by the second author in the general court indicated that physical abuse, which took the form of beating, kicking, pushing, and shoving, and which sometimes occurred when the woman was pregnant, was the ground for divorce.

In customary law, it is rare for wives to challenge the husband's right to chastisement when victimized by physical maltreatment, nor as a rule would they question its reasonableness. In the exceptional case where a wife feels she has been either excessively or improperly chastised, she may complain to her parents or family, who may apply their judgment as to the "reasonableness" of the physical abuse. If they find it was excessive, the husband may be asked to make some reparation. Physical maltreatment per se is not a ground for divorce in customary law.

Other Forms of Female Victimization

The subordinate and submissive status of women in Sierra Leone, particularly within the tribal culture, produces other related forms of female victimization in Sierra Leone. They include female circumcision, incest or sexual abuse, child marriage, and child labor.[3]

The fact that a "native" woman in Sierra Leone is deemed to be the property of some man (father, husband, or some other male head of the family) has one other far-reaching implication for a woman's interpersonal and sexual relations and rights: if she is unmarried, the father or some other male head of the family or guardian has responsibility for preparing her for marriage. In this regard, her legal guardian may not be criminally liable for any form of abuse, short of homicide, to which he may subject her, so long as the act in question is regarded as a social custom approved by customary law. One important social custom in point practiced in Sierra Leone is female circumcision (Thompson and Thompson, 1993:37). Generally, the phrase "female circumcision" refers to an operation involving physical damage to the female sexual and/or reproductive organs, or clitoridectomy—the removal of part or all of the clitoris as well as part or all of the labia minora.

Assaad (1980:6) has observed that "in societies where women's and men's roles are clearly delineated, where marriage is seen as an economic necessity, and where a woman derives her value from her family role of wife and mother, childbirth is of the utmost importance." In Sierra Leone tribal culture, marriage enhances a woman's social and economic status, and childbirth is the fulfilling experience of marriage. Therefore, a strong social stigma is attached to women who are either unmarried or infertile, or both. Female circumcision is considered a prerequisite for marriage and childbearing and a core requirement of customary family law.

It is difficult to estimate the size of the problem because there are no documented statistics on the number of adult females and girls circumcised at any given period of time. The only study ever undertaken on the subject is that by Fran P. Hosken (1980). Based on field research in Africa, interviews with medical personnel and midwives, and government information, Hosken estimated that 80 percent of the females in Sierra Leone have been circumcised. This proportion translates into 1.40 million females, assuming the female population of Sierra Leone to be 1.75 million out of a total population of 3.5 million as of 1982. Taking into account the rapid population growth rate of Africa, Kouba and Muasher (1985:100) maintain that the number of women and female children subjected to female circumcision in Africa is indeed significant, and prevalent among the majority of tribal women in Sierra Leone.

Among the group of Westernized females in Sierra Leone (Krio or Creole women), who enjoy a measure of autonomy and are not viewed culturally or legally as the property of males, female circumcision is rare. Circumcision is not perceived by this group as a cultural imperative for marriage and childbearing, nor is it a general-law, normative prescription for marriage. The inherited general-law system, however, has no special penal legislation proscribing female circumcision; nor is there any particular statute criminalizing the activities of the secret institution that practices it. Under the general law it is unlawful to assault, inflict physical harm, or cause the death of another person.

Under the existing general law, where an initiate dies during a female circumcision operation or as a result of it, those who performed the operation may be guilty of manslaughter. Where an initiate sustains serious bodily injury in consequence of the operation, the person who performed it may be criminally liable for causing grievous bodily harm, or assault occasioning actual bodily harm. Instructively, in the only known contemporary case ever brought before the High (then Supreme) Court of Sierra Leone on the subject of female circumcision, the chief female elder and head of the local "Bundo Society" (the secret society responsible for performing the operation) was tried for murder following the deaths of two initiates during the operation. She was convicted of the lesser offense of manslaughter and sentenced to five years imprisonment. Despite numerous injuries or fatalities resulting from this widespread practice, no further criminal prosecutions under the general-law system have been initiated. The law's response to the practice of female circumcision in Sierra Leone is thus one of apathy, indifference, or acquiescence.

Female circumcision may be perceived as a form of victimization akin to child abuse or spousal abuse. It is a deeply entrenched cultural practice which defies any attempt to apply notions of personal autonomy for females. In Sierra Leone, as in other African societies, it highlights the constant conflict between the modernization process and the traditional way of life, and the significance of the cultural context for perceiving a social custom as abusive.

Another form of female victimization in Sierra Leone is incest. Incest is neither documented nor a publicized problem in Sierra Leone. No official or unofficial statistics on the incidence of incest are available in the country. In the tribal society, the minimal publicity it receives is usually in the form of rumors. Alleged cases of incest either go unreported or are settled *en famille*; they do not attract the general law's intervention because of difficulties of proof resulting from the aura of secrecy that usually surrounds the incestuous relationship. In the Westernized segment of the Sierra Leone population, whenever it is rumored or alleged that incest occurred in a family, the influence, status, and prestige enjoyed by the family would often militate against the disclosure of the alleged incident or its reporting to the police. The known cases, based on rumor, reveal a continuing pattern of abuse rather than a single, isolated incident, as often is the case with incest.

Incestuous relationships are prohibited by both customary law and general law. Even though under the former law a parent (or guardian) cannot commit an offense against his own child, based on the customary-law doctrine that offspring of customary-law marriages are the property of their parents or legal guardians, parents nonetheless are prohibited from engaging in incestuous relationships with their children. Smart (1983) asserts that incest between a parent and a child that occurs when the parents are not married to each other is regarded as more serious than incest which occurs when they are within the marriage bond, but in the former case the offenders are seldom punished. According to Smart (1983:179), however, "it is generally believed that the violators will die." In effect, despite the customary-law prohibition against incest, it does not attract any penal sanction.

Under the general (English) law, incest is a common-law offense. Incest is committed when a man has sexual intercourse with a woman whom he knows to be his granddaughter, daughter, sister, or mother, with or by her consent (Butler and Garcia, 1966:1084). As the general law recognizes consent by women as necessary for legal sexual relationships, it is also incest for a woman to have sexual intercourse with a man whom she knows to be her grandfather, father, brother, or son, with or by his consent (Butler and Garcia, 1966:1085). Incest is a felony punishable with a maximum term of imprisonment for life if committed against a female child under the age of 13 years, and a maximum of seven years imprisonment if committed against a female of 13 years of age and upward (Butler and Garcia, 1966:1519). Police or court records, however, disclose no alleged incest cases in Sierra Leone in recent times.

Child marriage may be regarded as another form of abusive behavior toward girls. The harmful effects of child marriage have been long recognized. Oyebanji (1981) has argued that "it is wrong that the burden of performing the role of a wife, which includes sexual intercourse and childbirth, should be imposed on a child who is both mentally and physically unprepared for it" (p. 151). He emphasizes that this could shorten the child's life expectancy.

Although most Western cultures legislate against child marriage, Uzodike (1990:88) has recently pointed out that in Nigeria, girls as young as eleven years are given away in marriage, sometimes to men who are old enough to be their grandfathers. The same is true of Sierra Leone, where child marriage is permissible under customary law. Consequently, parents often give away their daughters to suitable men, those able and willing to pay the dowry, at as early an age as nine or ten (Erez and Thompson, 1991:203). In spite of the fact that the Prevention of Cruelty to Children Act (a general-law statute) punishes carnal knowledge of a girl (under the age of 13 years as a felony, under the age of 14 years as a misdemeanor), it is not unlawful to have sexual relations in the context of child marriage, between a man and a girl to whom he is married.

This statute law approbates and reprobates at the same time: on the one hand, it seeks to protect children under 14 years; on the other hand, it denies such protection by recognizing child marriages. It should also be noted that both the prevailing customary law and the exception to the general-law prohibition contravene international agreements to which most African countries, Sierra Leone included, are parties: the United Nations Convention on the Rights of the Child (1989) and, more specifically, the African Charter on the Rights and Welfare of the Child. The latter expressly (Articles 21 and 27) prohibits child marriage as a harmful social and cultural practice. At the national level, the Christian Marriage Act (1960) and the Civil Marriage Act (1960) of Sierra Leone prescribe 18 years as the minimum age at which "a person whose personal law is customary" can contract a marriage under both acts without parental consent. By contrast, the acts stipulate 21 years as the minimum age at which a person whose personal law is not customary can contract a marriage without parental consent. Under customary law, a female cannot validly contract a marriage until she has attained puberty. This means that a female whose personal law is customary law can marry in the customary manner much below the age of 18 years if she has attained puberty (Thompson, 1989:395). Although statistics are hard to come by, it is common knowledge that child marriages in Sierra Leone are performed on a large scale.

Child labor is another form of female abuse in Sierra Leone. Article 15 of the African Charter on the Rights and Welfare of the Child proscribes child labor by protecting children "from all forms of economic exploitation and from performing any work that is likely to be hazardous or to interfere with the children's physical, mental, spiritual, moral or social development." Obikeze (1986:39) states that child labor may be "exploitative and abusive or nonexploitative and societally approvable." Exploitative labor is defined by Rodgers and Standing (1984) as the engagement on a regular basis of a child in some productive or income-yielding activities for which the "primary beneficiaries are persons other than themselves." According to Uzodike (1990:89), exploitative child labor as distinct from nonexploitative child labor is abusive.

Despite Sierra Leone's contractual obligation under the African Charter on the Rights and Welfare of the Child, the country abounds in exploitative child labor. Child labor exists on a wide scale in three main areas: street-trading and hawking, work on farms, and work as domestic servants or maids (in the last case, especially for middle-class urban dwellers). A substantial number of child street-traders and hawkers are females, aged between 7 and 15 years. Most of them work daily from early morning to late evening. In tribal society, there is a perception that girls' formal education is superfluous. As girls are expected to become wives and mothers, formal education remains a male privilege only. Girls, particularly from socially disadvantaged and economically deprived backgrounds, are also expected to contribute their available time to help the family economy. This expectation translates to hours of work by young girls. The problem of child labor, which largely affects females, has not been defined as exploitative or abusive and so far has not attracted the concern of officials or agencies in Sierra Leone, despite the government's official commitment to protect children from all forms of economic exploitation and hazardous tasks. Like female circumcision and child marriage, child labor in Africa raises the sensitive issue of cultural relativism. In light of Africa's prevailing socioeconomic conditions, generated by seemingly intractable problems of development, it may not be easily dismissed as irrelevant or untenable.

Conclusions

The inferior status of women in African countries such as Sierra Leone, particularly among the tribal society subscribing to customary law, results in various forms of female victimization: rape and sexual assaults, wife sexual and physical abuse, clitoridectomy, child marriage, and child labor. These practices are viewed as male normative prerogative, female obligation, or expected duties as daughters, wives, or mothers.

The deeply entrenched beliefs in male superiority and men's divine privileges vis à vis women have rendered attempts to apply Western standards to the treatment of women futile. The general (English) law, with its conception of women's autonomy and independence, is regarded as external "white-man law." It has been at best ignored, or at worst used as a weapon to enforce the indigenous customary law. The conflict between the sexes in African society is not likely to be eased so long as the balance between its dual legal systems tilts heavily in favor of the traditional customary-law beliefs about women's inferiority.

Notes

[1] Physical abuse of both male and female children is also common in Sierra Leone because in tribal African society, children are regarded as the property of their parents. Parental authority is perceived in almost absolute and exclusive terms. However, the conception of

children as property and consequently their vulnerability to physical abuse is similar for boys and girls; sexual abuse of girls is an added form of abuse typical to girls only.

[2] This prohibition attempts to protect young children and other members of the extended family from seeing the private parts of parents or family members. Sexual intercourse in customary tradition has to be a private, almost secretive act between the parties.

[3] A recent report published by the World Health Organization estimates the number of such victimizations in Africa and Asia in the millions.

Bibliography

Assaad, Marie B. (1980). "Female Circumcision in Egypt: Social Implications, Current Research and Prospects for Change." *Studies in Family Planning* 11: 3–16.

Butler, R. F., and M. Garcia (eds.) (1966). Archbold Pleading, *Evidence and Practice in Criminal Cases*, 36th ed. London: Sweet and Maxwell.

Dobash, R. E., and R. P. Dobash (1992). *Women, Violence and Social Change*. London: Routlegge.

Erez, E., and R. B. Thompson (1991). "Rape in Sierra Leone: Conflict Between the Sexes and Conflict of Laws." *International Journal of Comparative and Applied Criminal Justice* 14: 201–10.

Harrel-Bond, B., and U. Rijinsdrop (1974). *Family Law in Sierra Leone: A Research Report*. Leiden, Netherlands: Africa Studicentrum.

Hazou, W. (1990). *The Social and Legal Status of Women: A Global Perspective*. New York: Praeger Publishers.

Hommes, Regina W. (1978). "The Measurement of the Status of Women." In Marry Niphius-Nel (ed.), *Demographic Aspects of the Changing Status of Women in Europe*. Hinghan, MA: Kluwer Boston.

Hosken, Fran P. (1980). "Female Sexual Mutilations: The Facts and Proposals for Action." Lexington, MA: *Women's International Network News*.

Kouba, Leonard J., and Judith Muasher (1985). "Female Circumcision in Africa: An Overview." *African Studies Review* 28: 95–110.

Obikeze, D. S. (1986). "Agricultural Child Labor in Nigeria—A Case Study of Anambra State." In *Child Labor in Africa*. Enugu, Nigeria: (ANPPCAN Publications) Chuka Printing Company.

Oyebanji, M. B. (1981). "Proposals for Reform of Marriage Laws in Nigeria." In T. A. Agenda (ed.), *The Marriage Laws of Nigeria*. Nigeria: The Nigerian Institute of Advanced Legal Studies.

Palmer, Craig (1989). "Is Rape a Cultural Universal? A Re-Examination of the Ethnological Data." *Ethnology* 28: 1–16.

Rodgers, G., and G. R. Standing (eds.) (1981). *Child Work, Poverty and Underdeveloped Countries*. Geneva: ILO.

Sanday, Peggy Reeves (1981). "The Socio-Cultural Context of Rape: A Cross-Cultural Study." *Journal of Social Issues* 37 (4): 5–27.

Smart, H. M. (1983). *Sierra Leone Customary Family Law*. Freetown, Sierra Leone: Fourah Bay College Bookshop.

Taylor, O. P. (1975). "The Position of Women Under Sierra Leone Customary Law." In T. O. Elias, S. N. Nwabara, and C. O. Akpamgbo (eds.), *African Indigenous Law* (pp. 195–231). N. Nsukka, Nigeria: Institute of African Studies, University of Nigeria.

Thompson, R. Bankole (1989). "Internal Conflicts in Marriage and Inheritance Laws in Sierra Leone: Some Anachronisms." *African Journal of International and Comparative Law* 1: 392–406.

———— (1990). "Child Abuse in Sierra Leone: Normative Disparities." *International Journal Of Law and the Family* 5: 13–23.

———— (1992). "Africa's Charter on Children's Rights: A Normative Break with Cultural Traditionalism." *International and Comparative Law Quarterly* 41: 423–44.

Thompson, R. Bankole, and Adiatu Thompson (1993). "Female Circumcision in Sierra Leone: Medico-Legal Perspectives." *World Medical Journal* 39: 36–43.

Uzodike, Eunice (1990). "Child Abuse and Neglect in Nigeria-Socio-Legal Aspects." *International Journal of Law and the Family* 4: 83–96.

Walker, L. E. (1979). *The Battered Woman.* New York: Harper and Row.

4

International Terrorism
in Historical Perspective

Jawad L Barghothi

In recent years, much has been written and said about terrorism, especially that of Middle Eastern origin. People throughout the world are asking, Where will it all end? When will it stop? One must recognize that terrorism has become an international affliction. Increasingly, the use of terrorism by groups and governments is being tolerated and even legitimized.

Terrorism in the international arena is not a new phenomenon. Having survived through the centuries, it has manifested itself in many guises, on all parts of the globe. Each successive generation has witnessed some form of terrorism by numerous groups using different strategies and tactics, each claiming a higher purpose, be it political or religious. Yet, all terrorist groups are using violence as a means to achieve their aims. Writings and discourse on terrorism are substantial, and there has been a wealth of research on the subject.

This article reviews some of the existing literature and traces the development of some of the early terrorist movements, as well as more modern incidents of terrorist activity. We will try to determine which era of terrorism, historical or modern, has been the most effective in achieving the professed aims of the various terrorist groups. We will also look at the effect of modern technology, such as the media and improved transportation capabilities, on terrorism and will determine how important these resources are to terrorists. Finally, we will look at the delineation between revolutionary terrorism and state terror.

One of the distinguishing hallmarks of all of the discourse on terrorism seems to be the inherent difficulty in defining terrorism. Writers often invoke the well-known quote, "One man's terrorist is another man's freedom fighter" (Wardlaw, 1982:3). The acts committed by a certain group, while regarded as terroristic by many, are viewed by others as natural and necessary violence needed to reach a legitimate political aim or end.

Prepared especially for *Comparative and International Criminal Justice, 2/E.*

> Thus, for example, the PLO is seen by some nations as a terrorist group having no political legitimacy and using morally unjustifiable methods of violence to achieve unacceptable ends. On the other hand, most nations view the PLO as the legitimate representative of an oppressed people using necessary and justifiable violence to achieve just and inevitable ends. (Wardlaw, 1982:5)

The crux of the matter lies in the fact that the legitimacy of the terror is in the eye of the beholder and therefore may be indistinguishable to the observer or victim of the act.

Terrorist acts and revolutionary insurrections often have been condemned during their promulgation, only to be praised or legitimized later in history. For example, the state of Israel was born out of terrorism against Great Britain and the people of Palestine, yet now Israel is viewed as a legitimate sovereign state, despite the fact that its violence was widely condemned during its occurrence. Instances such as this are common throughout history. In the final analysis, acts of terrorism will continue to be rationalized and legitimized by those initiating the terror and condemned as irrational and illegitimate by the victims. The right or wrong of acts of terrorism is simply a matter of personal preference and will likely continue to be so in the future.

Another common problem encountered in the study of terrorism is the distinction between terrorism conducted by the state, such as the bombing of the Greenpeace ship by France, and terrorism conducted by individuals or groups against the state. "A particularly thorny problem in all the major contributions to the literature on terrorism has been the relationship between terrorism by factions and state acts of terror" (Wilkinson, 1981:467). Many scholars fail, or do not wish, to make a distinction between the two. They say that terrorism is terrorism, regardless of who initiates the terror. Others take the view that actions taken by the state are justifiable on the grounds of "law and order" and are a reaction to terrorism conducted against the state. We take the view that a clear delineation between the two can and should be made, and we will make this distinction later in this article.

Before looking at its history we need to define terrorism, to set a framework within which we can place terrorist acts. Terrorism can be defined as any act or threat of violence conducted against a civilian population, whether undertaken by a state or by a group against a state, with the purpose of creating fear and anxiety in the hearts of the civilian population. Although by no means a perfect definition, it does serve to provide a framework that encompasses acts of terrorism both by states and against states.

Historical Terrorism

Throughout the remainder of this discussion, we will refer to incidents of terrorism as being either historical (occurring before the twentieth century) or modern (occurring during and after the twentieth century). Most of the violent acts of the historical terrorist groups had religious overtones, founded on the belief that "only a transcendental purpose which fulfills the meaning of the universe can justify terrorism" (Wilkinson, 1981:467). Although some modern terrorist groups also exhibit a religious fervor, seldom are their actions strictly religious (although often cloaked in religious trappings), and more often than not they are politically motivated.

Another striking feature of historical terrorist groups is the length of time these groups were able to sustain themselves. By modern standards, most historical terrorist groups lasted a very long time, usually hundreds of years. Even though they did not have the advantages of modern transportation, communications, and other types of modern technology, they were extremely successful. Many conclude that such modern advantages do not necessarily give modern terrorists an edge. We have selected a number of historical terrorist groups to examine, taking into consideration each group's purpose, strategy, and degree of success, as well as their effect on modern terrorist organizations and movements.

The first historical terrorist group we will look at is the *Sicarii*, "a highly organized religious sect consisting of 'men of lower order' in the Zealot struggle in Palestine (AD 66–73)" (Laqueur, 1978:7). The Sicarii were one of the first documented terrorist groups that actually achieved their stated aims. "By means of provocation they were successful in generating a mass insurrection, an aim of most modern terrorists but one that has probably never been achieved" (Rapoport, 1984:660). By historical standards the Sicarii did not last a relatively long time, but their effect on the Jewish community was enormous, later influencing Menachem Begin and others.

The Sicarii lasted about twenty-five years and strived for maximum publicity in their acts of violence. They not only promulgated violence against the civilian population but also engaged the military if necessary. Sicarii violence was religiously motivated, inspired by hope for a messiah.

> The nature of their messianic doctrines simultaneously suggested the object of terror and permitted methods necessary to achieve it. Jewish apocalyptic prophecies visualize the signs of the imminence of the messiah as a series of massive catastrophes involving whole populations, the upsetting of all moral order to the point of dissolving the laws of nature. (Rapoport, 1984:669)

The Sicarii doctrine used these prophecies to speed the process of mass insurrection:

> In all apocalyptic visions God determines the state of redemption. Still, these visions often contain some conception that humans can speed the process. Prayer, redemption, and martyrdom are the most common methods. When these do not produce results and a period of unimaginable woe is perceived as the precondition of paradise, it will only be

a matter of time before they will act to force history, or bring about that condition. Jewish terrorist activity appeared to have two purposes: to make oppression so intolerable that insurrection was inevitable, and subsequently, to frustrate every attempt to reconcile the respective parties. (Rapoport, 1984:669)

In this fashion the Sicarii, sometimes called the daggermen because they used the dagger to dispense their terror, effectively caused a mass insurrection that engulfed the Jewish community.

Another historical terrorist group appearing on the scene possibly as early as the seventh century were the Thugs. "They intend their victims to experience terror and to express it visibly for the pleasure of Kali, the Hindu goddess of terror and destruction" (Rapoport, 1994:660). Unlike the Sicarii, the Thugs avoided publicity, but they persevered longer (over six hundred years) than any other terrorist group. Like the Sicarii, the Thugs used a particular weapon—the noose—for their acts of terror, and they dismembered the bodies of their victims. They usually preyed on unsuspecting travelers, posing as travelers themselves, then ambushing their newfound "friends."

By modern standards, the Thugs killed many more people than possibly any other terrorist group, with estimates of as many as one million victims. Most modern terrorist groups (with the exception of al Qaeda) have killed a relatively small number of people in comparison, with one hundred victims being a large number. Murder was the main objective of the Thugs, although they did confiscate material goods from the travelers on which they preyed in order to further the organization. Exempt from Thug attacks were certain kinds of travelers, such as women, vagabonds, lepers, and the like, who were seen as descendants of Kali, the Hindu goddess:

> The reinterpretation of a cardinal Hindu myth and theme provided the Thugs with their peculiar purpose and method. Orthodox Hindus believed that in early times a gigantic monster devoured humans as soon as they were created. Kali killed the monster with her sword, but from each drop of blood another demon sprang up, and as she killed each one, the spilled blood continued to generate new demons. The Thugs believed that Kali sought assistance by making two men from her sweat who were given handkerchiefs from her garment in order to strangle the demons, that is, kill them without shedding a drop of blood. The Thug understood that he was obliged to supply the blood that Kali, his creator, required to keep the world in equilibrium. (Rapoport, 1994:662)

In this fashion, the Thugs served Kali by strangling their victims, without shedding a drop of blood. They even felt that they were doing the victims a favor by dispatching them to paradise. The Thugs were able to maintain themselves by acquiring international sanctuary from princes in return for confiscated booty. They were also well versed in deception, getting in the good graces of prominent Indians citizens only to murder them later in the name of Kali. "The paradox is that unlike modern terrorist groups, they did not or could not threaten society for the simple reason that their doctrine made them attack individuals rather than institutions" (Rapoport, 1984:662); yet they existed longer than any other known terrorist group and killed more victims than most modern terrorist groups. "By our standards, the durability of the Thugs is enormous; the IRA, now in its sixth decade, is by far the oldest modern terrorist group" (Rapoport, 1994:665).

The Assassins were another long-lived historical terrorist group who survived two centuries (1090–1275). Their main purpose was religious but also political: to purify and fulfill Islam. "The Assassins developed a distinctive, systematic Gnostic theology which promised a messianic fulfillment of history in a harmonious anarchical condition in which law would be abolished and human nature perfected" (Rapoport, 1984:665). Martyrdom was a large part of the Assassins' doctrine, with the idea that those who become martyrs would be delivered into paradise. In many of their beliefs, this group was a forerunner of present-day terrorists in the Middle East.

The Assassins, like the Thugs and Sicarii, had a particular weapon of terror, in this case the dagger. "Assassin education clearly prepared assailants to seek martyrdom. The word used to designate the assailants— *fedayeen* (consecrated or dedicated ones)—indicates that they were considered religious sacrifices who freed themselves from the guilt of all sins, and thereby gained entry into paradise" (Rapoport, 1984:665). The Assassins were sometimes referred to as "hashish eaters" in reference to the drugging of young disciples, who were made to believe they had experienced paradise:

> The Old Man, according to Marco Polo, used to drug his disciples and transport them while they were asleep to his secret pleasure garden, persuading them when they awoke in it that it was paradise itself. Drugging them again, he would transport them back to the everyday world while they slept. Never afterward did they doubt that their Master could and would reward them with eternal paradise after death if they did his killing for him while they were alive. And so they did do his killing for him. (Fromkin, 1975:698)

The Assassins were one of the only terrorist groups to build their own state, or a loose coalition of city-states, to buttress their organization of terror. "The state provided the means for the creation of an efficient, enduring organization that could and did recover from numerous setbacks" (Rapoport, 1984:666). So, like the Thugs and Sicarii, the Assassins showed a flavor for international terror—terror across state lines. While they did not wreak the havoc of the Sicarii or kill as many as the Thugs, they did threaten a number of governments—namely, those of Persia and modern-day Syria—and maintained themselves for nearly two centuries.

In review, all three of the historical terrorist groups participated in incidents of international terror. Also, each of the three had a specific *raison d'être* involving religion, as well as political purposes in the cases of the

Sicarii and Assassins. All three were extremely successful in their aims, with the Sicarii provoking a mass insurrection, the Thugs lasting for seven centuries, and the Assassins threatening foreign governments. All three would have to be termed extremely successful by modern standards, and without the advantages of modern mass communications and transportation.

Modern Terrorism

The *Narodnaya Volya* was an important modern terrorist movement that operated in Russia between January 1878 and 1881 (Wardlaw, 1982). (Although this group operated in the nineteenth century, for all practical purposes it will be treated as a modern terrorist group.) The Narodnaya Volya was among the first of the early modern terrorist groups to develop a specific policy of terrorism conducted against the state. Terrorism was seen as a way a small group with limited resources could combat the Russian czar while forestalling a mass insurrection, causing much more human suffering than sporadic acts of terrorism. "Terrorism was ethically a better choice than allowing a mass insurrection. If innocent people died as a result of terroristic activity, it had to be accepted as an inevitable consequence of war. It was, however, preferable to the slaughter which would accompany a mass struggle" (Wardlaw, 1982:19).

The Narodnaya Volya only lasted about three years, a short time even by modern standards, but it planted the seeds of later revolutionary struggles. Its support came mainly from the *intelligentsia*. It did not enjoy mass support but provided the impetus for further revolutionary struggle in Russia twenty years later.

Two writers prominent in early modern terrorist thought are worthy of mention. One of these is Nechayev, a Russian revolutionary generally credited with the writing of the *Revolutionary Catechism*, a how-to manual in terrorist strategy and tactics. "The revolution knows only one science: the science of destruction. The object is the same: the prompt destruction of this filthy order" (Rapoport, 1984:675). The Catechism wanted to make terror rational and has influenced almost every modern terrorist organization since then. "Nechayev's work is simply an exercise in technique, suggesting devices for provoking government to savage the people until the latter can bear it no longer" (Rapoport, 1984:675).

Another early writer, the anarchist Michael Bakunin, was concerned with the destruction of the prevailing social order everywhere. According to Bakunin, violence and bloodshed are the only ways to purge society. Bakunin seized upon the phrase, "propaganda by the deed," which is sometimes erroneously credited as his original phrase. Actually, it can be traced back to the Italian, Pisacane. "Simply stated, this concept advocates the necessity for members of the revolutionary vanguard to undertake acts of violence as individual revolutionary statements" (Wardlaw, 1982:21).

Bakunin disagreed with his contemporary, Karl Marx, on many aspects of revolutionary thought. Whereas Marx blamed the ills of society on capitalism, Bakunin placed the blame on the state as a concept. All of these early writers made a contribution to later terrorist thought, but none were extremely successful in achieving their desired aims.

Throughout the twentieth century and into the twenty-first, there have been numerous modern terrorist organizations, all with varying aims, strategies, and techniques. The list is too numerous to catalog here, but some of the better known are the German Red Cells (Baader-Meinhoff Gang), the Italian Red Brigade, and FALN. The one striking feature of almost all these terrorist groups has been their lack of success in achieving their professed aims. Compared with the historical terrorist groups, the modern terrorists' rate of success is rather dismal. In addition, the modern terrorist groups' length of dominance is usually limited to years rather than centuries.

The modern terrorist group also relies highly on the mass media (a subject which will be covered later) and seem to aim for maximum publicity in their acts of terror. We now look at two modern terrorist groups that were successful in achieving their professed aims: the *Irgun Zvai Leumi* and the *Algerian National Liberation Front* (FLN). These two groups were unique in that propagation of terror did indeed become a means to an end, which was ultimately achieved.

The Irgun Zvai Leumi (hereinafter referred to as the Irgun) consisted of about one thousand members who desired Israeli independence for Palestine from the state of Britain. The best known member of that group is, of course, Menachem Begin, who went on to become prime minister of Israel. The strategy of the Irgun was as follows: ". . . attack property interests. This would lead the British to overreact by garrisoning the country with an immense army drawn from stations in other parts of the world" (Fromkin, 1975:687). As the British were already weakened militarily, this would force them to commit scarce reserves of troops until the costs of these actions would tax an already burdened Britain to the breaking point. The strategy was very effective, the British response was just as the Irgun had anticipated, and the intended outcome followed. The British had to pull out, giving the Irgun their independence and their own sovereign state.

The Algerian FLN used terrorist tactics in their struggle for independence against the French colonial regime. They sought to disassociate themselves from the French and convince them that the Algerians were a distinct people, justified in their demand for an independent state. "By itself, terror can accomplish nothing in terms of political goals; it can only aim at obtaining a response that will achieve those goals for it. What the FLN did not demonstrate was the unreality of the claim that there was no distinct Algerian nation" (Fromkin, 1975:689). Through the FLN's campaign of terror, the French government was prompted to be suspicious of any people who were not French. By doing so, the French authorities were shown that the Algerians were a distinct people, completely removed from the French and deserving of their own nation. Again, the strategy was very effective. The French disassociated themselves from the Algerians, and the Algerians obtained their own state.

The successes of these two modern terrorist groups probably do not match that of the historical terrorists, either in effect on the government or ability to maintain themselves for long periods of time. The successes achieved by the Irgun and FLN were in large part due to their use of strategy and tactics, an integral part of any terrorist organization.

Since the events of September 11, 2001, terrorism has taken on a new significance—arguably a whole new dimension. The devastating attacks on U.S. soil that killed an unprecedented amount of victims brought Osama bin Laden to the world's attention as the leader of a terrorist organization calling itself al Qaeda. The goals of this group were stated as

> . . . establishing a pan-Islamic Caliphate throughout the world by working with allied Islamic extremist groups to overthrow regimes it deems "non-Islamic" and expelling Westerners and non-Muslims from Muslim countries . . . saying it was the duty of all Muslims to kill U.S. citizens—civilian or military—and their allies everywhere. (terrorism files, n.d.)

Al Qaeda's headquarters were in Afghanistan, under the patronage of—as opposed to under the direction of—the Taliban (the country's Muslim fundamentalist rulers who harbored bin Laden and his followers). After the 9/11 attacks, although the U.S.-launched war in Afghanistan succeeded in overthrowing the Taliban and dislodging al Qaeda's headquarters there, it did not kill or capture bin Laden. In fact, its actions actually seemed to fuel the fire of this fundamentalist Islamic terrorist movement. Under the banner of *jihad*, al Qaeda was in the unique position of fostering a global terrorism network, united in its hatred of all things Western (particularly the United States).

The subsequent decision by President George W. Bush to invade Iraq as part of the U.S. "war on terror" and to install an interim U.S.-backed government there escalated jihad-based terrorism to an unprecedented level. Islamic terror groups have been increasing in size and number inside Iraq since the U.S.-led invasion in April 2003 (Murphy, 2004). Abu Musab al-Zarqawi, one of the most prominent of the Iraqi insurgency leaders, was rumored in 2004 to have formed an alliance of mutual interests and convenience with Osama bin Laden:

> By combining their resources, Zarqawi and al Qaeda could further amplify their message of total war against the U.S., the Middle Eastern regimes it favors, and Israel, with an expanded Internet reach and ongoing attacks against U.S. and Iraqi forces. (Murphy, 2004)

Via audiotape, bin Laden urged Muslims to attack the United States and any Iraqis that work with the interim arrangements, including voters and election workers. He referred to what he sees as "the third world war," led by the "Crusader Zionist Alliance" against Muslims who, in turn, "have a rare and precious opportunity to get out of the dependency and slavery to the West" (Murphy, 2004). Nearly all the new jihadist groups claim to be receiving inspiration, if not actual leadership, from al-Zarqawi, the suspected al Qaeda operative who the United States believes has masterminded the insurgency's embrace of terrorism (Ware, 2004).

According to *Time* reporter Michael Ware:

> . . . the militants are turning the resistance into an international jihadist movement. Foreign fighters, once estranged from homegrown guerrilla groups, are now integrated as cells or complete units with Iraqis. Many of Saddam's former secret police and Republican Guard officers, who two years ago were drinking and whoring, no longer dare even smoke cigarettes. They are fighting for Allah, they say, and true *jihadis* reject such earthly indulgences. . . . Their goal now, say the militants interviewed, is broader than simply forcing the U.S. to leave. They want to transform Iraq into what Afghanistan was in the 1980s: a training ground for young jihadists who will form the next wave of recruits for al Qaeda and like-minded groups. (2004)

The effectiveness of this newest and most unique group of terrorists still remains to be seen.

Terrorism: Aims and Purposes

While different terrorist groups or organizations use different tactics to achieve their aims, their purposes and strategies seldom deviate greatly. Terrorist groups try to divide the masses of people from the government in power, disorient the public, and instill fear and panic in the hearts and minds of the civilian population. Terrorists want to show the public through their acts of violence that the government is unable to provide for the safety and security of its citizens. It is hoped that the incumbent government will react harshly to the acts of terrorism, responding with increased repression, acts of counterterror, or curtailment of civil liberties. Theoretically, the state will react irrationally, imposing strict controls and harsh measures on the citizens, ultimately showing the true colors of the state. "Whatever their undoubted advantages, liberal democracies are not embodiments of rationality. For one, proper adherence to democratic practices coupled with widespread inequality, suffering, and the anarchy of production might, on other criteria, be thought less than fully rational, if not positively irrational" (Bishop, 1978:55). This is probably the greatest danger confronting democratic states in dealing with acts of terrorism: to guard against becoming repressive in response to acts of terrorism.

Carlos Marighella writes about this strategy of terrorist organizations:

From the moment a large proportion of the population begin to take his activities seriously, his success is assured. The government can only intensify its repression, thus making the life of its citizens harder than ever: homes will be broken into, police searches organized, and innocent people arrested, and communications broken; police terror will become the order of the day, and there will be more and more political murders—in short, a massive political persecution. . . . The political situation of the country will become a military situation. (quoted in Wardlaw, 1982:188)

Another aim in the strategy of terrorism is to receive massive publicity on a worldwide scale. Through modern technology and transportation a terrorist act, if well orchestrated, can draw the attention of the whole world, plead the case of the group, and possibly gain sympathy for their cause. "Terrorism is not simply what terrorists do, but the effect (the publicity, the alarm) they create by their actions" (Jenkins, 1978:119). To achieve maximum publicity, the terrorists must choose the location and timing of the incident carefully. A terrorist incident staged in a developing country would receive far less publicity than in America or Western Europe. Also, actions taken in a developing country would not likely receive maximum media coverage, which many argue is vital for terrorist organizations. The same is true for incidents occurring in the country or rural areas. "Public perceptions of the level of terrorism in the world appear to be determined not by the level of violence but rather by the quality of the incidents, the location, and degree of media coverage" (Jenkins, 1978:119). Utilizing modern transportation capabilities; manipulating such factors as timing, possible media coverage, and publicity; and taking advantage of the increased availability of tools of destruction, a terrorist group can gain concessions or sympathy for its cause.

Not only do terrorists strive to gain publicity for their cause and to disrupt and confuse the government and public, they also hope to get the support of some or all of the people. With this support, the terrorists could cause a general lack of legitimacy of the political system, eroding the political stability of the incumbent government. If the situation gets bad enough, it is then possible for the terrorists to realize the establishment of an alternative political system, the ultimate and seldom-achieved goal of most terrorist organizations.

A final aim in the strategy of terrorism is to try to extract concessions from the government in power. This can be in the form of release of incarcerated terrorist-group members, changes in policy output, or simply the publication of the terrorist group's aims or philosophy. The use of hostages as a bargaining lever creates a dramatic situation, ensuring that the terrorists' demands are noticed and often providing the group with some measure of success.

Many scholars and writers on terrorism are convinced of the enormous effect the media have on terrorist operations. The element of publicity for the terrorist group's cause relies highly on effective use of the media. As one writer put it: "The media are the terrorist's best friend. The terrorist act by itself is nothing; publicity is all" (*Harpers*, 1976:104).

Terrorist groups by their very nature are highly dependent on the mass media to further their cause. The reasons are evident. Terrorist groups are small in nature, usually consisting of very few actual members, and must rely on their organizational abilities. The resources available to terrorists, while sometimes adequate, are still no match for the power and resources of the government they wish to replace or change. The odds are stacked unequally in favor of the state, but the media are the trump card of the terrorist group.

Terrorist groups use the media to achieve two aims:

> First, to enhance the effectiveness of their violence by creating an emotional state of extreme fear in target groups, and thereby, ultimately alter their behavior and dispositions, and bring about a general or particular change in the structure of government or society, and second, to draw forcibly and instantaneously the attention of the whole world to themselves in the expectation that these audiences will be prepared to act or in some cases, to refrain from acting in a manner that will promote the cause they presumably represent. (Knight and Dean, 1982:144)

Terrorists achieve varying degrees of success in these aims, and if the terrorist incident is sufficiently spectacular, chances are the media will aid the terrorist in achieving these aims by publicizing, and in some cases even becoming a participant observer to, the terrorist act itself. The media, usually labeled the manipulators, are manipulated by the terrorists, who receive publicity to promote their aims.

Another major consequence resulting from extensive media coverage of terrorism is the exportation of violent techniques which, in turn, often triggers similar extreme actions by other individuals and groups (Bassiouni, 1982:128). Through the publicity a particular terrorist group might receive, other groups gain valuable knowledge concerning terrorist strategies, methods of attack, and the timing of a particular incident in the hopes of similar success or publicity.

Through the media, terrorists try to incite terror in the public. By constantly living in fear, citizens become increasingly paranoid, demanding either that the terrorists be contained or that their demands be met. According to M. Cherif Bassiouni:

> In terrorism the psychological impact is more media-created than intrinsic to the act. That explains in part the reason for the choice of a given target and the means by which a given act is accomplished: to attract the media's attention and thus insure the dissemination of the act, the message of the perpetrators, and hence the terror-inspiring effect. (quoted in Alexander, 1978:102)

Bassiouni suggests that in order to achieve the desired psychological impact created by the incident, terrorists choose their target, time of action, and strategy with extreme thought and consideration in the hopes of achieving the desired outcome. The decisions of where and how to strike, as well as what type of coverage the act will likely receive, become major considerations of the terrorist group.

Because of their devotion to getting "the whole story," the media are often criticized for giving the terrorist group the impression that they support their actions, creating a climate congenial to further violence (Alexander, 1978:110). By trying to bypass the police or other authorities, media personnel often contact the terrorists directly and, in return for the story (the terrorists' demands and aims, name of the organization, and purpose), publicize the cause of the terrorists. To the terrorist, this comes across as tacit approval of further actions.

One of the first to see the advantages of using the media as a terrorist weapon was Carlos Marighella, who wrote on the subject (1985):

> These actions, carried out with specific and determined objectives, inevitably become propaganda material for the mass communications. The war of nerves or psychological war is an aggressive technique, based on the direct and indirect use of mass means of communication and news transmitted orally in order to demoralize the government. In psychological warfare, the government is always at a disadvantage since it imposes censorship on the mass media and winds up in a defensive position by not allowing anything against it to filter through.

In this fashion, terrorists effectively play the media against the government. The media cry abridgement of freedom of the press or of the public's right to know, and the government finds itself fighting both hostile media and a hostile terrorist group. This "double jeopardy" greatly reduces the government's chances of effectively dealing with acts of terrorism and gives terrorists the feeling that the media are on their side. In addition, it encourages other terrorist groups and organizations to undertake similar acts to publicize their aims.

In the past, some scholars have frowned on the notion that modern conveniences are needed for effective terrorism and have disputed the effects of the media and modern technology. To them, the media, although helpful to the terrorists, are not the key determinants of success for terrorist groups but "rather the purpose and organization of particular groups and the vulnerabilities of particular societies to them are decisive factors" (Rapoport, 1984:672; Wilkinson, 1981:467). According to this view, earlier terrorist groups, without the benefit of modern communication or technology, achieved by their terrorism gains that far surpassed any of the modern terrorist groups. Such groups as the Thugs and Assassins relied on word-of-mouth communications, primitive (but effective) weapons, and limited transportation capabilities; yet they were well organized, dedicated, and successful in achieving their aims. Although this school of thought that plays down the importance of the media may still have its proponents, they are clearly in the minority. Today it is difficult to argue that the media's effect is anything less than sizable.

Notable in the twenty-first-century is an unprecedented increase in the usage of the media by terrorist groups to further their ends. There can no longer be any question that terrorists today find an easily accessed global audience for their messages, both verbal and visual. Several audio and videotaped messages from bin Laden were initially broadcast locally by *al Jazeera* (an Arabic news organization) but were almost immediately given global coverage via the Internet. Iraqi insurgents subsequently made and forwarded to al Jazeera videotapes of gruesome beheadings of Western hostages. Worldwide Internet exposure made certain that these graphic messages of terror hit their targets with devastating accuracy. The Internet and e-mail also enable speedy communication among isolated terrorist cells, facilitating the possibility of a global network of terror. However, a case can still be made that the key determinant of success for terrorist groups may be the purpose and organization of such groups, and particularly the vulnerabilities of the societies in which terrorist acts occur.

Revolutionary Terrorism vs. State Terror

Before closing, one more aspect concerning terrorism should be addressed—that of the distinction between terrorism conducted *against* the state (revolutionary terrorism) and terrorism conducted *by* the state (state terror). As mentioned earlier, there should be a distinction between the two. "It is unreasonable to insist on encompassing analysis of the complex processes and implications of both regimes of terror, and factional terrorism as a mode of struggle within the same covers" (Wilkinson, 1981:467). With this in mind, we have defined both: State terror can be defined as violence undertaken against a civilian population, be it the citizens of that country or of another country. Any actions taken by the state of a violent nature, directed toward civilians of any kind, can be termed state terror (e.g., Saddam Hussein's Iraq). Revolutionary terrorism can be defined as terroristic actions of a violent nature taken against the state or citizens, undertaken by individuals or groups, with the purpose of publicity toward a professed end or cause (e.g., the Iraqi insurgency against the U.S.-backed interim government). If an established regime, such as the United States or the former U.S.S.R., precipitates or aids a group, individual, or other regime in the dissemination of violence against a civilian population, they can be said to be involved in acts of state terror. On the other hand, actions taken by a group of a violent nature, such as acts of violence committed by the Red Brigades or German Red Cells (aimed at destruction of property, government, or human life), would be considered acts of revolutionary terrorism.

Still the question remains: When is terrorism justifiable? The actions of states, under our definition, are fairly obvious: no violence precipitated against innocent civilians by the state is ever justifiable. Only violence in self-defense is acceptable, and only then as a last resort. Acts of revolutionary terrorism are more problematic. When are terrorist acts of this sort justifiable, if ever?

> Some would argue that there are circumstances when it might be morally justifiable as a weapon against tyrannical, oppressive regimes. For example, it is sometimes held that terrorism is the only weapon left to the opponents of such governments, or that the terror of the state "forces" the opposition groups to resort to terrorism in self-defence, or that terrorism is more effective than other forms of struggle and is a "lesser evil" because it may gain victory without costing so many lives. (Wilkinson, 1981:468)

Conversely, others may make the opposite argument. Can the use of terrorism, by definition a means of violence involving the killing of the innocent, ever be morally justifiable? The fact that regimes are frequently guilty of initiating the vicious spiral of terrorism and counterterrorism does not exonerate either side. We are not, as apologists for state terror and factional terrorism often pretend, forced to choose between the torturer and the bomber (Schlesinger, 1981:80).

Ultimately, the justice of a certain act of terror is in the eye of the beholder. "In the public discourse of the West, those who oppose established orders are the terrorists, while state terrorism is a category virtually never employed, unless it refers to the communist bloc" (May, 1974:279). Countries of the former Eastern bloc would claim the above statement a falsehood. They would say that the West is the terrorist, while they themselves are above suspicion. Consequently, the justifiability of a certain act eludes implicit identification and will likely continue to be a thorn in the discourse on terrorism.

The regime of terror is in an extremely advantageous position. It commands immediate access to all of the instruments of mass communication, as well as considerable resources at its disposal. For states engaging in state terror: ". . . the technology of modern information systems increases the possibility of rule by terror" (Bishop, 1978:55). With complete control of the tools of the media and other communications, states are in a position to use these resources to their advantage against the civilian population, dissidents, or other political enemies within the state. Revolutionary terrorists do not command these resources and must plan their actions so as to utilize whatever resources are available to achieve their desired aims. Many revolutionary terrorists try to cause the state to overreact and hopefully display its "true colors" (those of repression and hatred). The idea is to ". . . provoke oppressive countermeasures to deprive the government of popular support by turning it into a police state" (May, 1974:287).

Unfortunately, the strategy is far from perfect and seldom achieved by revolutionary terrorists. While government response to terrorist acts is sometimes harsh, society often welcomes and applauds such actions. In the face of a crisis a society is willing to tolerate a certain element of lawlessness in its law enforcers. Its agents are permitted to exceed the bounds of the lawful in the name of the law, to proceed without limits against those who exceed the limits. In most attempts, terrorist groups fall far short of the desired objective. Although they may attract attention, seldom do states become the repressive autocratic societies envisioned by the terrorists.

Conclusion

Terrorism as a mode of political struggle is likely to persist. It has been present in societies almost as far back as documented history and will likely exist in future societies. This article clarified the differences between terrorist groups of the historical and modern ages and examined which were more successful in achieving their desired aims. Although historical groups did not have the advantages of modern technology, they were very effective in achieving their aims, arguably even more so than most modern terrorist groups. In terms of length of time the movement maintained itself, numbers of casualties or deaths inflicted, and actual success in achieving a desired aim, the historical terrorist groups seem to have the better track record, although the twenty-first century terrorists' accomplishments remain to be seen. It is clear that modern technology, including communications and transportation, do play a role in modern terrorist operations on an ever-increasing scale. The distinction was also made between revolutionary terrorism and state terror, and the differences between the two were examined. It was demonstrated that the two are and should be separate, and that it is difficult to determine the justifiability of such acts of terror. In essence, it depends on which side of the looking glass one peers through—and even then, the picture is a bit blurred.

Bibliography

Alexander, Yonah (1978). "Terrorism, the Media, and the Police." *Journal of International Affairs* 32 (1): 101–13.

Bassiouni, M. Cherif (1982). "Media Coverage of Terrorism: The Law and the Public." *Journal of Communication* 32 (2): 128–43.

Bishop, J. W., Jr. (1978). "Can Democracy Defend Itself Against Terrorism?" *Commentary* 65 (5): 55–62.

Fromkin, D. (1975). "The Strategy of Terrorism." *Foreign Affairs* 53: 684–98.

"The Futility of Terrorism" (1976). *Harpers* 252 (March): 104–5.

Jenkins, Brian M. (1978). "International Terrorism: Trends and Potentialities." *Journal of International Affairs* 32 (1): 115–24.

Knight, Graham, and Tony Dean (1982). "Myth and the Structure of News." *Journal of Communication* 32 (2): 130–44.

Laqueur, Walter (1978). *The Terrorism Reader: A Historical Analysis.* New York: New American Library, Inc.

Marighella, Carlos (1985). *The Terrorist Classic: Manual of the Urban Guerilla.* Chapel Hill, NC: Documentary Publications.

May, W. F. (1974). "Terrorism and the Liberal State." *Social Research* 41: 277–98.

Murphy, Dan (2004). "In Iraq, A Clear-cut bin Laden–Zarqawi Alliance." *The Christian Science Monitor,* Dec. 30. Available: http://www.csmonitor.com/2004/1230/p01s03-woiq.html (accessed January 15, 2005).

Rapoport, David C. (1984). "Fear and Trembling: Terrorism in Three Religious Traditions." *American Political Science Review* 78: 658–77.

Schlesinger, Philip (1981). "Terrorism, the Media, and the Liberal-Democratic State: A Critique of the Orthodoxy." *Social Research* 48: 74–99.

terrorismfiles.org (n.d.). Encyclopaedia of Terrorist Organizations. Available: http://www.terrorismfiles.org/organisastions/al_qaida.html (accessed January 15, 2005).

Wardlaw, Grant (1982). *Political Terrorism: Theory, Tactics, and Counter-Measures.* New York: Cambridge University Press.

Ware, Michael (2004). "Meet the New Jihad." *Time* archives, WORLD (July 5, 2004). Available: http://www.time.com/time/archive/preview/0,10987, 1101040705-658290,00.html (accessed January 15, 2005).

Wilkinson, Paul (1981). "Can A State Be 'Terrorist'?" *International Affairs* 57: 467–72.

5

International Terrorism in the Name of Religion
Perspectives on Islamic Jihad

Hamid R. Kusha & Nasser Momayezi

Since the 1960s, we have witnessed a dramatic increase in both domestic and international terrorism. Indeed, our modern concept of terrorism dates from this decade. The number of terrorist groups increased tenfold since 1968 (Medd and Goldstein, 1997:281), accompanied by a sharp increase in the total number of acts of terrorism. Between 1968 and 1989, 35,150 acts of international and domestic terrorism were recorded worldwide, representing an incident rate of approximately 1,673 attacks per year (Jongman, 1992:33). By comparison, 30,725 incidents were recorded for the relatively short period spanning 1990–1996 (Chalk, 1999:152). Simultaneously, there has been a virtual explosion of identifiable *religious* terrorist groups. While none were identifiable in 1968, today nearly a quarter of the 50 or so identifiable terrorist groups currently active throughout the world are motivated predominantly by religious concerns (Hoffman, 1996:211). These groups appeared with a distinct and full-fledged organizational apparatus. Since 1982, religious terrorist groups have been responsible for nearly a third of the deaths caused in international terrorist attacks (Hoffman, 1996:211).

Unlike their secular counterparts, these terrorists are obviously, by their very nature, largely motivated by religion—but they are also driven by day-to-day practical political considerations within their context-specific environment. Nowhere is this more clear than in Muslim terrorist groups, as religion and politics cannot be separated in Islam. For example, the Hizb'allah or Hamas groups operate within the framework of religious ideology, which they combine with practical and precise political action in Lebanon and Palestine.

Prepared especially for *Comparative and International Criminal Justice, 2/E.*

71

Several Islamic fundamentalist groups have equated the use of terrorism with the Islamic concept of *jihad*. The term is frequently translated in the West as "holy war." Although jihad does not mean the use of terror or violence, religious terrorist groups have employed the concept to morally justify their terrorist activities against real and perceived enemies. This article reviews the Islamic concept of jihad, which has its epistemological and historical justification in Islam's sacred text, the Qur'an. It then explores the question of whether jihad in modern times can be equated with the Qur'anic Holy War that any Islamic state and/or group can wage against non-Muslim states and/or groups of people. Finally, it examines whether any Islamically valid perception of jihad allows for unbridled violence to be employed by Muslims against non-Muslims—in other words, whether jihad allows for terrorism to be employed in its propagation.

The Etymology of the Jihad

In its Qur'anic etymology, jihad is derived from the Arabic root *jahd*, or "a great striving." Other derivations are *jahed* (one who wages jihad) and *mujahed* (the wager of jihad). The term is repeated in its various forms in the Qur'an (for example, in the chapter on *al-Taubah*: Repentance, verse 20, which refers to those Meccans who left their abode and joined the Prophet Muhammad in Medina to propagate the new faith, Islam) [italics added in all Qur'anic quotations]:

> Those who believe, and have left their homes and *striven* with their wealth and their lives in Allah's way are of much greater worth in Allah's sight. These are triumphant.[1]

Verse 78 of the chapter on *al-Haj*: Pilgrimage witnesses the validity of Muhammad's claim to prophecy. Muslims believe that Allah gave Muhammad the same message given to Abraham, Noah, Moses, and Jesus:

> And *strive* for Allah with the endeavour which is His right. He hath chosen you and hath not laid upon you in religion and hardship; the faith of your father Abraham (is yours). He hath named you Muslims of old time and in his (Scripture), that the messenger may witness against you, and that ye may be witness against mankind. So establish worship, pay the poor-due, and hold fast to Allah. He is your Protecting Friend. A blessed Patron and a blessed helper![2]

In verse 52 of Chapter XXV (*al-Furqan*: The Criterion) we find: "So obey not the disbelievers, but *strive* against them herewith with a great endeavor."[3] Verse 69 of Chapter XXIX (*al-Ankabut*: The Spider) reads: "As for those who *strive* in Us, We surely guide them to Our paths, and lo! Allah is with the good."[4] Another example is verse 11 of Chapter LXI (*al-Saf*: The Ranks): "You should believe in Allah and His messenger, and should *strive* for the cause of Allah with your wealth and your lives. That is better for you, if you did but know."[5] Verse 75 in the chapter *al-Nisa* (The Women), one of the most compelling verses in the Qur'an, ponders why a believer should strive in the cause of justice for the weak in society, stating:

> How should ye not *strive* for the cause of Allah and of the feeble among men and of the women and the children who are crying: Our Lord! Bring us forth out of this town of which the people are oppressors! Oh, give us from THY presence some protecting friend! Oh, give us from Thy presence some defender.[6]

It is a central belief in Islam that these and similar verses were revealed to the Prophet Muhammad during his tenure that covers two separate periods, the Meccan (610–622 CE), and the Medinan (622–632 CE). During these periods, especially the Meccan, the Prophet suffered much hardship at the hands of Meccan idolaters as he tried to introduce Islam as a universal, monotheistic religion. In doing so, the Prophet struggled (jahd), and therefore he was a struggler (mujahid) in the path of Allah. However, Muhammad did not conduct Holy War when he was in Mecca. He warned the Meccans of the doomsday that he proclaimed was near, admonishing them for their vile ways of life and mannerisms.

Muhammad's warnings were not heeded and were never taken seriously by Meccans, who first looked at his preaching as that of an overzealous puritan (for he was known among the Meccans as Muhammad the Honest [*al-Amin*]). With the passage of time, however, the Meccans became less tolerant of his preaching, at first ridiculing Muhammad and eventually intimidating and threatening him with violence. The Qur'an alludes to this harsh period in the Prophet's life in Mecca and reminds him that those who struggle (jahd) in the path of Allah should not fear any oppressor *(jabbar)*, for Allah is indeed the "Oppressor of the Oppressors" *(Al-Qasim Al-Jabbarin)* at the same time that Allah is The Bountiful and the Kind *(al-Rahman al-Rahim)*.

Although jihad means "holy war against infidels," the Qur'an has characterized the Jews, Christians, Sabi`ins, and Zoroastrians as the People of the Book *(Ahal al-Kitab)* and not as infidels *(Kuffar, Ahl al-Kufr)*. In fact, the Qur'an considers both Jews and Christians as Muslims, in that Islam is the most complete and correct version of both Christianity and Judaism, according to the Qur'an.

The respect and love that the Qur'an shows for Jesus and Moses is beyond reproach. The Qur'an bears witness to the high moral standing of Mary, mother of Jesus of Nazareth, and to the miraculous birth of Jesus, characterizing Jesus as Allah's Spirit *(Ruhaallah)*. Those who argue that Jesus is God's Son are chastised by the Qur'an for attributing anthropocentric qualities to the God of Abraham, who is the God of Noah, of Janus, of Moses, of Jesus, and of Muhammad as well. This God is Allah. The Qur'an shows the same love and respect for Moses, characterizing him as on par with Jesus and Muhammad as one of the three Grand Prophets of Allah, and calling him the *Kalim-Allah*.

The Qur'an has never called upon Muslims to resort to wanton violence and bloodshed against their Christian and Jewish brothers and sisters, just as the Prophet Muhammad never waged jihad against any Jew or any Christian because they adhered to Judaism or Christianity. The Constitution of Medina is a historical document to that effect (Williams 1971; Hodgson 1974; Rahman 1979). The Qur'an, however, advises Muslims to wage "jihad in God's Route" *(jihad fi sabilallah)* against those who stray from God's values and resort to injustice, in order to propagate peace, justice, and Godly values.

Finally, the Qur'an advises Muslims to defend themselves if they are subjected to aggression. Even at that, however, the Qur'an recommends a peaceful and just settlement of conflicts. Irrational and wanton violence such as mutilation *(muthlah, taqtil)*, bloodshed, aggression *(ta`arruz)*, and injustice *(zulm, ta`addi, tajavuz)* are strongly condemned in the Qur'an. It reminds Muslims time and again not to deviate from moderation in their social affairs, be it in their rage or in their despair, in their sorrow or in their joy, in attending to worldly affairs or the affairs of the next world to come. The yardstick for such moderation is the Qur'anic "balance" *(mizan)* from the famous Qur'anic motto that the most bountiful road is that which is balanced.

The Prophet Muhammad and Jihad

It is an established historical fact that after the Prophet Muhammad emigrated to Medina, he made a pact with the people there, among whom were various Jewish and Christian tribal groups. The pact, known as the Constitution of Medina, allowed the Prophet to establish the first Islamic state in that city. There were some Jewish tribes (e.g., Bani Qurayzah) who made a pact with the Prophet but later conspired against the state in spite of the pact, and therefore the Prophet moved against them. In the Islamic view, this was not a jihad but rather a calculated political move against a party who had violated a pact. These tribes had collaborated with the Meccan enemies of the Prophet to destroy the Islamic state. Although this move of the Prophet has been criticized among some Orientalist circles, not one reputable Muslim scholar has said that the Prophet waged jihad against these Jewish tribes because they were infidels. In other words, even the most hypercritically analyzed events in the life of Prophet Muhammad leave no room for wanton destruction and wars of aggression against others. The kind of violence that occurs in the Middle East and North Africa today in the name of Islam and jihad appears in sharp contrast.

State and Revolution: The Transmutation of Jihad

Jihad, in its traditional context, has been used as a form of holy war against infidels from the time of the so-called "Four Rightly Guided Caliphs" (632–661 CE) to the time of the Ottoman empire (AD 1299–1924). It was in the twentieth century, however, that the concept of jihad found a new meaning—first in the Algerian Revolution and subsequently in the Islamic Revolution, as a concept that has legitimated every means in its propagation, including state-sponsored terrorism. Algerian revolutionaries argued that the French had occupied Algeria, an Islamic land, and therefore every Algerian patriot should wage jihad against French colonial forces. This definition of jihad meshed well with the Qur'anic notion that if aggressed upon, Muslims are duty bound to wage jihad against the aggressors. The same argument was used by the Afghani Mujahedin in the 1980s as they waged jihad against Soviet occupation of Afghanistan.

From the early 1980s to the present, thanks to the rise of the Iranian Ayatullah Ruhullah Musavi Khumaini, jihad has gone through a bizarre transformation. With the rise of Khumaini to power in Iran, this concept seemed to have acquired a new and radical anti-Western connotation. In this new context, jihad began to be utilized as a grandiose and all-out battle cry against the West in general—the United States and Israel in particular. More ominous, according to some scholars, is the transformation of the whole concept of jihad into a quasi-foreign policy apparatus among some Middle Eastern and North African states (e.g., Iran, Syria, Iraq, Sudan, and Libya) (Pipes 2000; U.S. Department of State 2000; Emerson 1995).

Following Khumaini's cues and rhetoric, these states created and financed into their proxies jihadi-type movements, who wage a "War of Liberation" against Israel, against U.S. domination of the region, and sometimes against each other's regional interests. In large measure, though, depending on who finances them, these movements seem to function as quasi-extraterritorial tools of policy in the region. The most radical, anti-Western and violence prone among them have been identified by various police and anti-terrorist intelligence-gathering organizations in Europe, Asia, North America (the U.S. and Canada), and even in Latin America.

Naturally, one cannot characterize all jihadi movements as purely terrorist organizations, although some resort to terrorism every now and then, and there are those jihadi movements that have resorted to unbridled terrorism more often than not. It is plausible, however, to propose that each of these states has its own rationale as to why jihad is not terrorism per se, but instead a legitimate political movement. Under the Islamic regime of the Ayatullah Khumaini in the 1980s, and now under his successors, anti-Western jihadi movements in the Middle East purportedly represent the propagation of the ideals of the Islamic Revolution. However, scholars agree that these movements (e.g., Islamic Jihad, the Hizbullah, Al-Dawa, Ansar-e Hizbullah—and more recently Al-Qaeda under Osama bin Laden, and its Iraqi offshoot [the former Jama'at al-Tawhid wal-Jihad] under Abu Musab al-Zarqawi) are *mutatis mutandis*, "realpolitik" tools in the region—especially against Israel, the United States, the Middle East peace process, and particularly against the democratization of U.S.-occupied Iraq. At the same time, these pro-Khumaini jihadi movements are capable of undermining secular regimes in the region. For example, it was the rise of the Ayatullah Khumaini that facilitated the birth of the pro-Iranian Hizbullah, which subsequently proliferated in the Persian Gulf Sheikdoms (e.g., Kuwait, Bahrain, Qatar, United Arab Emirates) as well as in the Middle East proper (i.e., Pakistan, Turkey, Lebanon, Saudi Arabia, Sudan, and Algeria) (Mohaddesin 1993; U.S. Department of State 2000; *Jerusalem Post International* July 13, 1996).

For Syria, these movements (e.g., Hamas and Hizbullah operating in the Bakka Valley) seem to serve the Syrian realpolitik objectives against Israel, including the Syrian desire to reinstate sovereignty over the Golan Heights, which were lost to Israel during the 1967 war. If the old adage is true that one cannot wage war without Egypt in the same manner that one cannot make peace without Syria, this war in which Syria has engaged by proxy against the peace process should remind us of Syria's irrevocable place in any comprehensive peace process in the region—specifically peace between the Palestinian authority and Israel.

For Sudan, immersed in a decade of low-level civil war, turmoil, and instability, support for these movements is a sign of the regime's dedication to its own brand of Islamic and revolutionary credentials. Sudan, now under the grip of a new Islamic regime, takes its ideological cues as well as financial backing from Tehran. These movements also allow the Sudanese regime to wage its own war of proxy against its neighbors, especially against Egypt, the military giant of the Arab world. Sudan also serves as a conduit for other revolutionary groups and movements in the region.

For Libya, these movements have helped to propagate the Colonel Maumar al-Qazzafi's views of Islam in his *Green Book*, wherein he explains his Islamic revolutionary ideals. Naturally, these movements are sympathetic to Qazzafi's anti-American and anti-Israeli propaganda as well as to his brand of Arab Nationalism and Arab Socialism.

In Afghanistan, whose Taliban had harbored bin Laden's Al-Qaeda prior to the 9/11 attacks, the Al-Qaeda movement first entered the public consciousness as state-harbored (if not state-sponsored) terrorism but evolved into the major forerunner of what many proclaim as a global jihad movement (Hayes, 2005; Murphy, 2004).

Finally, for Iraq, these movements—especially under Zarqawi's leadership—have given increased vigor to and sharpened the radicalism of insurgents in that war-torn country. In the aftermath of the toppling of Saddam Hussein's regime, anti-American violence and propaganda have escalated at an alarming rate.

Common Characteristics of Modern Jihadi Movements

One common characteristic of the pro-Khumaini jihadi movements is their "puritanical" view of Islam, a view that apparently has attracted them to a Khumainist view of Islam and struggle against the West. These movements, therefore, argue that to succeed in their war against Israel and against U.S. dominance in the region, they have to grab state power and create an Islamic state modeled after the Islamic Republic of Iran.

To achieve this stated objective, these movements often utilize a circular and yet superficially coherent logic that can be summarized as follows: to establish a puritanical Islamic state, one has to start with a purely Islamic agenda for political action because Islam, devoid of its puritanical politics, is devoid of those promises that Allah made to Muslim believers. What are these promises? Allah, through the Qur'an, encourages Muslim believers to wage jihad against the Infidel Oppressors *(al-Mustakbaran)*; Allah advises Muslim believers to fear none other than Allah and assures them that the final victory belongs to of the "Oppressed of the World" *(al-Mustazafan)*. Following this advice in what has been considered a political reading of Islam (Voll 1982; Taheri 1987; Kusha 1998), these movements argue that the sorry political plight of Islamic societies stems from oppression of Muslims at the hand of a powerful and arrogant "infidel oppressor"—the West. The rhetoric runs: Because the West utilizes its hellish powers to oppress Muslims; because the West does not follow the principles of a just war; because the West employs every conceivable means of terror and violence, it is only fair and just for Muslim jihadi combatants to resort to any means— including terrorism—even if it means losing one's life, limb, or property.

Not only is this rhetorical analogy turned into a powerful puritanical Islamic agenda of political action and struggle against the oppressing West. In addition, because most Islamic societies are governed by quasi-secular states and laws, these states are portrayed in the pro-Khumaini jihadi anti-state literature as being governed by Western-dependent mini-oppressors who have to be removed from power one by one (Siddiqui 1983; Algar 1981, 1983; Hussain 1985). The alternative is, of course, an Islamic state modeled after Iran.

We already see this Islamically based political agenda finding hard-core adherents in some parts of the Islamic world, as for instance in Algeria, where a bloody civil war has been waged against the state by the Algerian Islamic forces. Pro-Khumaini jihadi movements also appeal to the economically and sociopolitically marginalized segments of the population in other Middle Eastern and North African states. The appeal stems from the idea that by returning to an Islamic form of governance and the rule of Islam's Sacred Law (the *Shari'ah*), various social, political, and economic problems will be ameliorated. That is why, argues Peterson (2000), it is "cash" and "caution" that keep Saudi Arabia stable. There is no doubt that economic marginalization in the midst of real and perceived affluence is one strong reason for the internal appeal of anti-state jihadi movements. However, there are other factors that ought to be considered.

Another common characteristic of the jihadi movements is that they ideologically pose a serious challenge to other movements premised on modern Western ideologies. The battle cry of the pro-Khumaini jihadi movements is that the political agenda for action has to be cleansed from alien and Western-inspired influence and ideologies such as nationalism, liberalism, socialism, and communism. As a result, the movements pose not only an internally based challenge to secular Middle Eastern states (e.g., to the moderate Arab camp), but also a strong challenge to legitimate Western interests in the region.

A third common characteristic of pro-Khumaini jihadi movements is their misogynous tendencies (Azari, 1983; Moghadam 1993; Stowasser 1994; Kusha 1987, 1990; 2002). Although it has been argued that this misogynism has its base in these movements' fundamentalist view of Islam, it is actually of a secularly constructed nature, born of a puritanical, masculine esprit de corps arguing that woman has a definite (but limited) place in society: the home. Women are basically good only for household chores and reproductive activities. This misogynism, according to some scholars, is not a by-product of Shi`I Islam per se, but is instead concocted, structured, and ideologized by pro-Khumaini-movement views of Islam, be it in the Shi`I or Sunni creed. That is why the Sunni Taliban movement's first order of business has always been the suppression of Afghani women's civil and political rights, argues Moghadam (1993), in the same manner that Shi`I Ayatullah Khumaini's suppressive measures once targeted Iranian women.

The Objectives of Jihadi Movements

Based on the available literature, it is plausible to argue that the pro-Khumaini jihadi movements have two intertwined objectives: (1) grandiose puritanical objectives, and (2) realpolitik objectives. A synopsis is presented below.

Grandiose Puritanical Objectives

These objectives are usually of a rhetorical nature, wrapped in the context of a "clean sweep" mentality. The epistemological mindset of this mentality is that one must get rid of the present state of affairs in order to fill the void with a set of puritanical Islamic values. This mentality was gradually constructed in the course of Iran's Islamic Revolution, based on the rationale that Iran, as one of the most important constituents of the world of Islam, has been deeply exploited by the "Corrupt West"—a monolithic construct whose primary function is to exploit the World of Islam (another monolithic construct). This alleged exploitation is of a continual and one-sided nature—the roots of which go as far back as the rise of colonialism in the seventeenth and eighteenth centuries and has since been enhanced by modern capitalism, market economy, and imperialistic schemes. As a result, this "Corrupt West" has enjoyed unequal and stratified economic prosperity while simultaneously propagating poverty, exploitation, and a culture of corruption and immorality in the World of Islam.

However simplistic this perspective is, it is plausible to argue that it has had, and continues to have, a powerful impact on the worldviews of those undereducated and socially and politically disenfranchised segments of the populace throughout the Islamic world. The most corrupting among these Western values and constructs, argue the jihadi movements, are Western-style democracies as well as concepts such as political pluralism, human rights, and gender equity. These values and constructs are "corrupting" because Western democracies are devoid of "religious" values. In other words, whereas the Western world adheres to superficial values, Iran is a model for the Islamic world because it adheres to "true" democracy, human rights, and liberty—based on the Islamic rhetoric of the Ayatullah Khumaini. Judging from pro-Khumaini jihadi literature, it is plausible to argue that these movements have been empowered by this type of rhetoric, a point addressed later in this article.

Realpolitik Objective: How to Assume State Power

For the jihadi movements, Khumaini represented a liberating and revolutionary Muslim personality, one who had his historical legacy in the Twevler Imami Shi`I Islam's legacy of Awaited Mahdi. The historical significance of Mahdi stems from the Shi`i belief that he will appear one day to rid the world of corruption and injustices by waging the ultimate Grand Holy War *(al-Jihad al-Akbar)* against Islam's diabolical enemies; Khumaini characterized this enemy as monolithic, in the context of the so-called "global arrogance" *(al-Istikbar)*. Naturally, a true believer must expedite the return of Mahdi by engaging in jihad, sacrificing his or her ordinary life in the cause against al-Istikbar, argued Khumaini during his reign in Iran.

The term *Istikbar* is derived from the Qur'an, with the root word *kibr,* which connotes arrogance, the opposite of the humility that is so much stressed in the Qur'an. Khumaini popularized this term in the political discourse of his Hizbullahi followers by arguing that the Western world, under the direction of United States, has attained that status of arrogance. Its diabolical purpose is to exploit the Oppressed of the World, the so-called Mustazafan. Khumaini pondered: Who is more oppressed than the Iranian people, who have risen against the tyrant Shah—the servant of America, the Great Satan? Who is now more oppressed than the Palestinian people? Who are the oppressors but America and Israel? This discourse was a powerful and lethal rhetorical weapon that Khumaini utilized quite effectively in his war of words against the West at the height of his power in early 1980s.

The Question of Leadership

This enmity with a monolithic West and its "evil" offspring Israel, the "Zionist Entity," has created the need for political leadership that must be Islamic to it core in terms of values and worldview. In the past, and prior to the rise of Khumaini, this leadership cadre came from Nasserite Arab nationalist or Baathist socialist circles. The Nassirite Egypt and the Baathist Syria and Iraq of the 1960s and 1970s adhered to this type of realpolitik rhetoric as they confronted Israel on behalf of Palestine. Egypt, under President Anwar al-Sadat, left the Camp David Accords in the late 1970s to set the Egyptian polity into a difficult and yet rewarding rapprochement with the West and Israel. With Egypt having switched sides to the Western camp, neither Syria nor Iraq was in a position to fill the leadership vacuum. As most students of the Middle East will agree, Egypt historically has filled the position of leader in the Arab world thanks to that country's rich history, culture, and a large and industrious population as well as to its strategic location in the Old World. With Egypt having left the Arab radical camp, the position of leader of the oppressed masses throughout the Middle East now needed an alternative ideological anchor that could replace the powerful Arab nationalistic fever with yet another widely appealing one—Islam.

The Khumainist Challenge

Prior to his rise as the leader of the Islamic Revolution in Iran, the Ayatullah Khumaini had argued that the world of Islam needed a uniting leader (Siddiqui 1983; Algar 1983; Rose 1984; Hussain 1985). This leader had to have the loftiest human qualities as well as being well-versed in Islam and its laws. Others argue that Khumaini was a charismatic leader who utilized various social and political factors to assume the position of leadership (Fischer 1980; Jabbari and Olson 1981; Algar 1981; Keddie 1981; Bakhash 1984; Arjomand 1988). During his tenure (1979–1989), Khumaini managed to change the overall balance of power in the Middle East, a balance that the post–World War II American diplomacy had created in the region. This balance had been anchored on four pillars of stability: Iran under the Pahlavi regime, Saudi Arabia under the Ibn Sa`ud regime, and Turkey and Israel as the only two secular democratic and parliamentarian regimes in the region. Following American directives, these four pillars emerged gradually, stabilizing their base of legitimacy as pro-Western regional powers that acted in concert with American diplomacy in the region in order to (1) contain the spread of Soviet communism; (2) ensure the free flow of crude oil through the Persian Gulf; (3) contain radical states such as Nasserite Egypt, Syria, Iraq, South Yemen, and later the Qazzifite Libya from subverting the status quo; and (4) protect Western interests in the region. The demise of the Pahlavi regime in 1979 was the most serious threat to these pillars of stability and has proven detrimental to the Pax Americana in the region. One American remedy was to contain the Islamic Revolution from spreading through a kind of rapprochement with the emerging power in the region, the secular-Baathist regime in Iraq under Saddam Hussein. American policy makers now argue, quite openly, that they sought to engage Iraq for this containment purpose ("Iran-Contra Puzzle," 1987). This policy proved to be reactive and shortsighted.

The eight-year war gave Khumaini a much-needed theater of action to refurbish a complex anti-Western social psychology of resentment in Iran and in the Middle East. Khumaini argued that because the Islamic Revolution represented a strategic challenge to American hegemony in the region, the United States had conspired with Iraq to contain Islam's revolutionary appeal to the masses. He argued further that his campaign against American hegemony was a jihad, requiring all Islamic forces in the region to come to the help of Iranian Muslim revolutionaries under unified leadership of the Muslim clergy, the `Ulama*. In turn, the `Ulama, whether Sunni or Shi`I, should put aside their differences and accept the leadership of the Khumaini, the Imam, for this final jihad against America, the Great Satan. In this struggle, every tactic and means ought to be utilized, argued Khumaini, because the Great Satan is not bound by any principles of a just war. Thus, jihad turned into an all-inclusive panacea of struggle, including terrorism both individual and state sponsored.

The Pro-Khumaini Jihad and the Question of Islamic Identity

The battle cry of Khumaini in opposition to the pro-Western Pahlavi regime was that Iran and the Islamic world must reject Western values in order to return to Islam's superior fundamental values. This reject-return motto was, of course, a very powerful and tempting theme for the Iranian masses because it engendered an alternative identity that, in most Islamic societies, was believed to have been lost to an alien Western version. It also engendered a yearning for a blueprint of social action: how to get rid of the Western identity so that a superior, pure Islamic identity could first be installed in Iran and then exported to the rest of the Islamic world. The question was how? The answer was, of course, through the application of Islam and its fundamental values.

There were, however, both real and imaginary obstacles to this plan of action, as for example the omnipresence of the Western cultural products (cinema, TV shows, modern arts and music, laws, the economic and educational system, industry, market economy, and telecommunication networks). Whether through revolutionary fervor or through genuine fear of other social and political forces that had participated in the Revolution, Khumaini gradually started calling for an anti-West mentality that found expression in an almost irrational wholesale enmity toward the Western culture's most precious and enduring contributions to human civilization: democracy, pluralism, the parliamentarian form of governance, and human rights. To abolish Western influence, first, all remnants of social and political freedoms were suppressed in favor of the "superior" Islamic values under the total grip of the `Ulama.

This plan was augmented with another irrational and vociferous argument, namely, that Islam condones Holy War (jihad) against one's enemies regardless of time, space, and pretexts. Based on this rationale, taking American diplomats as hostages was portrayed as the most important step in the direction of getting rid of the West; in fact, it was characterized as the Second Revolution and as a manifestation of Iran's revolutionary Islamic identity building (Sullivan 1981; Beeman 1983; Rose 1984; Algar 1981, 1983; Taheri 1987). Khumaini argued that the Second Revolution was even more important than the first because the Great Satan had now been humiliated in the hands of Iranian Muslim revolutionary youths. Hyperbole aside, the one tangible result of this Second Revolution, argue many scholars, has been the rise of a new type of state-sponsored, extralegal, and extraterritorial war of attrition through proxy. For example, it is an almost established school of thought that the hostage crisis initiated the Iran-Iraq war.

Scholars also have argued that, unlike its secular counterparts, state-sponsored terrorism has spawned another ominous, international trend: legitimation of terrorism in the name of Islam and its fundamental values (Bakhash 1984; Taheri 1987; Mohaddesin 1993; U.S. Department of State 2000, 1997). This is in spite of the fact that Islam's Sacred Law does not allow the use of such unbridled violence against noncombatants; neither does it allow the violation of diplomatic immunity, which has a long and cherished history in the Islamic world. For example, among Bedouin Arabs of the pre-Islamic era, known as the *Jahiliyah*, anyone seeking refuge in a house, a tribe, or a sanctuary was immune to harm and even to legally proscribed prosecution. The Qur'an reminds the Prophet Muhammad time and again of the importance of not harming those who seek refuge in sanctuaries. It is common knowledge that the Prophet Muhammad sought refuge in the city of Medina in AD 622 as he could no longer conduct the affairs of Islam in his birthplace, the city of Mecca. In addition, the Iranian culture, one of the oldest among human civilizations, has a cherished legacy of diplomatic immunity that extends as far back as the Achaemenid Empire (550–330 BC).

Diplomatic immunity has a long tradition in International Law as well, and it has been accepted by members of the United Nations who have put their signatures under various conventions to that effect. Iran under Khumaini was, and remains, one such signatory. One justification for the taking of hostages was that the American diplomatic core was allegedly a bastion of C.I.A. operatives who conducted spy missions in Iran. However, if such were the case, the appropriate remedy would not have been storming the embassy compounds in contradiction of every norm of diplomatic immunity, but instead to declare the diplomatic core as a collection of personae non-grata and ask them to leave Iran. With the passage of time, however, the battle cry against the Great Satan was turned into another realpolitik objective: to liberate Palestine from the grip of Israel by waging Holy War against Israel, and thus the extension of the rationale that jihad means Holy War against one's enemies.

Osama bin Laden's Al-Qaeda (and its more recent Iraqi offshoot under Zarqawi) carry the Khumainist challenge even further. Al-Qaeda does not depend on the sponsorship of a political state (Hayes, 2005):

> Instead, Al-Qaeda operates as a franchise. It provides financial and logistical support, as well as name recognition, to terrorist groups operating in such diverse places as the Philippines, Algeria, Eritrea, Afghanistan, Chechnya, Tajikistan, Somalia, Yemen, and Kashmir. . . . The principal stated aims of Al-Qaeda are to drive Americans and American influence out of all Muslim nations, especially Saudi Arabia; destroy Israel; and topple pro-Western dictatorships around the Middle East. Bin Laden has also said that he wishes to unite all Muslims and establish, by force if necessary, an Islamic nation adhering to the rule of the first Caliphs.

Jihad as a Factor in Personal Empowerment

There is a powerful perception in Islam that a believer has to wage a personal struggle *(al-jihad fi al-nafs)* before attempting to ameliorate the sorrows of the world. Personal jihad includes purification of one's soul, deeds, thoughts, and daily life. One has to fight one's lowly inclinations *(al-nafs al-`amarah)* in accordance with the Qur'an, which maintains that a believer's first duty is toward him- or herself in so far as the purification of one's soul and material life is concerned. Islam under no circumstance allows an otherwise corrupt and vile person to declare jihad upon others. Put simply, to wage true jihad, one has to start from within. Once this is done, the believer is bound to take other steps in the direction of bettering the plight of the Muslim believers in other parts of the world. In other words, in Islam personal is political to a very large extent, in that one fights one's lowly inclinations to get ready to face his or her social and religious obligations, including struggle in the path of righteousness for the sake of God's satisfaction.

In addition, there is a notion in Islam that one moves from micro-struggle *(al-jihad al-saghir)* to macro-struggle *(al-jihad al-kabir)*. Naturally, all pro-Khumaini jihadi movements have used this rhetoric, notwithstanding what their real political motives might have been in the past regarding this very difficult Islamic test of purity in thought and in action. One has only to check the sorry state of personal freedoms and human rights situations in Iran, Libya, Syria, Sudan, and Pakistan (and even in post–"liberation" Afghanistan and Iraq), argue both scholars and various human rights organizations, to gauge the extent of discrepancies that exist between deeds and claims (Azari, 1983; Taheri 1987; Kusha 1987, 1994; Mohaddesin 1993; U.S. Department of State, 1996).

According to many Western scholars of jihadi movements, the issue of personal empowerment can be explained by a combination Islamic fatalism and fanaticism, hatred of the socioeconomic accomplishments of Western democratic societies, and the sense of despair and political impasse that thrives in the Middle East and North Africa (Kidder 2000; Sederberg 1991; Benesh 2000; Kusha 2002). That is why these movements, observe these scholars, revert to unbridled violence, such as the suicide bombings of Western targets as well as against Israeli soldiers and installations in the occupied territories.

Although some of these factors prevail among a number of pro-Khumaini jihadi movements, in my judgment these scholars miss the fact that Islam has never legitimated martyrdom for the sake of martyrdom, nor does the Qur'an advise the use of aggression for any purpose, let alone for moral struggle in the path of Allah. Most important of all, the Qur'an has never condoned the use of unbridled violence, which is perhaps the Qur'anic equivalent of the term *terrorism* in modern political discourse. In fact, the only concept found in the Qur'an that is close in definition to the term *terror* is perhaps the concept of *khawf*, which means fright and has many connotations. The biggest fright for a Muslim true believer is to be standing before the Judge of all Judges *(al-Qadi al-Qudat)*, Allah, on the Day of Judgment *(al-Youm al-Qiyamah)*, to be judged for crimes against oneself, humanity, and Allah. Allah inculcates this fright in the hearts of believers in order to control extremism in every realm of social behavior. Under this assumption, a true believer who wages jihad cannot—and should not, under any circumstance—revert to harming innocent bystanders. In other words, the very rationale of jihad, as a legitimate struggle against injustice and oppression, should be to refrain from resorting to terrorism against civilians, be it in Tehran, Damascus, the Occupied Territories, Tel Aviv, or Baghdad.

Western observers of the jihadi movements conceptualize the jihad as a manifestation of lowly inclinations. For example, Benesh (2000) describes Arab boys recruited by Hamas as Islamic jihad suicide bombers who are seduced with the promise of 72 virgins to serve them in heaven. Another observer, naming poverty as the main interlocutor for the Lebanese Hizbullah's resorting to terrorism, writes: "The photos always show young, smiling faces—ordinary people who one day decide to leave their miserable lives and get involved in the holy war against Israel" *(Jerusalem Post* January 18, 1997). The list of such observations is almost endless.

Such tactics are political, although employed in the name of Islam, the Qur'an, and jihad. Many scholars of Islam have argued that these tactics are anti-Qur'anic and therefore anti-Islamic. The Qur'an does not allow juveniles to be sent into harm's way, let alone allowing them to carry out suicidal missions, which unfortunately continue to rise in number. Those who promote these political tactics are abusing the concept of jihad. The same goes for other scholars who see various motives such as revenge, personal glory, and martyrdom in these movements.

This said, one should ask the question: Why is it that Hamas, the Hizbullah, Al-Qaeda, the Islamic Jihad, and others have resorted to such desperate measures? One simple answer is the level of frustration that these movements feel in the face of the hard-core realities that surround them:

social, economic, and political marginalization at the hands of a mighty West that seems to be the source of all troubles in the region. Another reason is the presence of Israel, backed by the mighty America, both of which are perceived to espouse a one-track political aim: the destruction of Islam.

The Oslo Accords to some extent changed this perception. Nonetheless, the image of a diabolical Israeli-American trickster as the root of all misery in the region is a very powerful tool in the pro-Khumaini jihadi movements' promotion of the idea that jihad necessitates every means and ways for struggle, including terror. However, going back to the very Qur'anic rationale of the jihad, true believers would not reach a level of despair that would justify such extreme measures in waging a struggle that ought to be just in the first place. The Qur'an portrays Allah as the Mightiest *(Al-Qasim)* of all Tyrants *(Al-Jabbarin)* who helps true believers in their just cause. According to the Qur'an, Allah's range of powers is unlimited, and He literally laughs at those who in their arrogance fathom that they can deceive Him, let alone those who foolishly believe that they can triumph over His designs. Because Allah is portrayed as such a majestic, moral, and just being in the Qur'an, despair is an almost impossible state of affairs for a true believer.

Accordingly, if one were a true believer, he or she would never despair and therefore would never utilize terrorist measures against civilian targets. In fact, it is the very premise of the Qur'an that Allah deliberately throws seemingly insurmountable difficulties in the path of true believers to gauge the strength of their patience, compassion, righteousness, kindness and graciousness, equity, resourcefulness, and most important of all, their belief in Allah. Therefore, sending a juvenile into a suicidal bombing mission not only is against the Qur'anic concept of jihad but also is against the very thrust of the Islamically-based notion of a just struggle *(al-jihad al-haq)*. For this reason, these tactics are condemned universally by all enlightened and educated political Muslims, including this author.

Jihad as an Organizational Factor

From its inception to the present, Islam has remained a powerful organizer and builder of civilization. Under Islam, a very sophisticated world culture bloomed in an extensive part of the Old World, a culture that has functioned to this date as a powerful, common heritage in binding together various peoples and races as far as Indonesia in the East and Tangier in the West. The Muslim social and political mind has been formed and refined throughout centuries of cyclical glory and civilizational eclipses, with a view of society, economy, and polity that values community next to individuality.

However, until the rise of European hegemony in the late eighteenth and early nineteenth centuries, Islam never went through the social and political stagnation that Medieval Christianity did. Because there was no Medieval Dark Ages in the world of Islam, there was never an Islamic Renaissance, per se, comparable to the European Renaissance that gradually divorced God from human organization. In the post–Renaissance Western thought, God was gradually replaced with such concepts as liberty, equality, and fraternity in their humanistic contexts. In contrast, the telocentric Islamic notions of humanity (Insaniyah, Bashariyah, al-Naas), liberty (Ikhtiyar, Mukhayyir), and fraternity (Ikhwah) have to this date never acquired the Western anthropocentric connotation. The concept of jihad has never lost its connotation to God, while at the same time it has played a significant social and political role in uniting believers in a common cause.

The concept of jihad easily lends itself to organizational logic for the simple reason that one cannot attempt the Grand Jihad (al-Jihad al-Akbar) without the participation of others. To say this is to state the obvious. What is noteworthy is that almost all jihadi movements, because they are religious in nature, adhere to the notion that participation in the organization of the jihad is a God-ordained duty with both worldly and other-worldly rewards (e.g., achieving Paradise through martyrdom, receiving God's appreciation, obtaining communal glorification, etc.). To organize, or to be organized, is to adhere to one's Islamic duty, which seems to be the motto of many jihadi movements, although not stated in so many words. This is not, however, something to which one can aspire if the attempt is based upon ignorance, hate, revenge, lust for power, or worldly glory. In other words, the question here is not the organization per se, but the *purpose* of a jihadi movement and/or a jihadi organization. Jihad for the sake of revenge, lowly inclinations, terrorism, or wanton destruction is anything but true jihad.

Many pro-Khumaini jihadi movements use the mosque as their starting place to recruit and organize socially and economically marginalized youths. The Iranian experience has shown the mosque to be a potentially fertile ground for the fermentation of jihadi movements because no state in the Islamic world can ban mosque-related social gatherings (e.g., the Friday Jamat Prayer and various religious celebrations such as Ramadan). The mosque has always acted as a conduit for clandestine quasi-political and anti-state activities in the past. As witnessed by the manner in which the Ayatullah Khumaini gained power in Iran, the organizational power of the mosques presents a formidable challenge to many quasi-secular states in the region. The rise of the Islamicist Necmeddin Erbakan in Turkey, one of the strongest secular states in the Middle East, ought to be a sobering experience for those Western democratic governments who foolishly believe that the greater the amount of conventional weapons and weapons of mass destruction they sell to these states, the more secure they become in the face of various challenges that the jihadi movements pose there.

Jihad as a Factor in State Empowerment

The pro-Khumaini jihadi movements aim at grabbing state power for the simple reason that an ideal Islamic state has always, at least in theory, combined individual and communal values for bettering the plight of humanity, regardless of race, color, and ethnicity. At the same time, the sorry state of affairs in the Middle East peace process in this author's judgment has given the impetus to many anti-Western, anti-American, and anti-Israeli sentiments throughout the Islamic world. To combat the West's perceived, well-organized, and cynical anti-Islamic plan, it would follow that the Islamic World should follow the example of the ideal model of Islamic state. In the collective consciousness of all pro-Khumaini jihadi movements, that state is the Islamic Republic of Iran. The ideological and political leadership of Tehran is now viewed as the Heart of the Islamic World *(Um Al-Qara')* in the jihadi rhetorical literature. Because of this, other Islamic nations seek to build similar political structures.

To grab state power, the flawed argument goes as follows: one has to use each and every means available to the believer, including legitimate struggle, al-jihad, as one vies for power. The main problem with this rationale is that most of these movements take jihad as an Islamically legitimated form of violence in the context of Islam's past history, and yet that very history belies the terror tactics that these movements espouse in promoting their cause. For example, although the Prophet Muhammad waged jihad against his enemies, he never argued that unbridled violence *(tavah-hush, khawf,* or *qatl)* was an acceptable means for grabbing power or promoting Islamic ideals. In fact, there is a rising school of thought that the Qur'an does not condone aggression and violence in *any* shape, form, or context (Hodgson 1974; Ahmad 1988; Rahman 1991; Kusha 1990, 1999; Al-Ashmawy 2000). It follows that because Allah despises aggressors, those who aim to grab state power ought to refrain from the argument that the end justifies the means.

This school of thought, of course, rejects the state-sponsored terrorism to which a number of Middle Eastern states resorted in the 1980s and 1990s as well as the Iraqi insurgency's terrorism in the twenty-first century. In fact, from an Islamic historical perspective, there is not one single document showing that the Prophet Muhammad condoned any use of unbridled violence against his enemies during his Jihad Campaigns *(Ghazawat)* as he established the first Islamic state in the city of Medina (622–632 CE). On the contrary, many authentic documents portray the Prophet as constantly reminding his followers that:

- Allah despises wanton violence and aggression;
- a true believer prefers peaceful means for conflict resolution;
- Allah carefully observes those who misrepresent His teachings for their vile and lowly inclinations;
- a true Muslim should refrain from using force as much as possible if the door to peace is not closed; and
- force ought to be considered as a last resort and used only for defensive purposes.

There is a qualitative difference between jihad as a multifaceted struggle in which a believer engages in order to be free of the yoke of sociopolitical backwardness and jihad as revenge, unbridled use of terror, and intimidation. In short, jihad in no way indicates that the end justifies the means. Every means has to be just, legitimate, and appropriate.

Jihad and Western Conspiratorial Schemes

The pro-Khumaini jihadi movements, including that of Osama bin Laden and Al-Qaeda, frequently allege a conspiracy to deny Islamic societies their rightful places in the modern world, including their share of political power. There are three central players who have conspired with one another in this alleged scheme: the West, spearheaded by America; International Zionism, spearheaded by Israel; and Secularism, spearheaded by the Intelligentsia (a broad category of Western-educated academicians, civil service personnel, journalists, state apparatchiks, and lay intellectuals who run the "secular" states in the Islamic world). Each of these players, consciously or otherwise, is believed to be involved in this conspiracy to harm Islam—to open the Islamic world to the corrupting influence of Western culture and its purely materialistic values. The Ayatullah Khumaini considered America, the Great Satan, to be as evil as the "Godless" Soviet Union. Khumaini characterized Great Britain as the brain in the conspiratorial schemes whose manifestation is the creation of the state of Israel, that "Zionist entity" whose main mission is to destroy Islam and its third holiest place, the *Qods al-Sharif* (Jerusalem) (Algar, 1981).

This enmity with Israel has created among various pro-Khumaini forces in the region a powerful bond in the context of the Islamic Fundamentalism that various scholars have characterized as an international and/or global threat. The more Western democracies become impervious to the points of conflict in the region (e.g., creation of a Palestinian state; the seemingly endless death and destruction in Iraq; the problems of Kurdish self-determination; the proliferation of nuclear, biological, and chemical weapons of mass destruction; and ignoring the question of human rights for the sake of economic considerations), the more adherents the jihadi movements will recruit to their simplistic conspiracy views. The recent United States–Iraqi confrontation is seen as one such conspiracy in which all the military might of the United States is directed against Islamic Iraq, while America's mighty shield covers Zionist Israel from any harm. The double standard is bolstered by the fact that both America and Israel have weapons of mass destruction.

Naturally, both sides have their supporters and detractors in regard to systematic violations of human rights (e.g., Iraq's treatment of its Kurdish and Shi`I population versus Israel's treatment of the Palestinian population; Iraq's invasion of Iran and Kuwait versus Israel's invasion of Lebanon; and violations of internationally recognized norms of conduct, such as the bombing of Southern Lebanon or the bombing of Iraqi nuclear facilities in the 1980s, and various state-supported assassination attempts). Whether justified or not, Israeli conduct has given much ammunition to the pro-

Khumaini jihadi movements' view that there is a Western and Zionist-inspired Grand Conspiracy against the world of Islam.

Conclusion: Does Islam Condone Terrorism?

To provide even a rudimentary answer to this very complex question, we do not attempt to argue that "terrorism" has different and conflicting definitions. The adage that one man's terrorist is another man's hero does not help our purpose here. Our argument is that the concept of jihad, no matter how one is to approach it, does not equate the "any means" argument that we hear from jihadi movements in Khumainist context. Jihad negates terrorism in any shape, form, or context. One cannot stage jihad against innocent civilian bystanders by killing them with bombs and crying, "Allah is great *(Allahu Akbar)*!" This, of course, is our personal belief, and every Muslim scholar does not necessarily adhere to this view of jihad. However, at the same time we argue in this article that our definition of jihad is supported by a wealth of historical Islamic documentation.

The Lesson for Western Democratic Governments and Law Enforcement

In the rhetoric of the pro-Khumaini jihadi movements, one can easily discern deep dissatisfaction over various issues in the Middle East and North Africa. In particular, as we have discussed, these movements perceive a Western conspiratorial scheme against the world of Islam. The issue of Palestine and the peace process is seen as a manifestation of such a conspiracy. The U.S. invasion of Iraq has provided more fuel to the conspiracy fire. Added to this is the issue of socioeconomic marginalization of a large segment of the population (in various oil-rich Middle Eastern states) at the expense of a corrupt minority in power who, in strategic collaboration with the West, reap the benefits of exploitation of the regions' riches.

Although these may all be legitimate concerns, resorting to terrorism in the name of Allah as an alternative to peaceful political dialogue with the secular and semi-democratic states in the region (Egypt, Jordan, Lebanon, Israel, Kuwait, Bahrain, Algeria, Morocco, and others) will hardly ameliorate the situation. It is time for Western democratic governments to make a concerted effort to fight state-sponsored terrorism in any shape, form, or pretext. The first step is to identify those genuine modern Islamic forces that believe democracy is not a Western monopoly but is an internationally cherished way of attending to the business of law, state, and economy. This requires support for universal human rights, as has been delineated by the United Nations; recognition and support of women's, religious, and ethnic minority rights to self-determination within the internationally recognized boundaries of any state in question; and support for the recognition of various conventions related to prosecution and punishment regimes throughout the world's criminal justice systems.

In short, there must be a unified struggle to abolish state-sponsored terrorism, and let us not hear this ugly voice that human rights are only valid in Western democracies. Let us reiterate our belief that terrorism is not acceptable under any form, context, or pretext—especially when it is waged in the name of Islam, Christianity, or Judaism and claims legitimacy in the name of such venerable personalities as Muhammad, Jesus, and Moses.

Notes

[1] See *The Glorious Qur'an*, text and explanatory translation by Mohammad M. Picktahall (New York: Mostazafan Foundation of New York, 1984), p.181.
[2] Ibid., p. 347.
[3] Ibid., p. 375.
[4] Ibid., p. 421.
[5] Ibid., p. 622.
[6] Ibid., p. 84.

References

Ahmad, Mirza Tahir (1988) *The Holy Qur'an, Vol. 1*, Introduction. Islamabad, Pakistan: Author.

Al-Ashmawy, Sai'd (2000) "Israel's Real Agenda," in Bernard Schechterman and Martin Slann (eds.), *Violence and Terrorism 98–99*, 4th ed. (annual eds. series). Guilford, CT: Dushkin/McGraw-Hill.

Algar, Hamid (1983) *The Roots of the Islamic Revolution*. London, UK: The Open Press Limited.

Algar, Hamid (trans) (1981) *Islam and Revolution: Writings and Declarations of Imam Khomeini*. Berkeley, CA: Mizan Press.

———. (1983) *The Roots of the Islamic Revolution*. London, UK: The Open Press Limited.

Arjomand, Said A. (1988) "Ideological Revolution in Shi`ism," in Said A. Arjomand (ed.), *Authority and Political Culture in Shi`ism* (pp.178–209). Albany: SUNY Press.

Azari, Farah (1983) "Islam's Appeal to Women in Iran: Illusion and Reality," in Farah Azari (ed.), *Women of Iran: The Conflict with Fundamentalist Islam* (pp. 5–25). London, UK: Ithaca Press.

Bakhash, Shaul (1984) *The Reign of the Ayatollahs: Iran and the Islamic Revolution*. New York: Basic Books.

Beeman, William O. (1983) "Images of the Great Satan: Representation of the United States in the Iranian Revolution," in Nikkie R. Keddie (ed.), *Religion and Politics in Iran: Shi`ism from Quietism to Revolution* (pp. 191–217). New Haven, CT: Yale University Press.

Benesh, Peter (2000) "Many Terrorists Are Seduced by Thoughts of Becoming a Martyr," in Bernard Schechterman and Martin Slann (eds.), *Violence and Terrorism 1998–1999* (Annual Eds. Series), 4th ed. (2000) (pp. 29–31). Guilford, CT: McGraw-Hill/Dushkin.

Chalk, Peter (1999) "The Evolving Dynamic of Terrorism in the 1990s," *Australian Journal of International Affairs*, (53) 2.

Davis, Douglas (2000) "Iranian Terror: At Rafsanjani's Door," in Schechterman and Slann (eds.), *Violence and Terrorism 98–99*, 4th ed. (annual eds. series), pp. 54–56.

Emerson, Steven (1995) "Islamic Terror: From Midwest to Mideast," *Wall Street Journal*, reprinted in Bernard Schechterman and Martin Slann (eds.), *Violence and Terrorism 1998–1999* (Annual Eds. Series), 4th ed. (2000) (pp. 126–129). Guilford, CT: McGraw-Hill/Dushkin.

Fischer, Michael M. J. (1980) *Iran: From Religious Dispute to Revolution.* Cambridge, MA: Harvard University Press.

Hayes, Laura (2005) *Al-Qaeda: Osama bin Laden's Network of Terror.* Available: http://www.infoplease.com/spot/terrot-qaeda.html (accessed January 7, 2005).

Hoffman, Bruce (April 1996) "Intelligence and Terrorism: Emerging Threats and New Security Challenges in the Post-Cold War Era," *Intelligence and National Security*, 11 (2).

Hussain, Asaf (1985) *Islamic Iran: Revolution and Counter Revolution.* New York: St. Martin's Press.

"Iran-Contra Puzzle" (1987) Washington, DC: *Congressional Quarterly.*

Jabbari, Ahmad and Robert J. Olson (eds.) (1981) *Iran: Essays on a Revolution in the Making.* Lexington, KY: Mazda Publishers.

Jongman, Alex (1992) "Trends in International and Domestic Terrorism in Western Europe, 1968–88," *Terrorism and Political Violence*, 4 (4).

Keddie, Nikkie R. (1981) *Roots of Revolution: An Interpretive History of Modern Iran.* New Haven, CT: Yale University Press.

Kidder, Rushemworth M. (May 13, 1986) "The Fear of Fear Itself," *The Christian Science Monitor*, reprinted in Bernard Schechterman and Martin Slann (eds.), *Violence and Terrorism 1998–1999* (Annual Eds. Series), 4th ed. (2000) (pp. 11–15). Guilford, CT: McGraw-Hill/Dushkin.

Klare, Michael T. (2000) "Redefining Security: The New Global Schism," in Schechterman and Slann (eds.), *Violence and Terrorism 98–99*, 4th ed. (annual eds. series), pp. 32–37.

Kusha, Hamid R. (2002) *The Sacred Law of Islam: A Case Study of Women's Treatment in the Islamic Republic of Iran's Criminal Justice System* (Introduction). Aldershot, UK: Ashgate Publishers.

——— (1999) "Islamic Jihad: Is Terror Condoned at the Service of the State?" *Crime and Justice International*, 15 (29):7–8.

——— (1990) "Minority Status of Women in Islam: A Debate between Traditional and Modern Islam," *Journal: Institute of Muslim Minority Affairs*, 11 (10):58–72.

——— (1987) "Iran: The Problematic of Women's Participation in a Male Dominated Society," *Working Papers of the Office of Women in International Development,* 136.

Medd, Roger and Frank Goldstein (1997) "International Terrorism on the Eve of a New Millennium," A *Studies in Conflict and Terrorism*, 20.

Moghadam, Valentine M. (1993) *Modernizing Women: Gender & Social Change in the Middle East.* Boulder, CO: Lynne Rienner Publishers.

Mohaddesin, Mohammad (1993) *Islamic Fundamentalism: The New Global Threat.* Washington, DC: Seven Locks Press.

Murphy, Dan (2004) "In Iraq, a Clear-cut bin Laden–Zarqawi Alliance," *Christian Science Monitor* (December 30). Available: http://www.csmonitor.com/2004/1230/p01s03-woiq.html (accessed January 7, 2005).

Peterson, Scott (2000) "Cash, Caution Keep Saudi Arabia Stable," in Schechterman and Slann (eds.), *Violence and Terrorism 98–99*, 4th ed. (annual eds. series), pp. 75–76.

Pipes, Daniel (2000) "The Paranoid Style in Mideast Politics: From Gulf War to Somalia, Fear of a Sinister Uncle Sam," in Bernard Schechterman and Martin Slann (eds.), *Violence and Terrorism 1998–1999* (Annual Eds. Series), 4th ed. (pp. 38–39). Guilford, CT: McGraw-Hill/Dushkin.

Rahman, Fazlur (1979) *Islam*, 2nd. ed. (pp. 30–42). Chicago: The University of Chicago Press.

Rose, Gregory (1984) "Velayat-e Faqih and the Recovery of Islamic Identity in the Thought of Ayatollah Khomeini," in Nikkie R. Keddie (ed), *Religion and Politics in Iran: Shi'ism from Quietism to Revolution* (pp.166–188). New Haven, CT: Yale University Press.

Sederberg, Peter C. (1991) "Terrorism: Contending Themes in Contemporary Research," reprinted in Bernard Schechterman and Martin Slann (eds.), *Violence and Terrorism 1998–1999* (Annual Eds. Series), 4th ed. (2000) (pp. 24–26). Guilford, CT: McGraw-Hill/Dushkin.

Siddiqui, Kalim (ed.) (1983) *Issues in the Islamic Movement, 1981–82*. London, UK: The Open Press Ltd.

Stowasser, Barbara (1989) "Religious Ideology, Women and Family: The Islamic Paradigm," in Barbara Stowasser (ed.), *The Islamic Impulse* (pp. 262–296). Washington, DC: Georgetown University Press.

———. (1994) *Women in the Qur'an, Traditions and Interpretations*. New York: Oxford University Press.

Sullivan, William H. (1981) *Mission to Iran*. New York: W.W. Norton & Company.

Taheri, Amir (1987) *Holy Terror: The Inside Story of Islamic Terrorism*. London, UK: Adler & Adler.

U.S. Department of State (1997) "Patterns of Global Terrorism:1996," in *Annual Editions Violence and Terrorism, 1998–1999, pp. 18–21*.

Voll, John Robert (1982) *Islam: Continuity and Change in the Modern World*. Boulder, CO: Westview Press.

Williams, John A. (1971) *Themes of Islamic Civilization* (pp. 11–15). Berkeley: University of California Press.

6

Organized Crime in South Korea

Dae H. Chang & Ronald G. Iacovetta

Organized criminals are found in every society, and Korea is no exception. However, its increasing impact is a function of the changing nature of Korean society, commensurate with an improved economic base and rapid industrialization. The former Eastern bloc communist nations (China, Russia, etc.) have also witnessed a surge of organized crime for similar reasons. Organized crime in Korea has been in existence since the end of Japanese occupation in 1910.

The overall level of criminal activities declined somewhat following the May 16, 1960, political coup d'état and the beginning of the fifth republic in 1980, because of the roundup-style arrests of many violent career criminals along with members of the major organized crime families (Chung, 1993:11–14, 49). However, these events marked only very short-lived reductions. The period that followed resulted in an increase of criminal activity of all types. Along with the increasing economic stature of the country, the Asian games in 1986 and the Seoul Olympic games in 1988 have created an escalation of "pleasure seeking"; and desire for immediate gratification has fostered the growth of pleasure-oriented businesses, which increased opportunities for criminal organizations. Societal discord has also become increasingly acute, especially among the young with their greater involvement in criminal activity.

According to statistics issued by the Korean National Police in 1990, there were 118 crime families dispersed widely in Korea with a total of 3,093 hardcore members. Among these members, 1,222 have been arrested, 869 have left their families, and 1,002 were under investigation by the police (Ministry of Internal Affairs, 1990:5). The 1992 data indicate that the number of families may be more than 300 and the number of members more than 6,500. It is also known that ten crime families maintaining nationwide networks in such places as Sehbang and Yangeun have gained power over extensive regions and have begun to control the underworld throughout South Korea.[1]

Prepared especially for *Comparative Criminal Justice, 1/E.*

In addition, the crime families have become exceedingly strong financially in the growing economy, have developed wide networks of influence over social organizations and business interests, and have threatened the integrity of the Korean social and political structure. Economic and political power has allowed organized criminals a much better opportunity to expand their empires and protect themselves from detection and prosecution. In order to develop a broad-based and effective work force, the recruitment of teenagers and young offenders is becoming more common, thereby increasing the impact on the youth of the nation.

The changing and expanding economy and the shift to pleasure-seeking among those who have been successful have created a very fertile ground for organized crime families throughout Korea. The sheltering of organized criminals by political organizations is also becoming a major concern. Political organizations that should stand against crime often use the services of crime families to gain or keep political power. In return, they are committed to sheltering and protecting the criminal activities of these organized criminals and are compelled to support their interests in whatever form they may take.[2]

In 1990, the Korean government declared, once again, "a war against crime." For a brief period theft and other crimes against property slightly decreased. However, more violent crimes such as homicide, rape, kidnapping, and drug abuse did not show significant decreases. Government statistics released in 1989 reveal about eleven million reported incidents of crime (National Police Agency, 1990). This represents a rate of 2,534 crimes per 100,000 population, and there is evidence that the rate has increased substantially since this data was released.

South Korean Organized Crime

Organized crime in Korea must be distinguished from ordinary violent crime that occurs every day on the streets and in the homes of South Koreans. While organized crime often involves violence in carrying out its objectives, it represents a collection of continual and habitually violent acts such as kidnapping, intimidation, coercion, blackmail, and extortion directed against others by a group of individuals for the purpose of achieving a collective goal (*Police Dictionary*, 1987:776).

While the multiple components of organized crime in South Korea cannot be detailed here, the nature and characteristics of the key players, the organizational rules, and the hierarchical structure will be addressed. For the purposes of this discussion, organized crime in South Korea is defined as criminal acts committed against society for the sole purpose of increasing profit and influence, even by use of violent means (Cho, 1986:53, 209).

According to current law in South Korea, organized crime is regulated by the Penal Code, Article 114, and Article 4 pertaining to the punishment for violent crimes.[3] The Supreme Court defines a criminal organization (codified in Article 114 as "a group of people organized for a common criminal goal with a systematic control [chain of command, organized structure, and division of labor]") (Supreme Court, 1976:[4.13, 76 Do 340]; Supreme Court, 1977:[5.24, 77 Do 1015]). In addition, the Court also defines and organization for criminal purposes, regulated in the Penal Code pertaining to violent crime (Article 4) as: "(1) A group of people in the same place at the same time organized to commit violent crimes; (2) need not be a self-perpetuating group; (3) has commanding structures such as boss, staff, and members; and (4) the consummation of the crime begins when he members get together" (Supreme Court, 1976:[12.14, 76 Do 3267]). Therefore, an organized criminal act can be defined on the basis of these Supreme Court rules as a crime committed by criminals who are members of a certain group that is organized with a common goal and commanding system to commit specific criminal acts continuously and systematically.

Chronological Development

The roots of organized crime in South Korea go back to Sabum Kim and Huok Kim, who lived during the Japanese occupation era (1910 to 1945). Huok Kim is considered the father of organized crime in Korea. As a youth he roamed Korea and Manchuria and trained to be a master of judo and boxing. He purportedly had a problem with the Japanese police and subsequently kicked a Japanese policeman into a river for revenge. Sabum Kim was a muscular man who lived outside of Dongdaemun (Seoul's East gate) and was an expert in Taikwando (Gweon, 1990:547). Immediately before Korea gained independence from Japan in August 1945, Sabum Kim organized a chivalrous criminal family that protected Korean businessmen from the threat of Japanese organized criminals and differed from modern organizations in this respect (Lee, 1990:9–10).

In the 1950s, criminal territory in Seoul was divided into South and North by the Cheonggye River. The northern part was controlled by four families: (1) Jeong Jae Lee's Dongdaemun family (East gate), (2) the Aomas family in Jongro, (3) the Changsoo Choi family in Sudaemun (Seoul's West gate), and (4) the Youngmin Chang family in Kwangwhamun. The southern part was controlled by the Meongdong family, which was divided into three subfamilies: Hwaryong Lee, Yip Jung, and Sowe Alm. Among all the families (north and south) Jeong Jae Lee's Dongdaemun family was the strongest and largest. Lim Whasoo, Cho Beongryol, and Yoo Jikwang were the key members of Jeong Jae Lee's family. At the time the Lee name was synonymous with "political henchman" (Choi, 1986:166).

After the coup d'état of May 16, 1960, the military junta attempted to eradicate violent criminals (including the organized crime families). As a result, Jeong Jae Lee and Lim Whasoo were sentenced to death and subsequently executed, and other leaders were transferred either to prison or to "hard labor" camps that have become known as national construction camps. However, in 1965, S. H. Shin (nicknamed Sergeant Shin), a sub-boss in the Meongdong family, formed an independent criminal family with about one hundred devoted members (Lee, 1990:3). The areas they controlled were in prime business districts with high population densities that contained a large number of entertainment establishments.

From 1967 to 1972, about two hundred new, smaller criminal families were organized and reorganized. During the period, the new families were busy establishing commercial concerns for economic stability while avoiding involvement with political organizations. According to government sources in Korea, the majority of organized criminals became engaged in the entertainment industry—dance halls, game rooms, restaurants, etc. (Chung, 1993:18). Some families became exceptionally versatile, using violence as a means of getting what they wanted (Kang, 1968:9–10).

In 1965, another new family, called Honam, was formed in Seoul by people from the southwestern provinces under the leadership of Baikhak Shim. After Youshin (the new reform movement), numerous leaders of this family were arrested and a new leader, Park Jongsuk (nicknamed Thunder), was finally selected. Park's interests conflicted with those of "Sergeant Shin's family" for power. The first major conflict occurred in 1975 over a managerial position in a nightclub, and Sergeant Shin's men caught some Honam men in a sudden attack and won the first battle.

In January 1975, after Honam family members were beaten by Sergeant Shin's men, the opportunity was created for sweet revenge. Three commanders and dozens of members of the Honam family attacked the Savoy Hotel coffee shop, the headquarters of Sergeant Shin's family, and gained primary control over the central part of Seoul.

About this time in the historical record, Kim Taechon was introduced to the underworld. Kim and a friend formed a new family called Suhbang, named after their hometown. At the beginning, Kim Taechon was under the control of Oh Kijun, the head of the Honam family, but later took control over the entire family by overpowering and defeating Oh Kijun.

In 1976, Kim Taechon attempted to fulfill his dream of unifying all the major crime families throughout South Korea. Members of his organization marched to Chungjangro in Kwangju City, where most of the businesses were controlled by the OB family, and which was the supply route for the Honam family's recruits. There was fierce fighting between the OB family and the Suhbang family, and Kim came a step closer to unifying the crime families. However, in 1977 he was arrested by police and his dream collapsed. As a result, the boss of the OB family, Cho Yangeun, regained control and became the "boss of bosses."[4]

Cho expanded his territory from Kwangju City to Seoul and reorganized a new family called the Yangeun family. In Kwangju, Lee Dongjae, a commander in the OB family, ordered his men to eliminate his boss, Cho Yangeun. However, this plot, reminiscent of many Mafia gangland plots in New York, was detected by police, and Lee Dongjae was forced to flee with his men. However, he formed a new OB family in Seoul in 1978. Through these conflicts and warring factions emerged three new families—the new OB family, the Yangeun family, and the Suhbang family; and a new era of organized crime known as the "era of the three families" commenced (Baik, 1990:198–99).

In 1980, under martial law, the commanding headquarters dispatched Samchung No. 5 to clean up organized crime from August 1980 to January 1981. Eventually, five bosses known as godfathers of organized crime in South Korea (after Mafia tradition) were arrested and sent to prison or to the Samchung Labor Camp for rehabilitation and hard labor. When this loss of leadership occurred, other members of the families ran away, or left their families, to escape detection and criminal sanction.

The withdrawal of curfew hours by the fifth republic in 1982 liberating public gatherings and events, and the hosting of the Asian games in 1986 and the Seoul Olympic games in 1988, created a renewed fervor and desire for pleasure-seeking by the population and allowed pleasure oriented businesses to prosper once again. This also created renewed opportunity for organized crime elements, waiting in the wings for a more liberal policy, to recommence the building of their power and influence.

Increased economic and political leverage fostered a new era of influence that posed a threat to the Korean social order. Organized crime activity began to increase and new, larger, organizations with more sophisticated networks of operation were formed to cover the entire area of South Korea, with Seoul becoming the undisputed center of organized crime activity. Renewed economic and political power created better opportunities for organized crime families to cover up their crimes and avoid prosecution through loopholes in the system. The recruitment of teenagers and young offenders also became common to broaden the reach of the organization and to provide insulation from law enforcement authorities.

Throughout the 1980s many small criminal organizations continued to form in cities all over South Korea, taking advantage of the opportunities that the new liberalism and prosperity offered. From 1988 to early 1989, many of these newly formed organizations were struggling in competition with other groups, and many were absorbed by other groups or combined with each other to form larger criminal syndicates.

Characteristics of Korean Organized Crime

American and Japanese organized crime families have had significant influence on Korean organized crime in the accumulation of large sums of black-market money. This accumulation has enabled Korean organized crime to broaden its opportunities to gain power and influence with political groups and law enforcement agencies in a fashion similar to the American and Italian Mafia and the Japanese Yakuza. Korean organized criminals have maintained close relationships with Japanese criminal families, which has afforded the opportunity for further expansion of their operations in Korea and beyond. After all, more than half of the total Japanese Yakuza members are descendants of Korean ethnic background.

Territorial Expansion

Throughout the history of organized crime's existence in Korea, the various families have attempted to expand their territory and power. The primary area of success of Korean organized crime families has been the successful exploitation of the entertainment business in the following ways: (1) by securing jobs in the industry ensuring a fixed income and by taking over the management of the business by threat and intimidation;[5] (2) by dominating the supply routes for entertainment employees, such as dancers and showgirls, and by extorting profit from them;[6] (3) by seizing exclusive sales of liquor, fruit, and other food supplies to entertainment businesses and reselling them for excessive and monopolistic profits;[7] and (4) by operating secret gambling houses and lending money at high interest rates (loan sharking). When the debts plus interest are not reimbursed in full as required, kidnapping, assault, and other means of extortion are used to compel payment.

Recently, criminal families have begun to manipulate public construction bids and have gained control of the supply of construction materials. Once control of the supply of materials is secured, control of the businesses is secured and profits are assured. Crime families have also influenced the real estate business significantly in recent years. Via strong-arm tactics and intimidation, they purchase real estate at prices lower than current market values and sell them at much higher prices. Korean organized crime, much like other organized crime confederations with widespread networks of power and influence, has penetrated everywhere profits can be realized. Korean organized crime has recently expanded its territory abroad (to Macao and elsewhere), taking its cue from the Mafia and the Japanese Yakuza. Some organized families have also become involved in labor and religious disputes and are often retained at handsome prices to help in their resolution.[8]

In conclusion, the past indicates that while organized crime families in Korea were primarily connected to myriad opportunities afforded by the entertainment business, they have expanded and ventured into new territory with a fury. There appear to be no restrictions on violence, extortion, and various forms of racketeering to achieve their broader objectives.

Relationship with Japanese Organized Crime

In late December 1990, news of a New Year's Eve party held in Pusan, Korea, by Korean gangsters and one hundred members from the Yamaguchi-Gumi (the largest Yakuza family in Japan) astonished the Korean people and raised major public concern over black-market money exchange and the import of a new form of violence in Korea (Cho, 1991:297). Nevertheless, it is well known that Korean and Japanese crime families have maintained a close historical relationship since the large-scale cooperative ventures of smuggling methamphetamine and gold bars in the 1960s and 1970s. In particular, Chilsung (New Stars), 20 Sehki (Twentieth Century), Shin Chilsung (New Seven Stars), and Sjin 20 Sehki (New Twentieth Century) families in Pusan have maintained such relationships with Japanese criminal families for some time. Recently, the Paikho (White Tiger) family in Soonchun and some other crime families have been reported to have close ties with the Japanese Yakuza (Kim, 1991:297).

Most Korean organized crime groups have received some form of training and assistance from the Japanese Yakuza, mainly from the cities of Osaka and Kobe, where a substantial majority of Yakuza members are known to be Korean Nisei or Sansei (second- or third-generation Koreans born in Japan). The government of Korea is aware of this form of Japanese "foreign aid," and law enforcement agencies in Pusan Harbor and Kum Hae International Airport are directed to observe and investigate airline passengers from Osaka and Kobe. Through a close relationship with the Yakuza, Korean organized crime families have inherited Japanese techniques of organization and operation with regard to training new recruits, crime techniques, financial management skills, and so on.[9]

Relationship between Organized Crime, Politics, and Business

The history of the symbiotic relationship between organized crime families and political or law enforcement agencies goes back to Jeong Jae Lee and Jikwang Yoo in the first republic (*Daily Chosun*, 1990). At that time, some corrupt politicians conspired with crime families to terrorize rival political parties. During the Korean War from 1950 to 1953, Paek Gol Dan (meaning "White Skeleton") and other families disguised themselves politically as extreme right-wing organizations and terrorized anyone who spoke against the government. On occasion they even unlawfully occupied the Korean Congress and threatened to persecute anyone opposing the government.

In 1955, the *Taegu Daily* newspaper was terrorized by political henchmen, and in 1960 students of Korea University who opposed the government in power were attacked (Kim, 1990:292). Many other instances of such intimidation are on record. Recently, in 1976, the New Democratic Party's convention was broken up and, in 1987, a convention designed for the formation of a new opposing political party, the Unified Democratic Party, was interrupted by political henchmen (*Daily Chosun*, 1990:23). Some Congressmen who belonged to a party in power from Inchon submitted a petition for the release of an organized crime family boss. In Daejeon, judges, public prosecutors, police chiefs, and gangsters belonged to the same party, raising speculation about the possibility of conspiracy. This evidence suggests a close symbiotic relationship between organized crime and law enforcement authorities (*Weekly Chosun*, 1990:9–10).

A more serious problem is the fact that organized crime families and political organizations have maintained employee and employer relationships that have served the vested interests of the families. Recently this relationship has changed somewhat to an increasingly consensual one, with each group "scratching the other's back" where necessary to maintain and protect mutual group or individual interests.

Increasing Number of Teenage Gangsters

While there are large and small organized crime families with nationwide networks in Korea, some criminal families consisting of mainly teenage gangsters have gained significant power in recent years. According to the Korean National Police, there are about one hundred teenage criminal families in Korea, including the San-e-Sul ("Mountain Dew") family (Kim, 1990:293).

In 1979, Boss Chang selected ten of the best members of his informal violence circle and formed a teenage criminal family called the San-e-Sul family. In October 1986, after failing to gain the upper hand in an ongoing territorial dispute with the Jinsung family, about 30 members of the San-e-Sul family were involved in a major, well publicized riot, in which 50 stores were destroyed in an hour. Arrested for the mayhem they caused, they were subsequently charged with extorting 10 billion Won ($1,400,000) in three years from Shiheung City businessmen in protection fees. In August 1989, Chang and eleven more teenage members of the San-e-Sul family were arrested. Fifty-nine members remain wanted by the police.

In 1990, investigators from the Shinjung police station in Seoul arrested nineteen Dolsan (meaning "Stony Mountain") family teenage gangsters. Surprisingly, the boss was only 16 years old, and members were either ninth graders or junior high-school dropouts. The organizational structure was so professional and intricate that everyone was astonished, not expecting that teenagers could structure a criminal organization with such a clear division of labor and chain of command. Further investigation revealed that this gang habitually engaged in assault, rape, racketeering, blackmail, theft, and other crimes in order to earn money for entertainment and parties. This example is just one indication of the increasing prevalence of violence and criminal activity by youth in today's Korean society.

Politics and Korean Organized Crime

Contrary to popular belief, Korean organized crime is rather conservative with regard to politics. One seldom finds members, either as individuals or as a group, engaging in terrorist acts, participating in popular social movements, rioting, or demonstrating for social causes. A majority of its members maintain an apolitical stance and endorse the status quo, because changes in the political guard or law enforcement leadership would create uncertainty and possible jeopardy for ongoing operations that are well insulated and protected. This is also true of the Mafia and most other elements of organized crime around the world.

Maintaining the status quo is crucial for the well-being of organized crime. Change creates instability and uncertainty. History has also revealed that when the Korean political pendulum shifts significantly, criminal elements often become the first targets of those who wish to achieve "clean government" in Korea. Moreover, in order to operate their activities effectively, it is essential to "buy" political influence and protection, which has been developed over time through great effort and cost. Changes in politics and social policy are viewed as threatening to these valuable long-term alliances. Calls for a "new order," "law and order," "economic and political reform," or the like are not viewed positively by organized crime elements in Korea.

General and Individual Characteristics of Korean Organized Crime

Most Korean organized crime groups are characterized by the following:

1. Most members originate from relatively low socioeconomic classes;

2. Most are found to be high school dropouts and are less than adequate in school performance, even though some of the organization leaders are believed to be exceedingly bright;

3. Induction into organized crime follows two forms: (a) recruitment directly into a group without having to undergo relatively complex ritualistic and ceremonial steps and (b) most commonly, recruitment from among ex-convicts or former affiliates of other rival gangs;

4. Almost exclusively, Korean organized crime activities are found in the larger cities. Perhaps the largest concentration is found in the capital city of Korea, metropolitan Seoul (containing more than eleven million people);

5. Unlike those of Japan where the organization is large (Yakuza-Gumi membership exceeds 20,000), the Korean organized crime groups rarely exceed 300 in number and usually contain 100 members or less (although the size of organizations continues to grow);

6. Organizational structures follow a very simplistic feudal system of boss, second boss, and a number of soldiers and workers;

7. Most organized crime members leave their hometowns for other communities. A majority of Seoul's organized crime members originate in the South Eastern provinces of Korea (Chulla North and South provinces);

8. Korean organized crime was not formally recognized until 1949, when the provisional South Korean government was established. After the Korean War of 1950, the successive internal political tur-

moil (including the takeover of the government by the military) helped to generate the organization of individuals into protective criminal enterprises. Many were imprisoned or executed during these periods of political turmoil, and as a result organizations have been unstable until recent times; and

9. Korea's organized crime is in its infant stages of development in comparison to the Japanese Yakuza and the American Mafia's sophisticated, broad-based operations. Investment revolves primarily around the entertainment business, such as nightclub operations, protection rackets, prostitution, liquor, pornography, real-estate speculation, and control of construction businesses. However, through these activities and recent diversification into other areas in a period of rapid industrialization, Korean organized crime is fast becoming a significant force. With the country's burgeoning economic growth, a large crime wave is anticipated by the government, especially in connection with black-market trafficking in arms and drugs.

Summary and Conclusions

If current trends continue in the development of organized crime in Korea, (1) fierce territorial disputes will likely continue to increase in the future; (2) the use of lethal weapons will prevail, and new and more intelligent crime techniques will be introduced; (3) for more economic benefit, organized crime will penetrate even deeper into normal, legitimate business transactions and will increasingly interrupt the daily life of the people; (4) the chances of developing close relationships with other criminal organizations from abroad will continue to increase as new opportunities are explored; and (5) teenage gangsters may develop an even closer relationship with politics and business.

As in many countries of the world, Korean organized crime represents an eclectic collection of many different faces and identities performing different (although often complementary) roles. Korean organized crime frequently serves a "financier" role in money lending—usually cash—ranging from simple money lending to high-interest loan sharking to debt collections in connection with million-dollar money laundering. Those involved are known as "expert" money investors in manipulative and speculative business ventures, such as "dual purpose" entertainment establishments, which may serve as fronts for illicit activities. These investors are also involved in real estate and construction, not only to buy and sell land and buildings for profit, but also to influence and "penetrate" labor unions. In this context they are clearly involved in labor racketeering.

Organized crime elements are also involved in various forms of illegal gambling, owning and maintaining illegal casinos that take in huge amounts of tax-free money. They are also involved in debt collections, numbers rackets, prostitution, extortion rackets, infiltration of legitimate business, blackmail, protection rackets, and similar ventures, which net millions of dollars. Innovation and diversification is recognized as the key to success, and nothing is considered to be off limits, with the growing economy offering many opportunities for new ventures.

Korean organized criminals have been known to pose as police officers and as daily tax-collecting agents, collecting servicing fees from business establishments. The networking system between organized crime and the law has been further established by those who act as a *hyongnim* ("big brother") for local police officers or detectives, frequently providing them with minor, and sometimes major, crime related information and intelligence reports on a friendly basis in exchange for leniency in the event that they get caught committing serious illegal acts or violent crimes. Such questionable liaisons exist at all levels of law enforcement and government.

Organized criminals often play golf with high-ranking government officials who are known for their political influence. After a day of golf they may treat such officials to exclusive baths and massages at major hotels and escort them to drinking and sex establishments, for the purpose of negotiating deals. This illustrates the fact that members of organized crime in Korea are often shrewd businessmen who know how to influence and corrupt through the delicate art of promoting reciprocity for favors received. In short, the process of corruption of law enforcement authorities and public officials is well developed and is likely to mature and expand as new ventures are undertaken.

Members of organized crime, through their corrupt influence of businessmen, establish networks for the movement of contraband, such as diamonds, gold, and drugs (which ultimately lead to investment in pornographic films), arms trading, and other illegal goods in the Korean black market. Furthermore, construction firms controlled by organized crime are able to purchase government-owned land or government-controlled real estate (known as Greenbelt) for a fraction of its actual worth and realize huge profits by building apartment complexes or commercial buildings. In Korea, land values often outstrip other commodities.

The symbiotic relationship between organized criminals and the police is, in part, functional. Crime members often aid the police in apprehending notorious criminals on the run, provide police with intelligence information crucial to capturing terrorists, and prevent unexpected riots or other outbreaks. It has been reported that members of Korean organized crime round up street beggars and use them as construction-site laborers, paying normal daily wages for their work. They are also known to provide security services when police response becomes a factor. Current research and evidence suggests that in areas where organized crime is well established, the territory in question contains less crime, particularly violent crime, due to their effective surveillance and the chilling effect of their presence and control. Rapes, for example, are rare in specific districts where organized crime controls the entertainment establishments.

Organized crime in Korea has developed, and continues to grow and prosper, because it is highly profitable and possesses minimal risks. Effective insulation of operations currently exists through an effective system of patronage and corruption. Output is far greater than input (or investment). Conversely, it is understood that if loss exceeds profits, a legitimate business cannot continue to operate. If illegitimate, it may serve as a front for other operations and is profitable in this sense, even though the business proper may be operating at a loss.

When legitimate businesses suffer losses they frequently file for bankruptcy. Organized crime has more leverage, given the illegal operations that the business may be fronting and, therefore, are less vulnerable financially in comparison to legitimate businesses. For this reason, businesses operated by organized crime can weather "hard times" and survive while others cannot. This leverage allows for greater capitalization and ownership of a wide variety of legitimate businesses that may prove very profitable in themselves.

Organized crime also has a "trump card": violence, intimidation, and extortion of rival businesses with a goal of driving them out of business or "taking over" the competition. However, it should be noted that organized crime elements in Korea generally shy away from activity that may lead to police or media attention and often prefer a "sweetheart" or "soft" approach in accomplishing business objectives, where possible. Nevertheless, violence between rival organized crime groups is common and is likely to continue in the future, given the maneuvering for territory in an era where immense profits can be amassed by crime families who successfully control the expanding markets.

Notes

[1] Right after the proclamation of the "War against Crime," on October 13, 1990, the Seoul branch office of the Public Prosecutor's Office announced the discovery of organized crime families: Suhbang, Yanguen, OB, Thunder, Chilsung, Youngdo, Jeonju, Paechajang, Kunsan, and Mokpo families. However, the Junsul family, which was famous for throwing a party with some judges and organized criminals in a salon in Daejeon City, and the Ggolmang family, which was known for filing clemency for a boss by two national congressmen in Inchon City, were not on the list.

[2] The definition of violence can be divided into four categories in the Korean Criminal Code: (1) the broadest definition which includes the crime of sedition (Article 115) and that of not complying an order to disperse (Article 116), (2) that which includes a crime of interference with a government official in the execution of his duties (Article 136) and the crime of assault against a head of a foreign country (Article 107), (3) the narrow definition which includes the crime of assault against a person (Article 260) and the crime of private lynching and cruel treatment (Article 225), and (4) the most narrow definition which includes robbery (Article 333) and rape (Article 297). However, according to popular view, violence implies the narrow definition. Therefore, violence means the exercise of direct or indirect force against a human. Jeong, Youngsuk (1980). Detailed *Criminal Code* (Seoul: Bubmoonsa, pp. 224–25).

Organized Crime in South Korea

[3] A crime of organizing a criminal body for the purpose of burglary or robbery can be punished on the basis of Special Law on Additional Punishment for Major Crimes, Article 5. However, in this article, it is not related with violence and will be excluded.

[4] The background for a war in organized crime can be of three types: (1) conflict within the organization, (2) conflict among groups, and (3) conflict with law enforcement agencies. A criminal can survive and receive higher rank within an organization by continuous fighting and winning in these three types of conflict.

[5] Fighting for the right of management among organizations is fierce whenever a new entertainment business is opened. As a result, in 1988, the owner of Lotte Hotel in Seoul gave up his plan for opening a video game room in his hotel because of fighting between two rival criminal organizations.

[6] According to Seoul City Hall, there were about 250 entertainment productions in 1986. However, in 1990 there were about 100 productions, about 90 percent of these the main illegal supply for nightclub dancers. In January 1990, the police arrested criminals who exploited several singers and comedians by force. The criminals compelled the singers/comedians: (1) to perform by kidnapping, (2) not to perform in a competing business, (3) to pay protection fees, and (4) to buy paintings and antiques. Even though the victims were very popular entertainers, they did not report their involvement to police because they were afraid of revenge by the criminals.

[7] On June 13, 1989, a stabbing murder of a liquor wholesale businessman by four members of a criminal organization took place. The victim supplied liquor to some 160 nightclubs and salons and was known as a sub-boss of the Suhbang family. A competing organization asked to take over the wholesale business and the victim refused.

[8] According to Haebum Ji's report (1989:440), it is assumed that roughly two to three billion won (about three to five million in U.S. dollars) is paid by religiously motivated people to settle certain disputes.

[9] The main points of training are the following: (1) loyalty until death, (2) don't bother ordinary people, and (3) avoid fighting with other members if possible.

Bibliography

Baik, Sungil (1990). "Situations of Organized Violence and Countermeasures Against Them." *Korean Criminological Review* 1: 198–99.

Cho, Gabjei (1991). "Korean Connection of Japanese Organized Crime." *Monthly Chosun* (October): 297.

Choi, Myoungsuk (1986). "Research On Organized Crime." Unpublished doctoral dissertation, Seoul National University.

Chung, Jin-Soo (1993). *Jojik Pokryok ui Siltae Wa Taechek* [A study on organized violent crime in Korea]. Seoul: Korean Institute of Criminology.

"Dangerous Stage: Violence and Political Power." (1990). *Daily Chosun* (December 4–8): 1–5.

Gweon, Suntaik (1990). "Violent Organization," *Sindonga* 3 (March): 547.

Jeong, Youngsuk (1980). *Detailed Criminal Code.* Seoul: Bubmoonsa.

Ji, Haebum (1989). "Organized Violence in Korea." *Monthly Chosun* (August): 440. Kang, Jaedong (1968). "Legal Issue on Roundup Arrest and Hard Labor Camp." *Administration of Justice* 92 (August): 9–10.

Kim, Jonghyuk (1990). "Organized Crime in Korea." Paper prepared for the IACP Asian-Pacific Area Conference (July).

Lee, Palho (1990). "Organized Crime in Korea." Paper prepared for the IACP Asian-Pacific Area Conference (July).

Ministry of Internal Affairs (1990). *Guideline for a New Order, A New Life Practice* (October 18).

National Police Agency (1990). "White Paper on Crime." Seoul: Ministry of Home Affairs.

Police Dictionary (1987). Seoul: National Police Headquarters. Supreme Court (1977). 5.24, 77 Do 1015.

Supreme Court (1976). 4.13, 76 Do 340.

Supreme Court (1976). 12.14, 76 Do 3267.

Weekly Chosun (1990). (December 9).

"Yakuza Is Coming" (1990). *Daily Korean* (December 4–10): 1–7.

PART II

Policing and Social Control

7

Democratizing Police Organizations from the Inside Out
Police-Labor Relations in Southern Africa

Monique Marks

Throughout Southern Africa, governments profess to be moving toward greater democratization. This move involves (among other things) a stated commitment to the participation of citizens in matters that affect their daily lives, establishing processes and structures of accountability as well as more effective service delivery. The police, as the most public face of the state, must be seen to reflect and defend this "new" democratic ethos.

As part of this purported state democratization project, police forces in Southern Africa profess to a shift toward the practice of democratic policing. State police agencies, following their colleagues in Western democracies, now have formal documentation which commits them to "community-oriented policing" (Brogden, 1999). Accompanying this philosophic shift is a move away from being a "force" toward being a "service"—away from brutal and discreditable policing legacies and toward international conventions of democratic policing.[1]

While there may be some attempts on the part of governments to democratize, in reality a substantial number of governments in Southern Africa remain autocratic and intolerant of popular mobilization and protest (Cole, 1999). This is most evidenced in police repression of demonstrations and protests in recent years, particularly in Zambia, Zimbabwe, and Swaziland. The continued repressive and discriminatory responses of the police in countries that have undergone transitions from authoritarian rule to democratic governance are not isolated to Southern Africa, however. Indeed, Mitchell and Wood (1998) have argued that in Brazil, Argentina, Chile, and Uruguay, despite the demise of authoritarian rule, police forces have continued to subvert democratic principles.

Prepared especially for *Comparative and International Criminal Justice, 2/E.*

Mitchell and Wood contend that a transition to democratically elected governments is not in and of itself a sufficient condition for the creation of democratic institutions. What is needed, according to them, is "the reconstruction of state institutions . . . and the dismantling of antidemocratic forms of exercising power, which may be authoritarian, corporatist, or plainly coercive in nature" (1998:1015). For this to occur, rights and responsibilities need to become "embedded features" of institutional life and part of the fundamental "cultural assumptions that organize and inform daily life" (Mitchell and Wood, 1998:1005). The question is, however, how can new cultural assumptions about citizenship be created within police organizations?

New conceptualizations of citizenship, stressing rights and freedoms alongside responsibility, are central to the invention of new cultural assumptions. In particular, the rights of freedom of association and expression, the right to join representative organizations, and the right to actively participate in daily governance decision-making processes are key citizen rights in post-authoritarian societies. This article argues that, in order for police to ascribe to and protect these rights, they need to experience the benefits of these same rights directly. This demands the democratization of police organizations themselves.

Tyler and Huo (2002) make a point about police and the courts cultivating respect of and compliance from community members. They argue that if the community is to voluntarily accept the decisions and directives of the police, it is important for community members to be treated fairly and respectfully by authorities. People take actions, Tyler and Huo argue, that are "consistent with their own intrinsic values. . . . People's behavior [is] shaped by their judgments of what is right and what is wrong, just or unjust . . ." (2002:49). Similarly, the way that the police respond to the public will in many ways depend on how they are treated within the police organization. Just as community members cannot be expected to respect police authority if they are not treated with respect by the police, police cannot be expected to treat communities in just and fair ways if these value systems are not cultivated within the cultural practices of police organizations themselves. Such cultural practices can be cultivated by providing police with means to actively participate in decision making, both as individuals and as collectives, as well as avenues for advancing their own interests and needs.

While Southern African police services recognize the need for reform or change, this pertains more to *external* democratization (improving service delivery) than to *internal* democratization (encouraging active participation by police and enhancing service conditions within the police organization itself). Police management and government in most Southern African countries have failed to see the link between internal and external democratization in police agencies. The police are viewed fundamentally as security personnel who are part of essential services, rather than as professional workers with industrial-based needs and interests.

In countries where democratic governance is lacking, such as in Southern Africa, police labor relations remain despotic. Despite attempts to transform (or more appropriately reform) police agencies in these countries, neither police management practices nor police labor-relations legislation have changed significantly. Rank-and-file police members are unable to influence policy-making and planning processes, and they have little control over their conditions of service.

I argue that the lack of democratization within the police labor-relations arena reflects the lack of democratic governance that exists more generally in Southern Africa. Furthermore, I argue, if public police bodies in Africa are to become more community and service oriented (as they claim to be), it is crucial that police experience democratic technologies and mentalities within their own organization. This means that, at the very least, police should be allowed to form and join representative employee organizations that are able to collectively bargain, and they should be encouraged to participate in police organizational decision-making processes and planning.

The Southern African Context

In 1991, political scientist Peter Vale optimistically (and perhaps prematurely) commented:

> Almost everywhere in Southern Africa, change is in the air. Political authority is under siege. . . . Long entrenched totalitarian states like Zambia's Kenneth Kaunda and Zaire's Mobuto Sese-Seko are facing demands for political pluralism. In one-year-old Namibia, a new university will soon open its doors in Windhoek, confident that the country's constitution will guarantee its autonomy. . . . In Mozambique and Angola, countries which for nearly three decades have been wasted by strife, there is hope for peace. . . . In Tanzania, one of the continent's poorest states, a commission of inquiry is probing the possibilities of introducing a multi-party system. . . . (1991:697)

Twelve years later, a very different analysis of Southern Africa had emerged. Although the initial years of independence in Southern Africa were accompanied by optimism, this sentiment has, it seems, been replaced by pessimism (Shaw, 1991). Denis Venter, in reviewing democracy and multiparty politics in the region, argued that:

> the SADC [Southern African Development Community] member states had been reluctant to exercise regional leadership in issues related to good governance. One reason for this reluctance has been that certain heads of state have themselves been facing severe criticism for authoritarianism and intolerance in their own countries, and, as a consequence, have been coming under intense pressure to allow a greater degree of accountability, freedom and democracy . . . the greatest defi-

ciency within the SADC remains the absence of integrated systems, processes, mechanisms to deal with human rights abuses, and the advancement of democracy and good governance. . . . Swaziland is regarded as non-democratic and is still frozen in time on the political dead-end road of a no-party, feudal monarchy, Zambia and Zimbabwe are accused of being undemocratic in election related practices and flaunting the principles of good governance; Angola and the DRC may now finally be able to extract themselves from a state of anarchy. . . with tentative moves toward finding lasting peace; Namibia and Malawi are characterised by growing authoritarianism. (2003:35)

While there is a new tolerance of pluralism in some countries such as Mozambique and Angola, in other countries "endangered states and structures, especially paranoid presidencies, have resorted to militarization in a last ditch effort to reverse the indigenous 'winds of change' now blowing across the continent" (Shaw, 1991:194). In a number of Southern African countries, Zimbabwe being the most notable at present, governments have "acted to obtain a monopoly of formal political office, manifesting a consistently authoritarian tendency justified by the rhetoric of security and national unity" (Van der Walt, 1998:90). As part of this project, police forces have been used to secure presidential and regime survival (Shaw, 1991; Hills, 1996).

Amadife has argued that in most instances, the appearance of democratization has "masked . . . the reality of the continuation of autocratic governance" (1999:621). At best, Southern Africa has achieved partial liberalization, but in all instances (though to a lesser extent in South Africa), this liberalization has not led to a full transition to democracy. Rather, Hills (1996) suggests, the introduction of multiparty democracy and structural adjustment policies have managed only to rearrange existing elites.

While the term *democracy* may not be applicable to states in Southern Africa, Southern African countries are nevertheless undergoing political and economic change. On the political front, parliamentary government is being promoted. At the economic level, more liberal systems are being advanced and the state is taking on more of a regulatory than interventionist role (Gbossa and Gauthe, 2000). The end of apartheid in South Africa also has had a significant impact on the region—it has led to fundamental changes in security and political concerns. What is currently being called for within the region is a framework of cooperation whereby peace and security can be assured. A Southern African Development Community (SADC) Treaty has been drawn up that commits the region to creating common political values, systems, and institutions (Cilliers, 1999).

There are two important spin-offs for police labor relations that result from regional cooperation agreements such as the treaty. First, the Southern African Regional Police Chiefs Co-operation Organisation (SARPCO), constituted in August of 1995, was envisaged as a forum for enhancing cooperation and meeting common goals between public police agencies in the region. It was created essentially to facilitate collaborative combating of crime in the region. However, its activities also include interstate assistance with regard to training, technical assistance and expertise, advice, improvement, and development of organizations and administration. Given the relatively advanced technical and administrative resources of South Africa, the South African Police Service is likely to provide a model for administrative restructuring, including structures and processes for addressing labor-relations matters.

Second, the Southern African Trade Union Coordination Council (SAT-UCC),[2] which was formed in the mid-1980s, has become an influential body in the region in the recent years. In 1992, SATUCC developed a Social Charter for Fundamental Rights. The charter calls for uniform labor laws across the region and for, among other things, the right of workers to organize and form independent unions. SATUCC has also called for worker rights to negotiation and collective bargaining in order to establish agreed-upon employment conditions.

Both of these initiatives are crucial if any kind of stable democracy is to be created in Southern Africa. The creation of secure and safe communities is essential to democratic governance (Hutchful, 1995:5), as are the fundamental rights of workers to organize and to collectively bargain. In order to invigorate democracy, it is important to move beyond the formal act of voting. What is required is a continuous engagement in policy making and implementation by communities, co-operatives, and unions. This is crucial if states are to move away from centrism toward more open political and economic cultures and practices, and the state police need to secure these new freedoms.

State Police in Africa

Despite the highly politicized and public role of the state police in Africa, African scholars have paid scant attention to the police as an institution, particularly in the post-colonial context (Cole, 1999). Two reasons can be suggested for this absence. First, the dominating presence of the military in Africa has led on the one hand to a conflation in understanding the role and function of the police and the military, and on the other hand to a preoccupation with the military as an institution in understanding governance issues (Hutchful, 1995; Honwana, 1997). Second, African scholars seem to believe that in trying to understand change in Africa, paying attention to the police represents a "statist" (even modernist) approach to developing a new social order (Mbaku and Kimenyi, 1995), or that such an approach assumes a narrow and limited conception of security (Obi, 1997).

There has, however, been a fair amount written about policing in colonial Africa. Anderson and Killingray demonstrate that almost uniformly, the police were the

> most visible public symbol of colonial rule, in daily contact with the
> population and enforcing codes of law that upheld colonial
> authority... the colonial policeman—be he European officer or local
> native recruit—stood at the cutting edge of colonial rule. (1991:2)

These police organizations during colonial times in Africa were paramilitary forces whose key goal was to suppress internal resistance (Sall and
Sallah, 1995). Instead of providing security and combating crime, police in
the colonies assisted the state in seizing land and provided the force
needed to enforce the property rights of minority owners (Mbaku and
Kimenyi, 1995).

In post-colonialism, it would seem, most police forces in Africa have
remained unchanged for many years in terms of personnel, equipment,
and even governing legislation. Cole has argued in this regard that:

> In many cases, the control of the police has merely changed hands
> from one authoritarian government to another.... Many African lead-
> ers have been able to continue in the colonial tradition of using the
> police for political ends. These have included the use of the police to
> oppress and intimidate political opponents and dissidents, trade
> unionists, university lecturers and students; and to control the work-
> ing class generally. (1999:98)

When, for example, Tanganyika attained independence in 1961, the new
Tanzanian government attempted to reform the criminal justice system.
This "reform" process seems to have resulted in a perpetuation of the colonial heritage of the police force and, in fact, new forms of authoritarianism
and social repression emerged. The new government refused to accommodate any opposition to its policies, and anybody who dissented was criminally charged. This severity in the implementation of law and order was,
according to President Nyerere, in the "national interest" of a newly
emerging state. The state police in Tanzania have since been accused of
carrying out procedures without regard for due process, corruption and
abuse of power, and the torture of offenders (Shaidi, 1989:254).

The Tanzanian case unfortunately is not exceptional. Weak states
throughout Africa, lacking legitimacy, mechanisms for delivery, and consensual means of social control, have resorted to awarding excessive powers to the security forces. The police and military have become almost
indistinguishable from one another in many African countries, raising serious concerns about the use of force and the lack of a civilian-based security body (Honwana, 1997; Hutchful, 1995). At the same time, there has
been an increase in private security, both in the form of corporate organizations and self-arming by civilians, all adding to increasing militarism
and spiralling violence.

It is in the policing of public order, however, that the repressive nature
of policing in Southern Africa is most evidenced. This is so, Hills (1996)
suggests, for the reason that public disorder remains a constant threat

because the political order is fragile. Reports of the policing of protests and demonstrations provide clear evidence of the lack of democratic technologies and mentalities within public police agencies in Southern Africa. Following are a few examples of the repressive policing of social movements in Southern Africa in recent years.

In Swaziland, the brutality of the police toward trade unions and other social movement organizations is well documented. Recently, for example, the police broke up a three-day protest action by the Swazi Labor Federation. Unionists were beaten by baton-wielding police officers, and one unionist was killed. The demonstrations were in protest of King Mswati III's anti-democratization statements and his banning of political parties in Swaziland (AllAfrica.com, 2003).

In Zimbabwe, the police are notorious for their brutal treatment of any anti-government activity. In June of 2003, Tim Butcher, BBC news correspondent in Bulawayo, commented:

> Encouraged by President Robert Mugabe's increasingly despotic regime, the security forces in Zimbabwe now treat any street gathering as a potential protest march. . . . Swish go the sjamboks, their heavy animal-hide whips, as the police beat anyone who gets in their way, and hiss go tear gas canisters. Under the draconian Public Order and Security Act recently passed by the regime . . . a gathering of three people is not just a crowd, but a potentially political event that needs explicit police authority. (Butcher, 2003)

In Angola, restrictions on freedom of assembly, association, and expression continue unabated according to Amnesty International's annual report of 2002. Activists have been detained and police reportedly have beaten and arrested peaceful demonstrators. In Malawi, in recent years police opened fire on a wide range of groups of demonstrators, including Rastafarians and students (BBC News, 2001) as well as Muslims protesting the deportation of suspected members of extremist groups (AfricaOnline, 2003).

In Mozambique too, despite various interventions from international human-rights bodies and governmental pressures for police reform, reports of police brutality are ongoing (Seleti, 2000). Police continue to carry out abuses when policing demonstrations or strikes. In January of 1997 police killed one man and wounded four others as they attempted to disperse 250 security guards who demonstrated for better pay (Human Rights Watch, 1999).

Similar reports are available from Afronet, based in Zambia. Afronet has argued that despite the fact that Zambia is party to various international human-rights conventions, police action clearly demonstrates a lack of commitment to human-rights principles on the part of the Zambian government. Interestingly, Afronet links the brutal nature of protest policing to the lack of employee rights and the poor working conditions of police members. According to them:

A large part of the problem confronting the police is the lack of independence from the executive, which is directed by the President of the republic. . . . The police service is charged with the responsibility of exercising its power to maintain law and order without violating the law or altering its meaning to suit the police force. This, however, has not been the case. . . . The police have on several occasions acted to curtail the rights and freedoms of citizens, especially if those citizens are perceived to hold dissenting views from those of the ruling political leadership. This has reinforced the public perception of the police as a militia force. . . . This culture is mainly exacerbated by two imperatives, namely, (a) the poor working conditions of the police and (b) individual officers' own bitterness at their poor conditions of service. (Afronet, 2001)

The reasons for the continual abusive treatment of the public by the police in Southern Africa are numerous.[3] They include poor police training; lack of adequate mechanisms to monitor, detect, and correct abusive behavior; deficient selection criteria; inadequate political will and direction with regard to police democratization; and derisory police leadership and supervision, as well as a civic population who lack the political and social rights to contest police abuses. However, as the Afronet report (2001) points out, cultures of impunity, derision, and militarism are likely to persist as long as police conditions of service remain deplorable and as long as police members are denied the right to freedom of association and to participate in the determination of organizational policy and planning.

It is only through directly experiencing freedom of expression and association that police can be expected to appreciate the value of such freedoms for the broader community in which they operate. As long as police members are treated as subordinates who are unable to influence decision making and determine the conditions of their working environment, they will be unlikely to apprehend the benefits of democratic participation in daily governance issues.

For any democratization of public policing to occur within Southern Africa, police require a work environment that emphasizes equity and human dignity. What is required, then, is a liberalization of police labor relations that allows police to participate in representative organizations and collectively bargain for improved working conditions and for more general organizational change. The reality is, however, that police labor relations in Southern Africa (with the exception of South Africa and to a limited extent Lesotho) have maintained an autocratic labor-relations framework.

Current Police Labor Relations Arrangements in Southern Africa

The link between external and internal democratization is not new, nor is it peculiar to Africa. Indeed, Thomas Feltes, in arguing for reform in German policing, states:

> By reorganising the police force into a community oriented, decentralised and independent organization with participatory management we can get both satisfied customers and satisfied employees. (2000:7)

Feltes is implying that police reform and more participatory police management practices go hand in hand. In recent decades attempts to reform public police agencies (generally in line with more community-oriented philosophies and practices) have given considerable weight to transforming management and work structures. Advocates of police reform, including the police themselves, have come to realize that the success of change efforts within police organizations depends heavily on the extent to which police feel motivated and valued and are able to influence policy and practice. This has led to recommendations that police organizational structures be flattened to allow for more participatory forms of management (Lafferty and Fleming, 2000; Bayley, 1994).

Police organizations, particularly within Western democratic societies, have been concerned with ensuring high-quality police management, what Reiner (1993) terms a "corporate management style," that incorporates a participatory management dimension.[4] This has coincided with "the emerging consensus around a service-based, consumerist-approach to policing" (Reiner, 1993:267). Community policing perhaps best encapsulates the most recent philosophic policing transition. The shift toward a more localized, community-oriented policing style thus demands more participatory types of police management and more flexible responses to community problems. Police supervisors need to promote rather than restrict creativity and problem-solving approaches (Birzer, 1996).

As police organizations increasingly construct their labor relations on the corporate model, police representative organizations (unions, federations, and associations) have become institutionalized, and collective bargaining processes have become commonplace. The resulting structures and processes differ from country to country, but within established democracies it is widely accepted that industrial rights should be extended to police, who are awarded the dual status of workers and professionals. Police managers are also increasingly realizing the importance of employing participatory management practices rather than the autocratic management systems that characterize more traditionally bureaucratic and hierarchical policing organizations. These shifts in management styles and the extension of rights of association to police, however, have not taken place in Southern Africa. Until very recently, no research had been conducted on the state of labor relations within public police agencies in this region.

In June of 2001, the Police and Prisons Civil Rights Union in South Africa commissioned researchers (including myself) from Natal University to investigate the state of police labor relations in Southern Africa. Between August of 2001 and February of 2002, six countries in Southern Africa were visited (Zambia, Namibia, Lesotho, Swaziland, Zimbabwe, and Malawi). Police heads of labor relations, human resources, discipline and grievances, and other related departments were interviewed, as were rank-and-file members of the police agencies (where this was allowed). A number of conclusions drawn from this research were later corroborated at a conference on Police Labor Relations in Southern Africa held in October of 2002 in Durban.[5] The conference was attended by senior police representatives and trade union officials from all SADC countries, with the exception of Angola, the Seychelles, and the Democratic Republic of Congo. A number of key conclusions were drawn from the research, all of which were buttressed at the conference.

In general terms, police labor relations in Southern Africa remain out of sync with current international trends in police labor relations and management practices. It is only in South Africa, and to a lesser extent in Lesotho, that police labor relations are comparable to those in Western democracies where, in broad terms, police are accorded the right to organize and to collectively bargain. Police labor relations in South Africa were formally liberalized with the promulgation of the first South African Police Labor Regulations in November of 1993.

At present, there are three main police representative organizations in South Africa—the Police and Prisons Civil Rights Union (POPCRU), the South African Police Union (SAPU), and the Public Service Association (PSA). The police are covered by the newest (1995) Labour Relations Act and share the same rights, responsibilities, and protections with other workers in both the private and public sector. These representative organizations, while not permitted to engage in strike actions, are permitted to engage in collective bargaining and political pressure activities.

The police unions were formally recognized in 1993 and have since played an important role, not only in determining officers' salaries and fringe benefits but also in determining policies pertaining to promotions, assignments, discipline, and other conditions of work. More importantly, perhaps, the police unions in South Africa, particularly POPCRU, have been concerned about the external democratization of the police force. They have initiated campaigns centered on building police professionalism and were one of the first advocates of community policing in South Africa.

While most other Southern African states claim to be democracies, basic employment rights (and arguably citizen rights) have not been extended to the state police. Although the nature of the police agencies differs in each country in Southern Africa, a few general observations can be made as to the current state of police labor relations in the region.

While police documentation in most Southern African countries refers to the civilianization and demilitarization of police forces, there is no mention in their policies, legislation, or annual reports of the need for internal democratization of these police forces or the need to liberalize police labor relations.

South Africa remains an exception with regard to police labor relations in the Southern African region. Lesotho has also made considerable headway toward aligning its police labor relations with those of Western democracies, particularly Britain. Police in the rest of the Southern African region are prohibited from joining representative organizations. Rank-and-file police have no forums or process available to them to participate in decision making about service conditions or about broader policy and planning.

Unlike in South Africa, police in the rest of the Southern African region are excluded from existing labor relations acts. Police labor relations are governed by police acts and police standing orders, which often are not in accordance with the more liberalized labor legislation governing the private sector or even the rest of the public sector. In every Southern African country surveyed in this study aside from Lesotho, police are denied access to collective bargaining forums and grievances are dealt with by means of an autocratic ranking system.

The Royal Swaziland Police (RSP), for example, are excluded from the Industrial Relations Act of 2000. Police Act No. 29 of 1957 covers their labor relations separately. Individual officers may file a grievance with their officer-in-charge, which is then taken through the chain of command up to commissioner level if need be. Individual police officers have no right to legal representation or assistance during this process and are expected to accept any decision made by the commissioner. They are, however, free to take the RSP to court if they wish, but this seldom (if ever) happens.

Police associations do exist in Swaziland, but they are not allowed to contest the commissioner's decision and are not authorized to represent officers facing disciplinary action. Should the charged officer be unsatisfied with the outcome of the hearing, he or she can appeal to the prime minister, who then makes a final judgment. If the charged officer is still not satisfied, he or she can take the matter to a civilian court.

In Zimbabwe the labor standards of the police are dictated by the 1996 Police Act and by police standing orders, which dictate every facet of the organization including the conduct of the police and conditions of service. The Zimbabwe Republic Police are exempt from key constitutional passages. As part of the "disciplined forces" they are not protected from forced labor practices, employment discrimination, or treatment amounting to violations of human rights. To change this, a two-thirds vote of parliament would be required.

Collective bargaining in the public sector is fairly new in Southern Africa (including South Africa). It is, therefore, not surprising that collective bargaining structures do not exist for the police except in Lesotho. This means that police have no forum in which to voice their collective concerns or to negotiate their conditions of service. At the most basic level, police officers are denied any power to influence police policy or economic interests.

Zambian Police Force members do not have access to direct collective bargaining. The Zambia Police and Prisons Service Commission deals with issues of a collective nature, including appointments, promotions, transfers, retirement, and compensation in cases of death. Salaries and other conditions of service are determined by central government whenever there is a general-salaries and conditions-of-service review in the civil service. During these review processes, unions represent other civil servants. A police association does exist but is not eligible to negotiate collective agreements.

Police unions are taboo in the Southern African region. South Africa is the only country in the region that legally provides for the unionization of the police. The South African experience, however, appears not to have had a positive impact on the rest of Southern Africa, where police management and government perceive police unions as troublesome and as a threat to police professionalism. Belonging to a trade union is viewed as antithetical to membership in a military-like organization.

Police are allowed to join associations in all of the countries visited, except for in Namibia. However, police associations tend to focus on issues of recreation and benefits, to the exclusion of issues pertaining to working conditions and the professional development of police officers. In Swaziland, the police associations are not even allowed to raise questions related to promotion or issues pertaining to politics and discipline. Police associations play no role in the formulation of policy or in shaping the general philosophy or practice of police agencies in the region.

The continued autocratic labor relations frameworks and practices in Southern Africa have serious consequences for both the morale and the commitment of police officers themselves as well as for the development of more community-oriented policing. As Brogden (1999) correctly points out, where there are very clear lines drawn between police managers and rank-and-file officers, the implementation of community policing is improbable. "New forms of participatory management" (p. 180) are crucial if community-policing initiatives are to become feasible.

The Case for Police Representative Organizations

Policing, Finnane (2002) has argued, is both an industry and a workplace. Reiner suggests that police are as concerned about working conditions and wages as any other employee: "When [police] have experienced pressure on their economic and other interests, [they] have (in all liberal democratic societies) developed collective means of defense, in the form of police unionism" (Reiner, 1978:5). It is not surprising, therefore, that in most liberal democratic countries, police have representative organizations either in the form of unions, associations, or federations.

As early as 1947, Australian labor historian and civil libertarian Brian Fitzpatrick concluded that if police had full political rights—including the right to unionize—"it would be harder for them to be used in the service of political repression" (cited in Finnane 1999:13). Fitzpatrick defended the rights of police to unionize as "consistent with the advancement of democracy and good governance" (p. 13). Police unions were legitimated relatively early on in Australia (in the 1920s), and the rights of police to assert their collective interests was won far earlier than in many other countries. Today, almost 99 percent of police members in Australia are unionized.

The road to police unionization in the United States was longer and more difficult than was the case in Australia. However, according to Cox (1996) and Gammage and Sacks (1972), with the exception of perhaps teachers and firefighters, police are the most unionized of public-sector employers in the United States today.[6] In Canada, police associations operate at the local, state, and provincial level.[7] Most, but not all, enjoy "statutorily designated bargaining units, the legislated ability to negotiate with their employers, and binding, independent and impartial third-party dispute resolution" (Griffin, 2001:4). The Canadian Police Association maintains that good police labor-management relations are crucial to safeguarding the public. This is because, they argue, "where relations break down and the organizations become dysfunctional, issues begin to spill into the public domain" (p. 2).

This tendency for police to form employee-representative organizations and demand the right to collective bargaining is unlikely to change. Rather, police demands for industrial rights are likely to increase. As Finnane (2002) notes, the history of police administration in the twentieth century has made police more like other workers in their rights and aspiration. And, he argues, it would be wrong to anticipate that changing structures of workplaces and industrial relations will weaken the authority of police unions. Police organizations, in fact, start from a position of comparative advantage with regard to unionization potential. While technology continues to supplement some fields of policing, policing remains a labor-intensive industry.[8]

Despite the propensity for police to form unions (or associations), collective representative police organizations are not welcomed in many instances by police managers and supervisors. This is because police are viewed as a symbol of authority, and police organizations are required to display an image of smooth operating that requires a "hierarchical and disciplined body" (Reiner, 1978). Time spent organizing collectively is viewed as negatively impacting police work, especially the ability to perform essential services. Police unions are also seen as interfering with the ability of police chiefs to manage their own departments; managerial prerogatives, it is believed, are undermined by police unions and collective-bargaining rights (Fogelson, 1977).

The general (if not always accurate) perception is that the collective organization of police officers into a union generates industrial action and disunity within the workplace and has led police management to advocate for police associations rather than unions. Associations are viewed as organizing in the professional ambit, while unions are viewed as organizing workers with somewhat separate interests from those of employers and managers. In a number of countries, therefore, police are allowed to form professional associations (sometimes called federations) rather than unions. While this distinction has become somewhat tenuous, associations may have limited rights with regard to collective action (both within the police and in sympathy with other workers), affiliation to other union bodies, and collective bargaining. These limitations, however, are generally determined by political and industrial climates rather than by the chosen terminologies allocated to police-employee representative bodies.

Skepticism with regard to police unions/associations is not, however, limited to the disruptive nature of collective industrial action. Police representative organizations can be extremely conservative in their outlook and the campaigns in which they engage. They have, across time and space, demonstrated preference for law-and-order approaches and are known to obstruct reform process. Police unions/associations have opposed civilian reviews of the police, have called for stricter sentencing of offenders, have disapproved lateral entry programs, and have contested increased training requirements (Fogelson, 1977). A further concern of those who oppose police unionization is that police unions have tended to exploit the political arena rather than the collective-bargaining arena in dealing with law enforcement policy (Juris and Feuille, 1973; Burpo, DeLord, and Shannon, 1997; Finnane, 2002).

The conservative bent and political maneuvering of police representative organizations are serious concerns. However, police stakeholder groups in Canada have come to realize that, "if police managers foster respectful and collaborative relations with police unions/associations, there will be less likelihood of labor conflict and less reason for the association/union to take extraordinary measures to present their issues" (Biro, Campbell, McKenna, and Murray, 2000:15). Furthermore, police associations/unions may provide police managers with the only forum by which to communicate with police officers as a group. Police representative organizations also can be a vehicle for gaining support for change processes, and they may even provide platforms for the formulation of policies oriented toward greater professionalism and improving partnerships with communities and other stakeholders. Support for reform processes is likely to occur only if police feel that they are able to participate in the formulation of change programs.

There are a number of other positive roles that police-employee representative organizations can play. First, they "furnish employee representation which serves as a necessary internal check against bureaucratic usurpation" (Gammage and Sacks, 1972:102). They are capable of posing a challenge to the culture, the decision-making processes, and the traditionally austere atmosphere of public police agencies (Guyot, 1979; Burpo, 1971). The demand that police employee organizations make on managers—to refrain from autocratic, bureaucratically determined practices within the police organization—has the potential to spur a new disposition among both high- and low-ranking police officers in dealing with constituencies other than the police.

Second, if police members are part of cohesive representative organizations, they are more likely to readily support new policy. Unions and associations play a "fundamental role in translating the aspirations of workers into coherent and structured strategies at the national, continental and international level" (ILO, 1999:15). As David Griffin (2001) of the Canadian Police Association has argued, police are more likely to resort to external pressure to resolve concerns when there is no recourse to independent third-party resolution and when they are not afforded an appropriate role in decision-making processes.

Third, police employee-representative organizations act as a deterrent to the fraudulent/corrupt minority often found in a police department. Police employee organizations tend to keep a careful watch over the behavior of managers and supervisors. They also have the potential to keep the conduct of their own members in check. While these organizations may attempt to defend members against disciplinary processes, it is in their interest to ensure that the mendacious action of their members does not bring the organization into disrepute by behaving in disreputable ways.

Fourth, police unions/associations provide a channel for real consultation and negotiation with police (Gammage and Sacks, 1972). Collective bargaining, which often falls within the ambit of rights of police unions/associations, restricts the ability of police management to make policy decisions unilaterally (Levi, 1978).

In South Africa, police managers, employers, and employees have jointly negotiated to resolve a number of issues ranging from wages, to promotion policies, to policing priorities. In so doing, the police unions have played a key role in shaping both the service conditions of police and the direction that public policing has taken. Indeed, the Police and Prisons Civil Rights Union placed community policing on the agenda as early as 1989, long before it was formally legislated as policing policy in 1995 (Brogden and Shearing, 1993; Marks, 2000a). POPCRU's formation and agenda is without doubt unique to the political, social, and industrial environment in South Africa (Marks, 2000a, 2000b). However, its very existence and the programs it has initiated demonstrate the potential that police employee organizations have to identify with the communities that they serve and to place the need for external and internal police democratization firmly on the agenda of police agencies.

Finally, and by no means least importantly, police unions/associations are best known for campaigning to improve morale by achieving better salaries, fairer procedures, and improved lines of communication (Cox, 1996).

While police unions of earlier decades were concerned mostly with traditional issues of collective bargaining and internal discipline, the focus of these organizations now has widened and their approaches have become much more proactive in recent years. Griffin states that his organization has come to the realization that:

In order for 21st century police associations or unions to be effective, they must engage in strategic activities which position the organization as an influential and respected stakeholder on issues concerning the safe and effective delivery of police services to in their communities. (2001:17)

The social, political, and economic environment in which police unions/associations operate demands a reconfiguring of their relations with management, the skills that members cultivate within these organizations, and the campaigns that are embarked upon. Police unions/associations need to be able to contribute constructively to debates on the future of policing. Privatization, new forms of crime and public disorder, reconfigurations of nations and states, and contested practices of democracy are all going to demand ongoing reform of public police agencies. Police services in Southern Africa are going to confront a huge burden with regard to reform, given the incomplete nature of state democratization at present.

If police unions/associations (whether in Africa, America, Asia, or elsewhere) are to be authoritative and respectable policing stakeholders, they will need to seriously consider the new challenges facing the policing enterprise. While they will always have to safeguard police members' interests, they must also be part of organizational enterprises to improve service delivery and respond to issues of local and global reorganization.

In the Southern Africa context, police representative organizations have important roles to play in promoting police reform and keeping its membership in check. As was the case with POPCRU in South Africa, police unions/associations can lead the way in devising new (more progressive) policies. Most importantly, perhaps, police organizations can play a key role in redefining notions of citizenship, informed by their own quest for rights and freedoms within the organizations themselves and by their identification with members of communities they serve.

Police representative organizations will have to become, to borrow a term from Martin Godfrey, "swords of justice" rather than merely "protectors of vested interests" (Godfrey, 2003:29). This is in fact already taking place within the labor movement in countries as diverse as Brazil, Mexico, South Africa, and the Philippines that have embraced a "citizenship frame." In so doing, the labor movement is increasingly taking on "issues of democracy, human rights and social justice not only in the context of labor relations but also in the larger society" (Johnston, cited in Webster and Lambert, 2003:4). Police-employee representative organizations in Southern Africa (and beyond) may benefit from the trends in social movement unionism, which stresses alliances with nongovernment organizations and community groupings as well as a strong focus on social justice issues (Munck, 2002).

In years to come, public police agencies worldwide are likely to evolve from their traditional organizational structure. Contract employment and an emphasis on performance measurement will replace tenured employment.

Civilians increasingly will be employed in police organizations in nonoperational functions. Female and minority-group representation is likely to increase. Public police agency members are likely to be better educated, more aware of their individual rights, and more concerned with issues of equal treatment and even affirmative action (Grabosky, 2001). Consequently, they are likely to be more demanding of police employers regarding working conditions, wages, benefits, and rights. They are more likely to challenge authority and to be captains of their own organizational destiny. The rights to join police associations/unions and to engage in collective bargaining are likely to be viewed increasingly as basic rights of the police.

In turn, police representative organizations will have to "up the ante" to meet the needs and expectations of this changing social base of public police agencies. They will have to be adept in problem solving and in providing visions for policing's future. A balance will have to be struck between traditional industrial concerns (which will always be a focus) and broad policy making and planning within police organizations. Furthermore, since the public police increasingly will compete with private policing agencies (Bayley and Shearing, 1996; Grabosky, 2001), both police managers and police unions/associations will have to expend considerable effort in devising innovative and effective means of combating crime, maintaining/creating public order, and strategies for reducing risks and insecurity. These efforts need to be framed by a human-rights, partnership-building framework.

Conclusion

Southern Africa is emerging from decades of authoritarian rule, and democratic institutions in the region have yet to take hold. Most [Southern] African countries have made considerable progress in the establishment of democratic rule of law, marked by enhanced political and union activities and the existence of a free press (ILO, 1999). However, the democratization process has been characterized by many weaknesses, including the sluggishness of institutional change and the unhurried pace of the review of labor laws (ILO, 1999). While institutional change needs to take place in all public (and private) institutions, police institutional change is most urgent. This is because the police "represent the very face of state power" (Della Porta, 1995:1). How the police act, particularly in regard to the policing of public order, is in many ways a reflection of state governance technologies, practices, and mentalities.

If the governance of Southern African states is to become more democratic—as Southern African governments claim is the case (Hyslop, 1999)—state policing needs to become less oriented to state protectionism and more oriented toward community needs and equitable service delivery. Policing, in line with the rhetoric of community policing, needs to emphasize practices of partnership building, joint problem solving, and equitable service delivery as well as mentalities of social justice (Bayley, 1994; Goldstein, 1990). But the police are only likely to shift toward such mentalities and practices if they themselves experience these things within the organization in which they spend most of their time.

While community-oriented policing may call for more participatory (even corporate) styles of management, there are also intraorganizational rationales for introducing such management styles. Like any work-based organization, it is crucial to bring all members of the police organization on board during processes of change or transition. Goldstein (1990) argues that participatory management is in fact fundamental to police organizational change. Change must make sense to those on the front line. If this does not occur, rank-and-file police officers are likely to feel threatened by change and feel that it is not necessarily in their best interest. More participatory management styles lead to a greater understanding of change processes, and this in turn makes change more acceptable to police officers (Washo, 1984; Sykes, 1986). High morale promotes pride, efficiency, and harmony, and this in turn enhances the acceptability of the profession and the quality of the service rendered (Van Heerden, 1982). Excluding rank-and-file members from information and from decision-making processes regarding change may leave them feeling disillusioned, manipulated, frustrated, and lacking motivation.

Police leaders in Southern Africa will continue to face new challenges and demands that will test the resolve of their labor-management relations. Meeting these challenges requires police organizations to develop a committed workforce which shares a vision, and in which conflict between management and the rank-and-file is minimized. This is only likely to occur if the police themselves have direct experience of the right to collectively organize and to influence decision-making processes. The form these representative bodies will take and the rights they are awarded will differ from country to country, depending on cultural and institutional traditions.

In order for the democratization of the police to occur, the transformation of the police labor-relations arena must be accompanied by a host of other mechanisms. These include instituting a change in the policy environment, increasing citizen rights generally in regard to governance issues, retraining police officers, increasing management capacity, and employing new recruitment processes as well as lateral entry programs and civilian oversight mechanisms. Without these accompanying mechanisms, democratic policing is unlikely to occur. It is difficult to determine which of these mechanisms, including the liberalization of police labor relations, is most crucial in effecting police transformation. However, it is clear that fundamental challenges to the authoritarian traditions within police organizations in the region are required if democratic governance of security is to take hold.

Notes

[1] While there is no easy definition of democratic policing, Marx (1995) argues that democratic police systems share some basic ideals such as that police powers should be used according to the rule of law, that police power should be used in a restrained manner, and that policing should take place through consent.

[2] SATUCC is a body formed to coordinate trade union activities of the Southern African Development Council. All major national trade union centers from the Southern African region are affiliated to SATUCC.

[3] It should be noted that these problems are not limited to the southern region of Africa. See for example, Marenin (1985) regarding policing in Nigeria. Interestingly, Marenin concludes that the police in Nigeria are

> not that useful as a tool of the state. Their routine work seems oriented more to self-interest and the avoidance of problems than the strict enactment of organizational policy. . . . A police officer is not likely to resist a specific command openly, whatever its content, but will attempt evasion or avoidance if the duty is unpleasant or dangerous. (1985:83)

[4] Goldstein (1990), however, argues that attempts to introduce more participatory management styles have been modest, at least in the United States.

[5] A full report of these findings can be found in Marks (2002).

[6] For a detailed account of the history of police unions in the United States of America, see Kadleck (2001).

[7] The Royal Canadian Mounted Police, however, do not have the right to unionize.

[8] Despite this, police scholars have paid scant attention to police unions. Robert Reiner (1978) has suggested that this is because the notion of police striking is viewed as antithetical to the policing role. This is particularly the case if police are defined as an essential service, as they often are. Secondly, Reiner argues, police are generally alienated from the labor movement and play a repressive role regarding collective action on the part of the labor movement, as the Southern African case clearly demonstrates.

References

Africa Online (2003). Malawi: Police fire on Muslim demonstrators. Available: http://www.africaonline.com/site/Articles/1,3,53388.jsp (accessed February 11, 2004).

Afrol News (2003). Slow progress in Botswana's labor rights. Available: http://www.afrol.com/News2003/bot003_labor.htm (accessed February 11, 2004).

Afronet (2001). Zambia: Human Rights Report 2001. Available: http://afronet.org.za/Human%20Report/zhrr.htm (accessed February 11, 2004).

AllAfrica.com (2003). Strikers beaten by police, 13/08/03. Available (password protected): http://allafrica.com/stories/200308130770.html.

Amadife, E. (1999). Liberalization and democratization in Nigeria: The International and domestic challenge, *Journal of Black Studies* 29(5):619–645.

Amnesty International (2002a). Amnesty International Report 2002: Angola. Available: http://web.amnesty.org/web/ar2002.nsf/afr/angola?open (accessed February 11, 2004).

Amnesty International (2002b). Amnesty International Report 2002: Zambia. Available: http://web.amnesty.org/web/ar2002.nsf/afr/zambia?open (accessed February 11, 2004).

Anderson, D. and Killingray, D. (1991). Consent, coercion and colonial control: Policing the empire, 1830–1941. In D. Anderson and D. Killingray (eds.), *Policing the Empire: Government, Authority and Control, 1830–1940*. Manchester: Manchester University Press.

Bayley, D. (1994). *Police for the Future*. New York: Oxford University Press.

Bayley, D., and Shearing, C. (1996). The future of policing, *Law and Society Review* 30(3):585–606.

BBC News (2001). Malawi police shoot protesters, World Africa Front Page, 12/12/ 01. Available: http://news.bbc.co.uk/1/hi/world/africa/1705577.stm (accessed February 11, 2004).

BBC News (2003). Police disperse Nigerian strikers, News Front Page, 30/06/03. Available: http://news.bbc.co.uk/1/hi/world/africa/3033648.stm (accessed February 11, 2004).

Bent, A. (1974). *The Politics of Law Enforcement*. London: Lexington Books.

Biro, F., Campbell, P., McKenna, P., and Murray, T. (2000). Police executives under pressure: A study and discussion of the issues, Police Futures Study Group Series No. 3, published by the Canadian Association of Chiefs of Police.

Birzer, M. (1996). Police supervisors in the 21st century, *FBI Law Enforcement Bulletin* 65(6):1–3.

Bolinger, H. (1981). Police officers' views on collective bargaining and the use of sanctions. In H. More (ed.), *Critical Issues in Law Enforcement*. Cincinnati: Anderson.

Brogden, M. (1999). Community policing as Cherry Pie. In R. I. Mawby (ed.), *Policing Across the World: Issues for the Twenty-First Century*. London: UCL Press.

Brogden, M. and Shearing, C. (1993). *Policing for a New South Africa*. London: Routledge.

Burpo, J. (1971). *The Police Labor Movement: Problems and Purposes*. Springfield, IL: C. G. Thomas.

Burpo, J., DeLord, R., and Shannon, M. (1997). *Police Associations, Power, Politics and Confrontation: A Guide for the Successful Police Labor Leader*. Springfield, IL: Charles. G. Thomas.

Butcher, T. (2003). Zimbabwe's brutal police tactics, BBC News, front page. Available: http://news.bbc.co.uk/1/hi/programmes/from_our_own_correspondent/ 3027072.stm (accessed February 11, 2004).

Cilliers, J. (1999). Building security in Southern Africa: An update on the evolving architecture, Institute for Security Studies Monograph series, Institute for Security Studies, Pretoria.

Cole, B. (1999). Post-colonial systems. In R. I. Mawby (ed.), *Policing Across the World: Issues for the Twenty-First Century*. London: UCL Press.

Cox, S. (1996). *Police Practices, Perspectives and Problems*. Boston: Allyn and Bacon.

Della Porta, D. (1995). Police knowledge and public order: Some reflections on the Italian case. In D. McAdam, T. McCarthy, and M. Zald (eds.), *The Dynamics of Social Movements*. Cambridge: Cambridge University Press.

Feltes, T. (2000). Community policing—Training and education: How to break the wall. Paper presented at the Brussels 2000 International Conference on Evaluating Community Policing, Vrije Universiteit, Brussels, August 16–19.

Finnane, M. (1999). Police unions in Australia: A history of the present. Paper presented at the History of Crime, Policing and Punishment conference convened by the Australian Institute of Criminology in conjunction with the Charles Stuart University, Canberra, December 9–10.

Finnane, M. (2002). *When Police Unionise: The Politics of Law and Order in Australia*. Sydney: Institute of Criminology, University of Sydney.

Fogelson, R. (1977). *Big-City Police*. Cambridge: Harvard University Press.

Fogelson, R. (1978). Unionism comes to policing. In. R. Larson (ed.), *Police Accountability: Performance Measures and Unionism*. Toronto: Lexington Press.

Gammage, A. and Sacks, S. (1972). *Police Unions*. Springfield, IL: Charles C. Thomas Publishers.

Gbossa, L. and Gauthe, B. (2000). From humanitarian aid to sustainable protection in Africa. In ILO, *Social Protection: What Workers and Trade Unions Should Know, ILO Labor Education Brief No. 121*, Geneva.

Godfrey, M. (2003). Employment dimensions of decent work: Trade-offs and complementarities. Discussion paper (DP/148/2003) for the International Institute for Labor Studies, Geneva.

Goldstein, H. (1990). *Problem Oriented Policing*. New York: McGraw-Hill.

Good, K. (1997). Accountable to themselves: Predominance in Southern Africa, *The Journal of Modern African Studies* 35(4):547–573.

Grabosky, P. (2001). Crime control in the 21st century, *The Australian and New Zealand Journal of Criminology* 34(3):221–234.

Griffin, D. (2001). Police association advocacy—A strategic priority: Police associations, political activism and public opinion. Paper presented at the Police Employment in 2001 conference, Toronto, February 27.

Guyot, D. (1979). Bending granite: Attempts to change the rank structure of American police departments, *Journal of Police Science and Administration* 7(3):253–284.

Hills, A. (1996). Towards a critique of policing and national development in Africa, *The Journal of Modern African Studies* 34(2):271–291.

Honwana, J. (1997). Civil military relations in the transition to democracy: The case of Mozambique. Paper presented at Codesria Governance Institute on the Political Economy of Conflicts in Africa, Dakar, August.

Human Rights Watch (1999). Available: http://hrw.org/worldreport99/africa/mozambique.html (accessed February 11, 2004).

Hyslop, J. (1999). Introduction: African democracy in the era of globalisation. In J. Hyslop (ed.), *African Democracy in the Era of Globalisation*. Johannesburg: Witwatersrand University Press.

ILO (1999). Ninth African Regional Meeting: Decent Work and Protection for All in Africa. Geneva: International Labor Office.

Juris, H. and Feuille, P. (1973a). The impact of police unions: Summary report. Review for the U.S. Department of Justice, Washington.

Juris, H. and Feuille, P. (1973b). *Police Unionism*. Lexington, MA: Heath and Company.

Kadleck, C. (2001). Police unions: An empirical examination. PhD dissertation, University of Cincinnati.

Killingray, D. (1991). Guarding the external frontier: Policing the Gold Coast, 1865–1913. In D. Anderson and D. Killingray (eds.), *Policing the Empire: Government, Authority and Control, 1830–1940*. London: Palgrave Macmillan.

Lafferty, G. and Fleming, J. (2000). New management techniques and restructuring for accountability in Australian police organizations, *Policing: An International Journal of Police Strategies and Management* 23(2):154–168.

Levi, M. (1978). Conflict and collusion: Police collective bargaining. In R. Larson (ed.), *Police Accountability: Performance Measures and Unionism*. Toronto: Lexington Books.

Marenin, O. (1985). Policing Nigeria: Control and autonomy in the exercise of coercion, *African Studies Review* 28(1):73–93.

Marks, M. (1999). Policing for democracy? The case of the public order police unit in Durban, *Africa Development* 24(1&2):222–270.

Marks, M. (2000a). Transforming police organizations from within: Police dissident groupings in South Africa, *British Journal of Criminology* 40:557–573.

Marks, M. (2000b). Labour relations in the South African Police Service. In G. Adler (ed.), *Public Service Labour Relations in a Democratic South Africa.* Johannesburg: University of Witwatersrand Press.

Marks, M. (2002). Organising the blues: Police labor relations in Southern Africa, *African Security Review* 11(2):51–63.

Marx, G. (2001). Police and democracy. In M. Amir and S. Einstein (eds.), *Policing, Security and Democracy: Theory and Practice, Vol. 2.* Huntsville, TX: Office of International Criminal Justice.

Mbaku, J. and Kimenyi, M. (1995). Rent seeking and policing in Africa, *Indian Journal of Social Science* 8(3):225–250.

Mitchell, M. and Wood, C. (1998). Ironies of citizenship: Skin color, police brutality and the challenge to democracy in Brazil, *Social Forces* 77(3):1001–1020.

Munck, R. (2002). *Globalisation and Labour: The New "Great Transformation."* London: Zed Books.

New York Times (2003). Swaziland Quells Protests over Commonwealth Summit Meeting. Late Edition 14/08/03, page A8.

Obi, C. (1997). Oil, environmental conflict and national security in Nigeria: Ramifications of the ecology-security nexus for sub-regional peace. Paper presented to the Programme in Arms Control Disarmament and International Security, University of Illinois, January.

Punch, M. and Markham, G. (2003). Animal rights protest, public order and police accountability: Analysis of the Brightlingsea demonstrations. Unpublished paper.

Reiner, R. (1978). *The Blue Coated Worker: A Sociological Study of Police Unionism.* London: Cambridge University Press.

Reiner, R. (1993). *The Politics of Policing.* New York: Harvester Wheatsheaf.

Sall, E. and Sallah, H. (1995). The military and the crisis of governance: The Gambian case. Paper presented at Codesria General Assembly on Conflicts and Transitions, June, Dakar.

Seleti, Y. (2000). The public in the exorcism of the police in Mozambique: Challenges of institutional democratisation, *Journal of Southern African Studies* 26(2):349–354.

Shaidi, L. (1989). Crime, justice and politics in contemporary Tanzania: State power in an underdeveloped social formation, *International Journal of Sociology and Law* 17:247–271.

Shaw, T. (1991). Reformism, revisionism and radicalism in African political economy during the 1990s, *The Journal of Modern African Studies* 29(2):191–212.

Sykes, G. (1986). Automation, management and the police role: The new reformers? *Journal of Police Science and Administration* 14(1):24–30.

Trojanowicz, R. and Bucqueroux, B. (1990). *Community Policing: A Contemporary Perspective.* Cincinnati: Anderson Publishing Co.

Tyler, T. and Huo, Y. (2002). *Trust in the Law: Encouraging Public Cooperation with the Police and Courts.* New York: Sage.

Vale, P. (1991). The search for Southern Africa's security, *International Affairs* 67(4):697–708.

Van der Walt, L. (1998). Trade unions in Zimbabwe: For democracy, against neo-liberalism, *Class and Capital* 66:85–108.

Van Heerden, T. (1982). *Introduction to Police Science.* Pretoria: University of South Africa.

Venter, D. (2003). Democracy and multiparty politics in Africa: Recent elections in Zambia, Zimbabwe and Lesotho, Project Muse. Available: http://muse.jhu.edu/search/pia.cgi (accessed February 11, 2004).

Washo, B. (1984). Effecting planned change within a police organization, *The Police Chief* November:33–35.

Webster, E. and Lambert, R. (2003). What is new in the new labor internationalism: A southern perspective. Paper presented as part of the sociology seminar program at the Rand Afrikaans University, Johannesburg, March 7.

8

Historical Trends and Recent Developments in International Drug Policy and Control

Charles B. Fields, Matthew Holt, & Gregory Ferrell

The illicit trade in narcotics is one of the most serious problems currently facing the world community. While there have been numerous international attempts at control, none have really been too successful; the world is currently experiencing a drug explosion. It seems that every aspect of the drug market, whether manufacturing, distribution, or consumption, is escalating. Not only is this occurring in the wealthy, consumer-driven West, but in almost all countries around the globe.

Despite increased efforts at stemming both the supply and demand sides of the illegal drug trade, recent years have only witnessed an increase in the size of the illegal drug business. In 1991, it was estimated that world production in metric tons was more than 23,000 for marijuana, 337,000 for coca, and 3,400 for opium, up from the 1987 estimates of 13,600, 291,000 and 2,242 respectively (*International Narcotics Control Strategy Report*, 1991:22). The Office of National Drug Control Policy (ONDCP) estimated that in 1990 U.S. citizens spent $18 billion for cocaine, $12 billion for heroin, $9 billion for marijuana, and $2 billion for other illegal drugs. The Select Committee on Narcotics Abuse and Control estimated the total amount spent at $140 billion on illegal drugs (1988 figure) (Bureau of Justice Statistics, 1992:36).

The sheer magnitude of the number of people employed makes the problem of drug trade even greater. While data show that hundreds of thousands of Americans sell drugs illegally in the United States, the greatest number of those involved in the drug trade live outside the United States. In Peru, Bolivia, and Colombia, an estimated one million people grow, produce, and export cocaine (Collett, 1989:48). In Peru, the number

Prepared especially for *Comparative and International Criminal Justice, 2/E.*

includes about 60,000 families; in Bolivia about 6 percent of the population depend on the cocaine trade (Bureau of Justice Statistics, 1992). In Burma, Thailand, and Laos—the Golden Triangle—there are hundreds of thousands employed in the heroin industry (Cooper, 1990:59). The impact of the illegal drug trade on the economies of the individuals and on their respective countries is enormous, with little incentive for them to turn toward other means of subsistence.

The response by the international community and most of the international leaders has been a strict adherence to the status quo system of universal prohibition of all illicit substances. Support is often demonstrated through a variety of criminal sanctions, from death to lengthy prison terms. As we know, the response to the application of these criminal sanctions has been skyrocketing crime and corruption in epidemic proportions. Meanwhile, the international community and the international drug-control organizations have proven largely ineffective in most areas. With the entire world focusing on drug problems, it has become increasingly clear that there needs to be a restructuring of these organizations in order to meet the increased demands being placed on them.

This article addresses the history of various international efforts at drug control. First, beginning with the 1909 Shanghai Opium Conference and the League of Nations' efforts in the 1920s and 1930s, several approaches are examined in historical context. These initial, fairly successful multinational efforts were the precursors to modern control attempts led by the United Nations. Focusing on several recent United Nations Conventions and Declarations, the next section addresses modern post–1984 international drug-control strategies.

International Drug Policy and Control: 1900–1984

The international effort to end the world's illicit drug trafficking is not a recent phenomenon. The movement of opium from India into China hit crisis proportions in the early 1900s, and the British and Chinese governments signed an anti-opium crusade agreement in 1906 to eliminate this trade. This led to the first international effort in 1909 at the Shanghai Conference, where thirteen countries began discussing a formal drug-control treaty (McAllister, 1991). The treaty was signed by twelve countries following a U.S.-led conference, later known as the 1912 International Opium Convention at The Hague, to restrict the consumption and trafficking of illicit drugs (Donnelly, 1992). This was the first time that international cooperation in the control of narcotics occurred (Rolley, 1992:416).

League of Nations

The League of Nations held its first assembly in 1920, at which time an Advisory Committee on Traffic in Opium and Other Dangerous Drugs was established to aid the League. The committee's expressed purpose was to assist and advise the League on drug-trafficking issues and to develop legislation in the area (Rolley, 1992:416). Under the direction of the League of Nations, three international conventions were coordinated regarding drug control. The first strengthened existing guidelines regarding the exchange of narcotics (Walsh, 1988:102). On February 19, 1925, the Geneva Convention was signed, and information from each member country on the transfer of narcotics was to be submitted annually from participating countries:

> Governments were required to submit to the newly created Permanent Central Opium Board annual statistics concerning production of opium and coca leaves; the manufacture, consumption, and stocks of narcotic drugs, and quarterly reports on the import and export of such drugs (not including opium and coca leaves). [The convention] also established the system of import certificates and export authorizations requiring governmental approval of each import and export. (Bassiouni, 1973:539)

The 1931 Convention for Limiting the Manufacture and Regulating the Distribution of Narcotic Drugs, the second League of Nations convention, was the first action to place limitations on the production of licit medical and scientific drugs. Members were obliged to restrict the quantity of these drugs to be manufactured in and imported to their particular country (Rolley, 1992:416). It should be noted that both the United States and China refused to sign because the agreement was not strict enough (McAllister, 1991:497). In contrast, Turkey and Switzerland, among others, refused to adhere to the document because it was seen as *too* strict!

The last League of Nations treaty, the Convention for the Suppression of the Illicit Traffic in Dangerous Drugs, was signed in Geneva in 1936. Provisions were written that specifically targeted the offenders of trafficking who legally had been able to bypass prosecution based on the previous standards (Rolley, 1992). The Second World War began shortly after this was to take effect, so it was rendered somewhat ineffective for several years (McAllister, 1991:498).

Following World War II, all of the League's functions and responsibilities regarding control of narcotics were transferred to the United Nations, in particular the Commission on Narcotic Drugs (CND) (Bassiouni, 1990:317). Established by the Economic and Social Council as the primary policy-making organ of the UN with respect to drug matters, the commission was comprised of 15 member states (out of 54 UN members) and currently consists of 53 members who periodically review the overall world drug situation and sponsor related international conventions (UNODC, 2004). During the commission's session in 1948, the World Health Organization (WHO) was given regulation over all addictive drugs. In 1953, guidelines (the Opium Protocol) were written by the commission and the

World Health Organization addressing the specific medical and scientific purposes for which opium could be used (Rolley, 1992:417).

The 1961 United Nations Single Convention on Narcotic Drugs

This convention met in New York and was attended by 115 state parties. It debated four main issues: First, it distinguished which substances were considered dangerous drugs. Second, it arranged estimated requirements and limitations regarding licit production and cultivation. Third, it made drug crimes international offenses. Fourth, it provided for the prevention of drug abuse, including education and treatment (Bossard, 1990:105–6). The most striking of these issues were the third and fourth. The third, discussed thoroughly in Article 36 of the convention, designated each illicit drug-related act occurring in different countries as a distinct offense that may be prosecuted separately. Article 38 of the Single Convention, addressing the fourth issue, was the first attempt to incorporate the handling of demand for illicit substances as a part of drug control (Bossard, 1990). This convention received the most support from UN member states at any time before or since, with more than half of the members ratifying it. For those members, this treaty merged all former treaties into the 1961 Single Convention on Narcotic Drugs, simplifying the multinational drug-control effort.

As a result, the International Narcotics Control Board (INCB) was created to monitor the illicit cultivation, production, and manufacture of drugs for medical and scientific purposes (Jamieson, 1990:36), and given the following responsibilities:

- Enforcing the provisions of the convention
- Securing estimates of drug requirements, existing stocks, production and consumption statistics, and statistics on seizures of unlawfully held drugs, and publishing the results
- Requesting information, explanations, and public declarations by governments
- Recommending embargoes on imports and exports
- Gathering and publishing texts of laws and regulations concerning narcotics from signatory states (Rolley, 1992:417)

The board also works closely with the Commission on Narcotic Drugs and other international agencies.

By 1970, it was apparent that the 1961 Single Convention on Narcotic Drugs was not comprehensive enough to control growing drug problems. The Single Convention relied heavily on each member country to oversee the enforcement of its new treaty, with no structured means of enforcement on the country. The majority of the member countries had domestic laws that contradicted this new UN treaty, but the treaty had no jurisdiction to influence a change in these domestic laws (Bassiouni, 1990; Rolley, 1992). In 1973, Bassiouni (see Rolley, 1992) summarized these problems:

- [The convention] rests essentially upon faithful cooperation by all parties in the context of their national decisions rather than upon effective international measures;
- The limited authority given the international control bodies—the Commission on Narcotic Drugs and the International Narcotics Control Board—is apparently inadequate to halt or even slow down the increasing drug traffic;
- The Convention lacks a precise obligation, machinery, and incentives for prevention of overproduction of drugs;
- It fails to clearly prohibit production of certain medically and scientifically unnecessary substances and drugs;
- It has no direct controls over the execution of any treaty provision, particularly with respect to production controls, which are very indirect;
- It has no assignment of production quotas or production ceilings;
- It does not prevent countries from entering into the production market;
- The denunciation of the Convention is rather facile and operation outside its ambit is possible;
- There is no international enforcement machinery (INTERPOL has no jurisdictional authority); and
- There are no international sanctions applicable to individual offenders. (pp. 417–18)

One area of rapid growth with no drug policy to use as a control mechanism was in pharmaceutical substances that were being manufactured in Western industrialized countries. Prior to this, drug-related issues had centered around the producing Third World countries and the consuming Western countries. These two issues—amending the 1961 Single Convention and controlling for pharmaceutical substances—were handled through two separate processes: the 1971 Convention on Psychotropic Substances and the 1972 Amending Protocol.

The 1971 United Nations Convention on Psychotropic Substances

Another major deficiency of the 1961 Single Convention was that it did not cover psychotropic drugs. Accordingly, in 1991, the Convention on Psychotropic Substances was put into place at a United Nations conference in Vienna (Rolley, 1992:418). This was also due in part to the increasing numbers of psychotropic medications being abused with few mechanisms for control. More than 32 "hallucinogenic" substances, including LSD, mescaline, and certain barbiturates, were covered under this new convention.

The 1971 convention adopted measures that increased the number of substances under international drug control to 180. While 115 state parties attended the 1961 convention, only 87 agreed to the stricter guidelines of the 1971 convention (Walsh, 1988:104).

The World Health Organization was designated as the agency responsible for determining whether a substance should be included in the four schedules of proscribed drugs. The basic criteria follow.

- The substance must have the capacity to produce a state of dependence and it must stimulate or depress the central nervous system, resulting in hallucinations or disturbances in motor function, thinking, behavior, perception, or mood
- The abuse of the substance must produce ill effects similar to those caused by a substance already included in one of the four schedules. WHO must also establish that the substance is being or is likely to be abused so as to cause a public health and social problem (Jamieson, 1990:35).

The 1972 Amending Protocol

Also known as the Geneva Protocol, the 1972 Amending Protocol to the 1961 Single Convention on Narcotics produced a much stronger drug-control system than the 1971 convention had indicated. Due to the expanding regulations surrounding drugs and their control, as well as the stricter measures associated with the amendments, numerous former supporters withdrew from the process. The 1972 protocol was confirmed by only 83 state parties (Rowe, 1988).

Both the 1971 and 1972 conferences served to expand the number of substances considered dangerous by the United Nations, and they created more stringent regulations over these substances. So while both alluded to stricter measures, neither of these amendments to the Single Convention of 1961 dealt with the creation of a unified multinational enforcement mechanism to oversee the implementation of these new regulations. However, with each step toward more stringent drug policy, the United Nations lost much of the support of many of its member states.

United Nations Efforts: 1984–1994

International organizations and agencies had been established throughout this period of time to focus specifically on drug control. Four such organizations play key roles in either the implementation of drug policy, the creation of drug policy, or both. They were designed as independent bodies for a specific purpose and are subject to the control of separate entities. In no way were they required to coordinate activities with one another; however, they frequently do so. Those four organizations are the UN Division of Narcotic Drugs, the International Narcotics Control Board, the UN Fund for Drug Abuse Control, and the World Health Organization.

The United Nations Division of Narcotic Drugs was established as the administrative office of the UN Commission on Narcotic Drugs (CND). It provides assistance to the CND that includes implementation guidelines and regulations, and it publishes various documents as needed for international treaties and reports (Bassiouni, 1990). The International Narcotics Control Board (INCB) was established through the 1961 Single Convention to gather data related to the estimation of licit drug production that each country could maintain. The INCB places limitations on cultivation, production, and manufacture of all substances in each country. This agency is given the function of enforcing the guidelines set by the 1961 Single Convention (Rolley, 1992; Schroeder, 1980). The first step toward promoting financial aid and technical assistance to the countries engaging in the war on drugs was the creation of the UN Fund for Drug Abuse Control (UNFDAC) in 1971. The significance of the UNFDAC program is the effort directed toward hands-on assistance instead of relying on written agreements between member nations. However, this body operates according to voluntary contributions from participating countries; therefore its level of aid and assistance directly relates to the amount of donations received (Bassiouni, 1990).

The World Health Organization, as mentioned previously, was brought into the international drug policy arena in 1953 to control addictive drugs. Under the 1971 convention, WHO functions were expanded to arrange the pharmaceutical substances into the four categories established by the convention (Bassiouni, 1990; Rolley, 1992).

In 1984, the United Nations General Assembly adopted a Declaration on the Control of Drug Trafficking and Drug Abuse to establish a new international means for law enforcement and government agencies to handle the increase in illicit drug trafficking. This developed into a draft convention in 1986, which was designed to concentrate on those issues that were not designated in previously existing conventions or amendments. This draft convention was coordinated by the Division of Narcotic Drugs (Rowe, 1988), leading to two international meetings in 1987 and 1988.

The 1987 International Conference on Drug Abuse and Illicit Traffic

This conference established a set of regulations and recommendations to address abuse and trafficking, entitled the Comprehensive Multi-disciplinary Outline of Future Activities in Drug Abuse Control (CMO). The CMO dealt with the problems of demand, supply, trafficking, treatment, and rehabilitation (Donnelly, 1992). The 35 targets of the CMO address a wide range of factors, but most impressive is their emphasis on demand and treatment. The goals emphasize the importance of focusing on all aspects of the illicit drug crisis. Additionally, the CMO demonstrates significant changes of policy even in the traditional areas of supply and trafficking. For example, while earlier efforts were directed at forced eradication, new policies have addressed the concept of financial incentives for the production of legal crops. The rural development programs are a sign that the international community is beginning to understand the context of the problem better.

The 1988 United Nations Convention against Illicit Traffic in Narcotic Drugs and Psychotropic Substances

The second meeting of significant importance was the 1988 United Nations Convention Against Illicit Traffic in Narcotic Drugs and Psychotropic Substances, provisions of which were adopted in 1990. Quite obviously, this convention dealt primarily with drug trafficking. The 1988 convention strengthened the previous CMO agreements, especially in the areas of customs, extradition, law enforcement, and penalties (Donnelly, 1992). While the actual efforts may seem to offer few new provisions, they do lead to an increased level of cooperation and action regarding the member states. For example, prior to this convention many UN regulations directly contradicted some signatory countries' domestic laws. The treaty recognized through this convention obligated each member country to enact domestic laws reflective of those adopted by the UN (Rolley, 1992). Furthermore, the requirements of the convention explicitly state the rules and regulations concerning membership, and it allows almost all states to become members of the international crusade against drugs.

The convention imposed the following responsibilities:

- The provision of adequate sanctions for offenses relating to drug trafficking
- The identification, tracing, freezing, seizure, and confiscation of proceeds and property derived from trafficking
- The extradition of offenders for drug trafficking charges (i.e., no safe havens)
- Mutual legal assistance in terms of investigations and prosecutions (banking secrecy not to be invoked)
- Other forms of cooperation, especially among law enforcement agencies in fields such as training
- International cooperation and assistance for transit states
- The law enforcement technique of controlled delivery
- The monitoring of precursor chemicals
- Prevention of trade in a diversion of materials and equipment for illicit production and manufacture of narcotic drugs and psychotropic substances
- Measures to eradicate illicit cultivation of narcotic plants and to eliminate demand for narcotic drugs and psychotropic substances
- The suppression of illicit traffic by sea, in particular in free trade zones and ports, and by air (Jamieson, 1990:36).

By 1990, 89 nations had entered into the agreement and nine countries had ratified (Jamieson, 1990:35–36; see Donnelly, 1992). As of January 2005, 170 countries were parties to the convention (UNODC, 2005a).

Throughout the 1980s, as the resulting convention and conference resolutions reflect, a growing emphasis on law enforcement emerged with regard to drug control. Several agencies evolved during this period to assist with the new and more restrictive drug laws. The first agencies emerged out of the UN Commission on Narcotic Drugs specifically as liaisons for regional and interregional cooperation. They are the Sub-commission on Illicit Drug Traffic and Related Matters in the Near and Middle East, and the Heads of National Drug Law Enforcement Agencies (HONLEA). HONLEA currently exists in the Asian and Pacific region, the African region, and the Latin American and Caribbean region (Rowe, 1988). Regional organizations are included in these meetings, such as the Association of Southeast Asian Nations, the Colombo Plan Bureau, the South Pacific Commission, and the Pan-Arab Bureau for Narcotic Affairs of the League of Arab States, among others (Rowe, 1988). These organizations have been the primary influence on law enforcement mechanisms, including training methods, and have also increased the support for the UN and for the development of new member states, and increased funding opportunities for the drug war.

The 1990 Special Session of the General Assembly

The principal policy emerging from the 1990 Special Session of the General Assembly was the Political Declaration and Global Program of Action (Donnelly, 1992). The declaration by member states of the United Nations showed significant steps toward a comprehensive and joint measure to confront the drug problem and all its complexities. The Program of Action reaffirmed the directives set forth in the 1961 Single Convention, the 1971 Convention, the 1972 Protocol, and the 1988 Convention (Rolley, 1992) and addressed new, innovative approaches to solving the problems associated with the illegal drug trade. For example, it stressed international support for programs designed to create alternative modes of income for Third World countries that rely on the economic outputs of the illegal trade (Brown, 1994). Also, the declaration placed international efforts at controlling drugs as a top priority, since without top priority any attempts by the UN or other multilateral organizations will almost surely fail (Donnelly, 1992). The Program of Action is a continuously evolving document, which was designed with the overall goal of intensifying international efforts through successive monitoring of progress and implementation (Rolley, 1992).

The most recent developments in drug policy have occurred due to the growth in money laundering accompanying the trafficking of illicit drugs. In an effort to mount a vigorous attack against this new enterprise, three previously mentioned organizations were combined in 1991. The Division of Narcotic Drugs, UNFDAC, and the INCB are now the single organization known as the United Nations International Drug Control Programme. This new agency is a first step toward what the UN refers to as a reorganization of its drug activities. One area for which the UN has been criticized regards duplication of services. By combining agencies and reducing duplication, the UN hopes to increase its membership and its funding (Rolley, 1992).

International Action to Combat Drug Abuse and Illicit Production and Trafficking (1993)

Controlling the illegal drug trade has steadily increased in global importance, but the true gauge of success will be measured in the amount of financial assistance each state gives to the effort. In the Seventeenth Special Session of the UN General Assembly, the secretary-general emphasized that considerable funding will be needed to ensure that the United Nations International Drug Control Programme reaches its projected goals. Funding has been a pressing concern for the UN, whose total budget of $1.76 billion in 1989 only allocated about $37 million toward the drug effort, about .0074 percent of the $500 billion drug trade in 1989. In 2004, that increased to $168 million. Therefore, the primary issue may not be who is cooperating, but whether the UN can successfully contribute the necessary funds to implement their often grandiose plans to end this international crisis (Fact Sheet, 2/18/91; Rolley, 1992).

In 1993, the United Nations General Assembly reaffirmed its previous drug-control efforts and adopted Resolution 48/112. Reaffirming the 1990 Global Program of Action, this resolution further emphasizes the necessity for international cooperation in the fight against drug production and trafficking. The document also requests the secretary-general to promote and monitor the United Nations Decade Against Drug Abuse, 1991–2000 under the theme, "A global response to a global challenge."

Recent Developments, 1998–Present

United Nations Convention against Illicit Traffic in Narcotic Drugs and Psychotropic Substances

A United Nations General Assembly Special Session (UNGASS) convened in 1998 to again address the issue of drug manufacture, production, and traffic. This session proposed a compromise between countries traditionally known for producing drugs and those who traditionally consumed those drugs. The producing countries desired an international declaration on demand reduction in response to what they considered unfair criticism by historical non-producers of drugs. The consuming states refused to come to the table formally on demand reduction, arguing that the issue was one of domestic policy and that international regulations would violate their sovereignty (Fazey, 2003:157).

In the end, the convention adopted a political declaration and outlined guiding principles for demand reduction. It also enacted two action plans—addressing trade and use of amphetamine-type substances (ATS) and endorsing crop eradication and alternative development. Furthermore, UNGASS 1998 formally advocated the control of chemical precursors, judicial cooperation, and action against money laundering (United Nations 1998). In a January 2005 meeting of the UN Interregional Crime and Justice Research Institute, Antontio Costa, executive director of the United Nations Office on Drugs and Crime, reiterated the organization's position that the perspective of law enforcement must be global (UNODC, 2005b).

Criticism of United Nations Policy Making

At least one former member of the UNDCP argues that the prospect for change in United Nations policy regarding drugs is minimal (Fazey, 2003:155). The UNDCP takes its money primarily from "the Fund," which is the descendant of the United Nations fund for drug-abuse control (established in 1971). Seventeen member nations are the main donors to this fund (one of which, the United States, remains in arrears for its contribution). Organizationally, the Commission on Narcotic Drugs (a component of the UNDCP under the 1991 merger) serves as the UN's ultimate policy-making body. It takes its money from the United Nations budget, however, and therefore essentially can implement only policies for which finances exist unless the major donors find money for them. Practically, this means that the major donors control the process by which policy becomes action. Furthermore, the major donors—Italy, USA, England, Japan, Sweden, European Commission, Germany, France, Canada, Denmark, the Netherlands, Switzerland, Norway, Spain, Australia, Belgium, and Finland—meet independently of CND with senior UNDCP staff in closed meetings. These sessions basically decide policy outside the UN realm, as the donors evaluate existing policy and agree on how to spend existing and future money. Fazey (2003:165) claims that most of the money goes to supply reduction and suppression of illicit traffic with only Scandinavian countries contributing to demand reduction.

Finally, two components of UN bureaucracy itself contribute to policy conservatism. Outside and independent funding translates to a short leash for forward-thinking leadership. Pino Arlachi served as the UNDCP's executive director from 1998 until 2002; he stated publicly in 1997 that he wanted to make the body more active and implementation oriented. The major donors quickly reminded him, however, that his authority was limited (politically and pragmatically) (Fazey, 2003:163). This no doubt played a role in the decision not to renew Arlachi's contract in 2002. In addition to individual constraint, member states come to resent the UNDCP for its inability (financially and politically) to assist them in paying for field projects.

Generalists in diplomacy and international politics usually receive preference in high-level appointments at the UNDCP (as in all UN organizations). Internal politics, therefore, contribute significantly to paralysis, as staff members spend a great deal of time lobbying for their jobs rather than disposing of them. The constant shifting of financial and human resources perpetually threatens nonpermanent positions, even those held by long-term employees of the UN. Specialists who challenge their generalist superiors are the first dispensable personnel, Fazey states; punishment postings were not uncommon either during her tenure (p. 163).

Regional Affiliations: Strength in Numbers?

The advent of organizations that unite states geographically has demonstrated efficacy in the realms of trade/economy, security, health services, and general international influence. These groups, however, also implement policies that concentrate on cooperation between members on the issues of drug production and consumption. Two such networks have orchestrated and committed action plans that address the shared concerns of their members related to drugs.

The European Union

The third Action Plan to Combat Drugs was approved in 2000. It continues in the spirit of its predecessors in stressing four key elements of collective European policy: demand reduction, supply reduction and the fight against illicit trafficking, international cooperation, and coordination at the national and Union level. It embraces "a global, multidisciplinary and integrated strategy to fight illicit drugs" (COM 239, 1999:6). Evaluation of Union policies heads a list of concerns that informed the 2000–2004 action plan. The list includes a need to increase monitoring of the drug issue in order to facilitate greater responsiveness to new challenges as they present themselves. The document itself identified several new challenges. Cannabis, amphetamine, and ecstasy; urban delinquency as it relates to illicit drug marketing; health, social and criminal justice challenges (i.e., hepatitis, synergy, social exclusion, alternatives to punishment, drug use in prisons, and vocational and social resocialization); and accession of new members are included as emergent challenges for which the Union must rapidly prepare strategies.

The Treaty of Amsterdam, in concert with the Maastricht Treaty, establishes the legal framework under which the action plans operate. They permit inclusion of drug-control measures as public health priorities, as a focus of cooperation in the field of justice and home affairs, and as a priority for international cooperation. Five nuclei comprise the action intended by the plan: information; demand reduction; reducing trafficking in narcotics and psychotropics; international cooperation; and co-ordination, simplification, and integration.

Demand reduction. The European Union (EU) set two objectives for evaluation before the current action plan expires in 2004: a five-year significant reduction in the use of illegal drugs by persons under 18 and a five-year substantial reduction in the number of drug-related deaths. As achievement of these two goals relates to public health, the sector is charged with improving prevention through early intervention, improved public awareness of drug challenges and problems, confrontation of behavior related to drug use, and encouraging local efforts (both isolated and complementary). Education and the use of schools in spreading information about drug use are also emphasized, as are media campaigns. Research will focus on: the establishment of factors relating to the socioeconomic and psychological factors relating to drug abuse, understanding the long-term social and health-related consequences of drug abuse, and the development of effective treatment strategies. The fields of biomedicine, criminology, neuroscience, economics, and sociology all receive specific mention in the plan as vanguards for research. Drugs and driving, though not included in the 1995–1999 action plan, garners attention in the current plan as a desired area of refinement in research measures and data collection. Doping in sports will be addressed in terms of public consequences, physician awareness, legislative coordination and action, clear and standard lists of forbidden substances, and protection of young athletes.

Reducing trafficking in narcotics and psychotropics. The plan identifies six elements related to trafficking. They are: the control of chemical precursors diversion within the EU and in Third-World countries; the prevention of and fight against money laundering; the effective cooperation between police, customs, and judicial authorities; the implementation of the EU Action Plan on Organized Crime; the prevention of the use of new communication systems (e.g., the Internet) as means of developing drug abuse, production, and trafficking; and the international cooperation in the fight against illicit drug trafficking. Coordination and cooperation represent key elements for the successful implementation of these policies (COM 239, 1999:22).

The plan acknowledges the need for a balance between law enforcement and other concerns as part of this action strategy. Industry, for example, is a prime target in controlling precursor chemicals. It also serves as a prime economic engine in the Union, however, and as a link with other state economies as well as the global economy; care must be taken to cultivate a symbiotic relationship between enforcement and development interests.

A common policy on avoiding exploitation of financial systems for money laundering has been ratified by member states; external mechanisms also serve to increase cooperation between member states and the international community. Communications technology is seen as a positive factor in spreading information about the risks posed by drug abuse but can also serve to facilitate illicit manufacture or glamorize drug abuse. Other EU documents provide legal and legislative support for cooperation among the enforcement mechanisms of member states and Europol.

International cooperation. The action plan calls for renewed international cooperation on drug enforcement. It emphasizes the utility of master plans at the national and regional levels that share guiding principles. The EU itself can employ a wide array of tools to reduce the international market for drugs. The external policies of development and trade should be used in eliminating production of illicit crops; technical and financial assistance can also be connected to regional or national action on drug production and trafficking. The common foreign and security policy (CFSP) possessed within the EU facilitates the plan's goals by presenting a common position, framing political dialogue, and enabling joint action by member states. The main targets of this international effort are countries applying for accession to the EU, Latin America/Caribbean, and central Asia.

Because the EU has described the drug problem it faces as multifaceted and responds to it on a number of fronts, synchronized efforts are critical for comprehensive success. The Horizontal Drugs Group, set up in 1997, serves as a connection between the agencies and commissions working on the drug issue for the EU. It establishes the presence of relevant groups within the target regions and nations and facilitates interagency dialogue and coordination.

ASEAN (Association of South East Asian Nations)

The members of this group (Brunei Darussalam, Cambodia, Indonesia, Laos, Malaysia, Myanmar, Philippines, Singapore, Thailand, and Vietnam) have formulated a plan called ACCORD (ASEAN and China Cooperative Operations in Response to Dangerous Drugs). It has four primary objectives.

Proactively advocating civic awareness on dangers of drugs and social response. The plan of action begins with the development by each member of a strategy for communicating and sharing information with its fellow members and citizens by 2005. This strategy will integrate the threat posed by illegal drugs with other criminal activity that preys on society in Southeast Asia and China: transnational organized crime, corruption, money laundering, and human trafficking. Social partnerships between government and nongovernment organizations are encouraged, as is exploitation of the media in spreading the benefit of drug-free lifestyles and developing culturally appropriate messages. An ASEAN Media Award for Drug Awareness Promotion will be established in concert with the UNDCP toward this end. The private sector is to incorporate education about the dangers and impact of drugs in the workplace and will play a part in public information programs.

Building consensus and sharing best practices on demand reduction. The region has witnessed a rapid increase in the use of ATS like methamphetamine and ecstasy, particularly among certain groups within society. The action plan in this area will first emphasize the collaboration and/or consolidation of national data-collection systems concerning ATS use. Regional clearinghouses will spread information about abuse and prevention through the media, Internet, and special reports. Schools are to begin educating children about the dangers of ATS, and ASEAN and UNDCP will cooperate in creating measures to assess the response to this action. Furthermore, treatment and rehabilitation for ATS abuse is to be specialized and dispersed across the region along with mechanisms for reducing intravenous drug use. Once again, nongovernmental organizations and community groups will play a role, and governments will create policies that nominally prioritize reducing demand for ATS.

Strengthening the rule of law by an enhanced network of control measures and improved law enforcement cooperation and legislative review. Resources in the region historically focus on law enforcement. The action plan urges the need to handle the demands on the rule of law in overwhelmed judicial systems, while increasing training for law enforcement. The UNDCP and ASEAN are to assist in facilitating a regional project aimed at strengthening control over precursor chemicals in drug production through regulation and legislation. International cooperation and information sharing will occur through regional networks and exploitation of existing mechanisms. Judicial capacity is to increase as a result of programs instituted by individual members to educate judges in international drug law and UN conventions on mutual legal assistance among regional and international colleagues. Money laundering is to receive renewed legislative attention, and by 2008 all countries hopefully will have a dedicated authority in the control of money laundering.

Boosting alternative development programs and community participation. Although complicated, UNDCP experience indicates that alternative development strategies (reducing raw materials for illicit drugs) achieve their desired goals when implemented in an integrated way. By the end of 2003, member countries developed and tested a methodology (national and subregional) for monitoring and verifying poppy cultivation. Best practice networks—for alternative development approaches, farmer experience, and development effectiveness—was in place in 2004 with a stated goal of the elimination of illicit poppy cultivation by 2008. Furthermore, ASEAN and UNDCP have agreed to create a secure computer network of drug agencies in the region to monitor progress in the action plan (ASEAN, 2000:1–3).

Conclusion

Consensus exists that alternative development presents a viable way to move impoverished countries and their agrarian economies away from reliance on drug production. Investment by outside states and agencies becomes irrelevant, however, if not applied globally (as simple displacement of producing regions will occur) and if investment does not result in tangible and sustained improvement for citizens. The main organ for directing this movement remains the United Nations. Reform must occur within its walls, however, before meaningful and widespread action can begin.

Fazey (2003:166) cites three options for increasing the efficacy of UNDCP policy. First, a suitable contingent of countries could demand a new conference with the goal of drafting a new convention to replace the Single Convention of 1961. Attempts have been made in the past to do just that, but states that would bear the financial burden of such a conference objected on financial grounds. An earmarked fund could help offset costs to individual members.

As a second option, states can follow the "quiet path" (Fazey, 2003:167) of interpreting the conventions to meet their specific needs. Especially as it relates to HIV/AIDS, the control of drugs has been de-emphasized in some states in exchange for policies aimed at preventing the spread of disease. Despite the fact that the UN (specifically, the INCB) protests in writing, no accountability can be forced upon the judiciaries and legislatures of member states.

Opening up policy debate related to the level of decision making serves as Fazey's third choice (2003:167). Consuming countries blame producing countries for their problems of crime and addiction, but producing countries argue that consumption drives their production. Furthermore, they insist, domestic circumstances vary widely enough that global policies do not pertain to most locations contingent on culture, religion, and social convention. In this realm, administrative decisions are distilled to the lowest possible level to permit the greatest local relevance.

As the previous discussion illustrates, there should be no doubt as to the seriousness of the global drug trafficking problem. But while there have been many international attempts over the years to combat narcotic production and distribution, success has not been evident. Politics and financial concerns continue to bog down policy formation and implementation while the drug epidemic continues. New attention is being paid to links between drug trafficking and terrorism, although such a link has existed in South America (particularly Colombia) for more than twenty years. As the global community becomes more integrated economically, hope emerges that through enfranchisement of all pertinent countries progress can be made. One fact remains, however: the international effort against drugs will continue indefinitely.

References

Albrecht, Hans Jorg, and Anton van Kalmthout (1989). "Introduction." In Hans Jorg Albrecht and Anton van Kalmthout (eds.), *Drug Policies in Western Europe* (pp. 1–6). Freiburg, FRD: Eigenverlag Max-Planck-Institut.

ASEAN and China Cooperative Operations in Response to Dangerous Drugs (2000). Unpublished paper.

Bassiouni, M. Cherif (1973). "The International Narcotics Control System." In M. C. Bassiouni and V. Nanda (eds.), *Treatise on International Law*. New York: Practicing Law Institute.

———. (1990). "Critical Reflections on International and National Control of Drugs." *Denver Journal of International Law and Policy* 18 (3): 311–37.

———. (1991). "A Border Lined with Gold." *The Economist* 319 (7701) (April 6): 31–33.

Bossard, André (1990). *Transnational Crime and Criminal Law*. Office of International Criminal Justice, The University of Illinois at Chicago.

Brown, Lee P. (1994). "The International Drug Problem: Law Enforcement, Education, Treatments and Economic Development." *Office of National Drug Control Policy—Vital Speeches* 1 (60): 489–93.

Bureau of Justice Statistics, U.S. Department of Justice (1992). *Drugs, Crime, and the Justice System*. Washington, DC: U.S. Government Printing Office.

Chang, Dae H. (1993). "Drugs and Punishment: An International Survey." *International Journal of Comparative and Applied Criminal Justice* 17 (1/2) (spring/ fall): 1–28.

Chatterjee, S. K. (1989). "The Limitations of the International Drug Conventions." In Hans Jorg Albrecht and Anton van Kalmthout (eds.), *Drug Policies in Western Europe* (pp. 7–20). Freiburg, FRD: Eigenverlag Max-Planck-Institut.

Collett, Merrill (1989). *The Cocaine Connection: Drug Traffickers and International American Relations*. New York: Foreign Policy Association Headline Series (fall).

COM 239 (1999). *Communication from the Commission to the Council and the European Parliament on a European Union Action Plan to Combat Drugs 2000–2004* (1999). May 26: Brussels, Belgium.

Committee on Government Operations (1990). *Clandestine Manufacturing of Dangerous Drugs*. Washington, DC: House Report.

Cooper, Mary H. (1990). *The Business of Drugs*. Washington, DC: Congressional Quarterly Press.

Donnelly, Jack (1992). "The UN & Global Drug Control Regimes." In Peter Smith (ed.), *Drug Policy of the Americas*. Boulder, CO: Westview Press.

"Fact Sheet: International Aspects of 1991 National Drug Control Strategy" (1991). *U.S. Department of State Dispatch* 2(7) (February 18): 115.

"Fact Sheet: 1991 Progress in the International War Against Narcotics" (1992). *U.S. Department of State Dispatch* 3(20) (May 18): 393.

Fazey, Cindy S. J. (2003). "The Commission on Narcotic Drugs and the United Nations Drug Control Programme: Politics, Policies, and Prospects for Change." *International Journal on Drug Control Policy* 14 (2) (April): 155–169.

Hamowy, Ronald (1987). *Dealing with Drugs*. San Francisco: Pacific Research Institute for Public Policy.

International Narcotics Control Strategy Report (1991). Washington, DC: U.S. Department of State, Bureau of International Narcotics Matters (March): 22.

———. (1994). Washington, DC: U.S. Department of State, Bureau of International Narcotics Matters.

Jamieson, Alison (1990). "Global Drug Trafficking." *Conflict Studies* 234: 1–41.

Johns, Christian J. (1992). *Power, Ideology, and the War on Drugs*. New York: Praeger.

Krauss, Melvyn B., and Edward P. Lazear (eds.) (1991). *Searching for Alternatives: Drug-Control Policy in the United States*. Stanford, CA: Hoover Institution Press.

Liang, Debra A. (1992). "The Golden Triangle: Burma, Laos, and Thailand." In Scott B. MacDonald and Bruce Zagaris (eds.), *International Handbook on Drug Control* (pp. 363–86). Westport, CT: Greenwood Press.

MacDonald, Scott B., and Bruce Zagaris (1992). "Introduction: Controlling the International Drug Problem." In MacDonald and Zagaris (eds.), *International Handbook on Drug Control* (pp. 3–18). Westport, CT: Greenwood Press.

McAllister, William B. (1991). "Conflicts of Interest in the International Drug Control System." *Journal of Policy History* 3 (4): 494–517.

McCoy, Alfred W., and Alan A. Block (eds.) (1992). *War on Drugs: Studies in the Failure of U.S. Narcotics Policy.* Boulder, CO: Westview Press.

Nadelman, Ethan A. (1993). *Cops Across Borders: The Internationalization of U.S. Criminal Law Enforcement.* University Park: Penn State University Press.

Office of National Drug Control Policy (2000). *Estimation of Cocaine Availability, 1996–1999.* Washington, DC: Authors.

Rolley, Robin (1992). "United Nations' Activities in International Drug Control." In Scott B. MacDonald and Bruce Zagaris (eds.), *International Handbook on Drug Control* (pp. 415–32). Westport, CT: Greenwood Press.

Rowe, Dennis (ed.) (1988). *International Drug Trafficking.* Chicago: Office of International Criminal Justice.

Schroeder, Richard C. (1980). *The Politics of Drugs: An American Dilemma*, 2nd ed. Washington, DC: Congressional Quarterly Press.

Trebach, Arnold S., and Kevin B. Zeese (1990). *Drug Prohibition and the Conscience of Nations.* Washington, DC: The Drug Policy Foundation.

Tullis, LaMond (1991). *Handbook of Research on the Illicit Drug Traffic.* New York: Greenwood Press.

United Nations (1998). *Special Session of the General Assembly Devoted to Countering the World Drug Problem Together.* June 8–10, New York.

United Nations Econonomic and Social Council (2003). "Consolidation Budget for the Biennium 2004–2005 for the United Nations Office on Drugs and Crime." New York: UN Commision on Narcotic Drugs.

United Nations Office on Drugs and Crime (UNODC) (2004). "CND Membership." Available: http://www.unodc.org/unodc/en/cnd_membership.html (accessed January 21, 2005).

United Nations Office on Drugs and Crime (UNODC) (2005a). "Monthly Status of Treaty Adherence." Available: http://www.unodc.org/unodc/en/treaty_adherence.html#1988 (accessed March 14, 2005).

United Nations Office on Drugs and Crime (UNODC) (2005b). "UNODC Executive Director Visits UNICRI," UNIS/CP/506 (10 January). Available: http://www.unis.unvienna.org/unis/pressrels/2005/uniscp506.html (accessed January 21, 2005).

Walsh, Stephen (1988). "Some Aspects of International Drug Control and Illicit Drug Trafficking." In Dennis Rowe (ed.), *International Drug Trafficking* (pp. 101–13). Chicago: Office of International Criminal Justice.

9

A Comparative Model of Democracy, Respect for Human Rights, and the Rise of Democratic Policing Reforms

Salih Hakan Can

Is there a relation between the rise of democratic policing reforms, such as community policing, and other indicators of a country's level of democracy and respect for human rights? And if there is such a relation, what specific democratic policing reforms tend to increase a country's level of respect for human rights and democracy?

Comparative analyses of democracy have given little attention to police and policing organizations (Marenin, 2000). Analyses of democracy by international organizations, scholars, and human rights activists have become sophisticated and look shrewdly beyond the actions of a country's government or legislature, to reflect on the reality of daily life. Daily realities obviously include the everday actions of police in citizens' lives, such as arresting or detaining individuals, protecting voting and speech rights, protecting elected officials from violence, and so forth (e.g., Bayley, 1997). But political scientists and other scholars analyzing comparative democracies give little attention to police and policing organizations within democracy, ignoring the most important and obvious coercive power of the state. Even human rights activists have not analyzed the police in their discussions of the violations of human rights and dignity (Das, 2000; Marenin, 2000).

Criminal justice analyses of police and democratic policing reforms have given little attention to cross-national analyses of the relationship between police practices and democracy/respect for human rights. The concept *democratic policing reforms* describes a variety of policing methods and practices intended to lower crime rates, diminish bribery and corruption, end brutality, and maximize community satisfaction with organizational reforms (e.g., problem-oriented and/or community-oriented policing). Scholars who

Prepared especially for *Comparative and International Criminal Justice, 2/E.*

advocate democratic policing reforms have identified several basic defining tenets, such as an emphasis on the rule of law, public accountability, open and public decision making, minimal use of force, public involvement, respect for human rights, and internal organizational democracy (e.g., Das, 2000). A wide body of qualitative case studies of individual countries identifies the policies used to implement these tenets, including the presence of civilian oversight boards, ombudsmen, civilian complaint boards, and police unions; decentralization; increased demographic representation within the police organization, increased use of high technology, and other problem-oriented and/or community-oriented policing techniques (e.g., Das, 2000; Kratcoski, 2000; Marenin, 2000; Stone & Ward, 2000).

This study is a cross-national exploration of the relation between democratic policing reforms and levels of democracy/respect for human rights. It is based on an explanation of the rich comparative field studies of police organizational structures, comparative analyses of different types of regimes, reports of governmental and nongovernmental international organizations (NGOs), and other secondary data analyses. The results of this analysis show significant positive correlations between the rise of democratic policing reforms within a country and its level of democracy and respect for human rights. It also strongly implies that scholars in the comparative study of criminal justice, public administration, and politics may underestimate the power exerted by policing institutions within democratic societies.

Democracy and Democratic Policing Reforms

What is democracy? The minimalist definition, from the original Greek meaning of the word, posits that democracy is the "rule of the people" (Herodotus, in Hornblower, 1992). Widely used by social scientists from Alexis de Tocqueville to Robert Dahl, this definition focuses on public participation in selecting governments by competitive, multiparty elections.

Beetham (1999) explained democracy more precisely. He combined the insights of the liberal and Marxist traditions in order to arrive at a definition of democracy that supports the basic principle of autonomy. His definition has three parts: first, substantial participation in local community institutions as well as the self-management of cooperatively owned enterprises; second, a bill of rights that goes beyond the right to vote, providing equal opportunity for participation; and third, social and economic rights to ensure adequate resources for democratic autonomy. Thus, democracy by this definition requires a high degree of accountability from the state as well as a democratic reordering of civil society (Beetham).

Hegemony has emerged among political scientists in the three main categories of a definition of democracy: competition, participation, and civil and political liberties. *Competition* refers to the popular election of legislatures and government heads (Sorensen, 1998; Dahl, 1971). *Participation* refers to an open and accountable government, with a variety of political, legal, and financial devices for accountability directly (Beetham, 1999; Sorensen, 1998). *Civil and political liberties* refers to freedoms to vote, dissent, associate, assemble, move, and to access due process of law (Beetham, 1999; Sorensen, 1998). A "civil society" is one that responds to all three categories of democracy (Diamond, 1992; Lipset, 1960; Beetham, 1999).

However, countries like Germany, the United States, and Denmark have been targeted by Amnesty International for their violations of human rights, even though they receive the highest scores in all of the democracy indexes based on the above definitions. Some political scientists argue that this is so because democracies do not necessarily promote human rights (Huntington, 1993). Reports from both Amnesty International and the U.S. State Department place the blame on police for the greatest portion of human rights violations in these and other countries, yet social scientists still give little attention to policing in their analyses of democracy. How can policing practices be made more accountable and supportive of democracy *and* respect for human rights?

Crawshaw, Devlin, and Williamson (1998), Das (2000), and Marenin (2000) agree that in a democracy, effective policies are developed and implemented in a manner acceptable to the people affected by the policies. This requires an informed debate within the community, and police make objective, rational, and reasonable contributions to public debate on policing matters, avoiding exploitations or moral panics about "law and order" concerns for political ends. It is a function of police to enable democratic political debate by ensuring that the processes are constitutional and peaceful.

International organizations in recent decades have been increasingly active in urging a role for policing that is more accountable and supportive of democracy and respect for human rights. In 1979, the United Nations adopted a "Code of Conduct for Law Enforcement Officials" that includes the idea that police should be representative of and accountable to the community as a whole. In 1994, the United Nations proclamation of 1995–2004 as the "Decade for Human Rights Education" focused extensively on human-rights training for police. In 1997 the Council of Europe, Directorate General of Human Rights, launched a program on "Police and Human Rights, 1997–2000" in the 41 member states of the Council of Europe and followed up with "Police and Human Rights—Beyond 2000."

While these human rights efforts tend to focus on the socialization of police, the organizational structures of policing are given little attention. Actions to preserve human rights can only be realized through the democratic behaviors of police, and we may promote democracy in policing by making the police organizational structure more democratic. From the consensus of scholars and diplomatic representatives at the "Theme of Challenges of Policing Democracies" symposium at the Institute of the Sociology of Law in Spain, Das (2000) identified seven criteria (i.e., democratic polic-ing reforms) to promote democracy in policing: rule of law, public account-ability, transparent decision making, public participation, minimum use of force, support/training in human rights, and internal organizational democracy. This "explanatory and co-operative" police accountability to democracy (embodied in the philosophies of community-oriented and problem-oriented policing) requires neutral police-to-citizen explanations and information (Chan, 1999; Miller, Blackler & Alexandra, 1997).

An ample number of well-documented scholarly case studies of indi-vidual countries has emerged, identifying the policies necessary to imple-ment these seven criteria. Within many comparative jurisdictions, civilian oversight and complaint boards are staffed by international and national NGOs to ensure independent findings on police wrongdoing. Ombudsmen, as representative citizens, are independent and impartial arbiters appointed by police authorities to investigate citizen complaints and sug-gest solutions. Police unions give individual officers the chance to help democratically govern their organization (see Berkley, 1969). Attempts to make police more representative by aligning the racial, ethnic, religious, gender, and political demographic profiles of police with those of the citi-zens they serve also may generate a more democratic police organization. The increased use of high technology may enhance the effectiveness and neutrality of policing activities with tools such as geographic information systems, electronic surveillance, computer information sharing, and bio-logical and electronic monitoring.

Yet, the broad assumption that democratic policing reforms help to increase respect for human rights and the level of democracy in a given country remains untested. Further, scholars typically focus only on police organizational practices in a single country at a time, without cross-national analyses.

Data and Methodology

This research explores two different questions: First, to what degree are democratic policing practices correlated with democracy in a given coun-try? Second, which specific policing applications are most likely to be corre-lated to high levels of democracy, especially with respect to human rights?

Phase I—Democracy and Democratic Policing Practices

Conceptualizing democracy. According to Sorensen (1998), the degree to which a country is democratic can be determined by the level of government responsiveness to the preferences of its citizens. Political equal-ity is therefore a key characteristic of democracy. However, a great number of physical manifestations, or institutions, can be observed within a country to measure its level of democracy. Sorensen borrows from Dahl (1971), who refers to democracy as *polyarchy* and outlines seven institutions that together define it: elected officials, free and fair elections, inclusive suffrage, eligibility for public office, freedom to form and join organizations, alternative sources of information, and freedom of expression.

Sorensen (1998) asserted that these institutions or conditions are physical manifestations of the three different categories, or ideological characteristics, of democracies: competition, participation, and civil and political liberties as human rights. The concept of human rights includes civil and political rights (as well as economic, social and cultural rights, according to Western thought). Sorensen believed that given the framework of the criteria listed above, the best instrument to measure democracy today lies in the Freedom House Index (defined in the section on measuring democracy, below). Its particular utility stems from its use of one dimension to measure competition and participation and another dimension for civil liberties. Consequently, it addresses all three of Sorensen's ideological characteristics of democracy.

Since the purpose of this research is to discover whether a correlation exists between democratic policing and democracy, the Freedom House Index is best used to represent the reality of daily life—including interaction between police and the community—for it is the police who protect and defend the civil and political rights of the people.

Defining democracy. This research is intended to draw a road map between democracy and the democratization of policing. In this map, *democracy* is limited to the definition provided by Dahl (1971). Obviously, this definition does not cover every aspect of democracy in depth. However, many political scientists add or remove various concepts when defining democracy. For instance, Daniel Lerner (1968) and Seymour M. Lipset (1959, 1960) connect democratization to economic growth and modernization. While Gary Marx and Larry Diamond (1992) were generally supportive of the work of Lerner and Lipset, they emphasized the Human Development Index (an expansion of the Physical Quality of Life Index constructed by Morris D. Morris [1979] that takes into account national rates of literacy, infant mortality, and life expectancy at age one) as having a stronger correlation with the combined index of political freedom than does economic growth.

Robert Dahl (1971) emphasized causal factors of democracy, including the historical, social, external, political–cultural, and political leadership of a country in addition to its economic development. Like Dahl, Samuel Huntington (1993) saw multiple preconditions for democratization, with no single condition being sufficient to cause democratic development. However, he does assert that a central prerequisite appears to be the elites' perception that their interests are served by the introduction of democratic institutions.

Mancur Olson (1993) argues that democracy will most likely emerge when those who lead in the overthrow of an autocracy are incapable of establishing another autocratic system. In contrast, Raymond Gastil (1985) argues that democratization might depend more on the diffusion of democratic ideas than on socioeconomic factors. However, Arat (1991) argues, "As long as social and economic inequalities persist, developing countries that go through a process of democratization today are doomed to return to some form of authoritarianism" (p. 112).

Accordingly, this study will not give attention to those arguments and will remain limited to Sorensen's definition of democracy. His standard approach operationalized a complex concept of democracy within the borders of common law and civil law (Gastil, 1985; Arat, 1991; Olsen, 1993; Sorensen, 1998).

Measuring democracy. The Freedom House Index is a product of The Survey of Freedom (designed by Freedom House, an international NGO). Since 1955, Freedom House has monitored the progress and decline of the political rights and liberties of 192 nations and several major related and disputed territories. The survey is based on the principle that a country grants its citizens political rights when it permits them to form political parties that represent a significant portion of the range of voter choice, and when the leaders of those parties can openly compete for and be elected to positions of power in government. The survey is also based on the principle that a country upholds its citizens' civil liberties when it respects and protects their religious, ethnic, economic, linguistic, and other rights. These also include gender and family rights; personal reforms; and freedoms of the press, of belief, and of association (Freedom in the World, 2001–2002, p.10).

The Survey of Freedom evaluates political rights and civil liberties around the world, and reviews a country's freedom by examining and rating each country on a seven-point scale for both political rights and civil liberties. One on the scale represents a high degree of freedom, and seven a low degree of freedom. These scores are combined to form three more general categories: "Free" countries receive a rating of less than three; "partly free" countries are rated from three to just less than five; and "not free" countries have a rating of five or more.

This seven-point scale represents the level of democracy a country has achieved, according to the findings of Freedom House. However, for the purpose of this study, the scale has been inverted so that "7," the highest number on the scale, corresponds to the highest level of democracy a country can achieve, with the lowest level represented as "1." By inverted recoding of the Freedom House scale, the author hopes to make visually meaningful and readily understood comparisons between the index and other measures of democracy. When the author states, for example, that the United States has a rating of 7 on the index, this indicates that the United States has the highest degree of democracy possible according to the information produced by Freedom House.

Reliability and validity of data. The Freedom House ratings both review the conduct of governments and reflect the reality of life. In compiling these ratings, a country with a benign government facing violent forces that oppose open society would be graded on the basis of the actual on-the-ground conditions that indicate whether the population is able to exercise its freedoms. This survey enables scholars and policy makers both to assess the direction of global change annually and to examine trends in freedom over time. Scholars can also make comparisons of varying political systems across regions (Freedom in the World 2001–2002, p.10).

The survey project is a yearlong effort produced by regional experts, consultants, and human rights specialists. The survey receives its information from a wide range of sources, including human rights activists, journalists, editors, and political figures around the world who provide information about their respective countries. The survey is also reviewed by an advisory board consisting of very well-known political scientists.

In the present study, only fifteen countries were selected from among the 192 included in the Freedom House Index. Originally, this researcher planned to select twenty countries at random, including ten "free" countries, five "partly free" countries, and five "not free" countries. This selection would have included four countries each from five geographic regions of the world (Western Europe, Eastern Europe, the Far East and Oceania, the Americas, and the collective Middle East and Africa). However, after careful screening, several countries were rejected due to unavailability, insufficiency, and/or untrustworthiness of their data on democratic policing and its operational variables. As a result, fifteen countries were selected for this study: three from the Americas (Brazil, Colombia, and the United States), three from Eastern Europe (Russia, Slovenia, and Hungary), four from Western Europe (the United Kingdom, The Netherlands, Sweden, and France), two from Africa and the Middle East (South Africa and Saudi Arabia), and three from the Far East and Oceania (Australia, China, and Japan).

Conceptualizing democratic policing. Data on policing and democratic practices in policing were collected from cross-national field studies of democratic police practices in each respective country as well as comparative studies on major criminal justice systems, policing, law enforcement, and social control. Case studies on civilian oversight systems were also used, in addition to a European Survey of Selected Police Organizations (Becker, 1980) and the available annual country reports (Amnesty International, 1999, 2000, 2001).

For the purpose of this study, democratic policing is characterized by the institutionalization of the rule of law, accountability to the public, transparency of decision making, popular participation in policing (categorized as *representativeness* in the following discussion), minimum use of force, an atmosphere facilitating the learning of human rights, and internal democracy of the organization. These concepts are outlined by Das in his evaluation of the findings of the symposium on the "Theme of Challenges of Policing Democracies" held at the Institute of Sociology of Law in Spain on May 17–20, 1995 (Das, 2000). In this symposium, officials from the field and scholars from thirteen countries participated in discussions on the definition and conceptualization of democratic policing. Das's conceptualization of democratic policing agrees with other literature in the field and is consistent with findings of the 2001 report of the Vera Institute of Justice (Stone & Ward, 2001).

This conceptualization of democratic policing can be operationalized, according to a review of the literature. Twenty-four democratic policing practices have been identified. However, while collecting data on those operational variables it was determined that data regarding the variables were either unavailable or insufficient to evaluate for the countries selected for this research. Consequently, those variables were eliminated and, as a result, fourteen variables were examined: centralization/decentralization; representativeness; community policing; problem-oriented policing; presence of ombudsmen; oversight performed by legislatures, elected officials, or the courts; civilian oversight by NGOs; civilian complaint boards; internal police control; effective disciplinary structure; use of advanced technology for crime investigation; unionism; use-of-force training; and human-rights training.

In addition, media–police relations were evaluated separately to understand the degree to which the inner workings of police are visible to the public (i.e., transparency). This assessment was based on the frequency of police organizations to give detailed information about general operations (those that do not involve intelligence work) to the media. The degree to which the police respond to media feedback in general was also evaluated.

Measuring democratic policing. The operational variables of democratic policing were applied to a simple content-analysis process defined by Zito (1974), who established a system to tally the number of variables present in a given policing system. The absence of a particular variable resulted in a count of "0"; a "1" was given if a variable was present. For the purposes of this research it was intended that the presence of each variable would be verified using at least three different sources. However, very obvious and easy-to-identify variables were counted based on one source, such as centralization/decentralization, unionism, internal police control, and the presence of ombudsmen. On the other hand, in two countries where data sources were inconsistent regarding one of the variables, majority reports were assumed as final.

Phase II—Democratic Policing and Human Rights

In order to address the second phase, a cross-tabulation was arranged between the datasets, comparing the democratic policing of the individual countries with the human rights applications of those countries.

Human rights measurements are based on the reports of NGOs like Freedom House, Transparency International, and World Bank, as well as governmental agencies like the U.S. State Department, European Commission, and European Parliament. Many researchers have proven these sources to be relatively unbiased in their reports (Poe, Vasquez, & Zanger, 2001). In terms of human rights issues, the research conducted by Poe et al. showed that the Political Terror Index produced by Purdue University (Gibney & Dalton, 1996) was the most reliable available. This scale was prepared by evaluating the reports of both Amnesty International and the U.S. State Department (Poe, et al., 2001).

Conceptualizing human rights.   Based on the Political Terror Index (PTI), countries are coded on a scale of 1 through 5. In "Level 1" countries, there is a secure rule of law, no political imprisonment, and torture is extremely rare. In "Level 2" countries, there exists a limited amount of imprisonment for nonviolent political activity, torture is unusual, and political murder is rare. "Level 3" countries have widespread political imprisonment; torture and brutality may be common, and unlimited detention with or without trial for political views is accepted. "Level 4" countries experience murders, disappearances, and torture as a common way of life. In "Level 5" countries, there is an extended level of violence among all populations. The leaders place no limits on the means or thoroughness with which they pursue personal or ideological goals (Gibney & Dalton, 1996).

Reliability and validity of the data.   In the PTI coding process, Gibney and Dalton indicate that coders were instructed to ignore their own biases, give countries the benefit of the doubt, consider the size of the country being coded, and view the various levels as part of a continuum. The weakest point of PTI was in differentiating between countries at the highest level. The countries that received Level 5 ratings exhibit a wide range in the number of violations. However, as the authors state, in either case the situation in a country that receives a score of 5 is very undesirable. Inter-coder reliability was ensured by using two different coders for the same report. If conflict arose, another coder reviewed and coded that report. Overall, reliability was about 70–90% (Gibney & Dalton, 1996).

However, there are some problems in the scale. For example, several countries, including the United States, Sweden, The Netherlands, and Australia, were not added to the scale. The explanation for their exclusion was that reports regarding these countries did not reveal any violation large enough to code. Consequently, they were assumed to have a score of 1. Incidentally, there was no other dataset available that contained information regarding all of these countries that was helpful for this study.

Generalizability and Limitations of the Study

The cross-nationality of the study ensures the generalizability of the findings. Field studies, case analyses, and comparative studies used in this research were prepared by the experts in the field or scholars considered as reputable social and political scientists. Their findings have been tested several times, and in many cases policies based on their findings have produced fabulous results in practice. While this research will not take into account the historical, economical, sociocultural or other effects, which may affect the internal validity of the study, the cross-nationality of the study should compensate for the omission.

Limitations. In terms of democratic policing, the operationalized variables used for this research may not ensure that police accountability, responsiveness and representativeness alone will promote democratic policing. Caution is needed when applying policies. Also, the effectiveness of any policy that adopts the assumptions presented in this study basically depends on the personal characteristics, perceptions, principles and fairness of the individuals who work in the organization. The police subculture is not the main issue of this study. Because of the existence of controversial terminology on democratic policing applications, definitions of the operationalized variables used in this study are defined at the end of this article.

Secondary information is an inexpensive data source that facilitates the research process in several ways and can be used for generating hypotheses for further research. It is useful to compare the findings from different studies and to examine trends. In this study, secondary data were used solely to help general arguments and to shed light upon commonly accepted international perspectives. The inherent bias due to the structure of certain datasets was unavoidable. In particular, the PTI arguably is biased because it did not even evaluate some countries based on commonly held views of their inherited democratic tradition. In short, the overall findings of this study are limited by the nature of those secondary datasets.

This research does not attempt to produce a perfect model that meets all expectations in all communities. The author does not claim that this model will lead to democratic policing through the exchange and importation of certain methods or procedures. No police organization can be transformed from top to bottom unless the society it serves is transformed as well (Goldsmith, 1999). This research simply intends to shed light on the various policing characteristics that correlate to democratic societies.

Results and Discussion

Using the Freedom House Index Classification of Free Countries, fifteen countries were selected for this study by measures of freedom.

Democracy Ratings in Selected Countries

Four countries (Australia, The Netherlands, Sweden, and the United States) are classified as democratic, with an average rating of 7. Six countries (France, Hungary, Japan, Slovenia, South Africa, and the United Kingdom) are classified as democratic countries with an average rating of 6.5. Three countries (Brazil, Colombia, and Russia) are classified as partly democratic, with average ratings of 5, 1.5, and 1, respectively. Two countries (China and Saudi Arabia) are classified as not democratic, having average ratings of 1.5 and 1, respectively.

Ratings of Democratic Policing Variables

Table 1 shows the rating of each country, extrapolated from the content analysis of democratic policing variables in the literature, with a detailed explanation of the scores of each country based on the democratic policing variables identified earlier. In addition, the *transparency to media* category was added for both combined and separate evaluations. Each of the variables is discussed in the following sections.

Centralization/decentralization. There is no clear consensus in the literature regarding the promotion of centralization or decentralization of policing as a democratic policing practice. While some scientists argue that centralization is essential, others accept decentralization as a key concept. Consequently, the correlation between democratic policing and democracy was explored considering both centralization and decentralization as separate variables.

Centralized police departments exist in countries at every level of democracy. However, decentralized police departments are found only in highly democratic countries such as Australia, Japan, The Netherlands, Slovenia, the United Kingdom, and the United States.

According to Bayley (1985), centralized police departments have often been the tools of authoritarian, repressive, and totalitarian regimes. He explains that some countries, such as Japan, Finland, and France, were exceptions to that rule and added that their centralized police forces were the heritage of their rich organizational background. On the other hand, Berkley (1969) claimed that countries like Sweden returned to centralized systems after experimenting with decentralized systems in order to allow the public a more powerful and more exact control of the police. Such countries were very successful with their centralized organizations at controlling and bettering police practices.

Many countries with highly centralized police organizations have upheld democratic values for many years. Variables other than centralization/decentralization, such as the existence of an effective disciplinary structure and the presence of ombudsmen, could be the reason. After a careful inspection, the links between democracy and democratic policing reforms show a positive correlation. Some deviations occurred in analysis of Hungary, Slovenia, and Saudi Arabia. In the cases of Hungary and Slovenia, their previous domination by communist regimes is the likely reason. Terrill (1996) indicated that eastern, formerly "iron curtain" countries

Table 1 Content Analysis of Democratic Policing Practices

Countries / Variables	Australia	Brazil	China	Colombia	France	Hungary	Japan	Netherlands	Russia	Saudi Arabia	Slovenia	South Africa	Sweden	United Kingdom	United States
Centralization	0	1	1	1	1	1	0	0	1	1	0	0	1	0	0
Decentralization	1	0	0	0	0	0	1	1	0	0	0	1	0	1	1
Community policing	1	1	0	0	0	0	1	1	0	1	0	1	1	1	1
Representativeness[1]	1	1	0	0	1	0	0	1	0	0	0	0	1	1	1
Problem-oriented policing	1	0	0	0	NA	0	1	NA	0	1	0	0	NA	1	1
Presence of ombudsmen	1	1	0	1	1	1	NA	1	1	1	1	1	1	1	1
Oversight[2]	1	1	1	1	0	1	1	1	1	0	1	1	1	1	1
Civilian complaint board	1	0	0	1	0	0	1	1	0	0	1	1	1	1	1
Oversight[3]	1	1	0	1	0	0	1	1	0	0	1	1	1	1	1
Internal police control	1	1	1	1	1	1	1	1	1	1	1	1	1	1	1
Effective disciplinary structure	NA	1	NA	1	1	1	1	1	1	1	NA	0	1	1	0
Advanced technology use	1	0	1	0	1	NA	1	1	1	0	0	0	1	1	1
Unionism	1	0	0	0	1	1	1	1	0	1	1	1	1	1	1
Use-of-force training	1	1	1	1	1	1	1	1	1	1	1	1	1	1	1
Human rights training	0	1	0	0	1	1	0	1	0	1	1	1	1	NA	NA
Transparency to media	1	0	0	0	1	0	1	1	0	0	0	0	1	1	1
TOTAL	13	10	5	8	10	8	12	14	7	9	9	10	14	14	13

[1] Popular participation in policing
[2] Legislative, executive, or judicial oversight
[3] Civilian oversight by NGOs

transformed into full democracies very quickly, without time to adapt their laws and organizations to coordinate with democratic principles and organizational culture. Although transition from authoritarian traditions to democratic applications requires time and patience, it is still necessary to build a stable democratic police organization. Otherwise, the transition to a democratic police organization could cause unexpected and unfixable damage in society, such as lost of trust and fear of crime, and in the case of many nations in the former Soviet bloc, a substantial rise in organized and occupational crime (Terrill, 1996).

However, our hypothesis proves invalid in the case of Saudi Arabia, which implements most of the democratic policing applications yet has the lowest score in democracy of the countries analyzed. Perhaps this dilemma may be explained by the limited amount of data used in our measurement of the efficacy and efficiency by which democratic policing reforms are rigidly controlled by the country's political regime. There is also a slight deviation from hypothesized correlation in the case of South Africa that resulted from the historical fear of violence between whites and blacks. A strict and fast-moving police organization is needed to prevent possible future violence during this time of transition from apartheid to democracy (Mokotedi & Koitsioe, 1997).

Evaluation and Discussion of Cross-Tabulations of Variables

Table 2 summarizes the cross-tabulation of the 14 variables, plus the *transparency to media* category. A more detailed discussion on this cross-tabulation follows in this section.

Centralization/Decentralization. As discussed earlier, decentralization seems preferable over centralization as a model of police organization in democratic countries, and it seems more consistent with democratic values and actions.

At this point, it is necessary to explain the unique situation of South Africa. Even though it was evaluated as a democratic country in the Freedom House Index, South Africa is classified by PTI as a level-four country, which indicates that murders, disappearances, and torture are a common part of life there. Although new, global policing practices have been adapted to the South African police organization in order to combat high crime problems, the results do not yet reflect a high level of improvement. However, the future of the country looks promising (Lever & Van der Spuy, 2000).

Community policing/Problem-oriented policing. Community policing is a widely-known approach to democratic policing reforms, emphasizing greater community involvement in police activities in: a dedication to crime prevention, public inspection of police, accountability of police actions, customized police action, and community organization and co-production of order (Swanson, et al., 2001). Problem-oriented policing is a democratic policing reform that similarly advocates community-police

Table 2 Cross-Tabulation of Variables

	PTS	1	2	3	4	5
Centralization	1	2	1	1	3	1
	0	5	1	-	1	-
Decentralization	1	5	1	-	1	-
	0	2	1	1	3	1
Community policing	1	5	1	1	2	-
	0	2	1	-	2	1
Problem-oriented policing	1	3	1	1	-	-
	0	1	-	-	4	1
Presence of ombudsmen	1	7	2	1	3	1
	0	-	-	-	1	-
Legislative, executive, or judicial oversight	1	7	1	-	4	1
	0	-	1	1	-	-
Civilian complaint boards	1	5	1	-	1	1
	0	1	1	1	3	-
Civilian oversight by NGOs	1	6	1	-	2	1
	0	1	1	1	2	-
Internal police controls	1	7	2	1	4	1
	0	-	-	-	-	-
Effective disciplinary structure	1	5	2	1	3	1
	0	-	-	-	1	-
Advanced technology use for crime investigations	1	5	2	1	2	-
	0	-	-	-	2	1
Unionism	1	6	2	-	1	-
	0	1	-	1	3	1
Use-of-force training	1	7	2	1	4	1
	0	-	-	-	-	-
Human-rights training	1	2	1	1	2	-
	0	3	1	-	2	1
Transparency to media	1	6	-	-	1	-
	0	-	-	1	2	1

collaborative efforts, or co-production, but emphasizes problem-solving teams focused broadly on community concerns rather than simply responding to crime incidents (Goldstein, 1990).

In terms of community-oriented and problem-oriented policing practices, there are two different findings. As seen in table 2, community policing became widespread in the democratic world. Although countries like France have not adopted any policy *called* "community policing," nevertheless their overall historical policing practices center around community relations (Gleizal, Domenach, & Journes, 2000). In addition, although

Hungary and Slovenia still have not adopted a specific policy of community policing, feasibility studies are currently underway (Videtic, 2000).

On the other hand, problem-oriented policing does not find widespread support among democratic countries. This is due in part to its complicated nature. Goldstein (1990) indicated that problem-oriented policing is a complicated policy that requires substantial resources, highly educated personnel, and long and difficult training that many countries cannot afford. In addition, the resources used in this study did not provide enough data on this particular policy application.

Ombudsmen/Judicial, executive, or legislative oversight. The use of ombudsmen and oversight by legislatures, elected officials, or the courts are widespread in all levels of democracy. However, their efficacy and efficiency are questionable based on the character of the individual regime.

According to Mendes (1999), conversion democracies and nondemocratic countries are using such policies as security valves to rid themselves of mass protests around the country. The nature of those kinds of applications tends to change over time in the midst of a democracy, and they are in reality the product of democracy (Walker & Luna, 2000).

Civilian complaint boards/Oversight by NGOs. These two variables receive almost the same rating on the PTS; they operate in basically the same way and stem from the same legislations. Both applications exert control over the police and are the most recently applied police reforms in democratic countries. Civilian oversight mirrors the growing movement of all countries toward a better democracy, not only by helping to better policing practices but also by developing policies and procedures that help police do their job.

According to the individual reports of each country and several independent sources, even conversion democracies and non-democratic countries tend to adopt democratic applications in response to the pressures placed on them by the international community. Certain political, trade, and security agreements depend on the existence of democratic programs (Kratcoski, 2000; Szikinger, 2000; Silva, 1999; Gleizal et al., 2000; Terrill, 1996).

Internal controls and disciplinary structure. Internal police controls and effective disciplinary procedures that are established by law and implemented by ordinances or rules are generally considered to be the primary structure in police agencies in every type of regime or country. As indicated by Bayley (1985) and Berkley (1969), the organizational structures of police organizations have these mechanisms to hold police accountable, not only to the community they serve but also to the stakeholders of the governments.

Use of technology. Modern and advanced scientific policing techniques are highly desired and recommended by scientists as well as governments. However, due to the rapidly changing nature of today's technology, its considerable expense, and the need for highly trained personnel to use it, the technology level used in each country varies along a huge continuum. Most of the countries use at least some level of technology and some degree of advanced scientific policing techniques in their police organizations.

On the other hand, some scientists—including Marx (1998), the leading figure to support technological methods as a way to better democratic policing—have also indicated that high levels of caution must be exercised when police work and science are combined. Technology can be used by police to invade individual privacy, and privacy is a central element of democracy.

Unionism.   Police trade unions are seen as a catalyst within the police organizations. They foster the democratization of the organization in principle (Berkley, 1969; Skolnick, 1966). Police trade unions in Russia serve as an example of such theory. According to Gilinskiy (2000), even the inefficient structure of their police trade unions helped on some level to democratize Russia's policing in the country.

Gleizal et al. (2000) in France as well as Morgan and Newburn (1997) in England state that police trade unions, like any other trade union in a democratic society, both encourage and promote the democratization of the police organization, as well as help with the overall democratic stabilization of the country itself.

Use-of-force/Human-rights training.   For the purposes of this study, this variable was intended to measure whether intensive training helps officers to understand when the use of force is appropriate and yet not disrespectful of individual human rights. However, the term *use-of-force training* is also used to describe simple "how to" classes used to teach recruits and/or officers how to operate weapons and how to physically overcome and combat a suspected criminal. It was, in some cases, difficult to tell how the term was being applied. For this reason, extreme caution should be exercised when evaluating use-of-force training. Because it is classified as one of the necessary requisites of basic police training, all countries have such training at some level.

Human-rights training, however, is another matter. The United Nations Office of the High Commissioner for Human Rights designs the standards of human-rights training programs to be consistent with the UN Decade for Human Rights Education Program. In addition, the European Council Directorate General of Human Rights designs parallel requisites in its Report on Police and Human Rights 1997–2000. Both international organizations have established access to check the situations in each country and publish reports regarding the current situation in each country. The results reflect real numbers on the existence of human-rights training programs.

Direct human-rights training is not considered necessary by democratic countries, even though the programs of international agenda require and insist on such implementations. There could be two reasons for this refusal to comply. The first, explained by Trautman, is that human-rights training could be infused into other different training programs, such as criminal procedure, the use of force and firearms, decision making, armed conflict, police administration, police investigation techniques, and police liability training sessions. Furthermore, most training programs incorporate human-rights training activities throughout the programs, without any *specific* training in this area (Trautman, 2000). In the second possible explanation for a lack of human-rights training, Das (2000) notes that most of the countries view separate and blatant human-rights training as embarrassing or find it repressive to their current, allegedly democratic and successful systems.

On the other hand, other countries have adopted human-rights training policies easily and promptly, expecting financial help from the UN or perhaps the European Council. A proper conclusion is impossible in these cases (Bayley, 2001).

Transparency to media.   In addition to the variables explored above, several social scientists state that the media do a great deal to control the police by bringing public attention to their antidemocratic wrongdoings (Goldsmith, 1999; Lewis, 2000; Marx, 1998; Goldstein, 1990.) Many police agency administrators have adopted new policies like keeping the society well informed on a timely basis and making police operations "transparent" in order to increase their reliability and accountability. Consequently, policies have been adopted to establish transparency to the media in regular and routine police operations. The results in table 2 show that most of the democratic countries have these types of policies in order to help increase their level of accountability. The media represent a powerful tool that can be used to combat crime. In order for police to wield this tool successfully, their operations must be open to the media (Windlesham, 1998; LaFree, 1998).

On the other hand, according to the Vera Institute's 2001 report, particularly in countries where community-based or nongovernmental structures do not have open relationships with police, the media can give voice to society's concerns about crime or police responsiveness. Accordingly, the media also play a role in exposing police misconduct and pressuring police to reform (Stone & Ward, 2000).

Conclusions and Implications

Many scholars assume that police organizations can help democratize a country. However, they also believe that this help is limited. For example, Bayley (1997) indicated that unless a regime is dedicated to becoming democratic, there is little that the reform of police can accomplish on its own to bring about greater democracy. Others (e.g., Marenin, 2000) insist that police can be de-politicized and removed from partisan control through a subservience to the rule of law, organizational regulations, professional norms, and democratic culture. If the police support democracy then democracy must, in turn, keep the police in check. The people must ensure that the police do not overstep their autonomy, and that they avoid the corruption and misuse of force that may result from exceeding their bounds (Marenin, 2000).

This study has shown an interrelation between democracy and democratic policing reforms with a significant positive correlation. Democratic policing reforms tend to promote democracy. Democracies, in turn, tend to promote policing reforms that maintain, consolidate, or stabilize the democracy of the country.

Decentralized police organizations were more likely than centralized police organizations to promote democracy. All democratic police reforms focused on oversight are associated with significant support and promotion of democracy (e.g., internal controls, effective disciplinary structures, unionism, and the use of advanced technology in crime investigation). However, while community policing is often adopted in democratic countries, problem-oriented policing is not.

It should be noted that most of the democratic policing variables that focused on police operations (e.g., community policing and problem-oriented policing) and some of the variables that focused on organizational structures (e.g., civilian oversight by NGOs and police trade unions) were consistent only with a *decentralized* police organizational structure. In fact, decentralized police organizations are more dynamic and adaptive. They are open to newly developed techniques and are very quick to adopt these new techniques and abandon old ones.

Some democratic policing reforms were chosen only by democratic countries, such as unionism, civilian complaint boards, and civilian oversight by NGOs. Although unionism and civilian control boards were never chosen by transition democracies or antidemocratic countries, new democracies such as Hungary, Slovenia, and South Africa have adopted at least one of these applications.

In itself, the presence of human-rights training did not positively correlate to the levels of democracy in the countries studied. Human-rights training was present in all European democracies, but this may be due to the mandates of European Union Regulations (Anderson, Boer, denCullen, Gilmore, Raab, & Walker, 1995). In a contradiction in the literature, scholars report that many democratic countries have little faith in the ability of human-rights training to make a difference in overall rights violations—yet many of these same countries revise their police training curriculums to teach respect for human rights in the hope of changing the police mentality (Shearing, 1997; Hazenberg, 2001; Sheptycki, 2000; Bayley, 2001).

In democracies, governmental agencies must represent the community they serve by race, ethnic background, religion, gender, and political profile. Our analysis has confirmed that belief. All established democracies have representative police organizations. Research has shown that some nation-states like Japan still do not meet this requisite. Even though the member countries of the European Union presented in this study have representative organizations, before the regulations were adopted and required by the European Union, the situation was the same in Europe. The countries, then, are forced to change their national laws to establish more representative police organizations. However, that change covers only the citizens of member states. In fact, some counties (e.g., Germany) decided not to adopt such policies (Anderson, et al., 1995). On the other hand, the nationality laws of those countries are still in conflict with European Union regulations. This conflict is not likely to be resolved in the near future. Since those laws are in force, it seems illogical to expect countries to be representative, not only in Europe but in any part of the world.

In this analysis, internal police control mechanisms and effective disciplinary structures received the same level of support from all levels of democratic countries. Because the literature emphasizes that internal police controls and an effective disciplinary structure promote democratic policing, it was obviously intended that these controls and the system, laws, and regulations were arranged and forged within democratic beliefs. Namely, if the laws and regulations were not designed within democratic structures, the meaning of these two variables was just imposition of a coercive and antidemocratic government. In order to avoid such confusion, in this study it is better to look at those variables together, considering either civilian oversight or transparency to the media in addition to control and discipline. The combination, then, can show the intended purpose. The situation is exactly same for the variable of legislative, executive, and judicial oversight. If one cannot assume an overall democracy in a country, this variable means nothing at all and can be manipulated by the government in question. Consequently, extreme caution is needed when analyzing such variables and forming a conclusion. On the other hand, since there were many other variables used herein that are not consistent with any kind of coercive power or antidemocratic behavior, the combination of all the variables together can offer a reliable conclusion.

Many scholars believe that technology use in policing will diminish the antidemocratic, suppressive and discriminating behaviors of police (Marx, 1998; Coleman, 2001; Broderick, 1987). However, many also agree that the uncontrolled use of technological improvements will have the ability to increase the suppressive power of the police by diminishing individual privacy (Serpico, 1998). In this analysis, it is observed that all countries use technology in policing. However, some countries like Colombia, Brazil, and South Africa did not have enough resources to use technology in policing. In this analysis, especially, the availability and usage of AFIS (Automated Fingerprint Identification System) and criminalistics laboratories (with DNA analysis capability, for example) have been examined and accordingly evaluated. In the end, it was found that there is no clear correlation between democracy and the use of advanced technology to investigate crime.

An additional variable, transparency to the media, showed that there is a strong correlation between police–media relations and democracy. In democracies police operations are transparent to the media; thus, society can demand accountability and establish stricter control over police. Without any exception, this conclusion was verified by the analysis of this research.

All of the policies that were chosen here have to do primarily with crime reduction. Beyond that, they are operational, organizational, administrative applications. The purpose of democratizing policing is still the same: to lower crime rates using democratic means. Some people claim that such policies tie the hands of police while not effectively combating crime. Administrators from transition democracies in particular seem to feel that initiatives such as civilian oversight and transparency to the media place too much pressure on police. As a result, police avoid confronting these types of systems and do not perform their primary duty, namely, pursuing criminals (Das, 2000). This is partly true. On at least some level, police officers think about the future of their careers. They are afraid of putting themselves in controversial situations. Consequently, they play it safe, not pursuing complicated situations even when they could legally go further.

This situation is not entirely true, however. Democratic systems do not obstruct police operations. To the contrary, they encourage and assist the police. In fact, they protect police officers from the accusations that are leveled against them (Walker & Luna, 2000; Lewis, 2000). The opposition to these systems stems mostly from a lack of officer training regarding the application and effectiveness of these policies (Marenin, 2000; Bayley & Shearing, 2001).

In terms of certain operational policies such as, for example, community policing, no research clearly shows these policies to decrease overall crime rates. However, because their main purpose is to stop crime before it is committed, there is enough evidence to indicate that policies such as community policing are more effective in certain neighborhoods and in certain types of crimes (Goldstein, 1990). Also, as Windlesham (1998) indicates, the benefits of these policies are long term. They are accompanied by radical, positive changes in the attitudes of the community toward the police.

In addition, when effective controls are placed on the police, corruption and brutality diminish. Consequently, the police become more effective and, more specifically, better able to prevent crime. Controls lead to a better organization and, accordingly, better policing (Sherman, 1978; Trautman, 2000; Knapp, Monserbat, Sprizzo, Thomas, & Vance, 1972).

This study has shown that several of the methods used in democratic policing agencies effectively reduce crime. In addition, democratic policing methods encourage police agencies to respect human rights, act within the scope of the law, be accountable to the public, and be representative of and responsive to the community. All of these by-products of democratic policing promote democracy in the society at large.

It is highly likely that the world can perhaps expect more from democratic policing than even these results. However, further research is needed to clarify the relationship between democratic policing and crime rates.

References

Anderson, M., Boer, M., denCullen, P., Gilmore, W., Raab, C., & Walker, N. (1995). *Policing the European Union*. Oxford, UK: Clarendon Press.

Amnesty International Country Reports Available: http://www.amnestyusa.org/ailib/aireport/ar99 (for 1999); http://www.web.amnesty.org/web/ar2000web.nsf/countries (for 2000); http://web.amnesty.org/web/ar2001.nsf/webamrcountries (for 2001). (Accessed May 11/June 9, 2002.)

Arat, Z. (1991). *Democracy and Human Rights in Developing Countries*. Boulder, CO: Lynne Rienner Publishing.

Bayley, D. H. (1997). Who Are We Kidding? Or Developing Democracy through Police Reform. In National Institute of Justice Research Report. (Eds.), *Policing in Emerging Democracies: Workshop Papers and Highlights* (pp. 59–64). Washington DC: U.S. Department of Justice, Office of Justice Programs.

Bayley, D. H. (2001). *Democratizing the Police Abroad: What to Do and How to Do It.*, NCJ #188742. Washington DC: U.S. Department of Justice.

Bayley, D. H., & Shearing, C. D. (2001). *The New Structure of Policing: Description, Conceptualization, and Research Agenda*. NCJ #187083. Washington DC: U.S. Department of Justice.

Becker, H. K. (1980). *Police Systems of Europe: A Survey of Selected Police Organizations*. Springfield, IL: Charles Thomas.

Beetham, D. (1999). *Democracy and Human Rights*. Cambridge, UK: Polity Press.

Berkley, G. E. (1969). *The Democratic Policeman*. Boston, MA: Beacon Press.

Broderick, J. J. (1987). *Police in a Time of Change*. Prospects Heights, IL: Waveland Press.

Chan, J. B. L. (1999). Governing Police Practice: Limits of the New Accountability. London School of Economics, *British Journal of Sociology*, 50(2): 251–270.

Coleman, V. (2001). Technology in Criminal Justice Administration. In M.A. Dupont-Morales, Michael K. Hooper; Judy H. Schmidt (Eds.), *Handbook of Criminal Justice Administration* (pp. 473–498) New York: Marcel Dekker, Inc.

Council of Europe Status Report. (2000). *Achievements under the Programme "Police and Human Rights 1997–2000" and the Future of Police and Human Rights Activities within the Council of Europe*. DW-AW-PO (2000) 10. Strasbourg, Austria: European Union Press.

Crawshaw, R., Devlin, B., & Williamson, T. (1998). *Human Rights and Policing: Standards for Good Behaviour and a Strategy for Change*. Dordrecht, The Netherlands: Kluwer Law International.

Dahl, R. (1971). *Polyarchy: Participation and Opposition*. New Haven, CT: Yale University Press.

Das, K. D. (2000). Challenges of Policing Democracies: A World Perspective. In K. D. Das & O. Marenin (Eds.), *Challenges of Policing Democracies: A World Perspective* (pp. 3–22). Amsterdam, The Netherlands: Overseas Publishers.

Diamond, L. (1992). Economic Development and Democracy Reconsidered. In G. Marks & D. Larry (Eds.), *Reexamining Democracy: Essays in Honor of Seymour Lipset* (pp. 179–221). London, UK: Sage.

Freedom In the World (2001–2002). Freedom House Index. Available: http://www. Freedomhouse.org/research/freeworld/2000/table1.htmp (accessed February 14, 2002).

Gastil, R. (1985). The Past, Present, and Future of Democracy. *Journal of International Affairs*. 38(2): 161–179.

Gibney, M., & Dalton, M. (1996). The Political Terror Scale. *Policy Studies and Developing Nations*, 4: 73–84.

Gilinskiy, Y. (2000). Challenges of Policing Democracies: The Russian Experience. In K. D. Das & O. Marenin (Eds.), *Challenges of Policing Democracies: A World Perspective* (pp. 173–194). Amsterdam, The Netherlands: Overseas Publishers.

Gleizal, J. J., Domenach, G. J., & Journes, C. (2000). *La Police: Le Cas des Democraties Occidentales*. Ankara, Turkey: Temiz Yayinlari.

Goldsmith, A. (1999). Better Policing, More Human Rights: Lessons from Civilian Oversight. In Errol P. Mendes, Joaquin Zuckerberg, Susan Lecorre, Anne Gabriel, and Jeffrey A. Clark (Eds.), *Democratic Policing and Accountability* (pp. 33–67) Brookfield, VT: Ashgate Pub. Ltd.

Goldsmith, A. J., & Lewis, C. (2000). *Civilian Oversight of Policing: Governance, Democracy and Human Rights*. Portland, OR: Hart Publishing.

Goldstein, H. (1990). *Problem Oriented Policing*. New York: McGraw Hill.

Hazenberg, A. (2001). Target Areas of Police Reform. In A. Kadar (Ed.), *Police in Transition: Essays on Police Forces in Transition Countries* (pp.177–186). Budapest, Hungary: Central European University Press.

Hornblower, S. (1992). Creation and Development of Democratic Institutions in Ancient Greece. In J. Dunn (Ed.), *Democracy: The Unfinished Journey* (pp. 1–16). Oxford, UK: Oxford University Press.

Huntington, S. (1993). *The Third Wave: Democratization in the Late Twentieth Century*. Norman: University of Oklahoma Press.

Kratcoski, P. C. (2000). Policing in Democratic Societies: A Historical Review. In K. D. Das & O. Marenin (Eds.), *Challenges of Policing Democracies: A World Perspective* (pp. 23–44). Amsterdam, The Netherlands: Overseas Publishers.

Knapp, W., Monserbat, J., Sprizzo, J., E., Thomas, F., & Vance, C., R. (1972). *Knapp Commission Report on Police Corruption*. New York: George Braziller Inc.

LaFree, G. (1998). *Losing Legitimacy*. Boulder, CO. Westview Press.

Lerner, D. (1968). *The Passing of Traditional Society: Modernizing the Middle East*. New York: The Free Press.

Lever, J., and van der Spuy, E. (2000). Challenges Facing Democratic Policing in South Africa. In D. K. Das & O. Marenin (Eds.), *Challenges of Policing Democracies: A World Perspective* (pp.224–247). Amsterdam, The Netherlands: Overseas Publishers.

Lewis, C. (2000). The Politics of Civilian Oversight: Serious Commitment or Lip Service? In A. J. Goldsmith,& C. Lewis (Eds.), *Civilian Oversight of Policing: Governance, Democracy and Human Rights* (pp. 224–247). Portland, OR: Hart Publishing.

Lipset, S. M. (1959). Some Social Requisites of Democracy: Economic Development and Political Legitimacy. *The American Political Science Review*, 53(1): 69–105.

Lipset, S. M. (1960). *Political Man: The Social Bases of Politics*. New York. Double-day Publishing.

Marenin, O. (2000). Democracy, Democratization and Democratic Policing. In D. K. Das & O. Marenin (Eds.), *Challenges of Policing Democracies: A World Perspective* (pp. 3–22). Amsterdam, The Netherlands: Overseas Publishers.

Marx, G. (2000). Police and Democracy Available: http://web.mit.edu/gtmarx/www/poldem.html (accessed January 14, 2002).

Marx, G. (1998). Some Reflections on the Democratic Policing of Demonstrations. Available: http://web.mit.edu/gtmarx/www/polpro.html (accessed January 14, 2002).

Marx, G., & Diamond, L. (1992). *Reexamining Democracy: Essays in Honor of Seymour Lipset*. London, UK. Sage.

Mendes, E. P. (1999). Raising the Social Capital of Policing and Nations: How Can Professional Policing and Civilian Oversight Weaken the Circle of Violence? In Errol P. Mendes, Joaquin Zuckerberg, Susan Lecorre, Anne Gabriel, and Jeffrey A. Clark (Eds) *Democratic Policing and Accountability* (pp. 13–22). Brookfield, VT: Ashgate Pub. Ltd.

Miller, S., Blackler, J., and Alexandra, A. (1997). *Police Ethics*. St. Leonard, NSW, Australia: Allen & Unwin.

Mokotedi, P., & Koitsioe, G. (1997). The State of Democratic Oversight. Secretariat for Safety and Security Discussion Document 1, No. 1 Available: http://www.gcis.gov.za/sss/evirosca.htm. (accessed May 14, 2002).

Morgan, R., & Newburn, T. (1997). *The Future of Policing*. New York: Oxford University Press.

Morris, M. D. (1979). *Measuring the Condition of the World's Poor*. New York: Pergamon Press.

Olson, M. (1993). Dictatorship, Democracy, and Development. *American Political Science Review,*87(3): 567–576.

Poe, S. C., Vasquez, T., & Zanger, S. (2001, August). How are These Pictures Different: Assessing the Biases in the U.S. State Department's Country Reports on Human Rights Practices. *Human Rights Quarterly,* 143–174.

Shearing, C. (1997). Toward Democratic Policing: Rethinking Strategies of Transformation. In National Institute of Justice Research Report. (Eds.), *Policing in Emerging Democracies: Workshop Papers and Highlights* (pp. 59–64). Washington DC: U.S. Department of Justice, Office of Justice Programs.

Sheptycki, J. (2000). Policing and Human Rights: An Introduction. *Police and Society,* 10(1): 1–12.

Skolnick, J. H. (1966) *Justice without Trial: Law Enforcement in Democratic Society*. New York: John Wiley & Sons.

Sherman, L. W. (1978). Controlling Police Corruption: The Effects of the Reform Plicies. *National Institute of Law Enforcement and Criminal Justice Summary Report*. Washington DC: U.S. Department of Justice.

Silva, J. D. (1999). Law Enforcement with the Community. In Errol P. Mendes, Joaquin Zuckerberg, Susan Lecorre, Anne Gabriel, and Jeffrey A. Clark (Eds.), *Democratic Policing and Accountability* (pp. 113–123). Brookfield, VT: Ashgate Pub. Ltd.

Sorensen, G. (1998). *Democracy and Democratization: Processes and Prospects in a Changing World*. Boulder, CO: Westview Press.

Stone, C. E., & Ward, H. (2000). Democratic Policing: A Framework for Action. *Policing and Society,*10(1): 1, 11–45.

Swanson, C. R., Territo, L., & Taylor, R. W. (2001). *Police Administration, Structures, Processes, and Behavior, 5/E*. Englewood Cliffs, NJ: Prentice-Hall.

Szikinger, I. (2000). The Challenges of Policing Democracy in Hungary. In K. D. Das & O. Marenin (Eds.), *Challenges of Policing Democracies: A World Perspective* (pp. 3–22). Amsterdam, The Netherlands: Overseas Publishers.

Terrill, R. (1996). *Policing in Central and Eastern Europe: Comparing Firsthand Knowledge with Experience from the West*. Ljulbljana, Slovenia: College of Police and Security Studies

Tocqueville, A. (2000). *Democracy in America*. Indianapolis, IN: Hackett Publishing.

Trautman, N. (2000). The Corruption Continuum. International City Management Association, *Public Management,*. 6(1): 2, 82–103.

Videtic, J. (2000). Policing Democracy: The Slovenian Experience. In K. D. Das & O. Marenin (Eds.), *Challenges of Policing Democracies: A World Perspective* (pp. 343–352). Amsterdam, The Netherlands: Overseas Publishers.

Walker, S., & Luna, E. (2000) Institutional Structure vs. Political Will: Albuquerque as a Case Study in the Effectiveness of Citizen Oversight of the Police. In A. J. Goldsmith & C. Lewis (Eds.), *Civilian Oversight of Policing: Governance, Democracy and Human Rights* (pp. 67–98). Portland, OR: Hart Publishing.

Windlesham, L. (1998). *Politics, Punishment and Populism*. New York: Oxford University Press.

Zito, G. V. (1975). *Methodology and Meanings: Varieties of Sociological Inquiry*. New York: Preager.

10

Public Support for the Police in Countries in Transition and Established Democracies

Sanja Kutnjak Ivković

The fall of the Berlin Wall and the ensuing collapse of the Iron Curtain symbolically marked the end of the communist era and the beginning of the democratization process in a number of former communist countries. The process of transition began in the late 1980s and intensified in the 1990s. The rate of progress in political, economic, and social environments differs across countries, but common features include attempts to change the political system (abolishing the one-party system and introducing a multi-party system), the economic system (changing from a state-controlled economy to a market-controlled economy; privatizing of public property), and social environments (changing the system of values).

The police in countries in transition are organized as national forces, with the ministry of the interior on the top of the hierarchy and the minister of the interior and/or chief of police as the top executive (see, e.g., Das and Marenin, 2000). While the rate of progress, specific nature of organizational changes, and conditions faced by the police tend to differ across East European countries (see, e.g., Abraham, 2001; Benke, 2001; Gilinskiy, 2000; Kutnjak Ivković, 2000; Leps, 2000; Plywaczewski, 2000; Stefanescu, 2001; Szikinger, 2000; Videtić, 2000), public support for the police is nevertheless one of the key ingredients of successful transition in virtually any country striving to be a true democracy.

The consequences of the lack of support for the police are adverse: when citizens do not have confidence in the police, they are reluctant to report crimes to the police and to provide any type of assistance. Over three decades ago, the U.S. President's Commission on Law Enforcement and the Administration of Justice (1967, p. 144) emphasized the impor-

Prepared especially for *Comparative and International Criminal Justice, 2/E.*

tance of citizens' strong support for the police as a necessary prerequisite for effective policing:

> Poor police-community relations adversely affect the ability of the police to prevent crime and apprehend criminals. People hostile to the police are not so likely to report violations of the law, even when they are the victims. They are even less likely to report suspicious persons or incidents, to testify as witnesses voluntarily, or to come forward and provide information. . . . Yet, citizen assistance is crucial to law enforcement agencies if the police are to solve an appreciable portion of the crimes that are committed. . . .

It has been more than a decade since the democratization process in countries in transition had started. This article studies the extent to which public support for the police in countries in transition is similar to the support prevailing in established democracies at the turn of the millennium. Using the data from the International Crime Victimization Survey, the results suggest that there is a sizeable gap in the extent of public support for the police between countries in transition and those with established democracies.

The Police in Transition and Public Support for the Police

Public support for the police is influenced both by the functions the police perform and by the manner in which they perform them. If the police functions were defined primarily as the protection of the existing totalitarian regime and/or if the police are enforcing unpopular, biased, or discriminatory laws, the level of support for the police would likely be low. Similarly, the way the police perform their functions could impact public opinion: overly aggressive, discriminatory, or corrupt police agencies generally would generate a lower level of public support. Indeed, U.S. studies suggest that respondents who perceive the police to engage in misconduct more frequently are less likely to express strong support for the police (see, e.g., Benson, 1981; Dean, 1980; Smith and Hawkins, 1973; Soo Son et al., 1997).

The idea of democratic policing is an abstract concept, but, as Marenin (2000, p. 321) argues, "the literature on democratic policing can be summoned up in six principles of good policing: effectiveness, efficiency, accessibility, accountability, congruence and general order." The actual operationalization of the concept is dependent upon the social, legal, and political context (see Marenin, 2000, p. 319). The police in established democracies do not fully conform to a uniform application of this concept, just like they do not experience exactly the same types of problems and challenges in the process (compare, e.g., Durston, 2000; Edelbacher and Norden, 2000; van de Meeberg and Aronowitz, 2000). Thus, although there are common guiding principles as to what constitutes democratic policing, the police in established democracies do not do police work in exactly the same way (see, e.g., Rosenthal et al., 2001; Sparrow, Moore, and Kennedy, 1990), nor do they have exactly the same accountability mechanisms imposed (see, e.g., Christopher Commission, 1991; Mollen Commission, 1994; Walker, 2001). Furthermore, their levels of integrity differ even within the same country (see Klockars et al., 1997), as does the extent and nature of their involvement in police misconduct (see, e.g., Chevigny, 1995; Christopher Commission, 1991; Mollen Commission, 1994; Skolnick and Fyfe, 1993).

The militia that carried out the police functions in the former communist countries had quite a different mission and means than the police in democratic countries. An important part of the police function was the protection of the communist regime (Mawby, 2001, p. 23), in addition to the range of other, less traditional police functions such as keeping up the national identity card system, licensing, or censorship (Mawby, 2001, p. 23). According to Matei (1994, p. 132), the political function in Hungary was more important than the more traditional police functions, such as crime fighting or order maintenance. The secret police, be they the Sigurimi in Albania, Stasi in the GDR, or KBW in Poland, were quite powerful, "with uniformed police organizations either formally or informally subordinate to them" (Mawby, 2001, p. 23).

Not only was the political function one of the key ingredients of policing during the communist regime, but policing during that period was also characterized by a different understanding of the boundaries of acceptable behavior toward citizens and the lack of appreciation for civil rights. Consequently, public accountability was not particularly important:

> . . . centralized and militaristic systems provided minimal local or civilian accountability, secret police were accountable to the party and ministry, not even—in many cases—to parliament, and the emphasis placed on political functions meant that those recruited to both police and citizens' groups were chosen on the basis of party loyalty rather than other qualities and came under direct political control. (Mawby, 2001, p. 24)

It would be interesting to compare the results of public-opinion surveys regarding these issues conducted in countries while they were still under communist regimes with the results of such surveys in established democracies. Unfortunately, public-opinion surveys from former communist countries are not available, and we can only venture an educated guess about the extent of public support for the police in these countries back then.

In the early days of the transition, changes to the criminal justice system, including the police, were considered crucial (see, e.g., Jasinski cited in Mawby, 2001, p. 24; Szikinger, 1999). Transformation of the police is driven by the desire to depart from the image of the communist militia, a military-style force in charge of protecting the communist regime, characterized by little accountability to the public, and willing to engage in gross violations of citizens' rights (see, e.g., Koszeg, 2001; Mawby, 2001), and instead to embrace the image of the democratic police, a modern professional force, accountable to the public, that serves the citizens and maintains public order.

Typically, the transition process included not only the changes in police functions (e.g., descaling of the political functions) and the structure of the police force (e.g., decentralization/centralization and demilitarization of the police; see Das, 2000; Mawby, 2001), but also changes in the applicable laws (see, e.g., Caparini and Marenin, 2003). These laws, substantive and procedural, as well as those regulating the work of the police, have been changed to better suit the current political, social, and economic conditions (see Das, 2000). In addition, professionalism, accountability to the public, and control of police misconduct are also viewed as basic elements of democratic policing (see, e.g., Das, 2000, p. 15–16; Caparini and Marenin, 2003). Consequently, the personnel reform at the beginning of the transition process (see Koci, 1996, p. 225) resulted in the dismissal or departure of a large number of police officers loyal to the communist regime (see, e.g., Das, 2000, pp. 5–6; Mawby, 2001, pp. 24–25).

However, the extent of success of the transition process remains an open question. For example, a 1997–1998 study conducted by Miller and colleagues (2001) indicated that approximately one-quarter of the respondents in the Czech Republic, Slovakia, Bulgaria, and Ukraine stated that the behavior of the street-level politicians (including the police) remained the same as it was during the communist period, while between one-third and three-fourths of the respondents (34% in the Czech Republic, 49% in Slovakia, 31% in Bulgaria, and 75% in Ukraine; Miller et al., 2001, p. 68) said that it actually *deteriorated* since the end of communism. In addition, over two-thirds of the respondents in Slovakia, Bulgaria, and Ukraine and close to one-half in the Czech Republic said that persons "seeking something to which they were entitled by law" from the police would "have to offer money, a present or a favour" (Miller et al., 2001, p. 73).

To what extent have the police in transition left their undemocratic pasts behind them? Does the public support for the police follow the actual changes and, if so, how closely? While these are interesting questions, the reality is, as Mawby (2001, p. 27) describes, that "very little research has been conducted on the police in societies in transition, at least partly because of the lack of tradition of academics carrying out research on policing issues." Several data sources provide more input into the public opinions about the police in the late 1980s and mid-1990s.

First, according to the 1989 International Crime Victimization Survey results, support for the police was weaker in Poland (the only country in transition included in the survey) than in any of the 15 industrialized nations included in the survey (van Dijk, Mayhew, and Killias, 1990, p. 71). The research team examined some of the variables that might have an impact on the respondents' opinions. Concluding that "there is no clear relationship between the national levels of victimization and judgments on the police," they reported that age and victimization experience were related with the respondents' opinions (p. 72).

Six additional countries in transition were surveyed in 1992: Estonia, Russia, Georgia, Czech Republic, Slovenia, and the Slovak Republic (Zvekic, 1996). It is difficult to evaluate the results of the public-opinion survey about the police because of the very high proportion of "unknown" answers (close to or well over one-half of the respondents in four out of seven countries selected the "I don't know" answer). Of the respondents who *did* provide an evaluation of the police ability to control crime in the area, the majority of the respondents in six countries (Slovenia being the exception) thought that the police were *not* doing a good job (see table 10 in Zvekic, 1996, p. 55). In the five countries (Estonia, Czech Republic, Georgia, Poland, and Russia) that participated in both the 1992 and 1996 surveys, the data indicate that the public opinion remained the same in three countries, somewhat improved in Estonia, and worsened in Georgia (see table 10 in Zvekic, 1996, p. 55). However, the key result is that the majority of the respondents in 10 out of 11 countries (Albania being the exception) surveyed in 1996 thought that the police were *not* doing a good job in controlling crime in the area (see table 10 in Zvekic, 1996, p. 55).

Second, several studies conducted in individual countries (e.g., Hungary, Czech Republic) reported that the public opinion about the police improved somewhat in the early 1990s. For example, Finszter (1994, cited in Mawby, 2001, p. 27) detects an improvement of 10 percent in the level of public satisfaction with the police between 1990 and 1992. Approximately at the same time, Zapletal and Tomin (1995) showed the results of a public-opinion survey conducted between early 1990 and late 1991 indicating that, while the level of satisfaction with how the police deal with order and safety improved slightly, the level of confidence in the police overall increased from 30 percent in May 1990 to 50 percent in December 1991.

Third, the analysis of the third wave of the World Values Survey data (1995–1997) (Kutnjak Ivković, 2003) yields support to the hypothesis that the police from the countries in transition and the police from the established democracies (still) enjoy different levels of support. In particular, while the majority of the respondents from 11 established democracies expressed a high level of confidence in the police, this was the case in only approximately one-third of the 16 countries in transition (Kutnjak Ivković, 2003).

Public Opinion about the Police and Contact with the Police

The type and nature of contact with the police seem to have an impact on public support for, or confidence in, the police. To begin with, the type of contact matters: empirical studies indicate that involuntary contact—in which the contact is initiated by the police (Decker, 1981, p. 83)—had a stronger impact on the opinion about the police than did voluntary contact—in which the citizens initiated the contact (Decker, 1981, p. 83). For example, Jacob's study (1971) suggested that, while involuntary contact worsened the individual's opinion about the police, voluntary contact did not substantially improve it.

Although the type of contact seems to be related to individuals' opinions about the police, an even more important factor tends to be the level of satisfaction with the interaction between the police and the citizens (e.g., Correia et al., 1996; Reisig and Parks, 2002). Correia and colleagues (1996, p. 19) report that "[i]n terms of whether or not the contact was voluntary or involuntary, the results show that, regardless of the type of initiation, unsatisfactory treatment of the individual decreases the likelihood of positive perceptions of the state police." The results of the British Crime Survey (Yeo and Budd, 2000) support this conclusion. Because the chances of unsatisfactory contact increase once any type of contact between the citizens and the police is established, it seems that having *any* contact with the police results in more negative opinions about them (Yeo and Budd, 2000).

One specific type of contact between citizens and police occurs when a citizen decides to report criminal victimization to the police. Both substantive-justice issues (e.g., whether the property was recovered, suspect charged) and procedural-justice issues (e.g., police lack of interest or care, providing feedback to the victim) could have an effect on victims' perceptions of the police. Poister and McDavid (1978) reported that overall satisfaction with the police was related to satisfaction with response time and satisfaction with the initial investigation, as well as the initiation and the quality of subsequent investigation and the possibility of arrest. Similarly, the results of the 1998 British Crime Survey indicated that the "police received higher ratings when they: recovered all or some of the victim's property (77%), charged the offender (73%), [and] had face-to-face contact with the victim (66%)" (Yeo and Budd, 2000, p. 3).

Based on the analysis of the 1989 International Crime Victimization Survey, van Dijk and colleagues (1990) write that approximately one-third of the victims were dissatisfied with their reporting experiences and that the main reasons for dissatisfaction were that the police "didn't do enough," "were not interested," "didn't find the offender," or "didn't recover my property." While the comparison with the 1996 results indicates that the fraction of victims who reported their victimization to the police and were dissatisfied with their experiences increased to over one-half, the main reasons for their dissatisfaction remained the same (van Dijk et al., 1990). Thus, victims who were dissatisfied with their reporting experiences provided reasons related to procedural justice (e.g., lack of interest in pursuing the case, impoliteness, slow to arrive), as well as substantive justice (e.g., the offender was not caught, the property was not recovered) (van Dijk et al., 1990, p. 39).

The analysis of the 1996 ICVS data indicated that the victims of burglaries and contact crimes in Central and Eastern Europe were less satisfied with the results of reporting the crimes to police than their counterparts in either Western Europe or the New World were (see figure 1.6 in van Dijk, 1999, p. 38). When asked the reasons for their dissatisfaction with their reporting experience, the most common reason for the respondents from Western Europe and the New World was that the police "did not do enough," while "[i]n Asia, Latin America, Central and Eastern Europe and Africa, where satisfaction was relatively low, victims were more likely to be unhappy that the police did not recover their property or apprehend the offender" (van Dijk et al., 1990, p. 39).

The procedural effect alone can explain the findings by Shapland and colleagues (1985, p. 85). They found that victims' opinions about police become more negative as their cases progress. As a consequence of the victims' "lack of knowledge of what was happening to the case and, for a few, the consequent feeling that the police did not care and were not doing anything—that the police were ignoring both the offence and the victim" (1985, p. 85)—the victims felt dissatisfied with their reporting experience. The impact of unsatisfactory experience with reporting a crime can have long-term consequences: if unsatisfied crime victims are victimized again, they may decide not to report the crime to the police (see, e.g., Carter, 1985).

Data and Methods

The International Crime Victimization Survey had been administered in 56 countries. It included more than 130,000 people across the globe. The first sweep of the survey in 1989, sponsored by the Dutch Ministry of Justice, included 15 industrialized nations (mostly from Western Europe), one developing country (Indonesia), and one country in transition (Poland; see Van Dijk et al., 1990). The second sweep, conducted in 1992–1994, co-sponsored by the Dutch Ministry of Justice, the UK Home Office Research and Planning Unit, and the United Nations Interregional Crime and Justice Research Institute (UNICRI), resulted in the inclusion of a larger number of countries, yielding a total sample of 12 industrialized nations, 13 developing countries, and 7 countries in transition. The third sweep (1996/1997) included 12 industrialized nations, 12 developing nations, and 20 countries in transition. The largest increase in participation occurred for countries in transition: from 1 in 1989 to 20 in 1996/1997.

Because of the potential changes in public opinion over extended periods of time, countries selected for the analyses should be surveyed within a short time frame. This is particularly true for countries in transition, in which the ten-year span from 1990 to 2000 encompasses extensive political, legal, economic, and social changes. Thus, the analysis included countries participating in the most recent wave of the ICVS for which the data are available (1996/1997). At the same time, the third sweep incorporated the largest number of countries in transition (20). Although a similar number of industrialized countries were surveyed in all three waves and a number of them participated in either two or all three waves, I limit the choice of established democracies only to those that participated in the most recent wave of the survey. The only exceptions are Belgium, Italy, and Spain, for which the most recent data available come from the 1992–1994 survey. The final sample consists of twelve industrialized countries, henceforth referred to as established democracies, and sixteen countries in transition (table 1).

Table 1   Established Democracies and Countries in Transition

Established Democracies		Countries in Transition		
Austria	Italy	Belarus	Latvia	Slovakia
Belgium	Netherlands	Bulgaria	Lithuania	Slovenia
Canada	Spain	Croatia	Macedonia	Ukraine
England	Sweden	Estonia	Poland	Yugoslavia
Finland	Switzerland	Georgia	Romania	
France	USA	Hungary	Russia	

In established democracies, the survey was conducted on a national sample by computer-assisted telephone interviewing (CATI). In most countries in transition, interviews were conducted face-to-face (for the description of methodology see, e.g., Nieuwbeerta, 2002; van Dijk et al., 1990; van Dijk, 1999; Zvekic, 1996). For the purposes of comparative analyses (e.g., established democracies versus countries in transition), country samples were weighted to carry equal weight (approximately 1,000 respondents per country).

The ICVS questionnaire contains one question that directly measures the level of specific support for the police. The question asks the respondents to specify how well the police are doing in controlling crime in the area. Possible answers ranged from doing "a good job" to "not [doing] a good job" ("don't know" answers were excluded from further analyses).

As previous research indicates, public opinion about the police and the public's willingness to report crimes to the police are related. The ICVS contains several variables that measure respondents' willingness to report crimes to the police and thus indirectly provide more information about the respondents' opinion about the police. For five typical street crimes common across the globe—burglary, robbery, assault, sexual offenses, and theft of property from a car—the ICVS questionnaire instructed the interviewers to ask the respondents more detailed follow-up questions about their experiences. In particular, the respondents were asked whether they had been victimized over the last five years, and, if so, whether they reported the crime to the police. If they did not report the victimization to the police, they were asked to state the reasons for not reporting. Some of these reasons are police-related (e.g., "police could do nothing/lack of proof," "police won't do anything about it," "fear/dislike of the police/no involvement wanted with police"), while others addressed a variety of non-police-related reasons (e.g., "not serious enough/no loss/kid's stuff," "solved it myself/perpetrator known to me," "inappropriate for police/police not necessary," "reported to other authorities instead," "no insurance," "didn't dare [for fear of reprisal]").

A separate series of questions applied to the respondents who did report the crime to the police; they were asked about the level of satisfaction with their reporting experience and the reasons for it. If they felt dissatisfied with the reporting experience, the interviewers asked follow-up questions about the reasons for dissatisfaction. The possible reasons from which the respondents could choose were: the police "did not do enough," "were not interested," "were slow to arrive," "gave no information," "were incorrect/impolite," "did not find offender," and "did not recover goods."

Results

One of the indirect indicators of the extent of public confidence in the police is the public's willingness to report crimes to the police. While the International Crime Victimization Survey contains questions concerning dozens of various crimes, the follow-up questions about reporting—crucial in the analyses that follow—were asked only for a smaller subset of crimes: theft from a car, burglary, robbery, sexual offenses, and assault. The starting point for examining victimization reporting patterns is observing how widespread the victimization is.

Table 2 presents the frequency of perceived victimization for the five types of crime. With the exception of theft from a car (shaded gray in table 2), the data indicate that fewer than 10% of the respondents from both countries in transition and established democracies experienced burglary, robbery, sexual offenses, or assault in the last five years. The only exception is theft of property from a car: the respondents from countries in transition seemed to be more likely to be victimized than the respondents from established democracies: 28.4% of the respondents from established democracies and 38.0% of the respondents from countries in transition said that they had experienced "theft of a car radio, or something else which was left in your car, or theft of a part of the car, such as a car mirror or wheel."

Despite the fact that the prevalence of victimization was similar across the two types of countries and that, overall, the respondents from coun-

Table 2 Frequency of Perceived Victimization

Country Type	Theft from Car[1] (N = 18,714)	Burglary[2] (N = 27,938)	Robbery[3] (N = 27,946)	Sexual Offenses[4] (N = 14,388)	Assault and Threats[5] (N = 27,845)
	% yes[6]	% yes	% yes	% yes	% yes
Established Democracies	28.4%	9.8%	5.2%	8.7%	11.1%
Countries in Transition	38.0%	10.7%	6.0%	6.9%	10.8%
χ^2	196.56***	5.66*	8.75**	16.38***	0.53
Phi	−.102	−.014	−0.18	.034	.004

* $p < .05$; ** $p < .01$; *** $p < .001$

[1] ". . . over the past five years, have you or other members of your household been the victim of a theft of a car radio, or something else which was left in your car, or theft of a part of the car, such as a car mirror or wheel?"

[2] "Disregarding thefts from garages, sheds, or lock-ups, over the past five years, did anyone actually get into your house or flat without permission, and steal or try to steal something?"

[3] "Over the past five years, has anyone taken something from you by using force or threatening you or did anyone try to do so?"

[4] "People sometimes grab or touch others for sexual reasons in a really offensive way. This can happen either inside one's house or elsewhere, for instance in a pub, the street, at school or at one's workplace. Over the past five years, has anyone does this to you?"

[5] ". . . have you over the past five years been personally attacked or threatened by someone in a way that really frightened you, either at home or elsewhere, such as in a pub, in the street, at school or at your workplace?"

[6] The answers offered to the respondents were "yes," "no," and "do not know." "Do not know" answers were omitted from further analyses.

tries in transition were no more likely to experience victimization than the respondents from established democracies were, the reporting patterns seem to have differed. In particular, as shown in table 3, the respondents from established democracies who were victimized were more likely to say that they reported burglary, robbery, sexual offenses, and assault to the police than their counterparts from countries in transition were. The only exception (therefore not shaded gray) is sexual offenses: over 80% of the victims from *both* types of countries said that they did not report the crime to the police.

Thus, while the prevalence of victimization for the selected crimes does not appear to differ (with the exception of theft from a car), the reporting patterns are divergent (with the exception of sexual offenses). An initial question is to what degree negative opinions about the police and their abilities affect victims' willingness to report a crime to the police. According to victims' own accounts, police-related reasons played one of the key roles (table 4).

The results in table 4 indicate that a strong minority of the respondents (sometimes even close to 50%) from both established democracies

Table 3   Frequency of Reporting Victimization to the Police[1]

Country Type	Theft from Car (N = 6,062)	Burglary (N = 2,803)	Robbery (N = 1,511)	Sexual Offenses (N = 1,073)	Assault (N = 2,993)
	% reported[2]	% reported	% reported	% reported	% reported
Established Democracies	64.7%	83.8%	58.8%	17.4%	36.2%
Countries in Transition	42.6%	64.3%	31.8%	10.3%	23.3%
χ^2	293.79***	129.21***	108.75***	11.29**	59.21***
Phi	.220	.215	.268	.103	.141

* $p < .05$; ** $p < .01$; *** $p < .001$

[1] "The last time, did you or anyone else report that incident to the police?"

[2] The answers offered to the respondents were "yes," "no," and "do not know." "Do not know" answers were omitted from further analyses.

Table 4   Frequency of Police-Related Reasons for Not Reporting

Country Type	Theft from Car (N = 2,125)	Burglary (N = 555)	Robbery (N = 650)	Sexual Offenses (N = 666)	Assault (N = 1,567)
	% police reasons	% police reasons	% police reason	% police reasons	% police reasons
Established Democracies	28.2%	17.0%	28.9%	12.8%	22.0%
Countries in Transition	47.0%	38.2%	46.5%	32.1%	31.7%
χ^2	73.70***	21.33***	17.96***	35.80**	18.10***
Phi	.182	.196	.166	.232	.107

* $p < .05$; ** $p < .01$; *** $p < .001$

and countries in transition decided not to report the crime because of the police-related reasons, though the percentages recorded for countries in transition exceeded those for established democracies by a margin on 10–20% Among the other, non-police-related reasons, not necessarily indicative of negative opinions about the police, the perceptions that the crime was not serious or that the victim solved it/knew the offender were the two most dominant reasons why victims decided not to report the crime to the police.

The police-related reasons can be further separated into three groups: "police could do nothing/lack of proof," "police won't do anything about it," and "fear/dislike of the police/no involvement wanted with police."

Table 5 presents a detailed frequency distribution by the category of police-related reason. With the exception of sexual offenses, fewer than 15% of the respondents who decided not to report for the police-related reasons decided to do so because they feared or disliked the police. The percentages were similar between established democracies and countries in transition.

Aside from the fear or dislike for the police, police ineptitude ("police could do nothing"), and unwillingness of police to do something about the crime ("police won't do anything about it") were virtually equally divided and strongly dominant for all five crimes for the respondents from countries in transition. By contrast, the majority of the victims of burglary, robbery, and sexual assault from established democracies who decided not to report because of police-related reasons did so because they perceived that the police "could do nothing"—that is, there was insufficient evidence to proceed with the case. For theft from a car and assault, the responses from established democracies were also almost equally divided between police ineptitude and police unwillingness.

Table 5   Police-Related Reasons for Not Reporting a Crime to the Police

Country Type	Theft from Car (N = 896)	Burglary (N = 181)	Robbery (N = 266)	Sexual Offenses (N = 149)	Assault (N = 433)
Established Democracies:					
could do nothing	51.2%	79.2%	72.4%	53.5%	49.7%
won't do anything	47.9%	20.8%	24.1%	20.9%	42.2%
dislike/fear	0.9%	0.0%	3.5%	25.6%	8.1%
Countries in Transition:					
could do nothing	44.6%	45.8%	42.3%	43.4%	45.1%
won't do anything	52.4%	45.8%	47.6%	40.6%	41.6%
dislike/fear	2.9%	8.4%	10.1%	16.0%	13.3%

How satisfied were the victims who actually reported their victimization to the police with their reporting experience? The results for all five types of crimes, from theft of property from a car to sexual offenses and assault, indicate that the victims from established democracies were much more satisfied with their reporting experiences than were the victims from countries in transition (table 6). With one exception (robbery), the majority of victims who reported the crime in established democracies seemed to be satisfied with their experience with the police, while the majority of the victims from countries in transition indicated that they were dissatisfied with their reporting experiences.

Table 6   Frequency of Being Satisfied with the Reporting Experience[1]

Country Type	Theft from Car (N = 2,587)	Burglary (N = 1,617)	Robbery (N = 516)	Sexual Offenses (N = 135)	Assault (N = 738)
	% satisfied[2]	% satisfied[2]	% satisfied[2]	% satisfied[2]	% satisfied[2]
Established Democracies	76.0%	73.9%	43.8%	63.1%	68.7%
Countries in Transition	40.3%	37.2%	31.8%	47.1%	44.0%
χ^2	340.35***	217.49***	7.81**	3.33	45.51***
Phi	.363	.367	.123	.157	.248

$* p < .05; ** p < .01; *** p < .001$

[1] "The last time, were you or were they satisfied with the way the police dealt with your report or reports?"

[2] The answers offered to the respondents were "yes (satisfied)," "no (dissatisfied)," and "don't know." "Do not know" answers were omitted from further analyses.

What aspect of police work or police attitudes is the strongest contributing factor to the victims' dissatisfaction with reporting? Why were victims not satisfied with their treatment by the police? The reasons offered to the respondents could be classified into three categories: lack of interest ("did not do enough," "were not interested," and "were slow to arrive"), substantive justice ("did not find offender" and "did not recover goods"), and procedural justice ("gave no information" and "were incorrect/impolite").

Although the percentage of victims who said they were dissatisfied with their reporting experience was larger in countries in transition than it was in established democracies, the most frequently stated reason for dissatisfaction was rather similar. Indeed, the lack of interest in the case (the police "did not do enough," "were not interested," or "were slow to arrive") was the group of reasons most frequently selected by respondents from both groups (table 7). However, a substantial proportion of respondents from countries in transition felt dissatisfied with their experiences of reporting theft of property from a car, burglary, and robbery because the police did not fulfill the primary role (and thus failed to achieve substantive justice): they neither found the offender nor recovered goods taken during the commission of the crime. These results were clearly related to the purpose of reporting; according to the respondents, the leading reasons for reporting were the possibility of recovering property and the opportunity to help the authorities apprehend the offender (there were no substantial differences between the two types of countries). It comes as no surprise that, once it becomes clear that the police will not fulfill the primary purpose of reporting, the victims feel dissatisfied.

Table 7 **Frequency of Reasons for Being Dissatisfied with the Reporting Experience[1]**

Reason	Theft from Car (N = 648)		Burglary (N = 389)		Robbery (N = 188)		Sexual Offenses (N = 49)		Assault (N = 225)	
	WD	EE	WD	EE	WD	EE	WD	EE	WD	EE
Lack of interest	72.6%	52.7%	61.7%	48.5%	68.3%	58.6%	82.1%	76.2%	83.3%	75.6%
Substantive justice	13.5%	41.8%	20.9%	43.1%	20.8%	36.8%	3.6%	9.5%	13.3%	12.6%
Procedural justice	14.0%	5.5%	17.4%	8.4%	10.9%	4.6%	14.3%	14.3%	3.3%	11.9%
χ^2	57.34***		19.56***		7.25***		0.75		5.08	
Phi	.297		.224		.196		.124		.150	

* $p < .05$; ** $p < .01$; *** $p < .001$

[1] Respondents were allowed to give more than one reason.

Finally, the respondents were also asked directly to express the extent of their specific support for the police by evaluating the police ability to control crime in the area. Figure 1 depicts the percentage of the respondents from each country who said that the police were doing "a good job" in controlling crime. While the percentages range from 16.1% in Estonia to 90.8% in Canada, there seem to be some common features.

The respondents from established democracies were more likely to give a positive report card to the police than the respondents from countries in transition were (χ^2 = 2,089.98; d.f. = 1; $p < .001$, *Phi* = .308); on average, 67.3% of the respondents from established democracies thought that the police were doing a good job in controlling crime, while only 34.9% of the respondents from countries in transition shared that opinion. In sum, while the *majority* of the respondents from established democracies agreed that the police were doing a good job in controlling crime, the *majority* of the respondents from countries in transition thought that the police were doing a poor job.

There were considerable country variations within both established democracies and countries in transition. In particular, in Italy and Spain— the two countries belonging to the group of established democracies— only a strong *minority* gave a positive report card to the police. On the other hand, in Croatia and Slovenia—the two countries from the group in transition—the *majority* of the respondents actually thought that the police were doing a good job.

Table 8 suggests that specific support for the police is strongly related to the victim's status: respondents who were not victims, victims who reported their victimization to the police, and victims who did not report

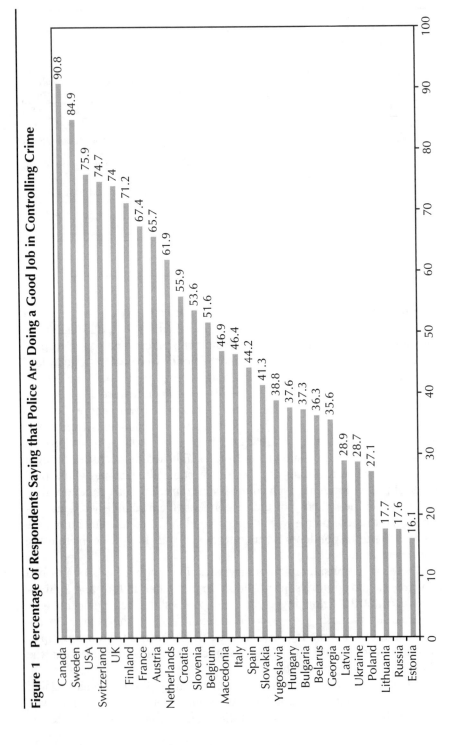

Figure 1 Percentage of Respondents Saying that Police Are Doing a Good Job in Controlling Crime

Table 8   Perceptions of Police Efficiency in Controlling Crime in the Area by Victim Status and Reporting

Victim Status and Reporting	Police Doing a Good Job in Controlling Crime	
	Yes	No
Not a victim	58.0%	42.0%
Victim who reported	48.9%	51.1%
Victim who did not report for *non-police*-related reasons	47.8%	52.2%
Victim who did not report for *police*-related reasons	29.3%	70.7%

$\chi^2 = 433.79$; *d.f.* = 3, *p* < .001, *Phi* = .148.

their victimization to the police for non-police-related reasons (e.g., "not serious enough/kid's stuff," "solved it myself/perpetrator known to me," "inappropriate for police/police not necessary," "reported to other authorities instead," "no insurance") were more likely to be more supportive of the police than were the victims who did not report their victimization to the police for police-related reasons ("police could do nothing/lack of proof," "police won't do anything about it," "fear/dislike of the police/no involvement wanted with police").

Conclusion

While striving to adhere to the standards of democratic policing, the police in countries in transition seem to continue to carry the heavy burden of their past. In the period preceding the late 1980s, various forms of communist militia, infamous for their blatant violations of civil rights, did not generate a high level of public support. Rather than being supported for their professionalism and success in enforcing the laws and maintaining order, they, especially the secret police, tended to be resented and feared by the public.

Although the transition process started more than a decade ago, the extent of public support for the police in countries in transition continues to differ from the extent of public support for the police in established democracies. The differences are striking: the majority of the respondents from established democracies responded that the police in their respective countries did a good job in controlling crime, while the majority of the respondents from countries in transition gave their respective police forces' efforts to control crime a failing grade.

Public confidence in the police is crucial for successful policing. In other words, the lack of confidence would result in citizens' unwillingness to cooperate with the police—neither reporting their own victimizations nor providing information about unsolved crimes. Indeed, the results indicate that the respondents who express a more negative opinion about police ability to control crime were also more likely to decide not to report their own victimization to the police.

Despite relative similarity of the extent of victimization from five typical street crimes in established democracies and countries in transition, the reporting patterns indirectly reflect general opinions about the police: respondents from countries in transition were less likely to report crimes to the police and were more likely to make such a decision because of police-related reasons. Among the respondents for whom the police-related reasons weighed heavily on their decision not to report, those from countries in transition were much more likely to perceive the police as unwilling to investigate crimes than were the respondents from established democracies.

As previous research studies imply (Poister and McDavid, 1978; Shapland et al., 1985; Yeo and Budd, 2000), even when crime victims decide to go through the process of reporting their victimization to the police, contact with the police during the process will probably impact their opinions abut the police negatively. For the respondents from countries in transition, the experience seemed to be primarily negative. Although the primary reasons for dissatisfaction seem to be the same for respondents from both groups, unlike the majority of the respondents from established democracies who felt satisfied with their reporting experience, the majority of the respondents from countries in transition nevertheless felt dissatisfied because the police neither caught the offender nor recovered stolen property.

The results of this study indicate that the public in countries in transition does not support the police to the same extent as the public does in established democracies. To what extent this is a consequence of the actual policing (e.g., not being able to catch the offender or recover stolen goods), or of predetermined public perceptions remains an open question. Learning the answer is crucial: if the police in countries in transition still have a long road ahead of them toward becoming democratic, then the way they perform their police functions needs a thorough adjustment. The results of the study Miller and colleagues (2001) conducted in Bulgaria, Czech Republic, Slovakia, and Ukraine indicate that the actual changes are not as dramatic as one would expect. On the other hand, if the discrepancy is between public perceptions and reality of police work in countries in transition, public opinion needs to be changed to reflect realistic expectations regarding the functioning of the new, more democratic police.

References

Abraham, Pavel (2001) The Romanian Police and challenges of transition. In Kadar, Andras (Ed.), *Police in Transition*. Budapest, Hungary: Central European University Press.

Benke, Miklos (2001) Policing in transition countries compared with standards in the European Union: Hungary—Where dreams are not fulfilled. In Kadar,

Andras (Ed.), *Police in Transition*. Budapest, Hungary: Central European University Press.

Benson, Paul R. (1981) Political alienation and public satisfaction with police services. *Pacific Sociological Review* 24:45–64.

Caparini, Marina and Otwin Marenin (2003) Comparative study of police reform in central and eastern Europe. Unpublished manuscript. (See article 12 in this book.)

Carter, David L. (1985) Hispanic perception of police performance: An empirical assessment. *Journal of Criminal Justice* 13:487–500.

Chevigny, Paul (1995) *Edge of the Knife: Police Violence in the Americas*. New York: The New Press.

Christopher Commission (1991) Report of the independent commission on the Los Angeles Police Department. Warren Christopher, Chair.

Correia, Mark E., Michael D. Reisig, and Nicholas P. Lovrich (1996) Public perceptions of state police: An analysis of individual-level and contextual variables. *Journal of Criminal Justice* 24:17–28.

Das, Dilip K. (2000) Challenges of policing democracies: A world perspective. In Das, Dilip K. and Otwin Marenin (Eds.), *Challenges of Policing Democracies*. Newark, NJ: Gordon and Breach Publishers.

Dean, Deby (1980) Citizen ratings of the police: The difference contact makes. *Law & Policy Quarterly* 2:445–471.

Decker, Scott H. (1980) Citizen attitudes toward the police: A review of past findings and suggestions for future policy. *Journal of Police Science and Administration* 9:80–87.

van Dijk, Jan J. M. (1999) The experience of crime and justice. In Graeme Newman (Ed.), *Global Report on Crime and Justice*. New York: Oxford University Press.

van Dijk, Jan J. M., Pat Mayhew, and Martin Killias (1990) *Experiences of Crime Across the World: Key Findings of the 1989 International Crime Survey*. Deventer, The Netherlands: Kluwer Law and Taxation Publishers.

Durston, Gregory J. (2000) The challenges of policing democracy: The British experience. In Das, Dilip K. and Otwin Marenin (Eds.), *Challenges of Policing Democracies*. Newark, NJ: Gordon and Breach Publishers.

Edelbacher, Maximilian and Gilbert Norden (2000) Challenges of policing democracies: The case of Austria. In Das, Dilip K. and Otwin Marenin (Eds.), *Challenges of Policing Democracies*. Newark, NJ: Gordon and Breach Publishers.

Gilinskiy, Yakov (2000) Challenges of policing democracies: The Russian experience. In Das, Dilip K. and Otwin Marenin (Eds.), *Challenges of Policing Democracies*. Newark, NJ: Gordon and Breach Publishers.

Jacob, Herbert (1971) Black and white perceptions of justice in the city. *Law and Society Review* 6:69–89.

Klockars, Carl B., Sanja Kutnjak Ivkovich, William E. Harver, and Maria R. Haberfeld (1996) *A Cross-Cultural Study of Police Corruption: A Final Report to the National Institute of Justice*. Washington, DC: National Institute of Justice.

Koci, Arianit (1996) Legitimation and culturalism: Towards policing changes in the European "post-socialist" countries. In Milan Pagon (Ed.), *Policing in Central and Eastern Europe: Comparing Firsthand Knowledge with Experience from the West*. Ljubljana, Slovenia: College of Police and Security Studies.

Koszeg, Ferenc (2001) Introduction. In Kadar, Andras (Ed.), *Police in Transition*. Budapest, Hungary: Central European University Press.

Kutnjak Ivković, Sanja (2000) Challenges of policing democracies: The Croatian experience. In Das, Dilip K. and Otwin Marenin (Eds.), *Challenges of Policing Democracies*. Newark, NJ: Gordon and Breach Publishers.

—— (2003) Shades of blue: Analyzing public support for the police. Unpublished manuscript.

Leps, Ando (2000) Estonian police. In Das, Dilip K. and Otwin Marenin (Eds.), *Challenges of Policing Democracies*. Newark, NJ: Gordon and Breach Publishers.

Marenin, Otwin (2000) Democracy, democratization, democratic policing. In Das, Dilip K. and Otwin Marenin (Eds.), *Challenges of Policing Democracies*. Newark, NJ: Gordon and Breach Publishers.

Matei, L. (1994) National police profile, Hungary. In Fogel, D. (Ed.), *Policing in Central and Eastern Europe*. Helsinki, Finland: HEUNI.

Mawby, Robert I. (2001) The impact of transition: A comparison of post-communist societies with earlier "societies in transition." In Kadar, Andras (Ed.), *Police in Transition*. Budapest, Hungary: Central European University Press.

van de Meerberg, Dann and Alexis A. Aronowitz (2000) Challenges of policing democracies: The Dutch experience. In Das, Dilip K. and Otwin Marenin (Eds.), *Challenges of Policing Democracies*. Newark, NJ: Gordon and Breach Publishers.

Miller, William L., Ase B. Grodeland, and Tatyana Y. Koshechkina (2001) *A Culture of Corruption*. Budapest, Hungary: Central European University Press.

Mollen Commission (1994) Commission report. Commission to investigate allegations of police corruption and the anti-corruption procedures of the police department. Milton Mollen, Chair.

Nieuwbeerta, Paul (ed.) (2002) *Crime Victimization in Comparative Perspective: Results from the International Crime Victims Survey, 1989–2000*. Den Haag, The Netherlands: Boom Juridische Uitgevers.

Plywaczewski, Emil W. (2000) The challenges of policing democracy in Poland. In Das, Dilip K. and Otwin Marenin (Eds.), *Challenges of Policing Democracies*. Newark, NJ: Gordon and Breach Publishers.

Poister, Theodore H. and James C. McDavid (1977) Victims' evaluations of police performance. *Journal of Criminal Justice* 6:133–149.

President's Commission on Law Enforcement and Administration of Justice (1965) *A National Survey of Police-Community Relations: Field Surveys V.* Washington, DC: Government Printing Office.

Reisig, Michael D. and Roger B. Parks (2002) *Satisfaction with Police—What Matters?* National Institute of Justice, Washington, DC. Available: http://www.ojp.usdoj.gov/nij

Rosenthal, Arlen M., Lorie A. Fridell, Mark L. Dantzker, Gyle Fisher-Steward, Pedro J. Saavedra, Tigran Markaryan, and Sadie Bennett (1996) *Community Policing: 1997 National Survey Update of Police and Sheriffs' Departments: A Final Report to the National Institute of Justice*. Washington, DC: National Institute of Justice.

Shapland, Joanna, Jon Willmore, and Peter Duff (1984) *Victims in the Criminal Justice System*. Aldershot, England: Gower Publishing Company.

Skolnick, Jerome H. and Jim J. Fyfe (1993) *Above the Law: Police and the Excessive Use of Force*. New York: Free Press.

Smith, Paul E. and Richard O. Hawkins (1971) Victimization, types of citizen-police contacts, and attitudes toward the police. *Law and Society* 8:135–152.

Soo Son, In, Chiu-Wai Tsang, Dennis M. Rome, and Mark S. Davis (1997) citizens' observations of police use of excessive force and their evaluation of police performance. *Policing: An International Journal of Police Strategy and Management* 20:149–159.

Sparrow, Malcom K., Mark H. Moore, and David M. Kennedy (1990) *Beyond 911: A New Era for Policing*. New York: Basic Books.

Stefanescu, Manuela (2001) Police governance in Romania. In Kadar, Andras (Ed.), *Police in Transition*. Budapest, Hungary: Central European University Press.

Szikinger, Istvan (1999) Law enforcement in Hungary during the transition to democracy. *Crime, Prevention and Community Safety: An International Journal* 1:71–77.

——— (2000) The challenges of policing democracy in Hungary. In Das, Dilip K. and Otwin Marenin (Eds.), *Challenges of Policing Democracies*. Newark NJ: Gordon and Breach Publishers.

Videtić, Jernej (2000) Policing democracy: The Slovenian experience. In Das, Dilip K. and Otwin Marenin (Eds.), *Challenges of Policing Democracies*. Newark, NJ: Gordon and Breach Publishers.

Walker, Samuel (2001) *Police Accountability: The Role of Citizen Oversight*. Belmont, CA: Wadsworth.

Winfree, Thomas L., Jr. and Curt T. Griffiths (1977) Adolescent attitudes toward the police. In Theodore N. Ferdinand (Ed.), *Juvenile Delinquency: Little Brother Grows Up*. Beverly Hills, CA: Sage Publications.

Yeo, Helen and Tracey Budd (2000) *Policing and the Public: Findings from the 1998 British Crime Survey. Home Office Research: Research Findings No. 113*. Available: http://www.homeoffice.gov.uk/rds/index.htm

Zapletal, Josef and Mikuláš Tomin (1995) Attitudes of the Chechoslovak public towards the police after 1989 in light of empirical investigations. In Shelley, Louise and Jozsef Vigh (Eds.), *Social Changes, Crime and Police*. Philadelphia, PA: Harwood Academic Publishers.

Zvekic, Ugljesa (1995) Policing and attitudes toward police in countries in transition. In Milan Pagon (Ed.), *Policing in Central and Eastern Europe: Comparing Firsthand Knowledge with Experience from the West*. Ljubljana, Slovenia: College of Police and Security Studies.

11

The Israeli National Police
A National Overview

Travis Morris

In order to understand the evolution of the Israeli National Police Force (INP), it is necessary to have a basic understanding of Israel's history and political evolution. Israel is a democratic republic, obtaining its current national identity on May 14, 1948, through a resolution passed by the United Nations granting the land to those of Jewish origin. The land was previously known as Palestine, an area administered by the League of Nations, formally mandated to the British government in 1922 after the British expulsion of the Ottoman Turks in 1918 (Shane, 1980). The resulting effect of the mandate to England led to a British system of government, economy, and way of life for the land known as Palestine. Immediately after the Palestinian declaration of independence, there were mass migrations of over two-thirds of the resident Palestinian population to neighboring Arab countries. This produced a problem of refugees that after a period of some fifty years has not been resolved (Shane, 1980).

Prior to the British removal of the Turks, the British government in November 1917 passed the Balfour Declaration, vowing support for the establishment of a Jewish national homeland and Jewish resettlement in Palestine (Bensinger, 1998). Approximately 13 years later the British drafted another document, the Passfield White Paper, that granted the same land to the Arabs (Shane, 1980). However, despite the Passfield Papers, Jewish legal and illegal immigration increased from the 1920s to the 1940s. After the end of World War II and after the Holocaust, vast numbers of peoples of Jewish decent began to immigrate to Palestine. As the percentage of peoples of Jewish nationality began to increase there, a movement of sympathy across the nations toward Holocaust survivors and the Jewish people intensified international pressure on the British government to relinquish control of Palestine to Jewish rule. Contradictory prom-

Prepared especially for *Comparative and International Criminal Justice, 2/E.*

ises made by the British to Jewish and Arab leaders while attempting to appease both groups led to internal conflicts. Internal pressure was placed on British management by Jewish resistance movements such as the Irgun, Stern Gang, and the Haganah, who used violent tactics resulting in the loss of life of numerous British soldiers and over 400 Palestinian police (Andrade, 1985). Therefore, in 1948, after a history of problematic governing in the region and bowing to international pressure, the British relinquished control of Palestine to Israeli rule.

The Provisional Council of the State issued the following Declaration of the Establishment of the State of Israel on May 14, 1948:

> The state of Israel will be open for Jewish immigration and for the ingathering of the Exiles; it will foster the development of the country for the benefit of all its inhabitants; it will be based upon freedom, justice, and peace as envisaged by the prophets of Israel; it will ensure complete equality of social and political rights to all its inhabitants irrespective of religion, race or sex; it will guarantee freedom of religion, conscience, education, and culture. (Bensinger, 1998)

Since independence in 1948, the nation of Israel has experienced a great deal of pressure both externally and internally. Five major wars have increased external pressure with the neighboring Arab nations, including the War of Independence in the late 1940s, The Suez campaign of 1956, the Six-Day War of 1967, the Yom Kippur War of 1973, and the Lebanon conflict between 1982 and 1985 (Brewer, 1988). Internally, the influx of massive waves of immigrants from North Africa, Europe, Russia, Ethiopia, and numerous other nations has created tremendous strain on the economy and on the nation-building process while creating new problems relating to national security, social climate, and crime.

Government of Israel

Israel emerged as a democratic republic with a parliamentary system of government known as the Knesset, or Israeli National Assembly. The democratic parliamentary system is based on three government branches: executive, legislative, and judicial. The nation of Israel does not possess a written constitution or a bill of rights; rather, the legislature serves as the absolute lawmaking body (Brewer, 1988). The constituent assembly, known as the First Knesset, agreed upon Israel's need for a constitution but postponed the matter for an indefinite period (Bensinger, 1998). Today's Knesset consists of 120 elected members, assembling in a single-chamber legislature convening in Jerusalem. Its members are charged to further the process of continued nation building through legislature and debate. The foundation on which the Israeli government is based has been derived from its legislation, administrative acts, parliamentary practice, and a multiparty system (Ebbe, 2000).

Basic Laws

The two Basic Laws passed by the Knesset in 1992 set forth a standard of behavior for the state and its agents that resembles certain tenets and phraseology of the U.S. Constitution. These two laws are considered the most significant of the Basic Laws with reference to progress toward a constitution and accompanying human rights. The laws set forth in specific terms the limitations of the INP as an element of national government, in respect to the reach of its authority. The governing rules established by the Basic Law of Human Dignity and Liberty (1992), and others enacted at earlier dates, laid the foundation for the authority of law in Israel over the government's conduct toward its citizens (Bensinger, 1998).

The Israeli president, who bears the ancient Hebrew title of *Nasi*, serves as the head of state. The Knesset elects the president for a five-year term, and he exercises limited powers. The office of president serves more as a ceremonial position and possesses no veto or executive powers such as those held by the president of the United States. However, the Israeli president does appoint civilian and religious judges, pardon offenders, appoint the state comptroller and the governor of the Bank of Israel, and consults with the newly formed government in order to form a new cabinet after elections (Weisman,1993). The president also has complete immunity from any legal process, during and after his term of office, to any matter associated with his presidency (Bensinger, 1998).

The prime minister is the leading figure for the nation, presiding over the both the cabinet and the government. He is an elected official of the executive branch, whose duties are similar to those of the president of the United States (Weisman, 1993). In 1992 the Knesset voted to declare a change in the procedure of the nation's electoral votes. The candidate for prime minister is required to win more than half of the popular vote and must form a government that controls the majority of the Knesset. If this process fails, new elections will be held within sixty days (Bensinger, 1998).

Legal Systems

Israel has two primary court systems. First are the religious courts, which carry jurisdiction in personal matters such as marriage and divorce. After the British took control of Palestine from the Turks they kept the religious court system established by the Turks. Subsequently, the new Israeli government kept but modified this earlier religious court system implemented by the British. Israel's other primary court system consists of ordinary courts that handle criminal and civil cases. This system is has three divisions: the Supreme Court, district courts, and magistrate's courts. These courts hold the responsibility for correctly reviewing actions of the government and individuals in accordance with Israeli law (Brewer, 1988).

At the birth of Israel as a nation in 1948 and during its early years of nation building, the primary influence on the formation of Israeli criminal law was the system of Common Law and criminal law that had been imposed by the British rule between the years of 1917 through 1948. In addition, the Knesset (whose members came from numerous countries and backgrounds) implemented provisions from other sources. These include the Italian Criminal Code of 1888, certain tenets of Ottoman Law that prevailed prior to British control (specifically in religious courts), the Indian Code (creating the offense of death by negligence), and the Sudanese Code (the defense of necessity) (Friedmann, Shadmi, & Kremnitzer, 1998). However, as the modern State of Israel progressed, a system of civil and criminal offenses evolved in an attempt to keep in step with its social problems and the pressures of nation building and progress. Therefore, portions of legal systems from various sources were altered and merged to form a system of law to meet the needs of Israel.

The Israeli National Police Force

Organizational Structure

The Israeli National Police Force is organized, directed, and controlled on both a national and a district level. The chief officer of the INP is the inspector general (commissioner), who commands from National Police Headquarters in Jerusalem (Bensinger, 1998). He reports directly to the public security minister within the Israeli Cabinet. The inspector general and the national headquarters are responsible for: direction of the INP, supervision of districts, long-range planning, operational and administrative services, and command and policy formation. At the national headquarters are six divisions: Operations, Investigations, Personnel, Logistics, Planning and Organization, and the Civil Guard (Bensinger, 1998).

In 1998, the INP consisted of 25,700 officers, of which about 80% are men, divided into 5 police districts (Ebbe, 2000; Moore, 1999): the Tel-Aviv district; Jerusalem; and the central, southern, and northern districts. These districts are further divided into 13 subdistricts, each with a commander who reports to the inspector general (Weisman,1993). The centralized nature of the INP was inherited from the British. This centralized model enables enforced discipline, an authoritative leadership style, carefully maintained distance between ranks, standardization of police actions, control of officer discretion, specific lines of communication, deployment anywhere in the country, and coordinated use of resources (Ebbe, 2000). However, although a police force controlled on a national level is advantageous, it also reduces the authority and discretion of the officers serving in local stations and the level of service it provides to citizens (Ebbe, 2000).

The duties and responsibilities of the police outlined by Article 3 of the INP manual (1971), as interpreted by Hovav and Amir (1979), are to: prevent crimes, discover and investigate crimes, apprehend criminals and carry out criminal prosecution, secure public safety and property, provide a secure environment for prisoners and detainees, and secure internal peace.

The goals of the INP for the twenty-first century were expressed before the United Nations Congress in the 1990s. New objectives were drafted in response to numerous attempts to reform the nature of policing in the nation of Israel. The goals outlined by the minister of public security were: (1) improving the quality of the service and the attitude to citizens in need of police service, (2) raising the feeling of security of the citizen, (3) increasing the citizen's faith in the police, (4) making crime prevention an initiated and active goal, and (6) dealing overall with the causes of crime. (UNCJIN, State of Israel, 2000).

Operations

The INP daily operations are similar to those in traditional models of policing. The tenets of random vehicular patrols and some foot patrols, rapid response to calls of service, and follow-up investigations characterize the major forms of Israeli policing. Since 1995 community policing has been embraced by the national headquarters and incorporated in several districts with the goal of a complete national integration in the coming years (Bensinger, 1998).

In addition to crime-related matters, the INP also maintains public order, enforces traffic regulations, executes warrants, guards personnel and facilities, and assists in medical emergencies. The INP also utilizes speedboats in patrolling the Gulf of Eilat, the Sea of Galilee, and the Mediterranean, while their helicopters assist in the enforcement of traffic laws, locating missing persons, and preventing illegal infiltration by air or sea (Bensinger, 1998).

Two specialized divisions, the Traffic and Bomb Divisions, perform essential services to the nation. Some estimated 20,000 fatalities have occurred on the road network of Israel since 1948. Israeli driving is notoriously disorderly and has led to a high ratio of accidents per citizen (Bensinger, 1998). This is attributed to the shortage of traffic police, poor road conditions, and a lack of self-discipline on the part of drivers (Kurian, 1989). In response to constant media attention and public outcry to lower the number of accidents and fatalities, the INP created the Traffic Division in 1991. The division uses innovative electronic equipment to apprehend speeders and violators who run red lights. Approximately 1,000 officers serve in the Traffic Division and are stationed in all districts across the nation.

The Bomb Disposal Division, formed shortly after the INP was granted the responsibility of internal security in 1974, is comprised of highly trained and specially equipped bomb disposal experts. The unit responds to an average of 80,000 calls per year from citizens reporting suspected explosive devices (Bensinger, 1998). The unit incorporates the use of two highly sophisticated robots, which were designed and developed in Israel. In 1995 the Bomb Disposal Division was awarded the prestigious National Prize for excellence in public service.

Personnel and Training

During past decades, employment as an Israeli Police Officer was perceived as an undesirable profession. The public's perception has changed over the years due to several reforms, including pay and benefit increases as well as improved training and recruiting procedures (Bensinger, 1998). Consequently, in 1994 the INP received more applications of qualified candidates than there were positions available—6,500 applied for only 1,320 positions (Bensinger, 1998). The recent alteration to the military's compulsory service policy was an important governmental change that has impacted the recruiting ability of the INP. Conscripts wanting to join the INP rather than enlisting for army duty attend basic training for the army and then transfer to INP for further training.

The recruitment qualifications for the INP are: being an Israeli citizen, being under the age of 35, completing military service (or legal exception), complying with compatibility test requirements, having a minimum of 12 years education (secondary degree), being in good health, and complying with security test requirements (Israel Police, 2003b). Newly recruited officers who possess military experience or have a college degree will be admitted into the corresponding INP rank. This process allows those with an education or relevant experience to enter the force at a level intended to maximize their qualifications and impact as officers.

After preliminary selection, recruits will undergo an assessment phase consisting of 2–3 days at a boarding school near Netanya to test their psychological, mental, and fitness levels. Upon successful completion of the assessment, the recruit is invited to the recruitment center and will be sworn in as an Israeli National Police Officer. During the first year the newly sworn officer will enter a training and trial period (Israel Police, 2003b).

The new officer will undergo a six-month training period at Israel's National Police Training Academy at Shefar-am about 12 miles east of Haifa (Kurian, 1989). Over the course of the training period the new officer focuses on elements of basic policing skills, technical skills, fitness training, operations, law, crowd control, firearms training, and conflict resolution (Bensinger, 1998). Fluency in the Hebrew language is not a prerequisite but is mandatory after an officer's acceptance, and Hebrew classes are offered for new recruits. Throughout the duration of the Academy training, officers also attend courses in police ethics, human rights, use of force, mediation, and conflict resolution (UNCJIN, 2002). Officers who enter a specialized field, for example the Intelligence Division, will then attend specific courses relevant to their field. Additionally, the National Police Training Academy houses a library, providing officers with research and training resources.

Ongoing education and training are required. Officers must attend professional training courses for 31–55 hours per year on topics ranging from drug-related crime, terrorism, child abuse, and arrest techniques to report writing, record keeping, and cargo examination (UNCJIN, 2002). Officers desiring promotion to the rank of sergeant must attend a voluntary six-month sergeants course that emphasizes leadership, psychology, computer skills, sociology, and statistics (Bensinger, 1998; Kurian, 1989).

Officers selected to occupy command positions within the INP attend Senior Officer College, a six-month course of education that exposes them to national policy, staff operations, criminology, and sociology (Kurian, 1989). The college is a partnership between the INP, the Institute of Criminology, and the Criminal Law Department at Tel Aviv University (Hovav & Amir, 1979). Some of the courses offered through the Senior Officer College accrue credit toward bachelor's or master's degrees (Bensinger, 1998). Moreover, officers are encouraged to attend educational and training programs outside those offered by the INP that assist in their professional development. The INP reimburses the officer for any expenses incurred in attending such programs (Bensinger, 1998).

The Civil Guard

The Civil Guard was created in 1974 in response to citizen demand for the INP and government to take a proactive role in decreasing the amount of terrorist activity across the nation. Its formation was intended to improve internal security by sharing the responsibility with citizens (Bensinger, 1998). This inclusion of citizens to assist the INP has empowered citizens in safeguarding their own communities and also serves as another method to improve community and national quality-of-life issues. The government's and INP's high regard for citizens willing to volunteer and for society's readiness to organize volunteer efforts are two characteristics of a healthy society with social solidarity. Volunteer work helps persuade citizens that they have a stake in controlling their own fate and that of their society (Israel Police, 2003f).

In 1974 there were approximately 108,000 volunteers, while in 1998 the numbers dropped to 50,000 (Shane, 1980; Bensinger, 1998). From the very first, the Civil Guard recruited Arab–Israeli volunteers in mixed Arab–Jewish cities. Then, in 1992, wholly Bedouin units were set up in Bedouin settlements, and likewise Druze units in Druze towns and villages. (Both the Druze and Bedouins are Israeli citizens living in various regions of Israel; however, their way of life and religion differs.) In 1996, the concept was extended to Arab towns (Israel Police, 2003d).

Today the Civil Guard remains the largest volunteer organization in Israel and is actively involved in Israeli society. The Civil Guard was incorporated into the INP in 1986 in order to become more efficient and effective, and the function of the volunteers was expanded. In 1974 volunteers patrolled their communities, neighborhoods, and certain rural areas.

According to the INP, Civil Guard patrols and roadblocks are intended to deter terrorist activity, report criminal activity, relay security information to the police, and locate wanted/missing persons (Ben Hamu, 2002). Members serve in general patrol duties, patrol on foot, on bicycles, in cars, and in all-terrain vehicles. In addition to general patrolling, volunteers also serve in specialized units. Some of these units include the Tourism Civil Guard, Victims of Disaster Identification Civil Guard, and the Interpreters Civil Guard (Ben Hamu, 2002).

Today's Civil Guard is comprised of citizens from numerous nationalities, age groups, and ethnic groups serving in both general and specialized volunteer units. Citizens active in the Civil Guard are required to serve a minimum of four hours each month, eight hours if serving in a special unit (Ben Hamu, 2002). Members of the Civil Guard wear specific uniforms or other clothing identifiers while on duty, are usually armed, and possess complete police authority (Bensinger, 1998). Volunteers are expected to have received weapon and other training from the INP, yet an evaluation by the comptroller in 1995 revealed that some volunteers were not being sufficiently trained. Despite any deficiencies noted in the comptroller's evaluation, the Civil Guard remains a pivotal organization to assist the INP in maintaining internal security and providing vital services to the community.

The Border Police

Since its creation in 1953 the Border Police (BP) have been an essential component in maintaining security along Israel's borders. The specially selected paramilitary force, numbering approximately 5,000 men, is intensely trained and has gained a reputation of being fearless and ruthless (Country Study and Country Guide, 1988). Its primary mission is to guard against guerrilla attacks along the northern border of Lebanon and Israel's shared border with Jordan. Members serving in the Border Police rather than in compulsory military duty number about one-quarter of the force (Frisch, 1993). The remainder of its officers are professionals who have completed their military service (normally in the infantry) and INP basic training course (Frisch, 1993).

After 1967, the Border Police were granted the task of patrolling Arab villages and settlements of the Gaza Strip and the West Bank (Bensinger, 1998). In the first year of the Arab *intifada* (an Arabic word that possesses two meanings: the first represents a shaking off or shivering because of fear or illness. The second refers to an abrupt and sudden waking up from sleep or unconcerned status. Politically, the word has come to symbolize the Palestinian uprising against Israel) in 1987, the Border Police accompanied the Israeli Defense Forces (IDF) in controlling riots and demonstrations. The Border Police constituted about 15–20% of the Israeli forces assigned to control Arab actions during the intifada. Throughout this time period the officers gained a reputation by using excessive force against Arabs during arrests. This matter was brought to national attention in an incident similar to the American case of Rodney King and the city of Los Angeles. Two amateur cinematographers documented officers of the Border Patrol beating and humiliating Palestinian workers caught in Israel without work permits (Herzog, 2000). The videotape showed BP officers kicking the Palestinians in the head and the groin. This led to a somber condemnation and pledge by the INP High Command and by governmental officials that such actions will not be tolerated.

A special unit using the acronym *Matilan* (translating as "intelligence, scouting, firing, combat, and mobility") was created in 1996. This elite anti-terrorist unit's primary responsibility was to track, stop, and apprehend anyone attempting to enter Israel illegally from the West Bank and Gaza (Ebbe, 2000). The unit is also activated in the event of a hostage situation or any other exceptional situation regarding terrorism or crime. In addition to their specific duties, members may also be employed in a traditional police role in order to bolster a community's police department resources in crime or public-order matters (Bensinger, 1998).

The ethnic makeup of the BP is more diverse than that of any other police unit. From its inception, the Border Patrol has recruited from Israel's Druze, Christian, and Arab populations to patrol predominantly Arab areas. In 1993, approximately 40% of BP officers were listed as being of Druze origin. The high percentage of Druze within the BP impacts the public's image to the point that the BP is equated with the Druze population (Frisch, 1993).

Community Policing

One of the greatest reforms undertaken by the INP occurred in 1995, with the advent of community policing. Brigadier General Dan Gimshi initiated the concept for an Israeli version of community policing. While a Wexler fellow at the Kennedy School of Harvard, he had been exposed to the American model of community policing and its strategies (Weisburd, Shalev, & Amir, 2002). The inspector general at the time, Asaf Chefetz, was interested in reducing the crime rate and was receptive to creative methods that also increased internal security. Moreover, due to the shortage of officers and increased responsibilities, most patrolling had been done from patrol vehicles, and a reconnection with the community was desired. The strategy of community policing appeared to accomplish both goals simultaneously.

Elements of community policing had existed in Israel since the nation was granted statehood in 1948. In the 1970s, the newly established Civil Guard recruited thousands of citizens to patrol their neighborhoods, borders, and ports (Friedmann, 1992). In addition, the police were given the task of helping new immigrants adjust to their new life in Israel by assisting them in language study and social adjustment. Despite a formal analysis of the impact of the Civil Guard and other programs on the community, the policy of involving the community and forming partnerships with citizens had existed since the formation of the INP.

However, the influence and impact of the American concept of community policing should not be ignored. An analysis of official INP publications conducted by Gad Bensinger noted that numerous American community-policing advocates were cited and included in the publications' bibliographies. Among those cited were: J. Q. Wilson, George Kelling, Robert Friedmann, Larry Hoover, Peter Manning, Robert Trojanowicz, and Herman Goldstein (Bensinger, 1999).

Since 1974, the dilemma of effectively sharing resources to manage the tasks of both traditional policing and internal security has been a constant challenge for the INP (Bensinger, 1998). As crime rates increased and terrorist acts became more frequent, local officials began to insist on better cooperation between the police and city organizations to increase the quality of life within their communities (Bensinger, 1998). Because local municipalities had no control over their local police departments, city leadership was receptive to the idea of mutual cooperation with their local police departments to implement more effective security measures and increase the quality of life for their communities.

The creation of a community policing unit (CPU) in 1995, falling directly under the control of the inspector general, marked the INP's move toward the philosophy, strategy, and methodology of community policing (Ebbe, 2000). The strategy involved changing the values, opinions, attitudes, and job perception of every police officer regardless of rank in the INP. The goals behind this monumental change were: decentralization of power to the individual officer and citizen, transfer of power to the local rather than the national level, improvement in service, and enhanced awareness of the needs of the community.

The partnerships between the community and area police officers involved several stages. First, members of the CPU were assigned to act as advisors to a particular station and community. Second, the CPU organized a series of workshops that included the community's leaders, local officials, the general public, and police officers. The topics of these workshops included the philosophy and strategy of community policing, establishing methods of collaboration, problem-solving skills, leadership, and the actual operational functions of community police officers (Bensinger, 1998).

A community-policing center (CPC) was established and manned by a neighborhood police officer (NPO) (Ebbe, 2000). This station was intended to be able to serve all the needs of the citizens. The NPOs were officers who had an average of 10–15 years of street experience, and most had held leadership positions (Friedmann, 1986a). The NPO devotes his time to public education, crime prevention activities, volunteer recruitment, organization of community events, and seeking solutions to neighborhood problems (Friedmann, 1992). Additionally the NPO was considered a personal ambassador to the community for any resources and problems that could not be acquired or solved at the community-policing center.

In the first year of the program, four CPUs were selected to serve as the preliminary experimental stations. After the initial startup period, a plan was developed to encompass all 70 police stations by the year 2003 (Weisburd, Shalev, & Amir, 2002). By mid-1997 more than 25 local police stations had implemented the strategy outlined by the initial four experimental stations. To date, approximately 347 community-policing centers are in existence.

According to official INP publications, some of the programs offered through the CPC are: safe-school prevention programs offered in 250 schools, criminology and police studies in high schools, police youth camps, Youth for the Advancement of Quality of Life and the Environment, self-defense courses for women, events and movies, a National Police Orchestra, and a police Web site (Ben Hamu, 2002).

The results, according to the INP, have been promising. Officers state that they are pleased with the response of the public, and the sharing of resources has been effective in crime prevention. Additionally, according to the INP and a study conducted by Robert Friedmann (1986b), officers expressed a greater sense of job satisfaction and felt they were empowered to target the problems within their communities (UNODC, 2003a). However, an evaluation by Amir, Shalev, and Weisburd (2002) states the opposite conclusion. In their initial observations they noted that no significant evidence was found to demonstrate that community policing had infiltrated the daily activities of patrol officers, though there have been significant changes in specific aspects of Israeli policing. The Criminology Institute of the Hebrew University in Jerusalem is currently conducting additional research covering multiple aspects of community policing to assess its impact on crime, officers, public perception, and internal security.

History of the INP

Pre-1948

The roots of the Israeli National Police can be traced to the transfer of governmental control of Palestine to the British after the expulsion of the Turks in 1917. After World War I, the League of Nations mandated Palestine to the British and granted them the responsibility of governorship. Through the British era of control lasting from 1918 to 1948, they maintained some of the laws and courts established by the Ottoman Empire, but the police experienced a complete renovation (Shane, 1980). The British first implemented a system of civil control through military units. However as time progressed the responsibility was transferred to police units, which continued to maintain a close cooperation between military and the civilian police (Hovav & Amir, 1979).

The early Palestinian police were exclusively British and did not incorporate the local population until a few years before the implementation of the British Mandate Police Ordinance of 1926, when the official and legal order for controlling crime and maintaining public order was declared. Prior to the Mandate Ordinance, the Criminal Procedure Ordinance of 1924 guided the organization, discipline, powers and duties of the police. The police of Palestine under British control were staffed using a combination of British, Jewish, and Arab officers. The force at the time of the Police Ordinance consisted of 120 British officers and 1800 Palestinian police (Shane, 1980). In 1929, as violence began to increase between Jewish and Arab inhabitants, the number of British officers and men from the local population was increased. The newly acquired British officers served in command and administrative roles, while the Arab and Jewish police continued to serve in the front ranks (Shane, 1980).

After the declaration of Independence in 1948, the British completely withdrew their officers and took with them equipment necessary to complete regular police duties, including vehicles of all sorts, armament, laboratory equipment, and police dogs (Cramer, 1964). After an almost total withdrawal, a skeleton crew struggled to adjust to the shift of control and the additional complication of the war of 1948–49. The British evacuation left large gaping holes in the new police organization because no Jewish officers had been promoted to command posts (Hovav & Amir, 1979). Yet even before the British withdrawal, members of Jewish Agencies were planning the early design of the INP (Israel Police, 2003d).

Those left to hold the reigns of the Israeli National Police had to endure the challenge of losing the best of its personnel to the Army, to fight for national survival (Andrade, 1985). However, those left to serve as police officers during the nation's first year coped with such issues as constraints on human resources, terrorist infiltrations, public disorder and demonstrations, traffic accidents, a growing crime rate, black markets, and the disappearance of children (Israel Police, 2003d). The challenges and shortages extended beyond the first year of a newly organized police force attempting to function during a time of war. These issues are addressed in the later time periods. However, the INP did survive and attempted to adhere to the mandates and example set by the British Colonial Police.

1948–1957

The years 1948 through 1957 were known as the formative years for the INP, according to their historical records. Throughout this time frame they had continued using the model and style of policing utilized by the British until the country attained some semblance of national stability. The 700 Jewish officers who had served under British control formed the core of the newly established Israel National Police (Brewer, 1988). Many of these early leaders were now serving in command roles, attempting to direct and build a national police force in a nation undergoing national turbulence and experiencing challenging social changes, including the migration of non-Western immigrants and Holocaust survivors, lack of national insecurity, war, economic difficulties, and violence and aggression on both political and interpersonal levels (Shadmi, 1998).

The officers of the Israeli National Police were entrusted with the following tasks:

- conventional police duties, including the apprehension of offenders, resolution of disputes, traffic enforcement, crowd/riot management, and random patrolling;
- security duties, including border patrol to assist in preventing attacks and illegal immigration; and
- nation-building tasks, including the education of new immigrants to the culture, laws, and democratic tenets, as well as establishing the authority of law and statehood to all citizens (Shadmi, 1998).

To fill the ranks of the INP, new immigrants were recruited to serve as officers from the thousands arriving in the country. Many of the new recruits did not speak Hebrew and were ignorant of the laws and culture in a democratic society. Therefore, a national training center was erected that not only instructed recruits in the elementary methods of policing but also provided language-study programs, culture and history studies of the land, and courses on the basics of civics and democracy (Hovav & Amir, 1979).

After the War of Independence in 1949, a cease-fire was enforced by the United Nations. Within its borders, the nation of Israel found itself facing a population of over 156,000 Arabs. Because of the threat of illegal border crossings to sabotage and attack Israeli citizens and property, the government made the protection of its borders a top priority. The formation of a special police unit to focus specifically on the protection of Israel's borders led to the creation of the Border Police in 1953 (Hovav & Amir, 1979).

By the 1950s the INP had already matched the number of personnel and officers of the old British Mandate Police Force (approximately 3,556 officers) (Andrade, 1985). These officers served in national projects to direct and assist Israel in the development of its government and society. The INP assisted in the formation of temporary camps for new immigrants. Acting as representative for the state, INP officers provided instruction in the camps to new immigrants for social customs and norms of Israeli society, work ethic, hygiene, dress, Jewish Holiday celebration, Western interpersonal behavior, and other socially dominant themes that those in authority wished to promote (Shadmi, 1998).

While many officers felt a sense of duty and loyalty to their profession, the INP still suffered from a high turnover rate, limited resources, and priority of governmental allocation. The high turnover rate existed because of the expanding economy and the low pay offered to officers. New immigrants would receive adequate language and cultural experience as an officer and, after becoming established, would leave the INP for better-paying jobs. Despite serving as an immigration absorption agency of positive influence and acculturation, the loss of trained experienced officers was detrimental to the INP's development. Due to the wars of 1948 and 1956, the priority of resources and attention was directed to the military for national survival (Brewer, 1988). This led to insufficient resources to accomplish the tasks required of the INP and the accompanying frustration at its lack of development.

During the War of 1956, the officers of the INP fell under the control of the military. The traditional methods and tasks of policing came to a halt during the war. Erella Shadmi, an officer serving in the INP for eighteen years, stated that almost all patrol, investigation and traffic tasks as well as staff work, with few exceptions, came to a halt. All officers were employed in war-related functions (Shadmi, 1998).

1958–1973

The transition from military to "regular" policing took place during the time period spanning 1958–1973. These years can be labeled as years of reform—of transition to a distinctive National Police Force with an Israeli rather than British character. The reform involved a transformation of police structure, doctrine, and operations. Regarding police structure, a reorganization of the division of labor granting a clear distinction between staff and operations was recognized as a necessity. The division of labor clearly articulated the duties, functions, and authority between central headquarters and those in district headquarters (Shadmi, 1998). Staff officers in headquarters assumed the responsibility of policy planning and decisions, research, advancing policing methods, and coordination between the districts (Hovav & Amir, 1979). The districts were granted the exclusive task of operations. This was a significant change, since district headquarters had previously been responsible for administration and services.

Numerous other alterations were implemented during this time period. According to Menechem Amir, Director of the Institute of Criminology, the following modifications occurred:

1. Five districts were reduced and combined into three (Northern, Tel Aviv, and Southern).

2. Districts and subdistricts became more independent.

3. The Border Police became a national force under the direct command of the inspector general.

4. Central headquarters was divided into planning and operations, public relations, judicial, human resources, training, transportation, administration, and investigations departments.

5. Ranks were Hebraicized, and the uniforms lost their British appearance.

6. The number of subdistricts decreased from 13 to 11.

7. Inside cities beat patrol was adopted, and police posts were established for rural areas.

8. Improvement was made in investigations in the areas of juvenile delinquency, fraud, and narcotics.

9. Scientific and research efforts were expanded, and intelligence doctrine was developed.

10. The Senior Command College was established in 1958, and a Junior Officer College in 1966 (Hovav & Amir, 1979).

An additional movement labeled the Rozolio Reform was implemented during this time period by Saul Rozolio, the newly appointed inspector general in the early 1970s, whose subtle and unpublicized reforms were never formally announced (Shadmi, 1998). The reform consisted of three major tenets. The first involved managing the human resources department, the second was the advancement in the use of technology and science, and the third was the development of the Multi-Level Recruitment System. According to Shadmi, all of the tenets are still functioning in the INP to this day.

The Multi-Level Recruitment System (MLR) was enacted to attract educated college graduates and professionals to serve in the INP. The objective was to infuse the ranks of the INP with personnel who could provide new vision and strategies and could further bolster the public's perception of the police. The implementation of the MLR resulted in ex-army officers and college graduates being transferred directly into management positions (Israel Police, 2003d). This reform was not without its problems. Senior officers who had been serving for years were disgruntled by "outsiders" with no background in policing now being assigned positions of authority. Even if the influx of professionals into the INP had a potentially drastic effect, those who accepted management positions lacked the process of socialization and the organizational knowledge and culture required in order to make valid decisions. A decline in morale was the result (Shadmi, 1998).

Throughout the Yom Kippur War of 1973, the INP again fell under control of the Israeli Defense Forces. After 19 days of bitter fighting, the United Nations declared a bilateral cease-fire (Israel Police, 2003d). Following the aftermath of the war, the multi-layered reforms that occurred from 1958 through 1973 laid the foundation for the new responsibilities of the INP. In addition to the effects of the war the readiness of the INP to accept its new responsibilities after 1973 was significantly impacted by the following events: the retiring of officers from the Mandate era, the increased requirement to protect Israel's borders and heartland from terrorists, and the development of a national police force that is distinctively Israeli.

1974–1981

The Yom Kippur War left the Israeli government in turmoil. Within a short time period, three governmental parties entered and exited office. The population of Israel was in a state of alarm and found themselves in disagreement concerning which political party was best suited to lead the nation securely. In May of 1977, the Likud Party was elected and was charged with forming the government. This was the first time since the founding of the State that a right-wing party had been elected. In 1974 the new government, after a short period of reorganization, handed over the responsibility of national internal security to the INP (Israel Police, 2003d). A portion of the reorganization directly impacted the INP. The INP and the inspector general reported to the position of the minister of police. However, after 1977 the inspector general reported to the ministry of the interior. The modification was implemented after political and police duties often conflicted (Hovav & Amir, 1979).

To accommodate the new responsibility the INP completed organizational changes and created several new units. The duties of the Border Guard were expanded, special bomb and terrorist units were created, the volunteer Civil Guard was created, and the operations division was formed to coordinate and streamline the work of all operational branches. The Civil Guard was organized to establish a national system of volunteers to patrol the streets and neighborhoods at night. The INP was responsible for training the volunteers and providing them with the necessary equipment to accomplish vigilant patrols. Many of the 100,000 volunteers were armed and worked regular volunteer shifts (Israel Police, 2003d). The Border Guard assumed control of guarding the airspace and seaports.

The task of internal security did not replace the INP's responsibility to manage crime. Allegations of organized crime existing in Israel led to the formation of an investigative committee. As the crime rate increased dramatically in the 1970s the newly elected Likud government established the Shimron Commission (named after its chairperson) to examine the topic of crime in Israel. The commission published a 136-page report on February 15, 1978, concerning its research (Bensinger, 1982). The Shimron Commission noted that the INP was understaffed, poorly trained, and had lost much of the confidence of the Israeli public. It recommended the following (Brewer, 1988; Bensinger, 1982):

1. strengthening the Bureau of Investigations;
2. creating several new units to combat organized crime, drug trafficking, fraud, and police misconduct;
3. establishing two high-level committees: the Cabinet Committee on Law Enforcement and the Central Committee for Integrated Operations against Organized Crime;
4. reintroducing foot patrols for police visibility; and
5. increasing measures to reduce the nation's high accident rates.

At the 1980 Independence Day celebration, the Speaker of the Knesset stated that Israel needed not only safe borders but also safe streets (Brewer, 1988). This placed a greater emphasis on the activities of the INP, and because of the renewed emphasis the Israeli government in 1980 appointed Herzl Shafir, a former deputy chief of staff of the Israeli Defense Forces, as the new inspector general (Brewer, 1988).

Shafir was the first inspector general to be appointed from outside the ranks of the INP. Immediately after his appointment, he initiated an extensive review of all levels of the INP, involving almost every police unit and rank (Shadmi, 1998). The review entailed officers from all levels and units to reevaluate, redefine, and streamline their police units, officers, and national structure. This process continued for five months and resulted in a proposed alteration of numerous facets of the INP. The proposal, known as the Tirosh Plan (Hebrew for *New Wine*), allocated five years for the INP to meet the stipulations as outlined. The plan, which was approved by the cabinet, outlined the following:

- increasing the number of officers to over 20,000;
- greater use of computers;
- routine rotation of personnel;
- radical changes in training
- increased patrolling;
- opening more police stations;
- increasing officers' ability to solve problems unconventionally; and
- increasing professional norms of conduct (Brewer, 1988).

The Tirosh Plan devised a strategy for better coordination and sharing of technology, ideas and personnel between elements of Israeli society, the military, and the police, creating a system of mutual intradependence. The plan called for a greater use and distribution of technology and training utilized by the IDF. The inclusion of volunteer agencies selected from Israeli society enabled the INP to become more aware of the social needs of communities and the social programs developed by such agencies. Some of the ideas would be incorporated in crime prevention efforts and in creating nontraditional methods of confronting crime. Subsequently, the Tirosh Plan called for wide-scale use of foot patrols into neighborhood communities to obtain such information (Reiser, 1983).

Another tenet of the Tirosh Plan called for the rotation of personnel. Shafir experienced firsthand during his military years what he labeled as "the erosion of professionalism" (Reiser, 1983) that occurred when a solider or officer spent extended time in the same position and location. An officer who had served in a location and position lasting longer than six years tended to become less sensitive to the needs of the community. Shafir asserted that the rotation of personnel every five to six years would keep police officers stimulated professionally and sensitive to the needs of the community in which they served (Reiser, 1983).

Tirosh also introduced a drastic change in the training of new recruits. The purpose of the change was to increase morale and performance, and to streamline the training methods as a time-saving measure. The reform called for a new recruit to enter the academy for 10 days and then spend a six-month internship in the field with experienced officers in two focus areas: (1) patrol, traffic, and internal security training; and (2) investigation and intelligence. The recruit then returns to complete a six-month course of academy training in which he will select one of the two focus areas for concentration. This selectively weeds out recruits not suited for police work, and it also enables them to obtain firsthand information on focus areas in order to select a concentration that is more suited to their abilities. This innovation was implemented because of the projected long-term impact for morale, re-attainability, and professionalization (Gurevitch, Danet & Schwartz, 1971).

Shafir wanted each INP officer to embrace the ideals of high-quality service in their communities and responsibility for public service. He was aware that for years the INP suffered from low morale and was poorly regarded by the public. Shafir desired to create an organizational personality of professionalism and exceptional performance that was embraced by every officer. According to the Tirosh Plan, this would come about through the leadership and example of higher- and middle-ranking officers (Reiser, 1983).

In order for the INP to efficiently provide internal security, the Tirosh Plan requested that the Border Police and Civil Guard be under the total control of the INP rather than the IDF. The INP would then be able to incorporate additional plans for extended police functions. Tirosh requested the establishment of 45 new police stations, the division of the country into 800 local beats patrolled by an additional 2,000 patrol officers, and a complete overhaul of police vehicles. The outlined actions, if fully implemented, would increase the effectiveness of the INP and further their transformation to an Israeli Police Force rather than remaining a colonial hybrid. (Most British police stations were on top of hills or mountains that provided the best field of view, yet most of these stations were not where the population resided (Reiser, 1983).

Despite the detailed analysis and clearly outlined proposal, the Tirosh Plan was never fully implemented. The resources required to accomplish the tasks were not available, and Shafir's superior dismissed him after one year of service. From its inception, Tirosh was intended as a five-year strategy. Some senior officers opposed some of the tenets of the plan, and after the dismissal of Shafir the strategy did not continue. However, some tenets did endure and impacted the professionalization of the INP (Shadmi, 1998).

1982–1990

The events of the following period can be described as developmental and problematic. This period was developmental because of the technological advances and other reforms implemented as a result of the Tirosh Plan. This was a time when the economy was affected by inflation, unemployment, the dismissal of Shafir, and immigration. The media were broadcasting internationally images of the first intifada (1986 through 1989). World audiences saw images of daily riots in Judea, Samaria, and the Gaza Strip, of masked rioters confronting the police and armed forces. Throughout the years of the intifada, acts of terrorism increased and many lives were lost, both Israeli and Arab. Additionally, over the course of these eight years, Israeli law was extended to the Golan Heights, the Sinai Peninsula was returned to Egypt, the IDF was ordered into Lebanon, and the Temple Mount disturbances occurred in 1990. The progress and development of the INP was in response to the national events surrounding them (Israel Police, 2003d).

The political climate was marked by a group of politicians whose views were labeled as extremist and who used forceful methods to obtain their agenda. In 1984, after a period of turmoil in the Knesset, a party obtained the majority of the 120-seat Knesset (97 seats) and began to attempt to confront the internal problems of the nation. The first decision of the majority party was the withdrawal of the IDF forces from Lebanon in 1985. The Knesset also passed an emergency economic plan in 1985 to scale down government spending, decrease inflation, and increase employment. Consequently, the economic plan placed a freeze on the recruitment of additional police officers (Israel Police, 2003d).

Some of the events affecting the INP as a result of the Tirosh Plan and the national events of the time period appear below:

1. A fourth police district—the Central District—was created in 1981.

2. Severe rioting occurred by the Ultra-Orthodox Jews, over Sabbath desecration and excavation of Jewish graves.

3. On November 11, 1982, an INP headquarters building in Tyre, Southern Lebanon, was targeted by a terrorist explosion that killed 34 police and Border officers.

4. The police uniform was altered from the British khaki uniform to a distinctive Israeli uniform.

5. Technological and scientific advances along with new equipment enhanced the effectiveness of forensics, bomb disposal/detection, and intelligence gathering (Israel Police, 2003d).

1991–Present

Several large-scale events occurred nationally and internationally that greatly impacted the internal security of the nation of Israel and the INP. Over the next 12 years the government of Israel and the INP experienced further challenges in national security, diplomacy, economics, and social affairs. The Gulf War of 1991, the collapse of the communist regimes in Eastern Europe and the Soviet Union, the Israeli–Arab peace negotiations, the Oslo Peace Accords in 1993, the resurgence of the second intifada, massive waves of immigration from the Soviet Union and Ethiopia, the

Cairo Agreement in 1994, the peace arrangements with Jordan, an increase in suicide bombings, the assassination of Yitzhak Rabin in 1996, the elections of Benjamin Netanyahu's right-wing Likud Party, and the rising crime and traffic accident rates all marked a challenging period (Israel Police, 2003d).

Internal security, a rising crime rate, and increasing deaths on Israeli roads indicated that changes in INP policy and enforcement also were a necessity. Efforts continued to improve the working conditions and morale of the INP through increased recruitment, increased pay, increased use of technology, and the creation of new units.

Regarding internal security a new police district was created, the Jerusalem District, with four police stations. The Southern District was reorganized and restructured with the intent of increasing patrols and the monitoring of the Gaza Strip and Israel's borders. The INP created three new units to counter the problems of a rising crime rate partially due to the influx of immigrants and the economy: the Community Policing Unit in 1995, the Anti-Drug Unit, and the Intelligence Department. The Civil Guard also was given greater responsibility and increased authority. The Guard was deployed into neighborhoods on regular patrol and was trained to serve in specialized units, with the intent of monitoring conventional crime and terrorism. To counter the rising fatality rate on Israeli roads, a National Traffic Police Unit was created in 1991. These newly created units further exemplified the INP's ability to adapt to the challenges of service of the time period (INP, 2003d).

A new Code of Ethics was created in 1997 as follows:

1. To uphold and enforce the law: Police Officers will act to enforce the law, to prevent and detect offenses, and to maintain public order, acting always within the powers and orders given them under the law.

2. To protect life and property: Police officers will protect, with courage and determination, the life and property of every individual.

3. To uphold human rights: Police officers will act so as to maintain individual rights; will treat every person with courtesy and tolerance; will conduct themselves so as to increase the public's confidence in the police; and will regard themselves as public servants, not the public's masters.

4. To set a personal example and maintain integrity: By their appearance and demeanor, police officers will set an example at all times and will avoid all unbefitting conduct; they will behave ethically and with probity; they will, at all times, display honesty, reliability, and discretion, and report fully and accurately.

5. Professionalism and responsibility: Police officers will be ready to carry out their duties at all times; will act with restraint and will do so, using appropriate and professional considerations; will keep

calm in times of danger; and take responsibility for the results of their actions (Israel Police, 2003c).

Conclusion

The events of the Middle East will continue to echo in headlines across the globe. The nation receiving unparalleled attention in proportion to its ratio in landmass and population is Israel. Yet a nation so small in square mileage sends ripples across the globe, warranting either defense or condemnation from nations almost on a daily basis. The Israeli National Police are responsible for maintaining public order and internal security of the nation's population in one of the most challenging political and social environments in the world. Despite the national attention on the nation and region, only a modest amount of information is available in English on the INP.

Today's INP officer traces his history to the British occupation of the region. The initial flavor of the INP was distinctly British; however, as the years progressed the INP began to shape itself into its own unique organization. The national events of the region and the social culture of the land serve as a source of the macro-forces that have influenced the INP. These forces have led the INP through several reforms, developing numerous programs in response to the challenge of maintaining public order and security. As a result, the INP have evolved into a police force that is uniquely Israeli.

References

Andrade, J. M. 1985. *World Police and Paramilitary Forces*. New York: Stockton Press.

Ben Hamu, H. R. "Community and Civil Guard: Israel Police." 2002. Communications Dept., Community and Civil Guard Division, Israel Police. Accessed on August 1, 2003, at http://www.police.gov.il/english/AboutUs/

Bensinger, G. J. 1999. "The Emulation and Adaptation of American Criminal Justice Concepts in Israel." *International Journal of Comparative and Applied Criminal Justice* 23(1):17–23.

Bensinger, G. J. 1998. *Justice in Israel: The Criminal Justice System*. Chicago: Loyola University of Chicago.

Bensinger, G. J. 1982. "Organized Crime Israel Style." *The Police Chief* 49(4):42–43, 67.

Brewer, J. D. 1988. *The Police, Public Order and the State: Policing in Great Britain, Northern Ireland, the Irish Republic, the USA, Israel, South Africa and China*. New York: St. Martin's Press.

Country Study & Country Guide—Israel. 1988. "The Israel Police."Accessed on August 1, 2003, at http://www.1upinfo.com/country- guide-study/israel

Cramer, J. 1964. *The World's Police*. London: Cassell & Company.

Ebbe, O. N. I. 2000. *Comparative and International Criminal Justice Systems: Policing, Judiciary, and Corrections*. Boston: Butterworth-Heinnemann.

Friedmann, R. R. 1992. *Community Policing: Comparative Perspectives and Prospects*. New York: St. Martin's Press.

Friedmann, R. R. 1986a. "The Neighborhood Police Officer and Social Service Agencies: A Working Model for Cooperation." *Police Studies* 9(4):175–183.

Friedmann, R. R. 1986b. "Transformation of Roles for Police Officers: Perceptions of a Community Oriented Role." *Police Studies* 9(2):68–77.

Friedmann, R. R., E. Shadmi, & M. Kremnitzer. 1998. *Crime and Criminal Justice in Israel*. Albany: State University of New York Press.

Frisch, H. 1993. "The Druze minority in the Israeli military: Traditionalizing an ethnic policing role." *Armed Forces and Society* 20(1):51–67.

Gurevitch, M., B. Danet, & G. Schwartz. 1971. "The Image of the Police in Israel." *Law & Society Review* 5(3):367–88.

Herzog, S. 2000. "Is there a distinct profile of police officers accused of violence? The Israeli case." *Journal of Criminal Justice* 28(6):457–471.

Hovav, M., & M. Amir. 1979. "Israel Police: History and Analysis." *Police Studies* 2(2):5–31.

Israel Police. 2003a. "The Commissioner of Police." Accessed on August 14, 2003, at http://www.police.gov.il

Israel Police. 2003b. "We Need More Special People." Accessed on August 14, 2003, at http://www.police.gov.il

Israel Police. 2003c. "Code of Ethics." Accessed on August 14, 2003, at http://www.police.gov.il

Israel Police. 2003d. "The Israel Police: 50 Years of History." Accessed on August 14, 2003, at http://www.police.gov.il

Israel Police. 2003e. "Structure and Organization."Accessed on August 14, 2003, at http://www.police.gov.il

Israel Police. 2003f. "Partnerships," ed. Maia Zisso. Accessed on August 14, 2003, at http://www.police.gov.il

Israel Police. 2003g. "A Very Special Job: Disaster Victim Identification," ed. Naomi Shapira. Accessed on August 14, 2003, at http://www.police.gov.il

Johnstone, P., & J. Mandryk. 2001. *Operation World: When We Pray God Works*. Carlisle, Columbia, UK: Paternoster Publishing.

Kurian, G. T. 1989. *World Encyclopedia of Police Forces and Penal Systems*. New York: Facts on File.

Moore, D. 1999. "Gender Traits and Identities in a 'Masculine' Organization: The Israeli Police Force." *Journal of Social Psychology* 139(1)49-68.

Reiser, S. 1983. "The Israeli Police: Politics and Priorities." *Police Studies* 6(1)27–35.

Shadmi, E. 1998. "Police and Police Reform in Israel: The Formative Role of the State." In *Crime and Criminal Justice in Israel,* ed. Robert R. Friedmann. Albany: State University of New York Press.

Shane, P. G. 1980. *Police and People: A Comparison of Five Countries*. St. Louis: C. V. Mosby.

Weisburd, D., O. Shalev, & M. Amir. 2002. "Community policing in Israel: Resistance and change." *Policing* 25(1):80–110.

UNCJIN (United Nations Crime and Justice Information Network). 2002. "Israel." Accessed on August 1, 2003, at http://www.uncjin.org/Standards/Conduct/ccl/israel.pdf

UNCJIN (United Nations Crime and Justice Information Network). 2000. "State of Israel Ministry of Public Security." Accessed on August 1, 2003, at http://www.uncjin.org/Documents/10thcongress/10cStatements/israel.pdf

UNODC (United Nations Office on Drugs and Crime). 2003a. "Country Profile: Israel." Accessed on August 1, 2003, at http://www.unodc.org

UNODC (United Nations Office on Drugs and Crime). 2003b. "Crime Prevention by the Israel Police: Recent Advances." Accessed on August 1, 2003, at http://www.unodc.org/egypt/en/country_profile_israel.html

Weisman, G. M. 1993. "World Fact Book of Criminal Justice Systems: Israel." Accessed on April 14, 2003, at http://www.ojp.usdoj.gov/bjs/pub/ascii/wfbcjisr.txt

12

Reforming the Police in Central and Eastern European States

Otwin Marenin & Marina Caparini

This article examines the experience of police reform in CEE (Central and Eastern European) states which rejected Soviet Union hegemony after the collapse of the Soviet Empire in 1989.[1] CEE states refers to the set of countries stretching from the Baltic Sea to the borders of Greece and Turkey, from Estonia, Latvia, and Lithuania through Poland, Czech and Slovak Republics, Hungary, to Slovenia, Serbia, Croatia, Bosnia-Herzegovina, and Montenegro—the five states which arose out of the disintegration of Yugoslavia—to Albania, Macedonia, Bulgaria, and Romania. I will argue that the path, speed, and substance of reforms in the criminal justice and policing systems of CEE states since 1989 have been shaped by the intersection of two political upheavals in the region and two developments in policing at the international level.

Introduction

Soviet control of the region was designed to protect the Soviet Union against possible aggression from the West by controlling and using CEE states as security buffers between East and West. Under Soviet influence and control, the CEE states had political, economic, and security systems that imitated, with local modifications (mainly in the former Yugoslavia), the Soviet model. After 1989, the need and desire by new governments to do away with the inherited models led to systematic and extensive attempts to change the criminal justice system, and the police, toward a system more in accord with democratic, nonauthoritarian values and practices.

The disintegration of the Soviet Union and its loss of control over Central European countries altered the political and security landscape of the

Prepared especially for *Comparative and International Criminal Justice, 2/E.*

region. The simultaneous and continuing political and economic integration of European countries into a larger union and community has reached the CEE states, who now are actively seeking to become members of the European Union. (Ten new countries, mostly from the CEE group, were admitted to the EU in 2004; current membership stands at 25 member states.) Concurrently, the forces and consequences of globalization—specifically transnational organized crime and the massive growth of transnational cooperation among police forces—as well as the emergence of an international police regime have influenced the form and substance of reforms of policing systems in the CEE states.

The question addressed here is whether the reforms that were adopted, in response to internally generated political demands and to pressures for reforms from the international and regional community, have led to more democratic systems of policing. This article examines the basic changes that have been attempted and draws some general conclusions about democratizing authoritarian policing systems. The reforms that have been accomplished are not yet sufficient to judge whether democratizing the police has succeeded. That goal requires a long and complicated process involving hard political work to overcome the objections raised and obstacles created by the police, civic society, and governments.

The examination of police reform in these countries can provide insights into the specific patterns and dynamics of reform in each country. Also, more generally, it highlights the difficulties faced when trying to reform authoritarian policing systems from within (i.e., through domestic politics) and by external assistance and advice.

Disintegration of the Soviet Union and the Balkans

The demise of the Soviet Union in 1989 led to vast economic, cultural, and political changes in the Central and Eastern European region. The successor states to the Soviet Union and the countries in the Central European region, which had been dominated by Soviet hegemony, inherited political systems tailored to the demands of Marxist ideologies as interpreted by Communist Party leaders and their associated *intelligentsia*. The criminal justice system was chief among the means to enforce ideological commitment; adherence to the demands of the state; and compliance with an extensive set of rules, laws, and expectations.

Socialist security systems throughout the region were characterized by powerful secret police and intelligence agencies; a centralized, militaristic, uniformed police (often called the militia); and an array of paramilitary forces. The main task of the secret police and state security apparatus was to sustain the political system and protect the party-state from insurrection, subversion, and political opposition (a function normally referred to as *political policing*). Regular police work involving the detection or prevention of crime was secondary to political policing and order maintenance. The regular police were formally or informally subordinate to party leaders, intelligence agencies, and the secret police. Public conformity with party guidelines was ensured by these coercive, intrusive, centrally guided and controlled policing systems, as well as by a pervasive system of informants and spies who told the authorities about suspicious activities, nonconformist behavior, any criticism of the ruling ideology and party, or evasion of party demands.

To survive within an economic and security system which had become increasingly bureaucratized, inefficient, and unable to meet the needs of the public, people had to evade state control through corruption, passive resistance, and evasion. Corruption became a necessary social lubricant for both state employees and citizens; corruption in all its forms enabled people to deal with the system by manipulating rules and regulations for organizational and personal needs. Evasion of state control (e.g., through an extensive informal economy) became a staple of Soviet life (Los, 1988; Shelley, 1984).

The inability of the state to meet its promises of a better life and the consequent corruption, coercion, and lies employed to hide the reality of failure ultimately delegitimized the state and the party. Initially, this led to underground critiques of party rule and of the corruption and personal aggrandizement of the leadership and its hangers-on. Ultimately, it resulted in open revolt against the dominant ideology and Communist system itself. The state and party collapsed, giving way to political struggles to gain control of the state and setting it on a new path toward economic betterment and political stability.

The disintegration of the Soviet Union and its hegemony model occurred in two stages. After 1989, former bloc countries embarked on the road to democratization, with Poland, Hungary, and Czechoslovakia leading the way. (Czechoslovakia later split, on the basis of ethnic identities and by mutual agreement, into two states—the Czech and Slovak Republics. That separation necessitated a division of criminal justice personnel and resources between the two states.) The second stage of the breakdown of socialist systems was the dissolution of Yugoslavia into separate, ethnically distinct republics—often accompanied by open warfare and extensive intercommunal violence. This prompted intervention in the region by the United States, European regional associations (EU, Organization for Security and Cooperation in Europe [OSCE]), and the United Nations to stop the killings, establish minimal conditions of stability and safety, and set the countries on the road to democratization and economic development. External intervention in the Balkans continues to this day, with a major focus on helping these new countries achieve stable, effective, and legitimate criminal justice and policing systems.

Not surprisingly, dismantling the state repressive apparatus and its infiltration of civic society enjoyed broad societal consensus. It was one of the first tasks advocated by democratic opposition during the transition period and undertaken by the first democratic governments after 1989–

1990. Dismantling the security system, in turn, created the need for new criminal justice and policing systems more in tune with the democratic aspirations of the new governments and civic society. The notion of Security Sector Reform (SSR)—a popular way to describe and analyze both the tasks which must be accomplished and the goals which must be achieved if the security of the state and citizens is to be assured—nicely captures the dominant aspirations and the search for new structures, or a new "security architecture," for CEE states (Caparini, 2002; Huisman, 2002). SSR argues that security is a basic pre-condition for democratization, and security requires an effective and fair policing system.

Integrating Europe

European integration, which began in the late 1950s, successively has led from small forms of economic cooperation to the current system, which has achieved a sufficient level of political integration that a European Constitution has been drafted and is being discussed. The CEE countries have sought to join the European Union, largely for economic reasons, but also as a means of ensuring that they will not again be dominated, as they were in the past, by the remnant of the Soviet Union, the Russian Federation.

To become eligible for accession to the EU, candidate countries must fundamentally transform their existing political and economic systems, moving from a state-controlled economy to a market economy, from a socialist political system to a democratic one, from a criminal justice system obedient to the demands of the ruling Communist elites to one which abides by the rule of law, respects human rights, and is accountable to civic society.

The demand by the EU that potential new members reform their criminal justice systems (as well as the economic and political institutions they inherited from their socialist past) is as much a moral and ideological statement as an effort to promote effective crime control. EU members think of themselves as having and promoting democratic values, institutions, and processes that new members must adopt as the price of admission. The success of democratization, and of crime control and order-maintaining policies, are judged and graded by criteria and standards set out in EU resolutions, codes of conduct, political objectives and goals, and training standards. The basic goals to be achieved before admission to the EU are: stable institutions guaranteeing democracy, the existence of a functioning market economy, and the ability to take on the obligations of membership in the EU. The category of stable institutions guaranteeing democracy includes the police.

Transnational police cooperation has been part and parcel of the expansion and integration of the EU (Hebenton and Thomas, 1995; Occnipinti, 2003). New countries, as they are admitted to the EU, must become integrated into these existing EU-wide policing systems. In addition to the basic structures—TREVI (Terrorism, Radicalism, Extremism,

Violence, Internationalism), Schengen, and EUROPOL—police cooperation within the EU now includes information exchanges through common
information systems; local trans-border institutions in which police from
different countries work together and are housed in joint facilities
(Nogala, 2001); advice and assistance provided by member states to each
other and to candidate countries; the development of a common police
training curriculum (AEPC, 2002), regional police academies (e.g., MEPA
[the Middle European Police Academy]), and hopes for a jointly operated
police command college, the European Police Academy; the stationing of
liaison officers in member countries and regional institutions (Bigo,
2000); and the growth of a vast set of common rules, regulations, and
laws (the *acquis communitaire*) to which the police of all member states
will need to subscribe.

The TREVI system was established in 1975 to coordinate the policies
of European states for the control of terrorism; private security issues and
football hooliganism; and organized crime (i.e., drug trafficking, money
laundering, or computer crime); and border security for an expanding EU.
Four working groups meet regularly to discuss these issues.

The Schengen Agreement (named after a small town where the agreement was signed by seven states in 1985) originally sought to coordinate
police cooperation at the existing borders and, later on, establish common
policies within the EU. Schengen seeks to develop common border control
policies on immigration, asylum, and the movement of goods; authorizes
interstate police practices, such as "hot pursuit" from one country into
another; and establishes the Schengen information system—an extensive
criminal data network linking all EU countries. One consequence of the
Maastricht Treaty of 1992, which formally established the EU, was a borderless Europe, the so-called "Schengen space." People, goods, services, and
finances are free to move anywhere within the EU without being stopped at
the former borders of member countries. Schengen now has 15 members.

EUROPOL began as the European Drug Unit, headquartered in The
Hague, the Netherlands, and has evolved into a general police coordination mechanism among EU countries, and between EU states and international organizations (such as INTERPOL), and bilaterally with non-EU
states. EUROPOL is staffed by delegated police officers from EU countries;
it runs an information system and offers advice and assistance to the
police of both member and nonmember states.

The most important of these organizations or systems for purposes of
this discussion is the Schengen Agreement. New members states will be
admitted to the EU only if they agree to all Schengen goals, priorities, and
expectations and agree to perform these at a level set by the EU. The reason is that the now borderless "Schengen space" within the EU will need to
be protected by states that exist at the expanding external EU borders—for
once legal immigrants, criminals, or terrorists have crossed the external
borders they are free to move anywhere within the EU.

European regional organizations—mainly the EU and the Organization for Security and Cooperation in Europe (OSCE)—have provided assistance to transitional states seeking to reform their police and border security, as well as conducted annual evaluations of progress achieved. One of many organizational vehicles for delivering aid and imposing judgment is the PHARE Program (http://europa.eu.int/comm/enlargement/pas/phare/index.htm), run by the European Commission (the executive bureaucracy of the EU). The OSCE has been actively involved in police reforms in the Balkan area, and sets priorities for assistance, coordinates donor activities, and oversees the implementation of police aid programs in the Balkans (OSCE, 2002).

Individual EU states and police forces have developed strong relationships with partner countries and agencies (Gregory, 1994; Lundberg, 1993; Mlicki, 2001). The Dutch police, for example, partner regional Dutch police forces with their Hungarian counterparts. Officers for Hungary visit and work with Dutch police and vice versa, and in the process exchange practical knowledge on how to conduct policing in a fair and effective manner (e.g., investigations, community relations, personnel practices). Scottish police forces partner with police in Baltic states. The West German police basically took over control of the East German police after German reunification; and they also have assisted Poland and Balkan countries in reforming their policing systems.[2]

Globalization and Transnational Threat

Globalization, most generally, refers to the increasing interconnectedness of international and local affairs, and to the forces and processes through which this integration is taking place and shape. The powers of technology, the coincident (and potential) conflicts of economic interests, the dispersion of cultural values attuned to consumption, and the convergence of political norms favoring democratic political processes have created conditions in which events occurring at a distance have an impact, for better or for worse, on local conditions. These global and local economic, political, and cultural dynamics are intricately connected and captured in the jargon term *globalization*.

One consequence of globalization is a vast increase in transnational communications, travel, and commercial activities. The ability to communicate instantly, and in secret, across international borders; the capacity to move money and information via cyberspace; and the inability of governments to stop the free exchange of information (or do so only with great difficulty)—all have undermined the state's control of the information available to its people. People now have the capacity to create and join informal networks of cooperation even in the most authoritarian systems. International borders designed to protect the sovereign domain have become porous and permeable, more difficult to close to illegal transactions without harming the legitimate movements of commerce and people.

The same global technology that enables legitimate activities also enables illegal and criminal acts. Domestic safety, order, and crime increasingly are impacted by events originating from outside countries. Organized crime routinely moves people, goods, information, and money between countries and continents. Millions of people are smuggled illegally across borders, seeking work or being lured into the sex service industry (often perpetuating the cultural patrimony of their place of origin); illegal goods (drugs, weapons, nuclear materials, heavily taxed goods, human body parts, protected animal species, pirated brands) cross borders in vast quantities; money is transferred electronically or through informal traditional financial networks in violation of currency regulations or to launder illegal profits; terrorists plot and carry out local attacks through globally dispersed and networked cells and organizations; streams of refugees and asylum seekers search for shelter from oppression and violence in safer havens.

Transnational crime poses a threat to European states, much as it does anywhere. With the creation of an internal free-movement zone within the EU (the Schengen space), the secure protection of governments, people, and property from transnational threats requires the fortification of the external borders of the EU. These borders are expanding and shifting outward as EU-qualified countries are admitted. The safety of all EU citizens and states will be, partially, in the hands of the police and border forces of newly admitted CEE states. The Germans, French, or Dutch have to trust that the security systems of the states at their external borders are efficient and effective in keeping out criminal actors, and that they do so in ways which can be justified by democratic values (Andreas and Snyder, 2000; Apap, 2001; Bort, 2002). Put differently, the existing states of the EU have a strong interest in reforming and upgrading the security systems at the EU borders in order to be and feel safe.

Much of the transnational crime in the CEE region consists of normal crime that happens to cross borders as part of its operations in terrorist activities. An example of normal crime is organized car theft (smuggling groups that steal luxury cars in Western Europe and transport them to Russia to be sold to the new economic elites, organized crime figures, and political leaders). Corrupt police and border forces are an essential part of these operations. Guns are smuggled from the Czech Republic, a major producer of small arms, to the Balkans; cigarettes and gasoline, which are heavily taxed, are sold on the black market at enormous profits. (Cigarette smuggling provided vast sums of black-market income to the Milosevic regime and required government cooperation with organized crime before it was overthrown.) Drugs and sex workers are transported along the "Balkan route," which winds from Turkey, Bulgaria, and Romania through the Balkans to service the demand in the West. An estimated half million women from the former Soviet Republic (e.g., Ukraine, Moldovia) are lured into sex servitude. Some end up as "sex workers" in European countries and others remain stranded, to service local Balkan populations and international soldiers/police stationed in the area, as for example in Macedonia. Again, the transport of these women requires cooperation by police and border forces, leads to corruption, and undermines reform efforts. In addition, large numbers of illegal immigrants and asylum seekers look for work and refuge in the West. For example, many illegal migrants from across the vast expanse of Asia can be found waiting in Hungary to cross into Austria, once sufficient numbers have arrived to make smuggling them worthwhile to organized crime. The land border between Hungary and Austria is remote and difficult to control and can be crossed without much risk of detection.

The Emergence of an International Policing Regime

International regimes embody widely accepted norms and standards of conduct which, though they do not have the force of law, guide the direction of reforms and provide the standards against which the success of reforms will be judged. Regimes emerge from the practical realities of transnational cooperation. In order to cooperate across borders, agencies such as the police, even though they exist within vastly different legal and political environments, must agree on minimal conditions for sharing information, working together, and assisting each other. Such understandings may be informal agreements to cooperate on particular problems; sharing common policies in specific situations; or formal agreements written and ratified in conference resolutions, Memoranda of Understanding (MOU), or legal documents.

At this point, it is fairly easy to specify what democratic policing should look like in principle. As Bayley (2001: 76) has noted, "the elements of democratic police reform are no longer problematic" and can be found in academic discussions of democratic policing; in codes of conduct for police officers produced by international and regional organizations (e.g., the Council of Europe code of ethics for police, the UN codes on police conduct and the use of force, OSCE guidelines, or the training standards proposed by the Association of European Police Colleges [AEPC, 2002]); in recommendations by reform commissions (e.g., Independent Commission, 1999); and in policy documents produced by NGOs (such as the "Budapest Recommendations" sponsored by the Helsinki Committee in Kádár, 2001).[3]

The specific terms and principles differ from document to document but tend to stress basic values and practices which democratic policing needs to embody. Most commonly, democratic policing:

- respects the human rights of all, including offenders;
- abides by the rule of law (i.e., treats all persons encountered in police work fairly, equitably, and without discrimination or arbitrariness);
- accepts an ideology of civil service to civic society rather than the state, the party, the powerful, or the well-connected;

- is politically neutral or nonpartisan in the exercise of its authority and power;
- is representative of the larger society in the composition of its personnel;
- is transparent in its operations and subject to effective external oversight and accountability (Council of Europe, 2000; Goldsmith and Lewis, 2000; Kádár, 2001; Mendes, et al., 1999; Perez, 2000; Stone and Ward, 2000);
- promotes the integrity of personnel and work through internal policies; and
- reflects in its working cultures and practices widely shared societal norms.[4]

Such principles may be classified as either non-negotiable or negotiable. Non-negotiable principles are essential traits of democratic forces, but they can be and will be adapted in multiple and diverse ways. Negotiable principles are valued but not essential. Every new democratic policing system created in every society will combine universal aspects (non-negotiable) and context-specific aspects (negotiable)—hence, no ideal model of institutions or policies can be specified as contexts of each system are always unique.

The basic non-negotiable principles are: representativeness, semi-autonomy, integrity management, transparency, and effectiveness. The essential nature of these characteristics is linked to the notion of *legitimation*. New police forces must gain legitimacy to be accepted, effective, and sustainable, and without these non-negotiable traits no policing system can do so. And if the police lack legitimacy, they have only force to fall back on.

Representativeness means simply that the composition of police personnel, at all levels, should be roughly proportional to or reflect the distribution of salient identity groups in society. What identities are salient will depend on each society—they may be determined by religion, ethnic identity, race, language, immigrant status, or gender. A non-representative police force, no matter how well it behaves, will always be suspect in principle (especially when identities are profoundly important to people); and every misstep, however excusable and minor, will be interpreted in the least favorable light as abuse of power, discrimination, or outright prosecution.

Semi-autonomy means that the police should have the right (and are expected) to exercise their professional judgments relatively free from direct societal or state directives. The police should not feel themselves beholden to those in power but instead to the normative system for order and justice which exists in their society (such as the notion of the "rule of law" or widely shared societal norms). They must have some autonomy, yet they cannot be a law unto themselves—they should only be semi-autonomous. Creating that delicate balance is difficult, but unless it is achieved the police will be either partisan or arbitrary in their actions.

Integrity is a necessary characteristic of police organizations and individuals, and it must be *managed*—that is, enforced though appropriate training, supervision, and accountability—to overcome the informal police culture that always exists in police organizations (Haberfeld, et al., 2000; Krémer, 2000; Kutjnak Ivkovich and Klockars, 1998). Accountability mechanisms can and should take many overlapping and reinforcing forms (Stone and Ward, 2000). If managed correctly, integrity will lead to rule-governed actions by the police; they will act in non-arbitrary ways, without discrimination, malfeasance, corruption, or abuse of power.

Transparency, or the ability of outsiders to observe and, ultimately, to participate in planning and evaluating the work and performance of the police, is an essential goal of police reform. The police should not able to hide behind their professional status, claiming that openness would compromise their work or that outsiders are incapable of judging it. They must be (and they must *feel*) obligated to explain themselves when asked by individuals or groups who have a legitimate right, in law or political standing, to ask.

Lastly, policing must be effective in protecting the routines of life on which people depend. An ineffective police force will lose legitimacy quickly and will drift into corruption and abuse of power to cover its shortcomings. *Effectiveness* requires skills, resources, and continuous training.

Democratic policing, like democratic politics, requires a balance of competing but equally legitimate values. Crime control and order maintenance must be effective but also fair; the collection of intelligence and information is essential yet must respect individual and group rights to privacy. The police, as trained professionals, must have some capacity for discretion and autonomy in their work but not so much so that they lose sight of their obligatory accountability. The specific manner in which these values are balanced (or not) will depend on local contexts. There is no one way of organizing democratic policing or one way of policing that is democratic (e.g., whether there exists only one or many police forces in a country), nor a specific ideology and practice which must be pursued (e.g., community-oriented policing, which may be inappropriate for local conditions; see Haberfeld, 1997). A basic principle of democratic policing is that each country needs to develop policing systems that fit its needs and norms.

Processes of Reform

The convergence of the disintegration of the Soviet empire, the widening of European integration, the explosion of transnational crime and threats to border security, and the emerging consensus on democratic policing regimes has structured the pace, direction, and extent of police reform in all CEE countries. Pressures for reform from the outside and the dynamics of political demands for change welling up from within have led to different paths of policing reform, some more successful than others.[5]

It should be noted, as well, that all CEE states experienced astounding increases in crime rates, particularly of serious crime and organized crime, which in some cases posed direct threats to the survival of the state. The police were expected to do something about threats to public order and personal safety. Undermined reform efforts that had stressed human rights and rule-of-law norms led to the perception by the public, and the police, that democracy and freedom equalled crime.[6] In some cases such thinking even fuelled nostalgic feelings for the socialist past, and political support for parties and leaders who advocated a (limited) return to strong and coercive rule.

The Goals of Reforms: The Three Ds

Despite the differences in territory, population, economic development (the CEE region has a more economically developed North and a poorer South, as does the rest of the globe), or experience with democracy prior to the imposition of Soviet hegemony, certain goals, trends, and problems have occurred in all CEE countries as they attempt to shift policing systems away from their socialist origins. The basic goals of reform can be summarized as the three Ds of decentralization, demilitarization, and depoliticization. The three Ds are largely a reaction to the policing systems typical of the socialist, state- and party-controlled, repressive, and politicized systems of the Soviet period. The three "D" processes seek to rid the policing systems of traits which made them instruments of state and elite power that were nonresponsive to civic society demands. Achieving the three Ds, it is argued, will go a long way toward preparing the ground for meaningful democratic practices. Without the three Ds, police reform cannot reflect democratic standards and practices.

Decentralization.   Centralization can refer to the locus of political control. In the centralized systems of socialist states, ultimate authority for all decisions rested in the national ministry, which itself was controlled by parallel party command bodies. Centralization also can refer to the organizational structure of the police, in which control and decision making rest in the apex of the police hierarchy while lower echelons carry out commands from on high.

In contrast, decentralization points to the ability of civic society and local communities to have some influence on the police, as it does in notions of community policing. It also refers to the dispersion or shift of authority and discretion to lower levels of the police organization. In a decentralized system, officers have the devolved capacity to make and implement policies and decisions (within broad legal and organizational limits) that reflect local conditions as well as their professional judgment.

In socialist systems, policing was highly centralized in terms of political control and command hierarchy. Nothing was done by the police that disregarded central, party-issued and approved directives and priorities.

Within the organization, officers were socialized into doing only what they were told, not taking initiatives, and certainly not doing anything that might go against central or organizational priorities without checking first with superiors. One of the most widely described aspects of policing in Western democracies—the ability to use discretion in their work—was rarely observed in socialist policing systems. Police organizations structured as highly centralized military-type hierarchies and command systems do not foster the individual responsibility on the part of police officers and the cultivation of professional discretion that Western police organizations have pursued.

Decentralization in practice requires a concomitant change in the way the police on the streets view their capacity for discretion, and in the perception of their efficacy among local communities and civic society. A mere change in formal structures and legal powers is not enough. Yet much of the police decentralizations that have occurred in CEE states has been at the organization-chart level. Reforms have occurred in reaction to the centralized nature of socialist systems rather than to the need for new capacities for civic control and street-level discretion. Coupled with the demands by the public that the police do something about crime, many of the initial attempts to limit the powers of the police through law were sidetracked and abandoned. Effectiveness became the priority, over and against the democratic values of due process and the protection of human rights.

At the local level, many reformers had argued that individual citizens and communities should be encouraged to take part in local law enforcement activities, should cooperate with the police, and should hold them accountable. However, in CEE countries many citizens previously had been involved in policing activities as informants or to carry out ideological directives. Arguments that the public should assist the police in crime control were often interpreted as calls to be informants for, rather than partners with, the police. In addition, many communist-era police forces had engaged in an intense form of community policing; certain officers walked the beat of streets or offices in the areas where they themselves lived. The proximity of these police officers and the active interest they took in the personal lives of citizens facilitated their surveillance activities, and the information they gathered could be passed on to the political police. Indeed, the model of community policing practiced in communist states (such as the German Democratic Republic or Albania) could be said to have exceeded that practiced in any other Western system—but it was done for very different reasons. New democratic, decentralized models of policing, such as community policing based on the notion that the public wants to have a say in police affairs, had little meaning to people not yet democratized themselves.

Demilitarization. As with decentralization, demilitarization can refer to different aspects of policing. It is generally accepted that the police, as a service that has civic society (especially victims) as clients and stakeholders, should be organizationally distinct from the military. But the militarization of policing can also refer to the mindset, ethos, and culture of the police. Military values, attitudes, and behaviors are inappropriate for a service organization. The military finds, fights, captures, and kills an enemy by whatever means it takes; the proper role for a civilian police force is to protect society, victims, and offenders in a legally circumscribed manner and turn their work over to other agencies. In contrast, a militarized police will treat its service clients as enemies who must be destroyed, eliminated, or immobilized by any means.

In most CEE states, the police were, by law and organizational affiliation, considered to be part of the military. After 1989, CEE states rewrote their police laws in order to stress the civil aspect of policing and to remove them from the structure of the armed forces; enacted laws regulating police procedures in crime control and order maintenance; prescribed new training procedures; and, in order to deal with crime threats, modified certain powers of the police, such as granting them authority for telephone taps or undercover work. As with organizational structure, changing the law was contested but relatively easy, since there was significant political pressure for reforms to do away with the most repressive and intrusive tactics and powers of the police.

But transforming the working culture of the new police has been another matter. There was a major practical problem. All states tried to remove or fire police officers who, tainted by their association with communist-era forces, had committed abuses, human rights violations or other crimes, and had engaged in corrupt practices. Almost by definition, most of them had been guilty of such actions while working within the socialist system, which placed little value on protecting the rights and privacy of individuals. All new police forces were vetted, especially at the upper levels of the hierarchy. The practical problem was that firing a large number of experienced police officers without first having newly trained officers to replace them left a vacuum in expertise and skills. In consequence, vetting was not carried out as thoroughly as initially intended, and many police who had worked in the socialist system continued working in the new system. These experienced officers then "infected" the new police with their old, authoritarian values. In consequence, the culture of policing changed little.

Creating a new police culture attuned to more democratic values is a difficult task. It is unclear what personnel practices (recruitment, education, training, discipline, and rewards), managerial strategies, organizational arrangements, and relational tactics (with civic society and other state agencies) will foster the needed cultural norms and attitudes. Much of the advice received from external sources has probably been of little value, given the vast differences in context that still exist between Western democracies and the transitional societies of the CEE states.

One practical problem was the low pay and the poor working conditions of the new police. Despite all efforts, the new democratic government simply did not have the resources to pay officers well, nor did external assistance compensate for the lack of local resources. Another development sharpened this dilemma. Since the new police forces did not seem capable of controlling the rise in crime, private police and security agencies proliferated, as did organized criminal groups. Many, and probably the most skillful and experienced police officers, left the service to work for private companies or organized crime, each of which offered substantially higher salaries and other benefits.

Progress on demilitarization has been much greater in the northern tier of CEE countries than in the Balkans. The dissolution of Yugoslavia into ethnic violence and atrocities (many of which were committed by police forces) and open warfare among the emerging states caused police across the region to become directly involved in violent conflict. The inter-ethnic character of conflicts and wars directly affected the composition of the police throughout the region, which went from being ethnically diverse to homogenous in each of the republics and enclaves. Police were usually drawn immediately into ethnic conflicts, aided by massive increases in strength, heavy arms and equipment, and deployment in military security-type roles. Hasty efforts to expand the police force resulted in loss of professionalism, as normal education and training requirements were shortened and standards were lowered. In Serbia, members of the special police units are known to have engaged in some of the worst war crimes on record in an attempt to suppress Albanian and Kosovar aspirations in Kosovo. In Macedonia Albanian ethnic separatist movements challenged the new government, leading to armed conflict that often involved the police.

In Croatia, police involvement in the war with Serbia in 1991–92 had the effect of reinforcing and strengthening the traditional code of silence and bonds of professional loyalty among police officers. As a result, rooting out police corruption or creating internal controls over police misconduct became more difficult. On the other hand, police support for the war that resulted in Croatia's independence helped legitimize the new police force and created high public esteem for the police (Kutjnak Ivkovich, 2000, 2004).

One consequence of open war and massive atrocities was the involvement of the international community to stop the violence in the region, create some political stability, and help in the creation of police and security forces. Soldiers, gendarmes from Italy, Spain, and France, and CIVPOL (civilian police from many countries working under the banner of the United Nations) were brought in to begin the reconstruction of the security system, implement necessary legal reforms, and create a functioning criminal justice system (i.e., courts, corrections) (Perito, 2004). As a consequence of both the war and violence and the presence of international soldiers and police, efforts to develop new democratic police forces started much later in the south than in the northern tier; therefore success and progress is much more difficult to assess.

Depoliticization.   The police in socialist systems were a tool of state and party power. They did what the political leadership ordered, regardless of rights enumerated in the Constitution, legal obligations and prohibitions, or local demands (unless approved by higher authority). Taking the police out of the political process has been a major goal of reforms. Depoliticization entails changing the function of the police from one of protecting the political regime or government to that of ensuring public safety, with their powers and responsibilities defined by law. The police should serve civic society and not the state, guided in their actions by law rather than political demands.

Depoliticization, establishing the political neutrality of the police, was and is a challenge confronting police organizations throughout the region. Given the history of Communist Party control and use of the police to protect the former political regime and persecute perceived enemies, depoliticization was, not surprisingly, one of the first reforms undertaken by many of the young democracies. The typical approach to depoliticization was to legally prohibit political activity by the police, including belonging to a political party or participating in party activity; and forming interest associations or unions. The one political right normally left to the police as individuals was the right to vote. Within the police organization, officers were given rights to file complaints and grievances, with their resolution typically left to police authorities themselves. While one could argue that depoliticization has freed police from accountability to any political authorities or police hierarchy that violated human rights or demanded the commission of criminal acts, this overreaction to the past has generally resulted in the almost wholesale deprivation of political rights for police officers and has had a detrimental effect on police performance and morale. The police see themselves as treated as second-class citizens, a perception which does not easily square with the notion of democratizing the state and civic society. It is likely, as has been argued in Western democracies, that if the police themselves are not treated with respect for their democratic rights they in turn will not treat citizens with such respect.

In sum, transforming the police from a coercive, corrupt, and politicized force into an organization that considers service to society as its primary mission has been the stated goal of domestic reformers, political leaders, civic society groups, and international advisors. The three Ds, while steps on the road toward democratizing the police, are not sufficient to achieve the final objective.

Lessons Learned for Police Reform

The three Ds can correct, and have corrected, some of the worst excesses of the former police, but these changes have not been enough to create the new desired policing systems. There are a number of reasons for this.

Talking the talk and walking the walk. There is a general sense among observers that police reformers and leaders in CEE countries have learned to talk the right democratic language but that they have not yet been able to translate knowledge of goals, values, best practices, and appropriate models into sustainable police progress. It is clear that progressive police leaders and political reformers have an intimate knowledge of international standards and human rights concerns, the basic notion that democratic policing is a service, the ideologies and practices loosely grouped under the rubric of community policing, and the importance of civic society involvement in accountability practices. Even when security conditions have deteriorated (as they have in all states), no current police leader talks the discredited policing rhetoric of the former socialist policing systems or advocates a return to practices which are now condemned. It is also clear that police leaders are serious when they use the new language and are committed to seeing it transformed into practice.

There are instrumental and almost philosophical reasons why the new policing ideology and its language are accepted. One pressure for reform, which can be observed in all CEE states, is the influence exerted by the regional and international community on the political and police leadership of CEE states. As noted earlier, gaining membership in the larger regional European community has been a basic aspiration. Pre-accession demands, guidelines, assessments, and assistance have mandated changes in CEE systems, and only if such demands are met will accession proceed. In some cases, such as Serbia and Bosnia-Herzegovina (and in Kosovo), international advisors effectively control the process of reforming the policing system. In short, the police of CEE states exist as if in a regional classroom, in which their performance is graded by existing members of the European community, using standards that reflect Western democratic concepts and values. Only if they achieve passing grades will these states be accepted into the European political community and their police forces be seen as peers by the international policing community. It is not surprising that police reformers in CEE states want to be associated with the latest, "cutting-edge" developments in policing. International models and examples may be imposed, but they are also objects of imitation and standards against which to judge the modernity and professionalism of police forces.

International pressure itself reflects the changing conceptions of policing that have crystallized in Western democracies in the last quarter century and have become enshrined in the international policing regime. International demands may be resented as a challenge to national sovereignty, but they have also provided internal reformers with a powerful argument and tool for reform. It has become practically impossible to speak of policing reforms in any other terms than those characteristic of Western democracies. Even a re-emerging nostalgia for the old times—when there was repression, to be sure, but also a greater sense of personal protection from ordinary crime—which arises routinely as crime explodes and organized crime takes over much of economic life, cannot hide the fact that the discourse of policing has changed. Although people want more security, they desire that it not be accompanied by a return of the repressive state apparatuses that used to be the police.

Philosophically, reformers know that the old systems needed to be replaced and reformed. There really is no choice, given the movement toward democratic governance and market reforms in the region. Democratizing the police is accepted by reformers as the basic goal, even when there may be some reservations about specific aspects of reforms, such as external oversight and accountability. In the long run, reformers expect that reforms will make the police more effective, will lead to greater acceptance of the police by the public, and make the job of policing easier—and that is all to the good.

The pragmatic question is how long the new rhetoric can be sustained in the absence of effective and visible reforms, and in the way the public is treated by the police in encounters, before the new conceptions and practices of policing lose their luster, before civic society and the state delegitimize the goals and policies of reform. At some point, reforms must become visible in the lives of ordinary people (especially marginal groups). If the police have not changed (or are not seen to have changed) in how they behave in the routines of their work, then other legal, organizational, or rhetorical reforms will mean little. The payoff for police reforms is on the street, and that requires, most fundamentally, a specific police culture.

Without a new culture, the new police forces will be empty institutions (Grugel, 1999). They will have all the attributes of structure, laws, and regulations typical of Western democratic police, but they will not be staffed by personnel who will (or can) bring the new ways of doing policing into practice.

The politics of reform.   Police reform is a political process. Analyses of attempted police reforms point to the inextricable connection of reform efforts to the larger political dynamics of a country. Policing is a form and manifestation of political power, whatever else it may be. Proposed reforms of policing systems will always be assessed, at least in part, by all internal actors (civic groups, political leaders, police managers, domestic and international reformers) in terms of the degree to which the reforms will redistribute control and power, as well as the criteria of justice and effectiveness. There is no neutral, apolitical way to talk about the police or to assess their roles and performance.

The police are part of politics everywhere. In CEE states, which are in the process of transition toward new forms of politics, economic practices, and changed state–society relations, the political role of the police and the impact of police reforms on the likely outcomes of transitions to democracy are apparent and understood by all internal actors, including the police. They understand that a democratic society cannot exist without a democratized police, and that both processes—creating democratic politics and democratizing the police—go hand in hand and are both achievable only by hard political work.

This tension of a police force that abides by the rule of law but is also responsive to demands from society (or influenced by politics) can have negative consequences. One harmful effect of politics on policing is what observers have called the "ceaseless innovation" in policing law (Plywaczewski and Walancik, 2004). New political leaders will try to "fix" what they see as inappropriate, biased toward the wrong values, and ineffective in past police reforms. The result is organizational instability and ineffective policing, as the police try to determine their responsibilities and priorities, as well as how to adapt and adjust to new demands and restrictions from the state and society. Another consequence is that competition for funds, which will be scarce in transitional societies, will limit the capacity of the police to recruit new members and equip themselves with needed resources. As noted before, a common occurrence in all CEE states is the temptation of police officers to move into private, and sometimes criminal, employment. The police become the training and proving ground, at the taxpayers' expense, for private security agencies. In addition, the ethnic, class, and gender composition of police forces becomes a political issue, whether reformers try to hire the best regardless of their background or whether political figures and civic groups try to stack the police with their "own" people. Merit will conflict with perceived political allegiance and group loyalties.

The crucial role of politics is understood by international and domestic reformers, but in an abstract and largely negative way. Reformers know that policing is subject to politics but think that political influence should be minimized. However, politics is part of the legitimation process of new policing systems. In short, police reform is a political process, not merely the creation or transference of technical skills and best managerial practices.

Transforming the police is not enough.   For police reforms to be sustained, laws have to be changed and the other institutions of the criminal justice system have to be democratized as well. Without a functioning courts system that is not corrupted or dilatory in its decisions, even good police work in crime control has little impact. If the courts cannot handle the load or are unwilling to convict even on best evidence, police reform will be ineffective. Similarly, a sanctioning system needs to be in place to hold, rehabilitate, and punish convicted offenders. And, most fundamentally, the public that observes the criminal justice system in action must see that justice is being meted effectively and fairly. There still exists the common perception in CEE states that the law does not treat all equally, that the politically powerful and the well connected are treated more leniently than regular people. It has been documented that the reality of discrimination against outsiders and marginal groups continues. For example, the Roma (Gypsies), which exist in sizable number in the Czech and Slovak

Republics and Hungary (or Romania), still are treated with suspicion and disdain by criminal justice personnel, a discrimination probably reinforced by most of the population. Other ethnic minorities typically suffer similar discrimination by the police and the public.

Gains and losses.   Reforms bring both gains and losses. The gains from implemented reforms are pretty clear. In the short run, there is a greater likelihood that the police will gain technical skills, public support and, in the long run, greater legitimacy.

Less clear is what has been lost. The explosion of crime, which the new policing system has been unable to curtail, has made the public less safe and has increased the fear of crime. Reforms also have meant a high degree of organizational turmoil, loss of personnel for various reasons (vetting, private employment, age and educational disqualifications), and increasing demands by civic society for harsher, more repressive, and less justice- or due-process-oriented policing. In the short run, such demands will be hard to resist by the police or political leaders, and supporters of due process (mostly international and local NGOs) will be ostracized and condemned (e.g., ICHRP, 2003; Kremplewski, 2001).

Conclusion

Fundamental and sustained reform of the civil policing system has proven to be one of the most difficult tasks faced by the new democratic regimes in Central and Eastern Europe. The police reforms attempted in the CEE countries raise the question of whether the reforms achieved so far—the changes in rhetorical aspirations, organizational arrangements, legal bases, and functional assignments of the police—amount to progress toward democratic forms of policing. On the whole, many institutional reforms have been implemented, but success in implementing democratic control and accountability of the police has been relatively modest.

Generally, reforms to police systems in CEE have been slow in taking place, have lacked coherence, and usually have not been guided in practice by a systematic plan or strategy to address all related components, such as the criminal justice system. Although the idea of democratic policing has begun to make inroads regarding certain formal structures, the legal protections of rights, and declaratory statements of various political and policing figures, it has not yet effected fundamental change toward a service mentality among police officers, acceptance of the notion of policing by consent, public accountability, and external oversight. Many police organizations throughout the region remain strongly influenced by the Soviet model of policing. Policing systems remain largely centralized, and many have remained militaristic until very recently (e.g., in Hungary, Bulgaria, Macedonia, or Serbia). These policing structures still tend to display certain authoritarian tendencies and lack public trust and confidence, factors exacerbated by chronic underfunding and lack of effectiveness in combatting crime.

One explanation for the slow and sometimes superficial reforms to policing systems in the region is that governments may have been reluctant to bring in radical change when social, economic, and cultural changes have put additional pressure on criminal justice systems—that is, when crime is increasing. Fear of crime is prevalent in these societies, and growing crime rates often lead to public demands for a return to repressive approaches to crime and social control. The sociopolitical context in many post-communist societies is such that increasing crime rates and fear of crime have made the maintenance of order and cracking down on crime the highest priority, with less concern for maintaining respect for human rights and civil liberties and little sympathy for accused criminals and prisoners. The growth in crime rates also has served to reduce the incentives for implementing more vigorous oversight and control mechanisms. Instead, efforts to make the police more effective and efficient have taken precedence over making them more democratic. In some countries, such as Hungary, the police are viewed by some as having successfully used the wave of public concern about increasing criminality to take control of the reform process (Benke, 2001; Szikinger, 2000). In other words, the primary concern of the public in environments characterized by high crime and public insecurity appears to be community safety rather than democratic policing. The police in these countries have not been averse to using the growth in crime rates and heightened public fears of crime as a justification for protecting their institutional interests and to resist calls for greater transparency and accountability.

Much of the success of reforms can be attributed to international pressures promoting democratic forms of policing. Yet those pressures must be supported by a local political will and by the mentalities of the police themselves in order to be sustainable over the long run. In CEE states, political will and police mentalities have consistently fluctuated in legitimate responses to crime problems; political demands made on the government by a newly empowered civic society; the desire by the police to achieve a professional, semi-autonomous status; and the congruence of new democratic norms with societal expectations. In many ways, such fluctuations in reforming the police are not surprising, given their political enmeshment in societies undergoing profound changes and in which security concerns and the status and powers of the police are major political issues. As with politics and policing anywhere, the road to reform is strewn with obstacles that are context specific, and outcomes are uncertain, unclear, and unpredictable.

Notes

[1] Much of the information and the arguments made here are based on work done while on sabbatical leave in the fall of 2002. I had the good fortune to be associated with the Geneva Centre for the Democratic Control of Armed Forces (www.dcaf.ch) and wish to

thank DCAF for giving me that opportunity. I was given the opportunity to sit in on workshops and conferences on police, border management, and Security Sector Reform in CEE states and elsewhere; listen in on donor conferences; help organize a set of papers and assessments of police reforms; and meet many academics, practitioners, and consultants working in CEE countries. It was an exciting and educational sojourn.

[2] EU countries are not alone in assisting CEE states. The USA has been a major player in specific assistance programs, participation in reconstructing criminal justice systems in war-torn societies (as in Kosovo), and in establishing an International Law Enforcement Academy in Budapest, Hungary. ILEA-Budapest (there are three other ILEAs across the world) trains mid-ranking police officers from CEE states and Soviet Republics (Marenin, 1998a).

[3] The principles that have guided assistance and evaluations to CEE countries also apply to police reforms in EU states themselves. A case in point is recent efforts to restructure the Royal Ulster Constabulary in Northern Ireland into a new police service. These efforts exemplify the emergent principles which underlie current thinking on what reforms are needed to convert a repressive, nonrepresentative police force into one which serves the public within a multicultural, multisectarian society.

The Committee on the Administration of Justice (O'Rawe and Moore, 1997), after studying a variety of police forces and reform efforts, concluded that there is "no single ideal model of policing but there are many interesting lessons to be learned from other jurisdictions" (p.18). The report concludes that "any proposal for re-structuring policing must be tested by its ability to: put respect for human rights at the heart of policing, provide accountability," lead to a civilian rather than military orientation in training and practice, cooperate with other forces, and "secure a diverse and representative composition of police personnel (pp. 208–209).

In a similar vein, the Patten Commission (itself international in the composition of its members), tasked to develop recommendations for reforming the RUC, applied these five "tests" when considering proposals: "Does the proposal promote effective and efficient policing? Will it deliver fair and impartial policing, free from partisan control? Does it provide for accountability, both to the law and the community? Will it make the police more representative of the society they service? Does it protect and vindicate the human rights and human dignity of all?" (Independent Commission, 1999: pp. 5–6).

[4] Informative discussions of the meaning of democratic policing can be found in Amir and Einstein, 2001; Bayley, 2001, 1995; Call, 2003; Das and Marenin, 2000; Das and Palmiotto, 2002; Independent Commission, 1999; Law Commission, 2002; Marenin, 1998b; Neyroud and Beckley, 2001; O'Rawe and Moore, 1997; OSCE, 2002a; UN, 1997; UN, Mission to Bosnia-Herzegovina, 1996; U.S. Congress, 1996; and WOLA, 1999–2000.

[5] General descriptions of police reform efforts, and of the policing systems to be reformed, can be found in Benke, 2001; Boda, 2003; Caparini and Marenin, 2004; Dimovné, 2004; Finszter, 2001; Fogel, 1994; Gottlieb, et al. 1998; ICG, 2002; Jenks, et al. 2003; Kutjnak Ivkovich, 2000; Los and Zybertowicz, 2001; Mawby, 1996; OSCE, 2002b; OSCE Mission, 2001; Pagon, 1996, 1998, 2000, 2002; Plywaczewski, 2000; Szikinger, 2000; and Wisler and Bonvin, 2002.

[6] For example, Joszef Boda (2003), director of the International Training Centre in Budapest, Hungary, notes that supporters for maintaining an effective and strong police ". . . might have been relieved to find that brutality is not alien to policing in democracy, [rather than] lying in the mechanisms of dictatorship, and at times, it is even accepted as a necessary evil. If every now and then an abuse occurs, public opinion is extremely understanding. Reforms protecting fundamental liberties would weaken the democracy's ability to defend itself" (p. 12).

References

AEPC (Association of European Police Colleges) (2002). Project Europol 118. European Curriculum for Police Training in Central and Eastern European Countries. Groningen: AEPC.

Amir, Menachem and Stanley Einstein, eds. (2001). *Policing, Security and Democracy, Volume 1: Theory and Practice; Volume 2, Special Aspects of Democratic Policing*. Huntsville, TX: Sam Houston State University, Office of International Criminal Justice.

Andreas, Peter and Timothy Snyder, eds. (2000). *The Wall Around the West: State Borders and Immigration Controls in North America and Europe*. London: Rowman and Littlefield Publishers.

Apap, Joanna, ed. (2001). "Reshaping Europe's Borders: Challenge for EU Internal and External Policy." Report and Policy Recommendations from the Conference on New European Borders and Security Cooperation. "Promoting Trust in an Enlarged Union." Brussels: Centre for European Policy Studies (CEPS).

Bayley, D. H. (2001). *Democratizing the Police Abroad: What to Do and How to Do It*. Washington, D.C.: National Institute of Justice.

―――― (1995). "A Foreign Policy for Democratic Policing," *Policing and Society*, 5, 2, 79–94.

Benke, Miklos (2001). "Policing in Transition Countries Compared with Standards in the European Union: Hungary—Where Dreams are Not Fulfilled." In A. Kádár, ed., *Police in Transition: Essays on the Police Forces in Transition Countries*. Budapest: Central European University Press, 89–102.

Bigo, Didier (2000). "Liaison Officers in Europe: New Officers in the European Security Field." In J. W. E. Sheptycki, ed., *Issues in Transnational Policing*. London and New York: Routledge, 67–99.

Boda, Joszef (2003). "Transformation-Cooperation of Police in the Security Sector Reform Context." Paper presented at the SSR-Track Panel of the 6th Annual Conference of the PfP Consortium for Defense Academies and Security Studies Institutes, Berlin, 15–17 June, 2003. Available as occasional paper: http://www.dcaf.ch

Bort, Eberhard (2002). "Illegal Migration and Cross-Border Crime: Challenges at the Eastern Frontier of the European Union." In J. Zielonka, ed., *Europe Unbound: Enlarging and Reshaping the Boundaries of he European Union*. London: Routledge.

Call, Charles T. (2003). "Challenges in Police Reform: Promoting Effectiveness and Accountability," *IPA Policy Report*. New York: United Nations; see also www.ipacademy.org

Caparini, Marina (2002). "Lessons Learned and Upcoming Research Issues in Democratic Control of Armed Forces and Security Sector Reform." In H. Born, M. Caparini and P. Fluri (eds.), *Security Sector Reform and Democracy in Transitional Societies*. Baden-Baden: Nomos Verlagsgesellschaft, 207–216.

Caparini, Marina and Otwin Marenin, eds. (Forthcoming, 2004). *Transforming the Police in Eastern and Central Europe*. Somerset, NJ: Lit Verlag/Transaction: Münster, Germany/Transaction Publishers.

Council of Europe, European Committee on Crime Problems (2000). *Police Powers and Accountability in a Democratic Society: Proceedings*. Reports presented to the 12th Criminological Colloquium (1999). Strasbourg: Council of Europe; see also http://www.coe.fr/index.asp

Das, Dilip and Otwin Marenin, eds. (2000). *Challenges of Policing Democracies: A World Perspective*. Amsterdam: Gordon and Breach Publishers.

Das, Dilip and Michael J. Palmiotto (2002). "International Human Rights Standards: Guidelines for the World's Police Officers," *Police Quarterly*, 5, 2, 206–221.

Dimovné, Éva Keresztes (Forthcoming, 2004). "The Hungarian Police Reform." In Marina Caparini and Otwin Marenin, eds., *Transforming the Police in Eastern and Central Europe*. Somerset, NJ: Lit Verlag/Transaction: Münster, Germany/ Transaction Publishers.

European Union (EU). Available at http://www.europa.eu.int (accessed February 6, 2004).

EUROPOL. Available at http://www.europol.net (accessed February 6, 2004).

Finszter, Géza (2001). "The Political Changeover and the Police." In A. Kádár, ed., *Police in Transition: Essays on the Police Forces in Transition Countries*. Budapest: Central European University Press, 131–153.

Fogel, David, ed. (1994). *Policing in Central and Eastern Europe—Report of a Study Tour*. Helsinki: HEUNI.

Goldsmith, Andrew and Colleen Lewis, eds. (2000). *Civilian Oversight of Policing: Governance, Democracy and Human Rights*. Oxford-Portland, Oregon: Hart Publishing.

Gottlieb, Gerhard, Karoly Krözsel, and Bernhard Prestel (1998). *The Reform of the Hungarian Police: Processes, Methods, Results*. Holzkirchen, Germany: Felix Verlag.

Gregory, Frank (1994). "Unprecedented Partnerships in Crime Control: Law Enforcement Issues and Linkages Between Eastern and Western Europe Since 1989." In Malcolm Anderson and Monica den Boer, eds., *Policing Across National Boundaries*. London: Pinter Publishers, 85–105.

Grugel, Jean (1999). "Conclusion. Towards an Understanding of Transnational and Non-state Actors in Global Democratization." In J. Grugel, ed., *Democracy Without Borders: Transnationalization and Conditionality in New Democracies*. London and New York: Routledge, ECPR Studies in European Political Science, 157–164.

Haberfeld, M. R. (1997). "Poland: The Police Are Not the Public and the Public are Not the Police," *Policing: An International Journal of Police Strategies and Management*, 20, 641–654.

Haberfeld, M., C. B. Klockars, S. Kutjnak Ivkovich, and M. Pagon (2000). "Police Officer Perceptions of the Disciplinary Consequences of Police Corruption in Croatia, Poland, Slovenia, and the United States," *International Journal of Police Practice and Research*, 1, 1, 34–51.

Hebenton, Bill and Terry Thomas (1995). *Policing Europe: Co-operation, Conflict and Control*. New York: St. Martin's Press.

Huisman, Sander (2002). "Transparency and Accountability of Police Forces, Security Services and Intelligence Agencies (TAPAS): A Comparative Assessment of the Effectiveness of Existing Arrangements in Seven Countries: Bulgaria, France, Italy, Poland, Sweden, the United Kingdom and the United States of America." Groningen: Centre for European Security Studies.

ICG (International Crisis Group) (2002). *Policing the Police in Bosnia: A Further Reform Agenda*. Balkans Report No. 130, Sarajewo/Brussels: ICG. Available at www.crisisweb.org (accessed February 6, 2004).

ICHRP (International Council on Human Rights Policy) (2003). *Crime, Public Order and Human Rights*. Draft report for consultation March 2003. Geneva: ICHRP.

Independent Commission on Policing for Northern Ireland (Patten Commission) (1999). *A New Beginning: Policing in Northern Ireland*. Available at www.belfast.org.uk/report/chapter02.pdf (accessed February 6, 2004).

Jenks, David, Michael Costelloe, and Christopher Krebs (2003). "After the Fall: Czech Police in a Post-Communist Era," *International Criminal Justice Review*, 13, 90–109.

Kádár, A., ed. (2001). *Police in Transition: Essays on the Police Forces in Transition Countries*. Budapest: Central European University Press.

Krémer, Ferenc (2000). "Comparing Supervisor and Line Officer Opinions about the Code of Silence: The Case of Hungary." In Milan Pagon, ed., *Policing in Central and Eastern Europe: Ethics, Integrity and Human Rights*. Ljubljana: College of Police and Security Studies, 211–219.

Kremplewski, Andrzej (2001). "The Police and Non-Governmental Organizations in Poland." In A. Kádár, ed., *Police in Transition: Essays on the Police Forces in Transition Countries*. Budapest: Central European University Press, 203–219.

Kutjnak Ivkovich, Sanja (2000). "Challenges of Policing Democracies: The Croatian Experience." In Dilip K. Das and Otwin Marenin, eds., *Challenges of Policing Democracies: A World Perspective*. Amsterdam: Gordon and Breach Publishers, 45–85.

——— (Forthcoming, 2004). "Distinct and Different: The Transformation of the Croatian Police." In Marina Caparini and Otwin Marenin, eds., *Transforming the Police in Eastern and Central Europe*. Somerset, NJ: Lit Verlag/Transaction: Münster, Germany/Transaction Publishers.

Kutjnak Ivkovich, Sanja and Carl B. Klockars (1998). "The Code of Silence and the Croatian Police." In Milan Pagon, ed., *Policing in Central and Eastern Europe: Organizational, Managerial, and Human Resource Aspects*. Ljubljana: College of Police and Security Studies, 329–347.

Law Commission of Canada (2002). *In Search of Security: The Roles of the Public Police and Private Agencies*. Ottawa: Law Commission of Canada. Available at www.lcc.gc.ca/en/index.asp (accessed February 6, 2004).

Los, Maria (1988). *Communist Ideology, Law and Crime*. London: Palgrave MacMillan.

Los, Maria and Andrzej Zybertowicz (2001). *Privatizing the Police State: The Case of Poland*. London: Palgrave Macmillan.

Lundberg, K. (1993). "The Czech Republic: Police Reform in a New Democracy." Cambridge, MA: Harvard University, Kennedy School of Government, Case Report.

Marenin, Otwin (1998a). "From IPA to ILEA: Change and Continuity in United States' International Police Training Programs," *Police Quarterly*, 1, 4, 93–126.

——— (1998b). "The Goal of Democracy in International Police Assistance Programs," *Policing: An International Journal of Police Strategies and Management*, 21, 1, 159–177.

Mawby, Rob (1996). "Comparative Research on Police Practices in England, Germany, Poland and Hungary." In Milan Pagon, ed., *Policing in Central and Eastern Europe: Comparing Firsthand Knowledge with Experience from the West*. Ljubljana: College of Police and Security Studies, 473–485.

Mendes, Errol P., Joaquin Zuckerberd, Susan Lecorre, Anne Gabriel, and Jeffrey A. Clark, eds. (1999). *Democratic Policing and Accountability: Global Perspectives*. Aldershot: Ashgate.

MEPA [Central European Police Academy]. Available at www.mepa.net (accessed February 6, 2004).

Mlicki, Pavel P. (2001). "Police Cooperation with Central Europe: The Dutch Case." In Daniel J. Koenig and Dilip K. Das, eds., *International Police Cooperation: A World Perspective*. Lanham, MA: Lexington Books, 217–228.

Neyroud, Peter and Alan Beckley (2001). *Policing, Ethics and Human Rights*. Cullompton, Devon: Willan Publishing.

Nogala, Detlef (2001). "Policing Across a Dimorphous Border: Challenges and Innovation at the French-German Border," *European Journal of Crime, Criminal Law and Criminal Justice,* 9, 2, 130–143.

Occnipinti, John D. (2003). *The Politics of EU Police Cooperation: Toward a European FBI?* Boulder: Lynne Rienner.

O'Rawe, M. and L. Moore (1997). *Human Rights on Duty: Principles for Better Policing—International Lessons for Northern Ireland.* Belfast: Committee for the Administration of Justice.

OSCE (Organization of Security and Co-Operation in Europe). Available at http://www.osce.org (accessed February 6, 2004).

OSCE (2002a). "Council of Europe and OSCE Joint Final Report on Police Accountability in Serbia." First Draft, Strasbourg: Co-operation programme to strengthen the rule of law, September 10. Report written by John Slater and Harm Trip.

——— (2002b). "Project Proposal for Police Reform, Republic of Serbia." Sponsorship Conference, June 5, 2002. Belgrade: Law Enforcement Department, OSCE Mission to FRY.

OSCE Mission in FRY (2001). "Study on Policing in the Federal Republic of Yugoslavia." Available at www.osce.org/yugoslavia (accessed February 6, 2004).

Pagon, Milan, ed. (1996). *Policing in Central and Eastern Europe: Comparing Firsthand Knowledge with Experience from the West.* Ljubljana: College of Police and Security Studies.

——— (1998). *Policing in Central and Eastern Europe: Organizational, Managerial, and Human Resource Aspects.* Ljubljana: College of Police and Security Studies.

——— (2000). *Policing in Central and Eastern Europe: Ethics, Integrity and Human Rights.* Ljubljana: College of Police and Security Studies.

——— (2002). *Policing in Central and Eastern Europe: Deviance, Violence, and Victimization.* Ljubljana: College of Police and Security Studies.

Perez, Thomas E. (2000). "External Governmental Mechanisms of Police Accountability: Three Investigative Structures," *Policing and Society,* 10, 1, 47–77.

Perito, Robert (2004). *Where Is the Lone Ranger When We Need Him? America's Search for a Postconflict Stability Force.* Washington, D.C.: United States Institute of Peace Press.

PHARE. Available at http://europa.eu.int/comm/enlargement/pas/phare/index.htm

Plywaczewski, Emil (2000). "The Challenges of Policing Democracy in Poland." In Dilip K. Das and Otwin Marenin, eds., *Challenges of Policing Democracies: A World Perspective.* Amsterdam: Gordon and Breach Publishers, 43–172.

Plywaczewski, Emil and Piotr Walancik (Forthcoming, 2004). "The Challenges and Changes of the Police System in Poland." In Marina Caparini and Otwin Marenin, eds., *Transforming the Police in Eastern and Central Europe.* Somerset, NJ: Lit Verlag/Transaction: Münster, Germany/Transaction Publishers.

Schengen. Available at www.eurovisa.info/SchengenCountries.htm (accessed February 6, 2004).

Shelley, Louise (1984). *Lawyers in Soviet Work Life.* Brunswick, NJ: Rutgers University Press.

Stone, C. E. and H. Ward (2000). "Democratic Policing: A Framework for Action," *Policing and Society,* 10, 11–45.

Szikinger, Istvan (2000). "The Challenge of Policing Democracy in Hungary." In Dilip K. Das and Otwin Marenin, eds., *Challenges of Policing Democracies: A World Perspective.* Amsterdam: Gordon and Breach Publishers, 115–141.

United Nations, Mission in Bosnia-Herzegovina, International Police Task Force, Sarajevo (1996). "Commissioner's Guidance for Democratic Policing in the Federation of Bosnia-Herzegovina," mimeo.

United Nations (1997). *Human Rights and Law Enforcement: A Manual on Human Rights Training for the Police. Professional Training Series No. 5.* Geneva: High Commissioner for Human Rights, Centre for Human Rights. Sales No. E.96.XIV.5.

United States Congress (1996). "Democracy, Rule of Law and Police Training Assistance." Hearing before the Committee on International Relations, House of Representatives, 100th Congress, First Session, Washington, D.C.: GPO.

Wisler, Dominique and Blaise Bonvin (2002). "Victimization in Bosnia and Herzegovina: Lessons for Police Training Reform." In Milan Pagon, ed., *Policing in Central and Eastern Europe: Deviance, Violence, and Victimization.* Ljubljana: College of Police and Security Studies, 479–504.

WOLA (Washington Office on Latin America) (1999–2000). *Themes and Debates on Public Security Reform: A Manual for Civil Society.* Washington, D.C.: WOLA. (This is a series of seven pamphlets on various aspects of reform. The focus is mainly on Latin and Central America and the Caribbean.)

13

The Prospects for Democratic Policing in the Third World
The Mauritian Model

Frederick P. Roth

The prospects for democracy in underdeveloped countries and for the establishment of democratic police agencies assigned to protect democratic institutions have seldom been less encouraging. Monetary resources in West and Central African states, for instance, are being squandered by widespread corruption and civil conflicts fueled by tribal and religious enmities. The violence that accompanied apartheid in South Africa has now been transformed into random criminal violence. Organized urban street gangs have forged links with international crime syndicates and are challenging the stability of a fragile democracy (Thompson, 2003). A dispirited Afghan people seek first and foremost the restoration of order provided by basic police services as predatory bandits and ethnic warlords have resumed pillaging (Bearak, 2003). The collapse of security in Iraq has spawned looting, banditry, and random violence, threatening destabilization and encouraging political fragmentation. Drug cartels in the Andean republics of South America have merged with anti-government guerilla movements to frustrate democratic aspirations. The appeal of religious orthodoxy has persuaded many of the disenfranchised that Western secular solutions to underdevelopment are irrelevant. Moreover, the demise of cold war "clientleism" (a style of redistributive politics) and the intensification of globalization have made the struggle to sustain democratic practices even more precarious for Third World nations.

The effort to understand the perils of establishing a Third World democracy and the security forces committed to its preservation has proceeded with little guidance from the police literature. In this regard the problem is both practical and theoretical. Attempting to establish contacts

Prepared especially for *Comparative and International Criminal Justice, 2/E.*

with government and police administrators and overcoming bureaucratic obstacles and suspicion is enormously expensive and time consuming. Consequently, there are relatively few studies of Third World police agencies, and little is known about policing in underdeveloped nations. The lack of theoretical reflections accounting for the various forms of policing that might result in developing several models commensurate with the social context that shapes the police institution, however, is more troubling. When confronted with the failure to explain why and how nation-states adopt similar or dissimilar police systems many criminologists merely acknowledge the diversity and eschew any attempt at analysis (Reichel, 1994:179). Recently, for example, Bayley (1999: 3–4) echoed the sentiments of many when he asserted that ". . . any classification scheme [of police practices] is bound to be limited, superficial, arbitrary, and problematic."

Sufficient resources and a commitment to the comparative study of crime and social control should suffice to rectify the knowledge deficit of policing in Third World nations. The absence of a theoretical architecture, however, to explain variable patterns of policing leads ineluctably to analytical inconsistency and makes policy initiatives vulnerable to error. As a corrective, an analysis of the evolution of democratic policing as it was enacted in Western liberal democracies is a useful point of departure. The model of democratic policing in these societies can serve as a comparative template for the prospects of establishing similar forms of institutional social control elsewhere.

The Western Model of Democratic Policing: The United States

The development of modern democratic policing in the United States was a by-product of the capitalist accumulation brought on by the Industrial Revolution that rationalized production, disrupted an agrarian social organization, and set in motion a breathtaking rate of social change. By mid-century, when professional policing was implemented in American cities, community social controls were strained by secularization and complexity as industrialization deepened. Although the cornerstone of democratic policing was the rule of law, the most pervasive theme of nineteenth-century American social control was the attempt to discipline social life, especially in the lower-class communities that formed the backbone of an emerging industrial labor force. As Monkonnen (1981) points out, the central task of the new professional police was the orderly functioning of cities, a mandate that markedly featured the regulation of the "dangerous classes." Most notably, this involved the restraint of the recreational habits, petty violence, and moral turpitude of lower-class citizens, a strategy Monkonnen (1981) refers to as "class-control" policing.

Although American police forces would continue to pursue a class-control pattern of policing throughout the nineteenth century, its form would be modified commensurate with the shift to industrial capitalism from small-scale mercantile capitalism. This transition entailed a fundamental transformation between labor and capital and required different forms of institutional social control to ensure the stability of capitalist relations. The composite portrait of democratic policing, therefore, is one intimately associated with the growth of American capitalism, an essential link to social organization that gives the changing face of American policing theoretical substance.

By 1848, when New York City inaugurated the first professional police force (Richardson, 1970), the rural character of America had been diminishing rapidly. Household manufacturing began to decline after 1815 wherever steamboats or railroads made the products of domestic and foreign manufacturers available. Beginning in 1820 and lasting till the outbreak of the Civil War, every Eastern state experienced an "urban take-off" fueled by the steady growth of manufacturing enterprise (Bruchey, 1990:149, 157). Nineteenth-century industrial development was made possible by the combined labor of native rural workers and an unprecedented influx of impoverished Irish immigrants. Employment in the mills and factories was casual, unskilled, poorly compensated, and most importantly, transient (Thernstrom, 1975; Jacoby, 1985), similar in many ways to the "floating" population of impoverished rural vagabonds uprooted by the advent of capitalism in Western Europe (Braudel, 1979). The nature of factory work was impersonal and insecure, producing substantial unruliness in American cities and industrial towns. In addition to public drunkenness, vagrancy, and disorderly conduct, assaults on ordinary citizens by organized bands of thugs had, by mid-century, become so commonplace in urban spaces as to create "a virtual epidemic of violence and disorder" (Steinberg, 1989:135).

Class-Control Policing

Clearly, the problem of order maintenance was a defining characteristic of early nineteenth-century urban life. Yet because the working class lacked consciousness of its common plight and failed to focus on its unprotected status, the disorder was unstructured and posed no threat to an ascendant capitalism. Since a mode of production dominated by a marginalized labor force seldom expressed itself in organized and protracted civil disturbances, the chief objectives of policing were to supervise lower-class communities, inhibit random disorder, and contain disreputable conduct. This pattern of regulation might be referred to as *intermittent proactive class-control policing* characterized by considerable, but irregular, involvement in minor public-order offenses. During this period, the control of crimes against persons and property, while not abandoned altogether, was of a lesser priority.

Even as metropolitan policing was becoming more common, from about 1850 to 1875, the ground beneath capitalist enterprise in America was shifting. In the decades straddling the Civil War, small craft shops, commercial establishments, and light industry were the most prevalent forms of entrepreneurial activity, often in the form of individual propri- etorships or partnerships requiring little capitalization. Although corporate structures and the factory system began to appear in the 1850s they did not yet represent the defining character of American capitalism. Small- scale enterprise dominated an American economy, a competitive capital- ism that required low- or semi-skilled labor without mediating institutions to negotiate working conditions. The typical small manufacturing business was operated by skilled craftsmen who were able to expand the volume of production per worker by instructing semi-skilled and immigrant workers in new production processes, and to delegate profits to materials (Bruchey, 1990). These structured relations, minimal skill levels, and regular wage employment differentiated this more mature capitalist social organization from the casual nature of the earlier mercantile mode of production.

As the self-concept of the working class became that of wage earners rather than potential entrepreneurs, the aim of social control shifted toward the creation of a disciplined and subordinate core of workers and the establishment of institutional hegemony. In part, this purpose was accomplished by a paternalistic organization of the workplace (Reich & Gordon, 1975; Edwards, 1979). The police, however, adopting what might best be described as *routine proactive class-control policing*, also had a role to play. The claim of legitimate authority based on impartial enforcement caused the police to eschew coercive measures that might encourage chal- lenges to that claim and promote instabilities in the accommodation between the police and the public. Instead, a protocol of surveillance was established that targeted suspect populations, intervening as circum- stances dictated.

To assure social integration, the preferred strategy was to conduct fewer arrests rather than maintain a forceful presence. The consequent pat- tern of policing consisted of moderate but diminishing prosecutions for petty public-order crimes and an augmented, but still negligible, concern for more serious criminal felonies. The police also contended with an increasing number of civil disturbances during this period, but "boom and bust" economic cycles that weakened labor-organizing efforts and the dis- ruption of the Civil War caused such events to be episodic (Raybeck, 1966).

Regulatory restraint, however, could not countenance the rapid growth of corporate industrial enterprise. Between the end of the Civil War and the outbreak of World War I, concentration became the hallmark of American capitalism. New production techniques contributed to the estab- lishment of new forms of industrial organization that reduced competition, increased the size of manufacturing firms, and engendered a contest with labor for control of the workplace. In areas where heavy industrial enter- prise took root, especially in the manufacturing cities of the Trans-Appala- chian region, labor-capital conflict was particularly acute and police were often called on to suppress militant worker resistance (Harring, 1983). In the initial stages of the corporate integration, the policing strategy could be characterized as *aggressive proactive class-control policing.* Collective protests, labor actions, and other forms of civil disturbances became markers of an intense mobilization for social justice. To restore order and nullify agitation, police intervention often took the form of paramilitary maneuvers, undercover tactics, and other coercive measures. Some of this ferment invariably spilled over into community routines, and police patrols in working-class neighborhoods became more alert for suspicious deviations from conventional behavior. The coercive policing of class conflict therefore also entailed increasing arrest rates for minor public-order crimes and limited enforcement of criminal felonies against persons and property.

Crime-Control Policing

Gradually, as labor's representatives were enfranchised, resources were reallocated in accordance with a new matrix of influence, and class conflict was eased by institutionalized power sharing, a crime-control pattern of policing emerged that resembled modern police practices (Monkonnen, 1981; Harring, 1983). An ideology of legitimacy, neutrality, and accountability embodied by the "rule of law" replaced the violent suppression of class relations, a strategy that might be identified as *routine reactive crime-control policing.* A stable accommodation allowed the police to disengage from contentious civil disturbances, devote less attention to public-order offenses, and focus instead on violent and larcenous threats to public safety.

The model of democratic policing in the United States represents a definitive pattern. When first established, the police organization was primarily concerned with maintaining orderly urban social relations to the relative exclusion of its obligation to prevent serious criminal felonies (*intermittent proactive class control*). During the latter part of the nineteenth century, the police were increasingly implicated in controlling the dangerous classes by the constant monitoring of public order (*routine proactive class control*) and, as class conflict became more manifest, by the naked expression of force (*aggressive proactive class control*). In both instances, reflecting its more narrowly specified duties, there was greater involvement by the police in crime control. When, by the turn of the century, the social relations of production stabilized and the capitalist class accommodated itself to a newly enfranchised labor movement, the contours of modern democratic policing were clearly evident, with a focus on criminal felonies and traffic control (*routine reactive crime control*).

The question that arises is whether the Western evolutionary model of democratic policing has any relevance for such a development in underdeveloped countries. While most Third World democratic institutions are fragile and social control often involves extra-legal measures, that question is best answered by identifying underdeveloped nations where capitalist economic development has flourished and the commitment to democratic practices and institutions is longstanding. The Indian Ocean republic of Mauritius exemplifies the development trajectory that corresponds, more or less faithfully, to the evolution of Western economic development. As such, it represents a potential path for democracies in underdeveloped countries where, without advantages or resources, a liberal democratic infrastructure and capitalist economy can be created based on democratic social control. The origins of the Mauritian model are located in the colonial legacy and the distinctive way the social and economic objectives of imperialism shaped the formal agencies of social control.

The Colonial Period of Mauritius: The Roots of Democracy

The island of Mauritius, at 720 square miles approximately the size of Rhode Island, is located some 500 miles east of Madagascar in the Indian Ocean. Originally uninhabited, settlement of the island began in earnest with the arrival of the French in 1721. Under French guardianship, the urban infrastructure and harbor facilities in Port Louis were established, access roads to the interior were constructed, and, most importantly, a sugar plantation economy was founded.

Presided over by an affluent Franco-Mauritian oligarchy, the social organization of the plantocracy and the colony's prosperity depended on forced African slave labor. By the early nineteenth century, the demographic features of Mauritian society reflected the distinctive contours of a feudal society. The island nation's population consisted of a small elite of wealthy white planters, an equal number of free colored, and a substantial majority of disenfranchised African slaves (Kuczynski, 1949:758).

Within the context of the Napoleonic wars, French dominion in the Indian Ocean became an irritant to an expanding British hegemony in the region. Considered a strategic resource, British imperialists determined to control the island to provide a safe harbor and protect British merchant vessels from French privateers operating in Mauritian waters. In 1810, a British amphibious force advanced overland to Port Louis where the French garrison, surprised and outnumbered, capitulated. The terms of surrender, however, were quite generous. The French planters were permitted to retain their property and the laws, religion, customs, and language of the local settlers received legal protections. Therefore, while the British formally administered Mauritius, the island remained French in manner and substance and the feudal social organization remained intact. Nevertheless, from that time forth Mauritius became an important colonial outpost in the region serving as a link between the British interests in southern Africa and the Indian subcontinent.

The feudal social organization was briefly disrupted when, in 1835, the British administration formally abolished the slave trade, forcing Mauritian planters to seek a source of cheap labor elsewhere. Within a short time, however, a system of indentured labor was instituted drawing primarily from the most impoverished areas of India. Beginning in the late 1830s, a substantial importation of indentured Indian laborers made Mauritius one of the leading sugar producers in the world. By 1866, about 340,000 Indian workers had immigrated to Mauritius to harvest the sugar crop laboring under conditions equal to the worst excesses of American slavery (Bowman, 1991: 20–22). This wave of Indian immigrants not only altered the demographic composition of the population but also stabilized a feudal social organization.

The demise of feudalism was precipitated by two developments that gradually marked the shift to a class-based stratification system. The first of these was known as *le grand morcellement,* or "the great breakup." Toward the end of the nineteenth century, declining prices and a more competitive global market for sugar compelled many wealthy planters to sell off some of their less profitable plots. Almost without exception, the land was purchased by Indian laborers who as overseers or job contractors had managed to acquire a small amount of capital. In the following decades, many of these immigrants prospered, forming a native Indian middle class that would ultimately challenge the political authority of the white propertied class (Carter, 1995).

Of equal significance was the emergence in the first half of the twentieth century of communal civic associations and a potentially potent trade-union movement. During the first three decades of the century, working-class aspirations found expression under the leadership of an increasingly educated Creole and Indian professional class. The demand for a greater share in the political and economic life of the nation culminated in a series of riots, violence, and labor unrest during the 1930s. Subsequently, trade and civic unions became a fixture of the Mauritian political process, constituting the core of the ruling Mauritius Labor Party. By 1948, the oligarchy's control of the political process was beginning to unravel in the wake of a new Constitution that permitted universal suffrage, which guaranteed that eventually political power would shift to the Indian majority.

In 1968, as the British prepared to withdraw, the Indo-Mauritian majority, under the banner of the Labor Party, was poised to wrest political power from the Franco-Mauritian planter class. Although the oligarchy retained economic influence, control of the institutional infrastructure was assumed by the Labor Party representing, in effect, a transfer of authority to a liberal bourgeoisie state (akin to a similar shift that occurred earlier in Western democracies). The final arrangement reflected a mutually convenient compromise: the white planter class would be assured proprietary rights to its estates while the Hindu majority would control the instruments of government. The Labor Party could thus be confident that the estates would continue to provide revenues and a source of labor while the oligarchy would rely on the Indian-dominated government to preserve public order and guarantee labor peace. Most important, however, the labor unions, sugar cane workers, and the Hindu middle class constituted the Labor Party and the base of an institutionalized civil society. This meant that feudal social relations had shifted to a social organization prepared to accept the discipline of industrial capitalism. Policing the new emergent social organization required a shift in strategy that was reflected in the shape of its institutional mandate. Official data sources and interviews conducted with current and retired police officers in the last half of 1999 provide a substantive account of the transformation.

Independence: Organized Resistance

During the global economic crisis of the 1930s, working-class discontent and the failure of the oligarchy and colonial officials to acknowledge the injustices of the feudal social organization culminated in a succession of riots and strikes. From July to September of 1937 plantations were set ablaze, communications were disrupted, pickets impeded normal work schedules, and violence left several dead and injured. The violence resulted in a series of ordinances that specified health and nutritional standards for workers, made mandatory the payment of cash wages, and, most importantly, legalized the right to unionize. Following another series of strikes and violence in 1943, the Mauritius Agricultural Laborers' Association and the Engineering and Technical Workers Union emerged as the most prominent trade unions, each intimately linked to the Labor Party. With its core support among the sugar cane workers, the Labor Party also extended its appeal to the predominantly Creole stevedores effectively consolidating both the urban and rural working class. By the time independence was declared in 1968, the most important sectors of the working class enjoyed protected status, and its interests were ably represented by the Labor Party. The central feature of the sugar industry, however, was that cultivation was seasonal in nature and could not absorb the labor of an expanding number of job applicants. Therefore, because the Mauritian economy remained solely dependent on sugar production, a large component of the labor force was chronically unemployed.

Consequently, the tensions inherent in holding together a largely unemployed rural agrarian society and a civil society divided along communal alliances began to unravel under the pressure of fashioning an independent republic. Prior to the proclamation of independence, ten days of sectarian violence between Muslims and Creoles erupted, leaving hundreds injured and 25 dead, forcing thousands of people to flee their homes, and ultimately requiring British troops to restore order (Simmons, 1982:186–188). As one former police officer recalls, the ethnic friction overwhelmed the ability of the police to contain it and threatened to evolve into civil conflict:

(M-4)[1] When independence was granted by the British the lights went off and there was conflict. Big conflict! . . . they [minority ethnic communities] knew that those people [the Hindu majority] would outnumber them and whatever they do, there wouldn't be any umpire or referee to say this is wrong, don't do that. . . . In Abercrombie and in Plaine Verte [Port Louis neighborhoods], the Muslims would fight the Creoles. There was a lot of killing. This is when the British came to Mauritius to establish order because we were on the verge of having a civil war. . . . It lasted about 4 months. The police started to control it but they couldn't do anything about it. We didn't have the kind of training needed. So that's when the British came on two occasions, the paramilitary forces, and they put down those disturbances.

Shortly after British forces withdrew, Mauritius was ravaged by a series of debilitating strikes fomented by a powerful labor union movement, some of whose leaders employed their organizations as a vehicle for their political aspirations. Between September and December 1971, a number of strikes sponsored by a radical new party, the Mouvement Militant Mauricien (MMM), disrupted the public transport, sugar, shipping, public service, and electricity sectors of the economy, forcing the government to declare a state of emergency (Bowman, 1991:72–73).

(M-6) . . . we [the police] were called to prevent illegal picketing—when some want to come to work and are prevented from doing so. We were also asked to protect property and prevent sabotage. The electrical workers, I remember, blew up substations and supply lines. There was never any labor peace at this time.

(M-4) In the 1970s, that was when the dockworkers went on strike. The syndicate prompted them to go on strike. This paralyzed the whole area, and merchandise coming from other parts of the world had to be left in a new island because they couldn't be left in Mauritius. We ran out of stock of milk and rice. So we [the police] were ordered to unload the dock. They thought you could just force the government to do whatever they wanted because they were handling the lifeblood of the country. And so the government had to give in to their demands because they knew that we had to ship our sugar.

Overwhelmed by constant ethnic violence and labor strife, in 1972 the government invoked the Public Order Act, declared a state of emergency, and cancelled the election that was to have taken place in 1973. The causes of these civil disturbances were not difficult to fathom. Clearly, the fear among the minority sectors of political and economic exclusion explains much of the communal violence that occurred. Most of the civil disorder, however, was aggravated by the critical state of the Mauritian economy. In 1968, reflecting a decline in world sugar prices, the gross domestic product (GDP) plummeted by 7% (World Bank, 1989). A 29% unemployment rate, inadequate wage scales, inflationary prices for goods and services, and population growth of about 3% per annum promoted a national mood of despair and fueled the violence and disorder (Alladin, 1993:104; Brautigam, 1999:142).

Beginning in 1972, however, economic prospects suddenly reversed course. Buoyed by a fortuitous increase in the price of sugar, conditions conspired to produce three successive years of superior crop yields (Bowman, 1991:116). The multiplier effect of this bounty was virtually instantaneous. Jobs were created, construction projects were initiated, domestic savings increased, investment growth in other economic sectors revived, and unemployment rates declined to about 15% (Alladin, 1993). Yet it was becoming increasingly obvious that consistent economic growth would have to be based on economic diversity and could not rely on this sort of anomalous productivity yield.

The MEPZ: Industrial Transformation

Government officials were astute enough to realize that sustainable development could not rest solely on a single-crop economy. As part of a long-term development strategy, therefore, the Mauritian government created the Mauritius Export Processing Zone (MEPZ) in 1971, offering incentives to investors in exchange for establishing labor-intensive export manufacturing enterprises. Despite international recession and rising energy costs during the 1970s, investment growth in the MEPZ was robust. The number of operating firms taking advantage of the generous terms of the program rose from 10 in 1971 to 85 by 1976, mostly small-scale textile manufacturing enterprises (Bowman, 1991). During the 1980s, the growth of the MEPZ was nothing short of extraordinary. By 1990, the number of MEPZ operations had risen to 574 (Ministry of Industry and Industrial Technology, 1991). By 1987, the MEPZ had assumed a greater sectoral share of the nation's GDP than sugar production and its contribution was double what sugar accounted for (Ministry of Economic Development, Productivity, and Regional Development, 1999).

The success of the MEPZ also helped the government solve the problem of unemployment caused by 10,000 annual entrants into the nation's labor pool and the fact that most of the available jobs "were unskilled and poorly paid, and many workers . . . were only seasonally or irregularly employed" (Bowman, 1991:114). In 1968 almost half (48.7%) of the total labor force was engaged in agricultural production, but that percentage has undergone a steady erosion, commensurate with the growth of the MEPZ (Ministry of Economic Development, Productivity, and Regional Development, 1999). By 1992, agricultural sector employment fell to 15% of the workforce, a 19% decrease from the previous 12 years with projections that "the attrition rate for this sector which is higher than the rest of the economy will increase further" (Ministry of Economic Development and Regional Cooperation, 1997:14). By 1995, as the MEPZ absorbed a

greater share of the available labor force, employment in the agricultural
sector diminished further as predicted to 13.7% of the total labor force,
almost half of what it had been in 1970 (Ministry of Economic Planning
and Development, 1996:114).

The so-called "Mauritian miracle," the transformation of the economy
from an agrarian society into a first-stage industrial mode of production,
was shaped by several factors with implications for formal social control.
When it became apparent that the MEPZ would be successful, the state
took measures to ensure investors of an inexpensive and compliant workforce by inhibiting legitimate organizing among MEPZ workers. The Industrial Relations Act of 1973 created a bifurcated labor force where the terms
of employment pertaining to unionized workers were subject to collective
bargaining while those for workers in the MEPZ industries were governed
by legislative enactment. The same arrangement that was so successful in
attracting the necessary capital to construct an industrial infrastructure
also discouraged MEPZ workers from petitioning for union representation.
To the present, labor relations in the MEPZ and in the manufacturing sector in general have remained unprotected except for some welfare benefits
and minimum wage standards established by the government.

Moreover, the diversity of firms in the MEPZ according to size has
remained relatively stable since the early 1980s. An analysis of the size of
manufacturing enterprise in the MEPZ suggests that there is a disproportionate clustering of small-scale operations. From 1982 through 1990,
most of the manufacturing enterprises in the MEPZ employed fewer than
100 employees. Of the 118 MEPZ firms operating in 1982, 65 (54%) corresponded to this category. The most pronounced growth during this
period occurred among those firms employing 10–50 employees (Ministry
of Industry and Industrial Technology, 1991:64). By 1997, MEPZ firms
tended to concentrate among those employing between 10 and 50 workers, and those whose labor force constituted fewer than 100 employees
represented 70% of the total (Ministry of Economic Development, Productivity, and Regional Development, 1999:62). The scale of the enterprise,
the minor skill levels of those employed, and the absence of negotiated
protections marked the formation of an industrial labor force that exhib-
ited similar characteristics to those of the working class that arose in the
early stages of the Industrial Revolution in the United States.

Meanwhile, despite the legacy of unionization among important segments of the Mauritian working class, a strong union presence began to
wane in the later post-independence period. By the 1980s, union membership among sugar workers, reflecting the concentration and mechaniza-
tion of production and the shift of capital from agriculture to
manufacturing, was only a fraction of what it had been a decade earlier.
Mechanical improvements at the harbor similarly had resulted in a
reduced workforce and diminished the prominence of the once powerful
stevedore's union. Furthermore, after the labor turmoil of the early 1970s,

the state made a concerted effort to integrate the leadership of the more prominent unions institutionalizing a consultative role and absorbing the leading figures under a state corporatist umbrella.

For some workers, the restructuring forced them to seek employment in the unprotected MEPZ and ancillary manufacturing firms. Others found work in the expanding tourism sector. For many, however, the only choice was casual or seasonal employment (mostly as laborers in the sugar cane fields) coupled with prolonged periods of enforced idleness. In effect, as organized labor's influence has waned, the dominant structure of the new industrial mode of production has taken on a cast reminiscent of the early stages of competitive industrial capitalism in the West. This has important implications for the police in mediating class relations. Where the social context involves an unprotected industrial labor force, the central objective is to construct an ideological consensus in support of a capitalist social organization—so that, concerning public order offenses, policing relies less on arrests, and petty disorders receive moderate but diminishing attention. To the extent that workers are compliant and labor peace is assured, the police are free to concentrate more of their resources toward establishing their legitimacy by focusing on the prevention and apprehension of criminal felonies.

By the end of the 1970s, much of the energy expended on civil disturbances had dissipated. The Hindu-led Labor Party had not trampled on the rights of ethnic minority communities and labor unions had accepted a benevolent state-corporatist arrangement in exchange for meaningful consultation on labor issues. The friction and violence that is so much a part of labor-capital relations came to be stabilized by the late 1970s, when it was generally acknowledged that a pluralist society like Mauritius would be better served by constructing a consensus through a process of accommodation. From that time forward, policy initiatives were subject to a process of consultations and discussions prior to implementation. This system of public consent reduced political and ethnic tensions, and no longer made it necessary for the police to concentrate its resources and priorities on the regulation of civil disturbances.

> (M-4) This violent period went off and on for approximately a five-year period. After that, it sort of reduced in importance. It was all over by 1980. There were isolated disturbances of a political nature after that but not as important as those we mentioned. These were sporadic outbreaks.

Many of the civil disturbances that did occur were neither well organized nor a threat to the capitalist social relations of production. Instead they tended to be short-lived, revolving around a single parochial grievance. The consensus regarding the legitimacy of the social relations of production and the state corporatist organization that came to institutionalize conflict generally tended to confine such outbreaks to impulsive agitations originating from some perceived problem. The police also were required to attend to such events, but the immediate objective in these instances was to disperse the assembly and restore order as quickly as possible. In the absence of any alternative ideological commitment or a meaningful change strategy this was usually all that was required.

> (M-19) There have not been serious disturbances. When I joined the force [1992], I was assigned to Fanfaron—you know, near the harbor. I knew many of the stevedores. During my time there were no serious disturbances. Maybe minor incidents. The same at the EPZ. There were some minor incidents but no violence. When we are called we go but it doesn't turn into turmoil.

> (M-21) For many years the people who live along the road are requesting a flyover to cross the road safely. So recently when two people died in an accident the people blamed the government for the accident. . . .
> People were very excited by the time the police got there. When we arrived, there were about 500 people collected. . . . They blocked the road and started throwing stones. They turned over police vehicles. Attacked an ambulance. . . . Every time we had an accident, we had these problems.

The nature of civil disturbances has changed since the early days of independence. The established members of the civic network, labor organizations, and political parties have been subsumed under the guardianship of a state corporatist forum of inclusion. This arrangement required power brokers to eschew methods of confrontation in exchange for access to influence. Consequently, civil disorder since the early 1980s has tended to be an exercise in popular discontent, generally of short duration, and inspired solely by local grievances. The police role in this instance has been irregular and negligible, allowing them to focus on more conventional law enforcement tasks.

Policing the Industrial Transformation

The social organization during the independence period was characterized by a well-established unionized sector, most notably the stevedores and the workers on the sugar estates, and a substantial segment of the rural working class that was idle for much of the time. In the absence of a manufacturing sector, however, an intractable unemployment problem could not be transformed into an industrial working class akin to the Western model during the nineteenth century.

The character of policing such a social organization was a combination of *intermittent* and *aggressive proactive class control*. In the period immediately before and after independence the police focused on maintaining domestic order and containing the challenges to state authority. The defiant confrontations posed by communal groups and labor organizations required police protection of fledgling state institutions when they were most vulnerable. Yet, in the matter of everyday affairs, policing what was mostly a rural agrarian society with a small urban core presented a more routine set of problems. The launching of the MEPZ made the ordinary functions of law enforcement exceedingly more complex as Mauritius attempted to recast itself as a model of Third World industrial development.

Public Order Offenses

For most citizens, living in Mauritius at the time of independence was a rudimentary affair involving modest means and a relaxed lifestyle. The lives of most of the island's rural inhabitants revolved around the bounty of land and sea and the companionship of family and friends.

> (M-6) Life was really very leisurely. But still now and then you'd get some people drunk and you have to take care of them. But no, it was leisurely. . . . No pressure, not tremendous pressure. I am using this term leisurely in that sense.

> (M-5) It was a simple society. We didn't have much nightlife. . . . The normal style of life for the laborers in the rural areas was go to the fields, work, come back home, go out and meet the friends on the street corner, or on the veranda, have a beer, talk. . . . There was never any problem. Never! Life for the police in the rural areas was a picnic.

It was only in Port Louis, the administrative and commercial hub of the sugar industry, where drunkenness, prostitution, and other forms of common disorder regularly took place. In the downtown area, merchant seamen on shore leave and Creole stevedores seeking to relax after a day's hard work would mingle in the shops, casinos, and restaurants during the evening. The nucleus of this activity was the Chinese section of the city where merchants offered casino gambling and sold food and alcohol at the "Chinese shops," prostitutes could find clientele, and a few hours in an opium den could be discretely arranged. In the period before and after independence, therefore, what constituted routine urban policing involved the maintenance of order in Chinatown.

> (M-5) Well, Port Louis was the main area where we had that sort of problem with drunk and disorderly behavior . . . what we called Chinatown. And the main problem was from the stevedores. They went to the restaurant after work around eight or nine when they worked the late shift. . . . That area was also very much frequented by all the sailors. We were very busy trying to keep it controlled. . . . Every night, you used to have problems there. In other areas like Abercrombie or Plaine Verte we didn't have much problem. Neighbors fighting, but not a lot.

> (M-8) We had problems in the streets and fights were often. The police were called. Street fighting. . . . We had to be called to maintain law and order. I remember our police chief chose to put one of our consta-

bles in front of the restaurant to control those alcoholics. . . . The Chinese shops too. They were allowed to serve up to 11 PM. These were places where they'd often fight. Especially Saturday night. Lots of disturbances. Sunday, too.

Official data from the period confirms these testimonials. The maintenance of public order most frequently involved the policing of minor skirmishes resulting from "common assaults" that might entail "simple wounds and blows." Excepting violations of traffic regulations, these two offense categories combined were the largest share of the police task. In 1968, 11,615 (146 per 10,000) minor assault cases were handled by the police. From that time forward, common assaults, the vast majority drunken brawls, were a constant element of the police function. Nevertheless, a decade later, the rate of police interventions for common assaults had declined to 122 per 10,000. By 1994, after a sustained rate of decline, the rate was 111 per 10,000.

In like manner, the rates of police intervention in cases of drunkenness were initially high, peaking at 52 per 10,000 in 1975. Thereafter, from 1977–1983, the rates subsided to slightly less than 20 per 10,000. During the mid 1980s, the rates expanded briefly again before declining steadily to a rate of 18 per 10,000 during the 1990s, the lowest rate of police involvement since independence. Thus, there was a clear trend of declining police intervention in cases involving alcohol abuse and simple battery and injuries sustained. The comments of currently serving officers suggest that alcohol-related disorder that might lead to common assault is not an important police priority.

> (M-15) I would say that people of all origins would drink but mostly people who live in the city. There was a housing problem some time back and the government built "sites" [low income, planned communities]. Most of the people who live there are from the lower class. I'm not trying to be prejudiced but they are the people who mostly abuse alcohol. . . . The police should be more vigilant but they are not. There are so many problems in the urban areas. If they are drunk on the street or somebody calls the police then we will make an arrest and put him in jail. But the problem is not widespread. The police usually only come when they are summoned. Otherwise they ignore the problem.

> (M-17) At the time [1984–1990], people didn't have much in the way of entertainment. They would go to work and then they go back home. Then they would go and drink, mostly in groups of men—just like a party. Only men. They would go to drink at the general retailer where they also get small things to eat. At that time we would attend to those shops. They patrolled and if they stayed open after the closing hour, they would be raided. But usually they [the police] were not too concerned about this problem.

As a port of call, among merchant seamen Port Louis was well known for its erotic charms. According to police records, however, there were few arrests for solicitation. The Port Louis waterfront was a gathering place for rough-hewn men who had the means at their disposal and a penchant for amusement. Under such circumstances, according to police informants, there was a thriving commerce in prostitution. Nonetheless, the police did little to interrupt this illegal trade. Prostitution was ubiquitous in and around the capital city, and as such, it was perceived as simply part of the urban landscape.

> (M-4) Prostitution was very common then. You could find these prostitutes on the outskirts of town, like Roche Bois and Abercrombie. Most of them were Creoles. We had quite a few ethnics, but most of them were Creoles.

> (M-5) We had quite a few cases of prostitution in Roche Bois where you used to have what you call pimps. . . . They worked together with the taxi drivers. And they knew where to go. The taxi drivers knew how to get the clients and where to get the girls.

> (M-6) There was no enforcement of prostitution because that would have been impossible. . . . Because being a port city, we should have some sort of escape plan for seamen, at least. It was rather accepted. . . . Whatever was happening was not under the close vigilance of the police.

After 1980, however, opportunities in the industrial sector, especially for women, expanded and provided a legitimate alternative to prostitution. Prostitution still continues but it has been marginalized considerably. Even so, the laws against prostitution are not strictly enforced and the police do not consider it an important component of their obligation.

> (M-21) We can't just arrest them. They are free to walk. An officer can make an arrest if he's heard a conversation. The sailors that come into the port they go outside. These women don't go to the port.

> (M-16) There is prostitution in my division. In Abercrombie. There are poor people there. On Royal Road it is very noticeable. We sometimes patrol for these women but manpower is a problem. . . . We do make arrests but they go right back on the street . . . there are other things we need to attend to. We care not to allow it, but you can't do anything.

The composite of urban disorder also included the consumption and trafficking of illegal drugs. Marijuana (known locally as "gandia") was locally produced and opium dens were operating in the Chinese section of Port Louis. The tropical climate and abundant rainfall were ideal conditions for growing the hardy cannabis plant. The isolation of many areas of the island and the ease of integrating the plants within the vast fields of sugar cane facilitated cultivation without detection. Chinese immigrants probably introduced opium to the island and its consumption was well established among the small Sino-Mauritian community. Policing the drug trade, however, was lackluster. Whatever the reasons, there was no sense of urgency and the police appeared to have no active control strategy to

curtail the consumption and trafficking of dangerous drugs, an enforcement policy that would have serious consequences by the 1980s.

> (M-8) I was a young constable. I didn't even know about the drug
> problem. It was rare. Only cannabis. Gandia. Only cannabis—it was
> grown locally. It was used for recreation. We had no trouble with gan-
> dia. . . . We had no trouble with drugs at that time. Only after the '70s
> did it start getting worse.

> (M-5) Opium, we had a few cases in Chinatown on the main street. We
> had a few opium dens there but they were discrete. Every now and
> then the police would go and raid these opium dens but the people
> there could get away by the back door, or they disappeared.

> (M-4) Most of the hard drugs that we had were gandia or anything
> made out of gandia. . . . For people to get things out of the ordinary
> you'd go to an opium den. The opium dens were concentrated in Chi-
> natown. . . . Of course, we knew where these places were but to
> arrest—there were complicated arrangements. Before you reached
> that place, everything would disappear. Access to that place was not
> easy. They took time to build the system—how to store it and how to
> dispose it and how to sell it.

Drug abuse, therefore, had been an element of Mauritian social life since
independence, but beginning in the early 1980s the problem began to spiral
out of control. To the extent that substance abuse threatens to disrupt capitalist social relations by discouraging the discipline and stability necessary for
orderly commerce, the police were obliged to make it a central component of
a social control strategy. By the mid-1980s, what had been a manageable
problem of gandia and opium consumption had grown to include a conspicuous population of heroin addicts and a lucrative drug market. The substance
abuse problem attained such visibility and grew to such magnitude that the
government moved to enact the Dangerous Drugs Act of 1986, which stiff-
ened penalties and led to the formation of an Anti-Drug Smuggling Unit
(ADSU) within the Mauritius Police Force. The center of the urban drug culture is the Muslim community of Plaine Verte, where the commercial acumen
of Muslim traders has been applied to drug trafficking. The corrosive effect of
the drug trade is evident in the comments of some of the junior officers.

> (M-21) Yes, drugs are a big problem here. They are mostly in Plaine
> Verte. Near the State Bank—by Kadaffi Square. Everybody knows that
> and still nothing happens. Maybe the police try to do something about
> it but major seizures have not been made. . . . There are regular checks
> at the airport. We've never arrested anyone with drugs at the port. . . .
> The major problem is heroin. Nearly all cases are imported from India.
> Here all the drug addicts are Muslims. About 90 percent.

> (M-20) It is very, very easy to get drugs here. It is really bad in the last
> six or seven years, especially heroin. It is coming in mainly from India.
> Maybe some by boat but usually at the airport. Maybe one flight in two

weeks brings in the heroin. The drugs are mostly from Muslims in Plaine Verte but now it is spread out everywhere—well, customers are getting rewards and policemen are getting rewards. A lot of them, they get tipped off by somebody. When we go there, to somebody's house, something's there but you don't get anything.

The order maintenance function of the police, in the aftermath of independence, was mostly concerned with the constraint of the evening revelry that took place in the Chinese section of Port Louis. The foreign sailors and Creole stevedores were drawn to the narrow side streets where the casinos offered games of chance, brothels provided erotic delights, opium dens induced fantasies, and the Chinese shops doled out generous amounts of food and rum. While these agents responsible for this urban commotion were left largely undisturbed, the many merchant seamen on shore leave and the Creole urban working class became the central focus of police efforts to maintain a semblance of order.

In the more recent period, the lax enforcement of public-order offenses underlies a *routine proactive class control* that has become the operative style of policing in Mauritius. Among the offenses repugnant to public morality, only drug abuse and trafficking have elicited any meaningful police attention. Common assaults, public drunkenness, and prostitution virtually are ignored. Of course, the police have not completely abandoned the battlefield to the enemy. Arrests are made when citizens violate laws governing standards of conduct, but except for drug offenses these contraventions do not directly threaten the system of capitalist social relations. Therefore, the police are inclined to overlook a good many infractions.

Violent Crimes

If the maintenance of order, collective and routine, was the central theme of policing during the immediate pre- and post-independence period, it is equally clear that the prevention of crimes against persons and property were accorded a lesser priority. To be sure, the tempo of rural life, which defined the character of Mauritius, did not lend itself to felonious conduct. According to official data, the absolute number of homicides averaged about 20 per annum. The rates for aggravated assault described a similar pattern, suggesting that violent crime was seldom a matter of much importance for the police. On the whole, the rates of police involvement for such offenses throughout the period under review have been negligible and stable. The testimony of police officers confirms this impression.

(M-9) This was an orderly society. Very, very quiet. It was not a tough problem to deal with. Violent crimes were not very serious. Maybe after drinking some would resort to violence . . . [but] it was not usually premeditated. . . . It was a very low rate of these kinds of things.

(M-4) Yes, we had those cases of violent attacks but not in big numbers. In most cases it would result from drinks or love affairs. Sometimes mischief. Two people would get very drunk—street fights turned very badly sometimes. Oh, you know, an accident, maybe you knock against somebody. Then, it comes to blows.

As for other crimes of violence, the police were seldom called on to attend to incidents of armed robbery. During the first decade of the independence period, annual rates of police intervention in larcenies involving force or the threat of force consistently declined. According to official data, from an initial rate of 2.3 per 10,000 in 1968, the rate of armed robberies trended downward incrementally to 1.4 per 10,000 in 1978. The commentary of police informants makes clear that these sorts of violent encounters, whether directed at individuals or commercial enterprises, represented a negligible fraction of the police obligation.

> (M-9) . . . cases of aggravated larceny were very light. A fraction of the people would still use violence to see if you have money in your pocket. That was all. I am not saying there weren't any such cases, but very rare, very seldom. Some person might attack somebody in the sugar cane field and steal a few rupees. Give them a knock on the head. But it was not common.

> (M-8) Yes, those people were people who had not been working. These were people who attacked on the streets. These were only a few in certain groups. Certain areas. But it was very low. I can't think of any bank robberies. I can't remember any. They might attack some small shops.

Since 1978, however, the rate of police activity for this offense category has increased sharply. As the police focused more intensively on armed robbery the rates continued to trend upward throughout the 1980s. By the mid-1990s a rate of almost 7 per 10,000 was twice what it had been a decade earlier. Official police data as well as the testimonies of police officers reveal that beginning in the early 1980s, robbery arrests notably increased with a steep rise during the 1990s.

> (M-16) Larceny-violence happens very often. Two or so a week. Women walking on the street and their jewelry is taken. They do this because they have no money to buy drugs. This is usually how it happens.

> (M-21) There is lots of larceny-violence. Many times it is working women with gold chains. They will come on motorbikes and just snatch them. They're armed with sabers and firearms. Small pistols. They also go after salesmen in vans, delivery vans. The salesman makes a delivery, takes the money, and keeps it with him. About 1 or 2 PM, he is attacked by these people on motorbikes. This happens maybe twice daily. When I started on the force [1989] there were holdups but they were not that regular. Maybe once a month. By 1996, maybe, it was regular.

> (M-15) There is now much larceny-violence in the urban areas. There is even larceny-violence in the banks. Banks pay persons to be in front of the bank. The officers are armed. . . . Also what is new is the larceny

of salesmen. This also is becoming more common. The guy goes to a certain place, then another, then another. At the end of the day, he is carrying about 40,000 rupees. Now they stop him and threaten him with revolvers. . . . These cases are increasing.

Except for armed robbery, the policing of violent crime in Mauritius has not occupied center stage. Coinciding with the maturation of the MEPZ in the early 1980s, the police became more involved with armed robbery. The wealth generated by industrial capitalism has enlarged the opportunity structure for armed robbery. Undoubtedly, some of the robberies being committed are drug-related. Most importantly, however, the social context for these kinds of violent and coercive thefts contributes to a climate of accumulation that encourages criminal innovation. If concern by the police for robbery is considered part of a matrix of property crime involvement, then low but ascending arrest rates are an indication of a pattern of Western-style policing.

Property Crimes

Regarding property offenses, the pattern of enforcement has followed a similar trajectory as violent felonies, although of a greater magnitude. The core of the police task focused on common thefts (e.g., simple larcenies, pickpocketing, etc.) though even here the rates of such offenses remained stable during the period following independence. From 1968 to 1978 the rate for common theft averaged about 48 per 10,000. The police response to burglary for the same period was almost negligible and indeed declined to less than 4 per 10,000 (1978) from 6.6 per 10,000 in 1968.

A partial explanation for the relatively high rates of petty theft lay in the persistent unemployment rates that afflicted the island's economy and impacted most especially on the Indo-Mauritian sugar workers. Yet those rates remained stable and along with declining burglary rates suggest other factors at work. More important was the general level of accumulated wealth. With the exception of the affluent proprietors of the sugar plantations, a relatively small per-capita income prevented most people from acquiring a generous store of material resources. The wealth that was most visible was modest and disproportionately urban in character. The Chinese shops, restaurants, general retailers, and other emporiums in the capital's commercial district were small in scale and hardly constituted attractive targets.

(M-9) It was hardly possible for them to steal valuable things. People didn't have valuable things. The likelihood of people coming to your place and stealing . . . what could they have stolen? Jewelry and money and that's all. They'd get so much rupees and be satisfied with this. These property crimes would occur more often than violent crimes but they were not a big occurrence. It was not an everyday occurrence in the police station. In rural areas, very seldom that you had such cases. It was more common in the urban areas.

> (M-6) There were some problems of larceny break-ins but it was a manageable amount. Not frequent how it is today. At that time, people were not so much crime prone, I suppose. We had some, still they were infrequent. At that time, it was not alarming.

A society in transition, however, from a rural agrarian mode of production to an economy based on industrial manufacturing should expect to see rising property crime arrests. The prosperity that accompanied industrialization created a flourishing middle class that embraced an expanding consumer market. Automobiles, electronic goods, appliances, and the like became a part of everyday life for the public servants, entrepreneurs, financiers, small sugar producers, and others who inhabited the middle stratum of Mauritian society. For those marginalized by the transformation, the evidence of increasing inequality was obvious, especially in Port Louis and the interior cities where the wealth was most visible. For most Mauritians who found themselves excluded from development, the prevailing assumption was that failure was an individual responsibility and that to succeed a greater effort must be made. A disadvantaged minority, however, perceived the solution to poverty and disenfranchisement to lie in acts of burglary and petty larceny.

Beginning in 1979, the moderate rates of common theft that had characterized the first decade of independence increased substantially, ascending to almost 75 per 10,000 in 1986. Although larceny rates declined over the next three years, they resumed a sustained increase thereafter to the previous levels of the early 1980s. By 1994, the annual rate for such offenses (86 per 10,000) exceeded all earlier rates by a wide margin. Concerning common theft, therefore, the pattern of police conduct has been in keeping with the configuration exemplified by Western industrial nations.

> (M-15) Swindling is very common here. People need to be educated so they don't get deceived by people when they are buying something. This has been increasing over the last few years. These and many other kinds of larceny as well. Bad checks that are issued. Passing bad checks. That happened frequently.

> (M-13) Pickpockets are here. You will find them in the Central Market. They are looking for tourists. They can also be found at the Champs de Mars on race day. Normally there are many police assigned to the races. They look for everything. Larceny, pickpockets, illegal bookmaking—this is all there at the Champs de Mars. Mostly they steal money. Sometimes jewelry too.

Police activity for the more serious forms of property crime describes a more eccentric motif. Unlike the response to common theft, the police response to burglary in the early independence period was negligible. In the early 1980s, however, policing of burglary cases increased notably to 11 per 10,000 in 1986 from a low of 4.8 per 10,000 in 1979. After a brief hiatus in which the burglary rates declined and leveled off, beginning in 1991 the rates began to spiral upward again. In 1994, a burglary rate of 11.6 per 10,000 was the highest for the entire post-independence period. Police respondents have taken note and provide confirmation of this development.

> (M-15) There are many cases where people have broken into houses where the owners were out . . . larceny break-ins, we have lots of those. They go for jewelry, money, TV's. Most of the larceny break-ins are in residences.

> (M-22) We have larceny break-ins in business areas and residential areas but more of these are in residential areas. We don't have large families living together the way it used to be. This has changed. There are more and more nuclear families. . . . When more and more people are working then nobody is home. This happens a lot in Port Louis. Many of the new houses being built, these are for nuclear families. This is why these offenses are increasing. Most of the larceny break-ins are in residences.

> (M-20) Hotels sometimes are targets from time to time. Many of these cases are in the bungalows that tourists rent for a week or two. They go to the beach and leave their stuff in the room. Tourists don't think about larceny break-ins. They are here to enjoy themselves so they don't always think to lock doors or windows.

The transformation of the social relations of production from a monocultural economy dependent on sugar production to small-scale, first-stage industrial production has provided new possibilities for innovation, both legitimate and illegitimate. For those excluded from participation in the new structure of institutional life, property crimes can serve as a functional alternative.

Conclusion

The inquiry that informs this article is whether the circumstances that gave rise to democratic policing in the West can be duplicated in the contemporary Third World, thus providing a viable model for constructing a democratic polity and establishing a context for democratic social control. Furthermore, it subscribes to the view that no inquiry concerning the changing role of the police can proceed without first considering how any transformation of the social relations of production will impact the exercise of public authority. The police are the most visible representatives of state authority and as such are intimately linked to the legitimacy of the state. An appraisal of the evolution of police operations, priorities, and strategies without a concomitant analysis of the social context in which those activities take place is inherently flawed.

Facilitated by an expansive literature on the history of policing as it evolved in Western liberal democracies since its advent in the nineteenth century, the Western model is now firmly established. As initially conceived, the primary task of a newly established, uniformed, publicly supported constabulary was to monitor, regulate, and if necessary, suppress the activities of the working class. It coincided with the appearance of an assertive propertied class that sought effective control over the forces of production, protection for commerce and manufacturing, and an orderly and stable social organization. The context in which democratic policing originated ". . . meant that policing could be 'socialized' only as part of an overall rationalization of social life: as a means to enforce the conditions and deflect the costs of capitalist growth" (Spitzer, 1993:331).

In Mauritius, while not an identical replication, the configuration of arrest patterns bears some resemblance to the paradigm of police development in the West. For the period surrounding independence the shape of Mauritian social control closely resembled the Western model. Prepared to assume power at the conclusion of the colonial period, an Indo-Mauritian bourgeoisie had to contend with a militant working class and a communally organized society for a share of the new nation's resources. The police were enlisted to preserve the compromise between the Franco-Mauritian elite and the new Hindu-dominated government by constraining challenges to state authority taking the form of aggressive proactive class-control policing.

Furthermore, the police were also called on to regulate routine public disorder. Official arrest data indicate that police involvement with public-order offenses, initially relatively high, has diminished notably as a police priority. The police interviews suggest that many of the arrests in the early period resulted from the festive evenings in the Chinese enclave of Port Louis. The recreational styles of foreign seamen and Creole stevedores required regulatory flexibility, but also direct intervention when the disorder became too unruly. Therefore, a social organization of production consisting primarily of unskilled and casual work in the sugar cane fields (coupled with substantial unemployment rates during this period) implied an intermittent proactive class-control style of policing.

Subsequently, this would change with the onset of a deliberate policy to cultivate industrialization, thereby transforming the foundation of the Mauritian economy. Almost coinciding with the launching of the MEPZ, the police, with few exceptions, became more inclined to enforce routine public-order offenses moderately. The gradual leveling of assertive police intervention in public-order offenses and a greater share of resources devoted to crimes against persons and property suggests a routine proactive class-control strategy that is a proximate correspondence to the Western model.

As implied, the incidence of police involvement in violent crimes also indicates some parallels with the pattern manifested in Western democracies. Official arrest data indicate that the policing of homicides and violent assaults has been both negligible and stable since independence, but police intervention in robbery offenses conforms to the classic Western pattern: a brief and gradual decline followed by a sharp increase beginning in the late 1970s, a period roughly contiguous with economic take-off and the success of first-stage industrialization in the MEPZ. Moreover, the qualitative nature of these events, revealed in field interviews, leaves little doubt that an increasing number, rather than opportunistic interactions, involved calculation and ambitious design.

Police interventions in property crimes delineate a similar though slightly more irregular trajectory. Burglary arrests do indeed decline marginally until the late 1970s, when an ascendant trend becomes evident, although the gradient is not abrupt. Reported larceny-thefts describe a similar pattern, but neither as pronounced nor as uniform. From the close of the 1980s to the present, cases of all forms of theft experienced a notable increase and in the latter period were more likely to entail craft and deceit. Furthermore, they appeared to be motivated almost solely by cupidity rather than the desperation of poverty, a function of rising incomes and the expansion of the opportunity structure. In general terms, therefore, for incidents of felonious criminal conduct, both violent and property, the pattern of policing in Mauritius closely duplicates the Western prototype.

The Mauritian experience suggests that it is possible to duplicate the evolution of Western-style policing in contemporary Third World countries and that Mauritius can serve as a model for other nations in their attempts to fashion democratic institutions of social control. Nonetheless, a cautionary note needs to be sounded. Democracy is a luxury, not a right, and in the present climate of globalization the prosperity of the Mauritian industrial economy, based on the success of its export platform, is a fragile foundation on which to construct democratic social control. Competitive pressures from similarly positioned nations make it imperative to restrain labor costs—something that, up to this point, the Mauritian government has accomplished by inhibiting MEPZ workers from organizing.

A legacy of militant labor organizations dating back to the pre-independence period, however, suggests that this strategy may be difficult to maintain indefinitely and presents Mauritius with a potential dilemma. A transition to social relations of production based on a fully protected industrial labor force would deprive Mauritius of its competitive position in the global marketplace. The turmoil such a reconstruction might entail would expose the coercive foundation of police power and undermine its legitimacy. If industrial capital investment were to abandon Mauritius, the island republic would find itself once again dependent on the sugar industry to sustain itself and provide sufficient employment, a position tantamount to a restoration of the pre-independence period. The dismantling of the industrial infrastructure and a retreat from prosperity is likely to unleash an exponential increase in public disorder, drug-related violence, and petty crime beyond the adequacy of current police resources.

Note

[1] Parenthetical notations refer to excerpts of actual interviews that were conducted in fall, 1999. To preserve confidentiality, the author has employed a simple coding system: The "M" stands for Mauritius and the number corresponds to the officer being interviewed.

References

Alladin, Ibrahim (1993). *Economic Miracle in the Indian Ocean: Can Mauritius Show the Way?* Rose Hill: Editions de l'Ocean Indien

Annual Report of the Mauritius Police Force (1968–1975, 1977–1983, 1985–1994). Port Louis, Mauritius: Government Printer

Bayley, David H. (1999). "The contemporary practices of policing: a comparative view" in Department of Justice (January, 1999). *Civilian Police and Multinational Peacekeeping—A Workshop Series: A Role for Democratic Policing.* Washington, DC: National Institute of Justice (workshop proceedings, October 6, 1997)

Bearak, Barry (2003). "Unreconstructed." *New York Times Sunday Magazine*, June 1, 2003: 40–47, 62–63, 96, 101–102.

Bowman, Larry W. (1991). *Mauritius: Democracy and Development in the Indian Ocean.* Boulder, CO: Westview.

Braudel, Fernand (1979). *The Structures of Everyday Life: The Limits of the Possible.* New York: Harper and Row.

Brautigam, Deborah (1999). "The 'Mauritius Miracle': Democracy, institutions, and economic policy" in Richard Joseph, ed., *State, Conflict, and Democracy in Africa.* Boulder, CO: Lynne Reinner.

Bruchey, Stuart (1990). *Enterprise: The Dynamic Economy of a Free People.* Cambridge, MA: Harvard University Press.

Carter, Marina (1995). *Servants, Sirdars and Settlers: Indians in Mauritius, 1834–1874.* Delhi: Oxford University Press.

Edwards, Richard (1979). *Contested Terrain: The Transformation of the Workplace in the Twentieth Century.* New York: Basic Books.

Harring, Sidney L. (1983). *Policing a Class Society: The Experience of American Cities, 1865–1915.* New Brunswick, NJ: Rutgers University Press.

Jacoby, Sanford M. (1985). *Employing Bureaucracy: Managers, Unions, and the Transformation of Work in American Industry, 1900–1945.* New York: Columbia University Press.

Kuczynski, Robert Renee (1949). *Demographic Survey of the British Colonial Empire.* London: Oxford University Press.

Map of Mauritius. University of Texas online. Available: http://www.lib.utexas.edu/maps/mauritius.html (accessed January 15, 2005).

Ministry of Economic Development, Productivity, and Regional Development (1999). *Digest of Industrial Statistics, 1997.* Port Louis, Mauritius: Central Statistical Office.

Ministry of Economic Development and Regional Cooperation (1997). *Vision 2020: The National Long-Term Perspective Study.* Port Louis, Mauritius: Ministry of Economic Development and Regional Cooperation.

Ministry of Economic Planning and Development (1996). *Mauritius Economic Review, 1992–1995.* Port Louis, Mauritius: Government Printer.

Ministry of Industry and Industrial Technology (1991). *Mauritius at Crossroads: The Industrial Challenges Ahead.* Port Louis, Mauritius: Ministry of Industry and Industrial Technology.

Monkonnen, Eric H. (1981). *Police in Urban America 1860–1920.* Cambridge: Cambridge University Press.

Raybeck, Joseph G. (1966). *A History of American Labor.* New York: The Free Press.

Reich, Michael & David Gordon, eds. (1975). *Labor Market Segmentation.* Lexington, MA: D.C. Heath.

Reichel, Philip L. (1994). *Comparative Criminal Justice Systems: A Topical Approach.* Englewood Cliffs, NJ: Prentice-Hall.

Richardson, James F. (1970). *The New York Police: Colonial Times to 1901.* New York: Oxford University Press.

Simmons, Adele Smith (1982). *Modern Mauritius: The Politics of Decolonialization.* Bloomington: Indiana University Press.

Spitzer, Steven (1993). "The political economy of policing" in David F. Greenberg, ed., *Crime and Capitalism: Readings in Marxist Criminology.* Philadelphia, PA: Temple University Press.

Steinberg, Allen (1989). *The Transformation of Criminal Justice: Philadelphia 1800–1880.* Chapel Hill: University of North Carolina Press.

Thernstrom, Stephan (1975). *Poverty and Progress.* New York: Atheneum.

Thompson, Ginger (2003). "Young, hopeless and violent in the new South Africa." *New York Times,* March 19.

World Bank (1983). *Mauritius Economic Memorandum: Recent Development and Prospects.* Washington, DC: World Bank.

World Bank (1989). *World Development Report.* Washington, DC: World Bank.

14

Civil Liberties and the Mass Line

Police and Administrative Punishment in the People's Republic of China

Dorothy H. Bracey

One of the functions of criminal law is to mediate relationships between the individual and the state. The criminal law is, therefore, an excellent avenue by which to explore the ways in which different cultures conceptualize those relationships.

Liberal Western law reflects the philosophy that individuals have certain rights of thought and action. Other individuals, groups, and the state itself may not interfere with these rights unless the possessor uses them to do substantial harm. The burden of proof is always on those alleging substantial harm. Both investigation and sanctions should be minimally intrusive. And criminal law, particularly the law of criminal procedure, exists not only to protect victims of harm and to punish those guilty of inflicting it, but also to protect the rights of the accused against the state (Ingraham, 1987:7).

In the People's Republic of China, law is considered to be one of a number of tools that the state may use to transform deviants into proper members of the socialist community, and rights are viewed as belonging to the community, not to the individual. It is not only deviant behavior that must be prevented, punished and corrected, but also deviant thoughts and attitudes, since such thoughts and attitudes will eventually cause deviant behavior. Because the deviant individual injures the well-being of the community, it is both the right and the duty of the community and the state to educate and rehabilitate deviant individuals.

Because Western criminal law attempts to prevent the state from intruding unnecessarily in individuals' lives, it defines criminal acts in a pre-

Prepared especially for *Comparative Criminal Justice, 1/E.*

cise manner, carefully differentiating "crime" from all other types of deviance. While the state is expected to use all its resources in identifying and responding to the former, it is forbidden to intervene in any way in regard to the latter. Strengthening this dichotomy between crime and other deviance is a trend within the last half-century to confine "crime" to actions, not to statuses or conditions. Thus, in the United States, being a prostitute is no longer a crime, although an act of prostitution is a crime in most jurisdictions. Ordinances against "public drunkenness" and "vagrancy" are among others that have been judged to be vague and overbroad because they refer to conditions rather than specific harmful acts.

To the Chinese, deviance is a continuum, not a dichotomy. In their view, deviant thoughts lead inevitably to deviant acts, and minor deviant acts lead to major deviant acts. This view underlies the commonly-heard medical analogy of crime; minor deviant thoughts, attitudes, and acts are like the early symptoms of a disease which, if left untreated, will develop into a potentially fatal condition. Early intervention is simple and has a high probability of success; later treatment necessitates heroic measures and the odds of success are far lower.

Organization

Crime and public order in the People's Republic of China (PRC) are the responsibility of the Ministry of Justice and the Ministry of Public Security. The former supervises courts, prisons, and the various methods of acquainting people with developments in the law. The latter directs the work of the professional and armed police.

The Ministry of Public Security is one of the ministries of the State Council, part of the central government located in Beijing. Its main activity is to make policy and to give guidance to the public security organizations in the twenty-two provinces, five autonomous regions, and the three municipalities that are under the direct control of the central government. These consist of public security departments at the provincial level, public security bureaus and sub-bureaus at the municipal level, and county public security bureaus and stations at the grassroots level. Each of these local public security organizations is responsible for crime control and public order in its locality, under the joint leadership of the government at its own level and the public security organization at the level above it (Dai and Huang, 1993:137–38.)

In addition to these "professional police," the Ministry of Public Security, together with the Central Military Commission, controls the more centralized armed police (the only public security personnel who carry weapons on a regular basis), who are in charge of border security; fire protection; and guarding embassies, consulates, residence compounds set aside for foreigners, prisons, power and utility centers, and public buildings.

The Chinese government assigns jobs to young people on the basis of the applicant's choice and performance on a competitive examination, as well as on the need for personnel in particular occupations and particular locations (Bracey, 1989a:131). In recent years, the growing opportunities to amass wealth in the private sector have made it more difficult to recruit applicants to public-sector jobs. At the same time, however, police training and education have improved tremendously. There are now twenty-four institutions of higher education, including the highly selective Public Security University in Beijing, police colleges in every province and major city, recruit schools, and ninety-five cadre schools designed for in-service training (Ward and Bracey, 1985; Dai and Huang, 1993). Although Chinese police duties in respect to crime prevention, investigation and public order maintenance are similar to those of their U.S. counterparts, the 1954 legislation stipulating police functions lists four additional activities. One is derived from the continental European model of policing, while the other three reflect particularly Chinese concerns.

The first activity refers to household registration. This involves keeping track of permanent residents, births and deaths, and individuals moving in or out. Through the early 1980s, registration duties were not a major burden, since transportation difficulties, a locally administered ration system, and the need for official permission to travel meant that the population was largely stable. Since the mid-1980s, however, the opening of the economic system has meant that many more people have been moving around the country in search of economic opportunity. This resulted in the institution of an identity-card system, making it far easier for the police to keep tabs on an increasingly mobile population.

A more uniquely Chinese provision directs the police to "take an active part in and give assistance in welfare projects for residents." Somewhat reminiscent of Western community policing, this provision calls upon the police to work with communities in identifying and solving problems. "Teach the residents to observe and abide by laws and respect social ethics" refers to the police role in community legal education-acquainting the people with provisions of the law, explaining the rationale underlying those provisions, and encouraging them to abide by both the spirit and the letter. Finally, "guide the work of public security committees" directs the police to work with the committees elected by members of factories, organizations, businesses and neighborhoods to act as liaison between police and people, to provide information, carry out patrols, implement crime prevention measures, assist mediation activities and supervise offenders returned to the community. Together, these provisions comprise the principle of "relying on the masses."

The Mass Line

Police training institutions teach that "the people's police are the servants of the people" and that the police must listen to the people and accept their supervision and criticism (Bracey, 1989a). This is one way of expressing the principle of "following the mass line" and "relying on the masses," a policy that applies to police as it does to all public officials (Johnson, 1983: 84–9).

Following the mass line demands that the police solicit and respect the opinions of the people, understand the conditions of their lives, and work closely with them. It requires the police to gather and analyze public opinion and translate it into policy. Ideally, this principle protects the people from police and bureaucratic abuse, since the police are subject to the direction of the people; in this way it may fill a function analogous to that of civil liberties or individual rights in liberal Western societies. There are, however, two differences.

First, there is nothing in the concept to protect an individual from the tyranny of the majority; if the masses feel that an individual or group must in some way be sacrificed for the common good, the principle of the mass line calls for the police to carry out their desire. Secondly, it is government officials—including police officials—who interpret the desires of the masses, who turn the "scattered and unsystematic ideas of the masses into concentrated and systematic ideas" (Mao, 1961:9). Thus, it is the job of officials to tell the masses what they "really" want.

If "listening to the mass line" refers to policy input, "relying on the masses" refers to implementation. Chinese police like to say that the police are like fish and the people are the sea in which the fish live. Mao Zedong used a similar analogy to describe the relationship between his army and the peasantry during the Chinese civil war.

The most common form of relying on the masses consists of working with the 1.2 million public security committees, whose more than 5.8 million members are directly elected for six-month terms. These committees have established lower-level public security groups, whose members are also elected; there are 2.6 million of such groups, with 6.3 million members (Dai and Huang, 1993:140–41). These organizations, made up largely of housewives and retired workers, act as the ears and eyes of the police by "taking every possible measure to enhance people's vigilance against the destructive activities of the lawbreakers; organizing people to assist the government and public security organs in exposing, supervising and controlling those endangering national security and public order; assisting people to take crime prevention measures to ensure the security of the area under their jurisdiction" (p. 141).

With almost twelve million people participating in this type of endeavor, it would seem that the police had ample assistance from the masses. Nevertheless, the burgeoning economy has recently produced a security industry that provides guards to factories and businesses and that are also mandated to work closely with the police and public security committees. By 1988, more than 200 such firms were flourishing throughout China (p. 142).

All of these private and popular groups share with the police information that might help in preventing and solving crimes. In addition, however, they look for signs of noncriminal deviance, the type of deviance that, if left unchecked, might grow into something harmful to other individuals, the community, or the state. This might include associating with bad *coåany*, mixing too freely with foreigners, laziness, or quarreling with family members, co-workers or neighbors. Should they find such signs, group members might discuss the deviant's behavior with him in private or within the group, ask family members or peers to reason with him, or suggest that quarrels be submitted to mediation.

If the deviant does not admit his faults and if the troublesome behavior persists, the police may be called in. Since no crime has been committed, the police will not be asked to make an arrest, but simply to add their authority and experience to the efforts to eliminate this minor deviance before it grows into something harder to handle. What Americans might see as unwarranted intervention into their private lives strikes the Chinese as logical, efficient, and effective crime prevention.

The Security Administration Punishment Act

Consistent with China's emphasis on early and efficient intervention in minor deviance is the Security Administration Punishment Act of 1986 (SAPA). SAPA enumerates offenses that are to be handled administratively, i.e., outside of the criminal courts. The act gives the police the power to impose warnings, fines of up to 200 yuan (approximately 28 percent of the average annual expenditure of an individual; Yang, 1994:61) or fifteen days of detention.

SAPA offenses lie somewhere between deviance and crime. The legislation is meant to provide a tool for the police to deal with those offenders who they believe can be easily corrected and reintegrated into the community. The procedure is quick and informal, the penalties relatively light, and because SAPA offenses are not crimes, the offender does not have the stigma of a criminal record.

The history of SAPA begins in 1914, when the Chinese government in Nanjing enacted a modification to the Penal Code dealing with "police violations." The police could handle such violations administratively rather than judicially by issuing summonses; making a finding; imposing a sanction of warning, small fine, or short period of detention; and supervising the carrying out of that sentence. Revisions to the Penal Code in 1928, 1935, 1957, and 1979 retained and sometimes modified the content, procedure and penalties defining "police violations." The changes often give a lively and colorful insight into the concerns of the moment.

For example, in the 1928 version, the section on violation of morals dealt with loitering without fixed purpose, asking for alms in a threatening manner (this applied to Buddhist and Taoist priests as well as beggars), defacing or damaging a tomb, secretly soliciting for prostitution, acting as a procurer, supplying a lodgings for immoral purposes, calling or staying in a house with a secret (unlicensed) prostitute, singing or performing lascivious songs or plays, going naked, making vulgar gestures, wearing clothes detrimental to good morals on a highway or in a public place, and scolding, mocking, or embarrassing another person in public (Bracey, 1989b:157).

Revisions in 1987 reflect the more contemporary concerns of the Chinese government. As China has increased its contacts with the rest of the world, it has seen an increase in infractions relating to vice and morals. Thus, this most recent revision contains an added number of provisions dealing with pornography, prostitution, gambling and drugs.

The concept of administrative punishment is not a Chinese invention. Japan introduced similar legislation in 1879 and abolished it only after the post–World War II occupation (Hess and Murayama, 1980). And both China and Japan were influenced by the European tradition of "police violation." Contemporary Sweden allows police, customs agents and prosecutors to advise, admonish, and impose fixed fines for minor offenses known as "breaches of regulations" (Terrill, 1984:212). In 1975, the Federal Republic of Germany decriminalized and transformed into "petty infractions" a number of offenses that were formerly included in the penal code; these are now handled administratively by any of a number of agencies, including the police (Yang, 1994:58; Fairchild, 1988).

Nevertheless, Yang (1994) suggests that SAPA offenses differ from European "police violations" in four important ways. First, while the European versions tend to deal with statutory offenses, SAPA offenses are most often are minor versions of crimes; for example, theft of 150 yuan is a SAPA offense while theft of 200 yuan is a crime. In this way, Chinese distinction between crimes and SAPA offenses is reminiscent of the distinction between misdemeanors and felonies in the United States. Secondly, Yang suggests that the distinction between SAPA offenses and crimes is fluid:

> The articulation of legal elements is often very flexible and subject to interpretation. For instance, the line between "criminal" and "noncriminal" sometimes depends on whether the "circumstances" are "serious" or the "amount" is "relatively large", while the circumstances and amount are not always precisely stipulated in law. (p. 58)

Thirdly, penalties in China are significantly harsher than those applied to analogous European violations, although less severe than those associated with misdemeanors in the United States. Finally, SAPA offenses are handled entirely by the police with no participation by lawyers or judges. It was only in the most recent revision that the SAPA procedure admitted any appeal to the courts, and this is only after appeal to a higher police authority has confirmed the original judgment.

Because the fluid line between crimes and SAPA offenses gives police great discretion in classifying unlawful actions, theoretically there is considerable temptation to designate an incident as a SAPA offense. This implies that the incident will be handled by the simple and expeditions SAPA procedures rather than by the longer and more complex rules of criminal procedure. It also means that attorneys will not be involved in either prosecutorial or defense roles and, unless the outcome is appealed to the highest level, it will not involve a judge.

Western students of crime and justice find two areas of concern with this situation. The first of these has to do with statistics. Classifying an incident as a SAPA offense means that it will not be included in the crime statistics that China has been reporting to Interpol since 1986. Yang (1994) suggests that this helps to account for the fact that Chinese crime figures, especially those for assault and property crimes, are so much lower than those of most other nations. He gives as an example incidents involving the commission of physical harm. Incidents classified as injuries are technically criminal assaults and are reported in the official crime statistics. On the other hand, incidents classified as "beating and injury" are SAPA offenses and are not reported. "In 1986 and 1988, the former (18,364 and 26,639) only equaled about 7 and 8 percent of the latter (268,306 and 326,552)" (p. 61). If the police do indeed have a consistent bias toward classifying incidents as SAPA offenses rather than crimes, China's crime rate may be significantly understated.

When China's crime statistics are compared to those of other nations, however, it becomes necessary to ask if other nations also underreport. In the United States, for instance, it is well-known that a substantial number of crimes are never reported to the police, while violations and misdemeanors are not always reported for comparative purposes. The reservations about Chinese crime statistics may simply remind us of the need for reservations about comparative crime statistics in general.

A more common and more important concern involves possible violation of human rights. Amnesty International (1991) suggested that SAPA sanctions, along with other and more serious punishments, are used to penalize vaguely defined forms of "antisocial" and "antisocialist" behavior or activities (p. 2). They are also disproportionately used against people of low social status: "vagrants, the unemployed, rural migrants and people regarded as 'hooligans' or social deviants; who do not have the status or social connections to protect them from wrongful arrest or other abuses which may occur in police custody" (See also Biddulph, 1993:337–54).

There is also the fear that police may use SAPA as a way of circumventing the safeguards of the criminal procedure. With no defense attorneys to protect the rights of the accused and no judges to worry about rules of evidence, and with a burden of proof lighter than that required for a criminal proceeding, both police and community might at times find it desirable to settle for a sure conviction and a lighter penalty than take the chance of going to trial in a criminal court (Dutton and Lee, 1993:324–25).

Police actions under SAPA reflect the "therapeutic" approach to deviance that is consistent with the medical model referred to above (Bracey, 1989c:133). According to this model of deviance, to which the police subscribe, "the deviant is someone whose conduct is abnormal and who needs help of some kind . . ." (Black, 1980:131). SAPA permits quick, informal intervention that leaves no lasting stigma; a fine tool for curing early symptoms of deviance before they have a chance to develop into full-blown crime.

Both the intentions behind SAPA and the reservations expressed about it are reminiscent of the United States system of juvenile justice. The theory of this system of justice, as it was developed at the end of the last century, was that juvenile crime was a symptom of a condition that could be cured by rapid and decisive intervention by an authority equipped with wide discretion. There was no need for a lawyer to protect the rights of the accused, since the juvenile wasn't being accused of anything—simply being examined for symptoms and was in no danger of being unjustly punished, because the system didn't mete out punishments, it dispensed cures. In less than 15 years, however, critics were suggesting that the informality and discretion of the juvenile court resulted in actions that might be meant as treatment, but were certainly perceived as punishment by the juvenile. A series of U.S. Supreme Court cases have introduced into the juvenile justice system much the same formality and procedural protections that exist in the adult justice system (Platt, 1977). Whether something similar happens to SAPA remains to be seen.

Bibliography

Amnesty International (1991). *CHINA Punishment without Crime: Administrative Detention*. New York: Amnesty International USA.

Biddulph, S. (1993). "Review of Police Powers of Administrative Detention in the People's Republic of China." *Crime and Delinquency* 39 (4): 337–54.

Black, D. (1980). *The Manners and Customs of the Police*. New York: Academic Press.

Bracey, D. H. (1989a). "The Police of the People's Republic of China." *World Encyclopedia of Police Forces and Police Systems*. New York: Facts on File.

——— (1989b). "The Regulations of the People's Republic of China Concerning Punishments for Disturbing Order: The Police and Administrative Punishment." *Criminal Justice Review* 14 (2): 154–65.

——— (1989c). "Policing the People's Republic." In R. J. Trover, J. P. Clark, and D. G. Rojek (eds.), *Social Control in the People's Republic of China* (pp. 130–40). New York: Praeger.

Dai, Y. S., and Z. Y. Huang (1993). "Organization and Functions of Public Security Agencies of the People's Republic of China." *Eurocriminology* 5-6: 137–43.

Dutton, M., and T. Lee (1993). "Missing the Target? Policing Strategies in the Period of Economic Reform." *Crime and Delinquency* 39 (3): 316–36.

Fairchild, E. S. (1988). *German Police: Ideals and Reality in the Post–War Years*. Springfield, IL: Charles C. Thomas.

Hess, A. G., and S. Murayama (1980). *Everyday Law in Japanese Folk Art*. Scientia Verlag Aalen.

Ingraham, B. L. (1987). *The Structure of Criminal Procedure*. New York: Greenwood Press.

Johnson, E. L. (1983-84). "Neighborhood Police in the People's Republic of China." *Police Studies: The International Review of Police Development* 6: 8–11.

Mao Tse-tung (1961). *Selected Works* (Vol. 3). Beijing: Foreign Languages Press.

Platt, A. M. (1977). *The Child Savers*. Chicago: University of Chicago Press.

Terrill, R. (1984). *World Criminal Justice Systems*. Cincinnati, OH: Anderson Publishing Co.

Ward, R. H., and D. H. Bracey (1985). "Police Training and Professionalism in the People's Republic of China." *Police Chief* 52 (5): 36–38.

Yang, C. (1994). "Public Security Offenses and Their Impact on Crime Rates in China." *British Journal of Criminology* 34 (1): 54–68.

15

Police in Developing Countries
The Case of Cameroon

David Chiabi

Policing is a costly and complex enterprise. It is a profession that entails interaction with people in every society for a variety of reasons ranging from civil order-maintenance activities to controlling serious crime. Every society needs police to control crime, to maintain order, to coordinate the smooth functioning of society, and to provide some solutions to social problems. In the performance of these functions, police regularly intervene in the lives of citizens they police. Different societies assign functions to their police in varying degrees. Using Cameroon as an example, this article examines the role of police in developing countries, on the premise that the current police organizational structure, training, and strategy in Cameroon (and probably in many other African countries) are corrupt remnants of systems imposed by the former colonial powers.

The organization of colonial police systems was in most cases tailored to maintain and protect colonial regimes and to thwart any resistance to colonial rule. Some policies and tactics were modified to combat resistance from groups within the colonized countries that were struggling for independence. Some of these groups, due to lack of legitimate access to voice their concerns, often resorted to the use of guerilla tactics[1] meant to disrupt colonial governments, often resulting in killing, destruction of property, and other forms of violence. Guerillas and other resistance groups were very willing to use all feasible tactics to disrupt colonial governments.[2] The colonialists responded by adopting repressive measures designed to combat rebellion and control emergency situations.

Long after independence and guerilla activities ended in Cameroon, current governments still maintain some of the same police structures and operating principles. Rather than reorganizing and properly training police to assume legitimate police functions in a civilian governmental structure,

Prepared especially for *Comparative and International Criminal Justice, 2/E.*

the old systems prevail. The present governments use repressive measures to advance political goals, and the police in turn use their offices for individual economic enrichment. This article maintains that these police systems are retained at great economic and social costs for these countries.

Police Functions

Clegg, Hunt, and Whetton's (2000) article, *The Policy Guide on Support to Policing in the Third World*, illustrates the distinction between police and policing. They define *police* as an entity, an institution comprised of values and ideals, having its own set of beliefs and doctrines. *Policing*, on the other hand, implies a set of procedures with specific social functions. It is the enforcement of ideals and social norms. Policing is the practical application of theoretical concepts and is unquestionably a societal expectation and norm for most functioning societies. It may be carried out in a variety of different processes and institutional arrangements.

The functions and responsibilities of police vary in different societies. This distinction is more apparent when comparing the industrialized countries with developing countries. In the industrialized systems, police agencies are undoubtedly the most visible exhibition of government power in most societies. Opolot (2001) calls them the gatekeepers of sovereignty for the purpose of social control and application of laws. They are the first criminal justice agency with which citizens have contact and, in turn, form opinions about the entire justice system. They represent the authority of the state, a symbol of state power. They are constantly under public scrutiny. Consequently their performance—particularly in crime prevention, control, use of power, and how they relate to the public—is constantly debated.

According to the American Bar Association (2003), the function of police in developed countries is to prevent and control conduct widely recognized as threatening to life and property. For example, American police prevent and control crime; aid individuals in danger of physical harm; protect constitutional guarantees; facilitate the movement of people and vehicles; assist those who cannot care for themselves; resolve conflict, whether it be between individuals, groups of individuals, or individuals and their government; identify problems that can potentially become more serious for the individual citizen, for the police, or for government; and generally create and maintain a feeling of security in the community.

Goldstein (1977), some decades ago, classified these functions into three main categories: order maintenance, law enforcement, and services. Order maintenance requires the engagement of police to prevent behaviors or actions that disrupt, threaten, and impede public peace. This could range from interpersonal conflict to conflicts between citizens and other groups in society. Basic techniques for these functions are patrol and calls for service. The law enforcement category calls for controlling crime by intervening when the law has been violated or preventing planned criminal activity from coming to fruition (p. 147). The performance of these functions requires investigative and other techniques. The service category entails general police services not related to crime prevention, although it has been realized in recent years that these activities help prevent crime (Watson, Stone, & Deluca, 1998). Goldstein's classification is typical of police functions in Western democratic and industrialized countries.

In developing countries, however, police function differently than in industrialized countries (Zveki, 1996). Opolot (2001) writes about the unique nature of the variation of police functions in developing countries. He classifies the transformation functions of police in developing countries of Africa into primary and secondary functions. One view holds that police should perform certain *primary functions*—specified duties that align themselves with the consensus view of the responsibilities of police. Such duties include arresting suspects, preventing and investigating crime, maintaining law and order, controlling traffic, patrol, and so on (p. 159). The purpose of the secondary function is to support and strengthen the primary functions—similar to the service category of police in industrialized countries. Opolot contends that the *secondary functions* are an important component of policing for developing countries because of the political nature of policing in these societies. Policing in developing African nations is affected by the political realities of their evolving histories and current existing conditions. The diversity of the different forms of government makes the application of policing ideals daunting. Governmental systems in Africa are constantly evolving. Although recently most African countries are experimenting with democracy, military and despotic regimes still exist in Africa.

Consequently, the police function of crime control in developing societies cannot be isolated from the socioeconomic, cultural, and political environment of these societies (Hills, 1996). For example, Clegg, Hunt, and Whetton (2000) identify two factors that illustrate the impact of crime in developing or transitional societies: (1) the poor are almost always the victims of crimes of violence, and (2) the poor suffer more heavily from the effects of all forms of crime (p. 5). Moreover, according to this view, if the political influences on the application of the law are ignored, the application of the law becomes problematic. Some of the practical realities of developing countries complicate the ability of the police to function properly. For example, Clegg, Hunt, and Whetton state how police in developing countries are often ill-equipped to respond to the demands for service because of limited resources and because they also have to contend with cultural practices that play an important role in people's daily lives (p. 19).

In developed countries, models of justice involve due process of law and enforcement styles. In developing countries police agencies are forced to deal with more basic forms of social control. For example, police find it difficult to address issues of violence and crime without addressing the equally large issues of poverty and hunger. Consequently, developed societies are generally more satisfied with police than are developing societies (Zveki, 1996). The effect of dissatisfaction and other influences is crucial to the understanding of policing in developing and transitional societies, because as Zveki (1996) states, the public's view of police reflects their concerns about crime, police behavior toward the public, and other issues that concern them.

Therefore, police actions are the basis by which the public often judge government's ability to control crime, right to privacy, and human rights abuses. Also, police misconduct is often viewed as government misconduct (*Monel v. Department of Social Services*, 1978; Peak, 1997). In this sense, public expectations of police in developed countries differ from those in developing countries. These distinctions are more obvious in Westernized, industrialized nations with well-developed judicial systems, where public expectations reflect public interests, including professional treatment, citizens' rights, and services. Expectations of the public in developing societies are more basic, ranging from simple recovery of stolen property and minimum protection to bringing offenders to justice (Zveki, 1996).

Each police institution in the world functions in a social milieu that has its own unique characteristics (Hart, 1996; Stojanovski & Sinadi-novska-Zdraveska, 1996; Reynolds, 1996). Because police in developing countries are affected by the political and cultural restraints of their respective societies, their functions and roles are a direct reflection of their history and evolution. The colonial legal model of policing imposed by the former colonial regimes is the standard in most African countries (Hills, 1996). These Western styles of policing are at times difficult to sustain in these developing countries because of their inherent formal qualities. Walker (1992), writing on the responsibilities of police, observes that the most important factor shaping the police role is their twenty-four-hour availability but observes that no police organization is immune to external influences. Many authors (e.g., Hills, 1996, 2001; Koch, 1996; Bayley, 1998) suggest other factors—most importantly, the culture of a society—that affect police and police institutions. For example, Hills (1996) states that the police institutions are affected by the history, customs, norms, values, and beliefs of the system.

Ivković and Haberfeld (2000) examine the evolution of police in Poland and Croatia. They conclude that cultural and other influences on police functions are not mutually exclusive to transitional societies. They state that the political nature of developing countries is the driving force behind future changes. They observe that countries that have had a militia face different circumstances when considering a change to a formalized police system, because in their past such nations were accustomed to police states where expectations are different (p. 196). In such nations, police were established auxiliaries of government, created to watch anti-government activities. Although the militia had law enforcement authority, their main function was to protect the interest of the regime in power. Ivković and Haberfeld's observations reflect similar circumstances in many developing nations where political stability is lacking. For instance, Nigeria, Ghana, and some nations of the Former Eastern and Soviet bloc facing constant changes are fairly unstable. The need to change philosophy and function is often central in any attempt to create a democratic form of police.

The fact that developing countries inherit police systems from their colonial regimes has often called into question the legitimacy of the police in these societies. This question of legitimacy requires consideration of the relationship between the purpose of the police and their mission in society (i.e., the philosophy of policing and the element of legitimate authority). When the community as a whole provides policing its legitimacy, as is the case in England, for example, it is called *policing by consent* (Koci, 1996). Often the legitimization of a type of policing is dictated by the cultural, socioeconomic, and political situation in a specific society. The justification for a certain style of policing is a means of acquiring legitimacy, which in turn determines police functions and structure. Thus, a change in a country's political philosophy entails the adoption of a new policing justification that matches new or amended governmental philosophies (Hills, 1996). As Koci (1996, p. 4) notes, King and Brearly (1996) illustrate this type of change in England, where the riots of the 1980s and 1990s necessitated changes in policing styles. The riots had illustrated a lack of support for police, creating a negative impact on their legitimacy. Because of these riots, the methods and tactics of dealing with public disorder underwent substantial revisions.

Most of the literature seems to demonstrate the impact of sociopolitical factors on police organization and their functions (see, for example, Hills, 1966; Walker, 1992; Ivković & Haberfeld, 2000; Opolot, 2001). Police organizations differ from one another in terms of equipment, use of force, efficiency, recruitment and training criteria, their status in society, and the tasks they perform (Bayley, 1998). Differences in the patterns of policing between countries also are attributed to the variations in their culture and history. For example, policing in America faced a crisis in the 1960s. The civil rights movement, antiwar sentiment, social unrest, and rising crime brought police under greater scrutiny (Dunham & Alpert, 2005). To cope with these crises the government created a commission that resulted in the Law Enforcement Assistance Administration. The events of the 1960s forced police and policy makers to reassess law enforcement because traditional methods of patrol, officer selection, and training were questioned.

Policing in the developing countries of Africa is particularly influenced by history. These countries inherited most of their police systems from some form of European occupying power. In cases when police legitimacy is provided by an occupying power, the police system hardly ever gains the public's trust and support. The method of policing that was imposed on the African countries by the British and French colonialists was highly coercive and militarized (Opolot, 2001).

The Case of Cameroon

Brief History

The Portuguese were the first Europeans to arrive in Cameroon in the 1500s, and it was not until around 1870 that many more Europeans began to arrive on the West Coast of Africa. By 1884, present-day Cameroon had become the German colony of Kamerun. After the First World War the former East Cameroon became French Cameroon, while the former West Cameroon became British Cameroon under the United Nations Trusteeship agreement. The two European powers ruled Cameroon until 1960–1961. French Cameroon achieved independence in 1960 as the Republic of Cameroon. The following year the British granted their own territory independence. Amadou Ahidjo[3] became the first president of the Federated Republic.

Cameroon is in West Africa, situated north of the equator on the Gulf of Guinea. It encompasses 185,569 square miles, roughly the size of California. It borders Nigeria to the west; Chad and Central African Republic to the east; and Congo, Gabon, and Equatorial Guinea to the south. Cameroon has a population of approximately 16 million people. The French occupied three-fourths of Cameroon, and French-speaking Cameroonians are known as Francophones. This explains the bilingual nature of Cameroon, with the Anglophone Cameroonians in the minority. There are ten provinces, and only two are Anglophone: Northwest Province and Southwest Province. (See Njeuma, 1989, for more details.)

Cameroon began its independence with a bloody insurrection that was suppressed only with the help of French forces,[4] followed by 20 years of repressive government under President Ahidjo. Like other African nations, the struggle for independence began in the middle of the 1900s. In 1955, the outlawed Union of the Peoples of Cameroon (UPC) began an armed struggle for independence in French Cameroon (U.S. Department of State, 2003) that continued until 1960 when French Cameroon became independent.[5] In 1961, following a UN-sponsored referendum, British Cameroon (at the time part of Nigeria)[6] rejoined the Republic of Cameroon to become the Federal Republic of Cameroon.

Over 200 ethnic groups make up the diverse population within the country. After gaining independence, Cameroon was ruled by former President Ahidjo until November 4, 1982, when he unexpectedly resigned and handed over his power (the presidency) to Prime Minister Paul Biya. Since 1982, Biya has continued to govern in his capacity as president of Cameroon, chairman of the Cameroon People's Democratic Movement (CPDM), and supreme commander of the armed forces.

Origins of Cameroon Police

The origin of the Cameroon police is attributed to both the former East Cameroon and the former West Cameroon. The former West Cameroon police force had its roots in the Nigerian police force, because Nigeria was a British colony. Under the League of Nations mandate of June 28, 1919, following World War I, Cameroon was partitioned between Britain and France. France received the larger East Cameroon and ruled it from Yaounde, its capital, while Britain ruled the smaller section bordering Nigeria from Lagos, the capital of Nigeria, one of its major colonial African countries. The plebiscite of 1961 (U.S. Department of State, 2003) led to West Cameroon's opting to rejoin the Eastern region. The new country, the Federal Republic of Cameroon, thus began with two separate police systems.

Most of the members of the first West Cameroon police force were members of the Nigerian police force. With the secession of West Cameroon from the Federation of Nigeria and the subsequent reunification of the two Cameroons, most of the West Cameroon indigents serving in the Nigerian police force returned home to serve in the newly created West Cameroon police force. Additionally, a special force was created to assume the functions of the retiring British security and defense forces that had been stationed in West Cameroon.[7] In July 1961, selected members of the special force were recruited and trained to take over from the British army. After their training, they were designated as the *Mobile Wing* of the police. West Cameroon police remained in force until a presidential order of 1969[8] merged the West Cameroon and East Cameroon police forces, creating the Delegation for National Security, a single police force for the country.

The role of the police in the former East Cameroon was based on the security needs of the French colonialists, the evolution of political events, and the conglomeration of people in urban centers.[9] The first police were created as early as 1925. The French High Commissioner's order of November 7, 1925,[10] created a police station in Douala. Two subsequent orders of June 28, 1930, and March 28, 1938, defined the modalities for the exercise of public security in urban areas such as Douala. The delineation of these modalities was necessitated by increases in trade unions and political unions. Another order of March 22, 1939,[11] outlined the structure of the police force and its functions in the fight against crime. Eventually police regional offices were created in all the areas of the country, particularly in the urban centers. In 1963, after East Cameroon obtained its independence from France, a presidential order of October 26, 1963,[12] created the *Surete Federal*, which maintained security within the federation. This Federal Surete existed until 1969, when the aforementioned Delegation of National Security was created after the reunification of the Cameroons.

Cameroon, like its former colonial master, has two types of police: the national security police and the gendarmerie. The gendarmerie is a paramilitary police force that performs some police as well as military functions—primarily a French type of police[13] operating out the Ministry of Defense, but unlike the French gendarmeries that only have conventional crime-control functions in the French rural areas (Fairchild & Dammer, 2001), Cameroon gendarmes operate nationally. As it is the case for other French colonies, the French created the Cameroon Gendarmerie shortly after the Second World War, when France was awarded part of Cameroon as a trust territory. After independence and the reunification of East and West Cameroon in the early 1960s, gendarme offices were extended to the whole country.

As stated earlier, police are to a large degree a reflection of societal norms. For example, Koci (1996) states that Alderson (1985) "attributes the emergence of the state police in Germany during the eighteenth century to the political and social turmoil prevailing in the country as a result of the Thirty Years War" (p. 4). Likewise, Stead (1983) found that in post-revolutionary France of the nineteenth century, fear of coups d'état and other revolutionary upheavals made possible the emergence of a highly centralized police, who had a clearly defined political character in safeguarding the regime (Koci, 1996, p. 4).

Similarly, in Cameroon, the type and nature of police forces reflect its historical past[14] and the cultural realities of the country. Originating mainly from the French and similar in structure, it has both the National Police and the Gendarmerie National. The colonial police in Cameroon were introduced to protect colonial political ideology and later modified in terms of organization and training to deal with indigenous resistance to colonialism and independence.[15]

The legitimacy or raison d'être for maintaining this structure after independence was that rebellious groups (e.g., the UPC, Marquisards[16]) continued their activities against the government of President Ahidjo[17] after Cameroon achieved independence. The Ahidjo government responded by attempting to crush the guerillas, using many tactics that were often as brutal as those used by the guerillas themselves, such as those practiced by the French to foil struggles for independence. During French colonial rule and the early years of Ahidjo's reign, police employed torture against those who threatened the government. Those subjected to these tactics were mainly members of the UPC (Awasom, 2000).

Other reasons for maintaining the status quo can be advanced, including the government's desire to strengthen its hold on power and police realization that their offices can be used for individual economic gain. Physical and psychological torture have proliferated (Mentan, 2002). Amnesty International reports over the last few years indicate that the routine torture and ill treatment of political detainees and criminal suspects are routine (Amnesty International, 2000, 2001, 2002, 2003). Cameroon's inherited colonial system of police still prevails. As Hills (1996) notes, Western concepts have continued to affect African policing long after independence, mainly by means of offered advice and training in the performance of functions (p. 274).

Organization of Cameroon Police

Surete Nationale

The present structure of the Cameroon National Police is outlined in Decree number 2002/003 of January 4, 2002,[18] under the name of the General Delegation of National Security. According to the decree, national security and its administrative officials are under the control of the president of the Republic. This function is shared by the National Intelligence Service, the Gendarmerie Nationale, the Ministry of Territorial Administration, Military Intelligence, the army, and to a lesser extent, the Presidential Guard. The police and the gendarmerie have dominant roles in enforcing internal security laws. The civilian minister of defense and the civilian head of police are also responsible for internal security (U.S. Department of State, 2002).

Article 5 of the decree states that police authority comes directly from the president. They execute orders as handed down by government authorities under the directives of the committee of defense and territorial administration. Police power extends to the national territory. Articles 6 and 7 of the decree detail the organization of *Surete Nationale*. Article 3 states the mission of national security as protecting the institutions, public liberty, people, and property; to maintain law and order; and to assure the defense of the nation. Article 4 outlines the functions of the National Police. They include:

- responsibility for the internal and external security of the State,
- investigating and arresting those who have violated the criminal laws and bringing them to justice,
- maintaining law and order, particularly in the urban areas,
- fighting national, international and transnational crime,
- crime investigation, and
- using public contacts to obtain information and to intervene for the security and protection under national defense.

Gendarmerie Nationale

According to decree number 2001/181 of July 25, 2001, the Cameroon gendarmerie is placed under the authority of the secretariat of state at the Ministry of Defense. The secretariat has two main functions: (a) administering the national gendarmerie, and (b) delineating the rules and regulations necessary in the accomplishment of the missions of the national gendarmerie.

The secretariat maintains both central services and territorial control. The central services consist of a private secretariat, a department of general affairs, and an inspectorate general for the national gendarmerie, a department for coordination, a department for administration and logistics, and some specialized units. The Gendarmerie is made up of units of territorial gendarmes, a company of specialized gendarmes, a gendarmerie brigade, and a special brigade. The general functions of the gendarme force include defense of the national territory, public security, maintenance of public order, execution of the law, and prevention and suppression of crime.

Assessment of Police Performance

The system of policing introduced in Cameroon during the colonial period was used to fight forces that were struggling for independence and to protect colonial administrations and goals. They used unconventional tactics including the *kale-kale*,[19] *laissez passer*,[20] administrative detention,[21] collective punishment,[22] burning of villages, arrest for challenging governmental authority, detention in underground jails,[23] curfews, and summary executions. Additionally, roadblocks were introduced very early in the history of Cameroon to control citizen movement, particularly in major cities like Douala. Thus, the French and early Cameroon indigenous governments legitimized the use of these tactics (brute force, roadblocks, etc.) under the pretext of combating guerilla groups, such as marquisards and other freedom fighters who used violence against colonial governments and even against their own citizens.

The practices and tactics used by Cameroon police prior to independence and in the years following independence are still currently in use. Unwarranted torture and other forms of abuse by the police and the gendarmerie are still widespread. As recently as 2003, anti-gang units using a mix of army personnel, police, and gendarmerie created under the direct authority of the Ministry of Defense (not subject to legal rules and operating outside the normal chain of command of law and order) were accused of carrying out extra-judicial executions. Critics of the government— including supporters of opposition parties, journalists, and human rights activists—are often harassed, arrested, and imprisoned (Amnesty International, 2000, 2001, 2002, 2003).

As noted earlier, after coming into power the Ahidjo government had to quell rebellion.[24] He needed French assistance and upon receiving it allowed the police to use the same tactics used by the French prior to independence. Long after the rebellion ended, Ahidjo and subsequent governments have maintained the same police structures, policies, and practices. This system does not serve any public need, but rather serves only the government's political agenda and the personal economic interests of the police. As Mentan (2002) states, the government continues to operate repressive machinery through its armed forces to impose constraints, terror, and coercion on its citizens. The systematic use of armed intimidation occurs under the pretext of maintaining law and order. Police (including the gendarmerie) and the military regularly arrest, torture, or kill those suspected of violating the laws of the state. A corrupt judiciary directly under the control of the president[25] passes judgment and determines punishment.

The desire of the government to exercise total control over police is obvious. Though complicated by attempts to convince the public and the rest of the world that it expects its police to respect the public and the law, the government has permitted police to use unacceptable practices in its attempt to eliminate opposition and to fight rising crime (Mentan, 2002). In a special United Nations report, Nigel Rodley[26] describes the practice of torture in Cameroon as widespread and systematic. Reports of the country's hard-handed paramilitary police troops committing unauthorized executions of alleged criminals are very common. An operational command of the forces[27] established to combat banditry, especially in Douala (the economic capital of the country), has often been accused of carrying out human rights abuses and arbitrary detentions.

According to U.S. government sources, arbitrary arrest and prolonged detention remain a serious problem in Cameroon. Government officials and security forces use arbitrary arrest to harass and intimidate members of opposition parties and other critics of the government (Guichi, 2002). Often, security forces subject prisoners and detainees to degrading treatment including stripping, confinement in severely overcrowded cells, and denial of access to toilets or other sanitation facilities. Police and gendarmes often beat detainees to extract confessions, as well as to obtain the names and whereabouts of alleged criminals. While the law provides for a judicial review of an arrest within 24 hours, the courts do not convene sessions on the weekend, so detainees arrested on Friday remain in detention until at least Monday (U.S. Department of State, 2002).

The government, under the pretext of maintaining law and order and providing security to its citizens, has granted police wide discretion in the use of police powers. Regrettably, the police largely abuse those powers, to the disadvantage of citizens. The real purposes of tolerating such misconduct are political. The present government—threatened by mounting opposition to its misrule, an epidemic of armed robbery (largely because of widespread unemployment and the attendant poverty), and attempts at cleansing political opposition—has allowed different groups of armed militia to torture and even kill at will, with little chance that they will be brought to justice.

Effects of Police Lack of Performance

Since police are the most visible component of government in most countries (Opolot, 2001) and represent the authority of the state (Wrobleski & Hess, 2000), their actions have consequences on the societies they police. Inadequate police performance in Cameroon has resulted in three main consequences: uncontrolled rising crime, economic cost, and social costs.

Rising Crime Rate

The crime rate in Cameroon has increased consistently since indepen-dence. This is to be expected, given the increase in the country's popula-tion from about 3 million at the time of independence to the present population of approximately 16 million. The population of the major cities is increasing on average by 5% each year (Tetchiada, 2002). The growth of urban centers is partly due to the natural increase in the population associated with major cities, but it is also due to the loss of land resulting from erosion, as well as to poverty and unemployment. People who move to the cities in search of economic and social opportunities are often met with frustration and contempt. Because of economic recession and gov-ernment incompetence and corruption, jobs are virtually unavailable. Generally, it is believed that urban problems in Cameroon were worsened by the government's economic policies in the 1980s and 1990s, policies mostly dictated by the World Bank and the International Monetary Fund (Nguekeng, 2003).

These urban problems have resulted in horrid consequences for the country. Social unrest is evident everywhere: a high crime rate; lack of security; corruption; the authorities' inefficiency; disparity in salaries; and, especially, the omnipresence of poverty (Nguekeng, 2003). In 2002, the government created Operation Harmattan (in reference to the hot, dry wind that blows southwards from the Sahara each year, sweeping northern Cameroon and other parts of the Sahel) in response to the wave of killings and armed attacks against senior state officials, as well as break-ins at pub-lic offices in the main cities of Yaounde and Douala. Major incidents of vio-lent crime against government officials (e.g., the assassinations of the commander of the mobile police unit in Bamenda in 2001, a magistrate in Yaounde in 2000, and a diplomat in Douala in the same year) often pro-voke some form of government response (United Nations, 2002). However, crimes against citizens do not often provoke a similar response. Crime has also become a political issue, with opposition leaders often issuing public calls to the government to find solutions to the ever-increasing problem.

Many recent sources confirm the problem of increased crime in Came-roon (U.S. Department of State, 2002, 2003; United Nations, 2002). The steady rise in the crime rate is an apparent consequence of the shortcom-ings of the police. Reasons for the high incidence of crime in Cameroon, according to observers, include inefficient police efforts at fighting crime, police corruption, lack of resources, the unchecked circulation of weapons, revenge killings, poverty, and unemployment (United Nations, 2002). The crime problem is so severe that in March 2003, the U.S. Department of State issued a warning to its citizens traveling to Cameroon, stating that all foreigners were potential targets for theft and possible violence. Petty crimes, crimes against persons, and thefts from vehicles are the most com-mon criminal activities. Armed banditry is a growing problem throughout all ten provinces. The risk of street and residential crime is high, and incidents of violent crime are on the rise throughout the country. Carjackings have also been reported on rural highways (U.S. Department of State, 2002). As late as February of 2004, the British Foreign Service issued a warning to its citizens to avoid carrying valuables or wearing jewelry in public. Petty theft is common on trains, in coaches, and in taxis (UK Foreign & Commonwealth Office, 2004).

Economic Cost

Evidence indicates that Cameroon police are not interested in performing police duties of deviance control within their own ranks. Most Cameroon police are deployed on state roads or highways as opposed to performing crime-fighting functions. The old tactic of mounting multiple blockades used in colonial and post-colonial periods to control the movement of rebellious groups continues. It is common to have police, gendarmes, and sometimes military blockades at main entrances and exits of cities and towns as well as on the few state highways, mounted under the pretext of checking for criminals and transportation of contraband, but functioning mostly to shake down motorists for bribes. The unofficial roadblocks are manned by military guards, who use them as a corrupt way to make money or to intimidate those passing through. The average Cameroon motorist knows the standard price for police or gendarme stops.

Moreover, the difficulties of travel are exacerbated by the extortion of bribes at these checkpoints. The sight of uniformed officers haggling with motorists over the amount of a bribe has become common on the state routes. Roadblocks usually include verification of identification documents, vehicle registrations, and tax receipts as alleged security and immigration control measures. Sometimes citizens are injured by police if they are perceived as attempting to evade checkpoints. Security forces also use roadblocks to disrupt opposition political activities (U.S. Department of State, 2002).

An article in *The Economist* (Trucking in Cameroon, 2002) narrates the account of a foreign correspondent regarding the burden that police activities are creating in the country. Although tourists who stay on the beaten path don't often have the experience this journalist describes, ". . . the people who actually live and work in countries with rotten infrastructure have to cope with the consequences every day. These are as profound as they are malign" (p. 75).

The narrative describes a ride hitched on a beer truck, on a delivery route that should have taken 20 hours but in fact took four days. The reason for the delay was simple: the truck was stopped at roadblocks 47 times. The roadblocks were jerry-rigged from old oil drums, tires, and planks with upturned nails protruding—the latter to be easily moved aside when police decided a vehicle was allowed to pass.

> Sometimes, they merely gawped into the cab or glanced at the driver's papers for a few seconds before waving him on. But the more aggressive ones detained us somewhat longer. Some asked for beer. Some complained that they were hungry, often patting their huge stomachs to emphasize the point. One asked for pills, lamenting that he had indigestion. But most wanted hard cash, and figured that the best way to get it was to harass motorists until bribed to lay off. (ibid.)

Taillights, axles, wing mirrors, and tires were inspected "in the name of safety," but the vehicle was allowed to pass when ample cash was offered. "One police officer decided that the driver did not have enough permits and offered to sell him another for twice the usual price. When he asked for a receipt, they kept us waiting for three-and-a-half hours" (ibid., p. 75).

> The pithiest explanation of why Cameroonians have to put up with all this came from the gendarme at roadblock number 31. He had invented a new law about carrying passengers in trucks, found the driver guilty of breaking it, and confiscated his driving license. When it was put to him that the law he was citing did not, in fact, exist, he patted his holster and replied: "Do you have a gun? No. I have a gun, so I know the rules." (ibid., p. 75)

The law allegedly provides for freedom of movement within the country. However, in practice, security forces routinely impede domestic travel. The author of the *Economist* article concluded that ". . . governments of poor countries ought to pay more attention to their roads. A good first step in Cameroon would be to lift those roadblocks and put the police to work repairing potholes" (Trucking in Cameroon, 2002, p. 75).

Social Cost

Although the social cost has never been estimated, the nature of police practices is an apparent barometer of the social costs of police performance—or lack of it. Injuries, human rights abuses, and loss of lives, property, and public support are just a few examples of the high social cost of police failure to perform their functions. Only a small percentage of police are engaged in crime prevention and resolution of crime. Judging from the attitudes of police and government officials, crime prevention seems to be secondary to other government policies and individual police gains (Mentan, 2002).

Like the economic cost, the social cost to the country is alarming. The failure to perform proper law enforcement duties leads to an increase in crime and jeopardizes individual rights. Because police seem most concerned with mounting roadblocks to collect money from motorists, little or no time remains to fight crime. Moreover, because criminals can bribe their way through police barricades, criminals are able to operate freely all over the country.

Blockades often result in confrontation between motorists and police. They allow police to shake down motorists and passengers for bribes resulting in unnecessary, degrading, and intrusive inspections. Moreover, the need for money and other forms of bribes also blind the police to traffic violations. Because there is little or no interest in enforcing traffic laws, accidents are common—some of which are fatal.

The legitimacy of Cameroon police, as well as police in many developing countries of Africa which inherited their police systems from European powers, has never been linked to public need (Opolot, 2001; Mentan, 2002). As Koci notes, how police acquire legitimacy is of fundamental importance in understanding their relationship with the state and with society in general (Koci, 1996, p. 3). Because Cameroon inherited its police from an occupying power, the resulting lack of legitimacy has resulted in Cameroonians' loss of faith in their police. As Mentan (2002) states, public perception of interaction between the police authorities and the population has become increasingly negative. Because of the way police treat citizens, the public's attitude is one of disrespect. According to one Cameroon journalist, "Bogged down by corruption, racketeering, torture and lack of discipline, Cameroon's police force does not have good press. The police pay a high price for its failings, so some kind of shock tactics are needed to set matters right" (Mihamle, 1998, p. 1).

Conclusion

We have examined the role of police in a developing country and how the creation of the police force in Cameroon has reflected the country's political past. As a United Nations trust territory following the First World War, Cameroon inherited two types of police systems from the British and the French, respectively, during the trusteeship period. Upon independence and reunification, the French form of policing became dominant, in all likelihood because the French ruled a larger portion of the country.

This author maintains that the effects of colonization and political greed are major factors influencing the country's current police system. The colonial powers used unconventional methods to subdue early independence movements and rebellious groups that used bloody insurrections to fight colonialism. The first independent government continued using tactics originally adopted by colonialists (Awasom, 2000) because anti-colonial movements such as the UPC continued to fight the first post-independent government. The public viewed the first postcolonial government as French stooges rather than as a truly independent government. The postcolonial governments have used police systems to perpetuate their power.

Cameroon's current government officials continue to maintain most of the organizational structures, training methods, and tactics used by the colonialists and the first governments. In fact, they have maintained

French advisors to a current police system that has failed to perform conventional police functions. Government officials continue to use police as an instrument of perpetuating their political staying power, and police continue to use their offices for individual material gain. The police force in Cameroon exists at great cost to the country in economic, social, and criminal terms—a fact that seems not to bother those in political power. A continued critical analysis is called for, followed by an intense and consistent pattern of reform.

Notes

[1] In 1955 the *Union des Population du Cameroun* (UPC) was banned. It subsequently went underground to engage the French colonial administration in a prolonged, ferocious guerrilla war under the leadership of Ruben Um Nyobe. In Cameroon, groups such as the *marquisards* (see note 16) used guerilla tactics to fight the French, their colonial masters, during the struggle for independence.

[2] Tactics employed by groups struggling for independence included arbitrary arrests, torture in the form of beatings to obtain confessions, extended detentions without charges, curtailment of freedom by the use of the *laissez passer*, and most notoriously, the use of roadblocks to harass passengers under the guise of controlling for weapons and other contraband.

[3] Ahidjo ruled Cameroon until 1982, when he ceded the presidency to Prime Minister Paul Biya, the current president.

[4] See U.S. Department of State, Bureau of Consular Affairs, Background Notes (2003). Ahidjo, relying on a pervasive internal security apparatus, outlawed all political parties but his own in 1966. He successfully suppressed the UPC rebellion, capturing the last important rebel leader in 1970. In 1972, a new constitution replaced the federation with a unitary state.

[5] These events influenced the type of police system adopted by the French in Cameroon. The French needed a force to suppress the bloody insurrection. Ahidjo, the first president, was facing similar problems and needed French assistance. He maintained the police system the French had created to deal with similar problems.

[6] Under the League of Nations mandate of June 28, 1919, this part of Cameroon became a trust territory of the British, who ruled it from the capital of Nigeria.

[7] The British were withdrawing their forces from British Cameroon. It became necessary to have some kind of force to assume the responsibilities of the retiring British forces.

[8] When the two Cameroons became a federal republic in 1961, two police systems operated in the two regions. In 1969 the two forces merged to form the Delegation of National Security.

[9] Douala, where the first police force was created, is the economic capital of the country. Because it is Cameroon's main port city, it was the first town that grew rapidly and consequently needed police services. Moreover, the main resistance to French colonial rule and the first Cameroon government centered in Douala and the surrounding area.

[10] Before the creation of the police, law and order and other police functions were exercised by French gendarmes.

[11] This order granted police extensive powers to investigate all conspiracies attempting to disrupt or compromise the political security of the state.

[12] The need to adapt to the new situation of the country (i.e., the Federation) required the reorganization of police. The decree created a dual police force. The federal police had charge over internal and external security, judicial functions, immigration, and emigration. State police acquired the responsibility of public safety. The dual police system remained in force until 1969, when another presidential decree created a single national police.

[13] The French police organization is unusual. There are two French police organizations, the Police Nationale and the Gendarmerie Nationale. The Police Nationale operates within the interior ministry and is responsible for deviance control in the urban areas. The Gendarm-

erie Nationale operates out of the Ministry of Defense and is responsible for small towns and rural areas.

[14] When Cameroon attained independence from Britain and France in 1960, French Cameroon adopted the French police system while British Cameroon adopted the English.

[15] On reunification of West Cameroon and East Cameroon in 1972, the West Cameroon police were replaced by the former East Cameroon police system. In his administration Ahidjo found resistance similar to that against the French, whose assistance was needed to crush the rebellion, and he maintained the inherited system of police from the French. The system remains virtually the same today.

[16] *Marquisards* was the label given the insurgents who fought the French and then the first post-independent government in Cameroon. They originated mostly from Douala and were members of the banned UPC.

[17] Amadou Ahidjo was the first president of Cameroon, coming to the helm of the country after independence in 1960.

[18] The decree is the latest among the many that from time to time reorganize the structure of the national police and outline police functions.

[19] Under this process, citizens were rounded up for no specific crime or violation and would be checked for identification. Citizens without proper identification or suspected of insurrection were often detained for extensive periods without charge.

[20] The *laissez passer* was a form of permit issued by police that allowed citizens to go from one section of the country to another.

[21] It is often used by high-level government officials to illegally detain those who challenge their authority.

[22] Collective punishments include arresting and detaining entire groups of people on the assumption that they were harboring suspects of various violations. Often, some would lie about others' criminal activities to gain release.

[23] A form of maximum-security prison used mainly for political prisoners (e.g., members of the UPC and other groups that practiced violent insurrection against the government), located primarily in noninhabited areas.

[24] When Ahidjo assumed the presidency after Cameroon independence, the Union des Populations du Cameroun continued to fight the government installed by the French, claiming the government was illegitimate.

[25] In Cameroon, members of the judiciary are appointed by the president and are directly answerable to the presidency.

[26] Sir Nigel Rodley is United Nations Special Rapporteur on torture. See *United Nations Convention against Torture and other Cruel, Inhuman or Degrading Treatment or Punishment*, 04/12/2000.

[27] These commands usually are combined units of the army, police, gendarmes, and sometimes other units of law of the state.

References

Alderson, J. (1985). *Policing Freedom: A Commentary on the Dilemmas of Policing in Western Democracies*. Plymouth: Macdonald and Evans.

American Bar Association (ABA) (2003). Available: http://www.sociology.ohiostate.edu/mlw/soc209/functions.html.

Amnesty International: Country Report, Cameroon (2000; 2001; 2002; 2003). Available: amnesty.org/library.

Awasom, N. F. (2000). The Reunification Question in Cameroon History: Was the Bride an Enthusiastic or Reluctant One? *Africa Today*, 47(2).

Bayley, D. (1998). *Policing in America: Assessment and Prospects*. Washington, DC: Police Foundation.

Clegg, I., Hunt, R. & Whetton, J. (2000). *Policy Guide on Support to Policing in Developing Countries*, Center for Development Studies, University of Wales.

Dunham, R. & Alpert, G. (2005). *Critical Issues in Policing: Contemporary Readings, 5/E*. Long Grove, IL: Waveland Press.

Fairchild E. & Dammer H. (2001). *Comparative Criminal Justice Systems*. Belmont, CA: Wadsworth/Thompson Learning.

Goldstein, H. (1977). *Policing a Free Society*. Cambridge, MA: Ballinger.

Guichi, M. (2002). Execution of Cameroon Youths Provokes Demonstrations. *Afrol News* Available: www.afrol.com/countries/Cameroon.

Hart, J. (1996). The Management of Change in Police Organizations. In Milan Pagon (ed.), *Policing in Central and Eastern Europe: Comparing First Hand Knowledge with Experience from the West*. Ljubljana, SL: College of Police and Security Studies.

Hills, A. (1996). Towards a Critique of Policing and National Development in Africa. *The Journal of Modern African Studies*, 34(2), 271.

Hills, A. (2001). Police Reform in Post-Colonial Sates. Paper presented for a Workshop on Democratic Control of Policing and Security Sector Reform, November 1–2, 2001. Geneva: United Nations Office for Coordination of Humanitarian Affairs.

Ivkovic, S., & Haberfeld, M. (2000). Transformation from Militia to Police in Croatia and Poland. *Policing: An International Journal of Police Strategies and Management*, 23(2): 194–277.

King, M. & Brearley, N. (1996). *Public Order Policing: Contemporary Perspectives on Strategy and Tactics*. Leicester: Perpetuity Press.

Koch, U. (1996). Intercultural Human Management for Police Cooperation in Europe. In Milan Pagon (ed.), *Policing in Central and Eastern Europe: Comparing First Hand Knowledge with Experience from the West*. Ljubljana, SL: College of Police and Security Studies.

Koci, A. (1996). Legitimization and Culturalism: Towards Policing Change in the European Post-socialist Countries. In Milan Pagon (ed.), *Policing in Central and Eastern Europe: Comparing First Hand Knowledge with Experience from the west*. Ljubljana, SL: College of Police and Security Studies.

Mentan, T. (2002). Democratization and Ethnic Rivalries in Cameroon: Colonial Legacies, Democratization and Ethnic Questions in Cameroon. *UNESCO. Ethno-Net Africa*. Yaounde, Cameroon: UNESCO.

Mihamle, J. (1998). Cameroon's Police Dishonored. *AND-BIA Supplement*, Issue/Edition Nr. 355. (1/11/98).

Monel v. Department of Social Services, 436 U.S. 658 (1978).

Njeuma, M. (1989). *Introduction to the History of Cameroon: Nineteenth and Twentieth Centuries*. London: Macmillan.

Nguekeng, G. (2003). Cameroon Urban Deterioration: Various Projects Are Afoot to Improve Home, Public Services, Security and Administration. *ANB-BIA Supplement*. Issue/Edition Nr 465, 01/11/2003.

Opolot, J. (2001). *Police Administration in Africa: Toward Theory and Practice in the English-Speaking Countries*. Lanham, MD: Rowman & Littlefield.

Peak, K. (1997). *Policing America: Methods, Issues, Challenges*. Englewood Cliffs, NJ: Prentice Hall.

Reynolds, C. (1996). *Producing Change in Police Organizations: The Story of the New South Wales Police Service*. Contemporary Issues, Butterworths. Oxford, UK: Butterworth-Heinemann.

Stead, P. J. (1983).*The Police of France*. London: Collier Macmillan.

Stojanovski, T. & Sinadinovska-Zdraveska, Z. (1996). Police Opinion about Their Own Organization. In Milan Pagon (ed.), *Policing in Central and Eastern Europe: Comparing First Hand Knowledge with Experience from the West*. Ljubljana, SL: College of Police and Security Studies.

Tetchiada, S. (2002). Cameroon Faced with Social Inequalities. Despite Progress Already Made, There's Still a Long Way to Go. *ANB-BIA Supplement*. Issue/edition Nr 430, 15/03/2002.

Trucking in Cameroon: The Road to Hell Is Unpaved (2002). *The Economist*, vol. 365(8304): 75.

UK Foreign & Commonwealth Office (2004). *Country Profile, Cameroon*.

United Nations (1999). International Covenant on Civil and Political Rights (CCPR/C/79/Add.115). New York: United Nations.

United Nations (2002). Office for the Coordination of Humanitarian Affairs. Cameroon: Crime-fighters Arrest Hundreds Amid Complaints of Rights Abuse. New York: United Nations Office for the Coordination of Humanitarian Affairs.

U.S. Department of State (2002). Country Reports on Human Rights Practices. Washington, DC: U.S. Department of State, Bureau of Democracy, Human Rights, and Labor.

U.S. Department of State (2003). Bureau of Consular Affairs. Background Notes. Washington, DC: U.S. Department of State, Bureau of Consular Affairs.

Walker, S. (1992). *The Police in America: An Introduction*. New York: McGraw-Hill.

Watson, E., Stone, A. & Deluca, S. (1998). *Strategies for Community Policing*. Riverside, NJ: Simon & Schuster.

Wrobleski, M. & Hess, K. (2000). *An Introduction to Law Enforcement and Criminal Justice*. Belmont, CA: Wadsworth.

Zveki, U. (1996). Policing and Attitudes towards Police Private in Countries in Transition: Preliminary Results of the International Crime (Victim) Survey. In Milan Pagon (ed.), *Policing in Central and Eastern Europe: Comparing First Hand Knowledge with Experience from the West*. Ljubljana, SL: College of Police and Security Studies.

PART III

Law and Justice
Judicial Systems—
Formal and Informal

16

The Elusive Search for Uniform Sentencing
A Look at Denmark and Scotland

Rudy Prine & Marc Gertz

The trend of globalization reminds scholars of the need to develop a world community outlook. As researchers delve into other political, economic, or legal systems, a better understanding of their own systems may be possible. In order to develop courtroom theory it is important to discover the similarities and differences in judicial systems. The level of generalization is severely limited if different theoretical approaches are restricted by politically defined national boundaries. An important task is the search for universal concepts within different judicial systems.

Common problems, such as the resolution of criminal cases and the application of appropriate punishment, plague all Western democracies. The search for the conditions under which uniform justice exists is an important issue, not only for criminological researchers but also for all jurists as well. If a system seems to have a legal model that applies uniform justice, then that model should be studied.

The original research in the Danish judiciary comprises the heart of this article; however, the analysis has extended to include another country. As the argument is outlined below Scotland was chosen for a variety of reasons. First, Scotland shares with the United States a Common Law heritage. Second, all too often Scotland, in terms of criminological research, is grouped together with England, Wales, and Northern Ireland, even though it has a distinct legal system. Third, English—our common language— makes it much easier for the authors both to understand written procedures and to interpret courtroom observations. Fourth, Scotland is similar to Denmark in that it has a relatively small, homogenous population.

Prepared especially for *Comparative and International Criminal Justice, 2/E*.

Why Study Denmark and Scotland?

Wilson and Herrnstein (1985) suggest a comparative approach as a way for criminologists to do research where genuine experimentation is difficult. Research within a cross-national context allows the criminologist a way to "experiment" with judicial process. Such a method frees observers from the tunnel vision of ethnocentrism and allows a clearer picture of their own system. If researchers truly are interested in making justice more uniform and humane, perhaps the key lies in comparative research. Friday (1988) considers Scandinavia to have the most progressive, innovative, and humane justice system in the world. Andenaes (1984) touts the Danish court system as applying uniform and lenient sentences.

This is not to say that all procedures and techniques can be transplanted from other countries to the United States. Langbein (1977) warns against copying procedures or institutions that may depend on other features of a country's culture. However, it certainly seems worth the effort to study in more detail court systems perceived to be both humane and progressive. The major issue this research addresses is the question of sentencing uniformity—whether it exists and, if so, what the contributing factors are. This is an important topic because the uniform application of justice is a goal of all systems. Sentencing uniformity is a demonstration of how close reality fits this ideal. An examination of the extent of variability in sentencing patterns is an empirical means of measuring the uniformity of justice in two different cultural contexts. Rather than depending on secondary statistics, this project penetrates into the actual court system. Sources utilized include actual participants in the day-to-day functions of the Danish and Scottish court systems.

Cultural Context

Culturally, politically, and geographically Denmark belongs to the group of nations that make up the area known as Scandinavia. Mead (1986) comments that the social scientist in Scandinavia can work with ease and greater effectiveness because of similar social structures, accessibility of statistical materials, lower thresholds of confidentiality, positive attitudes of bureaucrats toward such inquiries, and the familiarity of the public with investigations (p. 28). Scandinavia, or Norden, is comprised of Denmark, Finland, Norway, and Sweden. These countries are located on the outer northern perimeter of Western Europe. The term *periphery* is used by Nordic writers in reference to the social and cultural isolationism from mainstream Europe (Klinge, 1986). While an argument can be made for isolationism from Europe, at least geographically, there seems to be a great deal of cooperative effort among the Scandinavian countries. Some examples of inter-Nordic cooperation are common marketing and purchasing schemes, standardized methods of accounting, common labor market legislation, and transport agreements (Mead, 1986: 42).

Scotland is grounded culturally, socially, and politically within the United Kingdom, which is comprised of England, Scotland, Wales, and Northern Ireland. It too lies at the northern extremity of the British Isles but is well connected via major transportation routes to the more populated England in the south.

Denmark is indeed a unique environment in which to study criminal justice problems since it is a small country, about the size of West Virginia, with a relatively homogenous population of less than six million. Of the total, approximately one-third live in the Copenhagen area. Although Greenland is a Danish possession, its isolation and low population are reasons to exclude it from the current study.

In Denmark, a very small increase in total population is due to immigration (Nu-Serien, 1999). Over half of the new immigrants are from other Scandinavian countries. All Nordic countries make it easy for workers to move from one country to the other as far as receiving state benefits and obtaining work permits. Although Scotland shares a similar policy, more recently it has conveyed its sense of independence with the establishment of a Scottish parliament separate and distinct from England. However, its allegiance stays firmly grounded within the United Kingdom.

Economically Denmark is more socialistic in nature than the United States, but it has been characterized as the most capitalistic of the Scandinavian countries (Kyvsgaard, 1984). With economic and resource differences creating class lines, it is possible class differences might be a contributing factor to crime. However, Graubard (1986) comments that the differences in rank and fortune or the absence of extremes in wealth create a distinctive civilization. Dahl (1986) calls taxes (the inheritance tax especially) the great levelers. Jones (1986) adds that social legislation has given practically every Dane freedom from fear of poverty or hardship. He refers to the social welfare system as a "social security supermarket."

The counterargument is that even though people of the Nordic countries may place a high value on equality and equity, there are still general patterns of structural inequality. Pontinen (1983) studied social mobility and the inequalities of opportunity among the Scandinavian countries. His conclusions should sound familiar to the U.S. student—the best life chances go to upper white-collar children and the worst to the children of workers and farmers. Education, within limitations, seems to be the best ladder of upward mobility.

All of the above factors to a certain extent apply to Scotland. Students may think of a continuum with the United States as the more capitalistic, conservative, and socially heterogeneous country compared to the other two. Denmark is more socialistic, liberal, and socially homogenous, with Scotland in between, but in regard to public policy Scotland most likely is a bit closer to Denmark than to the United States. But this is one of the attractions of Scotland: a shared Common Law tradition yet a divergence on social policy compared to the United States.

It is tempting to speculate on the effects of social class in regard to crime and sentencing, considering Denmark's liberal social welfare system. However, the social stratification of Denmark and Scotland, although structurally an important issue, is beyond the scope of this discussion.

Legal History

An American observer is often in awe of the historical tradition found in European countries. Both Denmark and Scotland have a rich heritage in the study of law. For example, the University of Copenhagen, founded in 1479, offered legal courses by the end of the fifteenth century. Tamm (1982) states that by 1736 there was a formal legal university examination, especially relevant to the qualifications for judges and other key administrative officers.

The first Danish penal code came into existence in 1683. It was the first attempt at systematic arrangement of criminal law in Denmark. In it is the premise that all persons are equal before the law. Vagn Greve and his colleagues (1984) point out that in contradiction to the process of centralization there was not an attempt to "transfer the prosecution of criminal cases to the exclusive authority of the officials of the king." Such a process follows the history of the rise of power for parliament at the expense of the monarchy. Thus, history reveals no bloody revolutions in Denmark.

While Scotland's past indeed has had its share of bloody revolutions, in regard to the prosecution of cases the office of the Lord Advocate is indeed an ancient one. By the sixteenth century the Advocate prosecuted regularly in the public interest, and his right to prosecute was confirmed by an Act of 1597 (Crown Office: 2001).

A. S. Orsted, the father of modern Danish criminal law, was the author of four penal codes from 1833 to 1841. He was also influential in the construction of the 1866 penal code, in which judges were given discretion in sentencing depending on the seriousness of the offense and the circumstances of the offender, rather than being hampered by a set of mandatory statutory penalties (Greve et al., p. 4). Emphasis has been on the seriousness of the crime and the extent of the damage caused. Tamm (1981) notes that as far back as 1789 the punishment for theft was reduced to a system of minimum and maximum penalties. Tamm sees this as a development that went even farther than Beccaria's proposals calling for statutory penalties as a response to the arbitrariness of the courts. Indeed, a system of maximum and minimum guidelines has survived today and provides a framework from which perceived uniform sentencing emerges (Andenaes, 1984).

Court Structure

Basically, the court system in both Denmark and Scotland is three tiered (see table 1); however, there are several unique differences between the two models. In Denmark, level-one courts, the lower or city courts, resolve a majority of the criminal cases. In Scotland, level-one courts are designated as district courts. In the Scottish district courts, judges may be either justices of the peace or a legally qualified magistrate (only in Glasgow). Justices of the peace are the only non-lawyer judges in Scotland, and the maximum penalty that they may give is sixty days.

Table 1   Court Systems of Denmark and Scotland

Denmark	Scotland
Level One—City Court	Level One—District Court
Level Two—High Court	Level Two—Sheriff's Court
Level Three—Supreme Court	Level Three—High Court

At level two the Scots' sheriff's courts exercise a wide civil and criminal jurisdiction. The sheriff (or judge, by U.S. terminology) may sit with or without a jury. If a jury is present, the maximum sentence that the sheriff may impose is three years imprisonment. However, if the sheriff believes that a harsher sentence is called for due to aggravated circumstances, the case may be sent to the Scottish High Court for sentencing. Generally, a sheriff without a jury is limited to giving a maximum sentence of twelve months. The majority of criminal cases in Scotland are resolved in the sheriff's courts.

Level-two courts, designated the high courts in Denmark, try the most serious cases. Graver offenses have possible penalties of four years imprisonment or more, but even these offenses may be tried in a lower court if there is a confession. The high courts may hear appeals from both the prosecution and defense, but the court of last resort in Denmark is at level three.

In contrast, at level three in Scotland is the high court, which is established in Edinburgh. This court but may travel "on circuit" as required (e.g., it meets on a regular basis in Glasgow, which often is even busier than the court at Edinburgh). It is interesting to the U.S. observer that the high court serves as both a trial court for the most serious offenses and as a court of last resort in criminal cases. In Scotland, only civil cases may be appealed to the House of Lords.

At level three is the Danish Supreme Court, the court of last appeal, which serves to resolve constitutional questions. This court is located in Copenhagen. Denmark is not based on a common-law tradition with an emphasis on *stare decisis* (precedent law). However, Andenaes (1984) comments that the prevailing practice is to assign considerable weight to precedent from the Supreme Court.

An appreciation of precedent, even though not comparable with the common law concept in *stare decisis*, is important in understanding the value of encyclicals handed down by the Court on sentencing. U.S. observers might think it strange for the Supreme Court to hand down sentencing suggestions in regard to the role of blood alcohol content in drunk driving cases. However, such an example fits well with the Danish concept of *retspolitick*, which in English can mean either legal policy or legal politics. These guidelines, along with a weekly-published *UFR* (Journal of Justice) that reports on all sentencing activity, also contribute to a legal environment conducive to conformity. It seems clear that judges read the sentencing decisions about the cases currently before them. We believe the knowledge that a decision rendered will shortly be read by colleagues throughout the system induces judges to make uniform decisions in similarly situated cases.

Another important facet of the Danish courts is the inclusion of lay judges along with professionals. According to Gammeltoft-Hansen, Gomard, and Philip (1982), the use of lay judges was not widespread until the 1930s. This happened as an amendment to the Administration of Justice Act legislation, which established norms and rules governing the conduct of both civil and criminal cases.

Lay judges serve only on criminal cases. In the city courts lay judges participate in trials along with one professional judge. Obviously, the judge is the most influential member of this triad; however, guilt is decided by simple majority. The lay judges vote on both the verdict and the sentence.

Lay people also serve on criminal cases adjudicated by the high courts. In the most serious cases, i.e., rape, arson, and murder, three professional judges and twelve jurors decide the verdict and sentence. Jury trials do not require a unanimous verdict; a vote of eight to four is enough to convict a defendant. The professional judges may overrule a guilty verdict but, as in the United States, must abide by a jury vote for acquittal.

In sharp contrast to the United States, lay judges may participate in appellate cases. High court appeals are resolved by three lay judges and three professional judges. Each person has an equal vote. Another important distinction between Denmark and U.S. procedure is that appellate courts may resolve issues of fact and law; U.S. appellate judges may only consider issues of law.

Lay judges and jurors are selected by a committee from each separate local authority district. The members for these selection committees are elected during the general elections held every four years. Lay judges serve for four years. As a general rule, they will sit for four times per year.

Legal Training

Another important aspect of the legal community is the common legal training of all the participants. There are only two legal education programs in Denmark, one at the University of Copenhagen and the other at the University of Aarhus. The training for both prosecutors and judges is very similar. The law degree is awarded after a five-year formal education at one of the universities. Afterwards, there is a lengthy ten-year indoctrination process. A one-year probationary period follows, which finally results in a lifetime appointment. The important point is that these participants are trained to be judges and prosecutors, not selected on the basis of political whims. As the Crown Office notes, Scottish prosecutors are legally qualified civil servants—permanent officials who do not change with the government of the day (2001).

The Working Courts

An interesting component of the city courts process is the role of the police. Contrary to the U.S. system wherein the prosecutor and police are clearly separate, in Denmark the police can prosecute certain types of cases. Police cases do not include those where the outcome may be prison, fines, or perhaps simple detention. The police also have the authority to drop charges if the accused agrees to pay a fine. Such cases are tried without lay judges.

An important point made by Gammeltoft-Hansen, Gomard, and Philip (1982) regards the informality of procedures followed when a defendant confesses. If the defendant confesses, even if the offense has a possible penalty of prison, the court will proceed without lay judges. Such a scenario may seem alien to the American observer. However, to add clarity to the role of the police as prosecutors, a discussion of police training is in order. The training of police chiefs is remarkably different from such training in the United States. All Danish police chiefs are graduates in law from either Aarhus or Copenhagen University. According to Baun (1984), they have spent some ten to twenty years as assistant chiefs, mainly working in court for the prosecution.

The police chief is a state official who is not dependent on local politicians. Denmark has a national police force. Baun (1984) also notes, as a general rule, that police chiefs seem to enjoy a high degree of social esteem, ranking comparably with doctors and judges in Denmark. One is tempted to speculate on the quality of investigations and subsequent prosecutions that emanate from Danish police. It is important to have an understanding of law enforcement because, just as in the United States, this is the first line in the criminal justice system.

Legality vs. Opportunity Principle in Prosecution

As Vestergaard (1986) has noted, Danish prosecutors operate in the middle of a continuum with absolute discretion at one end and mandatory guidelines at the other. There is a principle of expediency written down in the official Prosecutorial Procedures, paragraph 735, that deals with discretion. According to Gammeltoft-Hansen, Gomard, and Philip (1982), the principle of relative prosecution or principle of opportunism means that the public prosecutor has wide authority to withdraw charges, even when evidence affords sufficient grounds for instigating proceedings (p. 388). Greve and his colleagues (1984) further elaborate on the "omission to prosecute" (p. 146). Even though enough evidence may exist to bring charges, the prosecutor is not bound to do so as long as omission will result in no harm to any "public interest" (p. 147). This can be defined as a principle of choice, or opportunity principle. This alternative is possible when legal proceedings are deemed unnecessary or for humanitarian reasons.

Another related principle is the withdrawal of charges. According to the Administration of Justice Act, Section 1, only the director of public prosecutions has the general authority to withdraw charges; in certain situations assistant public prosecutors may also do so. Greve and his colleagues (1984) note that provisions are wide enough so assistant prosecutors do in fact withdraw cases, and the involvement of the director is the exception rather than the rule (p. 147).

For the purposes of this article, it is noteworthy that withdrawals from prosecution may be conditional. Fines, for example, may be such a condition. This procedure is very similar to that of a suspended sentence. Greve and his colleagues (1984) offer some insight into the procedural difference between a withdrawal and a suspended sentence (p. 148). Withdrawals have the conditions laid down by the prosecutor and approved by the court. In contrast, suspended sentences have conditions proposed by the prosecutor and laid down by the court. In an examination of actual data from sample cases, Gertz (1990) found a very strong relationship between the prosecutor's recommendation and the actual sentence given by the judge.

Judicial Discretion

A commonly held view, expressed by Andenaes (1984), is that universal conformity and uniformity exist in the Danish judiciary. He comments, "We do not accept that judicial discretion in sentencing necessarily means disparity let alone arbitrariness" (pp. 190–191).

Historically, maximum and minimum sentences, instead of mandatory ones, have been (and continue to be) the primary guidelines. For example,

Tamm (1982) notes that the punishment for theft was reduced to a system of minimum and maximum penalties in 1789. Andenaes (1984) suggests that recent trends indicate a willingness of the jury to convict. The question remains regarding how sentences are perceived to be uniform with such broad guidelines.

A belief in the desirability of uniform application of justice gives rise to the empirical discussion of differentials in sentencing. There is a substantial body of literature indicating that cross-jurisdictional disparities exist; this is what Neubauer terms the "geography of justice" (2000). Gertz and Price (1985) uncovered sentencing discrepancies among Connecticut trial courts. In California, Pope (1975) found differences among rural and urban jurisdictions regarding sentencing type. Myers and Talarico (1986) explored rural and urban differences in Georgia and reported significant differences in regard to sentencing decisions. Austin (1981) found rural and urban sentencing disparities in terms of the importance of prior record and social background. Carp and Rowland (1983) found disparities between northern and southern trial courts. Lynch and Patterson (1990), concerned with the effects of race, uncovered significant jurisdictional differences among New Orleans, Norfolk, and Seattle regarding sentence length. Kramer, Lubitz, and Kempinen (1989) point to significant variations in sentencing policy among three states that have adopted sentencing guidelines. In Rengert's (1989) analysis of "spatial justice," significant disparities existed between metropolitan areas, small cities, and rural areas within Pennsylvania.

Britt (2000) examined Pennsylvania sentences during the period 1991–1994 and found that punishment severity varied by court jurisdiction, even after controlling for offender and case characteristics. Racial disparities varied by court jurisdiction, with controls for other offender and case characteristics. Within the European context Kuhn (1999) examined the period 1983–1996. The average length of incarceration in France and the United Kingdom increased while that in Finland and Germany have decreased, with Portugal having the longest. Given the extant findings the search for jurisdictions with sentencing uniformity seems illusory. However, Andenaes (1984), Friday (1988), Antilla (1984), and Selke (1991) indicate Scandinavian countries have in fact incorporated practices that approach the sentencing ideal. In comparing the United States and Scotland, McGhee and Waterhouse (1999) found that Scotland has retained a clear welfare focus whereas the United States followed a more conservative get-tough approach.

These two pilot studies empirically test the proposition that Danish and Scottish criminal courts have implemented strategies that produce uniformity in sentencing across jurisdictions. This work is exploratory in nature, and currently it is the only research to focus on Danish and Scottish trial-level courts. This project is an important step in laying the foundation for future research in both systems.

Both countries provide a unique "social laboratory" in which to examine criminal justice decision making. While Denmark is a bit left of Scotland in terms of social policy, the extremes of wealth and poverty that exist in the United States are missing in both countries. Instead of speculating on what effect a different social structure might have in the United States, the more appropriate task is to examine societies that already have progressive systems in place. The issue for comparative criminologists is objectively examining different legal systems while keeping the research findings within a social context.

An Examination of Sentencing Patterns

In both Denmark and Scotland, data were gathered from a variety of jurisdictions along a continuum of urban, town, and rural areas. In Denmark the communities were Copenhagen, a metropolitan area, Roskilde, a beautiful university town, and Ringkobing, a rural community. In Scotland, along the same continuum, the research sites were: urban Edinburgh, the town of Linlithgow, and rural Jedburgh. The populations within each category were approximately the same.

Key informants were crucial to both data collection and interpretation. This was especially true in Denmark since neither of the authors is fluent in Danish. In Denmark, Judge Niels Waage supervised the on-site case accumulation. In Scotland, retired Procurator Fiscal Robert Lees assumed the responsibility. In both countries the data reflect a purposive sampling strategy. While the cases were not the result of simple random sampling, they are comprehensive of the type cases dealt with in each jurisdiction. Since the data from Scotland were more recent, we were able to add a couple of variables that were not available from the Denmark files. Most noteworthy are employment status and marital status of the defendants.

Traffic and other minor offenses were excluded unless the maximum possible penalty included a term of jail. Also excluded were cases that involved mental competency. For all offices, in both Denmark and Scotland, cases were selected beginning with those that had been most recently adjudicated and ending once 100 files that met the admissions criteria had been scanned. The time period covered was longer in the rural courts than the urban ones (i.e., there were fewer serious cases in the outlying areas and thus it took a longer period of time to gather the 100 minimum cases). No "seasonal variation" occurred among crimes committed in the urban districts. However, since the primary purpose of the study is to examine court decision making rather than why crimes are committed, this should not be problematic.

The diversity of the courtroom workgroup in the rural districts was limited. In Scotland's rural Jedburgh, there was but one sheriff and one procurator fiscal (prosecutor or PF). While the PF in Jedburgh receives occasional assistance from the Edinburgh office, he is responsible for almost 100 percent of the decision-making process. In contrast, during the study period, the Edinburgh PF had 30 assistant prosecutors and their counterpart in Linlithgow had six.

Table 2 shows the frequency distributions of the 600 cases involved in the two studies. In the Denmark sample, 50 percent of the defendants received incarceration as at least part of their sentence, a statistic that by itself does not seem unduly lenient when compared to those of typical U.S. jurisdictions. However, the median sentence length is eight weeks, and the mean is nineteen weeks. Sentences ranging from one week to six months made up 78 percent of the cases that received a sentence involving jail time. Only 8 percent of those incarcerated drew sentences of more than one year; these figures add support to the proposition that Denmark has incorporated a fairly lenient policy of sentencing.

For comparison purposes it is noteworthy that the Scots courts were less likely to choose incarceration, only 28 percent of cases, but when jail was chosen the sentences were typically a bit longer than those given in Denmark. As table 2 shows, 46 percent of those sentenced to jail received more than six months.

As table 2 indicates, the primary offense charged generally fell into one of three categories: theft, DUI (driving under the influence), and some type of physical violence (generally, simple assault). The other category includes a wide variety of crimes including procedural violations (e.g., filing a false report, perjury, obstruction of justice, and drug-related offenses). In Scotland, the most frequent offense in the "other" category was for drug possession. In both countries there was a high correlation between incarceration and aggravated assault. In Denmark, there was a perfect correlation between DUI and jail, with all offenders receiving between 10 and 14 days.

The gender of the defendants was predominately male; only 10 percent in Denmark and 14 percent in Scotland were women. In both countries women were most likely to be charged with theft-related offenses. Table 2 reports interesting differences regarding prior record and prior detention. In Scotland defendants were more likely to have prior records compared to their Danish counterparts but were less likely to be detained prior to trial. Scot defendants were slightly less likely to have multiple charges filed against them.

While table 2 indicates that businesses were the most common type of victim in Denmark (e.g., shoplifting and vandalism) in Scotland the most common victim classification was male. Selke (1991) has noted that property offenses in Denmark were comparable with similar crime rates in Indiana. Therefore, it seems feasible that property crimes may indicate a stronger judicial response than would be expected in a jurisdiction noted for leniency. In the following analysis we isolated property offenses in order to examine the contextual effect of each jurisdiction.

Table 2   Frequencies Distribution for All Cases (in percentages)

	Denmark	Scotland
Incarceration		
Jail	50	28
No jail	50	72
Sentence Length		
1–6 months	79	54
7–12 months	14	22
More than 12 months	8	24
Primary Charge		
Theft	50	33
DUI/other driving	15	11
Physical violence	21	28
Other	14	28
Prior Record		
Priors	46	72
No priors	54	28
Prior Detention		
Detained	30	12
Not detained	70	88
Number of Charges		
Multiple charges	42	35
Single charge	58	65
Victim Injury		
Physically injured	24	27
Not physically injured	76	73
Type of Victim		
Business	40	30
State	31	23
Male	22	38
Female	7	9
Confessions		
Confessed	71	37
Did not confess	29	63
Average Age of Defendant	28	28
Median Age of Defendant	26	25

N = 600

Analysis of Discussion

First, we wanted to determine whether jurisdictional disparities could be caused by offense seriousness (i.e., does one jurisdiction have more serious offenses than the others?). In both datasets the seriousness of the crime as measured by maximum sentence possible seems to be fairly evenly distributed across jurisdictions. In five of the six courts the mean maximum sentence possible had a limited range of between 23 and 28 months. The exception was the rural court in Scotland: in Jedburgh the mean was only 6.3 months with a range of 2–36 months—about half the sentencing range for its rural counterpart in Denmark, Ringkobing. In fact, only 16 percent of the defendants received any jail time in Jedburgh, Scotland.

Independent Variables

The next step in the analysis measured the impact of the independent variables on sentence length. In all models the legally relevant independent variables are the most important. In Scotland this includes Unemployment and Marital Status (i.e., we found no "penalty" for being either unemployed or single) as well as the independent variables of Jail and Sentence Length.

The most influential variables proved to be the seriousness of the offense, pretrial detention of the defendant, and the prior record of the defendant. In order to avoid cross-cultural confusion on the relative seriousness of offenses (e.g., theft of $100 is more/less egregious than a simple assault), we constructed a scale based on objective criteria. We used the maximum possible sentence for each crime as the basis for a seriousness scale. By doing so, we were able to use a Danish and Scottish, rather than American, view on the relative harm of each offense. This technique also allows a quantitative approach to offense seriousness. A drug distribution charge with a maximum possible sentence of 120 months is 20 times as serious as filing a false report to the police, which carries a six-month possible sentence.

The only methodological concern here was how to calculate a life sentence. While not an issue in the Danish cases, this was a concern in both Edinburgh and Linlithgow, Scotland. After much discussion we finally settled on the somewhat arbitrary figure of 360 or the equivalent to 30 years. We felt this captured the spirit of the law and to some extent the judicial feeling on the "value" of a life sentence. It would be interesting to analyze actual time spent incarcerated for those who receive life sentences: is the time served closer to seven years, or would ten or fifteen be more accurate? Again, the dilemma we faced was to capture the "value" a crime associated with the maximum possible sentence of life.

Seriousness of offense and pretrial detention.   In the final analysis crime seriousness accounts for most of the sentence variation explained in both the aggregate and de-aggregated models (e.g., this variable alone explains 50 percent of the sentence variation in the Roskilde court). Another factor closely associated with the concept of seriousness of offense is pretrial detention. The legally relevant considerations regarding pretrial release are familiar to the U.S. student of criminal procedure: amount of evidence submitted to the court, the maximum possible sentence if the defendant is guilty, risk of flight, evidence that the suspect would attempt to intimidate witnesses or to continue in criminal behavior. While pretrial detention was seldom used in Scotland, it had the same impact on sentence as in Denmark, a substantial correlation with sentence length.

Prior record.   In the overall sentencing model, the defendant's prior record proved to be the third most important factor. Unfortunately, in Denmark we were not given any detailed information (e.g., the type of offense committed) concerning the prior record of any individual. We were only able to discern whether or not a defendant had been previously convicted. In Scotland we did have information as to the specific number of prior offenses. In one case in Linlithgow the defendant had 48 prior convictions! Including specific information about each prior conviction would have made for a rather bulky dataset. Prior record as a stand-alone variable had the greatest impact in the Roskilde, Denmark court. In Scotland, it emerged as most significant when combined as an interaction term with the maximum possible sentence variable.

Plea bargaining.   We were extremely interested in learning if the Danish system had incorporated the practice of plea bargaining, so widespread in the U.S. courts. We discovered in Denmark that most defendants (64 percent) did not request a jury trial but rather opted for a guilty plea and confession. This of course streamlines the adjudicatory process and saves the court time and money. However, in Scotland, only 37 percent of those accused confessed. Here again, we found no evidence of a trial "penalty" in sentence length.

Physical harm to defendant.   Another factor that did not emerge as an indicator of sentence length was physical harm to the defendant. In fact, in Denmark, the variable not only was insignificant but also had a negative impact on sentencing. There are several possible explanations for this result. Most of the violent offenders were youthful (25 years of age and younger) and the legally mitigating effect of age in the Danish system has been documented (Greve et al., 1984). Another explanation for the seeming lack of effect of physical harm may be the actual extent of the injury. Our data, even from Scotland, only indicate whether the victim was harmed; there is little information on the severity of the injuries sustained.

Nationality.   One noteworthy difference between jurisdictions regards the effect of nationality. Being a foreigner has a positive association with the length of sentence in Copenhagen but not in Edinburgh. In

Copenhagen, most foreigners tended to be of Middle Eastern origin. In Scotland, we classified defendants as Scots or non-Scots, and interestingly rural Jedburgh reported the highest percentage of foreigners. This may be due to a willingness of the Jedburgh court to view English residents as non-Scot. Even if this is the case, however, there was no sentence "penalty" attached to such a designation. In Denmark, none of the foreign defendants were listed as being from any of the other Nordic countries (i.e., Sweden, Norway, Finland, or Iceland). Nationality is the closest approximation we have to a racial or ethnic factor. However, even in Copenhagen, nationality was insignificant when compared to the legally relevant variables.

Property Crime: Rural/Urban Defenses

We noted earlier the Danish concerns with property crime. However, the effects of victim type were apparent in only one jurisdiction. Due to decreasing N size when examining crime categories, we only analyzed property crimes across jurisdictions. First, we isolated all the property offenses and then ran a regression analysis on those cases receiving an unconditional sentence. We entered the rural jurisdiction, Ringkobing, as a separate variable in order to draw a comparison with the urban and town courts. We were most interested in the effects of Ringkobing because of the contextual differences separating this court from the others. In the U.S., Myers and Talarico (1986: 385) reported significant rural/urban differences in regard to property crimes, with the urban judges sentencing more harshly than their rural counterparts.

There are several reasons why we expect to find differences, if any exist, to be most distinct between the rural and urban courts. Ringkobing is comparatively isolated from the other courts by its geographic location on the Atlantic coast; therefore the sole judge does not have the ease of access to other members of the judiciary found in Roskilde and Copenhagen. Gertz (1990) comments on the routine of judges gathering for a regular lunch meeting in order to discuss issues of common concern. Such collegiality may contribute, at least partially, to a common agreement on judicial practices. There also may be less of a social distance between the judge and offenders due to the small population of the community and fewer bureaucratic barriers between participants.

In contrast to the findings of Myers and Talarico (1986), the data reveal that in Denmark, rural court sentences property offenders more severely than the urban courts. In fact, in our sentencing model, property crime in Ringkobing proved to be just as important as the seriousness of the offense. Our findings indicate that property offenses within a rural jurisdiction are viewed more seriously than in the suburban and urban courts. In Denmark, this was the only real difference in sentencing practices that we discovered among the three jurisdictions. Again, this finding was not replicated in the Scotland model. The Jedburgh court demonstrated a consistently lenient sentence pattern when compared to its town and urban counterparts.

Conclusion

While some differences are present between the Danish courts (e.g., the impact of property crimes in the rural court) the similarities are most overwhelming. The legally relevant variables alone account for up to 70 percent, as in the case of Copenhagen, of the variance of sentence length. It seems that indeed the Danish model has succeeded in finding relatively uniform sentences.

With the invaluable assistance of PF (Retired) Robert Lees, we were pleased to have extended our analysis to include Scotland. We find a similar trend as depicted in Denmark, but with even fewer cases receiving incarceration. However, when incarceration was given, the Scottish courts tended to be slightly more punitive. The exception was the rural court that handed out consistently lenient sentences. We also find it informative to maintain a contextual analysis along an urban, town, and rural continuum. We hope in the future to include criminal courts from other countries.

References

Andenaes, Johannes (1984). "The Choice of Sanction." In Jorn Vestergaard (ed.), *Criminal Justice in Denmark*. Copenhagen: The Denmark International Study Program.

Andersen, Bent Rold (1986). "Rationality and Irrationality of the Nordic Welfare State." In Stephen R. Graubard (ed.), *Norden: The Passion for Equality*. Oslo: Norwegian University Press.

Antilla, Inkira (1984). "Control without Repression." In Jorn Vestergaard (ed.), *Criminal Justice in Denmark*. Copenhagen: The Denmark International Study Program.

Austin, T. (1981). "The Influence of Court Locations on Types of Criminal Sentences: The Rural-Urban Factor." *Journal of Criminal Justice*, 9: 305–316.

Baun, Arne (1984). "The Danish Police System." In Jorn Vestergaard (ed.), *Criminal Justice in Denmark*. Copenhagen: The Denmark International Study Program.

Britt, C. L. (2000). "Social Context and Racial Disparities in Punishment Decisions." *Justice Quarterly*, 17(4): 707–732.

Carp, Robert and C. K. Rowland (1983). *Policymaking and Politics in the Federal District Courts*. Knoxville: University of Tennessee Press.

Crown Office (2001). "The Prosecution of Crime in Scotland." Scottish Court Service, Edinburgh, Scotland.

Crown Office and Procurator Fiscal Service. (2000). *Annual Report 1999–2000*. Scottish Court Service, Edinburgh, Scotland.

Dahl, Hans Fredrik (1986). "Those Equal Folk." In Stephen R. Graubard (ed.), *Norden: The Passion for Equality*. Oslo: Norwegian University Press.

Eisenstein, J., R. B. Flemming, and P. Nardulli. (1988). *The Contours of Justice: Communities and their Courts*. Boston: Little and Brown.

Fairchild, E., and H. R. Dammer. (2001). *Comparative Criminal Justice Systems*. 2nd Edition. Belmont, CA: Wadsworth/Thomson Learning.

Frase, R. S. (2001). "Comparative Perspectives on Sentencing Policy and Research," In Michael Tonry and Richard Frase (eds.), *Sentencing and Sanctions in Western Countries*, 259–292. New York: Oxford University Press.

Friday, Paul C. (1988). "The Scandinavian Efforts to Balance Societal Response to Offenses and Offenders: Crime Prevention and Social Control." *International Journal of Comparative and Applied Criminal Justice* 12: 47–58.

Gammeltoft-Hansen, Hans, Bernhard Gomard, and Alan Philip (eds.) (1982). *Danish Law: A General Survey*. Copenhagen: GEC Gads Publishing House.

Gertz, M. (1990). "The Dynamics of Plea Bargaining in Three Countries." *Criminal Justice Review*, 14: 48–62.

Gertz, Marc and Albert Price (1985). "Variables Influencing Sentencing Severity: Intercourt Differences in Connecticut." *Journal of Criminal Justice* 13: 131–139.

Graubard, Stephen (1986). *Norden: The Passion for Equality*. Oslo: Norwegian University Press.

Greve, Vagn, Ole Ingstrup, Sv. Gram Jensen, and Martin Spencer (1984). *The Danish System of Criminal Justice*. Copenhagen: Department of Prison and Probation.

Jones, Glyn (1986). *Denmark: A Modern History*. Dover, NH: Croom Helm Publishing.

Klinge, Matti (1986). "Aspects of the Nordic Self." In Stephen R. Graubard (ed.), *Norden: The Passion for Equality*. Oslo: Norwegian University Press.

Kramer, John H., Robin L Lubitz, and Cynthia A. Kempinen (1989). "Sentencing Guidelines: A Quantitative Comparison of Sentencing Policy in Minnesota, Pennsylvania and Washington." *Justice Quarterly* 6 (4): 565–588.

Kuhn, A. (1999). "Are Periods of Detention Increasing in the European Union?" *European Journal of Crime, Criminal Law, and Criminal Justice*. 7(2): 197–204.

Kyvsgaard, Britta (1984). "Imprisonment in Denmark: Current Tendencies." In Jorn Vestergaard (ed.), *Criminal Justice in Denmark*. Copenhagen: The Denmark International Study Program.

Langbein, John H. (1977). *Comparative Criminal Procedure: Germany* (American Casebook Series). St. Paul, MN: West Publishing.

Lynch, Michael, and Britt Patterson (1990). "Racial Discrimination in the Criminal Justice System: Evidence from Four Jurisdictions." In Brian D. Maclean and Dragan Milovanivic (eds.), *Racism, Empiricism and Criminal Justice*. Vancouver, B.C. Canada: The Collective Press.

McGhee, J. and L. Waterhouse. (1999). "Comparative Juvenile Justice Policy: The Old Alliance Between Scotland and the State of Massachusetts Revisited." *Children and Youth Services Review*, 21(11/12): 967–985.

Mead, W. R. (1986). "Norden: Destiny and Fortune." In Stephen R. Graubard (ed.), *Norden: The Passion for Equality*. Oslo: Norwegian University Press.

Myers, L. and S. T. Reid. (1995). "The Importance of County Context in the Measurement of Sentencing Disparity: The Search for Routinization." *Journal of Criminal Justice*, 23: 233–241.

Myers, Martha and Susette Talarico (1986). "Urban Justice, Rural Injustice: Urbanization and its Effect on Sentencing." *Criminology* 24: 367–391.

Neubauer, D. W. (2002) *America's Courts and the Criminal Justice System*. 7th ed. Belmont, CA: Wadsworth Publishing.

Nu-Serien (1989). *Yearbook of Nordic Statistics*. Copenhagen: Nordic Council of Ministers and the Nordic Statistical Secretariat.

Pontinen, Seppo (1983). *Social Mobility and Social Structure: A Comparison of Scandinavian Countries.* Helsinki: Societas Scientiarum Fennica (Finnish Society of Sciences and Letters).

Pope, Carl (1975). *The Judicial Processing of Assault and Burglary Offenders in Selected California Counties.* Washington, DC: U.S. Government Printing Office.

Prine, R. and M. Gertz. (1993). "DUI Policy: Can the U.S. Learn from Scandinavia?" *International Journal of Comparative and Applied Criminal Justice* 17: 273–280.

Rengert, George (1989). "Spatial Justice and Criminal Victimization." *Justice Quarterly* 6: 543–564.

Scottish Office. (2000). "Fact-sheet Nine: The Scottish Courts." Edinburgh: The Scottish Office Information Directorate.

Selke, William L. (1991). "A Comparison of Punishment Systems in Denmark and the United States." *International Journal of Comparative and Applied Criminal Justice* 15(2): 227–242.

Sigler, R. T. and J. J. Williams. (1995). "Sentence Disparity in the Federal Courts and the Adoption of Sentencing Guidelines." *International Journal of Comparative and Applied Criminal Justice,* 19(1): 73–82.

Tamm, Ditlev (1982). "A Survey of Danish Legal History." In Hans Gammeltoft Hansen, Bernhard Gomard and Allan Philip (eds.), *Danish Law: A General Survey.* Copenhagen: GEC Gads Publishing House.

Tonry, M. (2001). "Punishment Policies and Patterns in Western Countries." In Michael Tonry and Richard Frase (eds.), *Sentencing and Sanctions in Western Countries,* 3–28. New York: Oxford University Press.

Vestergaard, Jorn. (1986). *Non-Prosecution in Europe* (HEUNI Publication Series 9: 163–72). European Seminar on Non-Prosecution in Europe. Helsinki, Finland: Helsinki Institute for Crime Prevention and Control (affiliated with the United Nations).

Wilson, James Q. and Richard J. Herrnstein (1985). *Crime and Human Nature.* New York: Simon and Schuster.

17

Banana Justice in Moroland
Peacemaking in Mixed Muslim—Christian Towns in the Southern Philippines

Timothy Austin

It is difficult to pinpoint the beginning of Muslim-Christian conflict. Disagreements and some violence occurred between advocates of the two religions during the four centuries after the death of Muhammad in AD 631. Nevertheless, much of the period was peaceful. The avid proselytizing of Christians likely compounded the intermittent state of belligerence between the two rivals. However, when Pope Urban II urged in AD 1095 that an all-out crusade be organized against the spread of Islam in the Middle East, the conflict increased in intensity and organization. To the great embarrassment of Christianity, the Holy Crusades dismally failed. Indeed, the Muslims took Constantinople in AD 1453 and thereafter generally managed to parallel the Christian expansion step by step. Today, various styles of crimes and atrocities continue between Christians and Muslims in such places as Bosnia, India, Iraq, Israel, and the Philippines.

In Mindanao, the southernmost large island in the Philippines, the two religious antagonists have been at each other's throats since Magellan, a Catholic, claimed the islands for Spain in AD 1521—even though Muslim colonies (referred to by the Spanish as *moros*) were already well organized there.[1] Today, nearly 500 years later, the two old foes persist in terrorizing each other. Daily reports graphically relate incidents of ambush, robbery, murder, and kidnapping. For instance, in 1992 at least 119 kidnappings involving religious extremists were reported by the news media (Anderson and Vokey, 1993; Feleciano, 1993a, 1993b; Flores and Agnote, 1993; cf., Austin, 1989, 1991).[2]

A substantial literature base has developed in recent years regarding the political and religious turmoil in the southern Philippines (See, for

Prepared especially for *Comparative Criminal Justice, 1/E.*

example, Austin, 1988; George, 1980; Gowing, 1988; Gowing and McAmis, 1974; Lacar, 1987; Macalangcom, 1974; Madale, 1990; Man, 1990; Molloy, 1988). These works and others generally emphasize historical, political, and ideological patterns of the conflicts in Mindanao. Conspicuously lacking are ethnographic accounts of the daily tensions and infighting at the local level, especially in mixed Muslim-Christian communities. Whereas nationally appointed task forces abound to address the peace-and-order crisis in the Philippines, the precise descriptive nature of the Muslim-Christian struggle at the small-group level receives only scant attention other than occasional newsprint features (Marapao, 1991; Rodriguez, 1993). Probably such grassroots personal accounts are implicitly understood by longtime village residents. Yet, the absence of such ethnographic detail in the contemporary literature prevents adequate qualitative analysis. This project partially fills the research void by furnishing case studies as models of local conflicts in which the Muslim-Christian variable is ingrained. The case-study approach provides an initial explanation of some of the styles of discord between Muslims and Christians in the research area and the manner in which hostilities are resolved. Particular attention is given to how locals attempt to peacefully manage grievances and lawbreaking without total reliance on official control agencies.[3] Such detailing of the conflict resolution process in a volatile Muslim-Christian region offers needed clarification of the precise role relationships between antagonists and mediators. Until now, this relationship in the southern Philippines has remained at best a gray area.

Setting and Concepts

This project was conducted in the coastal province of Lanao del Norte, situated in the northwestern corner of Mindanao in the southern Philippines, a mixed rural-urban region blanketed with banana and coconut plantations. The comparatively small province (100 kilometers north to south along the coast and 50 kilometers wide) has a single city (Iligan) and 23 smaller municipalities, about half stretching along the shoreline and others scattered in the inland mountainous region. Several of the highland towns are populated by Maranao (Muslim) Filipinos, whereas residents of the lowland coastal towns tend to be Cebuano or Hiligaynon (Christian).[4]

For centuries tempers have flared between the highland and lowland folk who typify distinct cultures, separated by language and, to a large extent, socioeconomic status. The Muslim groups are poorer and represent a minority population in the province. Over the years they have been stereotyped as the inferior culture by the lowland peoples. Yet, for centuries trade and commerce united the two regions, intermarriages occurred, and members of the different groups often competed for the same jobs. Several of the towns, as well as Iligan City, have sizable integrated communities.

Regardless, local skirmishes and intermittent military-style clashes have erupted between the antagonists.

Conflict between the rivals can be seen at two levels. On one level is the radical attempt of some Islamic groups and organizations to create an autonomous region and to press for secession from the Philippines.[5] This level of turmoil has bred in past years a civil-war atmosphere with the national militia (predominately Christian) joining the struggle against the Muslim secessionists. In recent years, exploding artillery shells were common in some areas of the province, and the region gained a well-deserved distinction as a terrorist-prone land. At another level, and of primary concern in this article, is the friction observable, not only on the battlefield but also among small groups in the form of intimidation, threats, and occasional hostilities in the daily workplace. The focus of this research centers on the strained interactions between Muslims and Christians in and around the offices of local government, both at the provincial and municipal levels. Here, heated relationships surface as Muslims and Christians seek elected offices and as the two cultures clash in everyday pressures of the job.

Procedures

Three strategies of data collection common to fieldwork were employed. First, interviews were conducted with a wide range of Muslim and Christian adult men and women over a five-month period. Among those interviewed were government workers, educators, lawyers, and merchants, as well as missionaries and students. Conversations combined open-ended and semistructured styles. In many cases, multiple interviews with respondents were extended for hours into the evening, only to be continued at a later date. Throughout the fieldwork, the researcher maintained daily contact with several influential citizens employed with the local government who were considered expert informants. Many of the respondents were well known to the researcher from previous research projects, which reduced or eliminated rapport-building time. In some instances the findings were available only because the researcher held active membership roles based on direct family ties to the area. Complete participant observation allowed probing questions otherwise possible only with extreme difficulty.

A second data-collection technique involved a scrutiny of two years (1991 to 1993) of issues of a small weekly newspaper, *The Mindanao Scoop.* Although the newspaper was typically only four or five pages long, it was filled with a rich amount of local editorials, reports, and minutiae relevant to the research area. Such archival data allowed ongoing review of themes pertinent to the research questions. Also, the news items provided a continuing range of Muslim-Christian issues for discussion with citizenry. Finally, observations of daily life in Iligan City and several municipalities allowed for detailed field notes, rounding out an understanding of the setting.

Findings

As anticipated, the field observations and extensive discussions with locals furnished a series of case studies. Some were more richly detailed and significant than others. However, at least four personal accounts clearly reflect how native grievances or lawbreaking may be further complicated in the southern Philippines by the addition of the Muslim-Christian variable. The first two cases illustrate styles of nonviolent intimidation, and the remaining accounts profile actual violence. Also, the personal accounts constructively reveal how attempts are made to resolve local conflicts informally and often outside the boundaries of official control agencies. Special care is made in each case study to highlight and contrast deviation style, political ramifications, resolution format, and outcome.

The Case of the Harassed Ballot Counter

My name is Nina and I work in the town of Palang, which has about 20,000 people and is more than 90 percent Muslim. I am employed in the office of local government, which has 52 employees and only 7 Christians. I am one of the Christians in the office and work as a bookkeeper. Jobs are hard to find in the province, and I have been reasonably content, although being very much in a cultural minority. In 1992, the election of the municipal council took place and I was assigned the task of tallying the votes. The election occurs every three years, and eight council members were to be elected. Being a member of the municipal council assures a monthly income of 8,000 pesos (about $300) and gives the counsel member a significant boost in social status. Also, a member could wield some influence on important municipal matters directly impacting the community.

Following established voting procedures, the top vote-getters out of more than 100 candidates were announced. All winners were Muslim and male. However, the candidate receiving the ninth most votes, a Muslim woman, was unwilling to admit defeat. She claimed improper tallying of the votes, which placed blame directly on me. The irate loser argued that I falsely tallied the votes in order to give the number-eight candidate sufficient votes to win; thus, bumping the number-nine candidate. The number-eight candidate, although Muslim, was the father of the town treasurer who was a *mestiza* (mixed Muslim-Christian heritage). The treasurer was my boss. It was implied that if I could please my direct superior by allowing her father to win a seat on the council I could myself gain a better position in the local government. Moreover, it so happens that the mayor is also a distant relative of the number-eight candidate, which makes it appear even more like political favoritism.

Rumors circulated that I had better watch myself, for the angry loser would seek revenge. I am not married and being alone could exert little or no influence in the community over the established Muslim family. I have heard that it was actually family members of the losing candidate who were the real instigators in seeking revenge against me. The pressure has become so great that I fear for my safety. The family of the successful Muslim candidate who received the eighth most votes tried to intervene on my behalf. Although I believe their intentions were sincere, their efforts had no effect on the angry candidate and her family. After all, according to the resentful candidate, the eighth vote getter was improperly declared a winner and as the father of my boss is not a trustworthy person to try to settle the grievance. The mayor, *barangay* (neighborhood) captain, and Muslim priests (Imams) of Palang, for whatever reasons, were not of much immediate assistance and did not pursue the case. As it turned out, the problem was coincidentally resolved by my accepting a temporary bookkeeping assignment in the nearby town of Tago. For a year I worked at this indefinite position. However, when a new mayor was elected in Tago, a shake-up occurred in the office of local government and my impermanent position was terminated. Now I find myself in the position of losing the Tago job but still feeling unsafe in Palang. To make matters worse, I have learned that if I do not return to Palang I risk losing that job also.

It was at this time in the sequence of events that Nina's problems came to the attention of the researcher. She was visiting the research setting to seek out a Mr. Manisco, who had many years in government service in the province and knew the town mayors in both Palang and Tago. Also, he was himself half Muslim and spoke the Maranao language. Furthermore, Nina was a distant relative of Mr. Manisco (a third cousin of Nina's father), which likely made her feel more comfortable approaching him. During the interview with Mr. Manisco, he outlined three potential remedies to Nina's plight.

As I see it, Nina has a college degree in accounting and holds government work experience. She ought to be able to compete successfully for vacancies in the provincial government. If she can be relocated, her problem could be solved without having to test the anger of the losing candidate and her family in Palang. I have written a letter to the regional director of local government proposing that Nina's position in Tago be reactivated or that she be fitted into some vacancy in that office. This would be one solution.

Second, I know that the municipality of Munoz has a vacancy for the office of Assistant Treasurer, for which Nina should apply. She is qualified for that position, although she would have to reside in that town for six months prior to taking office. Also, she would have to be endorsed by the town mayor and the municipal screening committee (*sangguinian*), a panel appointed by the mayor. If Nina were to be approved for this position, she could reside in the town for the six-month period and would be allowed by law to retain her salary from the Palang job until final appointment in Munoz.

As a third option, I will also accompany Nina to Palang and confront the angry Muslim candidate in the presence of the mayor. I will ask the chief of police of Palang, whom I know, along with several of the town council members (other than number eight) to sit in on the meeting. I would first send someone ahead of me to set up the meeting and to see if the bitter candidate is willing to attend the meeting. In such a setting it may be that the candidate and family will back down and promise to leave Nina alone.

Mr. Manisco related that ideally, Nina would return to Palang and await the outcome of the vacancy in Munoz. He also added that earlier he had provided a favor to the mayor of Munoz by recommending his son-in-law for the position of provincial treasurer. Assuming the truthfulness of Nina's account, as did Mr. Manisco, her case provides a distinct example of the power of intimidation and subtle threats in the research setting. Although the criminal nature of intimidation may be cloudy, it is plain that it can radically alter a person's lifestyle. It is both interesting and significant that the right of the provoked candidate to try to intimidate Nina was never questioned. Rather, it is as if such face-downs are simply part of the daily struggle for status, and that if the heat were too much for Nina, it would be her place to step back. Several key informants agreed that the action of the losing candidate and her family should not be surprising due to the need, or even duty, to protect a Muslim's self-esteem (or *maratabat*). If a Maranao Muslim believes herself to have been wronged, as in the case of the losing candidacy, she and her family can rationalize through the built-in cultural mechanism of the maratabat, taking a vengeful stance against any blameworthy opponent.[6]

Regarding conflict resolution, two important factors arise. The first is a strong dislike of official control agencies, especially the police, and the second is an active reliance on a third-party mediator. When possible, Filipinos avoid interaction with the government, especially police agencies. In such cases as intimidation, when hard evidence may be lacking, the necessity of resorting to unofficial solutions increases. Also, barangay officials or religious leaders in the community appeared ineffectual, probably because such functionaries also reside in the town and must consider any long-range ramifications of opposing a Maranao seeking vindication.[7] In essence, Nina, even as a permanent resident and government worker, was an outsider in the eyes of the Muslim majority and was in a weak position to exert influence.

On the other hand, Nina was lucky to have Mr. Manisco to call upon. The fact that he was a distant relative provided an additional stimulus for him to intervene. Searching one's own kinship lineage to locate people of influence, no matter how distant, is an established and acceptable practice among Filipinos. Loyalty to kin is generally regarded as a first line of defense and is relied on whenever possible. Also, Nina was fortunate that Mr. Manisco's many years of service in the provincial government had provided him with numerous personal and professional contacts who could be activated to assist Nina. Importantly, Mr. Manisco was willing to use his influence to create options for Nina, even to the point of setting the stage so that a local town mayor could help her and simultaneously return a favor owed to Mr. Manisco. Reciprocity in the form of giving and receiving favors (*utang kabubut-on* in the Visayan language) is strongly ingrained in the local culture. Favors not yet reciprocated can be called upon, even if very subtly, as bargaining chips. In a real sense, helping others increases one's personal influence or power by allowing the accumulation of favors which later can be called upon.[8]

In the province, the third-party mediator is commonly referred to as a fixer. Nina's fixer, being a bilingual mestizo, possessed qualities allowing him to straddle the fence between the two cultures. Still, he maintained that even if he could defuse the heated issue, it would be at best only temporary until Nina could be relocated. The mayor of Palang wished for the return of Nina but refused to guarantee her safety. The time frame for these resolution strategies extended over the duration of the research project, and the wait was frustrating for Nina. The fixer believed that patience may in the end pay off for Nina by providing a cooling-off period for the irate loser, permitting Nina to quietly and officially compete for the other vacancies. Also, time would allow for the utang kabubut-on to take its course. As a final note, it became clear that Mr. Manisco was not entirely happy with Nina. He had observed her in the office as relatively meek and unassertive. He felt that as a single woman, it would be best if she were ultimately relocated to Munoz, which was incidentally also closer to Nina's home, where she could be nearer to family. Being far from the extended family and vulnerable was, in the fixer's perspective, part of her original difficulty.

The Case of the Procrastinating Governor

Rico related the following scenario, describing how social interaction between government officials may become strained and lead to unseemly and possibly abusive behavior, due in part to mixed religious allegiances of the government workers.

> I worked in government service for more than forty years and am now anxious to retire. After so many years I have a sizable government bonus due me. Unfortunately, necessary approval of superiors is not

always automatic. In fact, I stopped receiving my regular government salary last October, and here it is nearly April and the final approval of my pension has been delayed. I was attached to the treasurer's office where I was an official. Persons who work with large sums of money must be audited carefully before they are allowed to go on pensions to make sure that all funds they managed have been accounted for. The books and financial transactions for which I have been responsible over the years have always balanced. However, the present provincial governor has chosen to delay signing final approval for my pension.

The governor argues that one piece of inventory which I had a hand in processing had never been officially cleared. That is, a certain speedboat . . . or actually a boat, an engine, and a trailer for hauling the boat were not fully accounted for by the usual process of vouchers and checks. An ex-governor who was an opponent of the present governor had arranged for a speedboat to be assigned to his office. The only role I ever played was to sign papers indicating that the engine had been borrowed from one government agency (Philippine National Police) to another (the Office of the Governor). However, the ex-governor kept the speedboat at his house, and when he met an untimely death some months ago his family did not return the boat. Because the deceased ex-governor, a Christian, and the present governor, a Muslim, carried on a fierce political rivalry it is not surprising that after the death of the Christian governor the family was in no hurry to return the property.

The governor has several reasons for delaying my pension. First, he wants me to file a legal suit against the family. This would make the keepers of the speedboat squirm and it would please the present governor. However, I really had very little to do with it and am in no reasonable way the person to file suit. Second, the governor wants me around to help settle a complaint filed against him by the ex-governor who believed the election was fraudulent. Since I was an official observer in the last election, the governor would like me to remain attached to the office to help clear up the complaint . . . which looks bad even if the person who filed it is now dead. The speedboat case is just being used as a controversial case to retain me.

A government worker who is party to a legal suit cannot receive terminal leave monies until the case is settled. It would be less appropriate for the governor to delay my retirement based only on his need for my assistance in the election law violation. That dispute is more of a political move against the governor and with no implication of me. The present governor is a Maranao Muslim from a very powerful political family in the province. I have some Muslim heritage but have long since converted to Christianity. Although we are cordial and respect each other, the governor would not likely delay my terminal leave bonus were I a full-blooded Muslim with close allegiance to the family.

Rico's plight illustrates a type of intimidation of a different style from Nina's. Whereas Nina was a young adult beginning a career, Rico was of retirement age, hoping to leisurely end a long and satisfying career in government service. It is a matter of perspective who was, in either case, the victim or offender (the Muslim or the Christian). Still, both Nina and Rico believed they were victimized by powerful Maranao individuals and families. Both suffered the disruption of career plans. Relatively little attention has been given to the concept of intimidation by criminologists, yet its emotional impact can be as disruptive and visceral in the lives of the victims as the more conspicuous forms of violence.[9] Distinctions can also be drawn between Nina's and Rico's circumstances in regard to the immediacy of interaction with their adversaries. Because Nina departed the area, she avoided confrontation with her perceived treacherous accuser. Rico's situation did not carry the same mood of hostility, yet often he was forced to interact agonizingly with his antagonist.

Methods used in attempts to resolve the two cases differ. Nina's situation involved a third-party intermediary, but one who first attempted to resolve the issue without forcing confrontation with the accuser by altering Nina's workplace. Rico did not have ready access to a third-party fixer. The introduction of a mediator might have inflamed a confrontation at a time when the governor would have denied that any problem existed with Rico. Instead, he chose to swallow his pride and avoided an open quarrel with the governor. At the same time, Rico combined accommodation with soft negotiation. That is, he agreed to work, even while no longer on government salary, to assist in clearing the governor's name of the voting fraud charge. However, Rico persisted in denying any fraudulent involvement in the speedboat incident. In fact, Rico did succeed in convincing a local fiscal (prosecutor) to write the governor, stipulating that Rico was not the appropriate person to bring formal charges against the family of the deceased governor. Rico resigned himself to relying on his personal qualities of perseverance combined with his wish to avoid any kind of formal judicial case against the powerful Maranao governor.

Key informants were vociferous in contending that Rico was not in any way directly involved in the wrongdoing of the deceased governor. However, because Rico could still be a political pawn to the present governor, the door was open for him to be coerced. Without question, Rico suffered both emotionally and economically. Having scheduled for many years to retire only to have his plans abruptly put on hold, Rico temporarily was forced to seek alternative funding for retirement. No official data is available on such cases in the Philippines, but respondents consistently report that dilemmas such as Rico's were widespread in the research setting. Locals were quick to recognize the need to stay in the good graces of a superior when approaching retirement age. One interviewee noted that problems could even arise "if one's friends or close associates were in disfavor with a superior, thus indirectly tainting their own image and possibly resulting in delayed clearance of retirement plans."

Although it is possible for a government official to be formally charged by a subordinate with "abuse of office," townsfolk vouch that such cases are notably rare. The formal judicial process could take years which, unless used as a last resort, somewhat defeats the purpose of a retiree awaiting a pension. Also, if a subordinate were to lose such an obviously sensitive case against a supervisor, which appears probable, the superior may find reason never to sign the clearance.

Rico's case was further complicated by both local politics and cultural alliances. Recent years have seen extreme bitterness between the families of two gubernatorial candidates, one being Maranao Muslim and the other Cebuano Christian. Rico's position was not a political appointment, yet he was required to work closely with and take orders from the governor. If he chose to remain totally independent and not indulge or accommodate the empowered governor, he would place himself in an insecure and vulnerable position. For example, if Rico refused to bend a few rules when requested by the governor, then he might have had to suffer the consequences of such a susceptible stance, no matter how honorable.

It is true that many interpersonal conflicts in the research setting persist as long-term and brooding intimidation. Others, however, reach a flash point where intimidation turns to more overt forms of violence. In northwest Mindinao, as illustrated in the following account, terrorist-styled property destruction and sometimes murder prevails, incorporating political and religious variables.

The Case of the Burning Bus

In a semirural region of Lanao del Norte during November of 1992, a modern, air-conditioned bus was hijacked by passengers, taken to a remote area, and firebombed. Although no one was injured, property damage was substantial and the dramatic event was a major news story for months. Mario, a native to the area and an expert informant, provided a summary of the political and cultural ramifications underlying the incident as well as his own involvement.

> For generations several factions in the province have antagonized each other, particularly around the municipality of Karomatan. The Maranao Muslims have been at odds with the Maguindanao Muslims, and both have generally opposed the Christian people of the area in various ongoing squabbles usually concerned with land rights and/or who has the greater political clout. In late 1992, the provincial governor, who was Christian, also happened to have maintained closer ties to the Maguindanaos. This angered the Maranaos, who were campaigning to win the governorship of the province in upcoming elections. A full-fledged feud developed between the Christian governor and a powerful and politically astute Maranao family of the area.

It occurred that when a member of the Maranao family was visiting Manila he was ambushed and fatally shot. The Maranao Muslim family presumed the Christian governor to be responsible. Some weeks later the bus-burning incident occurred. Although it was true that the Christian governor owned the land on which the bus terminal was located, he did not in fact own the buses. Thus, if the bus burning was an act of reprisal by the Muslim family as revenge for the ambushed family member, then they missed their target. However, the Christian family who leased and managed the buses suffered and wanted the matter resolved. As a mutual third party I was asked to intervene, but also because I work in the governor's office and speak the Maranao language.

Moreover, I am acquainted with the angered Muslim family as well as the owner of the buses. I spoke to several Muslim town mayors who resided near the location of the firebombing and knew the people who ostensibly ordered the burning. As it turned out, one of the mayors agreed that he would inform the responsible parties of the misdirected bus burning, but expected payment for such action from the owner of the buses. Not surprisingly, the owner refused to pay any money. I was also asked to inform the bus owners that if there were another bus incident the damage would be more extensive.

Mario further explained in the interview that it was certain that the Christian governor remained abreast of the highly publicized case and may or may not have been intimidated. From a purely economic point of view, the owner of the firebombed bus was the unfortunate loser. No more buses were destroyed, although some months later the Christian governor was shot dead at a local gasoline station. At the next election, a member of the powerful Muslim family was chosen as governor. Even though there were witnesses to the firebombing of the bus, the controversial and publicized case never made it to court and no arrests were made.

Clearly, the bus-burning case differs from the two less abrupt styles of conflict and deviation. An innocent bystander became entangled in a political clash between contesting political and cultural camps. Victimization of the owner of the bus was spontaneous and undoubtedly disruptive to the business. Disinformation (presuming the governor to be the bus owner) resulted in abuse to a previously uninvolved citizen. At the same time, the bus owner became resentful, fearful, and intimidated. Although the bus owner refused to give money to confederates of the saboteurs, unlike Nina he had the ability to opt for heightened security. Respondents later affirmed that private police could be seen stationed at the bus depot. Furthermore, the bus owner now keeps his house gates always closed, drives a van with fully tinted windows, and according to one interviewee, "drives directly from home to work with no side trips." Mario remarked that he believed that the bus owner, who also owned a gas station, was providing free gasoline to a police officer, suggesting a payoff for special protection.

This bus-burning incident was obviously a violation of law, yet barangay officials and local police were unsuccessful in resolving the politically connected case. The only recourse to the bus owner was to rely on a private fixer, and again the go-between had to be a mestizo who was allied to both sides. Mario defused the case in the sense that no more property destruction befell the bus owner, although he plainly remains intimidated as shown by his new private police. Indeed, it was Mario who suggested to the bus owner that it might be wise for him to seek additional security for the buses. The fixer could only call a truce between the bus owner and the vandals. He did not stop the fatal ambush of the governor.

The Case of the Benevolent Princess

Criminologists have given comparatively little attention to the act of kidnapping, yet from a social-psychological perspective few events are as damaging. In Lanao del Norte, and throughout the Philippines, anxiety over being nabbed off the street or from one's home for ransom, particularly for expatriates and wealthy merchants, demanded constant alertness. Although both Muslims and Christians were equally guilty of inflicting atrocities (in past years one antagonist bombing mosques and other churches), it was the Muslims who gained a reputation as skilled kidnappers.

As of 1993, the Philippine literature lacked any systematic examination of the recent flurry of kidnapping, whether of offenders or of victims. Local and national police forces seemed frustrated in attempts to solve kidnap cases, and strong warnings from government law-enforcement agencies and the military were customarily disregarded by organized kidnap gangs. Certain regions of the research setting were to be entered at one's own risk, and locals emphatically cautioned of impending capture if one were to ignore the warning.

The following personal account of a kidnap victim provides an example of how political and religious distinctions complicate an understanding of kidnapping in the Lanao del Norte vicinity.

> I had resided at a provincial university in the Lanao area for several years and worked as a Christian missionary. As an American working with the Maranao Muslims I was aware of the kidnap danger. The rule was not to risk opening the door to even your closest friends, for they may have a gun at their backs. We kept the gate locked and a dog to forewarn of intruders. Yet, late one night our front door was knocked in and I was taken at gunpoint and forced to walk to a nearby lake and board a boat destined for a small island hideout. There I was confined for six days while my kidnappers announced my capture. They apparently sought both publicity and money.
>
> As it turned out, my captors were angry because they had lost their university jobs due to political reorganization resulting from the dethroning of a Muslim university president, along with many of his

political cronies. Also, the Muslim kidnappers were furious that then-President Corizon Aquino had remarked in a speech that the real problem in Mindanao was the communist insurgency, not the Muslim uprisings. This comment slighted the Maranaos, who decided to send a return a message to Aquino and the nation through a series of kidnappings. Although the U.S. Embassy encouraged strong police and military intervention to gain my release, it was in fact the Muslim daughter (princess) of a powerful sultan who stepped in on my behalf. She had political aspirations and approached the tribal leaders of the kidnappers. She had reportedly collected a sum of money for my release, though I am unsure of the amount. I am not certain if it was the money or the fact that the negotiator was a sultan's daughter that won my release. I was only thankful to have gained freedom when I did, for I was beginning to suffer from loss of sleep and intestinal disorders.

As with the previous accounts, this case emerged from political unrest in the workplace. The fear of kidnapping, as well as the act itself, comprises aspects of intimidation. Any person thought to have money, and virtually any foreigner, was vulnerable. Kidnapping can have impact on the pocketbook and the body (through torture or fear of torture) and must be considered as a type of violence. Respondents emphasized that most kidnapping involves competition between political and religious factions. In such cases, some form of revenge against a perceived harm is apparent, and it is through kidnapping that the Muslim sufferer can seek vindication. When one Muslim group pursues revenge it is referred to in the research area as "redo," in the sense of "repeating" an earlier harm which had been inflicted by others. In fact, kidnapping may simply be one means to avenge prior hurt imposed by years of oppression. Theoretically at least, maratabat (see note 6) is at issue in the kidnapping cases and predictably in all acts of Muslim revenge.

The plight of the kidnapped missionary was eventually resolved through the efforts of a private fixer. In this instance, the fixer not only acted out of compassion but also had political motivations. Nonetheless, for the princess to intervene against an avenging Muslim group which was in allegiance with a powerful Muslim family required substantial fortitude. The kidnap victim related that in the months following his ordeal, he became friends with the Muslim princess who, utilizing her image of peacemaker, won the next election for provincial governor. Clearly a victim of a violent act, the missionary volunteered that he eventually realized his captors had meant no bodily harm. Though they did threaten his life to ensure his compliance, it was later revealed that his captors were willing to protect him from other renegade bands who may have wished to steal the prized missionary for themselves.[10] Interestingly, when kidnappers release their victims, the intimidation may linger on if the victim remains vulnerable. It is possible another group could target the same individual while avenging their own long-festering wounds. Whereas the missionary stated he "continued to pray a lot," others resorted to more secular security measures, such as carrying weapons and fortifying their homes.

Discussion

Three conclusions emerged from the data which, though at times only suggestive, do provide new insights and needed focal points regarding Muslim-Christian discord in Lanao del Norte.

Prevailing Mood of Prejudice and Hostility

Clearly, the research setting represents a region beset with prejudice between lowlanders and highlanders who stereotype each other as deficient, vengeful, and malicious. Simply stated, with few exceptions each side dislikes the other.[11] A condition exists which appears roughly analogous to the relationship persistent between American Indians and non-Indians, particularly observable near reservations where the two cultures daily intersect (compare Austin, 1984). In Lanao del Norte, religion has developed into a most unique negative label used mainly by Christians against Muslims. A Christian does not typically say, "There goes a highlander or a Maranao"; rather, "There goes a Muslim." That a person is acting "just like a Muslim" is frequently expressed with derogatory inflection.[12] Thus, the religious stereotype overrides other cultural distinctions of speech, residence, dress, or socioeconomic status. Being dirt-poor and living in squalor is associated with Muslim lifestyle by Christians, though many lowland Christians live in identical circumstances.

Although the Muslim individual also uses derogatory labels for Visayan lowlanders (dirty pigs, swine eaters or *kaper* in the Maranao language), the label "Christian" does not appear to be slurred in the same fashion as the label "Muslim." Yet, the religious terms Muslim and Christian as used in the research setting must be considered misnomers and their use illogical (Casino, 1988) because neither side is really much concerned with the theological or spiritual leanings of the other. Rather, over the years the religious label (of being either Muslim or Christian) has stuck and is used by each side as a symbol of inferior, offensive, and even criminal behavior. Except for a few local intellectuals, the early origins of the cultural conflict between Filipino Muslim and Christian groups extending back through the centuries seems to have been forgotten or of little concern to contemporary townspeople. There is no concerted effort to achieve proportionate representation of the two cultures in the workplace, especially in municipal or provincial government. Instead, representatives from each culture compete for influential government positions, such as mayor or governor, and citizens rely on political favoritism from the winning candidates to obtain jobs.

Nature of Muslim-Christian Deviance

The heated competition for lucrative positions in the workplace only adds to the prevailing backdrop of distrust and disrespect between the religious antagonists. The four case studies underscore diverse styles of deviant and sometimes illegal behavior in Muslim and Christian interaction. The accounts portray both similarities and differences in that all contain aspects of intimidation or harassment of one culture by another, while several cases illustrate specific styles of brutality (e.g., sabotage and kidnapping). Efforts to rank the types of rule breaking and victimization according to severity are awkward at best. Severity of victimization becomes blurred, and attempts to prioritize the degree of discomfort fails, depending on one's point of view. That is, from a purely legal perspective, kidnapping plainly results in steeper penalties than does destruction of property or intimidation. However, if long-term disruption of lifestyle in northwest Mindanao is of prime consideration, then severity of victimization becomes obscured. For example, as a victim of harassment and threat, Nina was compelled to seek job relocation elsewhere in the province, involving many months and potentially years of uncertainty and torment. Similarly, Rico's being denied his lifetime accumulated pension because of personal ploys of a government superior easily could be viewed as just as disruptive and perplexing as the typically fleeting but more sensational crimes of sabotage or kidnapping.

An understanding of deviance and crime in the research setting as portrayed in the four examples requires scrutiny of both political and religious allegiances. Each case involves a complex interplay of actors, some of whom are jockeying for political advantage and all of whom happen to have been born into either Muslim or Christian families. Religious persuasion or political aspiration alone appears insufficient as an explanation of conflict. Being Muslim or Christian does not in and of itself generally motivate one to wrongdoing. However, in the scramble for political office, if one's opponent is viewed as heretical, then ruthlessness is more easily justified. The case of the angry Muslim who sought revenge against a Christian to soothe a loss of self-esteem (maratabat) also illustrates a failed attempt to enhance one's political stance. The presence of the inflammatory religious component provides further pretext for initiating or perpetuating reprehensible behavior in the research setting—sometimes resulting in criminal victimization.

Key informants contend that the styles of friction observable at the local level are reflective of Muslim-Christian tensions and violence throughout Mindanao. Reportedly, a vast majority of the Muslim population continues to experience oppression, and most Christians residing in Muslim areas remain intimidated in the presence of Filipinos, who they fear will resort too quickly to violence if provoked. Throughout the field study, respondents and the daily print media corroborated such a conclusion. The brief profile of personal accounts in the specific research setting plausibly represents a microcosm of conflicts in the larger Muslim-Christian community in the southern Philippines. Longtime residents of Lanao del Norte concurred that infighting and anxieties at the interpersonal level as outlined in the case studies can spread quickly throughout the larger community (from barangay to town to city). Locals remarked that what may appear as office skirmishes involving Muslim-Christian factions competing for prized job vacancies may quickly ignite entire tribes and regions, eventually requiring military intervention (as illustrated in the case of the benevolent princess). Several of the seemingly localized accounts discussed here received periodic national coverage in Manila-based newspapers.

Resolution Strategies of Muslim-Christian Conflicts

The social organization of the dispersed and isolated Philippine islands from earliest origins appears to have resulted in the formation of a unique complex of tight-knit, village-based community networks (Jardiniano, 1989; Machado, 1979; Silliman, 1985; cf., Austin, 1988, 1989; Bunge, 1984; Vreeland, 1976). The cohesive and relatively independent island communities coincidentally furnished a social structure for resolution of local conflicts. Private management of Muslim-Christian skirmishes at the most local level has capitalized on these village-based networks, as illustrated in several important ways by the four case studies.

First, and rather ironically, in a region awash with interpersonal Muslim-Christian conflicts, a rich tradition of altruism lingers. Sources of self-help usually begin with kin and are likely followed by *compadreism* (among Catholics), *companionism* (friendship cliques), and finally work-group associates (*sakop* in the Visayan).[13] Kinship is of primary importance but, when necessary, victims may probe other potential sources of assistance. In some instances, relatives also may be sakop members, enhancing the likelihood of gaining another's assistance in resolving conflicts. Private fixers, who may act as negotiators or mediators, always appear to be available, but it is up to the victim to seek such operatives through word of mouth. Some victims have more extensive kinships or alternate networks than do others, placing them at an advantage when assistance is needed. Also, some fixers are more efficient than others. In the same way that one may choose a lawyer after much shopping around and then hope for the best, the outcome of seeking the private fixer is often uncertain.

Second, a fixer's accomplishments appear to be influenced in part by persuasiveness, believability, and connections (both private and official). Personal attributes of persuasion are difficult to assess; but believability of a fixer, at least in the research setting, was decidedly a function of being mestizo. Possessing mixed heritage and bilingual ability allowed for the immediate capacity to relate to Christian as well as Muslim antagonists. To both Muslim and Christian parties involved in conflict, the mestizo tended to carry an air of respect or a sense of being esteemed, probably resulting from having an intimate or exclusive knowledge of both cultures.

Although somewhat speculative, the data suggest that effective fixers are unbiased in their quest to achieve subjective understanding of each adversary and opposing perspective. In the research setting, fixers strive for reconciliation rather than retribution and avoid implying blame or favoritism. Even though a fixer may hold kinship or friendship linkages with one of the troubled rivals, no assumption is made that one adversary is necessarily right. Rather, the ultimate aim is to defuse the conflict, even if only through a temporary truce. A fundamental assumption is that one's closest allies should be most anxious to heal wounds rather than to seek retaliation. Since this appears to fly in the face of the maratabat attribute of Muslims, the fixer must be especially enterprising and realize the impermanence of any reconciliation.[14]

Several situational conditions common to the research setting surprisingly emerged as factors at least indirectly conducive to the conflict resolution process. Mindanao represents a low-tech region with poor quality electronic communications. Unreliable telephone and postal services forced locals to depend on somewhat primitive telegraph systems. Consequently, citizens relied heavily on personal interaction and indeed desired face-to-face contact for any consequential transactions. In the search for fixers and in any subsequent negotiations or mediations, much effort is spent by participants involved in the resolution process traveling with some difficulty throughout the province in order to directly, but informally, converse with one party or another. The meetings are time consuming and invariably call for the serving of refreshments (coffee, beer, rum, etc.). Notably, without sophisticated communications the necessity of multiple, on-site visits between functionaries in the private resolution process is required to iron out any details or to permit delivery of any new information or responses. This follow-up process is casually referred to locally as "follow apon" and has become institutionalized in almost all daily transactions. Nothing is automatic. Therefore, attempts to resolve Muslim-Christian clashes through numerous face-to-face dialogues, extending over weeks or months, appear to be fostered by what are usually unenviable low-tech conditions.

It is clear that while confidence in the government system of justice declines, a reliance on private and informal networks of control increases (as cogently argued by Black, 1976). This proposition is confirmed by the Lanao del Norte circumstance. The reputation of police agencies in the research setting regarding highly sensitive Muslim-Christian conflicts is that official control agencies either ignore the cases or do not vigorously mobilize all resources. Locals contend that among police agencies, when such delicate crimes occur, a lackadaisical mood of "round up the usual suspects" prevails. Such a near-anarchic atmosphere demands the emergence of informal controls if any semblance of peace and order is to be maintained.

This research only scratches the surface of a problem long set in motion, unlikely to see a quick cure. Yet, the study helps to pioneer overdue disclosure and interpretation of local Muslim-Christian conflict and efforts toward harmony in a tumultuous area of the world.

Notes

[1] The Moors, a warlike north African tribe of Arab and Berber extraction, invaded Europe, conquering Spain in the eighth century. Defiant natives of Mindanao (Muslims) appeared as fierce as the Moors and were called Moros by early Spanish troops in the Philippines. The region was stereotyped as Morolandia. The term Moro appears to have lost its earlier derogatory connotation and is used rather openly, sometimes with pride, in modern speech.

[2] With the election of a new president of the Philippines, the Philippine National Police in the early months of 1993 underwent extensive reorganization and purging of high-ranking officers. Estimates that at least 10 percent of the police force was corrupt were commonly reported. Crime data based on police reports were virtually nonexistent, and the suspicious statistics that were available led newspapers to keep track of major crimes such as kidnapping. Also revealing are the occasional reports of Amnesty International (Silliman, 1991).

[3] Perhaps as much as any cultural area, the Philippines reflects a long history of reliance on informal (out of court) resolution of disputes and even crimes (Austin, 1987; Machado, 1979; Silliman, 1985). During the Marcos regime the government provided funding for the construction of diminutive buildings in each village (barangay) where informal or semiformal conflict resolution could be sought (i.e., barangay justice halls). Many locals preferred to find shade from the equatorial sun under the nearest tree. On occasion banana leaves would be cut to provide ground cover where locals would sit for dialogue, hopefully resulting in some sort of amicable settlement.

[4] It should be noted that Muslims in Mindanao are also Filipinos. They distinguish among themselves based less on religion than on other ethnic lines (i.e., Maranao, Maguindanao, Taosug, etc.). However, the Visayan and Luzon Filipinos of the central and northern islands tend to lump all Arab-linked Filipinos together under the label Muslim. The Muslim (rather than Filipino) label carries a negative connotation perpetuated for more than 400 years of Spanish Catholic rule and nearly 50 years of American (Christian) occupation. Both colonial powers considered Muslims as foreigners in their native land (Casino, 1988: 43). The unfortunate religious-based dichotomy of Muslim versus Christian remains intact. Even if this logically may be viewed as a false dichotomy, it is firmly embedded as a reality in everyday speech and actions.

[5] In 1989, through a highly publicized and controversial open election, voters in four Mindanao provinces chose to create the Autonomous Region for Muslim Mindanao (ARMM). These provinces are Maguindanao, Sulu, Tawi-Tawi, and Lanao del Sur. The research site of Lanao del Norte, a mixed Muslim-Christian area, failed to approve entry into the autonomous region. Rather than providing a homeland, many Filipinos are fearful an autonomous region—in many ways still dependent on the national government—would create a situation similar to Native American reservations of the United States.

[6] No data exist on the frequency of use of the maratabat to neutralize vengeful reactions (such as intimidation) that may otherwise be inappropriate. Unquestionably, however, maratabat is alive and well among the Maranao, one respondent poignantly remarking, "It may be all we have left." Revenge is mandatory even though the time frame is secondary, illustrated with examples of children, once grown, avenging wrongs reportedly inflicted on deceased parents or even grandparents (Saber, Tamano, and Warriner, 1960). The phrase "We do not get mad, we get even," periodically heard in the province, takes on new significance. Were the situation reversed with a Muslim ballot counter in the minority, an angered lowlander (Christian), not having maratabat, would likely have to resort to civil court. Personal revenge would be more difficult to rationalize for Christians. Several pas-

sages in the Qur'an can be interpreted as justifying revenge: "Fight in the cause of God, those who fight you" (chapter 2: 190), and "Fight them on until there is no more tumult or oppression" (chapter 2: 193). Old Testament scriptures (Exodus 21: 26) suggest similar actions with the "eye for an eye" passage, but the doctrine is reversed for Christians in the New Testament "turn the other cheek" passage (Matthew 5: 39).

[7] Barangay (neighborhood) justice (*katarungang pambarangay* in the Tagalog) was signed into law by presidential decree during the Marcos regime in 1978 and has received mixed reviews (Austin, 1987; Jardiniano, 1989; Silliman, 1985). Whereas it does offer a rather ornate but clever system for managing small crimes and disputes, no comprehensive analysis addresses its nationwide effectiveness. Locals in the research setting appear to respect barangay officials but do not typically place much faith in their capability and regard their operations simply as an additional semiformal clerical barrier en route to official court. If true amicable settlement is sought, one must find a fixer (third-party mediator) with personal contacts.

[8] A sizable amount of attention has been given reciprocal gift exchange among Pacific islanders, but less focus has been given the offering and receiving of favors (see, however, the comments of Enriquez, 1988; Kaut, 1961; Gouldner, 1960; Morais, 1980). What appears unique in the research setting is that favors may be held somewhat in a back pocket, only to be pulled out when one is in need of assistance or if a favor can be used to help another (as in the case of Nina). Though indirect, the more favors one is owed due to previous altruistic acts toward others, the more secure one is. Such persons have at their beck and call persons who at least theoretically should rally to their defense. Also, one occasionally hears, "Do not accept anything from them because we will owe them utang kabubut-on." In the Tagalog and the northern islands the same phenomenon is referred to as *utang-na-loob*.

[9] Intimidation, as a disturbing force, likely parallels if not precedes the sequence of threat and assault foregoing battery. Regardless, it is clearly as emotionally wrenching as other modes of nonphysical harassment. Long-term intimidation appears analogous, in these Filipino accounts, to mental cruelty.

[10] When an individual is kidnapped by a small, loosely organized group of rebels, the victim may be held for only a short time. If ransom is not forthcoming, the victim may be turned over to a more powerful and better organized kidnap band who may have the means to care for the victim for an extended time as well as superior skills in negotiating for a ransom. Once a ransom is received by kidnappers, a kickback is paid to any rebel groups who previously may have held the victim or who may have made the initial capture. Such contracts between kidnap bands may involve up to three separate transfers.

Some rebel groups camping in mountain bivouacs are themselves quite destitute and barely able to care for and feed themselves, let alone to safekeep and feed a prisoner for any extended time. Respondents knew of some cases where unsophisticated kidnap groups appealed to victims' families for expense money if ransom was not going to be paid. Such networking between variously organized kidnap gangs provides opportunity for some impoverished but angry rebels to become a type of bounty hunter by snatching well-to-do persons off the street and handing them over to kidnap gangs in hope of receiving future kickbacks.

[11] Without question, interpersonal skirmishes between Muslims and Christians in the workplace are prevalent and diverse. Virtually all respondents could cite examples where they were directly or indirectly involved in religious-based discord. Whereas the four case studies furnish examples of conflict in workplaces linked to local government, many locals provided other illustrations of interpersonal conflict involving Muslim-Christian groups, corroborating the detailed cases presented. Also, much information pertaining to Muslim-Christian turmoil was interesting and important but was related to areas outside the specific setting of the workplace (e.g., marital and family problems, land-claim conflicts, vehicular accidents).

[12] Automobile passengers were overheard commenting about a jaywalker, "Don't hit that lady, she's a Muslim and her family will retaliate." On another occasion, a Muslim woman broke into a long grocery checkout line ahead of her turn. A bystander remarked, "She is Muslim and realizes that the others in line (Christians) will be afraid to interfere with her."

[13] Originating with hundreds of years of Spanish occupation, adult male citizens proudly boast of numerous compadre relationships resulting from being requested to sponsor a birth (act as godfather) or to officially witness a marriage. A compadre (*p're* to locals) provides additional associates who could reliably be called on for assistance (Hart, 1977). More general and less official is "companionism." In the research setting and apparently throughout the Philippines an adult male or female should not remain alone during daily routine activity. The remark, "Where is your companion?" is commonly asked of unaccompanied individuals. Same-sex companions provide friendship and, for outsiders, act as guides. The value orientation of disapproving solitary activity endorses companionship and indirectly provides ready access to assistance. On the other hand, being obligated to one's "in-group" work associates seemingly is a vestige of early feudal obligations felt by serfs to landlords. Theoretically, the larger the sakop, the greater one's security due to having at one's beck and call a cadre of persons ready and obligated to provide support.

[14] Admittedly somewhat of an interpretive leap, it appears that successful mestizo fixers tend to be what Richard Quinney described as seekers of the way of peace through compassion and service. The ability to feel the suffering of both antagonists must be viewed as a positive trait to contesting parties (see Quinney, 1991: 8–9). Following Quinney's argument, an acceptance of "patience" as a virtue appears to be of fundamental importance to the fixer ideology. Patience of the fixer implies slowness to anger and willingness to wait for the interjection of compassion and sympathy to take hold. This oriental ideal is elaborated by Udarbe (1989: 75–76).

Bibliography

Anderson, Harry, and Richard Vokey (1993). "A Make-or-Break Year: It's Now or Never if the Philippines is to Boom." *Newsweek* (February 8) CXXI (6): 11.

Austin, W. Timothy (1984). "Crow Indian Justice: Strategies of Informal Social Control." *Deviant Behavior* 5: 31–46.

Austin, W. Timothy (1987). "Conceptual Confusion among Rural Filipinos in Adapting to Modern Procedures of Amicable Settlement." *International Journal of Comparative and Applied Criminal Justice* 11 (2): 241–51.

——— (1988). "Fieldnotes on the Vigilante Movement in Mindanao: A Mix of Self-Help and Formal Policing Networks." *International Journal of Comparative and Applied Criminal Justice* 12 (2): 205–17.

——— (1989). "Living on the Edge: The Impact of Terrorism upon Philippine Villagers." *International Journal of Offender Therapy and Comparative Criminology* 33 (1): 103–19.

——— (1991). "Toward a Theory on the Impact of Terrorism: The Philippine Scenario." *International Journal of Comparative and Applied Criminal Justice* 15 (1): 33–48.

Holy Bible (1985). New King James Version. New York: Thomas Nelson Publishers.

Black, Donald (1976). *The Behavior of Law.* San Diego, CA: Academic Press, HBJ Publishers.

Bunge, Frederica (1984). *Philippines: A Country Study* (Area Handbook Series). Washington, DC: U.S. Government Printing Office.

Casino, Eric S. (1988). "The Anthropology of Christianity and Islam in the Philippines: A Bipolar Approach to Diversity." In Peter Gowing (ed.), *Understanding Islam and Muslims in the Philippines.* Quezon City, Philippines: New Day Publications.

Enriquez, Virgilio (1988). "Filipino Values: Towards a New Interpretation." *Philippine Studies Newsletter.* Center for Philippine Studies, University of Hawaii at Manoa (November), 29–34.

Feleciano, Jay (1993a). "Marines Kill 8 Moro Rebs in 2 Clashes." *Philippine Daily Inquirer* VIII (78) (February 11): 1, 11.

——— (1993b). "MNLF Areas Bombed; Marine General Sacked." *Philippine Daily Inquirer* VIII (67) (February 13): 1, 13.

Flores, Nelson F., and Mario Agnote (1993). "Government Ineptness vs. Crime Scored." *Philippines Daily Inquirer* VIII (71) (February 18): 1, 14.

George, T. J. S. (1980). *Revolt in Mindanao: The Rise of Islam in Philippine Politics.* Kuala Lumpur: Oxford University Press.

Gouldner, Alvin W. (1960). "The Norm of Reciprocity: A Preliminary Statement." *American Sociological Review* 25 (2): 161–78.

Gowing, Peter G. (1988). *Understanding Islam and Muslims in the Philippines.* Quezon City, Philippines: New Day Publishers.

Gowing, Peter G., and Robert D. McAmis (1974). *The Muslim Filipinos.* Manila: Solidaridad Publication House.

Hart, Donn V. (1977). *Compadrinazgo: Ritual Kinship in the Philippines.* DeKalb: Northern Illinois University Press.

Jardiniano, Pascual F. (1989). *Handbook on Barangay Administration.* Manila: Joris Trading Company.

Kaut, Charles (1961). "*Utang Na Loob*: A System of Contractual Obligations among Tagalogs." *Southwestern Journal of Anthropology* 17: 256–72.

Lacar, Luis Q. (1987). "Neglected Dimensions in the Development of Filipino Muslims." *Solidarity* 113 (July-August): 8–16.

Macalangcom, Capal M. (1974). "The Muslim-Christian Conflict in Mindanao and Sulu: Its implications to National Integration." *Philippine Military Digest* 11 (2): 70–77.

Machado, Kit G. (1979). "Politics and Dispute Processing in the Rural Philippines." *Pacific Affairs* 52 (92): 294–314.

Madale, Nagasura T. (1990). *Possibilities for a Peace in Southern Philippines.* Zamboanga City, Philippines: Silsilah Publications.

Man, W. K. Che (1990). *Muslim Separatism: The Moros of Southern Philippines and the Malays of Southern Thailand.* Singapore: Oxford University Press.

Marapao, Alan (1991). "Rebel Group Threatens to Blow Up NPC Plants, Burn Christian Workers." *The Mindanao Scoop* XXIV (8) (May 12): 1, 5.

Molloy, Ivan (1988). "The Decline of the Moro National Liberation Front in the Southern Philippines." *Journal of Contemporary Asia* 18 (1): 59–76.

Morais, Robert J. (1980). "Dealing with Scarce Resources: Reciprocity in Alternative Form and Ritual." *Philippine Sociological Review* 28: 73–80.

Quinney, Richard (1991). "The Way of Peace: On Crime, Suffering, and Service." In Harold E. Pepinsky and Richard E. Quinney (eds.), *Criminology as Peace Making.* Bloomington: University of Indiana Press.

Qur'an (1974). Hammondsworth, Middlesex: Penguin Books.

Rodriguez, Ben F. (1993). "Action Sought on Abalos Killing in Lanao." *Manila Bulletin* 242 (25) (February 25): 16.

Saber, Mamitua, Mauyag M. Tamano, and Charles K. Warriner (1960). "The Maratabat of the Maranao." *Philippine Sociological Review* 8 (1 & 2): 10–15.

Silliman, G. Sidney (1985). "A Political Analysis of the Philippine Katarungang Pambarangay System of Informal Justice through Mediation." *Law and Society Review* 19 (2): 279–301.

——— (1991). "Transnational Relations and Human Rights in the Philippines." *Pilipinas* 16 (spring): 64–80.

Udarbe, Proceso U. (1989). "The Transforming Power of Agape-Love." In Douglas J. Elwood (ed.), *Alternatives to Violence: Interdisciplinary Perspectives on Filipino People Power.* Quezon City, Philippines: New Day Publishers.

Vreeland, Nena (1976). *Area Handbook for the Philippines*, 2d ed. Washington, DC: U.S. Government Printing Office.

18

Political Challenges to Indigenizing Justice in Post-British Nigeria

Nonso Okereafezeke

Many post-colonial populations across the world are still struggling to reconcile their native systems of law and justice with the foreign systems imposed by colonialism and occupation. Nigeria provides a good example of this struggle. In considering the impediments to managing the conflicting native and foreign systems in Nigeria, this article focuses on the role of the country's post-independence civilian governments more than that of the military regimes. With eight military governments versus three civilian governments, the Nigerian Armed Forces have dominated politics and leadership in the country. Nonetheless, the civilians are presumed to be more responsible or accountable to themselves than to the military. Allegedly, Nigerian civilian governments freely elected Prime Minister Tafawa Balewa (1960–1966), President Shehu Shagari (1979–1983), and President Olusegun Obasanjo (1999–present) into office (in contrast to the civilian Ernest Shonekan, who was imposed by General Ibrahim Babangida's military junta). On the other hand, the military governments headed by generals—passing through eight different regimes from 1966 through 1999—were dictatorships imposed by armed forces, in many cases through bloody coups d'état. On the assumption that the civilian governments were elected, Nigerians have a right to expect more responsibility and accountability from their government in all aspects of the country's life, including law and justice reform.

The topic of this article[1]—the obstacles to reconstructing and indigenizing law and justice in Nigeria—is directly related to the issue of the place of Nigeria's native justice and law systems in the country's post-independence structure. The status of these systems has always been an issue since the British colonization of Nigeria (from the late nineteenth century through 1960). Decades after Nigeria attained political independence from Britain,

Prepared especially for *Comparative and International Criminal Justice, 2/E.*

the status question remains a critical issue, even though Nigerian post-independence leaders have swept it under the proverbial carpet. During its colonization of Nigeria, Britain sought to entrench British ideas and standards of law and justice. They succeeded, at least officially: Nigerian ideas and principles of law and justice are little more than official extensions of their British precursors. This situation prevails despite the irrefutable, well-documented conclusion by many researchers that most Nigerians, unofficially and privately, regulate their own lives and manage their own grievances, conflicts, and disputes through their native systems of justice, social control, and law rather than through the imposed English system (see as examples Okereafezeke, 1996; 2002). In Okereafezeke (2002), after having carefully evaluating scientific data, I conclude *inter alia* that:

> . . . Nigeria's native justice systems work. Based on the illustrations that the Igbo system provides, Nigeria's native systems are effective and efficient partners in the administration of justice in the country. The greatest obstacles to the native systems' assumption of their deserved and rightful position of primacy in Nigerian justice, law, and social control are negative official policies and attitudes. Since British colonial rule over Nigeria and up to the present post-independence government, there has been no meaningful effort to rescue and indigenize Nigeria's systems of justice and law. In particular, Nigerian post-independence leaders have lacked the nation-building vision, the intelligence, and the political will to reverse the present duplicate judicial path instituted for us by colonial Britain. Are we supposed to ignore or relegate our native and long-practiced systems of justice, social control, and law and continue to play by the rules imposed on us by our defunct colonizer? The British imposition of the English legal and justice system on Nigeria happened by means of political expedience. Thus, the reversal of the obnoxious British policy will involve Nigeria's contemporary political climate and the players. (p. 188)

This article is based on data concluding that average Nigerians tend to rely on their traditions, customs, and native laws more than on the British-imposed English law and justice, which Nigeria's post-independence governments have sustained and emphasized over native systems. And it should be noted that reliance on the traditional systems is not limited to minor grievances, conflicts, or disputes. It extends to very serious, complex cases (Okereafezeke 1996; 2002). The cases studied in the research for this article range from relatively minor issues, such as ostracism, to more serious violations like assault, theft, land-related issues, breach of contract, trespass, rape, incest, and homicide, among others. In short, the data demonstrate that any case, civil or criminal, major or minor, may be satisfactorily managed unofficially (outside the official governments' law and justice systems) through Nigeria's native justice and law system.

In addition, there are many avenues for case management under Nigeria's native systems. The avenues are often hierarchical, evidencing sophistication and organization in these systems. After comparing the relative effectiveness of "traditional" and "Christianized" Igbo[2] (Nigerian) control systems on behavior, Oli (1994) concludes: "Information tends to support the original hypothesis that traditional Igbo social control systems are more compelling [than Christian social control systems] on behavior" (p. 29). This is notwithstanding the fact that the official governments endorse the English law and justice system in Nigeria.

Research Procedures and Questions

The research supporting this article is based on a combination of methods: face-to-face interviews of native (unofficial) as well as official government justice personnel, such as judges, lawyers, and other actors in both the native and the official government justice systems in Nigeria. Available others (non-personnel in either justice system), whom the author believed could provide useful information, were also interviewed. Other research methods employed were archival searches of related documents, the author's personal observations of both the native and the official government justice systems, and a written questionnaire given to law students at a prominent Nigerian university located in the southeastern part of the country.

The findings and conclusions from previous and current research on the hindrances to indigenizing Nigerian law and justice elicit the following questions: Why has official post-colonial Nigeria retained and promoted Western ideas and principles of law and justice (English law) at the expense of Nigeria's native justice and law systems, even though the native systems, unlike the English system, are based on Nigerians' experiences, lifestyles, practices, and aspirations? Why does this situation persist despite the official declarations of law reform through several commissions, both ad hoc and standing, at the state and national levels? What roles have average Nigerians (as individuals and in groups) played (or should they play) to ensure the indigenization of Nigerian law and justice systems and to bring them in line with Nigerians' expectations? The answers to some of these questions may be traced to the structural dislocations engendered by the British impositions on Nigeria, while other answers may be found in the idiosyncrasies of Nigerian post-independence leaders.

Findings and Discussion

Several issues or "impediments" contribute to the continuing lack of appropriate justice and law reform in post-independence Nigeria. *Appropriate justice and law reform* should reflect Nigerians' post-British needs, preferences, and aspirations in procedural law and justice and should be based on and manifest, in theory and in practice, Nigerians' origins, cultures, languages, beliefs, customs, traditions, and historical circumstances. These essential ingredients ought to be entrenched in both the substantive and the procedural aspects of post-independence Nigerian justice and law. At the same time, this reform should be broad-minded enough to borrow from other societies when necessary to supplement the Nigerian native systems. Anything less is not good enough (see Okereafezeke, 2002, pp. 18–20).

The issues impeding indigenization of Nigerian law and justice are categorized into three broad groups: government-centered impediments, profession-centered impediments, and citizen-centered impediments. Some tend to overlap one another. However, each impediment is categorized and discussed in only one group in which, based on the research data, the impediment appears to be most concentrated.

Government-Centered Impediments

The following impediments are found mostly among the official local, state, and federal governments and their personnel.

Unpatriotic political leadership/lack of proper nation-building vision.   This impediment is one of the most notorious reasons for Nigeria's inability to effect appropriate reform to indigenize its law and justice systems over four decades after political independence from Britain. I have had occasion in another publication to analyze this phenomenon extensively (see Okereafezeke, 2003). Because the current discussion gives rise to the same elements I have addressed previously, I quote extensively from that publication:

> . . . a patriot in President Obasanjo's [1976–1979] position at this critical stage of Nigeria's existence would have led Nigerians much more purposefully and with a view to attaining nationhood. The way to do so is to be and remain faithful to [the] crucial characteristics of a patriot. To be patriotic is to be devoted. Regarding a country—especially a country like Nigeria that purports to be building toward a nation—a patriot is a person that is loyal and unwavering toward that country's overall best interests. Thus, a patriot recognizes and accepts that there are, and will be, many circumstances in which a person's or sub-group's well-being may conflict with the collective good. Even in such prevalent situations, a patriot resolves each inconsistency in favor of the collective interests of the country. The patriot renders individual and subgroups' advantages or perceived gains, however attractive they may be, subservient to the collective national welfare.
>
> From the perspective of political leadership, it seems that on every issue that confronts Nigeria a straightforward way to determine what is in the country's overall best interests is to ask: What official response will strengthen rather than weaken Nigeria? Associated with this question are other related, equally important questions, such as: What response will increase the citizens' sense of belonging and confidence

in the country? What response will most encourage the citizens to make their best individual and collective contributions toward nation-building? What response will demonstrate to the citizens that the country's leaders have a purposeful vision of the country's future and that these leaders are honestly pursuing that vision? . . .

. . . Patriotism is burdensome. It requires passionate and honest observance of, and adherence to, the innate [self] and societal control mechanisms to resist the temptations of behaving shortsightedly to serve personal or subgroup interests. Instead, patriotism evokes stead-fast focus on the long-term positive goals and overriding interests of the country. In Nigeria, patriotism should capture the great need to establish strong foundations for building the country into a nation. Such structures are embarrassingly lacking in this country that has so much and yet offers its citizens so little. In the present state of affairs, even hope in the Nigerian enterprise is in short supply because the leaders are very good at pontificating about the need for hope without giving the average citizen concrete reasons for hope. President Obasanjo in particular is good at exhorting the citizens to pray and to hope for a greater Nigeria. But, as Martin Luther put it, "prayer is a necessary supplement to human effort, but a very dangerous alternative." Unless Obasanjo takes the necessary practical steps to strengthen Nigeria by laying strong foundations for nationhood, Nigeria will remain an ad hoc contraption, which the British colonialists created to serve their desires and which now serves the desires of Nigeria's predatory post-independence leaders. (Okereafezeke, 2003)

President Obasanjo exemplifies the dearth of post-independence patriotic and visionary leadership necessary to midwife proper reforms to indigenize Nigerian law and justice. Such deficiencies are rampant at all levels of Nigeria's official government: local, state, and federal. Even the few leaders who appear to be aware of the need to indigenize still continue with the status quo, ostensibly because of the advantages they derive from it, some of which are discussed below.

Lack of political will to change the status quo.   Another   common problem with Nigeria's post-independence leadership is the leaders' unwillingness to formulate and execute a policy to indigenize Nigerian law and justice if they suspect that such policy would be unpopular among powerful and influential Nigerians. Fear of losing political power is a key reason for avoiding such a policy, even though research shows that it would be very popular among average Nigerians. The Nigerian elite's control of the country's politics and government, albeit illegitimate, is well documented. Since Nigerian independence, both civilian and military elite have succeeded in taking and keeping power, often by force of arms or election rigging, and excluding average Nigerians from the electoral process. Why would indigenization of Nigerian law and justice be unpopular among powerful and influential Nigerians? Retaining the English-based law and justice systems ensures continued advantages accruing to the country's leaders and other powerful and influential persons. One of these advantages is the powerlessness of English law and justice against the corruption among the Nigerian elite.

Ostensible ineffectiveness of English law and justice. One of the conclusions supported by previous research is that many (perhaps most) Nigerians follow their traditions, customs, and native laws in their private and public endeavors (see Oli, 1994; Okereafezeke, 1996; 2002). However, many of the Nigerian elite, who dominate the country's politics and leadership, prefer to maintain the existing British-imposed English law and justice system because, under the English system, the elite can more easily escape punishment for crimes than under the native systems. Social control among Nigerians who subscribe to the country's native systems, as in much of Africa, is predicated on strong belief in the omniscience and omnipresence of God, worshipped through various mediums. Most believers in the native systems accept that God is all knowing. Thus, God will identify and punish a transgressor, even if mortals are unaware of the transgression or are unable to identify the culprit, because God is present everywhere at all times. In this faith-based conviction there is no escape from accountability for one's conduct. Guilty persons would *voluntarily* identify themselves as responsible for wrongdoing without waiting for the system to do so, and they would come forward even if others were unable to identify them. This belief of those faithful to the native systems leads to increased social control, thus avoiding much crime and deviance. And, where crime does occur, there is a high likelihood that it would be solved. Oli (1994) has compared the following two groups of Igbos (a southeast Nigerian nation): Traditional Igbos (who believe in the native religions, customs, and traditions) and Christianized Igbos (who subscribe to Christian beliefs). The study compares the social control elements of the traditional (native) system and the Christian system. While pointing out that the Christian-based (English) law and justice system is officially endorsed over the native system, Oli concludes:

> The fear of spirits is gradually replaced by belief in expiation of sins, and an increased resort to devious means for achieving greatness. Control by tradition is replaced by police control. The English legal system notion that one is presumed innocent until detected and proven guilty, replaces fear of the omnipresence of spirits, admission of guilt and certainty of punishment. (Oli, 1994, p. 26)

Thus, without the comprehensive social control mechanism of Nigeria's native systems prior to British colonization, crime is likely to increase among the Christianized Igbos and other Nigerians (Okafor, 1978; Ogbalu, 1979).

There is a general perception that justice under the English system is slow or unattainable, that it is often inaccurate because it may be visited on innocent persons while the guilty escape sanction, and that it is not strict enough. Therefore, a person contemplating a criminal or deviant act can afford to take the risk of being identified and punished if there is a good chance that the reward accruing from the act will outweigh the punishment. Wealthy and powerful Nigerian leaders and elites have the means to conceal their crimes and, in cases where they have been identified and tried under the prevailing English system, have been able to escape with little or no punishment, being left to enjoy the fruits of their transgressions. Thus, the English law and justice system is perceived as an ineffective social control mechanism in the country. Many Nigerians, especially those who believe in the superior efficacy of the native systems, are convinced that the country's leaders would not get away with their crimes if the official government law and justice system were based on native institutions.

Lack of accountability. There is generally a low level of accountability by Nigerian public officials toward the citizens. Were it not so, the leaders would not be able to get away with a fraction of the things they do. Analysis of Nigerian politics and government since independence shows that most of the country's elite and government leaders do not regard average citizens as wielding sufficient influence to compel accountability for elite actions. Nor do the elite and leaders believe that the average citizens can hold the elite and leaders liable for bad public policies. In a true democracy, in which citizens have the electoral capacity to unseat a government or leader pursuing unpopular policies, the leaders usually try to formulate policies and programs that are consistent with the citizens' wishes. Nigeria, since independence, has not experienced a true democratic government. All of the country's governments instead have been military and civilian dictatorships. The military regimes have been results of coups d'état. Although the civilian governments have purported to be democracies, in reality they have been imposed on Nigerians through rigged elections, with the result that citizens have not had much say in choosing the country's leaders or in directing the course of policy those leaders pursue.

Inadequate knowledge of the native justice and law systems. The data also strongly suggest that some of Nigeria's leaders and elite are unaware or only minimally aware of the relative strength and effectiveness of the native justice and law systems in general social control. The limited knowledge on the part of these leaders and elite informs their lack of action to indigenize law and justice in Nigeria.

Most of Nigeria's contemporary leaders and elite—indeed, most contemporary Nigerians, whether educated in Nigeria or abroad—have not been sufficiently familiarized with native systems and processes, including the native justice and law systems. In Nigeria, pre-primary, primary, secondary, and tertiary school curricula are embarrassingly devoid of indigenous ideas and solutions to local problems. Instead, the designers and the implementers of the curricula usually focus primarily or exclusively on foreign (usually British, American, and other Western) ideals for solutions to local issues (Okereafezeke, 2002). Even the best-educated Nigerian leaders and elite fare no better than the less educated in this regard. The following statement accurately captures the dearth of knowledge about native justice and law among Nigerian leaders and elite:

> ... the British trained African lawyer appears to believe that English law is the embodiment of everything that is excellent even when applied to totally different social and economic conditions. Certain it is that no one who studies criminal law from Mr. Seidman's Casebook is likely to continue to believe that English criminal law makes complete sense when applied to African conditions. [African lawyers] merely substitute for a study of English law, a study of Nigerian, Ghanaian, Tanzanian, Zambian, or Malawi law. The received criminal law of all these countries is basically English criminal law. The statutory provisions in any of them closely resemble those in others. Yet at present relevant decisions in one are rarely cited in the others because the lawyers know English decisions best, their local decisions next best, and those of African states not at all. (Gower, cited in Onyechi, 1975, p. 270)

Neocolonialist craving for foreign ideas and ideals.   There is no doubt that leaders' and elites' limited knowledge of Nigeria's native systems fertilizes the unbridled craving for foreign ideas and ideals. The combination of limited (or no) education on the availability and efficacy of Nigeria's native justice and law systems—coupled with colonial teachings that the native systems are outdated and irrelevant while the imposed British model represents modernity—has given rise to neocolonialist reasoning, action, and omission by many of Nigeria's leaders and elite. As Gower has shown (Onyechi, 1975, p. 270), these leaders and elite demonstrate little or no original thought. Rather, they support and encourage what I have described as "substitutive interaction" (Okereafezeke, 2002, p. 19), resulting in a preexisting system or process being supplanted by another (foreign) system or process. The substitution may be enforced by a foreign or domestic power, with or without force. A colonizing or occupying foreign power can forcibly replace a set of native laws and customs with the colonizer's legal system, for example. Substitutive interaction also occurs when a domestic government supersedes an indigenous system of justice and law with a foreign system.[3] Thus, with the prevailing substitutive official policies and programs, Nigeria's native justice and law systems are denigrated while the foreign, English system is promoted.

Anomic leadership and a confused society.   The   prevailing   situation in Nigeria, in which the country's leaders pursue and promote an alien law and justice system even though, as research shows, most Nigerians would prefer of managing their cases traditionally according to their customs and native laws, creates confusion in the country. It is difficult to be certain of the guiding rules of conduct when the official government's laws and rules differ substantially from the citizens' traditions, customs, and native laws. In this situation, officially proscribed standards conflict with acceptable and expected practices among the people. Thus, a citizen who complies with a native law may be arrested, tried, convicted, and punished under the official English system without regard to tradition, custom, and native law. Apart from the confusion this situation fosters among the population, it ensures disrespect and contempt for the English system. The social instability created by this uncertainty and confusion, or *anomie*, unless corrected, could destabilize the country to a point where neither the English nor the native system is capable of controlling the population.

>   ***Lack of continuity in government, public policies, and programs.***

Since the end of British colonial rule, Nigeria consistently has failed to establish stability in its government and public affairs. Several attempts to streamline election procedures have failed woefully. Almost all elections organized in Nigeria to choose government officials have ended in chaos, with one or more political parties rigging the elections and installing its candidates into office regardless of the vote. Because of the resulting coups d'état, it is impossible to know with reasonable certainty how long a particular government will be in power. In addition, in most cases the incoming government abolishes all the major policies that the previous regime imposed on the population and replaces them with the current government's preferences. As an example, the governor of Osun State (one of Nigeria's 36 states), *by decree*, abolished all the customary courts in the state "with immediate effect . . . as the governor's *pronouncement* means that they have been scrapped completely" (italics added) (Adeoye, 2003, p. 1). Although state law had created the customary courts, the governor was able to annul them by simply pronouncing accordingly. There is no evidence that the governor consulted with, or relied on the recommendation of, the state legislature, nor is there any indication that the he sought and received citizen support for scrapping the courts. Such important matters should first be submitted to the state legislature for debate and vote, or to the citizens for a referendum. Considering the expeditious manner in which the customary courts were scrapped, what will prevent a future government in Osun State from restoring the scrapped courts? Imagine the resources that would be expended to develop a new customary court structure and personnel.

To be sure, even stable democracies experience shifts in policies and programs between administrations. However, there are three main factors that distinguish Nigeria's experiences. First, because of the unstable political culture, it is impossible to predict with reasonable certainty when a change of government will happen in Nigeria. Second, an incoming government usually does not derive its power from the citizens; in fact, the incoming regime takes power *in spite of* Nigerians' expressed wishes. Third, when a new government in Nigeria changes preexisting policies and programs, it hardly abides by the rule of law as a controlling standard. In a stable democracy, a new administration that seeks to change a policy or program of a previous administration has to ensure that the rule of law is maintained: the procedures for getting into and remaining in public office contain basic guarantees for the citizens, no matter who occupies a public office. Such basic guarantees are pitifully absent in Nigeria. The country's basic constitution (the 1999 *Constitution of the Federal Republic of Nigeria*) was really created by only a few military and civilian power usurpers led by General Abdulsalami Abubakar and foisted on the rest of the country.

Profession-Centered Impediment

This type of impediment is found mainly in the professional groups within Nigeria, especially the legal profession.

Intellectual and professional inadequacies of lawyers and judges.
Nigeria suffers from a shortfall in the levels of intellectualism and professionalism on the part of many of its lawyers and judges, especially those that make and implement policies and standards. Many Nigerian lawyers and judges, in legal education and practice, defer too much to the English legal system, such that in fundamental terms Nigeria's official law is little more than an extension of the British model. There is little attempt to build a legal system, and practice law, based on Nigeria's unique circumstances. Gower (cited in Onyechi, 1975, p. 270) has described this shortage of creativity as a "besetting sin"—in this case, of legal education and practice.

In the warped belief that "English law is the embodiment of everything that is excellent even when applied to totally different social and economic conditions" (ibid.), many Nigerian lawyers and judges routinely rely on and cite English laws and decisions to decide even those cases that Nigeria's native customs and traditions exhaustively cover. They adopt a dress code of English lawyers and judges, even in the hot, generally unfriendly Nigerian climate. Contrast the Nigerian lawyers' and judges' style of dress (black trousers, black shoes, white shirt, black tie, black suit, with wig and gown, for men; black skirt and black suit on top of white blouse, black shoes, with wig and gown, for women) with the much simpler, less formal dressing styles for lawyers and judges in the United States. Note that, like Nigeria, the United States is a former British colony, yet lawyers and judges there are not required to wear a wig and gown, even though the United States generally has much colder weather conditions than Nigeria.

Citizen-Centered Impediments

The following impediments arise from the general citizens' actions and omissions rather than from the conduct of governments and other groups.

Citizens' acquiescence.   An acquiescent culture exists in Nigeria. The average citizen does not want to know, or is not sufficiently enlightened to ask questions about, who runs the country and how public policies are made and implemented. Asking such questions should be every citizen's business. Unfortunately, however, the Nigerian leaders and elite have mostly excluded the citizens from the public processes, and citizens have generally imbibed the exclusion and, strangely enough, accepted it. The absorption and acceptance have led to a largely passive and politically alienated citizenry, even among the educated. In this negative culture the average citizen does not question whether the policies and programs implemented by Nigerian leaders are in the people's best interests. Most governments, especially those that are corrupt—as most of Nigeria's governments have been—would take advantage of the situation, which is exactly what has happened in Nigeria. Policies and programs that would benefit the citizens and strengthen the country, such as the indigenization of Nigerian law and justice, are not pursued partly because there is no citizen demand for the leaders and elite to do so.

Uninformed logics of "education," "native customs and traditions," and "modernity".   Many Nigerians (not just the leaders and other elite) believe that a person cannot be modern and well-informed if he or she believes in, or practices, any of Nigeria's traditions, customs, and native laws. It is particularly troubling to note that this view is commonly found among the educated population. At the November 2003 American Society of Criminology Conference in Denver, Colorado, a Nigerian-born, U.S.-based professor of criminal justice presented a paper in which he suggested that Nigeria's traditions, customs, and native laws should be discarded because they impede efforts to build a united, progressive, modern nation. In their place, he suggested, the English law and justice should be used exclusively for social control in the country. I challenged his idea by pointing out that there is abundant scientific evidence that Nigeria's traditions, customs, and native laws are working quite effectively for social control in the country, and that most Nigerians follow their native systems rather than the English system. On those bases, it would be most irresponsible and counterproductive to do away with the native systems and pretend that they no longer exist.

I am baffled that I have to defend Nigeria's traditions, customs, and native laws, especially to an educated Nigerian, but it happens fairly frequently. Many people have somehow reached the warped conclusion that an "educated" person living in a "modern" society cannot also believe in, or practice, his or her own traditions, customs, and native laws. That is a false and unfortunate belief. Even the so-called major law and justice institutions of the world—such as "common law," which is the basis of English law and justice—originated from the country's own traditions, customs, and native laws. There is therefore a need to rethink the way many Nigerians look at the role of the country's native systems and institutions vis-à-vis foreign systems. At present, the foreign systems and institutions enjoy too many advantages over their native counterparts.

Summary and Conclusion

More than four decades after its political independence from Britain, there has been no meaningful effort to effect "appropriate" law and justice reform for post-independence Nigeria. Appropriate reform would officially acknowledge, encourage, and strengthen Nigeria's traditions, customs, and native laws as the primary means of regulating relationships, thus indigenizing law and justice in the country. The argument that Nigeria's law and justice should be restructured to this end is based on scientific research activities,[4] which show the efficacy of the country's customary laws and the preference of citizens for their own traditions, customs, and native laws rather than the English-imposed law of colonial Britain. Despite the widely documented effectiveness and efficiency of Nigeria's native laws and customs, the country's successive post-independence governments and leaders have failed to adequately support the native systems of justice and law. Instead, these governments and leaders have consistently pursued the colonial-based English system of law and justice as the dominant, government-sanctioned system in Nigeria.

The data studied reveal several explanations for the continuation of the British colonial policies and programs in Nigeria. The explanations ("impediments") have been categorized into government-centered, profession-centered, and citizen-centered impediments to indigenizing Nigerian law and justice systems. Without downplaying the respective roles of the other two categories of impediments, the government-centered impediments should be treated as the most consequential because of the enormous powers and resources that the Nigerian governments command at the local, state, and national levels. These governments may make or break an issue, such as law and justice indigenization, depending on how they choose to respond. However, it seems that any meaningful effort to reform and indigenize Nigerian law and justice must begin with a full recognition of the need for such action. Thus, Nigerian leaders' understanding of this need and their willingness to develop and carry out such a revolutionary venture are central variables necessary to effect indigenization.

Finally, the importance of reforming and indigenizing law and justice for post-independence Nigeria lies in the need for the country's official governments to preach the same things that are important to the people and that the people follow. From the time of British colonial rule through the present, there has existed in Nigeria a deep chasm between the officially certified, encouraged, and financed system of law and justice (the British-imposed system) and the more relevant, more meaningful, and more commonly practiced systems of justice and law (the native systems). The gulf will remain—and may get deeper—unless official methods and procedures for managing grievances, conflicts, and disputes are brought in line and made consistent with the people's preferences. There is no doubt that the proposed indigenization of law and justice would improve social control in Nigeria because it would be an official endorsement of the people to regulate their lives in ways that most of them already do.

Notes

[1] This article is a part of research for an upcoming book titled *Reconstructing Justice in a Postcolony* by the same author. An earlier version was presented at the American Society of Criminology Conference, Denver, Colorado, USA, November 18–22, 2003.

[2] The Igbos (or Ibos) are located mainly in southeast Nigeria. With a population of roughly 30 million, they are one of the country's three largest ethnic nations.

[3] Contrast two other kinds of intersociety interaction: cooperative interaction and pluralistic interaction (see Okereafezeke, 2002, pp. 18–20).

References

Adeoye, Seun (September 8, 2003) "Osun scraps customary courts," in *The Guardian*. Available: http://odili.net/news/source/2003/sep/8/8.html (accessed October 26, 2004).

Constitution of the Federal Republic of Nigeria, 1999 (effective May 29, 1999).

Ogbalu, F. (1979) *Igbo Institutions and Customs*. Onitsha, Nigeria: University Publishing.

Okafor, F. (1978) *Africa at the Crossroads*. New York: Vintage Press.

Okereafezeke, Nonso (1996) *The Relationship Between Informal and Formal Strategies of Social Control: An Analysis of the Contemporary Methods of Dispute Processing Among the Igbos of Nigeria*. UMI Number 9638581. Ann Arbor, MI: University Microfilms.

———. (2002) *Law and Justice in Post-British Nigeria: Conflicts and Interactions Between Native and Foreign Systems of Social Control in Igbo*. Westport, CT: Greenwood Press.

———. (February 6, 2003) "Burden of Patriotism: Obasanjo, Leadership, and Nigerian Nation-Building," in *NigeriaWorld*. Available: http://nigeriaworld.com/articles/2003/feb/061.html (accessed February 11, 2004).

Oli, S. I. (1994) "A Dichotomization: Crime and Criminality among Traditional and Christianized Igbo," in Sulton, A. T. (ed.), *African-American Perspectives on Crime Causation, Criminal Justice Administration and Crime Prevention*. Englewood, CO: Sulton Books.

Onyechi, N. M. (1975) "A Problem of Assimilation or Dominance," in T. O. Elias et al. (eds.), *African Indigenous Laws: Proceedings of Workshop* (August 7–9, 1974). Enguru, Nigeria. Government Printer.

19

Islamic Legal Systems
Traditional (Saudi Arabia), Contemporary (Bahrain), and Evolving (Pakistan)

Richter H. Moore, Jr.

Islamic law, or *Shari'a*[1], is a major legal system distinct from both the civil and common law systems. Contemporary Western law, strongly influenced by Roman and Anglo-American common law, is law "expressly devised by men for men" (Karl, 1991:133). In contrast, the origins and scope of Islamic law are fundamentally different from any other. Although it takes many of its principles from religion, it is separate and distinct from religion; Islamic law is only one of the facets of the Islamic faith. The Shari'a is the method ordained by God whereby man is to conduct his life in order to submit to and realize God's will (Karl, 1992:135). From the time of the prophet Muhammad, a definite practical intent was inherent in the concept of Shari'a. It is a guide to all aspects of life, all behavior—spiritual, mental, and physical. All legal and social transactions are subsumed in the Shari'a as a comprehensive abiding principle (Weeramantry, 1988; Mayer, 1990:182).

The Shari'a originates from two primary sources (Karl, 1991:137). The first is the *Qur'an* (more commonly spelled *Koran*), which set out principles believed to have been revealed by God through Muhammad. The Qur'an is the final authority but requires authoritative interpretation since it contains many "layers" of meaning and ". . . more meanings hitherto unexpected keep revealing themselves in its pages" (Weeramantry, 1988:34). The second source, the *Sunna* or *Sunnah* (also called the *Hadith* or "traditions of the Prophet"), contains those decisions of the Prophet himself respecting circumstances not addressed in the Qur'an. Islamic writings often describe the Qur'an and Sunna as an "integrated whole, each supporting the other's primary purpose." In many instances, further interpretation is needed.

Prepared especially for *Comparative Criminal Justice, 1/E.*

There are also two secondary sources. In searching for additional guidance there arose a body of writings called the *Ijma*, a consensus of Muslim jurist decisions made in the absence of a ruling by either God or Muhammad. A major limitation of the Ijma is that it must not conflict with the Qur'an and Sunna. The final source is *Qiyas* ("reasoning by analogy"), a method of analysis whereby eminent jurists decided new legal principles by applying an established principle of the Qur'an or Sunna and sometimes recorded Ijma to a new, though similar, situation; the binding or precedented nature of the decisions rejected by certain schools of Shari'a interpretation (Karl, 1991:137–42; Weeramantry, 1988:30–45).

In Pakistan, a retired judge of the Supreme Court described Shari'a as follows:

> [The Muslims of Pakistan are] bound only by the divine law, i.e., the Shari'a. The Shari'a is the only law in this State, the status of the so-called remaining laws including the Constitution being only that of orders whose validity depends on their acceptance as Allah's will by the judicial Ulama or the judiciary, and that any order or so-called law including the Constitution which is in conflict with any part of the Holy Qur'an or Sunna including the directions relating to justice and righteousness is null and void. (quoted in Pearl, 1990:203)

Under the Shari'a there are three types of crimes: *Hadd* (that which is defined), *Qisas* (retaliation), and *Ta'zir* (discretionary crimes). Hadd[2] offenses are specifically prohibited and the punishment specified in the Qur'an; the court has no discretion in punishing these types of crimes. Qisas are crimes that give victims (or their families) the right of retaliation (i.e., murder, intentional amputation); these are specifically dealt with in the Qur'an and Sunna. Ta'zir offenses are those for which the punishment is not specified, and the judge may exercise a great deal of discretion (limited by the Shari'a) (Walker, 1993:867–68).

Although the Shari'a has dominated the lives of a large portion of the world's population, it has not been uniformly applied throughout the world because different schools of interpretation have periodically emerged. While the Shari'a undergirds the law and legal systems in all Islamic countries, as the world has changed each country has developed its own national legal system. All of the Islamic states' legal systems provide a recognition and a place for the Shari'a, in some a much more prominent one than in others.

This article will examine the legal and judicial systems of three Islamic nations—Saudi Arabia, Bahrain, and Pakistan—comparing the influence of the Shari'a on each. Of these, Saudi Arabia is the most pure Shari'a system. Bahrain, on the other hand, reflects substantial British influence and the influence of Egyptian civil law. Pakistan's primary influence has been the British judicial system, but it is currently undergoing several major changes. A brief discussion of judicial procedure in Saudi Arabia and Bahrain is also included.

Saudi Arabia

Under Islamic law, the Shari'a is the only permissible source of legislation in Saudi Arabia. Consequently, the ruler or civil government may not legislate. The ruler may issue regulations only in the form of royal decrees, which are consistent with and supplement the Shari'a. Today the regulations are formulated by a committee within the Council of Ministers that recommends them to the council. If the council approves, it recommends them to the king, who issues a royal decree that, when published, becomes law.

There is no law in Saudi Arabia other than the Shari'a. Authoritative acts and regulations, including the acts of the king, are valid only to the extent that they apply to and are consistent with the Shari'a (see Jones, 1992). It is the House of Saud's application of the Shari'a in Saudi Arabia that confers legitimacy on the regime, not right of birth.

Early in this century, King Abdul Aziz ibn-Abdul Rahman al Faisal al Saud (Ibn Saud) established the monarchy in Saudi Arabia, and the *Hanbali*[3] School was adopted as the official school of Islamic jurisprudence (Karl, 1991). This decreed the organization of the court system and the procedures to be followed by it, as well as the precedent for the king to regulate judicial functions and act as the final arbitrator in the kingdom. These actions led to the Civil Procedure Rules of 1936 and 1952, the Board of Grievances in 1955, and the creation of the Ministry of Justice in 1970.

At the pinnacle of the judicial system is the king, who may act as a final court of appeal and as a source of pardon. King Abdul Aziz was famed for personally dispensing justice in cases of every description, but he generally refrained from modifying legal interpretations of the *Ulama* (religious scholars and jurists) without first winning its members over to his view. His successors have exercised judicial power, but to an increasingly lesser extent.

The Ministry of Justice presides over the Shari'a judicial system, while almost every ministry has a committee system to adjudicate certain matters within its particular sphere of interest. The two most important committees are the Labor and the Commercial Dispute Settlement Committees. In addition, the Board of Grievances, essentially an administrative court, is now independent of the Council of Ministers and could become the nucleus of a more secular judiciary.

Since 1953 and especially after the creation of the Ministry of Justice in 1970, the judicial system has expanded rapidly, and elements of the judicial authority have been diffused throughout the government. Royal Decree M-64 (July 23, 1975) assured political autonomy of the judiciary. Article I reads: ". . . Judges are independent and, in their administration of justice, are subject to no authority other than the provisions of Islamic law and regulations in force. No one may interfere with the judiciary."

Shari'a Courts

The Saudi court system is made up of Shari'a courts, having jurisdiction over most disputes in the country, and specialized administrative tribunals whose jurisdiction is established by decree. The Shari'a courts are courts of general jurisdiction set up under the Ministry of Justice and as a result any matter, whether civil or criminal, may be heard in them. There is no formal division between civil and criminal matters, and the same judge may hear cases in both areas on the same day (Karl, 1991:144–45).

At the bottom level of the Shari'a judicial pyramid are the ordinary courts or courts of first instance, consisting of lower courts and general courts. The lower courts are found in almost every town and deal with minor domestic matters, misdemeanors, and small claims (i.e., less than 8,000 Saudi Riyals). They also deal with all crimes of Ta'zir involving discretionary penalties, and they have the power to adjudicate the *Huddud* (plural of Hadd) crimes of intoxication and defamation but have no power to try criminal matters carrying a sentence of death or mutilation. The proceedings are supervised by one Islamic judge, or *Qadi*. Jurisdiction in civil cases exists only in the home of the defendant, regardless of the location of the contract or property in dispute. There is no immunity from the court's jurisdiction; even the king is subject to it. General courts have original jurisdiction over all civil and criminal cases. Cases are heard by one judge, except in death penalty cases or sentences involving stoning or amputation, which are heard by a three-judge panel (Karl, 1991:145–46).

In order to file a claim, a plaintiff in a civil action processes the claim initially at the governor's office in the district of the defendant. In the case of a criminal action, the plaintiff processes the claim through the police in his own district or in the district of the defendant. In certain "private-rights" criminal matters or in matters of personal injury, the plaintiff files the claim directly with the court. In civil cases, the governor's office will attempt to compromise and if no consensus is reached, it then refers the parties to the court. In criminal cases, the police will investigate and the prosecutor brings the action; in "private rights" cases, the claimant initiates and prosecutes the action. Formal written pleas are not required. The claimant may dictate his claim to the clerk of the court at the start of the process (either at the governor's office or at the police station). The defendant is then notified and has the opportunity to dictate his basic defense to the clerk.

Since Shari'a is not case law, a judge is not bound by decisions of other judges or even by his own previous decisions in the same court. Nor is the judge bound by the decisions of other judges in a higher court. In civil cases, the judge sees himself first as a guide to the parties in seeking to settle and compromise. In criminal matters, he attempts to apply strict, long-accepted rules. To the extent the judge seeks binding precepts, he is bound only by the Qur'an and the Sunna. He may consult texts, including the jurisprudence of other Islamic countries, but his judgment of the oral testimony will be the overriding factor.

Once a Shari'a judge has held a hearing, he will usually make his decision the same day and dictate the decision to the clerk of the court, who records it and hands it to the claimant and the defendant. Objections to the decision must be filed within 15 days after the date the decision has been received by the objecting party. Appealable decisions from any of the Shari'a ordinary courts may be appealed to the next higher court, the high court of Shari'a law. The high courts of Shari'a law have exclusive jurisdiction over crimes of Huddud and Qisas and general jurisdiction to hear appeals from the lower court. The proceedings at this level are also controlled by one judge, except in cases calling for a sentence of death, stoning, or amputation, where the three-judge panel is required. Judgments from the high courts may be appealed, except where the amount in controversy does not exceed 500 riyals or where the penalty is no greater than forty lashes or ten days' imprisonment.

If a judgment is appealed, it is reviewed by a court of appeals. There are two of these courts: one in Riyadh, which hears appeals from lower courts in the Central and Eastern Provinces, and one in Mecca, which hears appeals from decisions issued in the Western Province. The appellate courts are divided into three departments: (1) criminal law, (2) personal status, and (3) cases that do not fall into the other two categories (Karl, 1991:146). The appeals court bases its decision on transcripts of the lower court proceedings but has the right to summon the parties and call witnesses. The court of appeals is required to hear appeals from:

- sentences imposing death or mutilation,
- convictions against trustees of endowments or guardians,
- decisions involving real estate,
- judgments awarded by default,
- decisions referred by another judicial authority, and
- decisions rendered against juveniles.

Cases on appeal involving sentences of death, stoning, or amputation must be heard by a five-judge panel as opposed to the normal three-judge appellate panel. For very serious cases, appellate courts may also sit *en banc* as a general committee made up of all members of the court. Except in the case of an en banc decision, decisions of the court of appeals are subject to review by the Supreme Judicial Council. This body consists of a president, who is a member of the Council of Ministers, and ten other members (Karl, 1991:146). The Supreme Judicial Council supervises the entire court system under Shari'a law in addition to serving as an appellate body. It is not, however, a court in itself; it cannot alter the verdict of a lower court but may only refer the case back to the court of appeals for reconsideration. The king has final review authority and therefore determines whether the verdict in fact conforms to the Shari'a. In criminal cases he also has the authority to pardon should he find that the verdict does not conform to Shari'a.

Administrative Tribunals

Administrative tribunals (called committees) have been established under the authority of various ministries to apply and enforce regulations enacted to cope with business/commercial, traffic, and labor matters in the kingdom—secular concerns. Established by royal decree, the jurisdiction of these specialized committees is limited to matters that come within the general purview of the Ministry's various activities and is concurrent with the general jurisdiction of the Shari'a courts (Karl, 1991:147).

Like the Shari'a system, the structure of the administrative tribunals is hierarchical, varying somewhat from ministry to ministry. There are committees of first instance and appeals committees at the intermediate level, all overseen by the relevant minister and the Council of Ministers. The Ministry of Labor and Social Affairs is responsible for the Committee for the Settlement of Labor Disputes. The Committee for the Settlement of Commercial Disputes and the Commercial Paper Committee were created under the Ministry of Commerce. The Ministry of the Interior supervises enforcement of motor vehicle regulations. The Ministry of Finance has a committee to deal with tax-related disputes. Most members of the various committees are Shari'a or ex-Shari'a judges. Generally, one member of each committee is trained in regulations law and has some technical background (i.e., familiarity with more sophisticated contract or commercial disputes). The committees almost always meet in the evening since the members usually have other full-time employment.

In the case of traffic violations, the Ministry of the Interior may impose modest criminal penalties (300 riyals or up to ten days in prison) for such offenses as speeding, driving through red lights, and illegal U-turns. However, where there is a combination of personal injury and illegal action, the police may refer the matter to the prosecutor's office, which in turn may commence legal action in Shari'a court. Property damage resulting from traffic violations is almost always settled by the police with appeal to a Ministry of the Interior committee. The police require the injured party to bring estimates of the property damage to them and then order the payment of all or such portion of the damages for which the police deem the party liable. Failure to pay may result in temporary imprisonment and civil prosecution.

Two of the more typical administrative tribunals are the Board of Grievances and the Committee for the Settlement of Labor Disputes. The Board of Grievances is an independent, quasi-judicial institution and perhaps the most important of these administrative tribunals. Established in 1955 as part of the Council of Ministers and later reorganized as an independent body whose chairman belongs to the Council of Ministers, it has investigative, review, and consultative branches. In 1982, new regulations

JUDICIAL SYSTEM OF SAUDI ARABIA

King of Saudi Arabia

Ministry of Justice

Shari'a Courts

Supreme Judicial Council

Courts of Appeal

High Courts *(Kubra)*

Ordinary Courts *(Musta'galah)*

Lower Courts   General Courts

Administrative Tribunals

Committee for the Settlement of Labor Disputes

Board of Grievances

Other Committees/Boards

altered the structure and jurisdiction of the Board of Grievances, making it an independent judicial body on a more equal footing with the Council of Ministers (Karl, 1991:147). The chairman of the board now answers to the king. By giving the board more independence and greater judiciary powers, the regulations have placed the Board of Grievances in parallel alignment with the Shari'a courts. Such an alignment leaves it to the king alone to determine whether the board's decision comports with the Shari'a.

The board hears almost all disputes involving a private entity (whether Saudi or foreign) and the Saudi government. They are also able to hear complaints regarding an administrative decision; a violation of judicial procedure; or the wrongful conduct of a Saudi official, including a Shari'a judge. The board does not generally review either Shari'a judgments or decisions made by specialized committees unless there is strong evidence that a decision was the result of incorrect evaluation. An extraordinary appeal similar to a certiorari may be made in the event that a party feels that a Shari'a court judgment was unjust, perhaps on grounds of judicial bias, but subject to the argument that judgment over cases involving judicial misbehavior is vested exclusively in the Supreme Judicial Council.

The Board of Grievances also has the authority to review foreign judgments that are brought to them for enforcement (Karl, 1991:148). The board is important not only for its new and respected position beside the Shari'a court but also as a modern example of *mazalim*—a tradition adopted by King Abdul Aziz of addressing individuals' grievances against the government personally. Mazalim derives from the notion that parties in dispute and even the government should "yield to justice."

Established in 1969, the Committee for the Settlement of Labor Disputes has jurisdiction (exclusive) over cases involving labor accidents and similar claims. Judgments are appealable to the Supreme Committee (Karl, 1991:148).

Procedures and Trial

The complaint, civil or criminal, must be a clear statement of charge, although there is no requirement that it be in writing or adhere to a specific format. It is generally directed to the court clerk so that hearing dates can be scheduled and notice served on the defendant. Once a hearing date is set by the clerk, notice, by way of confirmation to the claimant of the private right or the prosecutor of the public right and to the defendant of the charge, must be made. The claimant signs the summoning document, thereby receiving notice of the date set for the hearing. The defendant must be personally notified of the charge filed against him as well. Where the defendant is illiterate, two witnesses must testify that the defendant has received notice. There is no requirement that the defendant reply in writing (Karl, 1991:150–69).

The hearing, like the overall process, is informal as compared to trial procedures in the United States. The judge listens to the claimant or prosecutor while the clerk records the statement in writing. The judge then requires the defendant to admit to or deny the charge against him. His statement will also be recorded. If necessary, the defendant is given time to consult his records or other documents before answering. If he admits to being guilty of the charge, a judgment will be made summarily. If he retracts a confession, the retraction must be accepted and the claimant or prosecutor has the burden to introduce further evidence of culpability. The trial consists of oral statements and there is no jury.

According to Saudi jurisprudence and the general practice of the Shari'a courts, no legal representation is permitted in criminal proceedings regarding public rights where the accused is present. The defendant must defend himself but may request assistance of counsel. In practice, such assistance is permitted to foreigners but is discretionary. The choice of counsel is always left to the defendant.

In an action involving private rights, a party is entitled to be represented at trial by a Saudi attorney. The power of attorney must be notarized by the Ministry of Justice. Shari'a courts do not encourage legal representation, preferring that the defendant speak for himself. The administrative tribunals, on the other hand, have no objection to parties being represented by legal professionals, though the tribunals insist that such representatives be Saudi-licensed attorneys. There is no right to counsel in any pretrial proceeding. The accused is presumed innocent until proven guilty. The claimant or prosecutor has the burden of proof in trial.

In theory, a defendant is entitled to a public trial. However, the court may consider it "in the interest of morals" to hold the trial in secret, resulting in a closed proceeding. Rarely is permission granted to observe a criminal trial. The closed proceedings are viewed as protecting the accused from adverse publicity. In Saudi Arabia, the burden of proof is on the private claimant or the prosecution throughout the proceedings. The claimant or prosecution must establish the truth of the accusation only to the satisfaction of the judge.

The standards on which a judge bases his decisions are nowhere defined in a way that ensures a reasonable degree of predictability. A judge is not to draw on his personal experience or knowledge but is to rely on the evidence and testimony as produced by the parties and Shari'a principles as he knows them. He may consult legal sources and confer with his assistants. A Shari'a judge, as noted earlier, is not bound to precedent nor to his prior decisions. In addition, he is not required to follow the decisions of a higher-ranking judge. Thus, it is difficult to dispute his decision or even understand the basis of his decision.

There are no challenges for cause in Shari'a court. The judge cannot be changed during the proceedings and, if one feels the decision made was due to the judge's bias or a procedural error, the party may appeal the judgment on such grounds after the trial.

After judgment is rendered, the judge will ask whether or not the parties are satisfied with the outcome. If the defendant is dissatisfied, he must file his objection within ten to fifteen days from the date of the decision; otherwise he renounces his right to appeal. The prosecution in practice, but not by any clear regulation or Shari'a proscription, has the right of appeal as well. The court then submits the case record, including the record of the judgment, to the office of the chief judge for review. The period for review by the appellate committee is not to exceed 20 days for cases of normal difficulty, or thirty days if the case is especially difficult. The lower court judgment is automatically put into effect while the appeal is pending (Walker, 1993).

There are two kinds of appeals: automatic and ordinary. Sentences imposing death or mutilation are automatically appealed, as well as those involving real estate and other matters, as noted earlier. Ordinary appeal arises upon demand from a party who has the right to appeal. An appeal from an ordinary Shari'a court goes to a Shari'a high court. An appeal from a Shari'a high court will be received by the Supreme Judicial Council for review. The highest appellate authority is the president of the Council of Ministers or the king, who may receive an appeal from any judgment. The king or the president of the Council of Ministers must approve a sentence of death or mutilation. However, he cannot simply overturn an already determined penalty. Rather, he has the authority to request further investigation by the judicial authority.

In the Shari'a court, the court of appeals may affirm, remand, or reverse the lower court's decision. Appellate judges, however, do not have the authority to enter their own decisions. Instead, the court of appeals has the power to order a new trial with a new judge when the judge whose decision was reversed refuses (as is his right) to reconsider his decision in view of the appellate authority's recommendations. Thus, the court of appeals has the power to terminate the validity of the decision made below but not the case itself. Lower-court decisions can be revised for purely technical errors that have no effect on the judgment.

Unlike the Shari'a courts, most administrative appellate tribunals have the power to reverse the previous judgment below and declare a new decision. This is possible where the case has come up on appeal for its third time. With the two former appeals, the appellate tribunal can remand the case back to the lower level with instructions. The administrative tribunals can reverse or vary decisions for the same procedural reasons that reversals occur in Shari'a court.

Appellate proceedings are conducted in camera. Not even the involved parties are allowed to be present and there is no legal representation or oral argument. The cases are distributed among the judges, but only one judge will review a case file. After he has made his remarks, all the judges convene and discuss his comments. Most decisions are affirmed. The procedures in the administrative tribunals are similar.

Bahrain

Bahrain, as a result of its treaty arrangements with Great Britain, has been influenced by the British legal system to a greater extent than other Arab states. The Bahraini government, prior to withdrawal of the British and the enactment of the Law of the Organisation of the Judicature (Amin, 1985:36) in 1971, had adopted certain British laws by translation of the British-Indian text from English into Arabic. These laws include the Penal Code of 1860, the Criminal Procedure Code of 1861, and the Contract Act of 1872. After 1971, a legislative committee was set up by the Bahraini government to develop its own independent legal system (Khuri, 1980). The committee was led by Cambridge-educated Husain al Baharna, and the legal system that was established is based on a combination of the Egyptian and British legal systems and the Shari'a. The Egyptian influence brought with it elements of French civil law as well.

The primary sources of criminal law are the 1966 Code of Criminal Procedure and the 1976 Penal Code of Bahrain. Other laws are issued from time to time in the form of Amiri decrees from the ruler of Bahrain, the Amir. These decrees are published and have the full force of the law. The Judicature Law of 1971 was promulgated specifying a hierarchical structure when interpreting acceptable behavior: (1) provisions of law, (2) the principles of the Shari'a, (3) custom, and (4) natural law or the principles of equity and good conscience (Ballantyne, 1990:153). In 1973, a constitution for Bahrain was finalized and approved by the Constituent Assembly, and all Bahraini laws and Amiri decrees are presumed to follow the principles of the 1973 constitution.

Bahraini Courts

The courts of Bahrain are organized into two major divisions: the lay courts, consisting of civil, commercial, and criminal courts, and the religious or Shari'a courts. Each division is further organized into subdivisions based on, and determining, subject-matter jurisdiction and scope of competence.

At the top of the judicial pyramid is the High Court of Appeal (Court of Cassation), the highest judicial authority in Bahrain. It consists of a panel of five judges; a Bahraini judge serves as president, and Egyptian judges may reside on the court as well. The court is divided into two chambers with jurisdiction to hear appeals from judgments rendered by the civil senior and criminal senior courts involving non-Muslims and cases that carry the death penalty (*Middle East Executive Reports*, 1989:7).

The general jurisdiction level is composed of the civil senior courts and the criminal senior courts. The civil senior courts are composed of three chambers, each chamber having a president and two magistrates. These courts have jurisdiction in civil commercial disputes that are not within the jurisdiction of the minor courts. They hear cases involving personal status disputes of non-Muslim residents in Bahrain. In these cases, the courts apply the laws of the nationality of the parties to disputes involving marriage, divorce, alimony, maintenance of children, trust, estates, and inheritance. The civil senior court also hears labor disputes.

Criminal senior courts are also composed of three chambers, each with a president and two magistrates. The courts' jurisdiction extends to all criminal cases involving crimes for which the punishment is imprisonment for more than five years or a fine exceeding 5,000 Bahraini dinars. The senior court of appeals is also composed of three chambers, each with a president and two magistrates. This court receives all appeals from the minor, medium, and execution courts. The medium courts are composed of three chambers with one judge each. These courts hear all criminal cases for which the punishment does not exceed five years or a fine of up to 5,000 Bahraini dinars. The minor courts are composed of five chambers, each with one judge. These courts have jurisdiction over all civil and commercial disputes under 3,000 Bahraini dinars.

In addition, there are three special courts. The juvenile court, presided over by a single judge, tries all juvenile crimes. The traffic courts are composed of three chambers with one judge each. These courts hear all cases involving traffic offenses. The last of the special courts is the execution court. This court is composed of two chambers, each with one judge. Its purpose is the execution of all judgments of the civil and Shari'a courts.

The Shari'a courts are divided into two levels: the high courts of appeal and the Shari'a senior courts. The high courts of appeal are composed of two chambers, each presided over by a president and two magistrates. Because of the population division in Bahrain, in which approximately half the population is Shia while the ruling family and a substantial portion of the population are Sunni, one chamber of the court is Shia and the other Sunni. The Shari'a senior courts are composed of two chambers divided along the religious lines of the high courts. These courts hear all personal status disputes of Bahraini Muslims (Khuri, 1980).

The judges of the Bahraini civil, criminal, and commercial courts are almost exclusively Sunni. By and large they are highly trained and highly qualified. The judges are appointed by the Bahraini government for an indefinite term. At the present time there are nine Egyptian, two Jordanian, and two Sudanese judges on the bench; the remaining judges are Bahraini. The Egyptian judges, in particular, have brought much-needed expertise to the judicial system.

Judicial Procedure

As in Islamic and civil law countries, there is no right to a jury trial in Bahrain. All criminal cases are heard by judges alone, the number depending on the offense charged and the court to which it is referred. The law provides that civil damages can be awarded in a criminal case, but in actual practice this is virtually unknown.

There is no automatic appellate review of a conviction in Bahrain. No appeal is allowed from a guilty plea (a confession), except as to extent and legality of the sentence. Notice of appeal must be filed within thirty days of the date of decision. Such notice may set forth the grounds for appeal, with or without argument or narrative, and, as with all legal documents, it must be in Arabic. The appellate court may base its decision on the record of the trial court, may return the case to the trial court for a new hearing, or may order evidence or witnesses brought before it for a partial or complete trial de novo. The appellate court may increase a sentence on appeal. The public prosecutor may appeal an acquittal or the sentence, in the case of a conviction, and on appeal the accused may be found guilty and sentenced by the appellate court or the original sentence may be increased.

With very few exceptions, lawyers admitted to practice before the courts of Bahrain must be graduates of an approved law school; most are graduates of either Middle Eastern or United Kingdom law schools. A few nonlaw-school graduates are allowed to practice in the Bahraini courts, but those individuals have extensive experience and training, primarily in Shari'a law.

The Procedure Code provides that an accused person, as a matter of right, be defended by counsel before any criminal court. There is no provision in the code for providing counsel to indigents. As a matter of practice however, no indigent is required to stand trial without the assistance of counsel. The Ministry of Justice and Islamic Affairs will appoint a counsel in any case where the accused is not able to afford one. There is no provision in the code for counsel during those "critical stages" of the investigative process such as interrogation and lineups. The Bahraini Constitution, on the other hand, provides that counsel will be appointed for any person

JUDICIAL SYSTEM OF BAHRAIN

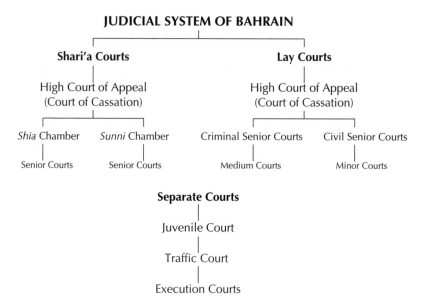

Shari'a Courts

High Court of Appeal
(Court of Cassation)

Shia Chamber   *Sunni* Chamber

Senior Courts   Senior Courts

Lay Courts

High Court of Appeal
(Court of Cassation)

Criminal Senior Courts   Civil Senior Courts

Medium Courts   Minor Courts

Separate Courts

Juvenile Court

Traffic Court

Execution Courts

accused of a felony and ensures the accused the opportunity to exercise his right of defense in all stages of investigation and trial.

While there is no set procedure for challenging judges for cause in courts of Bahrain, the Procedure Code provides that no person shall sit as a member of a court that tries any case in which he is a party or in which he has a personal interest. Presumably, bringing such information to the attention of the judge and putting it on the record of the court would result in the judge disqualifying himself from further participation. If not, this would be valid grounds for appeal. The Bahraini Constitution states that the accused shall be guaranteed a legal trial in which all the necessary provisions for the exercise of the right of defense are ensured.

The Procedure Code provides that the place in which any court is held shall be deemed an open court. All trials are open to the public, within the limits of courtroom capacity and the discretion of the court. Cases involving juveniles, seventeen years of age and under, are handled privately in closed court by the judge.

Pakistan

Pakistan has a highly centralized federal system (see Choudhury, 1988:194–204). The provincial territories of Pakistan are divided into small administrative districts, each under the control of a deputy commissioner who is responsible for maintaining law and order and collecting revenue and, as a district magistrate, is assisted by a large number of officers, including the police, in the execution of his duties. Pakistan has a codified

system of laws based on common law principles. Most of the existing civil and criminal statutes were enacted by the British before the independence of Pakistan in 1947 (Choudhury, 1988:221). An exception to this is found in the "personal laws" (i.e., the laws of inheritance, marriage, and divorce are decided between parties on the basis of their religious affiliation). Separate laws, therefore, govern Muslims, Christians, and Hindus. The judiciary in Pakistan remains in operation basically as established by the British, although the 1990 Criminal Law Ordinance perhaps was an indicator of a return to a more fundamentalist Islamic doctrine (Gottesman, 1992:435). Over the past 100 years the courts have interpreted the laws of the country. Their decisions have been included regularly in the law reports, as is the custom in England. The judiciary is supposed to be independent and insulated from the influences of the executive function, and the courts defend a citizen's fundamental rights (Choudhury, 1988:221).

Pakistani Courts

The courts are organized on the three-tier system, including an original court of facts and laws, which also records evidence, and a final court of appeal (Choudhury, 1988:221). They deal with all questions of personal laws, faith, and morals. In their interpretation and application of the laws, the courts look at original sources and follow a line of decisions, largely from courts in Pakistan and pre-partition India. The decisions of other common law systems, including those of the United States, the United Kingdom, and India, are also considered whenever similar language of a statute may be involved. In addition, the decisions of the Supreme Court of Pakistan are binding on all courts, and the high court decisions are binding on the subordinate courts.

In essence, Pakistan follows the British parliamentary system of government. Its legislative and judicial structure is modeled on that of the British. The similarities between the contents of the Pakistani statutes and the methodology of interpretation of laws by the courts suggest that Pakistan, having inherited the established British judicial system, continues to maintain it (for the most part).

In Pakistan, there is no distinction between state and federal courts. All courts administer and adjudicate on matters of state and federal laws. There are two constitutional courts, the Supreme Court of Pakistan and a separate high court for each province (Choudhury, 1988:227).

The Supreme Court consists of the chief justice of Pakistan and nine other judges, appointed by the president after consultation with the chief justice. For appointment to the bench of the Supreme Court, a person must have been a judge in a provincial high court for at least five years or must have practiced as an advocate of a high court for no less than fifteen years. A judge of the Supreme Court holds office until age 65.

The Supreme Court has original jurisdiction in any dispute between two provincial governments or between the federal government and state

government. It also has the power to issue appropriate writs, such as *certiorari* and *mandamus*. Appeals against the judgments of the high courts are made to the Supreme Court on matters involving the interpretation of provisions or on other matters of law. The Supreme Court is the final appellate court of decision in Pakistan.

Each province in the country has a high court consisting of a chief justice and court judges appointed by the president. A judge of the high court is appointed by the president after consultation with the chief justice of Pakistan and the governor of the province. A person will not be appointed to the high court unless he has served as a district judge for a period of at least three years or practiced at the bar for at least ten years. Unlike the Supreme Court, which primarily hears constitutional matters, high courts hear appeals both in civil and criminal matters originating in district courts. In civil cases, appeals to the high courts are regulated by the Code of Civil Procedure. Once an appeal has been filed in the high court, it has the power to determine a case finally, remand a case to the lower court and refer for trial, or take additional evidence or require such evidence to be taken.

The high courts, besides exercising appellate jurisdiction, have supervisory powers over the subordinate courts, both in criminal and civil matters. Most orders of the magistrates and session judges, depending on the sentence, are subject to review by the high courts. In the case of a death sentence passed by the session judge, the sentence must be confirmed by the high court before it can be carried out. The high courts also have the power of revision in criminal cases, which may be exercised through the issuance of a writ of habeas corpus or by transferring a case from one court to another.

Each province has a well-established trial court system at the district level. The major trial court is the district court. On the civil side it is broken down into the following classes of civil courts: (1) the court of the district judge, (2) the court of the additional district judge, and (3) the court of the civil judge. Each province is divided into small geographical districts, and a district judge is appointed to each district by the provincial government in consultation with the high court. Additional district judges may be appointed to discharge such functions of the district judge as the high court may decide to assign them. The district judge exercises powers of general supervision over the subordinate courts in the district. Assignment and distribution of the district judicial work is the responsibility of the district judge. The district court is the principal court of original civil jurisdiction. It has jurisdiction in civil suits without limit in regard to value. Orders of the district courts are appealable to the high court (see Choudhury, 1988).

The district court also has jurisdiction over criminal trials and, in that capacity, the court is designated as a court of session. The following are classes of criminal courts: (1) courts of session, (2) magistrates of the first class, (3) magistrates of the second class, and (4) magistrates of the third

class. The magistrate courts are courts of limited jurisdiction. The higher the class, the more serious the offense. The district and session judge are one and the same and comprise the head of civil and criminal justice in each district.

There are also special courts and tribunals that deal with specific types of cases (Choudhury, 1988:228). These include:

- special courts for trial of offenses in banks,
- special courts under the Banking Companies (Recovery of Loans) Ordinance 1979,
- special courts under the Customs Act 1969,
- special traffic courts,
- courts of special anti-corruption judges (at federal and provincial level),
- commercial courts,
- drug courts,
- labor courts,
- insurance appellate tribunal,
- income tax appellate tribunal, and
- service tribunals.

Appeals from these special courts are directed to the high courts, except for cases arising in the labor courts and special traffic courts, which have separate avenues of appeal (Choudhury, 1988:228).

A high court may pass any sentence authorized by law. Any session judge may pass any sentence authorized by law as well, but any death sentence passed must be confirmed by the high court. A court of session is the court of appeal from the orders of a magistrate in most criminal matters.

In order to implement the policy of having Pakistan strictly adhere to Islamic principles and traditions, President Zia in 1977 established a Shari'a appellate bench at the Supreme Court level and an independent federal Shari'a court (in 1980) at the high court level (Choudhury, 1988:131). Up until this time, there was a system of Shari'a benches on high courts (Weiss, 1986:12). Under Article 203(C) of the constitution, the powers and functions are delineated as follows:

(1) The Court may, on the petition of a citizen of Pakistan or the Federal Government or a Provincial Government, examine and decide the question whether or not any laws repugnant to the injunctions of Islam as laid down in the Holy Qur'an and the Sunna of the Holy Prophet, hereinafter referred to as the Injunctions of Islam.

(2) If the Court decides that any law or provision of the law is repugnant to the Injunctions of Islam, it shall set out in its decision
  (i) the reason for its holding that opinion; and
  (ii) the extent to which such a law or provision is so repugnant; and specify the day on which the decision shall take effect.

JUDICIAL SYSTEM OF PAKISTAN

```
                ┌────────────────────────────┴──────────────────────────────┐
        Shari'a Appellate Bench                              Supreme Court of Pakistan
                │                                                     │
        Federal Shari'a Court                             High Court (each province)
                                                                      │
                                                              District Court
                                                    ┌─────────────────┴──────────────────┐
                                                  Civil                               Criminal
                                                    │                                    │
                                        Court of the District Judge              Court of Session
                                                    │                                    │
                                            Court of the                        Magistrates of the
                                        Additional District Judge                   First Class
                                                    │                                    │
                                        Court of the Civil Judge                 Magistrates of the
                                                                                   Second Class
```

Special Courts

(3) If any law or provision of law is held by the Court to be repugnant to the Injunctions of Islam

(i) the president in the case of a law with respect to a matter in the Federal Legislative List or the Concurrent Legislative List, or the Governor in the case of a law with respect to a matter not enumerated in either of these Lists, shall take steps to amend the law so as to bring such law or provision into conformity with the Injunctions of Islam; and

(ii) such law or provision shall, to the extent to which it is held to be repugnant, cease to have effect on the day on which the decision of the Court takes effect. (quoted in Pearl, 1990:202–203)

The powers, functions, and jurisdiction of the court were further amended under President's Orders no. 1 (1980), no. 5 (1982), no. 7 (1983), and no. 14 (1985) (Choudhury, 1988:228).

The appellate bench consists of three Muslim judges of the Supreme Court, appointed by the president on the recommendation of the chief justice of Pakistan, and "not more than two Ulema . . . from amongst the judges of the federal Shari'a court" (Choudhury, 1988:230). The federal Shari'a court consists of not more than eight members, including the chairman, also appointed by the president (p. 229). Acting on the petition of a citizen of the federal government or any provincial government, these courts examine and decide whether any law is inconsistent with the Qur'an or Islamic tradition. If a law is found to be inconsistent, the court may declare the law void. In the matter of calling witnesses and receiving evidence, the Shari'a courts are vested with the powers of civil courts. Any decision of the federal Shari'a court is appealable to the Supreme Court (Shari'a bench) within sixty days of its decision. An appeal may proceed:

a. if the federal Shari'a court has on appeal reversed an order of acquittal of an accused person and sentenced him to death or imprisonment for life or imprisonment for a term exceeding 14 years; or, on revision, has enhanced a sentenced as aforesaid;

b. if the federal Shari'a court has imposed any punishment on any person for contempt of the court (Choudhury, 1988:229).

A legal practitioner is not permitted to appear or plead before these Islamic courts; however, a party may be represented by a jurisconsult[4] selected from a panel of jurisconsults maintained by these courts (Choudhury, 1988:132). No other courts may assume jurisdiction in matters for which the Shari'a courts are competent.

Conclusion

In the above sections, the legal systems of three Islamic countries have been examined. Each is very different, yet there is a common thread that binds them together—the Shari'a. If these three countries are somewhat representative, it is clear Shari'a plays a substantial role in the legal systems of Islamic countries, regardless of the social and political organization of each.

The legal system in Saudi Arabia is the closest of the three to a pure Shari'a legal system, but even it may be changing to meet the needs of modern society. After the invasion of Kuwait in 1990, a petition was presented to King Fahd of Saudi Arabia suggesting several reforms (Tarazi, 1993:261–62), some of which deal specifically with Saudi law and jurisprudence, among them:

• a commitment to the Shari'a but no limit on the questioning of scholarly opinions

• the issuance of a basic law

• reforming the judiciary so that it is not "biased towards a certain section of the people"

• establishing total equity between citizens

In 1991, the king drafted a basic law that has been characterized as "the beginning of an effort to supplement Islamic law to cover areas of modern life not addressed by Shari'a" (Tarazi, 1993:263). This is somewhat remarkable given the resistance to modernization "overly constrained by laws originating with the advent of Islam nearly fourteen centuries ago" (p. 263).

Bahrain is probably the most modern of the three systems examined. The legal system in Bahrain operates under a code of laws, major sections of which were adapted from other countries. Yet, its legal system is manned exclusively by Muslim judges and has separate religious Shari'a courts to hear the personal disputes of its country's Muslims.

Pakistan retains an almost pure British common-law legal system remaining from the days of British rule but, as discussed earlier, may be returning to a more fundamentalist orientation. The courts operate in an English mode and the law applied is basically English, but Pakistan too has established a Shari'a court to examine challenges to any law to decide if it is inconsistent with the Qur'an.

Notes

[1] Shari'a is used interchangeably with Shari'ah.
[2] The Hadd crimes (and their associated punishments) include:
- adultery (stoning)
- fornication (100 lashes)
- false accusation of adultery (100 lashes)
- apostasy; renouncing Islam (death)
- drinking alcohol (80 lashes)
- theft (amputation)
- highway robbery (amputation)

[3] The Hanbali School was founded by Imam Ahmad Ibn Hanbal (A.D. 780–855) and is the strictest of the four major schools of Islamic law. This and the other three major schools of jurisprudence *(Hanafi, maliki,* and *Shafi'i)* emerged as a result of the conflicting opinions among legal experts of the day as to the validity of Ijma (consensus among legal scholars) and Qiyas (analogical reasoning) (see, e.g. Karl, 1991:140–41; Weeramantry, 1988:52–53).

[4] For a discussion of the jurisconsult and jurisconsult concept, see Makdisi, 1990:121–25.

Bibliography

Aba-Namay, R. (1993). "The Recent Constitutional Reforms in Saudi Arabia." *International and Comparative Law Quarterly* 42: 295–331.

Amin, S. H. (1983). "Legal Systems in the Gulf States." *Lloyds Maritime and Commercial Law Quarterly* (February): 71–85.

——— (1985). *Middle East Legal Systems* (Chapter 2–Bahrain). London: Royston Limited.

Ballantyne, W. (1990). "A Reassertion of the Shari'ah: the Jurisprudence of the Gulf States." In Nicholas Heer (ed.), *Islamic Law and Jurisprudence* (pp. 149–60). Seattle: University of Washington Press.

Baroody, G. M. (1961). *Crime and Punishment under Islamic Law.* Author.

Brand, J. L. (1986). "Aspects of Saudi Arabian Law and Practice." *Boston College International and Comparative Law Review* IX (1): 1–45.

Choudhury, G. W. (1988). *Pakistan: Transition From Military to Civilian Rule.* Essex, England: Scorpion Publishing, Ltd.

Collins, D. P. (1988). "Islamization of Pakistani Law: A Historical Perspective." *Stanford Journal of International Law* 24 (92): 511–84.

Coulsan, N. J. (1983). *A History of Islamic Law.* Edinburgh: Edinburgh University Press.

Esposito, J. L. (1980). "Perspectives on Islamic Law Reform: The Case of Pakistan." *New York University Journal of International Law and Politics* 13 (2): 217–45.

Gottesman, E. (1992). "The Reemergence of Qisas and Diyat in Pakistan." *Columbia Human Rights Law Review* 23 (2): 434–61.

Hagel, G. (1983). "A Practitioner's Introduction to Saudi Arabian Law." *Vanderbilt Journal of Transnational Law* 16: 113–77.

Jones, M. (1992). "Islamic Law in Saudi Arabia: A Responsive View." *International Journal of Comparative and Applied Criminal Justice* 16 (1): 43–55.

Karl, D. J. (1991). "Islamic Law in Saudi Arabia: What Foreign Attorneys Should Know." *George Washington Journal of International Law and Economics* 25 (1): 131–70.

Khadduri, M. (1984). *The Islamic Conception of Justice*. Baltimore: The Johns Hopkins University Press.

Khuri, F. I. (1980). *Tribe and State in Bahrain*. Chicago: Center for Middle Eastern Studies, University of Chicago Press.

Lawson, F. H. (1989). *Bahrain: The Modernization of Autocracy*. Boulder, CO: Westview Press.

Makdisi, George (1990). "Magisterium and Academic Freedom in Classical Islam and Medieval Christianity." In Nicholas Heer (ed.), *Islamic Law and Jurisprudence* (pp. 117–34). Seattle: University of Washington Press.

Mayer, A. (1990). "The Shari'ah: A Methodology or a Body of Substantive Rules?" In Nicholas Heer (ed.), *Islamic Law and Jurisprudence* (pp. 177–98). Seattle: University of Washington Press.

Mehdi, R. (1990). "The Offence of Rape in the Islamic Law of Pakistan." *International Journal of the Sociology of Law* 18 (1): 19–29.

Metz, H. C. (1993). *Saudi Arabia: A Country Study*. Washington, DC: Federal Research Division, Library of Congress.

Middle East Executive Reports (1989). 12 (5): 7.

Ministry of Law and Parliamentary Affairs (1967). The Pakistan Code, 15V. Karachi: Government of Pakistan Press.

Moore, R. H., Jr. (1987). "Courts, Law, Justice, and Criminal Trials in Saudi Arabia." *International Journal of Comparative and Applied Criminal Justice* 11 (1): 61–67.

Pearl, D. (1990). "Executive and Legislative Amendments to Islamic Law in India and Pakistan." In Nicholas Heer (ed.), *Islamic Law and Jurisprudence* (pp. 199–220). Seattle: University of Washington Press.

Qur'an (1974). Harmondsworth, Middlesex: Penguin Books.

Saba, J. P. (1984). *Country Law Study for Saudi Arabia*. Washington, DC: Department of the Air Force, Office of the Judge Advocate General.

Sanad, N. (1991). *The Theory of Crime and Criminal Responsibility in Islamic Law: Shari'a*. Chicago: University of Illinois at Chicago, Office of International Criminal Justice.

Shapiro, M. (1980). "Islam and Appeal." *California Law Review* 68: 350–81.

Tarazi, A. M. (1993). "Saudi Arabia's New Basic Laws." *Harvard International Law Journal* 34: 258–75.

Walker, J. K. (1993). "The Rights of the Accused in Saudi Criminal Procedure." *Loyola of Los Angeles International and Comparative Law Journal* 15: 863–85.

Weeramantry, C. G. (1988). *Islamic Jurisprudence: An International Perspective*. New York: St. Martin's Press.

Weiss, A. M. (1986). "Implications of the Islamization Program for Women." In Anita M. Weiss (ed.), *Islamic Reassertion in Pakistan: the Application of Islamic Laws in a Modern State*. Syracuse, NY: Syracuse University Press.

20

Privilege against Self-Incrimination
A Comparative Perspective

Zoran Milovanovich

Examination of procedural models in both common law and civil law traditions reveals widely present concern for the prospect of innocent persons suffering punishment for a crime they did not commit, particularly if they incriminate themselves by their own words. For this reason, all legal systems typical of these two traditions have designed and implemented some sort of procedural safeguards to protect the right to silence. The core of this protection in almost all systems is the desire to prevent investigation or adjudication procedures from coercing unreliable confessions from the mouths of the accused persons. However, if we go beyond the core and explore the technical implementation of the privilege, its scope, and its underlying policies, differences begin to emerge.

Radical differences between civil law and Anglo-American concepts of the right to silence have led some American courts and legal commentators to incorrectly assume that the privilege against self-incrimination actually does not exist in civil law systems.[1] A system that relies on evidence "independently secured through skillful investigation" has been contrasted with a system in which "the defendant is presumed guilty and must prove his or her innocence." This latter system shows less respect for the individual, which raises concern because of "unlimited probing," and it resorts to inhumane practices of torture and coercion to extract confessions from suspects (*Miranda v. Arizona*, 1966). Consequently, proposals for reform in the American procedure addressing self-incrimination are often summarily dismissed for resembling the European inquisitorial method that conjures up "visions of torture, secrecy, and dictatorial government" to liberal democracy (Frankel, 1975, p.1053). However, such assertions rest on a smug, if not arrogant, confidence that the adversarial system is somehow inherently superior to other forms of criminal justice,

Prepared especially for *Comparative and International Criminal Justice, 2/E.*

and a parallel ignorance of the fact that the purely inquisitorial system is virtually extinct on this planet (Frankel, 1975; Van Kessel, 1992). Oddly enough, civilian jurists generally view the adversarial process as a clash of technicalities showing scant concern for the professed primary goal of criminal courts: to search for the truth (Frankel, 1975; Van Kessel, 1992).

The privilege against self-incrimination—the Fifth-Amendment guarantee that no person shall be compelled in any criminal case to be a witness against himself—has also been portrayed as an English invention intended to protect the indigenous adversarial criminal procedure against incursions of European inquisitorial procedure (Levy, 1968; O'Reilly, 1994). The truth is that the concept underlying the modern privilege originated within the European continental tradition, as a subprinciple of inquisitorial procedure, centuries before the integration of lawyers into the criminal trial made possible the development of the distinctive Anglo-American adversary system of criminal procedure in the later eighteenth century (Helmholz, 1990). The modern common-law privilege evolved from the medieval law of the Roman Church and was associated with the maxim *nemo tenetur prodere seipsum*, liberally translated as "no one is obliged to accuse himself" (Macnair, 1990). This maxim helped clarify the line between two spheres of Christian obligation. The believer's duty of penitential confession did not entail instituting criminal proceedings against himself: He could confess sin to a priest without being obliged to confess punishable offenses to judges and prosecutors (Helmholz, 1990). It has been established that the *nemo tenetur* maxim influenced practice in the English ecclesiastical courts long before anyone in England started complaining about Star Chamber or the Court of High Commission (Helmholz).

Self-Incrimination in Common Law Systems

The emergence of the right to silence was a landmark event in the history of Anglo-American criminal procedure. Earlier historical scholarship has found the origins of the common-law privilege in the second half of the seventeenth century, as part of the aftermath of the constitutional struggles that resulted in the abolition of the courts of Star Chamber and High Commission (Wigmore, 1891, 1902; Levy, 1968; O'Reilly, 1994). However, as Langbein (1994) explains, the true origins of the common-law privilege are to be found not in the high politics of the English revolutions, but in the rise of adversary criminal procedure at the end of the eighteenth century. The privilege against self-incrimination at common law was directly related to the work of defense counsel (Langbein, 1994).

From the middle of the sixteenth century until late in the eighteenth century, the fundamental procedural guarantee for the defendant was not the right to remain silent, but rather the opportunity to speak. The emerging concept of fair trial implied that the defendant should be afforded an opportunity to reply in person to the charges against him. Among the characteristics of the procedure that imported this character to the criminal trial, the most fundamental was the rule that forbade defense counsel. The prohibition upon defense counsel was relaxed in stages from 1696 until 1836, initially for treason and later for felony. Although persons accused of ordinary felony began to be allowed counsel in the 1730s, defense counsel did not become quantitatively significant until the 1780s (Landsman, 1990; Beattie, 1991).

In the later eighteenth century and especially in the nineteenth century, a radically different view of the purpose of the criminal trial prevailed. Under the influence of defense counsel, the criminal trial came to be seen as an opportunity for the defendant's lawyer to test the prosecution's case. The privilege against self-incrimination was introduced to common-law procedure (along with the beyond-reasonable-doubt standard of proof and the exclusionary mechanism of the modern law of criminal evidence) as part of this profound reordering of the trial. It was the criminal trial produced, directed, and dominated by lawyers for prosecution and defense that made it possible for the defendant to decline to be a witness against himself.

United States

The first American colony to give constitutional character to the right against self-incrimination was Virginia. The prototype of this right was contained in the Declaration of Rights, providing that "in all capital or criminal prosecutions" a man cannot "be compelled to give evidence against himself." Eight other states incorporated similar provisions in their constitutions, albeit with variations in wording in some instances (Levy, 1968). The first Congress, on a motion made by James Madison, incorporated the privilege in the Fifth Amendment of the Bill of Rights. The federal version differed from those adopted by most states, because it applied only to criminal prosecutions.

The American privilege against self-incrimination quickly became an integral part of the American political culture as an undisputed right of the free-born American. In 1821, Chief Justice Marshall asserted that the rights endowed by the Fifth Amendment were intended "for ages to come . . . designed to approach immortality as nearly as human institutions can approach it" (*Cohens v. Virginia*, 1821). The reach of the Fifth Amendment was not meaningfully tested, however, until the Supreme Court interpreted it liberally in 1886 (*Boyd v. United States*, 1886).[2] Six years later, this expansive interpretation was extended to all criminal proceedings (*Counselman v. Hitchcock*, 1892).[3] By 1936, the Supreme Court incorporated, through the due process clauses of the Fifth and Fourteenth Amendments, the common-law exclusion of involuntary confessions based on their inherent unreliability (*Brown v. Mississippi*, 1936). Thus began the era of fact-specific review of voluntariness, based on the totality of the circumstances.

The Supreme Court considered many factors in assessing the voluntariness of incriminating statements or confessions, including: age and education (*Payne v. Arkansas*, 1958);[4] deprivation of food and sleep (*Payne v. Arkansas*, 1958; *Ashcraft v. Tennessee*, 1944);[5] and infliction of psychological coercion (*Watts v. Indiana*, 1949). Over a period of more than 25 years and through a number of cases, the Supreme Court engendered "an elaborate, sophisticated, and sensitive approach to admissibility" that gave some recognition to "society's interest in suspect questioning as an instrument of law enforcement" (*Miranda v. Arizona*, 1966).

In *Miranda*, the Supreme Court made a radical step in reforming the procedural system for police interrogations, giving the right to silence a significantly new dimension. The system created by the *Miranda* decision involved four key elements: warnings, a right to counsel, a right to have a defendant's pretrial silence concealed from the trier of fact, and a right to cut off questioning at will. Each of these requirements was inconsistent with the position of the common law and with case law preceding *Miranda*.

At common law, there was no requirement that a suspect be advised in pretrial interrogation that he could remain silent or that his statements could be used against him. The use of warnings of this type did, however, come into play in connection with the abatement of judicial interrogation. As noted earlier, most jurisdictions had terminated the preliminary examination of suspects by magistrates by the mid-nineteenth century, and the remainder followed suit in succeeding decades. The only remaining vestige of the once central institution of pretrial questioning by a magistrate was a general practice of advising a suspect that he could make a statement on his own behalf at a preliminary hearing, but that he was not required to say anything and that anything he did say could be used against him. In this context, the function of the warnings was not to advise a suspect of his rights prior to interrogation, but to make effective a judgment that suspects should not be interrogated at all by judicial officers at preliminary hearings.

The Supreme Court had considered the question of whether warnings were required in pretrial interrogation as a matter of federal law in two early cases (*Wilson v. United States*, 1896; *Powers v. United States*, 1912) and had held that they were not. Following these early decisions, it was taken as settled that warnings were not required in pretrial interrogation as a condition on the admission of a defendant's statements. No contrary suggestion appeared in the Supreme Court's decisions prior to the case of *Escobedo v. Illinois*, 1964).

In *Miranda*, the Supreme Court also created a right to counsel in police interrogations. While this right was ostensibly based on the Fifth Amendment, the Court cited precedents relating to the Sixth-Amendment right to counsel, and to counsel rights in state proceedings that had been imposed as a matter of Fourteenth-Amendment due process. There was no right to counsel under the common-law procedure of preliminary examinations, and nothing in the history of the Bill of Rights or the colonial enactments that preceded it suggested a purpose to extend such a right to an early investigative stage at which it had not conventionally been recognized (*Cox v. Coleridge*, 1822). Rather, the contrary appears from the placement of the right to counsel in the Sixth Amendment, formulated by the Senate as a compilation of post-indictment and trial rights.

The historical understanding of the Sixth-Amendment right was altered by the Supreme Court in *Johnson v. Zerbst* (1938). This decision, authored by Justice Black, created a uniform right to appointed counsel in federal prosecutions and also created a novel constitutional rule that a defendant must "competently and intelligently" waive his right to counsel if a trial is to proceed without such representation. In relation to state proceedings, the Supreme Court also proceeded to create federal rights to counsel in a line of decisions running from *Powell v. Alabama* (1932) to *Gideon v. Wainwright* (1963). The concluding decision in *Gideon* made the Sixth-Amendment right to counsel applicable to the states. However, in relation to pretrial interrogation, the Court consistently rejected a right to counsel prior to the 1960s. A claimed right to counsel had initially been rejected in the context of a preliminary examination by a judicial officer in *Wilson v. United States* (1896). A number of decisions reviewing state cases in the late 1950s held specifically that there was no right to counsel in connection with pretrial interrogation by law enforcement officers (*In Re Groban*, 1957; *Crooker v. California*, 1958; *Cicenia v. Lagay*, 1958).

Despite the relatively recent vintage of these decisions, the Supreme Court proceeded to cast doubt on their continued validity in the early 1960s. Following two decisions that recognized right to counsel, in narrowly defined circumstances, in pretrial judicial proceedings at the state level (*White v. Maryland*, 1963; *Hamilton v. Alabama*, 1961), the Court took the major step of extending the Sixth-Amendment counsel right to purely nonjudicial pretrial contexts in *Massiah v. United States* (1964) and *Escobedo v. Illinois* (1964).

In addition to creating a requirement of warnings and a right to counsel in pretrial interrogation, the Supreme Court in *Miranda* prohibited the admission at trial of a defendant's refusal to answer questions in pretrial interrogation. The Court stated:

> In accord with our decision today, it is impermissible to penalize an individual for exercising his Fifth Amendment privilege when he is under police custodial interrogation. The prosecution may not, therefore, use at trial the fact that he stood mute or claimed his privilege in the face of accusation. (*Miranda*, p. 468)

At the time the Constitution was ratified, however, defendants were subject to questioning before justices of the peace, and any failure to respond to the justice's questions could be admitted in evidence. In later times, U.S. courts approached this issue in terms of the general rule of evidence, which holds that a party's pretrial silence in the face of accusations or statements to which he would naturally respond can be admitted at trial and made the basis for adverse inferences.[6]

The prohibition of adverse comment on a defendant's failure to take the stand, although the predominant approach in the United States, was frequently criticized by leading writers and law reform commissions, and was rejected in the formulation of model rules of evidence. By the 1960s, six states permitted adverse comment on a defendant's silence at trial.

The issue was brought to a head by the Court's "incorporation" of the Fifth Amendment against the states in *Malloy v. Hogan* (1964), which made it possible to address the Fifth-Amendment issue in reviewing state cases. The Court did so in the following year in *Griffin v. California* (1965). In a decision remarkable for its lack of any serious effort at justification, the Court held that adverse comment on a defendant's refusal to testify violated the Fifth-Amendment right against compelled self-incrimination (Osakwe, 1982). *Griffin* provided the essential precedent for *Miranda's* announcement in the following year of a corresponding rule barring the use at trial of a defendant's pretrial silence in custodial interrogation.

A final innovation of the *Miranda* decision was the creation of a right on the part of arrested persons to prevent questioning. The Court stated: "If the individual indicates in any manner, at any time prior to or during questioning, that he wishes to remain silent, the interrogation must cease. . . . If the individual states that he wants an attorney, the interrogation must cease until an attorney is present" (*Miranda*, pp. 473–474). The right not to be questioned was an addition to the traditional right to refrain from answering questions on grounds of potential self-incrimination. At the time of the ratification of the Constitution, suspects had no right to cut off custodial interrogation (Levy, 1968), and no right of this sort was recognized in the Supreme Court's decisions prior to *Miranda* (*Crooker v. California*, 1958; *Cicenia v. Lagay*, 1958).

In general character, the *Miranda* decision stood somewhere between a code of procedure with commentary and a judicial decision in the conventional sense. Chief Justice Warren, who devised the detailed set of rules announced in the decision, initially drafted the opinion of the Court so as to make these rules constitutional requirements. However, he was forced to accommodate Justice Brennan, who insisted that some latitude should be left to legislatures to develop alternative rules counteracting the pressures of custodial interrogation. Congress quickly repudiated the *Miranda* decision, and somewhat later the Supreme Court rejected its underlying rationale, following a change in the Court's membership. The legislative response was 18 U.S.C. @ 3501, a statute enacted in 1968 to overturn the *Miranda* decision and restore the pre-Miranda voluntariness standard for the admission of confessions. The Department of Justice attempted to establish the validity of this statute in litigation for several years with inconclusive results, but ultimately snatched defeat from the

378 Part III: Law and Justice: Judicial Systems—Formal and Informal

jaws of victory by terminating this litigative effort after an initial appellate decision (*United States v. Crocker,* 1975) that upheld the statute.

The Supreme Court's rejection of *Miranda* occurred in *Michigan v. Tucker* (1974), which took the position that no violation of the Fifth Amendment occurs if statements are obtained from a suspect without observing *Miranda's* rules or any other safeguards, so long as actual coercion is avoided. This view, which has been reiterated and relied on in later decisions, removed any intelligible doctrinal basis for applying *Miranda's* rules to the states, or for failing to give 18 U.S.C. @ 3501 effect in federal proceedings. Nevertheless, the Supreme Court continues to apply *Miranda's* standards in its decisions, apparently because no case has yet required the Court to confront the full implications of its rejection of *Miranda's* essential premise.

In its simplest form, the *Miranda* majority opinion adopted a per se exclusionary rule for all statements made by a suspect during the custodial interrogation in absence of a knowing and intelligent waiver of his Fifth and Sixth Amendment rights. On its face, Miranda purported to draw bright lines between the police and the suspect in custody, but a light scratch of the surface revealed some glaring problems and inconsistencies with this per se approach. The *Miranda* dissent argued that the majority's strict exclusionary rule was both under- and over-inclusive. Justice White pointed out that if the majority's goal was to eliminate the inherent coerciveness of custodial interrogation, then the exclusionary rule should be applied to all statements made by the accused while in custody, regardless of knowing waiver (*Miranda,* p. 533). Justice Harlan, also writing in dissent, posited the underinclusiveness of the majority's tack: the new per se rule does not stop coercion or even brutality because unscrupulous police officers will simply dissemble concerning knowing waiver, as they would have done previously concerning the circumstances of voluntariness. "The aim in short is toward 'voluntariness' in a utopian sense, or to view it from a different angle, voluntariness with a vengeance" (*Miranda,* p. 505).

At least three other related problems arise from the majority's per se rule. First, the majority placed great emphasis on their desire to end "police manual" interrogation procedures, but the per se exclusionary rule was not "sensibly tailored" to that end. What emerged is a situation where an assertion of rights leads to immediate cut-off of all questioning, including even brief or reasonable questioning. Conversely, coercive questioning may continue indefinitely after a waiver of rights. Second, if custodial statements are innately coerced, an accompanying warning will not preclude a finding of coercion, nor does the omission of warnings necessarily constitute any additional coercion (Department of Justice, 1989). Finally, the presumption that custody equals coercion may not be universally valid (Department of Justice).

England

In many ways the right-to-silence principles of English law parallel those in this country. However, in one fundamental respect the English right is more limited than the American right, with the result that police may subject the accused to greater pressures. The following basic English principles, known as Judges' Rules regarding police questioning, are substantially the same as the American:

1. Police may question any person, whether or not suspected of criminal activity;

2. A person questioned by the police is not legally obligated to respond, and the police have no legal power to compel answers. (This rule reflects the common-law right to remain silent, recognized in both countries, which guarantees that no one may be required to incriminate himself.)

3. Absent a proper arrest, police cannot take a person to a police station for the sole purpose of questioning. A citizen may be arrested and taken to the police station only upon reasonable or probable cause to suspect that he is guilty of an offense (Home Office, 1964; Kaci, 1982).

The Judges' Rules also provide that when there are reasonable grounds for suspecting that a person has committed an offense, he is to be given the following caution prior to questioning: "You are not obliged to say anything unless you wish to do so but what you say may be put into writing and given in evidence" (Kaci, pp. 109–112).

Absent from the Judges' Rules is a requirement that the accused be notified of his right to counsel. The Rules do provide that "every person at any stage of an investigation should be able to communicate and to consult privately with a solicitor." However, this principle is qualified by a provision that a person in custody need not be allowed access to counsel if that would cause "unreasonable delay or hindrance . . . to the processes of investigation or the administration of justice." As a practical matter, the police are free to deny access to counsel and to hold suspects incommunicado for questioning. There is also no offer of, or right to, free counsel for suspects who cannot retain counsel (Caplan, 1985; Zander, 1972).

Superficially, the Rules might appear to establish a restrictive standard for custodial police interrogations through the provisions that a suspect is to be charged or advised that he may be prosecuted without delay once there is sufficient evidence to do so, and that thereafter he is not to be questioned outside of "exceptional cases." However, this Rule does not significantly limit such interrogations in practice, since the police are free to make arrests on reasonable suspicion without formally charging a person or advising him of an intent to prosecute. As a practical matter, suspects are routinely interrogated by the police at the stationhouse following arrest. Few suspects remain silent in the face of such questioning, and most confess or make incriminating statements as a result (Caplan, 1985).

In England, the criminal courts apply, as their American counterparts did prior to *Miranda*, a "voluntariness" standard to custodial confessions and other self-incriminating statements by an accused (Van Kessel, 1986). Before the passage of the Police and Criminal Evidence Act 1984, judges considered two factors in determining whether a statement was voluntary: (1) whether the statement was obtained through threat or inducement; and (2) whether the statement was made as a result of oppression (Van Kessel). The most significant formulation of the voluntariness test was set forth by Lord Summer in *Ibrahim v. The King* (1914). According to Lord Summer, a judge determining voluntariness must ask: has the prosecution proven that the contested statement was voluntary in that it was not obtained by fear of prejudice or hope of advantage excited or held out by a person in authority, or by oppression? Determination that the statement had been obtained involuntarily led automatically to its exclusion regardless of its reliability.

With the passage of the Police and Criminal Evidence Act 1984, Parliament significantly modified the voluntariness rule. Under the Act, a confession must be excluded as involuntary unless the prosecution proves beyond a reasonable doubt that it was not obtained: (a) by oppression of the person who made it; or (b) in consequence of anything said or done which was likely, in the circumstances existing at the time, to render unreliable any confession which might be made by him in consequence thereof.[7]

The Act states that oppression includes such extreme measures as "torture, inhuman or degrading treatment, and the use or threat of violence," but no mention is made of threats of nonphysical harm or other psychological pressures. The old voluntariness rule looked to whether the action of the authorities sapped the free will of the suspect or excited hopes or fears of the suspect such that "his will crumbles and he speaks when otherwise he would have stayed silent" (*Regina v. Prager*, 1971).

The Act does not mention the aspect of the old voluntariness standard which asked whether the confession was obtained "by fear of prejudice or hope of advantage." Instead, the Act provides that a confession must be excluded only if it does not satisfy the reliability test.[8] This test was drawn from the recommendations of the 1972 Criminal Law Revision Committee.[9] That Committee regarded the rules relating to admissibility of confessions as excessively strict and considered two alternative approaches: (1) "to have no restriction on admissibility but allow all confessions to be proved before the jury or magistrates' court" and (2) "to preserve the general rule that a threat, inducement or oppression makes a resulting confession inadmissible but to provide that this should not apply to all threats or inducements but only to those likely to produce an unreliable confession" (Criminal Law Revision Committee, 1972, p. 41) The majority of the Committee approved a modified form of the second approach: "The right course is for the rule as to inadmissibility of a confession on account of a threat or inducement to be limited to threats or inducements of a kind likely to produce an unreliable confession, but for inadmissibility on account of oppression to remain" (Criminal Law Revision Committee, p.

43). Thus, the history of the Police and Criminal Evidence Act 1984 reveals the rejection of that part of the common-law voluntariness rule that would exclude all confessions induced by even slight threats or promises.

In England, until 1994, the right to silence did not permit the prosecutor to comment on the defendant's pretrial silence. The judge could, in an appropriate case, make a comment. However, the judge was required to make it clear to the jury that failure of the defendant to testify is not evidence of guilt and that the defendant is entitled to remain silent and see if the prosecution can prove its case (O'Reilly, 1994).

The new law that became effective March 1, 1995 imposed certain limitations on the right to silence.[10] It allows judges and juries to consider as evidence of guilt both a suspect's failure to answer police questions during interrogation and a defendant's refusal to testify during trial. The new law contains four sections describing situations in which adverse inferences can be drawn from silence. First, it allows such adverse inferences "as appear proper" to be drawn when the accused does not tell the police, during interrogation after being cautioned or informed of the law, any fact relied upon in their defense at trial if, under the circumstances, they would have been "reasonably expected" to mention that fact (O'Reilly, 1994). The rationale for such solution is seen in an effort to end terrorists' use of the "ambush defense," in which terrorist suspects would remain silent during interrogation, not reveal any details of their defense until trial, and thus prevent the police and prosecution from preparing a rebuttal to the defense claims (Royal Commission on Criminal Justice, 1993).

Second, under the new rule, the evidence may, in the words of a recent opinion from the House of Lords, "call for an explanation" (Jackson, 1993). If the accused fails to provide an explanation by testifying, then judges and prosecutors may invite the jury to make any inference which to them appears proper—including the "common sense" inference that there is no explanation for the evidence produced against the accused and that the accused is guilty. This is a significant departure from the common-law approach that permitted judges to instruct the jury that, where the accused does not testify, his or her silence means that there is no evidence from the defendant to undermine, contradict, or explain the evidence put before you by the prosecution. However, the jury still had the responsibility to decide whether, on the prosecution's evidence, the defendant's guilt has been established (Jackson).

The third section allows adverse inferences "as appear proper" to be drawn from the accused's failure to respond to police questions when arrested. This section applies when the accused is arrested in possession of any suspicious objects or substances, or when suspicious marks are found on the accused's person or clothing or in the place where the accused was arrested. Under this section, the accused must respond to questions if the police reasonably believe the presence of the object was attributable to the accused's participation in the offense (Jackson).

The fourth section allows adverse inferences "as appear proper" to be drawn from suspects' failure to explain to the police why they were present at a place at or about the time of the offense for which they were arrested. As with the third section, suspects must respond if the police reasonably believe that the suspect's presence was attributable to their participation in an offense.[11]

Proponents of the new law have argued that change was greatly needed because the right to silence was "a charade which has been ruthlessly exploited by terrorists" (Mills, 1993). They have also asserted that such measures will induce suspects to talk to police, to confess, and to reveal their defenses during interrogation, allowing the police to use interrogation techniques to break down their stories. Advocates of the use of adverse inferences believe that it would remedy the significant problem caused by the "ambush" defense, in which suspects remain silent during interrogation and do not reveal any details of their defense until trial (Jackson, 1993), and that unlimited use of the right to silence forces the police to drop a large number of cases.

Proponents have also diminished the significance of the proposed changes, contending that the accused's silence will simply become "an item of evidence . . . scarcely a major infringement of a defendant's liberty . . . [and that the change] . . . should dissuade offenders from thwarting prosecution simply by saying nothing" (Howard's Beginning, 1993; Mills, 1993; Zander, 1993).

Opponents of the new law argue that the benefits of using adverse inferences are illusory and that the costs are real (O'Reilly, 1994). According to them, the use of adverse inferences will erode or eliminate the right to silence and, in doing so, shift the burden of proof to the accused; in some cases it will reduce the prosecution's burden of proof and weaken or remove the presumption of innocence. These changes will undermine the accusatorial system of justice, moving the criminal justice system toward an inquisitorial model (O'Reilly).

Scotland

As a hybrid system of uncodified civil law with a 300-year-old common-law overlay, Scotland represents a very interesting model for the interaction of the two major legal traditions. Like all common and civil law jurisdictions, Scottish criminal law recognizes that an accused should not be compelled to convict himself from his own mouth. This assumption underlies the rather strict exclusionary rule for unfairly coerced confessions in Scotland (Hardin, 1964).

The Scots take a rather pragmatic view of law enforcement, recognizing that the people have some interest in effective police investigation. As in England, no privilege against self-incrimination attaches when an individual is merely questioned by police. Upon arrest, Scottish courts are quite strict: after a suspect is arrested, cautioned, and charged, police may undertake no further interrogations and any custodial confessions will be subject to a rigorous "voluntariness" review.

In 1980, the near per-se ban on police custodial questioning was relaxed somewhat with the adoption of the Criminal Justice Act, which sought to strike a more realistic balance between the rights of the individual and the interests of society in the detection of crime. The Act authorizes the police to detain a person on reasonable suspicion for up to six hours for purposes of interrogation and other investigation. The police are required to advise a person detained pursuant to this authority of the reason for the detention, and to inform him that he is not obligated to answer questions. Additionally, the Act featured a revival of a limited form of judicial examination. Although similar to an initial appearance or arraignment in the United States, the new judicial examination would allow the prosecutor to question an accused for the purpose of eliciting any explanation he may have to offer. This revived form of judicial examination was justified by the government as offering the accused an early opportunity to lay the foundation for challenging a confession or presenting an alibi. The Crown, in turn, could comment at trial upon an accused's refusal to answer questions at the judicial examination.

Although the ability of the Crown to comment on an accused's silence at trial was seen by some as a retrograde step in protecting the rights of the accused, it should be noted that judges were already permitted to make comment to the jury concerning silence by the accused (*Scott v. H.M. Advocate*, 1946).

Another interesting feature of Scottish criminal procedure concerns the scope of exclusion of evidence obtained by coerced statements. As in most civil law jurisdictions, if police are led to physical evidence by coerced statements from the accused, the evidence itself is admissible (Ewing & Finnie, 1982). The prosecution must, however, find some way of linking the evidence to the accused other than by the coerced statements.

Canada

The Canadian right to silence was based on the English right. In Canada, as in England, the privilege against self-incrimination is based on the absence of any right by the police to coerce statements from an accused rather than any absolute protection against self-incrimination. The Canadian courts adopted the English Judges' Rules in 1918, modifying them somewhat but still generally following the English line. The cautions which must be given, however, differ rather substantially. An individual taken into custody must be immediately notified of the charges against him and informed that he has an absolute right to retain counsel (Department of Justice, 1989). The police, however, are not required to advise a suspect or an accused of his right to silence, the implications of self-incriminating statements, the availability of appointed counsel, or his privilege to refuse questioning (Caswell, 1985; Pye, 1982; Ratushny, 1978).

The admissibility of statements made to the police generally depends on their voluntariness. The voluntariness requirement is interpreted as barring the admission of statements obtained through a fear of prejudice or hope of advantage held out by a person in authority. However, if real evidence is discovered as the result of an involuntary statement, the evidence is admissible along with the portion of the statement that it confirms (Ratushny, 1978).

With the declaration of the Canadian Charter of Rights and Freedoms in 1982, the privilege against self-incrimination and to access to counsel may rise to the level of constitutionally entrenched rights. As of May 1991, however, Canadian courts have declined granting an absolute right against self-incrimination (*Regina v. Woolley*, 1988).[12] Oblique references to a defendant's silence are allowed, and both triers and reviewing courts are free to draw adverse inferences from such silence (Pye, 1982; Ratushny).

Self-Incrimination in Civil-Law Systems

Judicial torture and different forms of compulsory interrogation prevailed in most countries on the Continent of Europe until the eighteenth century. Ordinary criminal courts regularly employed it in the prosecution of routine crimes (Langbein, 1977a). In the middle of the eighteenth century, however, the leading states of Europe abolished judicial torture. As a result of events set in motion by the French Revolution and the liberalizing influence of eighteenth-century writers, Continental systems discarded other pernicious aspects of old inquisitory trials and at the same time adopted many aspects of the English accusatory system (Schlesinger, 1977). Criminal proceedings in Europe do not feature any more compulsory interrogations, secret trials based on an investigating judge's written summary of the case, and presumption of guilt (Langbein, 1977a). In fact, they are so vastly different from those that characterized the Continent from the thirteenth century until the first half of the nineteenth century that the use of the label "inquisitory" is no longer appropriate.

Today, continental systems are accusatory in a sense that the power to institute the action against a suspect resides in the governmental agency (public prosecutor). They provide nearly the same array of procedural guarantees and safeguards that can be found in adversary systems. However, it has to be noted that these guarantees operate within historically and conceptually different legal and criminal justice environments and, consequently, may have different form, or their application in practice may vary.

In civil law jurisdictions, the privilege against self-incrimination first gained the statutory form in the 1808 *Code d'Instruction Criminelle* (the French Code of Criminal Procedure). Soon after, it was adopted by other civil law jurisdictions. Today, virtually all continental legal systems recognize and provide statutory foundation for exercise of some form of the

right against coerced interrogation. Also, many codes of criminal procedure (e.g., those of Germany, France, Italy, and the former Yugoslavia)
provide specific exclusionary remedy for the violation of due process,
including improper obtaining of evidence in a police interrogation.

In contrast to common-law concept of the protection, the continental
defendant is not free to decide whether to submit to questioning. He only
has the right to refuse to answer at all, or to refuse to respond to a particular question.[13] As a matter of formal doctrine the trier of fact is usually not
allowed to draw unfavorable inferences from the defendant's silence.
However, his quite realistic concern that such inferences will—consciously
or unconsciously—in fact be drawn acts in a typical case as a psychological
pressure to speak and respond to questions. Thus, it is of no surprise that
almost all continental defendants choose to testify.[14] The pressure to speak
is, undoubtedly, stronger than the parallel pressure on the common-law
defendant. One of the reasons for that is fairly obvious. It is very likely that
more immediate inferences will be drawn from refusal to answer specific
questions than from the general refusal to submit to questioning process.

As a reaction to these pressures, the guilty defendant will often resort
to lies in order to counter charges brought against him. However, recognizing and tolerating this frequently instinctive desire of the guilty defendant to act as an innocent person, most modern continental systems
generally do not put the defendant on oath. Nor do any adverse legal consequences will affect the defendant if it has been established that he was
making false statements,[15] though he will, of course, hurt his credibility as
an evidentiary source. It appears that the continental system is not concerned about exposing the trier of fact to the defendant's unsworn testimony. Namely, it is believed that precious information can be obtained
even from false denials, discovered inconsistencies, and other verbal and
nonverbal symptoms of guilt. The very moment this information is
received it becomes an integral part of cognitive picture that the trier of
fact forms about the case, and on which determination of guilt will eventually be made.

True dimensions of the difference in the approach of the two systems
to the use of the defendant as a source of testimonial evidence cannot be
fully appreciated if one ignores the time sequence. In the common-law
trial, of course, the defendant cannot take the stand, even if he wishes to
do so, before the prosecution has established a prima facie case. Before he
is given a chance to defend himself from the witness stand, he has already
heard evidence presented by the prosecution.

In the continental courtroom, the situation is completely different. As
there is no requirement that the prosecution establish a credible case
before the defense introduces its evidence, there is no obstacle to beginning the evidence-taking stage by questioning the defendant. In fact, this
is the rule in civil law. This may lead the common-law observer to believe
that civil law puts too heavy a burden on the defendant's shoulders and

that he has to answer for the crime even before the prosecution has established a credible case against him. However, such a conclusion would not correctly reflect the position of the civil-law defendant. During the course of pretrial judicial investigation, the defendant has ample opportunities, both to be informed of the precise nature of charges against him and to hear and challenge the evidence that the prosecution intends to present at the trial. Civil-law doctrine also states that the defendant's examination comes first because it is primarily a means accorded to him to contest the prosecutor's charges at the beginning of the trial. While the strategic value of this arrangement for the defense is a matter of some dispute, there is little doubt that is advantageous to the prosecution.[16]

France

Under the French Code de Procedure Penale (n.d., article 114), the accused is entitled to the right of silence, but only explicitly during his first appearance before the *juge d'instruction*[17] (examining judge) (Pieck, 1962). Traditionally, this right has been extended to include all judicial proceedings. However, this right does not extend to police interrogations (Pieck, 1962). A suspect may be held in investigatory detention for up to 48 hours without probable cause, judicial approval, or mandatory court appearance. During that time, he needs not be given the warning as long as an inquiry is of preliminary nature and conducted by the police. However, he is not legally obligated to answer questions, but the police are not required to advise him of this fact, and the defense attorney does not participate at this stage of the process. Any statements made by the suspect during preliminary investigation are entered in the dossier and admitted at trial.

A suspect is entitled to be advised of his right to remain silent when an official investigation by the prosecutor (*Procureur de la Republique*) begins. Once a suspect is charged, however, the examining judge must advise the accused of his right to know the charges against him, to remain silent, and to secure free counsel prior to any judicial examination. However, in cases of urgency the judge can exercise the authority to directly proceed to an interrogation and confrontation without giving the warning (Code de Procedure Penale, article 115, n.d.).

The accused's demeanor and attitude at the judicial examination will be commented upon in the dossier by the examining judge, obliging the accused to offer some explanation (Pieck, 1962). French law does not allow the trial court to draw an inference of guilt from the accused's silence, yet his reticence will generally reinforce the state's case and may be unfavorably commented on by the judge and prosecutor. Finally, the accused is never placed under oath at any stage of the judicial process. Therefore, the threat of perjury does not reinforce any desire to remain silent.

When the defendant is finally brought to trial, he is forced to play a much more visible role than his American counterpart. As already indicated, the right not to be questioned does not exist in civil-law systems. The trial normally opens with the questioning of the defendant by the presiding judge. In conducting questioning, judges have at their disposal a dossier containing the results of earlier investigative efforts, including the pretrial interrogation of the defendant. The defendant may refuse to answer but rarely does so, since this would involve remaining silent in the face of direct questioning in the presence of the trier of fact, and since such silence "exposes the defendant to whatever inferences the court chooses to draw" (Tomlinson, 1983). If the defendant decides to confess at trial, his confession is not binding for the trial judge. It will receive a treatment as any other important piece of evidence and will be evaluated along with all the other relevant evidence (Tomlinson).

In France, there is a statutory ground for the application of exclusionary rule if the suspect has not been advised of his rights, including the right to remain silent. Confessions obtained through physical abuse are clearly inadmissible, while lesser forms of pressure by the police do not affect the admissibility of a suspect's statements (Tomlinson).

The application of exclusionary remedy is a legal possibility, not a mandatory court action. There is a certain procedure that must always be followed regardless of the nature of the breach of rules governing the obtaining of evidence. After he or she determines that there are grounds for exclusion, the examining judge refers the question to the *Chambre d'accusation* (Chamber of Accusations). In reaching the decision, this judicial body will rely on the material received from the examining judge as well as on the opinion of the prosecutor. If the Chambre d'accusation finds that the exclusion is necessary, it will void the act and all part of subsequent proceedings, if any (Code de Procedure Penal, article 206, n.d.).

Germany

Under section 136(1) of the German Code of Criminal Procedure, the German police, prosecutors, and courts are required to respect an individual's right against self-incrimination. Various forms of overreaching are specifically prohibited by the law and automatically inadmissible at trial, including eliciting statements by "ill-treatment," fatigue, physical abuse, or deception.

The German police are authorized to arrest a suspect for purposes of interrogation and other investigation. Detention pursuant to this authority cannot extend beyond the end of the day following the arrest, after which the suspect must be released or brought before a judge. The police are required to advise the suspect of the presumed charges, the right to silence, and his right to counsel (Department of Justice, 1989). As a practical matter, the police usually engage in informal conversation with a suspect without warnings, "to get his side of the story," and are likely to defer giving the statutory warning until a later point in the interrogation (Schlesinger, 1977).

The German trial commences with either the presiding judge or the prosecutor reading the charges. The defendant then answers questions asked by the presiding judge, giving an account of his personal background, including his address, family, and employment history (Langbein, 1977b). The presiding judge then turns to the accusations, advises the defendant of his right to remain silent, and asks if he wishes to say anything. The defendant almost always agrees to speak. After the defendant has spoken, the presiding judge questions him extensively about the charges and evidence, referring often to the dossier with which she has familiarized herself in preparation for trial. After the examination by the presiding judge, the prosecutor and defense counsel may ask additional questions, either directly or through the presiding judge. Throughout the questioning the defendant may refuse to answer each specific question, and the court is prohibited from drawing a legal inference from such a refusal. However, if the defendant does answer some questions, but refuses to answer others, adverse inferences may be drawn from the refusal (Schlesinger, 1977).

Statutory exclusion of evidence in Germany is specifically required by section 136a of the Code of Criminal Procedure. This provision is based on the principles that "the dignity of man is inviolable" and that "everyone has the right to free development of his personality." It was originally aimed at involuntary confessions, but its use has expanded greatly over the last four decades. While in the 1950s German courts used this provision to exclude confessions obtained as a result of physical coercion, different deprivations (of sleep or of cigarettes), or the use of truth serum, in the 1960s they went further to include infliction of mental distress, coercion by third parties, and promises of advantage (Pakter, 1985). Since the 1970s, the Supreme Court of Germany (BGH) has increasingly relied on section 136a in a variety of other situations not necessarily directly related to due process violations.[18] Thus, in its relatively recent decision the Court excluded a confession from an accused who had been misled by the police to believe that they were investigating a "missing person" report when, in fact, they had already found the body and were investigating a murder.[19]

Japan

Japanese criminal law joined the circle of codified civil law jurisdictions during the late nineteenth century after the Meiji Restoration. Initially, the traditional elements of torture and the requirement of a confession for conviction were retained. Under European influence, the Japanese abandoned these practices in 1879 and adopted a system whereby convictions are based solely on the evaluation of evidence (Ramlogan, 1994). However, the abandonment of torture as a means of obtaining confession did not diminish the significance of confession. Japanese police and prosecutors, as well as Japanese society as a whole, place a high value on confessions and favor a pattern of confession, repentance, and absolution. If the defendant does not confess, the process of absolution and reassimilation into society cannot begin (Port, 1991).

After World War II, the Allied Powers were determined to further reform Japan's legal system and introduce Western-style human rights. Efforts were made to limit the importance of confession and undermine its role as the single most valuable piece of evidence. The problem was addressed on both a constitutional and a statutory level. The new Japanese Showa Constitution provides that no person shall be compelled to testify against himself; that confessions made under compulsion, torture, threat, or after prolonged arrest or detention shall not be admitted in evidence; and that no person shall be convicted or punished in cases where the only evidence against him is his own confession. Under the new Code of Criminal Procedure (Article 198), a suspect in a criminal case is entitled to the right to refuse to answer questions, as well as to the right to be advised of such a right before any questioning begins. The Code also provides for protection against the use of confessions obtained under conditions similar to those outlined in the Showa Constitution. Despite these efforts to break Japanese heavy reliance on confession, it still represents a centerpiece of the criminal justice process, thus reflecting a preference for a traditional Japanese method of administering justice.

One of the effects of the constitutional guarantee against the use of confessions is that a conviction cannot be based on a confession alone. As a consequence, a person may confess to having committed a crime but will nonetheless experience detention and extensive interrogation. Japanese investigators continue to use confessions not only to ascertain culpability but also to obtain corroborative evidence and other background information relevant to the building of their investigative dossier. The confession is often the cornerstone on which investigators build the case against the accused (Ramlogan, 1994).

Japanese police may detain and interrogate a suspect for 48 hours without approval from a prosecutor or review by a magistrate, and upon a showing of probable cause to a magistrate a suspect can be detained for ten days; those accused of serious crimes may be held for an additional ten days. Extended detention is the rule, resulting primarily from the police and prosecutors' great preference for confessions over any other form of evidence. Additionally, detained suspects have no access to bail, since they have not yet been charged. During detention suspects generally have access to counsel, but this right is subject to the "designation authority" of prosecutors and police (Ramlogan, 1994). This authority, amounting to time and place restrictions for suspect–counsel consultation, is systematically used to severely limit a suspect's access to his counsel to two or three 15-minute interviews during a ten-day detention.

In theory, any statements made after the expiration of the permissible detention period are barred from admission at trial. In practice, prosecutors have seldom, if ever, attempted to admit such statements, so the question is essentially moot. Even total denial of access to counsel extended beyond the prescribed period does not necessarily lead to exclusion, since confessions made after complete denial of counsel have been admitted.

The Japanese courts have largely ignored the constitutional and statutory restraints on the use of confessions and have placed more emphasis on the reliability of the confession rather than on its voluntariness (Foote, 1992). Lack of concern of courts for the nature and extent of the use of coercion in obtaining confession is viewed as one of the factors that could be used to explain a fairly large percentage of involuntary confessions in Japan today.[20]

Conclusion

The privilege against self-incrimination outlined in this survey suggests that it is the fairly well-established procedural protection in both common-law and civil-law traditions. The perception is almost universally shared that suspects and defendants should not be coerced into making incriminating statements, and extensive procedural rules are prescribed in most instances as safeguards against overreaching. A substantial body of judicial and academic opinion in this country assumes that the government's use of the suspect as a source of testimonial evidence through pre-trial interrogation is fundamentally wrong, and that even attempts aimed at questioning involve elements of compulsion and are therefore improper if not outright unlawful. However, the core of the protection in other surveyed countries does not expand to the point of preventing investigators from asking a suspect or defendant questions relating to the crime or of keeping the person from answering them.

The critical question in determining the admissibility of statements made by suspects is whether they are voluntary or uncoerced in some specified sense, and not whether the police observed the prescribed procedures. Moreover, most of the jurisdictions surveyed clearly share the view that society's choice not to compel a person to answer incriminating questions does not require that it also permit him to remain silent at no risk to himself. Rather, the common view is that the trier should be allowed to draw adverse inferences from a defendant's failure to tell what he knows at some stage in the process.

Beyond these common themes, the specifics of interrogation law and practice differ from country to country. However, they differ from the rules that have been imposed in the United States by the *Miranda* decision. Warnings may not be required at all at the initial stage of police interrogation, and any warnings that are required may be quite different from *Miranda*'s. Even where warnings are required, their omission need not result in the exclusion of subsequent statements. The countries surveyed also show that a substantive right to counsel may not be recognized at all in connection with police interrogation, and that any right that is recognized may be drastically narrower than the counsel right created by *Miranda*.

In sum, an examination of the law of other countries does not support the view that any of the features of *Miranda*'s system are essential to fairness to suspects and defendants. The prevalence of practices prohibited by *Miranda* in other civilized nations tends to substantiate the desirability of reconsidering the system employed in this country.

Notes

[1] In *Rogers v. Richmond* (1961), the Supreme Court declared: "Ours is an accusatorial and not an inquisitorial system—a system in which the State must establish guilt by evidence independently and freely secured and may not by coercion prove its charge against an accused out of his own mouth" (p. 541). Later, the Supreme Court in *Garner v. United States* (1976) pointed to "the preservation of an adversary system of criminal justice" and avoidance of inquisitorial practices. In *Andresen v. Maryland* (1976), the Court insisted that some of the most important characteristics which distinguish the accusatorial system from inquisitorial systems of justice are right to silence and the rule against admission of coerced confessions (p. 476). In *Arizona v. Fulminante* (1991), Justice White, writing for four members of the Court, emphasized that the rule against coerced confessions is founded on the distinction between accusatorial and inquisitorial systems.

[2] Applying the Fifth Amendment to the compelled production of business records.

[3] Applying the Fifth Amendment to grand jury proceedings.

[4] The Court held that the defendant, who had only a fifth-grade education, did not knowingly waive his Fifth Amendment rights.

[5] The Court held the confession inadmissible because it had been obtained through coercion (law officers had forced the defendant to stay awake for 36 hours).

[6] Note (1964), Adoptive Admissions, Arrest and the Privilege against Self-Incrimination: A Suggested Constitutional Imperative, *University of Chicago Law Review*, 31:556; note (1966), Developments in the Law—Confessions, *Harvard Law Review*, 79:935.

[7] Police and Criminal Evidence Act 1984, ch. 60, @ 76(2).

[8] Police and Criminal Evidence Act 1984, ch. 60, @ 76(2)(b).

[9] Criminal Law Revision Committee, 11th Report Evidence (General) @ 60, p.41 (1972).

[10] The Criminal Justice and Public Order Act, 1994 Part III, 27–31 (Eng.).

[11] Public Order Act, Article 37.

[12] The Court held that courts may exclude evidence obtained from a violation by police of the right to silence if admitting such evidence would "bring the administration of justice into disrepute."

[13] Medieval inquisitorial procedure not only required that the defendant testify but also permitted enforcement of this duty through torture. After the use of torture was outlawed toward the end of the eighteenth century, most continental procedural systems still provided that the defendant had the "duty to answer" and even threatened to impose punishment on those who would refuse to perform this duty.

[14] Refusal to answer any question at all are mostly encountered in political trials where such an attitude may be interpreted as defiance of the court and as a political protest.

[15] The fact that no adverse legal consequences affect the defendant even if he intentionally makes false statements has led some continental scholars to hypothesize that the defendant has a "right to lie." However, this hypothesis is analytically incorrect. More importantly, it overlooks the fact that as a practical matter, discovered inconsistencies or outright lies in the defendant's testimony will be assessed against him by the fact finder, the defendant will undermine his credibility, and his denials will lose probative value.

[16] It has been suggested that the continental practice of examining the defendant first has a "distinct" advantage of giving him the chance to make the "first impression" on the fact finder. This seems to have some support among behavioral scientists: a person exposed to adversary argumentation forms his opinion on the basis of the first argument, and this opinion cannot be easily dislodged.

[17] French Code de Procedure Penale, Article 114.

[18] For example, in the 1978 case that introduced a "fruit of the poisonous tree" doctrine, a confession obtained by an impermissible wiretap was held inadmissible even though the accused had not been mistreated during interrogation. The Supreme Court of Germany [BGH] drew an analogy to section 136a, which barred an involuntary confession even if the accused later consented to its use (Judgment of February 22, 1978, BGHSt, W. Germany, 27 Entscheidungen des BGHSt 355, 359, 1978).

[19] Judgment of May 31, 1990, 4 BGHSt 112.

[20] According to some sources, the number of forced confessions could be as high as 50% (Watanabe, 1992). It was reported that 7 convictions were overturned because of coerced confessions in 1988, 11 in 1990, and 6 during the time period between 1990 and May 1991.

Cases Cited

Andresen v. Maryland, 427 U.S. 463 (1976)
Arizona v. Fulminante, 111 S. Ct. 1246 (1991)
Ashcraft v. Tennessee, 322 U.S. 143 (1944)
Boyd v. United States, 116 U.S. 616 (1886)
Brown v. Mississippi, 297 U.S. 278 (1936)
Cicenia v. Lagay, 357 U.S. 504 (1958)
Cohens v. Virginia, 19 U.S. (6 Wheat.) 264 (1821).
Counselman v. Hitchcock, 142 U.S. 547 (1892)
Cox v. Coleridge, 1 B.& C. 37, 107 Eng. Rep. 15 (1822)
Crooker v. California, 357 U.S. 433 (1958)
Escobedo v. Illinois, 378 U.S. 478 (1964)
Garner v. U.S., 424 U.S. 648 (1976)
Gideon v. Wainwright, 372 U.S. 335 (1963)
Griffin v. California, 380 U.S. 609 (1965)
Hamilton v. Alabama, 368 U.S. 52 (1961)
Ibrahim v. The King, 1914 App. Cas. 599 (P.C.) (H.K.)
In Re Groban, 352 U.S. 330 (1957)
Johnson v. Zerbst, 304 U.S. 458 (1938)
Malloy v. Hogan 378 U.S. 1 (1964)
Massiah v. United States 377 U.S. 201 (1964)
Michigan v. Tucker, 417 U.S. 433 (1974)
Miranda v. Arizona, 384 U.S. 436 (1966)
Payne v. Arkansas, 356 U.S. 560 (1958)
Powell v. Alabama, 287 U.S. 45 (1932)
Powers v. United States, 223 U.S. 303 (1912)
Regina v. Prager, 56 Crim. App. 151, 161 (C.A. 1971)
Regina v. Woolley, 63 O.A.C.3d 333 (1988) (Ont.)
Rogers v. Richmond, 365 U.S. 534 (1961)
Schmerber v. California, 384 U.S. 757 (1966)
Scott v. H.M. Advocate, J.C. 3 (Scot. H.C.J.) (1946)

United States v. Crocker, 510 F.2d 1129 (10th Cir. 1975)
Watts v. Indiana, 338 U.S. 49 (1949)
White v. Maryland, 373 U.S. 59 (1963)
Wilson v. United States, 162 U.S. 613 (1896)

References

Beattie, J. (1991). Scales of Justice: Defense Counsel and the English Criminal Trial in the Eighteenth and Nineteenth Centuries. *Law and History Review*, 9:221.

Caplan, G. (1985). Questioning *Miranda*. *Vanderbilt Law Review*, 38:1417.

Caswell, M. L. (1985). The Law Reform Commission of Canada: The Proposed Canada Evidence Act and Statements by an Accused. *Canadian Bar Review*, 63:322.

Code de Procedure Penale. Accessed November 15, 2004, at http://translate.google.com/translate?hl=en&sl=fr&u= http://www.adminet.com/code/index-CPROCPEL.html&prev=/ search%3Fq%3D%2522code%2Bde%2Bprocedure%2Bpenale%2522%26hl% 3Den%26lr%3D

Criminal Law Revision Committee (1972). *11th Report Evidence (General)*. London: Home Office.

Department of Justice (Office of Legal Policy) (1989). Truth in Criminal Justice Series Office of Legal Policy: The Law of Pretrial Interrogation. *University of Michigan Journal of Law*, 22:437.

Ewing, K. & Finnie, W. (1982). *Civil Liberties in Scotland: Cases and Materials*. London: Sweet and Maxwell.

Foote, D. (1992). The Benevolent Paternalism of Japanese Criminal Justice. *California Law Review*, 80:317.

Frankel, M. (1975). The Search for Truth: An Empirical View. *University of Pennsylvania Law Review*, 123:1031–1059.

Hardin, P. (1964). Other Answers: Search and Seizure, Coerced Confessions, and Criminal Trial in Scotland. *University of Pennsylvania Law Review*, 113:165.

Helmholz, R. H. (1990). Origins of the Privilege Against Self-Incrimination: The Role of the European Ius Commune. *New York University Law Review*, 65:962.

Home Office (1964). Circular No. 31, Judges' Rules and Administrative Directions to the Police, Appendix A. London: Author.

Howard's Beginning (1993). Editorial, *The Times*, London, Oct. 7.

Ingraham, B. (1987). *The Structure of Criminal Procedure: Law and Practice of France, The Soviet Union, China, and the United States*. Westport, CT: Greenwood Press.

Jackson, J. (1993). Inferences from Silence: From Common Law to Common Sense. *North Ireland Legal Quarterly*, 44:103.

Kaci, J. (1982). Confessions: A Comparison of Exclusion under *Miranda* in the United States and the Judges' Rules in England. *American Journal of Comparative Law*, 6:87.

Landsman, S. (1990). The Rise of the Contentious Spirit: Adversary Procedure in Eighteenth Century England. *Cornell Law Review*, 75:497.

Langbein, J. (1977a). *Torture and the Law of Proof.* Chicago: University of Chicago Press.

—— (1977b). *Comparative Criminal Procedure: Germany*. St. Paul, MN: West Publishing.

———— (1994). The Historical Origins of Privilege against Self-Incrimination at Common Law. *Michigan Law Review*, 92:1047.

Levy, L. (1968). *Origins of the Fifth Amendment: The Right against Self-Incrimination.* New York: Oxford University Press.

Macnair, M. (1990). The Early Development of the Privilege against Self-Incrimination. *Oxford Journal of Legal Studies*, 10:66.

Mills, H. (1993). Tougher Policies Aimed at Helping Victims of Crime. *The Independent*, London, Nov. 19.

O'Reilly, G. (1994). Criminal Law: England Limits the Right to Silence and Moves Toward an Inquisitorial System of Justice. *Journal of Criminal Law & Criminology*, 85:402.

Osakwe, C. (1982). *The Bill of Rights for the Criminal Defendant in American Law.* In J. Andrews (ed.), *Human Rights in Criminal Procedure.* The Hague, Netherlands: Martin Nijhoff Publishers.

Pakter, W. (1985). Exclusionary rules in France, Germany, and Italy. *Hastings International & Comparative Law Review*, 9:1.

Pieck, M. (1962). The Accused's Privilege against Self-Incrimination in the Civil Law. *American Journal of Comparative Law*, 11:585.

Port, K. (1991). The Japanese International Law "Revolution": International Human Rights Law And Its Impact on Japan. *Stanford Journal of International Law*, 28:139.

Pye, L. (Autumn, 1982). The Rights of Persons Accused of Crime Under the Canadian Constitution: A Comparative Perspective. *Law & Contemporary Problems*, 45:221.

Ramlogan, R. (1994) The Human Rights Revolution in Japan: A Story of New Wine in Old Wine Skins? *Emory International Law Review*, 8:127.

Ratushny, L. (1978). Self-Incrimination: Nailing the Coffin Shut. *Criminal Law Quarterly*, 20:312.

The Royal Commission on Criminal Justice (1993). *The Right to Silence in Police Interrogation: A Study of Some of the Issues Underlying the Debate.* London: Home Office.

Schlesinger, R. (1977). Comparative Criminal Procedure: A Plea for Utilizing Foreign Experience. *University of Buffalo Law Review*, 26:361.

Tomlinson, E. (1983) Nonadversarial Justice: The French Experience. *Maryland Law Review*, 42:131.

Van Kessel, G. (1986). The Suspect as a Source of Testimonial Evidence: A Comparison of the English and American Approaches. *Hastings Law Journal*, 38:1.

————(1992). Adversary Excesses in the American Criminal Trial. *Notre Dame Law Review*, 67:403.

Watanabe, T. (1992). Victims of a Safe Society: Behind Japan's Low Crime Rate and Civilized Streets Is a Criminal Justice System Criticized as the Most Backward in the Industrialized World. *Los Angeles Times*, February 27, at A1.

Wigmore, J. (1891). Nemo Tenetur Seipsum Prodere. *Harvard Law Review*, 5:71.

———— (1902). The Privilege against Self-Crimination: Its History. *Harvard Law Review*, 15:610.

Zander, M. (1972). Access to a Solicitor in the Police Station. *Criminal Law Review*, 342.

———— (1993). Abandoning an Ancient Right to Please the Police. *The Independent*, London, Oct. 6.

PART IV

Corrections, Punishment, and Juvenile Justice

21

The Penalty of Hand Amputation for Theft in Islamic Justice

Sam S. Souryal, Abdullah I. Alobied, & Dennis W. Potts

There has been a great deal of skepticism regarding the severity of punishment in Islamic justice, particularly the penalty of hand amputation for the crime of theft. In the eyes of Western publics, and perhaps most Western scholars as well, imposing such a severe punishment for such an "insignificant crime" is too cruel and unusual, and carrying it out so blatantly in public validates the perception of Islamic justice as barbaric and backward. The Western observer may legitimately question why a thief in Islamic justice may have to lose a hand while rapists and most murderers in Western societies are punished by prison sentences. Implicit in this reasoning is clearly the broader view that severing a human limb as punishment for crime (any crime) is a repulsive thought that shocks the human conscience.

From the viewpoint of Islamic justice, however, rape and murder are so rare in Moslem communities precisely because of the imposition of severe punishments for seemingly less heinous crimes such as theft. As will be shown, the penalty of hand amputation for theft is a *Hadd* (a God-prescribed punishment), which was intended to be a particularly stern deterrent. The penalty was ordained by the Qu'ranic verse: "As for thieves, both male and female, cut off their hands. It is a recompense of their deeds, an exemplary punishment from Allah" (Chap. 5:41). As a Hadd, the penalty is absolute; it cannot be negotiated, altered, or forgiven as long as a set of rigorous rules of evidence are met. *Huddud* (the plural of Hadd) penalties are designed, on the one hand, to be so severe that people may not become complacent about committing crime but, on the other hand, to satisfy exceptionally stringent rules of evidence, which under normal conditions may render them inoperative. The purpose, of course, is to maximize their deterrent effect without allowing their casual manipulation by a reckless

Reprinted from *Journal of Criminal Justice*, vol. 22, "The Penalty of Hand Amputation for Theft in Islamic Justice," pp. 249–65,1994, with permission of Elsevier.

judge (Doi, 1984:13). Hence, in the crime of theft, if there is the slightest doubt in establishing the crime, the judge should refrain from awarding the Hadd penalty by not ordering the amputation (Siddiqi, 1985:13–14).

The theft Hadd was reportedly practiced by the Prophet twice, once when he cut off a male thief's hand and another time when he ordered the amputation of a female thief's hand (see Bukhari and Muslim, in El-Awa, 1982:2–3). This should, by no means, lead to the inference that during the Prophet's time only two thefts occurred, but that only two thefts were proven to be prima facie amputateable thefts. In support of the theft Hadd, a famous *Hadith* (saying by the prophet) states that "Allah curses a man who steals a *Bida* (an egg), and gets his hand cut off, or steals a rope and gets his hand cut off" (Doi, 1984:256). This Hadith reinforces the stern warning that "right from the beginning," theft is a wicked crime that is motivated by a sinister desire to exploit the toils and wealth of others, and that "thieves must be considered a menace to peaceful society who must be looked upon with terror" (see Auda, 1981:652; Siddiqi, 1985:127). Both the Hadd and the Hadith came to represent a "categorical impera-tive" against all acts of thievery and an injunction to socially disgrace all thieves. Indirectly, they also support general deterrence theory, which pos-tulates that unless deterred from committing small crimes, people will commit more serious crimes. In addition, as a reiteration of this emphasis on deterrence, a famous (albeit anonymous) Arab saying goes, "In order to train monkeys to do tricks, it may be necessary to slay a willfully disobedi-ent dog in their presence." Interestingly, the Hadd, the Hadith, and the Arab saying bear an uncanny resemblance to the "broken windows" crimi-nological theory—if mischief is not punished early, it will lead to much greater mischief (Wilson and Kelling, 1982).

In Islamic tradition, thieves are considered the "rapists and murder-ers" of society because they violate its most precious essence—spiritual communitarianism. The Qu'ran declares, "Do not devour one another's wealth by false or illegal means" (Chap. 2:188), and a prominent Hadith also states: "Your lives and properties are forbidden to one another until you meet your Lord on the Day of Resurrection" (Doi, 1984:254). Thievery atomizes society by laying personal property prey to indiscriminate viola-tion, thus keeping its members in fear for their freedom to own, trade, and worship. Not only does thievery victimize the individual, it impedes the formation and maintenance of a spiritual community by disrupting the fundamental ties—both formal and informal—that unite the *umma* (spiri-tual community), thus threatening its discontinuity.[1] Given this quintes-sential concern for interdependence and social utility within the paradigm of a spiritual umma, Islamic jurists reluctantly but cautiously justify the taking of a human limb for the transgression of theft.[2]

As to the Western allegations of barbarism and backwardness associ-ated with the practice of hand amputation, from an Islamic viewpoint they could be explained in terms of: (1) the notion of Western "squeamishness" combined with an unnatural urge to act "in a civilized manner," which are seen as inconsistent with the tenacity of Islamic law and the expectations of a robust spiritual community, and (2) the lack of familiarity with Islamic law and its rigorous rules of evidence, which may give the false impression that hand amputation is a casual penalty carried out on a daily basis. As will be explained later, Islamic law provides stringent safeguards that preclude hand amputation in all but a few prima facie cases. As such, the Western allegations are generally assumed to constitute unwarranted rhetorical exaggeration.

In this article we intend to: (1) explain the true relationship between the crime of theft and hand amputation in Islamic law (i.e., why theft is considered such a heinous crime and its penalty so severe), (2) present another view of the generally negative perception associated with the notion of severing a human limb as a criminal punishment, and (3) discuss the rigorous rules of evidence that must be met if theft is to become an amputateable crime. Before we can discuss the topic of theft, however, we believe the reader should first be exposed to a brief overview of Islamic justice and its social-supernatural origin as well as to the general typology of Islamic crimes.

Two important caveats must be stated before the goals of this article are to be misconstrued: First, it is neither a stated nor an implied goal of this article to advocate hand amputation for theft in the United States. Although a few jurists have discussed castration (chemical or surgical) for habitual rapists, we believe our justice system is unique and its social and moral foundation is powerful enough to accommodate such a proposition. Second, it is neither a stated nor an implied goal of this article to digress into a theological debate by implying the superiority of one religion over another. It would be utterly foolish to imply such a thought.[3]

Overview of Islamic Justice

Bassiouni (1982:xviii) stated that the Western world has all too often seen the wrong side of Islam. Although he explores several cultural and social reasons, he puts most of the blame on two educated groups: Western Orientalists whose distorted perceptions failed to grasp the social essence of Islamic justice, and the Moslem *Ulema* (scholars) who failed to convince the West of Islam's fair and equitable philosophy. To truly understand—and better still, to appreciate—Islamic justice, it is important to unlock the mask of positivistic thought, to allow for the metaphysical as well as the physical, to rely more on transcendentalist philosophy rather than on science, and to confront the "cunning of reasoning" that normally manifests itself so compulsively when religious beliefs are judged. As Bronislaw Malinowski remarked, the Western scientist must be able to "see in the lives of alien people," and before the beliefs of another culture are examined, one must first wear the minds of its people (Wilson and Hern-stein, 1985:439).

Justice, in Islam, can have several meanings. One meaning likens it to a sacred trust, a duty imposed on humans to be discharged most sincerely and honestly. This is to identify one's own interests with those of others and to administer the trust as if an act of devotion (Muslehuddin, 1979:101). As such, justice is the quality of being morally responsible and merciful in giving everyone his or her due. Another meaning is based on the notion of mutual respect of one human being by another. As such, a just society is one that offers equal respect for individuals through various social arrangements made in the common interest of all members (Doi, 1984:8; Muslehuddin, 1979:104–5; Bassiouni, 1982:14). A third meaning characterizes the bond that holds society together and transforms it into a brotherhood in which everyone becomes a keeper of everyone else and each is held accountable for the welfare of all (Qu'ran, Chap. 3:103). A fourth meaning identifies justice as "a command from God, and whosoever violates its tenets traces grievous punishment" (Qu'ran, Chap. 16:90). The third and fourth meanings of justice are probably the ones most commonly invoked in Islamic jurisprudence, especially when the topic of theft is discussed. Moreover, Islamic justice is considered to possess a much deeper essence than the formalistic justice enumerated in Roman law or stipulated in the works of the Greek philosophers. Moslems consider issues of justice to be much more penetrative because, as Moslems, they are expected to act as if they are always in the presence of God, to Whom all things, acts, and motives are known (Doi, 1984:5). Both the rich and poor, the powerful and the weak, are equals under God's protection as far as their legitimate interests are concerned, but neither group can be favored at the expense of the other.

There are numerous Qu'ranic injunctions that command justice within the Islamic community. Allah (God) is believed to have dispatched with his Apostles three gifts that characterize the Islamic community: "We sent aforetime our Apostles with clear signals and sent down with them The Book and the Balance and the Iron, that men may stand forth in Justice" (Qu'ran, Chap. 4:4). The Book, the Balance, and the Iron are the elements that effectively hold the Islamic society together: The Book is the body of revelation that commands good and forbids evil; the Balance is the essence of justice that gives each person his or her due; and the Iron is the arm of the law that deters and sanctions evildoers (Doi, 1984:2–3). As mentioned earlier, this third gift of God—the law—is one on which we will focus closely throughout the remainder of this article.

Like Jewish law, Islamic law has two primary sources: Shari'ah, which is a theocratic legal system based on a divine code revealed to the prophet Mohammed and expressed in the scriptures of the Qu'ran; and Sunnah, or acts of the Prophet. The former source will pervade this entire article; the latter will appear only when theft is discussed specifically.

In Islamic tradition, God is the only lawgiver, the sovereign who has the right to ordain all commands for the guidance of humankind (Qu'ran, Chap. 1–2). Shari'ah, which literally means a pathway but is invariably used to mean law, represents such commands identifying what is right and wrong, legal and illegal, proper and improper in the Moslem's life. Shari'ah combines within itself the "is's" and the "ought's" of society; the "is's" represent the prowess of the law, the "ought's" represent the benevolence of justice, the supreme end of the law (Muslehuddin, 1979:100). To accomplish this design, Shari'ah law regulates human conduct by demanding, authorizing, or prohibiting certain behaviors. As such, it provides an all inclusive scale of religious valuation of human conduct. Behaviors falling under the prescription of Shari'ah include all religious and secular conduct, without exception. All aspects of human behavior are classified as obligatory (*fard*); meritorious or recommended (*mandub*); indifferent, which means bringing neither reward nor punishment (*mubah*); reprehensible, which is not punishable but disapproved (*makruh*); and forbidden (*haram*).

The main body of Shari'ah, however, addresses issues of crime and punishment that are known as Huddud Allah, or divine limitations. For all practical purposes, Huddud serve as the Constitution, the Penal Code, and the Code of Criminal Procedure, all in one. Crimes in the Huddud category—which include theft—are offenses against God's community, and because community in Islamic jurisprudence takes preference over the individual, it is the interests of the individual that may have to suffer, and not vice versa (Doi, 1984:219). Huddud penalties are decreed by God; they are absolute, universal, nonnegotiable, and unpardonable—even under the sentiments of mercy (Qu'ran, Chap. 24:2). As such, Huddud cannot be subjected to interpretation by any judge or government official, regardless of power, rank, or status. By the same token, because they represent God's decrees, they are neither subject to rational consideration nor are they to be judged by human reason (Souryal, 1987:433).

In addition, as in Jewish tradition, social goodness in Islamic societies is claimed to be sustained and social evil resisted through a *nomos* (a set of norms) based on a spiritual commitment to social decency. When the nomos is internalized in the psyche of believers, it produces a collective moral conscience by which society, as a functional organism, can distinguish between right and wrong, abstain from criminal behavior, and adequately resist criminal endeavors. Reprehensible acts, therefore, do not shock the collective conscience of society because they are criminal; instead, they are considered criminal because they shock the collective conscience. When obligatory duties are thus internalized, they are seldom ignored, and it does not become necessary to make them manifest (Souryal, 1987:431).

In contrast to the neatness and precision of Western penal philosophy, which attempts to legislate morality through an exhaustive enumeration of secular prohibitions, Islamic justice is based on divine law. The Qu'ran states "Be just: that is next to piety and fear of God" (Chap. 5:9). Moslem jurists further argue that positive laws, despite their "politically correct" provisions, must fall short of rendering natural justice (Bassiouni, 1982:239; Muslehuddin, 1979:24–37). In its purest sense, natural justice is *justica virtutis*; it is asocial, apolitical, amoral, and cannot be subjected to the rules of science. As Plato declared, natural justice is the "perfect circle in the sky," which, if manipulated for any reason, ceases to be perfect. It cannot, therefore, be legislated, tailored to fit, or replaced by "technological" justice, as is the case in the West. Furthermore, although individual freedoms and amenities should be universally protected, in Islamic justice they cannot be allowed to take precedence over the benefits of communitarianism—the truism of God's plan for creation. Moslems believe that failure to observe this hierarchical order of justice can exacerbate social disorganization, encourage material hedonism, heighten ethnocentricity, and lead to the high rate of criminality and violence currently experienced in the West. For a spiritual community to be truly spiritual, it must be based on unadulterated natural justice, and because Shari'ah is God's natural justice as submitted to the umma, the entire umma must be committed to the administration of justice.

On the other hand, the Western philosophy of compartmentalizing human conduct into religious and secular, sacred and profane, or spiritual and material is contrary to Islamic doctrine because human judgment always falls short of God's purpose. In Islam, religion and behavior cease to be autonomous categories; they become two sides of the same coin. Each human act must reflect God's will and at the same time be regulated by His guiding command. Human activities receive a transcendent dimension: they become purposeful and sacred, earthly and heavenly, for this day and for the hereafter. Good deeds earn humans righteousness with God and bad deeds take away in the same manner (Souryal, 1987:431). That is probably why Shari'ah law establishes no court jurisdictions; a judge is a judge for every matter, whether it is civil, criminal, or military.

To establish justice in accordance with Islamic doctrine, the head of the Islamic state has a judicial responsibility consisting of two functions, one positive and the other negative. The positive function relates to the establishment of peace in the realm, the maintenance of accord among the various segments of society, and the protection of the weak against the strong. This negative function involves the punishment of offenders and the restitution of the rights of the injured. Toward that goal, the head of the state must appoint *Qadis* (judges) who are well versed in Islamic law, are God-fearing, and are of irreproachable character and sterling piety. Qadis, especially in orthodox Islamic countries, are perhaps the closest representation of Plato's philosopher-king concept. In conducting his court (Shari'ah prohibits female judges), the judge is expected to be upright, sober, and calm. Nothing should distract his mind from the path of rectitude. If he does wrong, he is not only held responsible to the community of believers, but also to God. He is not to feel mercy in the execution of ordained sentences for the prescribed crimes. The Qu'ran states, "Let not pity detain you in the matter of obedience to Allah if you believe in Allah and the Last Day" (Qu'ran, Chap. 24:2). Naturally, to be a just Qadi under such conditions must be an extremely difficult task. If he is slightly irresponsible and unjust, he will be judged on the Day of Judgment. On the other hand, if he administers justice strictly by the Shari'ah and the Sunnah, he risks making enemies with highly influential members of society. To illustrate this difficulty a Hadith states: "A just Qadi who administers justice among people is like a person slain without a knife" (Doi, 1984:12).

Punishment in Islamic Law

The perpetual task of Shari'ah law is to create and sustain a spiritual bonding committed to the perpetuation of religious beliefs, social order, and proper individual conduct. This task is not only entrusted to elders of the clergy and government officials, but to each and every believer in the commonwealth. The bond that results imposes a dual responsibility on believers: a commitment to do what is good and abstain from what is blameworthy, and a responsibility to directly or indirectly correct the behavior of nonconformists. The principal objective of Islamic jurisprudence (indeed of all justice systems) thus becomes determination of the proper balance between the interests of a spiritual society and those of the individual. To accomplish that social paradox, Western philosophers have searched for answers in the nature of humans; Islamic jurists have found their answers in the nature of God.

Given the Islamic view of Allah as an omniscient God who is stern but benevolent, jealous but compassionate, and militant but merciful, a theory of punishment that is both deterrent and forgiving fits perfectly the Islamic philosophy of justice. Punishment in Islamic justice is designed to be so severe as to deter the most corrupt in the community, but also so magnanimous as to accommodate their reintegration into the society of believers. To manifest its forgiving nature, Shari'ah law maintains the ultimate weapons of compassion and mercy by encouraging the forgoing of punishment. This is done in part by paying *diya*, or restitution (if one is able to), or in full if the offender comes forward and admits the act before apprehension by the authorities. By maintaining this duality of deterrence and forgiveness, Islamic justice attempts to sustain the chastity of religion and the safety of society without sacrificing the dignity of the individual (Lippman, McConville, and Yerushalmi, 1988:84).

Based on the Islamic view of God, punishment in Islamic justice is naturally harsh and its application is expedient because the "sword of Shari'ah" must take priority over social disruption. Furthermore, because punishment has a definite tangible impact, its effectiveness must be maximized by carrying it out in public. Severe punishments are, therefore, justified (if not indeed necessary) not only on the basis of retribution, as most Westerners believe, but more so on the basis of social utility. Examples of Islamic punishment include beheading for murder and robbery, stoning to death for adultery, and 80 lashes for public intoxication. It is important to note, however, that although severe punishments can have a devastating effect on the offender, they are systemic by-products of the "eternal triad" of God, society, and humans. In this relationship, punishment serves a three-tiered obligation: (1) the fulfillment of worship, (2) the purification of society, and (3) the redemption of the individual. If the interests of the individual—the least valuable component in the triad—have to be sacrificed for the wholesomeness and integrity of the encompassing justice system, then it is the natural and rational thing to do. This should, by no means, imply contempt for humans—God's most favorite creation—but simply their expendability if the sanctity of God is violated or the integrity of society is threatened. The imposition of capital punishment, for instance, underscores society's deep abhorrence of disorder and its innate affection for spirituality and social conformity. Beheading as a punishment for social corruption, the Prophet proclaimed, is "more effective than forty days of rain" (Souryal, 1987:433). In a sense, the Prophet's proclamation can be seen as a precursor to Bentham's (1963) "hedonistic calculus," by which he attempted to measure social utility and the prospects of the "greatest felicity" within society. Consistent with Bentham's thought, a calculus of Islamic justice can be summarized as follows:

1. The larger interest of society takes precedence over the interest of the individual.

2. Although "relieving hardship" and "promoting benefit" are both among the primary objectives of Shari'ah, the former takes precedence over the latter.

3. A bigger loss cannot be inflicted to relieve a smaller loss or a bigger benefit cannot be sacrificed for a smaller one. Conversely, a smaller harm can be inflicted to avoid a bigger harm and a smaller benefit can be sacrificed for a larger benefit. (Doi, 1984:8–11; Siddiqi, 1985:8–14)

Perhaps the most graphic display of the triadic fusion between God, society, and the individual is when hand amputation is applied. It is usually carried out in the center square of town and invariably within sight of the Mosque when worshippers conclude their Friday noon prayer. The condemned person is brought forth, the verdict is read loudly, and the arm is stretched on the surface of a regular table with the body of the condemned person turned backward. In a quick move, a professional executioner (in the presence of at least one male physician and a male nurse) exerts strong pressure, pulling the hand away from the wrist and severing the limb at the joint with a sharp knife. At that moment, the physician intercedes to stop the bleeding and bandage the wrist.[4] The amputation, which is usually watched by a multitude of worshippers, is always carried out with utmost solemnity. Unlike the carnival-like scenes depicted in English history books, the event represents a welcome solace in which the forces of religion, government, and community climax in a live experience of puritanical justice. The scene and memory of the event serve to reinforce in the conscience of believers the deterrent consequences and the horrible cost of betraying community standards. Tangible and severe as it may be, believers still find in hand amputation what amounts to an act of mercy, especially to offenders who have a strong tendency to commit thefts. It is further argued that when compared with a long prison sentence, which with subsequent thefts could lose its effectiveness, amputation offers obvious advantages. Besides serving as an act of penance and remission, it allows the offender to resume working within a very short period of time.

Severity in Islamic Punishment: Is Severing a Bodily Limb Justified?

Severity (the proportionality issue) in Islamic punishment constitutes the crux of contention by Western observers. Whereas proportionality of punishment is a relative concept that can be raised against virtually any system of justice, in Islamic justice the issue becomes purely academic for two reasons: (1) It cannot be viewed as a real issue because it is eschewed by divine ordainment, and (2) it is almost never raised because the punishment does not trouble the collective conscience of the spiritual society that practices it (Christie, 1970).

Throughout history, communities have determined severity primarily by indigenous measures, basically traditions, beliefs, and customs that form their sense of theodicy (Hegel's notion of philosophy of history) as well as the dialectics of their beliefs and experiences. Sovereign societies, even vanquished ones, rarely modify their views on how sacred is sacred or how severe is severe, even in the face of overwhelming exogenous forces. The case of world Jewry is a perfect example; despite continuous persecution, they held to their beliefs. Furthermore, when societies do change measurably, they normally follow a slow and arduous process of cultural evolution. If that were not the case, then the U.S. Supreme Court should rule against capital punishment without any delay because most civilized nations disfavor its use. Obviously, this cannot be decreed, because by the end of 1991 only sixteen states had made the cultural change. The remaining states, on the other hand, cannot be denigrated or ostracized for maintaining their social, legal, or moral stands. In spiritual communities, views on crime and punishment are even more deeply ingrained. What is just desert and what is not can be a dogmatic, if not fanatical, issue, and not without justification. As Durkheim remarked,

"There exists a unified system of beliefs and practices relative to sacred things set apart and forbidden" (Berger and Luckman, 1967; Durkheim, 1947; and O'Dea and Aviada, 1983).

The way Moslem law explains proportionality is in terms of *Quesas*, or retaliation. The term, which will be explained later, has its origin in the divine principle of *lex talionis*. Accordingly, Moslems are little bothered by the extent of severity as long as it ensures the equivalence of pain or loss inflicted on the victim. In addition, given the tribal practice of raids and counterraids over trivial matters in the history of Islam, Quesas came to be a perfectly reasonable alternative to greater retribution against the offender, his family, or his tribe. Furthermore, by carrying out a Quesas sentence, an Islamic community reaches the point of social finality by putting an end to disputes that otherwise would fester and cause greater harm to the parties involved as well as to the spiritual umma as a whole.

But how can modern societies judge the severity of a penalty that severs a human body part (i.e., a hand, an eye, a leg, or a tooth) as punishment for crime? Is carrying out such a penalty really barbaric and backward? What universal principles or moral guidelines can support this view? In responding to these questions, we believe the reader should be freshly reminded that the primary motive behind hand amputation in Islamic justice is not to punish the perpetrator vindictively, but to ensure the preservation of a benevolent community. Obviously, a thief with one hand can still commit theft and cause social harm, but at least the spiritual wholesomeness of the community will have been exonerated.

Now let us examine any universal principles or moral guidelines that may bear on the issue of severing a human limb as an act of punishment. History, of course, can be a reliable source because it is replete with events that confirm the presence of such acts in the West.[5] But history can also be a suspect source because (1) it is descriptive in terms of merely chronicling events without speaking for the principles or ideals that directed their occurrence, (2) it is unreliable because it is mostly written by those who had the power to mount events rather than by those upon whom the events were mounted, and (3) even if we were able to verify that severing human limbs had been common for millennia, history cannot justify why it ought to be continued or discontinued. Obviously, more reliable sources must be sought.

If natural law is to be considered a reliable source of judgment, then hand amputation may be as justifiable as pruning a tree, neutering a pet, or performing surgery. These practices are routinely carried out without any hesitation to salvage a weak plant, to redirect the energy of an animal, or to restore a patient to health. Circumcision, as a human example, may have been the longest of such practices that has been religiously commanded, socially accepted, and probably deemed hygienically necessary. Since the beginning of Jewish history, the practice has been perceived as necessary and proper despite the substantial pain involved in its exercise, especially in the earlier times. In applying the natural law view to the areas of crime, social control, and punishment, it is not too surprising to learn that in recent rape trials in the United States judges have indeed imposed chemical or surgical castration as a condition of probation to ensure the "proper" treatment of compulsive rapists and/or the protection of society.[6]

Moreover, if religious testaments are considered a valid source of judgment, then the practice of hand amputation may not be inconsistent with Judeo-Christian teachings, which state: "if thy right eye offend thee, pluck it out and cast it from thee" (Matthew 5:29) and "if thy right hand offended thee, cut it off . . . for it is profitable for thee that one of your members should perish, and not that your whole body should be cast in hell" (Matthew 5:30). References to removing a "sick" body part in these verses represent serious concern for rejuvenating life—in this case human spirituality. Although it is true that many religionists argue that these verses were only meant allegorically, the fact remains that religious allegories contain powerful fields of meaning and establish de facto realities, sometimes of quantum social implications. If this were not so, it would be laborious to argue that God, in His grace, would recommend to His chosen people practices that are intrinsically evil or wrong. Moreover, one would be at a loss to justify why it is reasonable to believe that when God refers to severing body parts He means it allegorically, but when He refers to stoning—which was reportedly carried out in the Bible and is obviously much more inhumane than amputation—He does not.

In the philosophy of Islamic justice, all human beings are considered salvageable, if not for their intrinsic value then for the benefit of society and the preservation of God's plan. Given this basic premise, it does not seem too contradictory or irrational for the Moslem believer to accept the amputation of a "sick" hand as a method of salvation rather than doing away with the entire person. The amputee, handicapped as he or she may be, will remain alive and Moslem. In the more serious crimes of murder or robbery, for instance, the Moslem believer would naturally not hesitate to condone public execution as the ultimate act of societal purification and redemption.

Based on what has been said, when the Islamic philosophy of penology is compared to its Western counterpart, an interesting analogy can be discerned: physical amputation versus societal amputation. In Islamic philosophy, although the offender suffers enormous physical loss at the initial stage, he (very few offenders are females) is immediately set free and reintegrated into society. He is accepted as a normal person who has paid his debt to the community—in full. He, by the grace of God, has become spiritually whole and the entire community acknowledges his reformation.[7] In Western philosophy, by contrast, the offender's freedom is restricted at the initial stage through a prison term, but the offender remains "socially amputated" perhaps for the remainder of his or her life. Western societies have often rejected ex-convicts, relegating them to the role of social outcasts.[8]

Perhaps the final argument against the severing of a human limb as an act of punishment is the repulsiveness of the act itself—it shocks the human conscience. From a psychological viewpoint, the notion of repulsiveness is basically an emotional state, which is independent from the utility of the act or the collective conscience that supports its adoption. It can be argued further that if the objection to hand amputation in Western thought is based solely on the issue of disproportionality (that it does not fit the crime of theft), it would be a fairly rational and logical objection, because if that is true (which we assume it is not), there ought to be lesser resentment if hand amputation were to be applied to more serious crimes such as aggravated theft, armed robbery, or terrorism. The notion of repulsiveness seems to be based on much broader sentiments than the single issue of disproportionality of punishment, perhaps involving paradoxical reasoning. It would seem illogical, if not outright contradictory, that some Western-minded penologists would continue to favor capital punishment and, at the same time, view the practice of hand amputation as repulsive. This contradiction can be analogous to one that states, "I can see perfectly in the dark, but I cannot see in dim light." The minor premise obviously negates the major one, and no logician can possibly reconcile the two without doing serious harm to human intellect.

One possible factor for this contradiction may be that when offenders are executed, they forever disappear, whereas amputated offenders remain ever visible. Although this may be a relevant factor, it would seem more germane to a condition of guilt (after the act) than to the validity or equity of the punishment itself. Other possible factors could be (1) the emotional vacillation in Westernized societies between the clichés of "law and order" and "waging war on crime" and the "appearance of civility," in light of one's concern for effective punishment and one's concern for political correctness; (2) the cultural repugnance of having to endure watching more people (perhaps many more people) roaming the downtown streets wearing prostheses; and (3) the sort of "pragmatic reasoning" in the West that seems inclined to interpret God's commandments either literally or allegorically, depending on the social romanticism of the time. If for no other reason, the contradiction could be explained in terms of the "cunning reasoning," the kind warned against in the beginning of this article. In Islamic jurisprudence, the response to crime is serious and straightforward: if deterrence is good, then maximum deterrence is better, especially if society, government, and religion share the same structural foundation—God's ordainment.

Typology of Crime In Islamic Law

Shari'ah is an extensive code of religious obligations that believers must fulfill, especially when no one is out there to enforce them. To pre-

viduals. Punishment for such crimes follows the principle of lex talionis. Quesas, which literally means "equal harm," is a generic category of crimes that includes (1) murder and its related areas of manslaughter and criminal negligence, and (2) assault, battery, and similar acts of violence against the person. Although these crimes are mentioned in the Qu'ran, their penalty is not specifically ordained. In addition, although prosecution of these crimes is mandatory, punishment could be negotiated or even for-given, in part or in full, by the victim or his or her family. It is necessary to explain at this juncture that although murder and aggravated assault are clearly of a graver nature than theft, the latter is a Hadd crime whereas the former are not. Accordingly, the punishment for theft is fixed whereas the punishment for murder is not. To the uninformed Western observer, this simply means that in Islamic justice the penalty for theft is more severe than the penalty for murder. However, this is an inaccurate assumption because a fixed penalty does not necessarily make the penalty more or less severe than a negotiable one, especially because the penalty for a prima facie murder is death by beheading. Negotiation, which may allow restitu-tion or forgiveness, can be of assistance for all practical purposes only when the murderer and the victim are related and/or a strong family con-cern favors saving the life of the perpetrator. Otherwise, negotiation in Quesas is invariably not used. The difference, therefore, between the pen-alty for theft and that for murder is not one of severity but of possible reprieve, and only if the victim's family cooperates.

As mentioned earlier, the punishment for Quesas crimes is equal retal-iation: "The life for life, and the eye for the eye, and the nose for the nose, and the ear for the ear, and the tooth for the tooth, and for wounds retali-ation" (Qu'ran, Chap. 5:48). As such, Islamic law continues the Judeo-Christian principle of *talion*, which allows diya, or restitution, if both par-ties approve. Whereas Jewish law insisted on retaliation and Christianity allowed compensation, Islam combined both. Although on the one hand, it allows the infliction of Quesas to attain justice without exacting a greater level of retribution against the perpetrator, on the other hand it encour-ages the acceptance of restitution as a means of augmenting one's favor with God (Bassiouni, 1982:204). Urging the acceptance of diya by trial judges has recently become a more popular practice because determining an exact Quesas in modern-day disputes has become increasingly difficult to judge, let alone apply.

Ta'azir (rehabilitation) crimes represent an open-ended category that can cover all other conducts . . . considered unacceptable in a spiritual society. They include three subcategories:

1. Acts that are condemned by Shari'ah or Sunnah but are not included in the inventory of Huddud or Quesas crimes such as the consumption of pork, usury, false testimony, bribery, breach of trust by public officials, espionage, and astrology.

serve the spiritual community, Shari'ah charges people with a dual resp
sibility: one in relation to God, best known as *taqwa* (the fear of God), a
the other in relation to society, consisting of a bill of social duties, rath
than of rights, as in Western laws. This latter category is the one mo
referred to when Moslems address issues of crime and punishment. I
accordance with this bill, crimes in Islamic justice are (1) Huddud crimes
(2) Quesas crimes, and (3) Ta'azir crimes. For the benefit of those who are
shocked by the penalty of hand amputation for the offense of theft, these
three types will be discussed briefly in this section.

Huddud crimes are grave crimes committed against Huqquq Allah, or
God's rights. They are mentioned specifically in the Qu'ran and the Sun-
nah while others are not. Huddud crimes are based on one of the Qu'ran's
most stern verses: "These are the limitations of God. Do not transgress
them" (Chap. 2:229). Prosecution in these crimes is mandatory and pun-
ishment is meted exactly as prescribed in the commandment. On the other
hand, due to the gravity of these crimes, judgment requires a rigorous set
of evidentiary rules that far exceeds the strictest rules in any Western code.
For the crime of adultery, for example, the rules require either confession
or the sworn testimony of four pious eyewitnesses that they saw the very
act of carnal conjunction as clearly as they could distinguish "a black
thread from a white thread"; for the crime of drinking alcohol, either con-
fession or the testimony of two male eyewitnesses; and for the crime of
theft, either confession or the testimony of two eyewitnesses to the com-
mission of the stealthy act (Siddiqi, 1985:53–69). Punishment for Huddud
crimes is characterized by three attributes: (1) It is prescribed in the inter-
est of a spiritual community—all Huddud crimes are committed against
God and His community of believers; (2) it is taken literally from the
words of the Qu'ran, and it cannot be mitigated, negotiated, nor made any
more or less severe; and (3) once guilt is established and punishment is
determined, it cannot be pardoned for any reason by a judge, by a political
authority, or by the victim.

Huddud crimes are seven: adultery (including fornication and illicit
sexual relations), defamation (slanderous accusation of adultery), drink-
ing alcohol (in public or in private), theft, highway robbery, apostasy from
Islam, and corruption in earth (mishandling of public trust). The punish-
ment for adultery is flogging, with both parties receiving 100 lashes fol-
lowed by stoning; the punishment for defamation is 80 lashes; the
punishment for drinking alcohol is flogging and/or exile from the land;
the punishment for highway robbery is death by crucifixion or cutting off
both hands and feet; the punishment for apostasy (after refusal to repent
and reconvert) is beheading; and the punishment for corruption against
the Islamic community is beheading (Aly Mansour, in Bassiouni,
1982:195–203).

Quesas (retaliation) crimes could actually be considered much more
serious crimes (since they include murder) but are committed against indi-

2. Acts that violate proper Islamic conduct such as obscenity, provocative dress, and disorderly conduct. Of course, traffic violations, zoning violations, school violations, and other administrative infractions have recently been added to the category of Ta'azir crimes.

3. All acts in the categories of Huddud and Quesas crimes that fail to meet the rigorous requirements of evidentiary rules as ordained, thus giving rise to doubt (Doi, 1984:221–26; El-Awa, 1982:96–100).

Ta'azir punishment is basically of a rehabilitative nature, and judges are allowed a wide range of discretion in determining punishment. Prosecution and the imposition of punishment is discretionary and is left entirely to the court and its religious elders to determine, in light of the amount and seriousness of the damage caused, the circumstances of the offender, and the social and spiritual significance of the offense. Penalties may vary from a long-term jail sentence to light corporal punishment (i.e., shaving off the long hair of an effeminate young man) or to the payment of restitution.

Theft in Islamic Law

In Islamic law, social control begins with the rudimentary causes of social disorganization. "Simple" theft is considered a serious predatory crime that can endanger the basic structure of an organized community. In a spiritual society, a lenient punishment might be even more detrimental. For example, during the time of Jesus, the penalty of a "proven" theft was crucifixion (Matthew 27:38). Moreover, there is always the fear that the commission of seemingly little crimes, if not deterred, would be the starting point for more serious and deadlier offenses such as robbery and murder (Doi, 1984:260). Given this basic premise, meting severe punishment for theft is considered a cornerstone of Islamic deterrence—one signaling that a spiritual community will not tolerate even the least offenses.

In Islamic jurisprudence, *Sariqa*, or theft, is defined as taking the property of another in a clandestine manner when such property is kept in custody. This definition, which also includes burglary, distinguishes theft from robbery, mugging, or purse snatching in terms of associating the act with the element of stealth rather than violence. Crimes of violence, after all, are ultra-predatory crimes that may be punished by beheading. The absence of distinction in Islamic law between theft and burglary (which requires breaking and entry) may have an interesting historical origin. In the early times of Islam, people did not ordinarily shut their front doors (if they had any at all) as a sign of hospitality, and all neighbors were welcome to enter peacefully. It is indeed the element of stealth that Islamic jurisprudence considered most betraying and bothersome. The intrinsic meanness associated with stealth—not the tangible loss inflicted on the victim—characterizes the perpetrator as a pariah in a communal sense. Furthermore, the motive behind committing the crime had no standing whatsoever; it did

not matter whether one was a rich kleptomaniac or an indigent with starv-
ing children (although Caliph Omar ibn El Khatab reportedly suspended
the theft Hadd in the year of the famine during his caliphate). This signifies
a deontological as well as an absolutist view of theft as an act that is reprehensible in itself. No other reasoning could be made that can justify violating the integrity of the Moslem home in a spiritual society. It is no wonder
the Qu'ran stated unequivocally: "Do not take another's property without
right . . . as to the thief, male or female, cut off his or her hand [as] a punishment by way of example from God" (Chap. 5:41).

Thus, whereas Shari'ah established the unequivocal punishment for
theft, it was left to Sunnah (public sayings, or Hadith) to specify the rules
of evidence under which this stern punishment could be meted. As a Hadd
crime, the punishment for theft cannot be enforced if doubt arises; this by
no means implies that the accused goes free, but that he or she would
become subject to Ta'azir law if found guilty (Al-Zurrair, 1980:283–86).
According to Sunnah, an act of theft is complete and amputation must be
carried out when the following elements are present: (1) The perpetrator
is an adult of sound understanding, (2) the property is movable, (3) the
property is in the careful protection of someone, (4) the property is taken
in a secret manner, (5) the thief has obtained full possession of the stolen
property, (6) the value of property amounts to the prescribed *nisab*, or
limit, and (7) the criminal intent is present (Siddiqi, 1985:123–38). In this
section, we will combine these elements into those regarding the offender,
the stolen property, and the victim.

Elements Regarding the Offender

To constitute a prima facie amputateable case of theft, the circumstances of the crime must satisfy three criteria:

1. The accused must have reached the age of puberty. This is supported
   by the Hadith: "Three classes of offenders are not subject for Huddud punishment; the child before coming to age, the sleeper until he
   wakes up, and the insane until he is cured" (Doi, 1984:226; Siddiqi,
   1985:123). Although Islamic Qadis of yesteryear determined
   puberty by traditional means, in modern times a physician's testimony is invariably required, especially when the issue is contested.

2. The accused must have committed the act voluntarily—any implication of coercion nullifies Hadd punishment. This is supported by
   the Hadith: "My community is excused for what it commits under
   duress" (Doi, 1984:227).

3. The accused must have committed the crime through an act of
   stealth. Therefore, if the victim is suspected to have had prior
   knowledge of the act, the Qadi is obliged to drop the Hadd punishment and to apply the provisions of Ta'azir law. In that case, a jail
   sentence or restitution would be a more likely punishment.

Elements Regarding the Stolen Property

This category is particularly significant because it places substantial responsibility on the victim. The element of stealth—the crux of culpability in Islamic philosophy—cannot be established and the Hadd cannot be imposed unless the victim is shown to have exercised reasonable care in preserving the property. This, in Islamic jurisprudence, institutes the concept of *al-hirz*, or proper custody, which has no similar counterpart in Western criminal law.

Hirz legally means that the property is kept in a place that is traditionally considered safe, such as a secure box or a locked cabinet. In this regard, amputation cannot be ruled for the theft of what cannot be guarded or is not worth guarding, such as dry wood, hay, grass, game, or fish. A Hadith states: "A hand is not to be cut off for fruit which is hanging outside the wall or sheep stolen from the mountain but when the sheep is in its fold or the fruit is in the place where it is dried" (Mishkat, in Siddiqi, 1985:124). Therefore, amputation is disallowed if the offender stole a bicycle or a lawnmower from the front yard of a house or a public property left in the open. It is the responsibility of the Qadi to determine when stolen property is kept in a safe place meeting the requirement of hirz. If this is not established, only Ta'azir punishment can apply.

The value of stolen property is another important element. It must have a minimum nisab, or worth, although there is disagreement among the four schools of Islamic thought regarding the amount. The Shaffi, the Hanbali, and the Maliki schools are of the opinion that the stolen property should equal or exceed three *dirhams* (about the equivalent of twenty-five cents in U.S. currency if valued sixteen centuries ago). The Hanafi school, on the other hand, is of the opinion that amputation cannot be imposed unless the value of the property is at least ten dirhams (the equivalent of seventy-five cents if valued sixteen centuries ago). More contemporary jurists prefer the Hanafi opinion because doubt must be resolved in favor of the offender (Doi, 1984:257; Siddiqi, 1985:125). It is noteworthy, however, to ask whether the seemingly insignificant value of the stolen goods would discourage victims from reporting the crime to the police, as is the case in Western societies. The most common view is that it does not, because reporting transgression in itself is a religious obligation that earns Moslems favor in the eyes of God and fellow believers. Furthermore, homeowner insurance policies, as a motivation not to report theft crimes in the West, were unknown in the Moslem world until recently and may continue to be unpopular today.

The third important limitation on hand amputation for theft is the question of ownership. There are three basic sanctions in this regard:

1. Amputation is disallowed if the property is owned by the father or the son of the accused. The rationale is concern for the ancestral cohesiveness and peace within the family, which, in Islamic justice,

is of much higher good than exacting punishment. This prohibition is based on an incident reported to the Prophet by a victim who alleged that his money was stolen by his father. The Prophet reportedly replied (thus establishing the act of Sunnah): "But you and your money belong to your father" (Alobied, 1991:72).

2. Amputation is also prohibited if the stolen goods are forbidden by Islamic law, such as pork or alcohol. One rationale is that these substances are not lawful property in accordance with Islamic law (Siddiqi, 1985:130). Another rationale is to rid society of illicit substances that present more harm to the community, if consumed, than does severance of the thief's hand. The assumption, of course, is that the accused is going to destroy the illicit substance.

3. Amputation is disallowed if the thief steals from *Bait al-Mal* (the public treasury) where community money is kept. Although this may sound particularly puzzling to the Western observer, the rationale is based on the fact that public funds are common property of all Moslems (thus the thief, as a member, has a share) and will eventually be distributed among them—thus, the crime is basically one of impatience.

Elements Regarding the Victim

As a Hadd crime, theft is a transgression committed against God and His community of believers, and it is therefore nonnegotiable and unpardonable. Yet the justice process cannot be initiated without a formal and voluntary complaint by the victim unless the accused is apprehended in the process of committing the act. This rule has been established by Sunnah in a case brought to the Prophet by Safwan bin Ummayah, who, after accusing his neighbor of stealing his sheet, changed his mind and forgave him. The Prophet, nevertheless, ordered the amputation, admonishing Safwan by saying: "Why didn't you forgive him before bringing him to me?" (Mishkat, in Siddiqi, 1985:125). This Sunnah apparently became another legal precedent upon which jurists rely in support of the nonnegotiability and unpardonability of the theft Hadd.

Rules of Evidence

As in most secular systems, the accused in Islamic justice is presumed to be innocent until proven guilty. The corollary to this principle is that the burden of proof is on the complainant. Furthermore, the graver the crime, the greater the number of eyewitnesses required to testify and the stricter the measures necessary to establish proof. Consequently, the rules of evidence required in the case of theft are more rigorous than those required in the case of murder, because the latter is a Quesas crime and might have a slim chance for negotiation. Furthermore, to ensure a high degree of reliability, the restricted view of evidence—especially in Huddud crimes—permits only two kinds: *iqrar* (confession) and eyewitness testimony (Bassiouni, 1982:111; Lippman, McConville, and Yerushalmi, 1988:68).

Iqrar, in Islamic justice, is the admission by the accused of having committed the act that incurs punishment. A single confession is considered sufficient, although the Hanafi school of thought requires a number of confessions equal to the number of required witnesses (Bassiouni, 1982:119). For a confession to be admissible, it should be made voluntarily, unequivocally, and in detail (indicating the confessor's awareness of what he or she has done and reaffirming an understanding of the legal consequences of the confession) in and during the court proceeding. Further, due to the grave consequences of confession in Huddud crimes, they can be withdrawn at any time—during trial, after the sentence has been passed, and up to the moment of execution. If the accused withdraws the confession (assuming it was the only evidence against the accused), the Qadi would be required to set aside the sentence and retry the accused in accordance with Ta'azir rules (Alobied, 1991:55). In such a case, the accused may end up with a harsher or a more lenient sentence based on the merits of the case.

Testimony in Islamic jurisprudence must begin with the word *Ashhadu* (I testify) because it indicates bearing witness, or seeing with one's eyes. No other word can be substituted because it would be less affirmative and might cast doubt on the testimony—a condition that absolutely nullifies the Hadd (Bassiouni, 1982:115). The number of eyewitnesses required to establish guilt in Huddud crimes may vary. Four male witnesses are required to prove guilt in cases of adultery and slander, but only two in the case of theft. Should there be fewer than two male witnesses, Sunnah permits a combination of one male and two female witnesses. On the other hand, a group of four female witnesses is prohibited (Siddiqi, 1985:136). Witnesses must meet rigorous criteria: (1) They must be persons of moral integrity whose credibility, righteousness, and sense of honor are above reproach; (2) they must be mature, over the age of puberty; (3) they must be sane both at the time of observing the offense and at the time of the testimony; and (4) they can never have been convicted of a serious crime or have engaged in deviant behavior. It is ultimately the responsibility of the Qadi to certify that the witnesses testifying in his court possess all these qualifications.

The Deterrent Effect of Hand Amputation in Saudi Arabia

In an attempt to examine the effectiveness of the penalty of hand amputation for theft, we wanted quantitatively and qualitatively to assess property crime rates across cultures. We chose the Kingdom of Saudi Arabia as the theater of examination for two reasons: (1) It is the country whose justice system is most consistent with orthodox Islamic law, and (2) coauthor Alobeid is a Saudi national and was instrumental in obtaining the Saudi data.

In attempting a quantitative approach, we expected property crime rates to be considerably lower in the Kingdom than the world average and, of course, the United States. Our objective was to synchronize three sources of data: United States data, worldwide data, and Saudi Arabian data. The American data were based on figures collected from the Uniform Crime Reports, the worldwide data were based on the Report of the Secretary General on Crime Prevention and Control, and the Saudi Arabian data were based on the Arab Crime Statistics.

We quickly found that while this task was not impossible, the data were incompatible to the extent that the resulting figures would lack substantive meaning. Difficulties regarding worldwide and Saudi figures, for example, arose because of the absence of verifiable data, since few countries besides the United States collect victimization data to offset the unreliable nature of official statistics. Worldwide data also would have to be disaggregated because they are reported every decade in aggregate form. The Saudi data (which included citizens as well as more than five million foreign workers and related only to Huddud thefts) differed from the others in the classification of crimes, because under Islamic law, theft and burglary are considered one and the same. Due to the lack of more discriminating data, it was difficult to determine whether the expected low rates of property crimes in the Kingdom were the product of the deterrent effect of harsh punishment or of other sociological factors, such as religiosity, family structure, social control, self-discipline, or routine activities.

Qualitatively, we found that the views of several Ulema (literary leaders) at the Mahad Al-Ali Liz Qada (the Higher Institute of Justice Studies) in Riyadh reflect their belief in the utility of Islamic punishment. These views were gleaned from the voluminous work by Doi (1984), which often has been cited in this article. Under the headline of "Punishment for Theft: A Comparative View" (pp. 250–63), one unidentified *alem* (singular of ulema) stated:

> Due to the harshness of punishment in Islam, both the hand of the thief and the life of the victim have been protected, at one and the same time, and tranquillity is secured for all. The execution, which is done publicly, serves to set an example.

Another alem (Dr. Dawalibi) stated:

> Harshness has made it possible for all of us to live in perfect security and tranquillity, and for those who are tempted to steal, to keep their hands whole. Formerly, when these regions were ruled by the French-inspired Penal Code, under the Ottoman Empire, pilgrims traveling between the two Holy cities—Mecca and Medina—could not feel secure for their purse or their life unless they had a strong escort. But when this country became the Saudi Kingdom and the Qu'ranic law was enforced, crime immediately disappeared. A traveler, then, could journey, not only between the Holy cities, but even from Dahran on the

Gulf to Jeddah on the Red Sea traversing a distance of more than one thousand and five hundred kilometers across the desert, all alone in his private car, without harboring any fear or worry about his life or property be it worth millions of dollars, or be he a complete foreigner.

Another alem (identified as the head of the Saudi delegation) stated:

In the Kingdom of Saudi Arabia where Islamic Law is enforced, state money is transferred from one town to another, from one bank to another, in an ordinary car without any escort protection but the car driver. In any Western state, even in the capital cities, no one would be ready to transfer money from one bank to another without the protection of a strong police force and the necessary number of armored cars.

Another alem (identified as the speaker of the institute) stated:

Only here, in this country, where Islamic Law is enforced, could the American Secretary of State, Mr. William Rogers, and his party dispense with the armored cars which had been transported by special planes and which accompanied them in their tour of ten countries. Only here did the government disallow its visiting dignitaries to go around in their own cars. Only here did Mr. Rogers decline the guards assigned to him and walk through the *soukes* (markets) by himself declaring that only in this kingdom, and this kingdom alone, could one have such a feeling of security that one no longer needs a guard.

Finally, another unidentified alem stated:

If you consider the striking results with regard to security, public order, and general tranquility which are the order of the day in the Kingdom, do you not agree that it is our duty to remain faithful to the commands of our religion in order to prevent social infraction? Stealing is almost unknown in our Kingdom, while people in the great capitals of western countries have no security for their lives or their possessions. I remember when I was in Paris in the summer, two years ago, a hold-up in one of the biggest restaurants, near the Champs Elysees: in front of hundreds of customers who were stunned and stood motionless, gangsters managed to take off the whole cash. The next morning, all Parisian newspapers published the news.

Conclusion

The issues raised in this article reveal that Islamic justice is certainly unique in itself as well as in its endeavors to create a peaceful society. Severe sanctions are ordained by God and hand amputation for bona fide theft is carried out in public as a Hadd penalty. Although the penalty is designed primarily as an instrument of social deterrence, its continuing and undisguised application serves as a powerful reminder of the believers' spiritual obligations toward God and society. Furthermore, the application of this penalty does not appear to be inconsistent with the principles of natural law or Judeo-Christian doctrine in their original versions.

Although the penalty of hand amputation is considered cruel by all concerned, including the Moslem jurists and believers, in the societies that apply it, it ceases to be "unusual" and is naturally accepted as a necessary deterrent sanction. This, we believe, is based on the unique blend in Shari'ah law of the need for a stern deterrent measure, as manifest in the practice of hand amputation, and the need for reintegration and forgiveness as is expected in Quesas crimes. When both needs are met and the justice process is safeguarded by rigorous evidentiary rules and nonnegotiable sentences, Islamic justice is not only able to all but eradicate theft—the most common crime in the history of humankind—but perhaps deter much more serious crimes.

Notes

[1] Note Braithwaite's (1989) emphasis on communitarianism and the informal mechanics of social disapproval, shaming, and reintegration.

[2] See Jabir's argument, Abu Salama's argument, and Rafi Ben Khadijs's argument in support of amputation, as cited in Siddiqi (1985:127–30).

[3] The reader should be aware that not all Moslem countries apply Islamic law as presented here. Indeed, at this time, the majority of them do not—we suspect only for political reasons. The practice is currently common in the Kingdom of Saudi Arabia, Pakistan, Iran, Afghanistan, and a few fundamentalist countries including the Sudan (until 1989). However, current events in North Africa and Egypt indicate that the practice might be reintroduced in a number of Moslem states. The substance of this article has been derived from a masters thesis completed by the third author in 1991, as well as from several research projects conducted in Saudi Arabia and other Islamic states by the first author, who is Christian.

[4] Personal observation by the principal author while in Saudi Arabia in 1984 (see also El-Awa, 1982:5). As to which hand is to be cut for the first amputateable theft, the Qu'ran does not say. Nevertheless, nearly all jurists agree that the thief's right hand should be cut first (El-Awa, 1982:5). A Hadith also states: "If a thief steals cut off his hand, if he steals again cut off his foot, if he steals again cut off his hand and if he steals again cut off his foot" (Mishkat, as cited in Siddiqi, 1985:128). In another interpretation, the order of amputation for successive thefts is hand-hand-foot-foot (Abu Salama, as quoted in Siddiqi, 1985:128). Similarly, Moslem jurists also differ in the case of a theft committed by many thieves. According to Immam Malik, if the stolen property reaches the nisab, or required limit, one hand of each thief should be cut off. In the Hanafi school of thought, if the stolen property is divided among them and the share of each one amounted to a nisab, then the Hadd will be applied. If the share does not amount to a nisab, only Ta'azir punishment should be applied (Doi, 1984:257; see also Al-Zurrair, 1980:91).

[5] Reckless (1973:348–50) noted some of the more creative methods, including lynching, electrocution, crucifixion, burning at the stake, flogging, branding, dismemberment, and drowning. In more recent times, Shover (1979:233–39) recounted other, more recent "civilized" instances involving incarceration in the United States, such as living in leaking human waste and slow starvation (1971), whipping (1968), rodent-infested solitary confinement cells (1970), and exposure to the elements without clothing (1967).

[6] See *State v. Brown*, 326 S.E. 2d, 410 (S.C. 1985) and *People v. Gauntlet*, 394 N.W.2d 437 (Mich.App., 1986).

[7] See Braithwaite's (1989) view on constructive reintegration and its imperative for communitarianism in society.

8 See Foucault's view of "social scapegoating" (1977); Lozoff and Braswell's view of "We Are All Doing Time" (1989); and Souryal's view of "The Camp of Outcasts" (1992:336).

Bibliography

Alobied, A. (1991). The Deterrent Effect of Shari'ah Law in Islamic Justice with a Special Application to the Crime of Theft. Unpublished Masters Thesis, Sam Houston State University, Huntsville, TX.

Al-Zurrair, Khalifa Al-Ibrahiem (1980). *Mukafahat garimat al-sariqua fi-al-Islam.* Riyadh, Saudi Arabia: The Maaref Library.

Auda, A. Q. (1981). *Al tashri at ginai al Islami.* Beirut: The Risala Institution.

Bassiouni, C. N. (1982). *The Islamic Criminal Justice System.* New York: Oceana Publications.

Bentham, J. (1963). In A. J. Ayer (ed.), *Philosophical Essays.* London: MacMillan.

Berger, P., and T. Luckman (1967). *The Social Construction of Reality.* New York: Doubleday.

Braithwaite, J. (1989). *Crime, Shame, and Reintegration.* New York: Cambridge University Press.

Christie. N. (1970). "Comparative Criminology." *Canadian Journal of Corrections* 12 (1): 40–60.

Doi, Abul Rahman I. (1984). *Shari'ah: The Islamic Law.* London: Delux Press (Ta Ha Publishers).

Durkheim, E. [1959] (1947). *The Elementary Forms of Religious Life.* New York: Free Press.

El-Awa, M. S. (1982). *Punishment in Islamic Law: A Comparative Study.* Indianapolis: American Trust Publications.

Foucault, M. (1977). *Discipline and Punish: The Birth of the Prison.* London: Allen Lane.

Lippman, M., S. McConville, and M. Yerushalmi (1988). *Islamic Criminal Justice Procedures.* New York: Praeger.

Lozoff, B., and M. Braswell (1989). *Inner Corrections: Finding Peace and Peace Making.* Cincinnati, OH: Anderson Publishing Company.

Mansour, A. (1981). "Huddud Crimes." In C. Bassiouni (ed.), *The Islamic Criminal Justice System.* New York: Oceana Publications.

Muslehuddin, M. (1979). *Philosophy of Islamic Law and the Orientalists.* Lashore, Pakistan: Islamic Publications.

O'Dea, T., and J. Aviada (1983). *Sociology of Religion.* Englewood Cliffs, NJ: Prentice Hall.

Qu'ran (1946). Trans. Abdulla Yusuf Ali. Cairo: Dar-Al-Kitab Al-Masn.

Reckless, W. (1973). *The Crime Problem,* 5th ed. Pacific Palisades, CA: Goodyear.

Report of the Secretary General on Crime Prevention (Report A/32/199) (1977). New York: United Nations.

Shover, N. (1979). *A Sociology of American Corrections.* Homewood, IL: The Dorsey Press.

Siddiqi, M. (1985). *The Penal Law of Islam.* Lahor, Pakistan: Kazi Publishers.

Souryal, S. (1987). "The Religionization of a Society: The Continuing Application of Shari'ah Law in Saudi Arabia." *Journal of the Scientific Study of Religion* 26 (4): 429–49.

——— (1988). "The Role of Shari'ah Law in Deterring Criminality in Saudi Arabia." *International Journal of Comparative and Applied Criminal Justice* 12 (1): 1–25.

———— (1992). *Ethics in Criminal Justice: In Search of the Truth*. Cincinnati, OH: Anderson Publishing.

Wilson, J. Q., and R. Hernstein (1985). *Crime and Human Nature*. New York: Simon and Schuster.

Wilson, J. Q., and G. Kelling (1982). "Broken Windows: Police and Neighborhood Safety." *Atlantic Monthly* 26: 29–38.

22

History and Development of Modern Correctional Practices in New Zealand

Greg Newbold & Chris Eskridge

New Zealand is a nation of approximately 3.9 million people, located about 1,200 miles southeast of Australia. The country consists of two principal land masses, known simply as the North and South Islands. The North Island has more than twice the population of the South Island.

Polynesian voyagers, later known as Maori, first discovered and colonized New Zealand around AD 900. However, the islands were unknown to Europeans until the voyage of the Dutch explorer, Abel Tasman, in 1642. Hostile natives deterred Tasman from landing, and European exploration was left to the British navigator James Cook, who first arrived in 1769. Sealers, whalers, and seafarers began to inhabit New Zealand's shores after 1792, and the first missionaries introduced Christianity in 1814.

Early relations between European and Maori were symbiotic, with the warlike Maori holding the balance of power. However, in 1839 a plan by private entrepreneurs to systematically settle New Zealand led to a decision by the British government to annex the country, ostensibly for the protection of the natives. A treaty was hastily drafted, guaranteeing protection of Maori rights and possessions in return for cession of sovereignty and the granting of equal status as British subjects. Known as the Treaty of Waitangi, this document was ultimately signed by the majority of tribal chiefs in 1840. New Zealand was then declared a Crown Colony. Although subsequent breaches of the treaty led to warfare between Maori and colonials, it now stands as an often controversial symbol of partnership between the two cultures.

In 1907, New Zealand became a dominion of the British Commonwealth. As such, it gained independence but retained the British Crown as

Prepared especially for *Comparative and International Criminal Justice, 2/E.*

the titular head of state. Then, as now, no law in New Zealand could be ratified without the approval of the Crown's local representative, the governor-general. New Zealand, in fact, has kept close links with Britain and has emulated Britain in many areas of its development. Its parliamentary system, for example, is similar to that of Britain, with a prime minister as head of government. Ministers of the Crown, who control areas such as finance, social welfare, and justice, are all elected members of Parliament. Permanent staff, who are appointed public servants, run the departments that ministers head.

For many years, New Zealand was a recognized world leader in social policy. In the late 1930s, in the wake of the Great Depression, a Labour government began to create a worker-oriented, social-democratic state. By 1940 such benefits as free health care, accident compensation, sick pay, old age and disability pensions, child-care, liberal unemployment benefits, and free college education had been instituted. These remained until 1984 when another Labour administration began to abandon Keynesian economics in favor of laissez-faire monetarism. One result has been increased economic efficiency and hugely reduced inflation levels. Another has been social dislocation and poverty in the lower strata. Between the mid-1970s and the early 1990s, unemployment rose steadily, exceeding ten percent in 1993. Unemployment has since dropped to about seven percent, but crime, particularly violent crime, continued to rise until about 1996 before stabilizing and even declining somewhat. As we shall see, harsher measures introduced to control violent crime have generated pressure on corrections that is still being felt today.

The History of New Zealand Corrections

Early Developments (1840–1909)

Before 1840, social control in New Zealand was maintained by native custom or by ad hoc measures that varied according to the power and interests of various groups (Hanson and Hanson, 1983; Owens, 1981). The signing of the Treaty of Waitangi brought all New Zealand inhabitants within the scope of imperial law, but it was not long before the new colony began drafting legislation of its own. Initially, following the laws of Britain, those sentenced in New Zealand courts could be publicly hanged, publicly flogged[1] (if male), transported (to the penal colonies in Australia), imprisoned with or without hard labor, or fined (Pratt, 1992a: 74–5). Transportation ceased in 1854, when the Secondary Punishments Act translated all sentences of transportation into terms of penal servitude (Engel, 1982: 12).

Lockups were locally administrated, but a prisons ordinance in 1846 attempted to standardize the running of New Zealand lockups by empowering the governor to set regulatory and administrative principles for the whole colony. A punitive model, similar to that of Britain, was followed. The Secondary Punishments Act was the country's first independent attempt at creating a national penal policy. This act required all prisoners to work at hard labor, often on public works, during the course of their sentences. Prisoners at work were generally forbidden to talk (Pratt, 1992a: 78).

In reality, the administration of prisons and sentences was disorganized, often chaotic. Legislation was unclear and contradictory. Management of lockups was inconsistent, incompetent, and corrupt. A procession of criticisms about these matters by government committees and judges in the 1860s led, in 1876, to a decision to centralize the penal system and to appoint an experienced overseas officer (Mayhew, 1959: 22–30; Pratt, 1992a: 109–130). Accordingly, in 1880 Captain Arthur Hume, formerly deputy governor of a number of British institutions including Dartmoor and Wormwood Scrubs, was appointed inspector-general of New Zealand prisons.

Hume rationalized the New Zealand penal system and laid correctional foundations, some of which remain today. Mt. Eden Prison, which served as the country's maximum-security facility until 1965 and still operates today, was designed and constructed under Hume. The first experiments with public-works prison camps were undertaken under Hume in 1890 and 1901. He ceased the use of ship hulks as prisons in 1891. Trade training, classification, and graduated privilege systems were introduced. These measures were supplemented by parliamentary activity. The First Offenders Probation Act of 1886, which established the first national probation system in the world, was passed. Also legislated was the Criminal Code Act 1893, repealing the Secondary Punishments Act. The Criminal Code Act abolished the sentencing of prisoners to solitary confinement and introduced the option of imprisonment with or without hard labor.

In spite of these advances, however, Hume's overall philosophy, following British tradition, was narrow, rigid, autocratic, and punitive. For him, the function of imprisonment was primarily deterrent. Accordingly, Hume reinforced the rule of prison silence. He reduced inmate rations. He opposed the abolition of corporal punishment in prisons. To add to their punitive effect, all prisons designed during Hume's time and for more than 60 years thereafter were built without toilets in the cells. Hume's overriding concern with discipline brought him many critics, whose numbers increased as his reign progressed. By the end of his tenure, the country was ready for change. Thus, when Hume eventually retired in 1909, Parliament wasted no time in freeing the penal system of its Victorian shackles.

The New Method (1910–1949)

The first move out of the Victorian Era was the Crimes Amendment Act of 1910. Following the example of Elmira Reformatory in New York, this act created the indeterminate sentence of reformative detention (0–3 years or 0–10 years, depending on jurisdiction) and established a prisons board to preside over matters of parole. Under what became known as "the new method," classification was refined and an emphasis was placed on educating, training, and treating inmates on an individual basis. Teachers were appointed, libraries were enlarged, and lighting and general conditions were improved. A rural work program was established, and between 1910 and 1922 tens of thousands of acres of land were purchased for development into prison farms. Overall, security was de-emphasized. By 1913, the general issue of firearms to officers had been discontinued and distinctive arrow-shaped markings were being removed from inmates' clothing. Between 1910 and 1923, the ratio of inmates employed in outside work schemes grew from eight to 70 percent.

Special programs were created for particular types of offenders, and eleven classes of criminal were identified (Pratt, 1992a: 204). In addition, there was provision for juveniles. Segregation of younger offenders had begun in 1910 and the first juvenile correctional facility, known as the *borstal*, was established in 1917. It was patterned on a youth institution that had opened in the village of Borstal, Kent, England, in 1908, itself influenced by Elmira. The borstal program featured a special emphasis on education, sport, recreation, and cultural activities (Webb, 1982: 37–44). In 1924, a specific borstal sentence was legislated. The borstal term became indeterminate, involving 2–5 years in cases sentenced in the Supreme Court; 1–3 years in those of the Magistrates Court. Borstal training was restricted to persons aged 15–21.

After 1924 New Zealand entered a fallow era, during which a conservative permanent head of prisons, the depression, and the Second World War effectively prevented further progress in correctional policy (Newbold, 1989: 5–13). The only major development was the abolition of capital punishment for murder in 1941 (see Newbold, 1990). This fallow era came to an end in 1949 with the appointment of a new permanent head of justice and prisons.

Later Developments (1950–1989)

In 1950 a period of penal reform, similar in its style and power to what had occurred after 1909, began. Energized by 25 years of stagnation, the 1950s brought some of the most imaginative penal developments that the country has seen.

Between 1950 and 1955, full-time welfare officers were appointed to prisons and inmate commissaries were established. Hours of cell confinement were reduced, recreation was increased, and education services were rationalized and improved. For the first time, newspapers were permitted into prisons. Unsupervised visits, communal dining, discussion groups, and inmate recreation committees were allowed in most institutions. The community was encouraged to become involved as well. Initially, sporting, recreational, and cultural groups met with inmates on their home turf, but by early 1952 outside excursions, even by maximum security inmates, had begun (Newbold, 1989: 34–39).

Alongside provision of better conditions for inmates, attempts were made to professionalize the prison service. Wages and uniforms were improved. A centralized staff training college was set up, and specialist classification committees were created within prisons. Full-time school teachers and psychologists were appointed, and each institution gained access to a chaplain (Newbold, 1989: 34–39).

These changes were administrative, but there were legal moves as well. The Criminal Justice Act of 1954 repealed the sentences of hard labor and reformative detention. A law called the Habitual Criminals Act of 1906, which had allowed persistent offenders to be incarcerated indefinitely, was repealed. In its place came preventive detention, permitting persistent offenders over the age of 25 to be held for between three and 14 years, or for three years to life in the case of sex crimes. The Criminal Justice Act also extended the powers of the probation service and made specific provisions for the custody and release of various categories of prisoners. It tightened restrictions on youthful incarceration, redefined borstal training as a sentence of 0–3 years for youths aged between 17 and 21, and created a similar sentence for those aged 21–30, called corrective training. In addition, the Criminal Justice Act legislated New Zealand's first boot camps, which were known as detention centers. When they were eventually established in 1961, detention center training involved a three-month term of rigorous activity and strict discipline for young men aged 17–21.

After 1955, rising prison numbers, leading to chronic overcrowding and crises within maximum security, and a timorous Labour government (1957–60) stultified further growth (see Newbold, 1989: 47–56; 63–67; 89–97). But in 1960 an incoming National government, together with a bold partnership between the new minister, J. R. Hanan, and the permanent head of justice, J. L. Robson, allowed the surge of reform to continue.

In the 1960s, some new developments evolved from measures created by the legislation of 1954. The establishment of detention centers in 1961 is one example. Another is home leave, which began in 1965. Initially restricted to married inmates only, since 1975 home leaves of 72 hours every two months have been generally available to minimum-security prisoners, who constitute 52 percent of the sentenced population.

But many of the initiatives taken in the 1960s were new. A release-to-work scheme for inmates nearing completion of their terms began in 1961. Within institutions, the general rule of silence, over a century old and by then seldom observed, was formally done away with the same year. A policy of full privileges for all inmates on admission was commenced. Group therapy and inmate counseling began. A model prison for adult first offenders was established at Wi Tako (later known as Rimutaka) in 1964. The borstal sentence was reduced to 0–2 years; and an extra one-twelfth remission, effectively increasing the standard remission of one-quarter to one-third of the sentence, was made available for exemplary conduct. Preventive detention for nonsexual offenders was removed but a ten-years-to-life term remained for adult sexual recidivists.

In 1961, the penalty of bread and water for prison misconduct was done away with and replaced by two, more liberal grades of restricted diet. Punishment diets were abolished completely in 1981. Also in 1961, the use of firearms to stop rebellious or escaping prisoners was limited and defined. The latter adjustment was particularly necessary at this time because of a change in the law relating to capital offenders. As noted, capital punishment for murder had been struck out in 1941, but community pressure forced its reintroduction in 1950. However, eight hangings in the 1950s dampened public fervor, and one of Hanan's residing passions was abolition. Accordingly, in the Crimes Act of 1961 the penalty was removed again and replaced by a mandatory life sentence with a ten-year minimum (see Newbold, 1990).

Apart from capital punishment, two other major changes occurred in relation to sentences. As a result of disuse through overcrowding, corrective training ceased in 1963. And in what was one of the world's first, a weekend imprisonment program began in 1963. Known as periodic detention (PD), the penalty was intended as a diversion from prison for nonserious male young offenders. Hostels were established for the purpose of holding detainees from Friday night to Sunday, with employment in community and public work. The scheme was extended to adult males in 1966 and to females in 1974. Adult PD programs were never residential and were restricted to Saturday work only. By 1980, due to expense, juvenile programs had merged with the adults' and became one-day-only as well. Notwithstanding, periodic detention proved one of the most successful innovations of the 1960s and became a major feature of New Zealand's correctional landscape.

In 1965, Mt. Eden Prison suffered a destructive riot, ending its role as the country's maximum-security prison. For the rest of the 1960s there was little more progress in corrections, as public attention and justice department energy became concentrated on the construction of a new high-custody facility at Paremoremo, north of Auckland. Hanan died in 1969, and Robson resigned the following year. But by the beginning of 1969, with Paremoremo receiving its first inmates, the structure of New Zealand's correctional program was set. Unlike the dynamic surges that had characterized the 1950s and 1960s, change now was slower and more piecemeal. In 1975, one-third remission became standard for all minimum-security prisoners, and parole eligibility at half sentence was given to those serving five years or more. The nonparole period for lifers and preventive detainees was cut from ten to seven years. It was raised back to ten years in 1987.

There also were some developments for youthful offenders. High recidivist rates prompted the abandonment of borstal training between 1975 and 1980. In 1980, all hitherto existing borstals became redesignated as youth prisons, with their inmates serving fixed terms. Detention centers were abolished too. Due to high levels of reoffending, detention center training was scrapped in 1981. In its place came an almost identical sentence of shock incarceration called corrective training (no relation to its namesake of 1954–63). The new corrective training proved even less effective than the detention center in curing criminality (Walker and Brown, 1983) and was repealed in 2002.

In the 1970s, home-leave provisions were gradually relaxed and work parole was expanded. Periodic detention was extended to include women, but rising costs eventually restricted it to daytime attendance. A variation of periodic detention, in the form of a sentence called community service, came in 1980. Less punitive than periodic detention, community service orders required an offender to do voluntary work in the community. The type and timetabling of the work was set in consultation with the justice department.

In 1985 the Criminal Justice Act of 1954 was replaced. The Criminal Justice Act of 1985 consolidated the extensive amendments to the 1954 statute and added some new provisions. One intention of the act was to cut a prison population that had grown by nine percent in the previous four years. A general restriction was placed on imprisonment of property offenders, who were not to be imprisoned other than in exceptional circumstances. To assist the courts in this endeavor, another community option was created: community care (later called community program), by which offenders could be sentenced to the custody of community organizations or private community-based treatment facilities. Finally, parole provisions were broadened. In October 1985, parole became available to all prisoners at half sentence, or after seven years. This caused an immediate surge of inmates into the community, so that by February 1986 the national muster had dropped to 2,217—its lowest point since 1970 (*NZ Herald*, February 13, 1986).

In the long run, though, the attempt to cut prison musters was a failure. The restriction on jailing property offenders never really worked. One reason was that many defaulted from community sentences and finished up in prison anyway (Spier and Luketina, 1988: 161). A second reason was the increasing sentences for violent crime after 1986 and a virtual removal of parole eligibility for violent offenders in 1987 (Newbold, 2000: 115–116). Third, although parole changes in 1985 caused a flush of early releases, many parolees soon reoffended and returned to prison (*NZ Herald*, May 13, 1986). Thus, within 13 months, prison numbers were higher than they had been when the law took effect in October 1985 (*NZ Herald*, November 14, 1986).

One intention of the new law had been to toughen up on violent offending, convictions for which had grown by 24 percent in the previous four years. So the act mandated imprisonment for nearly all violent and serious sexual offenders. But violence persisted and constituted a rising proportion of cases (see Newbold, 2000: 110–154). The amendment in 1987 that restricted violent offenders' parole eligibility also increased the nonparole period for murder and preventive detention from seven to ten years. But the violence continued, with overall convictions growing another 30 percent between 1984 and 1991 (Spier, Norris and Southey, 1992: 28). Accordingly, prisons began to fill with the accumulated bulk of violent and serious sexual offenders, so that by 1991 they constituted half of all prison inmates (Braybrook and Southey, 1992: 49). A further amendment in 1993 made preventive detention available for nonsexual violent offenders; allowed the parole board to keep in prison beyond their earned remission dates those serious violent and sexual offenders considered likely to reoffend; and allowed courts to sentence violent offenders, lifers, and preventive detainees to serve minimum terms longer than those set out in law. As a result, by November 1999, the percentage of inmates in prison for violent or serious sexual offenses had increased to 62 percent and the prison population was at an all-time high of 5,647 (Rich, 2000: 11, 18). Thereafter the percentage continued to rise; in fact, by early 2002 the prison muster of over 6,000 was nearly three times the low of 2,217 recorded in February 1986.

In 1999, yet another addition to what became known as the "violent offenses legislation" was made. This was the home invasion law, which mandated add-ons of three or five years (depending on the crime) to the sentences of violent criminals who committed crimes after having invaded a private home. Widely seen as a vote catcher for the 1999 general election, the home invasion law was dropped in new laws passed in 2002. These new laws were the result of a national referendum on violent crime that had accompanied the general election of 1999, in which 91 percent of respondents had favored even tougher penalties for violent offenders. Three years later, with another election looming, in 2001 the liberal Labour-Alliance coalition government attempted to respond to the referendum by drafting new laws relating to the sentencing and parole of offenders. Presented as "get tough" legislation, the Sentencing Act of 2002 and the Parole Act of 2002 tightened some aspects of law—for example, by extending the nonparole minimum available for some types of murder—but actually relaxed other laws (for example, by liberalizing parole provisions for many violent offenders). The two new acts repealed the majority of provisions contained in the Criminal Justice Act of 1985 and came into effect on July 1, 2002. Falling short of their expectations, it was received derisively by truth-in-sentencing hard-liners.

Current Trends in Community Corrections

The Criminal Justice Act of 1985 had attempted to modify the pressure that would be created by mandatory imprisonment of violent offenders by emphasizing noncustodial alternatives for the nonviolent. At the same time, rising unemployment in the 1980s made the courts likely to favor community sentences over fines (Spier, Norris and Southey, 1992: 42). This increased the pressure on what is now known as the Department of Corrections' Community Probation Service. Persons under the jurisdiction of the service more than tripled between 1985 and 1989, to 48,500 (*AJHR** E.5, 1987: 42; Statistics NZ, 2000: 251). In 1999, for every person in prison there were more than eight serving community sentences and more than six serving community sentences other than supervision or parole (Statistics NZ, 2000: 251).

The Community Probation Service administers a number of noncustodial or postcustodial treatment measures. In recent years these have included: probationary supervision, post-release supervision, periodic detention, community service, community programs, and home detention. It also oversees the administration of privately run habilitation centers.

Probationary Supervision

In 1985, the community sentence of probation was renamed *supervision*. Since then its use has declined slightly relative to other measures, as a result of an expansion in community-based options. Thus, between 1985 and 2001, the number of individuals sentenced annually to probationary supervision grew by only 37 percent to 8,313 (*AJHR* E.5, 1987: 41; *AJHR* E.61, 2001: 49).

A sentence of supervision in New Zealand can be set for any period of between six months and two years. Persons serving such sentences can live at home but are subjected to monitoring by probation personnel. Judges and probation officers can set rules that closely control an individual's activities and behavior: associates, spending, employment, and residency all can be regulated as conditions of supervision. Judges may prohibit alcohol consumption for probationers and require attendance at alcohol, drug, or other types of programs. Thirty-two percent of probationers fail to comply with the conditions imposed by the courts, and within twelve months 40 percent reoffend badly enough to be sentenced to further correctional control (*AJHR* E.61, 2001: 49).

New Zealand has a centralized offender supervision system that is divided into three regions, each with five areas. Sixty-nine percent of the 878 staff employed by Community Probation are probation officers.[2] These officers deal with all cases of supervision and parole, in addition to writing presentence reports and administering community sentences.

Probation officers are not sworn officers of the law. They can make summary arrests for parole violations, but they cannot obtain search warrants, order urine tests, or carry weapons. The majority liken their role to

---

* AJHR (*Appendices to the Journals of the House of Representatives*) are held in most large public and university libraries in New Zealand. The best way for an overseas person to access them is through library interloan.

that of social service brokers. As a whole, probation officers are highly respected by the courts, and about 80 percent of their sentence recommendations are followed by judges.

Post-Release Supervision

Since 1993, all inmates serving more than twelve months imprisonment who have been discharged before the expiration of their full terms have been released on conditions. There are two types of early release in New Zealand: remission (which is automatic) and parole (which is discretionary). Release conditions are administered by Community Probation and may apply up to the expiration of the full term and usually for at least six months. Those sentenced to preventive detention or life remain on parole for the rest of their lives. Release conditions are of two types: standard and special. Standard conditions apply to all sentences of over twelve months and involve regular reporting to a probation officer and compliance with his or her directions. Additionally, in all sentences including those of twelve months or less, a variety of special conditions may be stipulated. Among other things, these conditions may require an offender to live under home detention or in a residential treatment program.

Prior to July 2002, and provided they had not lost "good time" through disciplinary infractions, offenders sentenced to finite terms of more than twelve months imprisonment were automatically released on remission after two-thirds of sentence. If they were nonviolent offenders, they were also eligible for discretionary release on parole after one-third of sentence. In 1987 most violent offenders became ineligible for parole and thus served two-thirds of their sentences before being released. Under the Parole Act of 2002, automatic release has been abolished for all except those serving two years or less, who are released at half sentence. All other offenders serving finite sentences, including violent offenders, are now eligible for parole after serving one-third of their time or ten years, whichever is the shortest, unless a longer nonparole period has been set by the court. Those serving life are paroleable after ten years, unless a longer nonparole minimum has been imposed. In cases of murder, where at least one aggravating factor is present (such as lengthy planning, extreme brutality, or the victim being a police or prison officer), the minimum nonparole period is 17 years. Life imprisonment is mandatory for murder and is discretionary in the cases of manslaughter and trafficking in Class A drugs (such as heroin, cocaine, and LSD). Those serving preventive detention are paroleable after five years unless a minimum has been imposed. (Before July 2002 the minimum was ten years.) Preventive detention is available to offenders aged at least 18 who commit serious violent or sexual crimes and who are deemed by the court to constitute an ongoing threat to the community.

In recent years, 28 percent of parolees have breached the conditions of their parole. Of those paroled before their two-thirds remission dates, 17 percent reoffended seriously enough within twelve months of release to be sentenced to further correctional control. Of those denied or ineligible for early parole, 46 percent reoffended within twelve months and required further correctional control (*AJHR* E.61, 2001: 53).

Before the Parole Act of 2002, parole determinations in New Zealand were carried out by two separate authorities: district prisons boards for inmates serving less than seven years, and a national parole board for all others. From July 2002 these were replaced by a single authority known as the New Zealand Parole Board (NZPB), which is an independent statutory body appointed by the attorney-general. The chair is a sitting or retired high court judge supported by at least nine panel conveners, who are sitting or retired district court judges. In practice, parole hearings are generally heard by delegated parole panels of at least three members, including the panel convener, who presides.

Just as it decides over matters of release, the NZPB also adjudicates over recall. In doing so, it acts on applications made by the chief executive of corrections (in the case of nonfinite sentences) or by probation officers (in all other cases). Inmates on parole who reoffend, breach their parole conditions, or present an undue risk to the community may be recalled up to the expiry of their sentences. In addition, offenders convicted in court of breaching parole conditions can be imprisoned for up to one year and fined up to $2,000.

Although the consequences of breach are different, the conditions of probationary and parole supervision are quite similar. In June 1999 there were 9,945 persons undergoing probationary supervision in New Zealand and another 2,368 on parole: a quarter of all those under the jurisdiction of Community Probation (Statistics NZ, 2000: 251). This was a 50 percent jump on the numbers reported on probation or parole in 1985 (*AJHR* E.5, 1987: 42). These 12,313 individuals on supervision or parole yielded a rate of 1:309 mean population. As of December 1999, there were 3.8 million persons on probation in America and another 713,000 on parole (Mays and Winfree, 2002: 228; 230). Combined, these yield a rate of 1:60 mean population. In other words, in terms of population, the United States has roughly five times as many persons on probation or parole as New Zealand. The extension of parole supervision responsibilities under the new law means that New Zealand's ratios will almost certainly rise in the near future.

Periodic Detention/Community Work

Pioneered in 1963, periodic detention (PD) was the oldest and most successful of the country's noncustodial alternatives until its abolition in the Sentencing Act of 2002. It was also the most popular, accounting for over half of all those on community sentences. Approximately a quarter of all offenders convicted of an imprisonable offense received periodic detention (Triggs, 1999: 72). The sentence allowed a periodic detainee to be kept in PD custody for up to nine hours on any one day for up to 15 hours a week, during a period of up to twelve months. In practice, the bulk of periodic detainees reported at a PD work center. Accompanied by a PD warden, they went out in gangs of about ten to work, unpaid, on community projects such as scrub cutting, maintaining parks, and cleaning government buildings.

The number of persons sentenced annually to PD grew by 83 percent between 1985 and 2001, to 20,433. Approximately 70 percent of those who received periodic detention completed their sentences, and those who defaulted could have their terms extended or be sent to prison for up to three months. Because PD centers needed to provide transportation and food to workers, and because they hired wardens independently of probation staff to supervise, PD was one of the most expensive of all community programs to run. Sixty-nine percent of all periodic detainees successfully completed their sentences, and half reoffended seriously enough within twelve months of completion of sentence to require further correctional control (*AJHR* E.61, 2001: 50).

Although legally abolished, in practice periodic detention continues within a new sentence called community work. Community work is available to offenders convicted for an imprisonable offense, for whom prison is deemed too severe a penalty. It allows an offender to be ordered to perform between 40 and 400 hours of unpaid community work, much of which is organized through the former periodic detention centers (renamed community work centers), supervised by community work wardens.

Community Service/Community Work

Another sentence that has been abolished by the Sentencing Act but has been incorporated within the provisions of community work is community service. Designed as an alternative to PD in 1980, community service empowered the courts to order a convicted person to perform up to 200 hours of specified charity work within the community. There was flexibility over when the hours were worked and, because it was administered by probation officers, its per capita costs were only 40 percent of those of PD. Under the new sentence of community work, administration by probation officers remains, but it is they, not the courts, who decide what form of work an offender shall be assigned. As noted above, the maximum term of service an offender can be required to provide has been increased to 400 hours.

Community service could not be imposed without the consent of the offender, and in this respect it is different from community work. In other areas, however, it is similar, and probation officers make the decision about who should serve their sentence at a work center and who would be better suited to some other form of unpaid service. Certainly, community service was used increasingly as an option in its later years, and this may also prove to be the case with community work. Thus, between 1985 and

1999, use of community service jumped nearly fourfold. In June 1999, approximately 11,000 persons were subject to community service orders, about 23 percent of whom were serving community-based sentences. About nine percent of all offenders convicted of an imprisonable offense were sentenced to community service (Triggs, 1999: 84). Twenty-nine percent of all offenders who got community service failed to complete their sentences, and 19 percent reoffended seriously enough within twelve months of sentence completion to require further correctional control (*AJHR* E.61 2001: 46).

Community Programs

Established in 1985 as community care, this was another innovative type of sentencing in New Zealand's correctional repertoire. Community programs involved placement of offenders with groups or assigned them to individuals who provided supervision, education, or other assistance to help integrate them to society. The sentence required the consent of the offender and could be awarded for up to twelve months, with up to six months being residential.

Also considered a "soft option," community care/programs were not used to the extent that had been hoped for. The sentence was cheap to run, but the number serving such sentences fell considerably in the 1990s due to economic constraints and a decline in service providers. Whereas in June 1995 there were over 1,000 people on community programs, this had dropped by almost two-thirds by 1999, to 365 (Statistics NZ, 2000: 251). That year, community program clients accounted for less than one percent of those under the jurisdiction of the Community Corrections Division, and only one percent of those convicted of an imprisonable offense got the sentence (Triggs, 1999: 91). Twenty-nine percent of those given community sentences failed to complete their sentences, and 37 percent reoffended seriously enough within twelve months of completion of sentence to require further correctional control. Community programs were abolished in the Sentencing Act of 2002, although provision for offenders to be placed in residential care now exists under the terms of supervision.

Home Detention

A recent innovation to the community corrections repertoire has been home detention. First mooted in 1991, legislated in 1993 and piloted for two years commencing 1995, home detention originally allowed for the electronic monitoring of certain offenders in their homes toward the end of their sentences. In 1997, in spite of a Ministry of Justice report which found that home detention was relatively expensive and its benefits inconclusive (*Dominion*, June 9, 1997), the Minister of Justice decided to expand it. Further enabling legislation was passed in March 1999, and the scheme commenced in full in October. This allowed courts to give leave to apply for release on home detention immediately after commencement of sentence for offenders sentenced to two years imprisonment or less. In other cases, parole boards and district prisons boards were empowered to direct that an offender be subject to a term of home detention as a condition of release. These sentencing and parole provisions have remained under the new legislation.

Heralded as a success, by October 2001, 197 offenders were serving home detention sentences and 1,206 had completed such sentences since commencement of the scheme in October 1999 (*Corrections News*, October, 2001). Of the 388 home detentions granted in 2000, only three percent resulted in cancellation or recall (Spier, 2000: 145). Twenty-seven percent of those given home detention reoffended seriously enough within twelve months of completion of sentence to require further correctional control (*AJHR* E.61, 2001: 51).

Habilitation Centers

A less successful innovation has been the habilitation center. This came as a result of an idea floated in a Ministerial Committee of Inquiry report in 1989 and was established by an amendment to the Criminal Justice Act in 1993. Habilitation centers are small, privately run halfway houses that offer residential treatment programs for parolees released under special conditions and for some offenders sentenced to supervision. Funded on a not-for-profit basis by the Department of Corrections, the first habilitation center contract was awarded in 1996 to the Salisbury Street Foundation in Christchurch, which houses up to 17 residents for as much as twelve months each. Since then, no more than four habilitation centers have operated at any one time, and the majority have failed as a result of mismanagement. By 2002, Salisbury Street was the only successful habilitation center in operation. Fifty-seven percent of those sentenced to a habilitation center fail to complete their terms, and a quarter reoffend badly enough within twelve months of completion to require further correctional control. Part VI of the Criminal Justice Act, which contains provision for habilitation centers, was repealed by the new legislation and no specific reference to centers remains in law. However, the centers continue to be used under the terms of supervision and the operations of the parole board.

Breaches

If persons under the authority of Community Corrections fail to meet their sentence obligations, they can be breached. In the case of probationers and those sentenced to community work, violators can be fined a maximum of $3,000, be imprisoned for up to three months, and/or have conditions of supervision altered. As noted, parolees may be recalled summarily to serve the rest of their sentences.

Because the maximum penalties for breaching conditions of community sentences are small, sentences awarded tend to be lenient. In 2000, only twelve percent of all parole violators and twelve percent of PD violators received prison sentences averaging only two months or less (Spier, 2001: 57). In addition, serious or repeat violators of parole, including those who commit further felonies while on parole, could be returned to prison. Between 1987 and 1997, 40 percent of all lifers released on parole were reconvicted of criminal offenses. Thirty percent were returned to prison (*NZ Herald*, Nov. 28, 1997). Although this rate may seem high, it is in fact comparatively low, since approximately 80 percent of all those released from New Zealand prisons are reconvicted within two years (Spier, 2001: 183) and a third are reincarcerated (*AJHR* E.61, 2001: 29).

Current Trends in Penal Institutions

Operating alongside the Community Probation Service of the New Zealand Department of Corrections is the Public Prisons Service. As a whole, the Department of Corrections operated on a budget of about $447 million in 2001, of which about $396 million was devoted to prisons. Of the 4,317 personnel employed in corrections, more than 3,000 were working in prisons. The Public Prisons Service administers 15 male and three female institutions throughout the country. There are no jails in the American sense. Arrested persons may be held overnight in police cells, but if bail is denied, they are transferred to special remand sections within local prisons after their first appearance in court. In addition, since July 2000 Australasian Correctional Management PTY Ltd has operated a purpose-built 275-bed remand prison in Auckland. This is the only privately run correctional facility in New Zealand.

Compared with American sentences, prison sentences in New Zealand are short. Although average terms have increased by 75 percent since 1981, in 2000 79 percent of all inmates were given seven years or less and the average prisoner served about eight months (Spier, 2001: 75; Spier, Southey and Norris, 1991: 47). The average American inmate who is released actually spends about 30 months in prison. Approximately 8.6 percent of the New Zealand prison population is serving non-determinate sentences of life imprisonment (6.5. percent) or preventive detention (2.1 percent) (Rich, 2000: 17). The majority of these will be released after about twelve years. Although average life sentences are getting longer, in 2002 there were only 25 inmates in the entire New Zealand system who had done more than twelve years on their current terms, and only four who had served more than 15 years. In contrast, there are many American inmates serving very long sentences, approximately 100,000 of whom are serving life sentences (Bureau of Justice Statistics, 1994).

New Zealand prison administration costs vary between institutions and security levels, but in 2002–2003 they averaged NZ$58,000 per inmate, per year (*AJHR* E.61, 2003: 24). Excluding capital expenditures, adult state incarceration costs in America in 2001 averaged about US$26,500 per year

(American Correctional Association, 2001: 18, 42). The spending power of the NZ dollar in New Zealand is roughly equivalent to the spending power of the US dollar in the United States.

As in America, prison populations in New Zealand are at an all-time high. As noted, in 2002 there were 6,000 people in prisons in New Zealand. However, New Zealand penal facilities are small by American standards, with musters of between 41 and 690, and an average size of 333 (see table 1). By comparison, the average population of a correctional facility in the United States is approximately 800 (Bureau of Justice Statistics, 2001), and some, such as the California Institution for Men, have in excess of 6,500 prisoners (*California Department of Corrections Monthly Report*, March 3, 2002). Despite the population surge, New Zealand is committed to the construction of small, 60-bed minimum- and low-medium security units. These units operate as discrete entities within larger administrative complexes. While perhaps more expensive to operate, they are inexpensive to build and permit closer staff-inmate relationships. Such relationships fit in with policy for targeted programs within the case management concept and allow security to be relaxed.

In spite of growing populations, overcrowding has been far less of a problem in New Zealand than in America. This largely has been due to the fact that in 1987, the powerful New Zealand prison officers' union forced standardized wage increases of as much as 15 percent when prison musters exceeded agreed levels, and threatened to strike if they rose too high beyond those levels. As a result, officers were soon receiving between $6 million and $7 million a year in penalty payouts. Anxious to be relieved of the burden, in August 1993 the government bought out the contracted "muster allowance" clause in exchange for a one-off payment of $6,000 per officer. Conscious of the ongoing threat of industrial action and the negative publicity it attracts, the Department of Corrections has made efforts to ease population pressure. One example is the habilitation center; another is home detention. A further measure is the building program. In 2001/02, more than $450 million was projected for building new correctional facilities over the ensuing five years (*AJHR* E.61 SI [01], 2001: 19). Thus, the dormitory-type accommodation that is a feature of many American prisons is virtually absent in New Zealand. Nearly all inmates have their own cells. Partly because of this and partly because of home leave provisions, homosexuality is rare and homosexual rape is almost unheard of in New Zealand prisons (see Winfree, Newbold and Tubb, 2002).

Within prisons, decisions over security and institutional assignment are made by classification committees. Soon after being sentenced, and before being assigned to a particular facility, inmates are assessed in one of nine prisons that have classification committees.[3] These committees assign a numerical score to each prisoner over a range of categories (e.g., offense type, length of sentence, escape history, risk of reoffending) which is entered into a computer that gives the prisoner a security rating. Prisoners are then assigned to an institutional setting consistent with their security status. There are four major security classifications: maximum, high medium, low medium, and minimum. Reassessed every six months, most inmates gradually move to less secure units over time.

There is only one dedicated maximum-security facility in New Zealand. This is Auckland Prison's East Division (informally known as Paremoremo Maximum), built in 1968 on the model of Marion, Illinois. With a design capacity of 240, but seldom holding more than 200, Paremoremo once provided a range of programs and amenities for inmates (see Newbold, 1989). However, a radical policy change early in 1998 led to the introduction of a sentence management system, which involved removal of most freedoms and privileges along with large increases in hours of lockup. Today Paremoremo Maximum provides little more than custodial accommodation for its inmates. In addition, several of the medium-security facilities are over a century old and are limited in what they can offer.

As with community corrections, New Zealand has a history of liberalism in its prison program. Tower guards are never armed and inmates,

Table 1   New Zealand Prisons (as of November 18, 1999)

Men's Prisons	Muster
Auckland East/West	200/426
Mt. Eden	382
Waikeria	830
Hawkes Bay	508
Manawatu	267
New Plymouth	97
Ohura	99
Tongariro	470
Wanganui	407
Rimutaka	424
Wellington	120
Christchurch	712
Rolleston	252
Dunedin	51
Invercargill	147
TOTAL MALE INMATES	5,392
Women's Prisons	
Mt. Eden	45
Arohata	106
Christchurch	79
TOTAL FEMALE INMATES	230
TOTAL PRISON POPULATION	5,622

Source: Rich (2000: 11).

even those in maximum-security disciplinary segregation, are never routinely shackled, cuffed, or chained when they move. Only three percent are held in maximum security. More than half of all inmates are minimum security and as such are eligible, after serving one-third of their sentences or one year (whichever is sooner), to apply for 72 hours home leave every two months. Additionally, nearly all inmates can apply for leave during the final months of their terms.

In some units, flowers and potted plants are permitted, and prisoners grow their own vegetables. Since 1998 a small number of self-care units have been established, where selected inmates reside in four-person apartments inside the prison fences. They live as if at liberty but are employed in prison industries and remain within the perimeter fence. Granted a modest budget, once a week an elected representative is escorted to a supermarket to do the grocery shopping. The existence of incentives such as self-care gives prisoners a stake in stability and lessens prison tensions. The effect is visible in rates of escapes, suicide, and assaults. In 2000–2001 there were only seven breakout escapes (.12/100), five suicides (.08/100), and 48 (.47/100) serious inmate-on-inmate assaults causing serious bodily injury in the New Zealand prison system. These figures compare favorably with those of New Zealand's closest neighbor, Australia (*AJHR* E.61, 2001: 17–22).

A major focus of corrections in recent years has been drug control. In the past, marijuana use was often tacitly overlooked by prison staff, who concentrated on policing more disruptive activities such as alcohol and hard drug use. Gradually, however, policy tightened, with the establishment of trained drug-dog teams in 1996, the commencement of random compulsory drug testing of inmates in 1998, and a comprehensive drug-control strategy in early 1999. Inmates who are caught with drugs, submit a dirty urine sample, or refuse to supply a urine or blood sample for analysis suffer a short term of solitary confinement plus loss of remission, followed by loss of privileges for 27 days and placement on Identified Drug User (IDU) status for a year. IDU-status inmates are prohibited contact visits, are restricted in their movements about the prison, are drug-tested more often, and are more likely to be denied parole. Penalties increase with subsequent detections. In addition to these measures, in 1999 rigorous new visiting standards commenced, requiring all visitors to apply for written official approval before visiting any inmate. From time to time, police and/or prison staff search visitors and their vehicles for drugs, and if any are found, prosecution normally follows.

The consequences of the policy have been dramatic. When compulsory drug testing started in June 1998, approximately 35 percent of all tests were positive. Within five months, this had dropped to 21 percent but has remained about the same since (*Corrections News*, Feb. 1999: 2; Oct. 2000: 6–7; Sept. 2001: 3). A downside of the policy has been that visits have declined. Because of the hurdles placed in front of prospective visitors, there has been about a 25 percent drop in the volume of visitors since the new measures were introduced.

Officially, 34 percent of all prisoners are listed as unemployed, and a large proportion are underemployed. This situation has existed for at least ten years. Unemployment is largely caused by the cost of maintaining supervision and industries within a confinement context, as well as the difficulty in finding stable markets for prison produce in the external community. Apart from maintenance occupations such as in prison laundries, mechanical workshops, and kitchens, medium-security prisoners may be employed in gardening or small workshop enterprises, while the bulk of minimum-security employment is in farming and forestry. There is virtually no work beyond routine housekeeping duties for maximum-security inmates. Since 2000 a change in the focus of inmate employment has occurred, with the department endeavoring to provide employment that will increase an offender's opportunities for obtaining work after release. With the majority of inmates coming from urban areas and the bulk of prison employment designated as rural, it is unclear how this may be achieved. As of March 2002, unemployment levels had not been affected by the new policy.

Employed inmates are paid a small gratuity, usually about $3.00 a week. This money is put into a bank account that is administered by the state in the name of the inmate. Prisoners can access a portion of their savings while in prison, but the balance is paid out on release. Toward the end of their sentences, inmates may be granted up to twelve months (but usually four months) day-parole to work for real wages in the community. Some of these payments are retained by administration for maintenance, and some may be used to cover outstanding fines or reparation orders. The bulk of funds, however, are also paid out to inmates on discharge.

In 1992 a report prepared for the New Zealand Department of Justice concluded that program participation can reduce reoffending (McLaren, 1992). A number of programs are available in prisons, and inmates are encouraged to participate in them. Although they only account for about 14 percent of the nation's population, about half of all convicted inmates have Maori ancestry. Today, in an attempt to address the so-called Maori crime problem, a significant proportion of departmental resources are directed specifically at Maori programs. New Zealand is a highly integrated society, and it is doubtful whether any full-blooded Maori now exist. Moreover, few people speak Maori with any real proficiency. Nonetheless, due to a firm, albeit unprovable, belief within corrections that Maori offending is a result of cultural dislocation, most Maori programs emphasize language training and cultural re-awakening. In spite of well over a decade of experiment with this notion, Maori offending and reoffending rates are as high as ever, and still far higher than those of non-Maori (Spier, 2001: 155; Williams, 2001: 152). The department's latest response to what is known as the *tikanga Maori* (Maori principles) strategy has been to increase the number of Maori cultural programs available in prison (*Corrections News,* June 2000: 3; Department of Corrections, 2001a: 2). In 2001, the department spent $7.9 million on tikanga Maori programs alone (22 percent of the entire rehabilitative services budget), a further $10.23 million on running the Maori focus units within prisons, and $660,000 on other Maori therapeutic models (*AJHR* E.61, 2001: 15). In addition to tikanga Maori, the department also offers programs in "straight thinking," violence prevention, alcohol and drug treatment, sex-offender treatment, employment-skills education, and psychological services. Nationwide, $38 million—8.5 percent of the corrections budget—is dedicated to rehabilitative programs within prisons and community alternatives (*AJHR* E.61 SI [01], 2001: 26). Nonetheless, possibly due to rising inmate numbers and relatively static service provision, the percentage of inmates enrolled in programs has dropped from 68 percent to 43 percent since 1991 (Rich, 2000: 61).

Within prisons, a number of teachers are employed on a contract basis to provide educational services to inmates. In 2000, prison educational programs began to focus on the National Certificate in Employment Skills (NCES), providing $4.245 million a year to provide basic educational services to 800 inmates and vocational training to 1,120 inmates a year (*Justice Matters,* Issue 9, June 2000). Support for other forms of education—such as university study and distance education—was removed, on the basis that demand for such study was small and did not necessarily improve an inmate's employability.

Psychological services are another component of the New Zealand penal program, and use of psychological models to assess the security status of inmates and their risk of reoffending has taken center stage in recent years. The Psychological Services Division's 50 staff members are distributed through eleven separate offices, are actively involved in departmental policy planning and development, and also play a key role in specialist facilities for the treatment of child sex offenders. The first such facility, known as *Kia Marama* (Behold the Light), was opened in 1989 and boasts a 90 percent success rate—more than double that of untreated sex offenders (*Corrections News,* Dec. 2001: 7). A second unit, *Te Piriti* (The Bridge), opened in Auckland in 1994. As initiatives based on psychological models have developed for all types of offenders, reliance on psychological specialists has increased.

Recent Developments in Prisons

In 1990, responding to a Justice Department publication in 1988 and the results of a Ministerial Inquiry into the prisons system the following year, the department embarked on an innovative restructuring of its prison philosophy. Known as *He Ara Hou* (A New Way), the program was fostered by then Assistant Secretary for Justice Kim Workman, who had joined the department in 1989. He Ara Hou created a minor revolution in the organization of New Zealand prisons. With a strong emphasis on rehabilitation, He Ara Hou provided better programs for inmates and attempted a dramatic shift in the philosophy and management of the prison system itself. He Ara Hou had five major components:

1. The objective of rehabilitation was upgraded, to give it a status equal with that of security. Program managers were appointed to all institutions to work alongside security managers.

2. The old military-style prison organization, where five ranking officer levels were headed by a prison superintendent, was abolished. It was replaced with three management levels, headed by a general manager. The wearing of rank insignia by officers was discouraged, and inmates no longer had to wear uniforms.

3. A formal system of unit management was installed in all institutions. Unit management involved dividing prisons into small administrative units of about 60. Creativity in unit managers was encouraged. Managers were given considerable discretion in the way they ran their units, and they made the bulk of day-to-day decisions. This decentralization was designed to encourage teamwork and delegation of authority, and to allow greater line-level participation in operational processes.

4. Case management was formalized. Line staff were encouraged, in addition to maintaining security, to become involved with inmates and their programs. Many staff volunteered to act as case managers, signing contracts with individual prisoners to assist them in the achievement of specific goals. As a result, many officers took a personal interest in inmates and even signed them out for excursions on their days off. Staff and inmates sometimes played together on the same sports teams, organized plays and concerts together, and were often on first-name or nickname terms.

5. Finally, there was a major shift in expectations from inmates. Prisoners were actively discouraged from simply "doing their lags" while they were in prison. They were confronted with the implications of their crimes and urged to participate in correctional activities.

The task of administering He Ara Hou to a body of often cynical correctional officers was difficult and was not without problems. Resistance from some quarters and administrative screw-ups impeded the changeover process; however, significant progress was made. Senior management positions were redefined, and personnel had to reapply for them in terms of new job descriptions. Not all reapplied or were reappointed. One general manager was taken from outside the penal division, a pattern that has often been repeated since. In the case of some positions, inmates were informally consulted in the selection process. More women were hired. Women have worked in male facilities since 1985, and by 2001 women comprised 26 percent of the employment complement of public prisons. The first woman manager of a male institution was appointed in 1992.

The early results of He Ara Hou were encouraging. In its first year there was a threefold increase in the number of inmates completing educational course work. By 1991, nearly a quarter of prisoners were engaged in academic study (Braybrook and Southey, 1992). In addition, there was a 75 percent reduction in misconduct reports and escapes, and suicides fell to about 1.13 per 100,000 (Department of Justice, 1991; *Dominion*, May 15, 1993). In 1992–1993, there was a total of only 34 assaults by inmates on staff in the entire country (*Corrections Operations*, Dec. 1993). In addition, inmate governing councils were formed, segregation units were desegregated, and club activities—many involving outside participants—rose dramatically.

In truth, however, the effects of He Ara Hou were never systematically analyzed, and its real achievements were less illustrious than the department's publicity plugs suggested. Within the department there was a growing feeling that inmates were being given too much license and that prisons were being turned into holiday camps. Heedless of criticism, the idealistic Workman pressed on with his vision, but 1992 and 1993 brought a number of embarrassing scandals, of which two in particular rocked the prison system and drew the whole program into question. The first began at the newly established Hawkes Bay (Mangaroa) Prison in 1992, where allegations of criminal collusion between staff and inmates, sex between a female officer and an inmate, lax procedures resulting in escapes, and brutal treatment of inmates by staff necessitated suspensions and a series of highly critical inquiries. The second occurred in 1993 when two inmates—Brian Curtis (60), serving 18 years for importing LSD, and Michael Bullock (26), serving life imprisonment for murder—escaped from Auckland maximum-security prison. They were not recaptured for several years, and for some time it appeared they had got clean away. Together with a number of other smaller crises involving mismanagement, opponents to the changes successfully blamed He Ara Hou, which became the critics' whipping boy. Certainly, the new system was at least partly at fault, and at the end of 1993 Workman resigned. From there the project he had fostered soon died. Although many of the innovations Workman had encouraged have remained, security and procedures gradually tightened from 1994 onward, reaching a zenith in 1998 when a new and conservative minister of corrections, Dr. Nick Smith, introduced rigorous cell standards nationwide, even prohibiting inmates from having pet parakeets and goldfish in their cells. Inmates at Auckland maximum responded with the first riot the prison had seen in 25 years.

In 1995 the Department of Justice became the Ministry of Justice and a Department of Corrections was established as a separate entity. The chief executive of the new Department of Corrections is Mark Byers, who had previously been deputy secretary (Corporate Services) for the Treasury. The year after his appointment Byers's brainchild, Integrated Offender Management (IOM), was commenced. Combined with a computerized offender recording system (IOMS), IOM was first announced in October 1996 (*Corrections News*, Sept.–Oct. 1996). Since that point, IOM has received extensive and regular coverage in departmental publications and has become the flagship of modern corrections policy. Introduced gradually, IOM became fully operational in July 2000.

IOM retains many of the principles of He Ara Hou, with the difference that it is far more systematic in its application and objectives, and is driven by a psychological perspective. Complex in detail, the principles of IOM are that each offender is assessed on entry to the system, and a sentence management plan is drafted according to a criminogenic needs inventory (CNI) that is applied to meet his or her requirements. Interventions appropriate to the offender are designed with the specific objective of reducing his or her chances of reoffending. As the offender passes through the system, interventions alter to fit changing needs, ending with a reintegration plan to assist successful readjustment to civil life. Central to the plan is an intense 10-week CNI program, administered in the last years of a person's sentence.

Success of IOM rests in a yet-to-be-proven ability to reduce reoffending. The department expects that Maori prisoners and those identified as high reoffending risks (as measured on the department's Risk of reConviction index [RoC]) will be most responsive to IOM, and it is primarily these groups that are being targeted. According to one departmental publication, "offenders who are not ready to address their offending behaviour will receive services to increase their motivation and encourage them to take advantage of other services" (Department of Corrections, 2001b: 11). Exactly what services will be involved in increasing this motivation has not been detailed, although, no doubt, parole will be one tool the department will use to encourage compliance from reluctant starters.

Although IOM was originally designed for all offenders, high running costs have restricted its applicability. In fact, Byers now says that the program is inappropriate for short-termers, young offenders, low-risk offenders, and maximum-security prisoners (pers. comm., 3-20-02). In 2001, only 18 percent of eligible offenders were able to receive it, despite $12 million per annum in expenditure (*AJHR* E.61, 2001: 69). Somewhat optimistically, the department originally expected to cut the reimprisonment rates of those exposed to IOM by between 10 and 15 percent—an improvement of between one-third to one-quarter over existing rates (Department of Corrections, 2001a: 6). Preliminary results show IOM has had little effect, although Byers (pers. comm., 3-20-02) believes that this is because it was tested on a low-risk group. He still hopes to be able to reduce reoffending *among those exposed to IOM* by up to 10 percent. Many staff, recalling the hype and the subsequent failure of He Ara Hou, remain cynical about the new strategy. As this article was being completed, and reminiscent of what happened at Mangaroa ten years before, evidence of corrupt practices, vigilantism, cover-ups, unprovoked brutality toward inmates, and other serious misconduct by certain staff at Christchurch Prison was being heard in the Employment Court (*Press*, May 14; 15; 16; 17, 02).

The Imprisonment of Women

As seen in table 1, The New Zealand Department of Corrections operates three facilities for women: Christchurch (housing 79), which holds principally high- and medium-security intakes; Arohata (housing 106), which caters mainly to low risks and juveniles; and Mt. Eden Prison Women's Division (housing 45) for medium security, pretrial custody, and short stays. With a total population seldom exceeding 230, the female muster is only about four percent of the male. Unlike those of the male prison population, female numbers are quite stable and usually remain below the maximum manageable limit.

The main institution for women is Christchurch Women's Prison (also known as Paparua). This facility is divided into seven areas: maximum-medium security, minimum security, remand (pre-trial) custody, solitary confinement, education, work, and recreation.

The education and work areas at Paparua Women's Prison are very modern and are equipped with clean, spacious rooms fitted with computers or work stations. Recreational provisions include a modern gym as well as outdoor areas where prisoners have gardens. In general, the quality of the physical layout, cleanliness, and habitability of the prison is high. But there is one exception—the solitary confinement unit.

Known as the pound, conditions in solitary are primitive, albeit typical, of solitary confinement throughout the country. The pound at Christchurch Women's Prison consists of four cells in a block, arranged around a cement-floored yard, which is 24 feet by 27 feet in size. Only two of the cells are still used for punishment; the other two are reserved principally for administrative segregation. All cells are of standard size: eight feet by ten feet with a ten-foot ceiling. As in most segregation units, there are no outside windows, no light switches in the rooms, and the punishment cells have no toilets or sinks.

As in men's prisons, women in punitive segregation who wish to use the toilet must use plastic pots or try to attract the attention of an officer by yelling or banging on their doors. During the day, they have no furniture save a sheet of corrugated plastic and, at times, a blanket. Those in punitive solitary are confined 23 hours a day and are unlocked once a day for exercise. They can be held in these conditions for up to seven days by order of the prison general manager, or up to 15 days by order of a justice of the peace acting in the capacity of a visiting justice.[4]

Custody of Young Offenders

In New Zealand, a person under age ten cannot be prosecuted for any offense. Any person under 14 is classified as a child for criminal justice purposes, and children aged 10–13 can be prosecuted only for murder or manslaughter. Most children who commit criminal offenses are handled under the Children, Young Persons and their Families Act (CYP&F Act) of 1989. Offenders aged 14–16 are classified as young people and may be processed under the CYP&F Act, in a youth court, or in serious cases they may be tried and/or sentenced in an adult court. Under the Sentencing Act, offenders under age 17 can be imprisoned only for purely indictable (i.e., extremely serious) offenses. Between 1991 and 2000, the number of young people apprehended by the police for non-traffic offenses grew by 40 percent, to 1,583. A stable average of about 253 a year were convicted in adult courts during this period, with the majority being processed by youth courts. In the years 1991–2000, a total of 30 young people were convicted of murder or manslaughter.

For many years, the prison system of New Zealand has made special provision for young offenders. This began with the establishment of borstal training in 1924 and was followed by the boot camps, known as detention centers, in 1961 (renamed corrective training centers in 1980). Borstal training was abolished in 1980. Borstals were redesignated as youth prisons, but this only lasted a short while, as rising inmate numbers forced them to become used for general purposes, with youth offenders segregated in special units.

Until its abolition in July 2001, corrective training was a three-month sentence of intensive activity and strict discipline, specifically available for young offenders aged 15–20. One month remission was available for good behavior. Initially there were several corrective training centers, but, like borstal, high recidivist rates of between 70 and 80 percent caused them to fall out of favor with judges. Finally only one center remained, as part of the Tongariro complex, and for years it struggled to maintain viability. Between 1997 and 1999, an average of only 48 young offenders got corrective training, and in 2000 there were only 19.

However, since October 1999 four dedicated youth offender units housing 143 inmates have been opened, recognizing a need for young offenders to be dealt with separately from the adult population. Three of these units are smoke-free, and the percentage of positive drug tests returned from the units is close to zero. Although the principles of IOM are being applied in youth units, the chief executive of corrections believes that young offenders are unlikely to benefit from IOM; thus, its future in this context is uncertain.

Prison Population Trends

The approximately 6,000 New Zealand prison/jail population as of February 2002 translates to an incarceration rate of 158 per 100,000. While this ratio is only about one-quarter of the American figure (see Austin et al., 2001), New Zealand does rank high in comparison with other Western nations (Criminal Justice Policy Group, 1998: ch. 5). Of greater concern is the fact that the figures have been steadily increasing in recent years. The prison population as of 2002 (the most recent figure available as of this writing) nearly tripled that of February 1986, and it shows no sign of leveling off. Prison numbers are increasing by more than five percent a year.

One of the reasons for the rise is that more prison sentences are being delivered by the courts. But, as noted, sentence length is also growing, especially for violent offenders. Between 1985 and 2000, the length of the average sentence imposed on violent offenders doubled (Spier, 2001: 43; Spier and Norris, 1993: 62). Longer sentences and restrictions on early release have had little obvious impact on violent offending, convictions for which in 2000 had increased by 92 percent over that of 1985 when the Criminal Justice Act was passed. However, since 1994, convictions have stabilized (Spier, 2001: 14, Spier and Norris, 1993: 28). The proportion of those in prison for violence as their major offense grew from 41.9 percent in 1987 to 61.9 in 1999 (Braybrook and O'Neill, 1988: 41; Rich, 2000: 18).

A number of writers have attempted to explain this rise in prison commitments. Newbold (2000: 24–127; 111–114) argues for a relationship between economic decline and crime rates. Pratt (1992b) and Newbold agree that a combination of unemployment, high expectations, and visible affluence work together and lead to the root sentiments of crime—bitterness, resentment, and jealousy.

For some years, analysts have been detailing a clear ethnic dimension to this trend. Simply stated, Maori offend and are sentenced to prison in disproportionately large numbers. Between 1950 and 2000, the chances of a Maori being sent to prison compared to that of a non-Maori grew from 4.7 times as likely to 9.2 times as likely. At 14 percent of the population, Maori are convicted of 36 percent of all offenses and 45 percent of violent offenses. They are more likely to reoffend than any other ethnic group. As a result, Maori constitute 52 percent of those sent to prison (Department of Statistics, 1991: 19; Spier, 2001: 27, 81, 155).

Maori offending patterns and their subsequent overrepresentation largely have to do with social and economic factors. Maori are more likely to leave school without qualifications than non-Maori, they are more likely to be unemployed than non-Maori, and if employed they tend to work in lower-paid, unskilled occupations. They are more likely to come from large families where the father is absent, to be subjected to serial parenting, and to live in households where alcohol abuse and wife-bashing is a problem. Maori children are significantly more likely than non-Maori to be physically and sexually abused within their families, and they are more likely to be murdered before they reach 14 (Newbold, 2000). Herein lies a critical link in the cycle of Maori offending. Due to cultural and political sensitivities in New Zealand, these problems are seldom acknowledged openly and publicly and they receive little specific attention in the culturally driven, new-age treatment strategies of the Department of Corrections. Without recognition of and attention to these root causes, the solution to the much discussed "Maori crime problem" is unlikely to be found.

Discussion and Conclusion

As New Zealand progresses into the new millennium, its criminal justice system appears to be branching in two directions. On one hand, a scientific psychological treatment model has been devised in an attempt to cut recidivist rates through implementation of IOM. On the other hand, there is continuing public pressure for harsher measures to deal with violent crime, even though rates have stabilized and in some cases are falling. Since 1985 there has been significant toughening in the treatment given to violent offenders, with increased penalties and restrictions on parole. The overall result, we have seen, is a prison population that has continued to rise. By increasing parole recall periods, tightening the standard for prison remission, and lengthening maximum sentences, the violent-offenses legislation has boosted the incarceration trend. The growth in violent crime has not been visibly affected, but these initiatives have nonetheless won wide public approval.

In spite of some hardening attitudes, however, sentences in New Zealand remain quite short and prisons are comparatively benign. Penal institutions still offer a good range of recreational, educational, spiritual, and cultural programs. There is little tension within the walls. There are few escapes and suicides, riots are rare, and serious assaults are few. Overall, New Zealand's institutional programming, the quality of life within its prisons, and its range of community sentences would place it high in the scale of modern correctional systems.

These advances notwithstanding, it must also be noted that correctional programs can have little impact on national crime rates. Individual offenders may be assisted by reintegrative schemes, but the profile of crime itself is determined by political, economic, and social factors, not by correctional policy. Correctional officials, while they may worry about rising crime rates and their impact on musters, are not in a position to explain them. Their major concern is the effective provision of services.

It perhaps goes without saying that correctional officials should seek to maintain a sense of humanity, civility, and tolerance within the facilities and programs they manage. New Zealand's integrated offender management strategy is a serious, albeit untested, attempt to do just that. At the same time, the courts avoid custodial options when community sentences are appropriate. In spite of funding shortfalls, there is continuous attention to the provision of spiritual, recreational, vocational, and educational activity to those in correctional care.

These objectives will, of course, become increasingly difficult to attain if correctional numbers continue to grow without corresponding adjustments in funding. When the population surge occurred in America, security, custody, and operational management began to supersede programs and have continued to supplant them to this day. In New Zealand the quality of programs has likewise been compromised by client increases and sluggish budgetary responses. The impact of this has been mitigated by diverting many away from prison and by building new institutions. All correctional initiatives carry a price tag, and only time will tell if quality service delivery can be maintained in the future.

Notes

[1] Public executions were abolished in 1858. Flogging was abolished in 1941.

[2] The salary range for a probation officer is NZ$35,000 per year, rising to NZ$47,500 per year. For a corrections officer, the scale is NZ$32,825 to NZ$40,325. By comparison, starting police officers make NZ$46,125 per year, rising to NZ$56,246 within the constabulary rank. Note that the purchasing power of the New Zealand dollar in New Zealand is roughly equivalent to the purchasing power of the U.S. dollar in the United States.

[3] The nine facilities that have classification committees are Mt. Eden, Waikeria, Wanganui, Manawatu, Wellington, Christchurch, Invercargill, Auckland Maximum, and Auckland Medium.

[4] The legal situation is in fact more complicated than this because the Penal Institutions Act distinguishes between confinement to a cell (up to 7 days or 15 days in the case of a visiting-justice-ordered confinement), and nonassociated labor (up to 14 days or 28 days if sentenced by a visiting justice). In practice, the two are treated as the same. Nonassociated labor usually means solitary confinement without labor.

References

American Correctional Association (2001). *2001 Directory*. Lanham, MD: Author.

Austin, James, Marino Bruce, Leo Carroll, Patricia McCall, and Stephen Richards (2001). "The Use of Incarceration in the United States." *Critical Criminology*, 10: 17–41.

Braybrook, Beverley and Rose O'Neill (1988). *A Census of Prison Inmates*. Wellington, NZ: Department of Justice.

Braybrook, Beverley and Pamela Southey (1992). *Census of Prison Inmates 1991*. Wellington, NZ: Department of Justice.

Bureau of Justice Statistics (1994). *Comparing Federal and State Prison Inmates*. Washington DC: Department of Justice.

Bureau of Justice Statistics (2001). *Prisoners in 2000*. Washington DC: Department of Justice.

Criminal Justice Policy Group (1998). *The Use of Imprisonment in New Zealand*. Wellington, NZ: Department of Corrections.

Department of Corrections (2001a). *About Time: Turning People Away From a Life of Crime and Reducing Reoffending*. Wellington, NZ: Department of Corrections.

Department of Corrections (2001b). *Better Corrections Law for New Zealand: A Public Discussion Document*. Wellington, NZ: Department of Corrections.

Department of Justice (1986). *Submission to the Committee of Inquiry into Violence*. Wellington, NZ: Department of Justice.

Department of Justice (1988). *Prisons in Change: The Submission of the Department of Justice to the Ministerial Committee of Inquiry into the Prisons System*. Wellington, NZ: Department of Justice.

Department of Justice (1991). *Inmate Deaths in Custody*. Wellington, NZ: Department of Justice (unpublished).

Department of Statistics (1991). *Justice Statistics 1990*. Wellington, NZ: Department of Justice

Engel, Pauline (1982). *A History of Custodial and Related Penalties in New Zealand*. Wellington, NZ: Government Printer.

Hanson, Allan and Louise Hanson (1983). *Counterpoint in Maori Culture*. London: Routledge and Kegan Paul.

Mayhew, Peter (1959). *The Penal System of New Zealand, 1840–1924*. Wellington, NZ: Department of Justice.

Mays, Larry and Tom Winfree (2002). *Contemporary Corrections*. Belmont, CA: Wadsworth.

McLaren, Kaye (1992). *Reducing Recidivism: What Works Now*. Wellington, NZ: Department of Justice.

Newbold, Greg (1989). *Punishment and Politics: The Maximum Security Prison in New Zealand*. Auckland, NZ: Oxford University Press.

Newbold, Greg (1990). "Capital Punishment in New Zealand: An Experiment That Failed." *Deviant Behavior*, 11: 155–174.

Newbold, Greg (1992). *Prison Escapes and Prison Management*. Consultancy Report for the New Zealand Department of Justice (unpublished).

Newbold, Greg (2000). *Crime in New Zealand*. Palmerston North, NZ: Dunmore.

Owens, J. M. R. (1981). "New Zealand Before Annexation." In W. H. Oliver and B. R. Williams (eds.), *The Oxford History of New Zealand*. Wellington, NZ: Oxford University Press.

Pratt, John (1992a). *Punishment in a Perfect Society: The New Zealand Penal System, 1840–1939*. Wellington, NZ: Victoria University Press.

Pratt, John (1992b). "Unemployed Scapegoat in Violent Crime Debate." *Christchurch Press*, March 4, p.16.

Rich, Michael (2000). *Census of Prison Inmates 1999*. Wellington, NZ: Department of Corrections.

Spier, Philip (2001). *Conviction and Sentencing of Offenders in New Zealand: 1991 to 2000*. Wellington, NZ: Ministry of Justice.

Spier, Philip and Francis Luketina (1988). *The Impact on Sentencing of the Criminal Justice Act 1985*. Wellington, NZ: Department of Justice.

Spier, Philip and Marion Norris (1993). *Conviction and Sentencing of Offenders in New Zealand: 1983 to 1992*. Wellington, NZ: Department of Justice.

Spier, Philip, Marion Norris, and Pamela Southey (1992). *Conviction and Sentencing of Offenders in New Zealand: 1982 to 1991*. Wellington, NZ: Department of Justice.

Spier, Philip, Pamela Southey, and Marion Norris (1991). *Conviction and Sentencing of Offenders in New Zealand: 1981 to 1990*. Wellington, NZ: Department of Justice.

Statistics New Zealand (2000). *New Zealand Official Yearbook*. Auckland, NZ: David Bateman.

Triggs, Sue (1999). *Sentencing in New Zealand: A Statistical Analysis*. Wellington, NZ: Ministry of Justice.

Walker, Walton and Robert Brown (1983). *Corrective Training: An Evaluation*. Wellington, NZ: Department of Justice.

Webb, Patricia (1982). *A History of Custodial and Related Penalties in New Zealand*. Wellington, NZ: Government Printer.

Williams, Charlotte (2001). *The Too-Hard Basket: Maori and Criminal Justice Since 1980*. Wellington, NZ: Institute of Policy Studies.

Winfree, Tom, Greg Newbold, and Houston Tubb (2002). "Prisoner Perspectives on Inmate Culture in New Mexico and New Zealand: A Descriptive Case Study." *The Prison Journal*, 82 (2): 213–233.

23

Police in a Correctional Role
Cautioning by the English Police and Its Viability as an Option for Offenders in the United States

Bill Wakefield & J. David Hirschel

As interest in cross-cultural studies has increased, it has become fashionable to look at foreign nations as possible sources for innovations that might have significant practical applications for our own systems of justice in the United States. In particular, because of our shared heritage, many have suggested that we should consider the "lessons to be learned" from the English (Orrick, 1983). While many facets of the English criminal justice system merit attention, the authors of this article, long interested in the issue of transferring criminal justice practices from one country to another, focus on the distinctive English police practice of *cautioning*.

Although English law has long allowed the criminal justice system the option of issuing formal police cautions to juveniles, and since the passage of the Children and Young Persons Act of 1969 actively encouraged such action, research interest in its effects on the reduction of juvenile delinquency in England was not manifested until the 1980s (see, e.g., Farrington, 1980, 1984; Farrington & Bennett, 1981; Myren, 1985; Buchan & Edwards, 1991; Lee, 1994; Willner, Hart, Binmore, Cavendish & Dunphy, 2000; Johnson et al., 2001). Interest in its possible application to the juvenile justice systems in the United States is of even more recent origin (Wakefield, 1983; Wakefield, Caulfield & Kane, 1984; Wakefield & Hirschel, 1988). The key issue is whether the practice of police cautioning as used in England has practical potential for application to offenders in the United States. This article responds to this and other questions by examining the use of the police caution in England, exploring barriers to its transfer to the Unites States, and discussing the policy implications of such a transfer for both juveniles and adult offenders.

Prepared especially for *Comparative and International Criminal Justice, 2/E.*

Police and Juveniles in England

As in the United States, the police in England always have been and probably always will be the first line of contact for troubled youth. In many ways this can be an uncomfortable role for police in both the United States and England, especially when responding to complaints of relatively minor criminal activity. On one hand they are the backup for the major institutions of social control in society, providing assistance to those in need. On the other hand, they are assigned the responsibility for protecting society from delinquent youth when these agencies of social control fail. The decisions made by police officers on the street initiate the entire juvenile justice process in both the United States and England, and it is this application of police discretion in dealing with both juveniles and adults that makes the job of a police officer difficult at times.

The aforementioned conflict between care and control tends to be uppermost in the minds of police officers as they decide what action to take in response to a complaint of minor misconduct, and whether to refer a youth to some agency other than the juvenile court for treatment. In the United States, the practice of referring to other agencies has become known as *police diversion*. In England the police have one more option: the police caution. The practice of police cautioning has gained a great deal of attention on both sides of the Atlantic, primarily due to its distinctive nature and unique method of implementation (Ditchfield, 1976; Farrington, 1980; Farrington & Bennett, 1981; Landau, 1981; Landau & Nathan, 1983; Mott, 1983; Wakefield, 1983; Myren, 1985; Wakefield, et al., 1984, 1988; Pratt, 1986; Giller & Tutt, 1987; Wilkenson & Evans, 1990; Buchan & Edwards, 1991; Lee, 1994; Hirschel & Wakefield, 1995; Willner et al., 2000; Johnson et al., 2001).

The Police Cautioning Process for Juveniles

The police cautioning process in England was originally based on a highly traditional view of what was considered "proper" versus "improper" behavior for young people (Wakefield, 1983:7). Although "precise" police guidelines for its administration were not formulated until 1990 (Home Office, 1990a), the process, as implemented after the Children's and Young Persons Act of 1969, was described earlier as follows:

> When a juvenile is arrested for a crime, he is taken to a police station. The offense is then investigated by the station officer, who must satisfy himself that the charge is supported by credible evidence. The parents or guardians are requested to attend the police station, and in most instances the juvenile is released to their custody. The case is then referred to the juvenile bureau, which collects information about the

juvenile from relevant agencies, such as the probation, education and social services. An officer for the bureau usually visits the offender's home and interviews him together with his parents or guardians. Any police records on the juvenile are also checked. On the basis of all the information collected, the Chief Inspector in charge of the bureau decides whether to prosecute the juvenile in court, to issue a formal caution, or to take no further action. *A caution can only be administered if the juvenile admits the offense, if the parents agree that the juvenile should be cautioned, and if the complainant or victim is willing to leave the decision to the police.* A caution is administered to the juvenile in the presence of his parents at the police station by a senior officer (Chief Inspector or Superintendent) in uniform. The juvenile is warned about his future and reminded of the likelihood that he will appear in court if he offends again. (emphasis added) (Farrington & Bennett, 1981:27)

Cautions can, it should be noted, be cited in subsequent proceedings in juvenile court (Home Office, 1990a:7; 1994a).

As outlined in the 1994 Home Office Circular, there are three aims behind administering a caution: first, "to deal quickly and simply with less serious offenders"; second, "to divert them from unnecessary appearance in the criminal courts"; and third, "to reduce the chances of their re-offending" (p. 6).

The caution has for the most part been used with first-time offenders who have committed minor offenses. The predominant type of offense for which a caution has been issued has been some type of property crime—in particular, theft and handling stolen goods (Johnson et al., 2001). Until 1995 such offenses accounted for 50% to 75% of cautions (see, e.g., McClintock & Avison, 1968; Home Office, 1986:80, 1991:3, 1993:99–102, 1994c:5). Since 1995 that percentage has been declining (Johnson et al., 2001). Younger children have consistently been more likely than older children, and females more likely than males, to have cases resolved through the issuance of cautions.

Cautioning rates vary among the forty-three English police jurisdictions (see, e.g., Home Office, 1986:69, 1993:92–93; Johnson et al., 2001), an issue that has been of interest to British researchers (see, e.g., Ditchfield, 1976; Laycock & Tarling, 1985; Wilkinson & Evans, 1990; Evans, 1993a, 1993b; Lee, 1994). To an extent these variations may be explained by differences in crime rates and the proportion of first-time offenders in the jurisdictions (see, e.g., Ditchfield, 1976; Evans & Wilkinson, 1990) or by the willingness of offenders to admit offenses (Evans, 1993a). "Policy and practice," however, still play their part (Wilkinson & Evans, 1990:169). Evidence has indicated that between 1980 and 1990 the number of young persons cautioned "outstripped" the number found guilty in a court of law (Giller & Tutt, 1987:373; Home Office, 1990b). The 30 percent decrease in the number of those entering court between 1980 and 1985 together with the corresponding increase in cautions has been attributed to net widening and "geographic variations" in cautioning practices of individual police forces (Giller & Tutt, 1987). In addition, the "Home Office Circular 14/1985" issued to all chiefs of police outlining new guidelines for the cautioning of offenders was suggested as a reason for the increase in cautioning rates (Wilkinson & Evans, 1990). Further, these authors suggest that the impact of the 1985 circular led to a "slight narrowing" in geographical variations of cautioning rates (p. 175). While there were great increases in cautions administered in the 1980s and early 1990s, recent statistics indicate that from 1995 to 2000 cautions for all ages, and for both males and females, have been steadily decreasing. It appears that the increase in cautioning in the 1980s and early 1990s has leveled off at the turn of the twenty-first century (Home Office, 2001a; Johnson et al., 2001).

In the early 1990s, a streamlined version of the caution was adopted in a number of police jurisdictions. This version, known as an "instant" or "early" caution (Laycock & Tarling, 1985:25), was less time consuming and less expensive than the full version since it did not require a full investigation, only a record check. Initially, it was aimed at juveniles who had been arrested for the first time for very minor offenses; however, it began to be widely administered to offenders in all age groups. Often the early caution was administered only a few hours after the offense had been committed. Home Office Circular 59/1990 (1990a) discusses the circumstances in which the instant caution should be used, as well as outlining when an informal caution should be given or no further action taken by the police. The circular also notes that it may be helpful to provide formally cautioned offenders with referrals to other agencies or voluntary organizations for assistance with educational, social, and/or drug/alcohol problems (p. 4).[1]

The New Reprimand and Final Warning Scheme

Concerns about wide variations in cautioning rates among police forces and individual offenders receiving unlimited numbers of cautions led to a restructuring of the system for dealing with offenders under the age of 18 (Hine & Celnick, 2001:4). Under the Crime and Disorder Act 1998, a system of "reprimands" and "final warnings" replaced cautions (see sections 65–66). Instituted initially on a pilot basis in five selected jurisdictions, the new system began operating throughout England in June 2000.

"Reprimands" can be given to first-time offenders who have committed minor offenses, with reoffending triggering either a "final warning" or a formal charge (Crime and Disorder Act 1998, Section 65).[2] A final warning requires immediate referral for assessment by a "local youth offending team" and, unless considered "inappropriate," a rehabilitation/change program to treat the dynamics of the offender's behavior (Crime and Dis-

454   Part IV: Corrections, Punishment, and Juvenile Justice

order Act 1998, Section 66). This plan may include contact with the victim and some form of compensation for the victim and/or the community by the offender. The youth offending team, led by a team manager, is comprised of representatives from the police, probation, social services, health, education, drugs and alcohol, and housing agencies. The scheme generally allows for juvenile offenders to be dealt with a maximum of two times without going to court,[3] "but in a structured way that ensures they face up to their behaviour" (Home Office, 2003:4). The intent of the final warning scheme is to divert children and young people from their offending behaviour before they enter the court system by:

- ending repeat cautioning and providing a progressive, meaningful response to offending behaviour;
- providing appropriate and effective interventions to prevent re-offending; and
- ensuring that young people who do re-offend after being warned are dealt with quickly and effectively by the courts. (Home Office, 2002:5)

Unlike cautions, both reprimands and final warnings are classified as convictions.

Research on Juvenile Cautions

Although one study (Tweedie, 1982) found an unusually high rate (83%) of cautioned juveniles who had not re-entered the juvenile system for at least two years, research conducted in the 1980s and early 1990s on the effectiveness of a police caution versus a court appearance generally seemed to indicate that there were no significant differences between cautioned juveniles and court referrals when measured by reconvictions (see, e.g., Mott, 1983; Home Office, 1992:7). However, after passage of the Children and Young Persons Act of 1969 there was a "widening of the net" that resulted in a significant increase in the number of "officially processed" juveniles, even though they may not have ended up in court. In fact, as near as can be measured, there was a disproportionate increase in official processing after the introduction of police cautions when compared to the increase in juvenile delinquency (Farrington & Bennett, 1981:134; Giller & Tutt, 1987; Wilkinson & Evans, 1990). When viewed against the initial objective of reducing the negative effect an official court appearance would have on a juvenile, the upswing in the use of police cautions may have had the undesirable effect of bringing into the system youth who would not previously have been subjected to any type of official processing (i.e., net widening).

Myren (1985:11) suggested that the early research on both sides of the Atlantic yielded the following conclusions concerning police discretion in determining whether to refer the youthful offender to juvenile court or utilize diversionary methods: (1) younger boys (defined in England as under age 12) were less likely to come to the attention of the police and, if they did, were less likely to be prosecuted; (2) girls were less likely to be prosecuted than boys; (3) previous notice, and more certainly previous prosecution, increased the rate of prosecution in the instant case; and (4) there was a correlation between seriousness of the current offense and prosecution. More recent data published by the Home Office (1990b, 1992, 1993, 1994b) indicates that this picture has not dramatically changed. In his overview Myren (1985) concluded that "Police warnings and release in either formal or informal programs does not seem to retard delinquency any more than court processing" (p. 11). Finally, in a three-year study of police cautioning of juveniles, Lee (1994) raises questions about the extent to which the locus of the power to punish has shifted from the court to the pre-court decision makers (pp. 43–54).

After 1995 there was a dramatic decline in research specifically examining the effectiveness of police cautions. In one such study Willner et al. (2000) examined underage alcohol sales by businesses and the probability of future court processing after receiving a formal caution. While cautioning was found to have a minor effect on juveniles illegally purchasing alcohol, businesses were relatively unaffected by formal cautions as they were rarely subjected to criminal prosecution. In a second study, Hoyle, Young, and Hill (2000) found that employing cautions with a restorative element[4] resulted in lower subsequent reconviction and recautioning rates than traditional cautioning.

Another line of research has focused on the attitudes of police officers in England who have actually been involved in the practice of cautioning. Wakefield, Caulfield, and Kane (1984) surveyed a sample of London police officers who had been placed in a quasi-correctional role through their involvement with police cautioning of juveniles. Their perception of its effectiveness as a deterrent to further delinquent behavior yielded mixed results. Older officers involved in administering cautions felt positive about the effectiveness of this procedure and its potential for deterrence. Also, higher ranking, higher salaried, and married officers felt positive about the benefits of a police caution versus a court appearance. However, younger, unmarried police officers felt the practice of administering cautions to young delinquents was "too soft" and constituted a way to "get off" without going to court. The findings of this study appear to indicate that the effectiveness of police cautions may be influenced by the attitudes of the very people administering them: the police. This conclusion is supported by a study of the implementation of two young adult diversion schemes in London, which resulted in only a slight increase in cautioning rates because of negative attitudes displayed toward cautioning by the officers responsible for administering the schemes (Evans, 1993b). Appropriate training was also considered an integral element for success in the restorative cautioning study discussed above (Hoyle et al., 2000). All of this suggests that there is a need to include police training as a factor integral to a successful program of placing police in a quasi-correctional role.

Research on the effectiveness of a police cautioning policy in other countries has mostly indicated results similar to the English experience. In Canada, juveniles warned by the police about future delinquent behavior were just as likely to recidivate as those subjected to a court appearance (Kijewski, 1983). Similar results came about when police warnings were administered to delinquents in Victoria, Australia (Challenger, 1981). A negative result even occurred in a large western city in the United States. "Warned" juveniles were more likely to recidivate than those who had been subjected to a juvenile court appearance (Lincoln, 1976).

As the history of law enforcement has demonstrated, both England and the United States have developed separate bureaus/divisions for dealing with youthful offenders. In England, separate branches (Youth Specialization divisions) emerged where the personnel are trained in the sociopsychological dynamics of young people. New policies and practices were developed concerning cautioning, preventive patrol, and investigation (Tutt & Giller, 1983). Although the jurisdiction of the juvenile court has been modified by decriminalization of certain status offenses, and more offenses are sent to adult court where previously they would have been handled by the police, there continues to be a feeling in England that youthful offenders are unique and require different methods of intervention when they come into contact with the juvenile justice system.

The new reprimand and final warning scheme has not been in existence long enough to draw firm conclusions about its effectiveness. However, there are some encouraging signs in the research that has been conducted thus far. The Home Office reports that in 2001 28,339 young people received final warnings, 70 percent of whom received intervention programs (Home Office, 2001b:5). In addition, a one-year follow-up of a sample of offenders who had received final warnings indicated they committed fewer subsequent offenses than a comparison sample of offenders who had been cautioned. However, no statistically significant difference was found in "further criminal proceeding rates" among those whom the youth offending team had deemed "appropriate" for the "behavioural change program," those deemed "inappropriate," and those not seen by the youth offending team (Hine & Celnick, 2001).

Police Cautioning of Adults

Experience with juvenile cautions led officials in England to institute more widespread use of the caution with other offenders. Although evaluation research had not clearly demonstrated the effectiveness of the caution with juveniles, it was determined that the caution would be an appropriate device for certain adult offenders. In 1983 the Metropolitan

Police in London began using cautions for "drunkenness offenders" (Home Office, 1990b:86). Since 1985, there have been three circulars issued concerning the caution. The 1985, 1990, and 1994 Home Office circulars endorsed the principle enunciated in the Attorney General's report on guidelines for prosecution in 1983 that certain criminal offenses "should not automatically be the subject of prosecution" (Home Office, 1985:9). If sufficient evidence existed that prosecution could take place but would not be in the "public interest," a formal caution was stated to be appropriate (Home Office, 1994a:2). However, the situation would differ from the case of juveniles in that there would not be an automatic presumption in favor of a caution in these types of cases. The 1985 circular (affirmed in Home Office, 1994a:2) listed the following categories of adults as potentially appropriate recipients of cautions:

1. *The elderly or infirm.* The older or more infirm the offender, the more appropriate the use of the caution would be—especially if it were likely that upon conviction only a nominal penalty would be imposed. However, age by itself would not be the determining criterion. There would also be a subjective determination of the "fitness" of the individual to withstand the rigors of a court action.

2. *Young adults.* To be considered would be those between the ages of 17 and 20, especially those without previous criminal convictions.

3. *Persons at risk.* This category would primarily be intended for those suffering from some sort of malady such as mental illness or impairment; and in addition, where it is determined the shock of prosecution might prove fatal, severe emotional distress might result, or severe physical illness would emerge.

4. *Others.* A "catch-all" category, which would allow others not included in the above categories to be issued cautions. In determining the appropriateness of a caution, seriousness of offense, previous record, and the public interest would all be considered, although existence of a previous caution or even a conviction would not preclude a caution in the present case (e.g., if there had been a sufficient lapse of time since a previous caution had been administered to suggest there had been a positive effect on subsequent behavior) (Home Office, 1994a:6).

The 1994 circular reaffirmed the practice of cautioning adult offenders, stating that: ". . . properly used, cautioning continues to be regarded (by the Home Office) as an effective form of disposal, and one which may in appropriate circumstances be used for offenders of any age" (p. 2). Situations in which a caution might be issued could include sexual offenses where the female consented or was a willing participant in the act, minor "victimless" crimes, and minor property offenses. Also to be considered were the potential "deterrent effects" on the offender and the "formal mark" a caution might signify as a symbol of society's disapproval of the offender's behavior (Home Office, 1994a:6).

In addition to describing the target population, the 1990 circular also provided the following guidelines for deciding whether to issue a caution:

1. *Cautioning must not be used as an alternative to a weak prosecution case.*

2. *The offender must admit the offense.* If the offender does not make a clear admission of the offense, then a caution will not be administered.

3. *The offender must agree to being cautioned.* Before the offender can agree to a caution the significance of the caution must be explained; namely, that a record of the caution will be kept and may be used against him/her in a future court case, influencing both the decision to prosecute, and, in the case of conviction, the sentence imposed. It should be noted that a caution can be cited in a court proceeding for a period of up to three years after it was administered. However, careful attention is paid to the manner in which cautions are cited. This is done to ensure that a distinction is maintained between cautions and convictions, and there is no confusion between the two even to the point of not *listing them on the same piece of paper* (emphasis added).

4. *The interests of the aggrieved party will be considered.* This would appear to be consistent with current emphasis on "victims' rights" both in England and the United States. Efforts are to be made to determine the victim's view of the appropriateness of a caution; however, this is not mandatory before a decision is made.

5. *Social services and other agencies should be consulted where appropriate.* This is particularly important where issues of mental fitness and impairment may be involved (Home Office, 1994a:7).

Finally, the circulars detail the manner in which a caution should be administered to an adult offender and encourage consistency between police forces in their use and reporting of police cautions. In most cases, when dealing with the elderly, the infirm, and those suffering from stress, the caution will be administered by an officer of command-level rank in person, in a relatively informal setting (perhaps at the person's home), possibly with a relative or friend present. However, for certain offenders it may be deemed important to have a more "formal" setting (e.g., the police station) and have the caution issued by an officer of the Inspector rank or above (Home Office, 1994a:9). At the conclusion of the caution, the offender should be asked to sign a form confirming consent to the caution and that its significance has been explained. In fact, the 1994 circular particularly stressed the importance of better recording practices for cautions in order to prevent multiple cautions and to achieve greater consistency (Home Office, 1994a:4, 9).

To provide added flexibility to the cautioning scheme and allow for requirements to be tailored to fit the circumstances of the case, the Criminal Justice Act of 2003 provided for the establishment of conditional cautions and directed that the "Secretary of State must prepare a code of practice in relation to conditional cautions" (Section 25).

Examination of annual data on cautioning rates for adult offenders from 1979 through 1989 reveals a significant increase in the use of the caution for summary and indictable offenses[5] for both young adult (aged 17 through 20) and adult (aged 21 and over) males, and for indictable offenses for both young adult and adult females (Home Office, 1990b). The caution was most frequently used for young adults and adults who committed property or minor sexual or drug offenses (Home Office, 1990b:88, 1994c:5). The proportion of those cautioned who were adults (i.e., aged 17 or more) increased from one-fifth in 1985 to one-third in 1988 to over one-half in 1991 (Home Office, 1994b:5). Though these increases permeated the English criminal justice system in the 1980s and early 1990s, current data show that the overall number of cautions given out for all age groups and members of both sexes declined from 1995 to 2000. Indeed, the overall cautioning rate in this period dropped from 40% to 32% (Home Office, 2001a; Johnson et al., 2001).

Issues Affecting Transferability

It would seem appropriate at this point to speculate as to the transferability of the practice of police cautioning to the United States. However, two issues need to be considered before a discussion of another country's application of a police practice to the United States can be undertaken. First, the central features of the practice being considered for transfer need to be discussed. Second, barriers that stand in the way of executing the transfer need to be considered.

The essential features of the caution can be simply described. An offender is administered a stern warning by a senior police official for an offense that he or she has admitted committing. At this point in the process, it would appear as if the police are acting in what amounts to a correctional role. Although police in the United States have long been accustomed to issuing offenders warnings (e.g., traffic warnings, "field adjustments," and even "station releases" without charging), this practice has been carried out on an informal, individual basis by officers in the field. Moreover, the frequency with which such informal warnings have been issued has probably decreased as efforts have intensified to make the police more accountable for any action they take. Formalizing this process and requiring it to be approved through the chain of command might well meet, at least initially, with resistance at all levels of the police in the United States.

From the experiences of England and other countries that have utilized the practice of police cautioning of juveniles in place of a court
appearance,[6] the following items have emerged as significant factors
affecting the use of cautions: age, gender, prior record of the offender, seriousness of the current offense, and the attitudes of police and other criminal justice system personnel. In addition, cultural tradition and
environment would also seem to constitute influential components that
must be taken into consideration when contemplating any transfer of system practices (Wakefield, 1983; Wakefield & Hirschel, 1988). These factors would appear to apply as much to adults as they do to juveniles.

Although Myren (1985:11) noted that England and the United States
pursued similar policies in diverting young offenders in the two decades
prior to that study, there has recently been a shift in the United States in
prosecution practices for serious offenses—with states lowering the age at
which juveniles may be prosecuted in adult courts for such offenses. In
addition, juveniles have not been spared imposition of the death penalty:
consider, for example, the Carla Cooper case in Indiana and the McCleskey
case in Oklahoma, in which both teenagers were sentenced to death. However, it is somewhat ironic to note that in the Columbine, Colorado, High
School Shootings case in 1999, the two young men who committed this
tragic crime would probably have been candidates for a "formal caution"
when they committed their earlier offenses. Had authorities followed the
guidelines for cautions in place in England, the two boys' prior records
would have put them in the "caution" category. The aftermath of this case
and other similar cases suggests that a transfer of the cautioning technique
from England to the United States would require close scrutiny and would
probably encounter intense opposition from the populace as well as from
system officials. For some these cases may indicate the desirability of moving away from leniency for young offenders in the United States, with a
"trickle-down" effect militating against diversion even at the less serious
end of the offense continuum. In any event, there might be resistance from
both the system and society to this type of diversion for youthful offenders,
since it appears to allow them to "get off" with just a lecture from a police
officer as to the errors of their ways (Wakefield et al., 1984:23). Such
resistance might be expected to be even greater if adults were to be the
recipients of this technique of diversion.

When gender is considered, it has long been known that in both the
United States and England the young female offender is likely to receive
lenient treatment from the system. This may point to a viable area for consideration of the use of a caution in the United States. Instead of an outright release for certain types of young females (or males) caught up in the
juvenile (or, in some cases, the adult) justice system for less serious
offenses, the police might have an effective alternative to further court
action with the added tool of a police caution (or the replacement "reprimand" and "final warning" system) at their disposal. This would also

appear to be consistent with one of the goals of diversion, that of advocating less involvement in the formal process of the justice system.

The commission of previous offenses affects the decision to arrest and charge in both the United States and England. In both countries there is a higher probability of arrest and prosecution for those with prior records, and societal attitudes in the United States would appear to continue to support such an approach. However, with the use of a police caution, police in the United States could have another resource when dealing with certain types of juveniles and adults, particularly those with no prior record. The legislature would provide the legal authority and the framework for the issuance of cautions. It would be the task of the police to establish specific administrative guidelines and institute specialized training for officers involved in the decision-making process. In England, the 1994 Circular suggests that in cases where there is doubt about whether a prosecution should be brought, the Crown Prosecution Service should be consulted in order to avoid an offender escaping any censure at all, as the offender might be unsuitable for a caution as well (p. 4). In the United States, this situation could be similarly handled by cooperation between the prosecutor's office and the police.

As noted above, the attitudes of police and other system personnel toward new practices are of prime importance when considering the adoption of a practice from another country. In addition, the cultural and traditional attitudes of the society must also be taken into consideration. Combining these aspects with the variables discussed above, a schematic representation can be derived of factors affecting the potential effectiveness of implementation of the practice of police cautioning of both juveniles and adults in the United States (see figure 1). This gives rise to further discussion of the applicability of police cautions to the United States juvenile and adult criminal justice systems.

Figure 1   Factors Influencing Transferability of English Police Cautioning to United States Criminal Justice System

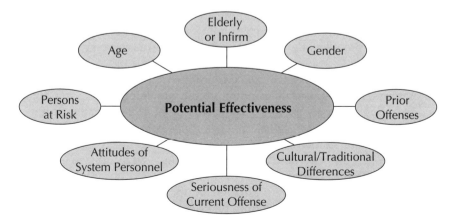

Discussion

The police caution has been used for many years by the English as part of the arsenal of measures designed to combat the incidence of juvenile delinquency and, more recently, crime by adults. It is a measure that is simple in nature and rather inexpensive to administer. Although its effectiveness as a deterrent to further delinquency by the individuals to whom it has been administered is inconclusive, it clearly appears to have met the goals of dealing "quickly and simply with less serious offenders" and "divert(ing) them from unnecessary appearance in the criminal courts" (Home Office, 1994a:6). Its initial popularity was evidenced by the periodic calls for its extension (see, e.g., Laycock & Tarling, 1985) and also by the cautioning statistics, which indicate a great increase in the 1980s and 1990s in use of the caution (see, e.g., Home Office, 1990 b:100–102, 1991, 1993:91; Giller & Tutt, 1987; Wilkinson & Evans, 1990). Of more than passing interest is the fact that of the 321,300 offenders cautioned in 1992 for non-motoring offenses, 216,200 received cautions for indictable offenses. This represents 41% of those charged with indictable offenses (Home Office, 1993:91–2). Though, as we have noted above, there has been a dramatic decrease in the use of the caution since 1995, the cautioning rate (down from 40% in 1995 to 32%: Johnson et al., 2001:1) is still significant. With these figures, it would appear that, given the very real problem of court congestion we face in the United States, even a small decrease in the number of court cases would bring some much needed relief to our criminal justice system. Therefore, it would seem prudent to explore the possibility of utilizing this method of case disposition in the United States.

Often, the social, cultural, political, or economic differences between two countries are so great that they prevent the adoption in one country of measures that have been employed in another. Although there are notable differences between England and the United States (consider, for example, the contrast in criminal homicide rates), the overall similarities between the two countries suggest that there are no such major barriers to the adoption of the English police caution in the United States. This is not to suggest that problems do not exist. Public support is more crucial for the implementation, as opposed to the continuation, of a process. Thus, similar levels of opposition to the police caution on the grounds that it constitutes too soft an approach to crime, while not impeding its continued usage in England, may prevent its adoption in the United States. Still, visits and presentations by English officials could help facilitate understanding and acceptance of the caution, especially if seasoned and respected English police officers, both line and command, were utilized in police training in the United States.

It should be clear that in England the police caution has only been used with any frequency for certain types of offenses and for certain categories of offenders. It has been aimed primarily at the first-time minor property offender. Nevertheless, all such minor offenses in England are not suitable for a caution, and the caution has not been employed as a panacea. Any offense may be considered too serious for a caution if it is racially motivated, caused too great a harm to the victim, involved a breach of trust, or was carried out in a systematic or organized manner (Home Office, 1994a:3). Obviously, the caution is not recommended for serious offenses such as murder, rape, or robbery and should only be used in exceptional circumstances when serious offenses have been committed, such as where a child has taken another's pocket money by force, which by law is a robbery (Home Office, 1994a:2). In addition to authorizing such use only in limited situations, the 1994 Circular emphasizes that the caution should never be used where there is no reasonable expectation that it will serve as a deterrent to further illegal acts (p. 3). Similarly, its adoption in the United States should not be advocated on broad grounds. Rather, its adoption should perhaps be viewed as providing the justice system with another possible disposition for a limited class of offenders.

In England juvenile sentencing options may be available for young people until they reach the age of 21, and cautions may be administered to juveniles who are as old as 20 and, indeed, to adults of all ages. In the United States, however, youngsters in their late teens generally come within the jurisdiction of the adult criminal court, and for a variety of reasons it is suggested that at the present time the caution may not be appropriate for this age group. First, on theoretical grounds it would appear most prudent to begin an experiment using the caution on a younger age group, since they are more likely to have less serious records and more likely (because of their age) to be deterred from subsequent delinquent activity by the deliverance of a stern warning. Second, public opinion is more likely to support the adoption of what may be considered a soft disposition when it is to be used with a young age group. Third, practical considerations make the adoption of the police caution more difficult in the adult criminal justice system. Both the philosophy and procedure of the adult criminal justice system are not as amenable as those of the juvenile justice system to the adoption of a police caution.

Despite these caveats about the adult criminal justice system, it must be noted that the elderly, like the young, constitute a group for whom the caution may be particularly appropriate. In view of the "graying" of the U.S. population, the caution may constitute a useful cost-saving option for elderly persons who have committed minor offenses and who, if convicted, are likely to receive nominal sentences.

It is thus being suggested that the police caution be considered in the United States as an alternative disposition for young, first-time offenders who have committed minor offenses such as petty theft, and for elderly offenders. The use of the caution as an additional method of case disposition could help alleviate some of the heavy burden currently placed on court systems and could prove more cost effective than the court processing of such cases.

The question arises as to what other dispositions the caution might replace. It could be used as an alternative for probation, an overworked disposition which is often given when nothing else appears suitable. It could take the place of fines, which can impose undue hardship, particularly on the elderly poor, or it could take the place of doing nothing. A major concern is that, as happened in England after passage of the Children and Young Persons Act of 1969, the introduction of police cautions in the United States would simply result in "net widening." Close monitoring of the new procedure would enable quick feedback to be given if this were to occur. Remedial action could then be taken if deemed appropriate. Arguably, some net widening may be beneficial. For it is possible that issuing a stern warning is more effective than doing nothing in terms of deterring an individual who has had his or her first brush with the law from indulging in further delinquent activity.

Conclusion

This brief examination of the English police practice of cautioning serves to take yet another step in the process of comparative criminal justice studies. As Adler et al. (1994) suggest, it is important to examine the successful (and unsuccessful) features of the criminal justice systems of other cultures to determine which features, if any, would be appropriate for transfer to our own systems (p. 541). That all countries share at least the commonality of dealing with human beings is reason enough to pursue the examination of comparative practices. The benefit to each system should be apparent if the alleviation of crime and its aftermath is the ultimate result. This should be sufficient motivation to undertake comparative criminal justice research. Concomitantly, this research should follow sound scientific methods and procedures so that, regardless of country of origin, the results can be compared in a standardized format.

Notes

[1] This type of action is referred to as a "caution plus" scheme. With this action, the 1994 circular encouraged the police not to involve themselves directly in negotiating reparation or compensation, but to assist the juvenile in securing support services as part of a more comprehensive program. This was implemented along with the caution (Home Office, 1994a:5).

[2] To assist police in assessing the seriousness of the offense, the Association of Chief Police Officers has established a "Gravity Factor System" under which all offenses are given a score of one, two, three, or four, with one denoting the least serious and four the most serious of offenses. Aggravating and mitigating factors may result in the score being raised or lowered (See Home Office, 2002: Annex D).

[3] There is, however, an exception in that if two years has expired since a previous warning and the offense does not require that the offender be charged, a second final warning may be given.

[4] This took the form of structured discussions of the impact of the offense and what might be done to alleviate that impact with the victim and offender—either meeting each other face-to-face or reading a victim statement to the offender.

[5] The English abolished the division of crimes into felonies and misdemeanors in 1967. They now have indictable and summary offenses. Indictable offenses are roughly equivalent to serious misdemeanors and felonies.

[6] In 2002, Canada implemented police cautions as a diversionary tactic (Youth Criminal Justice Act (Canada) c. 1 sec. 7, 2002). Canada's system is implemented only for youth at this time. In addition, Australia has experimented with many forms of diversion programs since 1980, one of which includes cautioning (Commonwealth Attorney General's Department, 2002). Research on all diversion techniques in Australia (including cautions) has revealed that they have little effect on upward crime trends (Willner et al., 2000).

References

Adler, F., Mueller, G., & Laufer, W. (1994). *Criminal justice*. New York: McGraw Hill.

Binder, A., Geis, G., & Bruce, D. (1988). *Juvenile delinquency: Historical, cultural, legal perspectives*. New York: MacMillan.

Bottomley, A. K. (1985). Guidelines on cautioning—Identifying the principles. *Justice of the Peace*, May 18, 1985, 311–312.

Buchan, I., & Edwards, S. (1991). *Adult cautioning for domestic violence*. London: H.M.S.O.

Cavadino, P. (1985). Two cheers for cautioning circular. *Justice of the Peace*, May 18, 1985, 310–311.

Challenger, D. (1981). Comparison of official warnings and court appearances for young offenders. *Australian and New Zealand Journal of Criminology, 14*(3), 165–169.

Commonwealth Attorney General's Department. (2002). *The review of the Northern Territory Agreement*. Canberra, Australia.

Crime and Disorder Act 1998. Retrieved from http://www.legislation.hmso.gov.uk/acts/acts1998/19980037.htm

Ditchfield, J. A. (1976). *Police cautioning in England and Wales*. London, England: H.M.S.O.

Evans, R. (1993a). Comparing young adult and juvenile cautioning in the metropolitan district. *Criminal Law Review*, 1993, 572–578.

———. (1993b). Evaluating young adult diversion schemes in the metropolitan district. *Criminal Law Review*, 1993, 490–497.

———., & Wilkinson, C. (1990). Variations in police cautioning policy and practice in England and Wales. *The Howard Journal of Criminal Justice, 28*, 155–176.

Farrington, D. P. (1980). La dejudiciarisation des mineurs en Angleterre. *Deviance et Societe, 4*, 257–277.

———. (1984). England and Wales. In M. W. Klein (Ed.), *Western systems of juvenile justice* (pp. 71–95). Beverly Hills: Sage.

Farrington, D. P., & Bennett, T. (1981). Police cautioning of juveniles in London. *British Journal of Criminology, 21*(2), 123–135.

Giller, H., & Tutt, N. (1987). Police cautioning of juveniles: The continuing practice of diversity. *Criminal Law Review*, June, 367–374.

Hine, J., & Celnick, A. (2001). *A one year reconviction study of final warnings*. Sheffield, England: University of Sheffield.

Hirschel, D., & Wakefield, W. (1995). *Criminal justice in England and the United States*. Westport, CT: Praeger.

Home Office. (1970). *Children and young persons' rules, rule #6.* London, England: H.M.S.O.

———. (1985). *Home Office circular 14/1985: The cautioning of offenders.* London, England: Author.

———. (1986). *Criminal statistics England and Wales 1985.* London, England: H.M.S.O.

———. (1990a). *Home Office circular 59/1990: The cautioning of offenders.* London, England: Author.

———. (1990b). *Criminal statistics England and Wales 1989.* London, England: H.M.S.O.

———. (1991). *Home Office statistical bulletin: Cautions, court proceedings and sentencing in 1990.* London, England: H.M.S.O.

———. (1992). *Home Office statistical bulletin: The criminal histories of those cautioned in 1985 and 1988.* Croydon, England: Home Office Research and Statistics Department.

———. (1993). *Criminal statistics England and Wales 1992.* London, England: H.M.S.O.

———. (1994a). *Home Office circular 18/94: The cautioning of offenders.* London, England: Author.

———. (1994b). *Home Office statistical bulletin: The criminal histories of those cautioned in 1985, 1988 and 1991.* Croydon, England: Home Office Research and Statistics Department.

———. (1994c). *Cautions, court proceedings and sentencing England and Wales, 1993.* London, England: Home Office Research and Statistics Department.

———. (2001a). *Criminal statistics: England and Wales, 2000.* London, England: Author.

———. (2001b). *Criminal statistics: England and Wales, 2000, supplementary tables.* London, England: Author.

———. (2002). *Final warning scheme: Guidance for the police and youth offending teams.* London, England: Author.

———. (2003). *Youth justice—The next steps: Companion document to* Every Child Matters. London, England: Author.

Hoyle, C., Young, R., & Hill, R. (2000). *Proceed with caution: An evaluation of the Thames Valley police initiative in restorative cautioning.* York, England: York Publishing Services.

Hullin, R. P. (1985). The cautioning of juvenile offenders. *Justice of the Peace,* May 18, 1985, 312.

Johnson, K., et al. (2001). *Cautions, court proceedings, and sentencing: England and Wales, 2000.* London: Home Office.

Kershaw, C. (1997). *Reconvictions of those commencing community penalties in 1993, England and Wales.* London: Home Office.

Kidner, D. H. (1985). Guidelines on cautioning—A justice clerk's view. *Justice of the Peace,* May 18, 1985, 308–309.

Kijewski, K. J. (1983). The effect of the decision to charge upon subsequent delinquent behavior. *Canadian Journal of Criminology, 25*(2), 201–208.

Landau, S. F. (1981). Juveniles and the police. *British Journal of Criminology, 21*(1), 27–46.

———, & Nathan, G. (1983). Selecting delinquents for cautioning in the London metropolitan area. *British Journal of Criminology, 23*(2), 128–149.

Laycock, G., & Tarling, R. (1985). Police force cautioning: Policy and practice. *Home Office Research and Planning Unit: Research Bulletin No. 19*, 23–26. London, England.

Lee, M. (1994). Police cautions of minors: In whose best interests? *Deviance and Society, 18*(1), 43–54.

Lincoln, S. B. (1976). Juvenile referral and recidivism. In R. M. Carter and M. W. Klein (Eds.), *Back on the street: The diversion of juvenile offenders* (pp. 321–328). Englewood Cliffs, NJ: Prentice Hall.

Mattinson, J., & Mirrlees-Black, C. (1999). *Attitudes to crime and criminal justice: Findings from the 1998 British crime survey*. London, England: Home Office.

McClintock, F. H., & Avison, N. H. (1968). *Crime in England and Wales*. London: Heinemann.

Mott, J. (1983). Police decisions for dealing with juvenile offenders. *British Journal of Criminology, 23*(3), 249–262.

Moore, R. H., Jr. (1982). *Juvenile justice in England: The magistrates' court as a juvenile court*. Paper presented at the annual meeting of the Academy of Criminal Justice Sciences: Louisville, KY.

Myren, R. A. (1985). Police handling of juveniles in England and the United States. *Criminal Justice International, 1*(3), 9–17.

National Association for the Care and Resettlement of Offenders (NACRO). (1993). *Supplementary guidance on cautioning* (Dec.). London, England: Author.

———. (1994). *NACRO criminal justice digest: Home Office circular on cautioning* (April). London, England: Author.

———. (2000). *Final warnings—Implementation issues*. London, England: Author.

Orrick, D. A. (1983). *A closer look: An examination of possible applications from England to America's criminal justice systems*. Paper presented at the annual meeting of the Academy of Criminal Justice Sciences, San Antonio, TX.

Pratt, J. (1986). Diversion from the juvenile court. *British Journal of Criminology, 26*(3), 212–233.

Shoemaker, D. (1995). *International handbook on juvenile justice*. New York: Greenwood Press.

Tutt, N. S. (1981). A decade of policy. *British Journal of Criminology, 21*(3), 246–256.

———, & Giller, H. (1983). Police cautioning of juveniles: The practice of diversity. *The Criminal Law Review*, 587–595.

Tweedie, I. (1982). Police cautioning of juveniles: Two styles compared. *Criminal Law Review*, 168–174.

Wakefield, B. (1983). *Gimme that ol' time religion: Some observations on value systems in British juvenile justice*. Paper presented at the annual meeting of the Academy of Criminal Justice Sciences, San Antonio, TX.

———. (1987). *Attitudes of London police officers toward the prosecutor's new role*. Paper presented at the annual meeting of the American Society of Criminology, Montreal, Canada.

———, Caulfield, D., & Kane, J. (1984). *Attitudes of London metropolitan police officers toward the practice of police cautioning of juveniles*. Paper presented at the annual meeting of the Academy of Criminal Justice Sciences, Chicago, IL.

———, & Hirschel, D. (1988). *Police in a correctional role: Police cautioning of juveniles in England*. Paper presented at the annual meeting of the American Society of Criminology Meeting, Chicago, IL.

Wilkinson, C., & Evans, R., (1990). Police cautioning of juveniles: The impact of Home Office circular 14/1985. *Criminal Law Review*, March, 165–176.

Willner, P., Hart, K., Binmore, J., Cavendish, M., & Dunphy, E. (2000). Alcohol sales to underage adolescents: An unobtrusive observational field study and evaluation of police intervention. *Addiction, 95*(9), 1373–1388.

Wright, A. (1990). Diversion for adults: Northamptonshire's initiative. *Journal of Probation, 37*(1), 18–22.

Youth Criminal Justice Act (Canada). (2002). Part 1. Extrajudicial measures: Warnings, cautions and referrals. Retrieved from:
http://web.lexis-nexis.com/universe/document?_m=
7abee8a9cc4520735c208bbdd1ddde7d&_docnum=1&wchp=
dGLbVlz-zSkVb&_md5=c2cbcf6d33b37ad4272806c59a984058

24

Local Welfare and Safety Planning in Finland
Critical Factors of Success

Hannu Kiehelä & Matti Vuorinen

The Finnish economy experienced a severe economic recession in the 1990s, which brought about large deficits in public-sector finances. Because of the economic slowdown, the relative size of the public sector increased to 60% of GDP. This led the government to embark on a radical reform of public-sector and economic policies, particularly the reform of social transfer payments. Throughout the 1990s public expenditures were cut, although efforts were made to retain much of the Welfare State. This was achieved through the use of public management techniques, including opening public services to competition, reform of the budget system, and performance management.

Municipalities are the only levels of local government in Finland, although there are a number of regional bodies that function as arms of the national government or collectives of municipalities. Duties of local authorities can be changed only by legislation. While meeting their statutory duties, municipalities may also assume duties such as recreational, housing, energy, public transportation, and port services at their discretion. The national crime prevention program represents a large number of actions overseen by the responsible actors at the local level, with the goal of creating extensive common policies to prevent crime and increase the feeling of safety. However, preventing local crime and addressing public security problems are challenges for public-sector authorities, even more so today than during the time of economic recession.

In comparison with many other European countries, Finland is a safe country, even though crime has increased considerably since the 1950s—in particular where opportunities for crime have expanded due to im-

Prepared especially for *Comparative and International Criminal Justice, 2/E.*

provement in the standard of living, changes in living environment, and increased internationalization. The majority of crimes are committed by a small group of people who in general have begun their criminal activity at an early age; this is connected with marginalization.

National Crime Prevention Program

The Council of State in Finland took a decision in principle on a national crime prevention program in March of 1999. The goal of the program was to create a common policy for action in the prevention of crime and the promotion of security, so that the impact of measures on crime was taken into consideration in public decision making. The idea of the program was that not only the state police but also municipalities, the business community, the Church, and nongovernmental organizations as well as private citizens would participate in crime prevention in a more purposeful and active manner. In principle the program covers all types of criminality; however, particular attention is directed against offenses that cause feelings of insecurity and that may occur in the everyday environment. The goals are to:

- prevent both crimes and damages caused by crimes and prevent the development of at-risk individuals into offenders;
- make it more difficult to commit a crime, and make crimes less profitable;
- develop criminal legislation;
- develop the functions of local societies by drawing up safety plans and creating co-operative networks to support local crime prevention;
- promote strategies aimed to deter economic crime; and
- prevent violence toward women through active support of the equality program.

Role of the Finnish Police

The sole centralized police organization in Finland comes under the jurisdiction of the Ministry of Interior. The Police Department of the Ministry of Interior acts as the Supreme Police Command, it has a three-tier line organization, and it coordinates police operations across the whole country. There are five provinces in Finland, each of which has a provincial police command, which, along with the national police units, are subordinate to the Supreme Police Command. Local police units operate under the provincial police commands. The local police administration is divided into state/local districts; there are currently a total of 90, each with its own district police force. The Police Department of the Ministry of the Interior also includes the Police Research Advisory Committee, which is appointed by the government. At the level of the state/local district police departments, local councils have their own police advisory committees. The local council appoints advisory committee members for their term of office. Their purpose is to follow developments in areas that affect police operations, to monitor police operations, to make proposals for improvement, to give statements on police matters, and to handle any other matters assigned to it.

This link between the "government-owned" police and the surrounding society, the municipality, was created to secure and strengthen the basis for mutual understanding and reciprocal actions. In general, however, the work of these advisory committees has not produced any significant foundation to evoke or promote fruitful cooperation, at least in part because the advisory committee has no decision power over meaningful matters in the police work. This situation is exacerbated by the fact that the political parties that are able to make the nominations to the committee are not too anxious to put "first row" politics in such an organization. Outside this connection, there is regular cooperation between the police and the surrounding society, created specifically by both parties, in every police district. It is notable that in the Finnish system, where the police are completely "owned" by the government, cooperation is always reciprocal; therefore, skills to ensure cooperation are always required.

Local Government and the Reorganization of Police Services

Finland is a signatory to the Council of the Europe Charter on Local Self-government. The Constitution divides Finland into municipalities, whose administration is based on the self-government of their residents. The 448 municipalities constitute regions and subregions, or provinces; these provinces are the grounds for the regional development in the country, and the authority for provincial development has been given to the provincial governments. Subregions serve as a context for local people and authorities to cooperate at the municipal level. The borders of the state/ local offices (police districts and police departments) have been arranged to coincide as much as possible with those of the subregions; thus, there are almost always several municipalities within the area of every subregion.

The Finnish Local Government Act of 1995 reiterated the constitutional autonomy of local authorities, and the legislation states that local authorities will strive to promote the welfare of their residents and sustainable development in their areas. The functions of local government are prescribed by legislation, and the operations and finances of local government are monitored by the Ministry of Interior, which is also required to ensure that municipal autonomy is taken into account in the preparation of legislation concerning local authorities.

The municipal council, composed of 17 to 18 members (depending on population) who are elected for four years each, is the most significant decision-making body in local government. It is not possible to be an official or have a supervisory task over municipal administration and simultaneously have a leading role in a municipality. The council is responsible for the local authority's finances and operations and makes decisions in all important issues; it can also delegate its power to an executive board or to committees. Each municipality has an executive board with a two-year term, appointed by the council. The executive board is responsible for the preparation and execution of decisions for permanent functions of the municipality, as well as the appointment of the boards of management for commercial or other utilities. The division of power and responsibility is legislation based, with the council itself being the highest decision-making authority. The municipal council is required by law to undertake matters of policy making and goal setting, finance, organization, budget, and elections of employees to subsidiaries or joint ventures.

A considerable amount of work has been done to improve services in Finland. Structurally, municipalities work in a collaborative approach for service delivery and improvement. Between 1993 and 2001, 150 multiservice centers (one-stop shops) were established, enabling citizens to access services in a single location from two or more service providers either separately or together. Some municipalities also participate in benchmarking activities. Councils are required to ensure that local residents and service users have opportunities to participate and influence their local authority operations. This can include electing representatives of service users to municipal organizations, providing information about local affairs, holding hearings to determine residents' opinions before making decisions, and helping citizens manage, prepare, and plan matters on their own initiative. To provide services the municipalities can function cooperatively with one another through contracts between municipalities, joint enterprises/utilities under private law, and joint municipal boards (which are public judicial bodies).

Subregional municipal administration is organized by subregional councils, which take care of area development and planning. The most important tasks are European Union structural funding and regional policy, environmental planning, and international relationships connected with their work.

Crime prevention is a task that has particular significance, since the Finnish police implemented a reorganization in 1997, spanning all local functions within the judicial administration. The goals for the reorganization were to improve the quality of services and legal protection of citizens, and to secure a sufficient level of and equal accessibility to services throughout the country. Furthermore, police services were prepared to meet the preconditions of consolidating administrative functions in order to increase decisive capacity and economical service provision on the local level. The preparations that undertaken by the law ten years ago laid the foundation of the reorganization, which put the police in a different relationship with the surrounding societies, the municipalities.

The reorganization reduced the number of units substantially, from 249 local units to 90 units, or state/local offices, to administer the functions of judicial administration on the local level. Every state/local office has its own general administration: the police, the prosecutor, distrait services, and register services. The reorganization thoroughly rearranged police duties, and accordingly the Finnish police have changed their ways of working in order to cope with this new situation. Reorganization of the local police has produced one prominent effect throughout the country: concentrating resources—particularly human resources. Today, the service net of the police consists of central and local offices. The central office is situated in the most significant municipality of the state/local district (and at the same time of the subregion). The size of a central office, which offers all the services a local police unit can have, is determined by population density. Local offices offer a variable and less comprehensive set of services as determined by their smaller size.

The Supreme Command of the Finnish Police decided in 1999 that all state/local districts should implement community safety planning according to the decision in principle by The Council of State of Finland. Safety planning is one of the pivotal goals set as the result of an agreement about preventive policing functions. The plans are scheduled to cover all municipalities by the end of the year 2004.

Safety As a Consequence of Welfare

Traditionally, the concepts of safety and security (as perceived by the public) have been defined in criminology as objective or subjective risk (fear or angst based more or less on earlier, direct or indirect experiences of crime). In a subjective sense, fear of crime is a psychological state that varies between genders, age groups, and living environments. Thus, the estimated risk of becoming a victim has more to do with subjective assessment of one's own vulnerability than it does with objective facts. The concept of safety can be considered an expression of *social* experiences, which can be seen in terms of a community's vulnerability or ability to defend itself from social risks in general. Consequently, safety is a human and social value that is linked with successfully minimizing the risks of modern society, decreasing criminality in a social and physical environment, and enhancing social welfare. Traditional safety, seen as an objective or subjective risk of crime, is linked fundamentally with welfare in its broadest meaning. Thus, in the crime surveys and screening of local communities that have been a part of Scandinavian welfare research tradition, neither human experiences nor crime statistics can be considered without framing the results in a socioeconomic background. In the research dealing with Finnish welfare and safety, the research group used a multidimensional model to describe the quality of life (Niemelä, et al., 1997).

The strongest dimension of social differentiation is clearly related to household structure, which characterizes mostly *neighborhood cohesion.*

The residential areas with loose social connections to their neighborhoods can be divided into two single-adult household areas: city centers housing elderly people, and single-parent families living in suburban areas. The second dimension of social differentiation is associated with *socioeconomic status*. The areas with private housing, high incomes, and high socioeconomic status are concentrated in certain locations easily and sharply distinguished from surrounding residential areas. The third dimension describes the *risks of modern society*, including community-based factors that have influence on people's well-being, such as traffic, pollution, and physical environment. The most immediate factor in the *environmental* dimension is the gradual destruction of neighborhoods. The physical environment, related to city planning and land-use, has impacted urban patterns and even criminality.

The fourth dimension of social differentiation—not empirically represented in the study and of only theoretical interest here—can be called *cultural acceptance*. The ethnic groups experiencing discrimination are at the core of this dimension. In Helsinki, the divided nature of the substance of this factor emerges when its spatial pattern is examined. High numbers of foreigners are located within both the most affluent areas and the low-income suburbs (Vaattovaara, 1998, 85).

Table 1 describes the key dimensions of welfare. These material and immaterial, objective and subjective factors are *causes* of crimes rather than effects, in the sociological sense. Many empirical findings support this fact; the social status and living environment not only affect the factual level of crime but also human experiences involving it. This means that safety issues cannot be considered without bearing in mind that there are no general safety levels in socially and culturally diverse communities. In addition, the experience of safety is strongly linked with an individual's control of life, which in turn is a sum of the above-mentioned factors. There is at

Table 1   The Dimensions of Welfare

Dimensions of Social Differentiation	Risk Groups/Areas	Emergent Problems
Socioeconomic (welfare model)	Unemployed people with low education and income	Economic insecurity, high crime rates
Cohesive	Single-parent families	Social exclusion, high crime rates
Health	Low-income urban areas	Spatial differentiation, vandalism, high crime rates
Safety/Well-being	Minorities	Discrimination, confrontation

least one obvious reason why these explaining factors have been ignored in strategic safety planning: security authorities (e.g. police, customs officers) are only loosely affiliated with what passes for the local welfare plan (if ever a plan existed). This has translated into ongoing efforts to keep streets safe by increasing surveillance, both formal and informal.

The surveillance strategy is now being challenged, and the information gathered using geographical welfare and safety analysis paints a different picture. As a method of promoting proactive city planning, focusing primarily on social and geographical variations and differences in the Forssa sub-region, this data also revealed the weaknesses of traditional safety planning. Many socioeconomic datasets are employed and integrated with data on crimes reported to the police and also with the results from victim surveys. The analyses of registered crimes focus on a selection of everyday offenses affecting private citizens. The victim questionnaire survey gathered information on victims of criminal activity as well as on perceptions of safety and other welfare problems regarding socioeconomic status, lifestyle, social cohesion, and satisfaction with the respondent's residential neighborhood.

However, problems exist associated with the use of sociogeographical data in Finnish communities—for example, the skewed nature of the variables employed in the analyses. Different methods were employed, including transforming the variables and using the same statistical area unit. This work served as a pilot project to show how general social differentiation and segregation (undesirable differentiation) is linked with safety in the traditional sense. On the other hand, the purpose of the project was to build a common database for safety and welfare planning at the community level. The results of this research can be used to formulate crime prevention strategies and to mobilize authorities and other stakeholders to implement them. The analytical strategy employed examines the significance of interactive effects between different explanatory characteristics of criminality.

The present findings suggest that in order to explain and understand crime level and fear of crime one needs to study covariation, the aspect of welfare that seemingly describes the process of residential differentiation (Niemelä et. al., 1997). This study takes into account those structural factors assumed to affect the municipalities' crime levels and citizens' fear of crime. The risk of social and spatial segregation is highest in the groups and areas where all these forms of social differentiation accumulate ("poverty pockets"). One can also hypothesize that actual victimization and level of criminality are the highest in these residential areas as well.

Forms of Spatial and Social Differentiation

The traditional, deterministic, environmental approach to social and spatial differentiation deals with urban areas as social organisms, where individual behavior and social organization are governed by a struggle for existence and a constant search for optimal physical location. Studies associate residential differentiation with households' choices of location and are in this sense related to the competition based on household choice models used in housing-market economics. The *classical optimization model* created by Alonso (1964) is based on a market curve (i.e., housing prices), while more recent research relates residential differentiation to individual lifestyle (Giddens, 1991).

At least three models of spatial differentiation can be distinguished. The first is the *managerial* or *administrative model,* in which spatial differentiation process is seen as a consequence of political discretion and environmental planning. (For example, during the 1960s and 1970s many public housing areas were built in Finland. These areas of low socioeconomic status have often been targets of neighborhood programs.) The second model stresses *rational choices* and household competition. From this perspective, residential differentiation is seen as a result of free housing markets. The most desirable housing areas are those featuring good transportation services to the city and easy access to outdoor recreation areas. Finally, in the *lifestyle approach,* spatial differentiation takes place in the process of social and cultural differentiation. People prefer residential areas that fit their own living conditions.

Does residential differentiation lead to other different social problems? To understand crime reports we must analyze and interpret figures of crime along with other socioeconomic statistical data. Crime figures should be seen as a part of welfare indicators. According to Per-Olof Wikström's model (1991), urban structure and physical environment are the key determinants of factual criminality and fear of crime (see figure 1).

Figure 1   Housing and Criminality

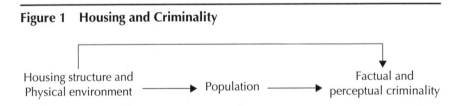

The *social disorganization theory* is undoubtedly the most significant model in the area of traditional ecological criminology and has provided the theoretical basis for a large number of studies in this research field. Similarly, the *routine activity perspective* has become a frequently cited model in modern criminological research. The two are not to be regarded as competing perspectives, however. The social disorganization model is used primarily to explain geographic variations in the residency patterns of criminal youths in metropolitan environments, but it also has been employed to explain variations in crime. The ecological applications of the routine activity perspective, in contrast, are intended to explain geographical variations in the situation of crime events (Wikström, 1990, 1998). Social disorganization is the most well-known perspective in the field of ecological crime, having originated in the Chicago School's extensive research into crime in a major city (Shaw & McKay, 1969). The contention is that socio-geographic variations in the residency patterns of offenders depend on variations in the ability of neighborhoods to sustain social rules and norms to exercise informal social control.

The *routine activity perspective* was developed as a reaction against the classical tradition in criminological research focusing on an offender; it focuses instead on crime and the situations in which crime takes place. The fundamental idea is that variations in the constituent elements of day-to-day life also create conditions that facilitate crime. The well-known principle that a crime results from the coincidence of a motivated offender and a suitable victim in the absence of capable guardians constitutes one of the central elements in this perspective (Cohen & Felson, 1979).

In recent years there has been a growing interest in the possibilities integrating different theoretical perspectives. Disorganization theory has been combined with the routine activities perspective in several instances. One reason for combining the two is that the routine activity perspective is quite often perceived to be incomplete. For example, the significance of the presence of a motivated offender is sometimes not taken into account, even though the theory states that crimes take place when a motivated offender and a suitable object are combined in the absence of capable guardians. The disorganization perspective may possibly serve as a complement to the routine activity theory by providing an explanation of geographic variations in the distribution of offenders (Bursik & Grasmick, 1993). Another reason for combining the two perspectives is the emphasis that they both place on the significance of informal control.

Robert Bursik and Harold Grasmick (1993) examined the relationship between economic deprivation and crime rates; the two competing explanations of this relationship are the *direct effect* and the *indirect effect* models. The direct effect idea is that poverty directly induces people to commit crimes because they want otherwise unattainable wealth. The indirect effect idea is that poverty encourages crime primarily by weakening a community's social ties. The strategy of the study was to see how social economic status and unemployment appeared to be related to the crime rate when regulatory capacity (the measure of social disorganization), or RC, was added to the equation. If adding RC produced negligible results, then economic deprivation would seem to directly cause crime, but if by adding RC it had significantly weakened the association between economic deprivation and crime rate, and then the indirect effect theory would be strengthened. These results provide important support for the indirect effect approach. RC clearly accounts for a considerable amount of the apparent direct relationship between economic deprivation and crime rates. Bursik and Grasmick (1993) say this holds true despite a decline in the kinds of social conditions that many early indirect-effect theorists blamed for the deprivation-disorganization link.

Defining and Explaining Crime

The literature in this area contains no consensus on the question of theoretical or empirical definitions of crime. Crime or offender distributions are very difficult to explain on the basis of the theoretical arguments contained in the original statements of the routine activities model or in the literature on disorganization theory (Maxfield, 1987). Despite the fact that disorganization theory is intended primarily to explain variations in the residency patterns of young offenders, one also finds this perspective used in studies of crime, offenders, exposure to crime, and perceptions of insecurity. Analyses of the routine activity perspective are subject to similar variation, although the majority of such studies are focused primarily on crime and exposure to crime. A relatively large portion of this research is therefore devoted to analyzing the significance of these perspectives for various different factors (i.e., crime, suspected offenders, and victims of crime, but also for geographical variations in perceptions of insecurity).

Decision makers are interested only in emergent welfare indicators; this is why only immediate welfare needs are satisfied. More diffuse and subjective dimensions of welfare, like the feeling of safety or more generally of happiness, are not considered. Even if they were, authorities could hardly see the complex connections between different aspects of welfare. The destruction of social norms, socioeconomic instability, marginalization, and social segregation are crime facilitators that cannot be tackled in terms of crime. In an urban social environment, where leisure-time activities, work, and social life are separated in time and space from each other, more crimes are likely than in rural areas because of individuals' distance from neighborhoods and also distance from informal social control.

Furthermore, it should be pointed out that the people who are committing crimes, especially violent crimes, are also very likely to be the victims of crimes themselves. The criminal lifestyle affects whole families, and it includes all the aspects of cumulative social problems, such as child molestation, sexual abuse, domestic violence, truancy, and drug trafficking and abuse. Unfortunately, authorities are not sufficiently prepared to meet these problems at local levels, not because of lack of political goodwill but because there is no common interest. Controversially, there is a continuing lack of resources and fierce competition among human-service agencies, fuelled by budget cutbacks during the last decade in Forssa. Compounding the problem, there is no common database among these agencies. Common problems of clients are cut into segments according to administrative boundaries, and after administrative tinkering the pieces of information are no longer compatible. In addition, strictly applied laws regulating professional confidentiality hamper the exchange of information between authorities. For these reasons, the welfare indicators do not give a comprehensive picture of welfare problems for the authorities.

Explaining Local Crime Rates

According to a study on socio-geographical structure and violence in Helsinki (Kortteinen, et al., 2001), violence was much more prevalent in the low welfare suburbs than in high welfare areas as well as in the city. Other factors affecting the level of violence were property crimes, number of drug users, and alcohol consumption. The study reveals two types of violent crimes in Helsinki: on one hand, so-called street violence can be explained by the number of restaurants, bars, and pubs serving the young public in downtown Helsinki. Typically, this type of violence is concentrated in the busy and crowded streets nearby the main railway station, the offenders and victims are young, and violence escalates between small groups of people in the early hours of Saturday and Sunday nights right after closing time. On the other hand, the probability of domestic violence is much higher in low-class areas with a lot of public housing.

In a study on structural factors explaining local crime rates (Heiskanen, Siren, & Rouvainen, 2003), welfare and crime statistics were combined throughout Finland. The explaining (predicting) factors were population structure, employment, socioeconomic welfare, and services in a municipality. The aim of the study was to explain the level of crime when different structural factors, assumed to influence the criminality, are controlled. The data comprised all 448 Finnish municipalities, which were divided according to their level of urbanization into three groups. A selective regression model was used to "predict" the level of property and violent crimes. For different types of municipality and crime, different factors are important in explaining the variation in crime rate. However, the proportion of married people, per-capita alcohol consumption, and variables describing the age structure of the municipality were the most common explanatory factors in estimated models, and also the number of available crime targets (measured by volume of retail selling), a usable factor in explaining property crimes.

According to how much the expected crime rate differed from the actual rate of recorded crime, the municipalities were classified into five groups (high, rather high, expected, rather low, and low). In Helsinki (the capital) and in Turku the level of violence recorded by police is high; however, taking into account the structural factors, the level of violent crimes was expected in these cities (Dolmen, 2002). In the urban municipalities, the regression model predicted the level of violence utilizing the following nine variables: percentage of people under 15 years of age in the population, percentage of 15–24-year-old males in the population, percentage of married people in the population, degree of education, mobility of a population, percentage of low-income population, and employment and alcohol consumption. In many of the rural municipalities (n = 305: the municipalities having less than 15,000 people and 60% of the population living in an urban area), the factors explaining the variation in crime rates were partly different from the factors affecting rates in urban municipalities; in cries of violence the voting activity, unemployment rate of men, and per-capita alcohol consumption are statistically the most important factors. The level of property crimes correlates, among other things, with the number of summer cottages, and with the percentage of divorced families in the municipality (Blixt, 2002).

In this classification, Forssa is an urban municipality, and all the other neighboring municipalities are in rural areas. In all types of municipalities the amount of retail and licensed trade of alcohol was a factor connected to the level of violent crime (Heiskanen, et al., 2003). According to the regression model, family structure is a factor influencing violent crime (a larger percentage of married couples are connected with a lower rate of violent crime). A large part of violent crime recorded by the police is "street crime" in areas with restaurants and other places of entertainment, where both the victims and the offenders are young, mostly unmarried men.

The statistics used by the police clearly show that reported house calls in the entire area concentrated heavily in the city of Forssa. During the period of 1997–2003, there were 531 house calls in Forssa, while in all other municipalities there was a total of only 137 house calls. During the last couple of years the numbers of house calls has not fluctuated. It looks like this trend may now be over, however, since in September 2003 there were already almost as many reports as there was at the end of the previous year.

In general, statistics indicate that there was a tremendous upsurge in nearly all types of crime in Forssa between 1980 and 1985. The growth of property crime was 110%, that of violent crime was 86%, that of traffic infractions was 53%, that of crime related to drugs and alcohol was 331%, that of drunkenness in traffic was 25%, and that of all crime was 82%. Also worth mentioning is that there were no narcotic crimes known to police before 1983. In the classification of property crime, Forssa is among the number of municipalities that have a rather high crime level. The rural municipalities of Humppila, Jokioinen, and Tammela, are all among the high-level group and Ypäjä among the expected-level group.

The increase in recorded crimes did not affect the surrounding municipalities in the same measure in 1980–1985; only a couple of years later the numbers began to grow in these municipalities. The different rate of increase can be explained at least in part by the growth of all kinds of crime targeted at vehicles (usually in connection with drug abuse). The offenders, many of them addicted to drugs, simply widened their area of action to cover the surrounding municipalities. The growth of criminality slowed between 1990 and 1995 and has continued to decrease. According to the model, precipitating factors are assumed to be per-capita alcohol consumption, family structure (in this case the high number of one-parent families), unemployment, and marginalization. The licensed trade of alcohol per inhabitant over 18 years of age in Forssa is clearly higher than average in the country. In the early 1990s the trade decreased to 11 liters per every inhabitant over age 18. In the entire economic region the licensed trade is below average in the country. Consumption outside the statistics is estimated to be about 15 liters per every inhabitant.

The proportion of the one-parent families has been notably high in Forssa during the last decade; the number is also higher than average in the country. The lowest number of one-parent families is found in Tammela and Jokioinen; the higher numbers in Forssa are also higher in comparison to nearby cities and have been high ever since 1997. The percentage of unemployment in the subregion has been higher than the average in Finland; the rate of unemployment in the subregion has clearly exceeded the regional unemployment level. The highest numbers in the province have been recorded in Forssa and the lowest in Tammela. During the past decade the numbers in the subregion were equal to those in the country. The rate of recorded crime in the subregion and all municipalities within it is clearly connected to the depression in the early 1990s. The depression caused a notable decrease in the number of jobs, resulting in cuts in public services and benefits and leading to increasing migration of the active population—particularly those able to find work elsewhere (e.g., on account of their education). The depression struck Forssa exceptionally hard, and the city that was once a booming industrial area fell into decline. The other municipalities were not so vulnerable and retained their economic stability.

In the early 1970s, Forssa built multi-story buildings and tenements in a highly concentrated area. Changing economic conditions have made this area vulnerable in crisis. Residents often have lower-than-average incomes, above-average unemployment, one-parent families, and are troubled with alcoholism, drug abuse, and marginalization. In other municipalities such problems have not been as prevalent. The notable amount of summer cottages within the subregion of Forssa creates a clear potential for burglaries and property damage, and an increase in the number of recorded crimes.

Welfare and Safety Planning in the Subregion of Forssa

Keeping the abovementioned figures in mind, plus the fact that a great deal of crime problems were played up by the local media, the Forssa subregion organized a so-called welfare and safety council in September 2001. The council was comprised of director members from five municipalities and covered social, health, education, and technical services. The chief of police in the Forssa state/local office represented the traditional safety sector in the council, and two expert members (the authors of this article) were chosen to initiate the project and evaluate its progress. The basic idea in strategy planning was to keep political decision makers and city mayors informed of the results by organizing discussion forums every six months. Strategy planning consisted of five phases: (1) defining the concept of welfare, (2) defining the measures that were fitting for the welfare model, (3) collecting and interpreting welfare data, (4) setting the goals for each welfare dimension, and (5) formulating the strategy and follow-up system.

Cooperative Partnerships in Municipalities

The subregion of Forssa consists of five municipalities, the biggest being the city of Forssa. There were 18,201 inhabitants in the city of Forssa at the end of 2002; at the same time there were altogether 17,353 inhabitants in the other four municipalities. The subregion is considered average in population density among the subregions. Forssa lies in the southern part of Finland, about 80 miles northeast of Helsinki; all its municipalities are part of the province of Southern Finland.

The municipalities of the Forssa subregion historically have been able to work together in many ways. This is an important consideration in creating the safety strategy for the municipalities. The most important area of cooperation is perhaps that of health services.

In the aforementioned reorganization, the Forssa state/local office was located within the Forssa subregion and was established by merging two police districts in the area. Resources were combined and concentrated in a central office situated in the city of Forssa. As a result, the needs of community under local police jurisdiction cover a wider area than before. For this reason, cooperation with other local authorities is crucial in order to gain positive results.

The cooperative potential in this situation offers totally new possibilities for police cooperation if realized, understood, and used skillfully. After the reorganization the police confronted the problem of regaining the confidence of those citizens in need of its services. The local police must reconnect themselves with the surrounding society, together with the municipalities. This brings the expertise of the police to bear on administrative decisions that define the well-being and safety of the citizens in the municipalities.

Participating in community safety planning enables cooperation between police and the community as partners. First, the welfare situation in a particular community must be determined. Second, police and community as partners must determine what should be done, and finally they must continue to work as partners to get the approval and resources from those who have the power to implement change. The community safety strategy for the Forssa subregion facilitates goal setting and political decision making by those responsible for the functions and procedures that promote and improve the well-being and safety of the citizens in the municipalities. Although it does not provide a forum for citizen debate as such, the themes it supports are hoped to provoke large-scale conversation about both the current situation and future well-being and safety by taking up various issues within the strategy.

The welfare and safety policy benefits from professional collaboration between administrative sectors based on partnerships among authorities, where different partners combine their expertise to set individual goals. The purpose of such networking is not to change duties or roles but rather to clarify the division of labor among local authorities in welfare sectors and to agree upon common goals in welfare and safety. The local authority network in Forssa defined the following strategic goals:

- to increase awareness about welfare and safety problems,
- to pinpoint safety problems in different welfare sectors,
- to analyze the benefits of collaboration in solving these problems,
- to define the common targets of the welfare and safety plan,
- to determine the means by which authorities can work to solve the defined problems,
- to set up a common cross-sectored instrument by which critical premises of success and results can be evaluated, and
- to create an administrative system that supports the continuity of strategic planning and its commitment to welfare policy.

Collaborative Networking

In the Forssa subregion the strategic goal is to improve the welfare and safety of citizens by taking care of their physical and mental health, increasing the integration and cohesion of communities, actively influencing the socioeconomic living conditions, and ensuring everyone's safety and well-being. The implementation of the strategy presupposes that subregional municipalities, governmental organizations, and nongovernmental organizations are exchanging information and allocating resources appropriately. The implementation of the strategy depends on political commitment, which must be obtained and gauged in meetings with local authorities, town council members, and other politically elected officials. Although this new alliance is still in its formative stage, the strategy has already obtained widespread political support. From the local police's point of view; the strategy has meant increasing opportunities to influence local political decisions on crucial issues in reducing crime.

The subregional collaborative network in Forssa is built on the mutual interrelationship between independent local authorities. Collaboration is sustained by effectively focusing activities and limited resources on constructive changes in the local environment. In Forssa a case has been made that safety problems originate from cultural, social, and material problems that reflect people's inability to participate in normal life. The welfare strategy proposes solutions that are social, physical, or economical in nature. Basically, crime prevention goals are twofold: to obstruct the marginalization process and segregation of high-risk groups, and to support offenders through positive diversion (i.e., through provision of jobs or suitable education) in order to prevent recidivism. In the former task, local public services need not be reorganized in accordance with service *sectors* but rather with service *processes* (chaining). In the latter task, the Forssa state/local office has taken its first concrete steps in collaboration with the probation center and local social and labor offices.

Welfare and Safety Databases

A comprehensive database is a critical factor for the welfare and safety strategy. The database is a combination of different datasets from welfare statistics, research studies, and other empirical findings on citizens' living conditions. The welfare and safety council agreed on the critical parameters and measures in common meetings. By using this database authorities can analyze, interpret, and apply the information in defining their annual or long-term plans. The database also can be used as a follow-up system by which alternative strategies are later evaluated. For example, the local police office can use combined information from demographic statistics on truancy rates, school dropouts rates, social security information, and employment information in order to analyze crime statistics. The following databases exist in the Forssa subregion:

Welfare and safety account. This account is an annual dataset including both quantitative and qualitative data combined from selected statistics describing the situation in each of four welfare dimensions (socioeconomic, cohesive, health, and safety/well-being). The following crimes were chosen as categories representative of the safety account: larceny, car theft, property damage, violence in public places, domestic violence, and house calls made by police. These categories were chosen to represent everyday crimes and different aspects of social problems—especially the domestic violence category, because emergency calls particularly reflect general welfare and safety problems. The majority of requests for house calls very clearly predominate in the "poverty pockets" of the area.

Welfare and safety barometer. This includes indicators describing the welfare and safety of local people. The indicators are constructed from selected raw statistics and presented annually in summarized form to elected members of municipal administration, providing a kind of cross-sectional picture of state tendencies and welfare dimensions.

Welfare and safety report. This report is presented every four years to newly elected members of municipal councils, to be used as a basis for welfare planning and budgeting. The welfare and safety report is comprised of information on changes in the welfare of the Forssa subregion and the factors influencing welfare and safety. It also includes critical information on welfare services. Basically, the report is a checkpoint of the accountability and effectiveness of public services. On the basis of this report, optional strategies will be defined for each welfare dimension and confirmed by elected members of municipal councils.

The welfare and safety report not only gives an overall picture about the cultural, social, and economic environment of the area but also describes the connections between different aspects of welfare. Based on this knowledge, the political accountability of the chosen strategy can be enhanced. The purpose of the report is to facilitate decision making and resource reallocations. Chosen means are part of a cross-sectional welfare program and budget. The results will be evaluated in the frame of commonly accepted indicators. Table 2 illustrates the critical factors of success, necessary measures, and the main partners in the safety plan.

Table 2   Critical Factors of Success, Measures, and Partners in the Safety Plan

Critical Success Factors	Measures	Partnerships Involved
Realistic information on public safety and criminality	• Cooperation with local media • A more active role for police	• Local radio • Local press • Welfare and safety council
Early intervention for young people with school problems and learning difficulties	• Aid for pupils with social problems through intranet • Early indication of problems and information exchange • Family support	• Local social services • Day care centers • Schools • Regional health services
Implementation of a program against domestic violence	• Organizing an expert group for the program • Statistical analysis of domestic violence based on police reports	• Local social services • Day care centers • Schools • Churches
An effective reintegration program for former prisoners of the subregion	• Active diversion and reintegration into society	• Probation offices • AA-clinics • Employment services • Social services
Welfare considerations in environmental planning and housing	• Mapping the needs of people concerning physical environment • New public housing projects • Integration of situational crime prevention in community planning	• Regional/community planning office
Implementation of a traffic safety program	• Safety account about traffic accidents	• Local engineering services

Conclusion

As in most Western democracies, in Finland there is a trend wherein citizens believe themselves to be distant from the political process. Attempts are being made to engage citizens at different levels in the communities. The government has introduced a financial equalization scheme to ensure that all citizens can receive an appropriate level of services, regardless of their geographical location. The welfare and safety plan has been designed to give public-service employees a more comprehensive knowledge of local welfare and safety, from its origins to future projections. It is essential that administrative personnel at the municipal level be well trained if they are to cope with the problems and complexities that accompany the rapid changes in the concept of safety. The sophistication of the system within which they must operate demands a deeper level of understanding and knowledge than can be gained through previous levels of experience and outdated information systems.

The welfare and safety plan's commitment to local government and its considerable independence from the state allows services to be tailored more appropriately to local needs. There has been an increasing trend to improve systems of regulation by the central government. The use of indicators and performance criteria in the Forssa subregion accompanies the allocation of state funds. At all levels there is recognition of a need to coordinate central policy as it impacts local government organizations, based on four welfare dimensions: socioeconomic, cohesive, health, and well-being and safety. For each of these dimensions the goals, critical factors, and evaluation system is defined separately. The purpose of the subregional welfare and safety-planning model in Forssa is to develop collaborative efforts among the existing local authorities in a more systematic and constructive way, and to link crime control issues more strongly with local welfare planning.

The implementation of a constructive safety plan is finally a political process and part of local welfare policy in Finnish society. The time span of the welfare and safety plan is four years, after which time new political members of municipal councils will take office. The plan has to be approved by political parties and budgeted and organized by new local authorities. There is still long way to go; the internal coherence of a plan is not enough. Welfare and safety planning requires changes in administrative culture. Many aspects of municipal collaboration and local bureaucracy must be re-examined, including cross-sectional budgeting, new results-based planning and evaluation, collaboration between state and municipal services, and information exchange between authorities. There is increasing pressure to reorganize limited public resources and improve administrative accountability in the future. The Forssa subregion can be the model.

References

Alonso, W. (1964). *Location and Land Use*. Cambridge: Harvard University Press.

Blixt, M. (2002). Municipal Crime Rates in Sweden. A Statistical Study. Report 2002: 5, Stockholm: BRÅ.

Bursik, R. J. & Grasmick, H. G. (1993). *Neighborhoods and Crime: The Dimension of Effective Community Control*. New York: Lexington Books.

Cohen, L. E. & Felson, M. (1979). Social Change and Crime Rate Trends: Routine Activity Approach. *American Sociological Review*, 44 (August): 558–608.

Dolmen, L. (2002). Brottslighetens Geografi. En analys av brottsligheten i Stockholms län. Kriminologiska Institutionen. Stockholms Universitet, Nr 6.

Giddens, A. (1991). *Modernity and Self-Identity in the Late Modern Age*. Cambridge: Polity Press.

Heiskanen, M., Siren, R., & Rouvainen, O. (2003). Rikollisuus kunnissa. Tilastollinen tutkimus Suomen väkivalta- ja omaisuusrikollisuuteen vaikuttavista tekijöistä. Poliisiammattikorkeakoulun tutkimuksia 16. Edita, Helsinki.

Maxfield, M. (1987). Lifestyle and Routine Activity Theories of Crime: Empirical Studies of Victimization, Delinquency and Offender Decision Making. *Journal of Quantitative Criminology* 3: 275–282.

Shaw, C. R., & McKay, H. D. (1969). *Juvenile Delinquency and Urban Areas*. Chicago: University of Chicago Press.

Vaattovaara, M. (1998). Pääkaupunkiseudun sosiaalinen erilaistuminen. Ympristö ja alueellisuus. Helsingin kaupungin tietokeskus. Tutkimuksia. 1998:7. Helsinki

Wikström, P. (1990). Brott och Åtgärder mot brott i stadsmiljö. BRÅ rapport 1990:5, Stockholm.

Wikström, P. (1991). *Urban Crime, Criminals and Victims. The Swedish Experience in Anglo-American Comparative Perspective*. New York: Springer-Verlag.

Wikström, P. (1998). Communities and Crime. In Tonry, M. (ed.): *The Handbook of Crime and Punishment*. New York: Oxford University Press.

25

Vital Questions Concerning the Rehabilitation of Offenders
A Scandinavian Perspective

Matti Laine

What Does Imprisonment Aim to Do?

Prisons have always fulfilled a variety of functions. Perhaps the most classic example is the idea that imprisonment as a form of punishment is a preventive measure. General *prevention* means that when a citizen is sentenced to imprisonment, it functions as an example and deters the rest of us from committing offenses. This idea can manifest itself in two ways: as direct general prevention, which refers to the deterrence effect of imprisonment, or as indirect general prevention, in which the aim of the punishment is to create a long-term universal morality toward the blameworthiness of certain acts. In Scandinavian criminal policies the latter has been predominant (Lappi-Seppälä 2003:45).

Another function that prisons fulfill is the *isolation* or *incapacitation* of the offender. The idea is that imprisonment prevents the offender from committing new offenses, thus protecting other citizens. Fulfilling this function often requires long, even indeterminate terms of sentence. An example of this line of reasoning is the preventive detention system and its history in Finland. The effectiveness of this function has been criticized, however, because imprisonment does not always prevent or indeed even diminish the criminal acts of some offenders. Many offenses are actually committed behind prison walls.

The ancient idea of just *retribution* is another function of imprisonment as well as other forms of punishment. In retribution, the goal is not beneficial effects, such as preventing recidivism, but rather restoring justice through the correlation of the crime and the punishment. Retribution

Prepared especially for *Comparative and International Criminal Justice, 2/E.*

is also known as *social revenge*. Our moral feelings and our objection to the committed offenses are involved in the punishment, whether or not we consciously want them to be. This was one of the basic premises of famous Finnish anthropologist Edvard Westermarck in his great study of the origins of moral ideas (1906–1908), although he recognized that the penal system also fulfills some utilitarian functions.

Yet another function can be demanded of prisons, namely, that of the *rehabilitation* of offenders. Rehabilitation has multiple meanings and can refer to a variety of concepts and functions. This is particularly true if we look at rehabilitation in light of the history of prison service. In short, the idea of rehabilitation can be defined as all of the measures used to influence an individual offender during imprisonment so that he or she will be less inclined to commit new offenses after release and will have a better chance of being a productive member of society. In this case we have to remember that prison service always has included various functions that are less justified from the viewpoint of diminishing recidivism alone than they are from other perspectives.

Which of the above, then, should we consider as the main function of imprisonment? Sociologically we have good cause to claim that despite the varying emphasis of different eras, all the above-mentioned views are in one way or another functions of the prison sentence of today. This is not always officially apparent, for instance in the legislation of different countries. The fact that prison service has to measure up to a variety of sometimes-contradictory demands and expectations causes certain inner tension and conflict, which are not always easily resolved within the parameters of everyday prison service today.

Is Rehabilitation a New Idea?

It is often suggested that in the past, the function of prisons was only to isolate, avenge, and deter, but that today the rehabilitation of individual offenders is a priority. However, the purpose of the modern prison is seen by many as intervention. In that respect it differs radically from the dungeons of ancient castles, which were mainly places of storage for prisoners awaiting trial or punishment. The modern prison was born around 1750–1820 in the United States and Western Europe. Americans consider Walnut Street Jail in Philadelphia, Pennsylvania, to have been the first modern prison (Grimes 1996:493–495). The function of the prison was to replace the cruel capital and corporal punishments and to affect individual prisoners through certain special methods. The Quakers were pioneers in developing the prison system, and it has been said that prison service was much influenced by their religious thought.

Many researchers who have studied the history of prison systems (i.e., Frenchman Michel Foucault [1979], American Thorsten Sellin [1944], and

Norwegian Thomas Mathiesen [2000]) have described how early the ideas of reform, treatment, and rehabilitation came to represent prison service. They already existed in the precursors of prisons—the workhouses—founded in England and Holland at the end of the sixteenth century. Workhouses were not actual prisons in which offenders were placed by court order. In addition to criminals, they housed other people perceived as troublesome to society, such as vagrants. As early as 1589 influential Dutchman Jan Laurenzsoon Spiegel wrote a memorandum that underlined the importance of rehabilitation, in which he proposed highly developed, specialized work and professional skills programs for inmates of the workhouses (Mathiesen 2000:32–34).

In the course of the nineteenth century, the following methods became central in preventing recidivism:

• Hard work

• School and religious education

• Reflection on one's guilt, penitence (solitude)

• Discipline and daily schedule

These methods spread worldwide, thanks to the Auburn and Philadelphia cell-prison systems that were developed in the United States. Accordingly, the first National Congress on Penitentiary and Reformatory Discipline held in Cincinnati, Ohio, in 1870 concluded that reformation, not vindictive suffering, is the purpose of imprisonment. Incarceration must reform offenders so that they will be diligent, respectable citizens when they are released (Pisciotta 1983:614–615). These ideas, and the progressive system, in which prisoners progress or "improve" gradually during their sentences, were developed further in the first International Penitentiary Congress in London in 1872. The cell and progressive (Irish) systems were widely accepted. The only exception was Russia, whose representative Count Sollohub declared that Russia would not accept the solitary-cell systems but instead would develop its own communal prison system (Pears 1872:186–199). This might be the reason why even today most prisoners in the Russian Federation serve their sentences in corrective labor colonies and not in cell prisons (and not as a by-product of the Soviet or Stalinist era). In the late nineteenth century, special institutions for young and first offenders—reformatories—were founded in the United States. They emphasized the importance of obtaining a professional education and finding employment. When it came to discipline, however, sometimes they were even stricter than the traditional state prisons (Pisciotta 1983).

The Principles of the Twentieth-Century Rehabilitative Ideal

The integral tools to influence individual offenders with the aim of completely preventing their criminal activities were created as early as the nineteenth century. These tools included, for example, special courts and prisons for young offenders, the progressive system and adjacent indeterminate sentences, probation, parole with supervision, and specialized rehabilitative institutions and reformatories. The still-ongoing discussion about whether it is possible to integrate controlling measures and methods of rehabilitation and treatment began in the nineteenth century, if not earlier. According to some views, controlling measures and punishment destroy the possibility of rehabilitation, and these should therefore be seen to by different authorities. On the other hand, there is support for the view that all methods of rehabilitation and treatment necessarily include elements of control and that a certain degree of control is a prerequisite for rehabilitation.

It can be said, nevertheless, that rehabilitative thought did not reach its high point until the twentieth century. One could go so far as to call it the century of the rehabilitative ideal, at least until the 1960s. Thomas G. Blomberg and Karol Lucken (2000:100–101) have summarized the rehabilitative ideal into the following four assumptions:

1. Human behavior is a product of antecedent causes. This is the fundamental principle of the whole rehabilitative ideal. Our individual personal histories determine who we are, how we think, and how we act. For example, one's domestic background can be seen as a major factor in shaping that individual's behavior later in life (e.g., in view of possible criminal activity).

2. It is possible to identify and discover the causes of human behavior (e.g., criminality), and behavioral science is the tool for doing so with all possible exactness. The antecedent causes can be found in one's past, and therefore particular attention should be given to an individual's personal history.

3. Knowledge of the antecedent causes of problem behavior enables the scientific treatment of such behavior. Once the causes of an individual's problem behavior are discovered and identified, they can be corrected with the help of specifically designed treatment.

4. The measures employed to treat a prisoner or an offender have a therapeutic function. Both the offender and society benefit from them. A successful reformation leads not only to a reduction in recidivism, but it also enables the offender's reintegration into society (e.g., securing employment, paying taxes, and having a normal family life).

As early as the 1920s, prisons began to employ professionals in rehabilitation. The objective was to form professional teams which, with the help of tests and interviews, assessed the prisoners and created suitable rehabilitation programs for them. The teams consisted of psychologists, social workers, studies instructors, vocational guidance counselors, and psychiatrists. At this stage there were mainly three types of rehabilitation programs: therapeutic, generally educational (elementary school), and vocational. The underlying principle was "the more the better." In other words, the chances of successful rehabilitation improved as the variety of activities inside the prison increased. This occasionally could lead to an attitude of "anything goes," wherein the usefulness or uselessness of the activities was never questioned.

Alongside the assessments, very specific classification systems were developed. The basis was not just how dangerous prisoners were deemed to be, nor their liability to escape, but was especially their need of and possibilities for rehabilitation. Different kinds of prisoners were placed in different kinds of prisons. One of the pioneers embodying this type of thinking was the famous Sing Sing (Ossining) prison in the state of New York. In Sing Sing, prisoners were extensively tested and assessed, psychologically and otherwise, as early as the 1920s. Bernard Glueck, doctor of psychology, founded a psychiatric clinic in Sing Sing in 1916, which the Rockefeller Foundation funded. The term *clinical criminology* was introduced (Callahan 1996:445–446). The idea was for Sing Sing to function as a general assessment and placement prison that allocated prisoners to other state prisons according to their varying needs of treatment. When looking back on the prison service of the era, however, a classic phenomenon can often be detected: it was more a matter of principles and objectives than it was the actual reality of the cell blocks. Prisoners usually served their sentences in dreary conditions in overcrowded institutions. Rehabilitation did not take place, and treatment was rarely even attempted. The prisoner was seen as a passive object who was treated with different kinds of methods.

The new rehabilitative ideas took a long time to come to Finland, if indeed they came at all. Group work methods began to be discussed in the early 1960s, but the first psychologists, for instance, only came to Turku and Helsinki central prisons in 1968. (Social workers had arrived in the late 1940s.) It can be claimed that the Finnish prison service system was based on the so-called coercive treatment ideology of the nineteenth century long into the 1960s, although the treatment ideology was never as strong as, for example, in Sweden. Generally, Finland stayed rather "classical" in its crime policy. The assessment and classification of inmates has arrived in Finland only recently. Traditionally, very different kinds of prisoners have served their sentences together in Finland.

Internationally, two ideologies began to form in the 1960s. Inkeri Anttila (1991) describes them as follows:

> One line of thought, represented by psychologists and psychiatrists especially, believed that increasing resources, testing inmates, founding assessment and distribution prisons, creating more effective methods of treatment, and in some cases, isolating prisoners in special institutions, lead to the rehabilitation of inmates and therefore decrease crime. On the other hand, the other ideological stance, represented especially by sociologists but also by certain lawyers, again and again brought up research results which proved the hopelessness of

the attempts of treatment in prison. In fact, many of the same people who were of the opinion that certain inmates needed treatment also admitted that a prison cannot be a place of treatment. (pp. 346–347)

The Crisis of the Rehabilitative Ideal: Does Anything Work?

Developments in behavioral and social sciences after World War II led to numerous studies that attempted to estimate the results of various methods of intervention in treating criminals. In 1974, American criminologist Robert Martinson and his colleagues (1974:22–53) summarized the results in a metastudy, on the basis of which he published an article that is considered to have deeply influenced not only American but also European criminal policies and prison service. Martinson's article sported the title "What Works?" but, in accordance with the results of Martinson's study, the title was soon modified among criminologists and criminal politicians into "Nothing works!" Martinson was by no means the first one to voice this opinion. In 1958, the famous criminologist Donald R. Cressey (1958:14–19) criticized the treatment in prisons. According to him, behavioral theory officially used a mixture of humanitarianism, middle-class values, and some psychiatric principles. Under such a system, institutions' success was impossible to measure. However, Martinson was the first one whose views won great publicity. For instance, he appeared on the popular American TV show *60 Minutes* on CBS.

According to the cliché "nothing works!", the methods employed in treating offenders have so far accomplished nothing—they do not rehabilitate anybody. Martinson reviewed over 200 different studies to assess the various methods of treatment, such as general and vocational education, individual counseling, group counseling, milieu therapy, medication, and activities that take place after release (such as supervision in parole).

Nevertheless, Martinson did *not* claim that nothing works. In a few studies, at least a minor positive effect on recidivism was detected. The idea that Martinson's metastudy sought to invalidate was that individual rehabilitative methods could considerably reduce recidivism. Martinson (1974) summarized his views thus:

> It may be, on the other hand, that there is a more radical flaw in our present strategies—that education at its best, or that psychotherapy at its best, cannot overcome, or even appreciably reduce, the powerful tendency for offenders to continue in criminal behavior. Our present treatment programs are based on a theory of crime as a "disease"— that is to say, as something foreign and abnormal in the individual which can presumably be cured. This theory may well be flawed, in that it overlooks—indeed, denies—both the normality of crime in society and the personal normality of a very large proportion of offenders, criminals who are merely responding to the facts and conditions of our society. (p. 49)

Therefore, all breaches of the norms of law cannot be attributed to the problems of an individual's persona; all criminals do not have a "deficit" that could be removed by the right treatment. Many offenders have had a relatively unproblematic childhood, they are not socially or intellectually incompetent, and yet they violate the law. Crime, especially in its level and structure, is a complicated social phenomenon that cannot in its entirety be explained by a criminal's psychological background.

When considering Martinson's views, we have to keep in mind what methods were being assessed more widely in the late 1960s and the early 1970s. The therapeutic ideal of that era was in many ways permeated with psychodynamic and psychoanalytic thought (and often nonsensical group sessions, the likes of which are depicted in the novel and film *One Flew Over the Cuckoo's Nest*). Probation could mean nothing more than a passive report to an officer once every month. Cognitive-behavioral methods and therapeutic communities were scarcely used at the time. At least in this respect Martinson's analysis was correct: few methods produced effective results from the viewpoint of recidivism. Martinson also revised his philosophy in 1978, acknowledging that he had been plagued by a kind of methodological narcissism that resulted in his ignoring several relevant studies in the meta-analysis due to some insignificant shortcomings in them. Had they been included in the metastudy, the chances of rehabilitation would have looked a little better (Martinson 1978).

In his original article, Martinson also considers the then topical question of the significance of risk assessment in the penal system. According to some views, the offense-centered idea of punishment should have been abandoned, and the sentence should have increasingly depended on a person's likelihood of recidivism and psychologically assessed level of dangerousness. Here Martinson, however, defended the classical view of criminal law: If assessing the risk for recidivism were a central element in imposing punishment, we would end up in an endless quagmire. It would then be logical to sentence a young, multiply-convicted car thief with an intoxicant addiction to a long imprisonment, while a middle-class jealousy killer could be released relatively soon or be sentenced only to probation with supervision (Martinson 1974:50). The blameworthiness of the offense should be the basis of the punishment. Exaggerated utilitarianism, where the punishment is viewed only from the point of rehabilitation, can easily mislead us.

We also have good cause to ask whether recidivism is too rough an indicator for assessing the results of different kinds of rehabilitative treatment. It may be that these methods of treatment have produced many positive results per se, but that positive factor is annulled in the circumstances in which the person finds him/herself after the release. In Finland, for instance, it can be very difficult to detect the positive results of rehabilitation when after release, a persistent offender—unemployed and with nowhere to stay—ends up living in a night shelter for homeless alcoholics. On the other hand, many of the results of rehabilitation only become visible after several years, not immediately during the first few months of freedom.

This problem is well illuminated in William McCord and José Sanchez's study on how well the young graduates of two different kinds of reform schools fared after their release (see Currie 1985:241–244). In the 1950s, Wiltwyck School was considered a progressive place where up-to-date methods in treating young offenders were employed. It provided a well-organized environment where punitive measures were avoided and self-control and self-esteem were encouraged. The researchers compared Wiltwyck with Lyman School, which was a traditional institution that favored punishment—in actuality a juvenile prison. These two establishments were exact ideological opposites.

Two comparable groups of former pupils were found and their situation was evaluated in the 1980s, when they were 30–40 years old. The former Wiltwyck boys were less inclined to recidivism during their first five years of freedom than the Lyman boys. It seemed apparent that the rehabilitation-centered treatment in Wiltwyck was much more successful than the punishment-centered program in Lyman. The Wiltwyck method had even been effective in the case of boys who had been labeled "psychopaths" or "impulsively aggressive."

After five years, however, the Wiltwyck graduates began to have serious problems with the police. At around the same time, the number of crimes committed by the former Lyman pupils diminished. According to the researchers, this paradox was due to the fact that the increase in recidivism was, almost without exception, only in the black and Hispanic pupils of Wiltwyck. For the majority of the Lyman pupils, who were whites of Irish, Italian, or French Canadian origin, it was easier to reintegrate into society and find permanent employment, among other things.

In other words, the rehabilitative methods of Wiltwyck worked, but they could not prevent the boys from committing new crimes because there were no legitimate ways for them to succeed in life, and the boys were pushed back into a criminogenic environment after their release. As a result, the discussion began to emphasize that the essential factor in making rehabilitative programs successful is the environment in which the methods are employed, not always so much the substance of the methods themselves.

The discussion centered around Martinson's views hardly gained attention in Finland. Some ten years earlier, a heated critical debate concerning the old-fashioned coercive treatment system of prisoners and criminals had begun in the country. The sharpest critique was directed at the preventive detention and progressive systems and at the lengthy terms of sentence in imprisonment. Thanks to the critique, the system was reformed in the early 1970s, and the main function of imprisonment became morality-inducing general prevention. Imprisonment should be employed considerably less because of its negative effects, and at the same time, those negative effects should be minimized. The term of imprisonment therefore should be utilized as well as possible by arranging activities for inmates that were useful from the viewpoint of release, such as work and studies. In Finnish prisons, activities designed to "utilize the term of sentence" became the talk of the day. But rehabilitation was not the main function of the prison sentence.

Soon after Martinson's study had received public attention, a great number of researchers and people who had experience with rehabilitative programs in practice expressed their differing views. Some important names are Paul Gendreau, Robert Ross, James Bonta, Francis Cullen, and Clive Hollin. They argued that more recent evaluations of rehabilitative programs indicated that many of them work well, for at least some offenders (see, e.g., Gendreau & Ross 1979, Andrews et al. 1990).

They also emphasized that rehabilitative measures in fact have never been given a fair chance to prove their effectiveness compared with other measures in treating criminals. In the majority of cases the substance of the rehabilitative programs was in reality very different from what it should have been. The personnel were incompetent and almost completely unmotivated. The counterargument strongly emphasizes the importance of the therapeutic integrity of the programs. Eventually, the term *structured rehabilitation* was introduced in the 1990s.

As we have seen, recidivism alone may be too unspecific an indicator in evaluating the change in an individual's behavior. It has been claimed, for instance, that we do not estimate the efficacy of a hospital according to how many of its patients become ill again at a later date, or intoxicant programs according to how many of the clients fall off the wagon at some later point. If absolute objectives do not work elsewhere, how could they work in rehabilitating criminals?

In the Finnish intoxicant treatment system, the point of departure has been a wider interpretation of the term *treatment result*, with several levels. Adapting this interpretation, we can reach a hierarchy of results, for example:

1. "Rehabilitation," no offenses, at least not serious ones
2. Partial improvement of the situation, diminishing number of offenses
3. The situation does not deteriorate, positive factors remain
4. The deterioration of the situation can be delayed
5. Pain relief

Such scaling, or even "lowering," of results naturally causes even greater difficulties for empirical studies that attempt to research the reduction of recidivism through different measures of treatment. On the other hand, we can ask whether "pain relief," especially when results and effectiveness are required, is sufficient grounds for arranging a form of treatment.

Rehabilitative Thinking at the Turn of the Century

During the last decades of the twentieth century, the publications in the field actively began to discuss rehabilitation and its possibilities, in prison as well as post-release. Martinson's question "What works?" rose to the surface again: Which kinds of treatment and programs have a significant effect in preventing recidivism? A large number of both old and new studies on the effectiveness of different types of treatment and programs have been placed in the foreground. The results are by no means self-evident or consistent, but several meta-analyses have at least partly reached the same conclusions.

The late twentieth century ushered in the Era of Structured Rehabilitation. This implies abandoning the former "anything goes" idea, in which the quality and consistency of the treatment was largely neglected. The treatment ideology of the new era requires that the offender, too, accept responsibility for the success of the treatment. Demands are set for the structure of the treatment: the programs must be uniformly and consistently realized by committed, trained personnel. Methods designed to influence learning, morality, and values have replaced classic psychotherapy and its derivatives. The new era also mandates that private enterprises sell treatment programs to the officials of the penal system.

Andrews and Bonta (1994:175–178) have presented four basic principles, which they think should be the points of departure of successful treatment programs: risk, need, responsivity, and professional discretion. The risk principle consists of two different components—being able to predict criminal behavior, and basing treatment on the level of risk. High-risk offenders should have more intensive and extensive services. The need principle means that we should be able to identify the criminogenic needs of the offenders. A significant amount of these needs are associated with pro-criminal attitudes and values.

The responsivity principle refers to the idea of delivering treatment programs in a style and mode that is consistent with the ability and learning style of the offender; and professional discretion means that not all offenders can be treated in exactly the same way, although they may share similar risk and need factors. There must be room for professional judgment, which can serve to override other principles of assessment in each unique case.

The new, structured rehabilitative idea has been justified by its concentration on the elementary factors of crime, which traditional methods of prevention, control, and intimidation cannot affect: antisocial values and attitudes, and the effect of peer-group participation.

Risk-assessment methods have come under criticism in recent years. Eric Silver and Lisa Miller (2002:138–161) consider the social and political implications of using actuarial risk-assessment tools for social control. They argue that actuarial tools are designed primarily to facilitate the efficient management of institutional resources rather than to target individuals or social conditions in need of reform. Second, they argue that the group-based nature of actuarial prediction methods may contribute to the continued marginalization of populations already at the fringes of the economic and political mainstream. Risk assessment and prediction can become self-fulfilling prophecies.

We have already seen that the new rehabilitation and treatment ideology especially emphasizes the importance of therapeutic integrity. Achieving this goal requires reformation in how the organization, personnel, and activities are structured in prisons. The realization of therapeutic integrity must meet the following prerequisites and demands as presented by Reppucci (1973; see also Hollin 1992:133–134). The author's personal professional experience in the 1980s in the special activity center of Finnish Probation Service strongly supports them.

- *There must be a clear guiding background philosophy understood by everyone involved.* The program cannot be based on some mysterious "occult science" that only a few special experts can comprehend and master.

- *There must be an organizational structure that facilitates communication and accountability.* Small groups of people with conflicting interests do not support integrity. Communication must be open, and responsibility must be delegated to the shop-floor personnel.

- *Personnel must be actively involved in decision making.* People only accept responsibility if they can affect matters under discussion before a decision is made.

- *A community orientation must be maintained.* Crime and the inmate community are in many ways essentially social factors. Thus, the idea of influencing offenders through individual therapy alone is often doomed to fail. In the case of substance abuse/addiction, for instance, social dependency can be as important a factor as physical and psychological dependency.

- *Time constraints must be set in developing and "tuning" rehabilitation programs*, so that the pressure of trying to achieve too much in too short a time can be resisted. Human behavior, and criminal behavior, too, are complex issues. There are no simple miracle cures.

What Works and What Does Not?

During the last few decades the literature and international conferences in the field have presented summaries of various methods and programs, some of which have an apparent influence on recidivism and others that do not seem to have such influence, or even a contrary effect. It is understandable that, due to the complexity of the issue, the results can be conflicting.

In one country, or in one prison, a certain method can produce good results in reducing recidivism in a short time, whereas such results cannot be detected in another place. There can be a variety of reasons for this, such as differences in how the program is carried out, differences in the target group, or differences in analyses of the results. A program can be effective in the case of certain types of criminals, for example property offenders, but may have no effect on violent offenders. It also has been discovered that a method can be reasonably effective when carried out in freedom, but the same results cannot be reached when employing the method in prison. Furthermore, the majority of the evaluation research has taken place in the United States and Canada, thus making it difficult to ensure that the conclusions are valid where other countries are concerned.

Generally speaking, it would seem that the percentages referring to the reduction in recidivism discovered in the evaluations vary between 0 and 40 percent. The question that arises, then, is how large the reduction should be in order to be considered significant. Despite the relative inconsistency and openness to various interpretations of the results, it is still possible to make a few generalizations when it comes to which methods have at least a short-term effect on recidivism, however it is measured. Positive results seem to be achieved by the following methods (see, e.g., MacKenzie 2000:464–469):

- *Programs and activities that include a cognitive component.* Cognitive here refers to concentrating on a person's patterns of thought and attitudes sustaining criminal behavior. It is a matter of concentrating on the offense itself and not just thinking that changing the environment and circumstances of the offender will reduce his or her recidivism.

- *Therapeutic communities in prisons and other institutional environments.* These work especially well for drug users. Therapeutic communities are a method where the people in rehabilitation are to a great extent responsible for carrying out the activities, but also for themselves and for the other members of the community. In Finland, the so-called Kisko-projects carried out in Kerava prison and the Helsinki work colony partly conform with the ideas of a therapeutic community.

- *High-quality vocational education programs, sufficiently versatile work- and professional programs in prisons, and employment-centered activity in aftercare.* This is a wide area, but many studies have concluded that these forms of rehabilitation have an influence in reducing recidivism, too, even though they are often well justified for other reasons as well.

Scientists also have published lists of the treatment methods that do not appear to produce results or may even produce negative results. There is general agreement that the traditional psychoanalytic and psychodynamic therapy models do not reduce recidivism. The same is true of many vague and unstructured, often nondirective methods. "Nondirective" refers to a form of individual therapy wherein the client's explanations and reflection are either largely neglected or not actively directed and corrected.

Some Vital Questions

As mentioned previously, in the area of prison service the tension created by the sometimes-conflicting targets set for prison today needs constant reflection. Many questions of principle related to the rehabilitation of offenders, too, necessitate theoretical and practical discussion. A few of the most common ones are presented here.

1. *When and where should rehabilitation take place?* The ideal would naturally be that active rehabilitation be carried out in all the places where criminals are treated. Because of the limitations on resources and possibilities, however, we must prioritize and make choices regarding where rehabilitation would work best. In principle, rehabilitation can be realized in three phases: before imprisonment, in prison, or after imprisonment. It is often suggested that treatment should start as early as possible, at school age even, to prevent the formation and strengthening of a criminal identity. Many studies have also concluded that some methods of treatment work best when carried out in freedom, for instance in connection with aftercare. Especially in countries where terms of imprisonment are very long, refocusing emphasis mainly on treatment programs carried out in the community has been discussed. Some scholars still have the view that rehabilitation and punishment should be separated (e.g., Logan & Gaes 1993). Some say that prison as a place of rehabilitative treatment has the advantage of being a location where a large number of offenders in need of treatment are already gathered.

2. *Is affecting recidivism the only criterion of prison activities?* The inmates' daily activities, the effects of which on recidivism are unknown or unquestioned, have always existed in prisons. Some activities have been intuitively considered to produce positive results, even though the matter has never been empirically studied. If inmate activities are selected only on the basis of effectiveness, it can lead to negative results in regard to the whole of prison service work. In this context it is often argued that prisoners should have a right to even those forms of activity inside the prison which cannot be proved to have an immediate effect on recidivism, such as health care, education, vocational activities, hobbies, etc. (Mathiesen 2000:179). The long-term effects of these activities are often unknown and not easily studied.

3. *Is effectiveness the only value?* Scottish criminologist David Garland (1990:291–292), among others, has suggested that legal systems include many values of a very fundamental nature that can collide with simple "efficiency" thinking. Examples are the fundamental concepts of law and justice. The realization of justice and the effectiveness ideal can be in contradiction. A certain treatment or activity can appear sensible, but we can nevertheless ask if it is just. This phenomenon reached its most acute stage at the time of the so-called old treatment ideology, when all consideration of justice could be abandoned. A minor offense could lead to decades in prison or other institutions, because the offender was being "reformed" and it was thought to be for his own good. From this point of view the famous Norwegian sociologist Thomas Mathiesen (2000:174–179) is still very critical about the new positivist rehabilitation ideal. Penal systems as a part of legal systems have other functions besides the aim of altering the behavior of an individual offender.

4. *Are we forgetting the inmate community?* Different forms of treatment often have been brought to prison from the outside. Various methods of individual treatment have not taken into account the environment in which they are carried out. In the course of history, the influence of the inmate community—both good and evil—as a rule has been ignored. In the most extreme cases, prison has been perceived as a collection of separate, isolated criminal individuals whose sole need and objective is to be rehabilitated. In most cases, rehabilitation is not an offender's principal objective, and his or her aim is not becoming a decent citizen (such as the personnel of the prison represent), but rather everyday survival in the inmate community and in the prison. The methods and strategies of survival often have an opposite effect to the aim of rehabilitation. Criminal identity and subculture are actual strategies of survival. The effects of rehabilitation can easily be annulled in a matter of minutes inside the inmate community. Methods based on therapeutic communities take the inmates into consideration and attempt to create an alternative, healthy sense of community, with norms of its own. It has been very difficult to realize these methods in such a way, however, to include the whole inmate community. Legal norms sometimes can also hinder the formation of a strong therapeutic community.

5. *Who is treated and who is not?* In all systems of treatment, there has been an inclination to select clients in a way that perhaps serves the interest of the rehabilitator rather than aiming at the original objective. Clients selected for treatment are the motivated, "easily" rehabilitated ones, who might do quite well even without treatment. The clients with the most problems are left without attention, because it is very difficult and unrewarding to try to treat them.

This danger is also apparent when we look at rehabilitation in the context of prison service or aftercare, even if we attempt to take into account the risk-assessment principle based on the above-mentioned model. Because most often only a small percentage of the inmate community participates in rehabilitative activity, it is vital to recognize the problem of selection. It is also possible that the different objectives set for prison service may conflict here. When it comes to security in a prison, for instance, decisions about such matters as placement, for example, can be taken with a very different perspective from that of the inmate's rehabilitative needs. In theory, the prisoner who is the most dangerous and the most liable to recidivism is also in greatest need of rehabilitation, when the interest of the community is considered. In practice, this ideal is often hard to realize, even though some countries emphasize, for example, that maximum-security prisons and wards should have the best rehabilitative programs, both in quantity and in quality.

References

Andrews, D. A. & Bonta, James (1994). *The Psychology of Criminal Conduct*. Cincinnati: Anderson Publishing Co.

Andrews, D. A., Zinger, Ivan, Hoge, Robert D., Bonta, James, Gendreau, Paul, & Cullen, Francis T. (1990). Does Correctional Treatment Work? A Clinically Relevant and Psychologically Informed Meta-Analysis. *Criminology* 28(3): 369–426.

Anttila, Inkeri (1981). Kansainväliset vaikutteet Suomen vankeinhoidon kehityksessä [International influences in the development of Finnish Prison Service], in Suominen, Elina (ed.), *Suomen vankeinhoidon historiaa, osa I: Katsauksia vankeinhoidon kehitykseen*. Helsinki: Valtion Painatuskeskus.

Blomberg, Thomas G. & Lucken, Karol (2000). *American Penology: A History of Control*. New York: Aldine de Gruyter.

Callahan, Lisa A. (1996). Sing Sing Prison, in McShane, Marilyn D. & Williams, Frank P. (eds.), *Encyclopedia of American Prisons*. New York & London: Garland Publishing, Inc.

Cressey, Donald, R. (1958). Contradictory Directives in Complex Organizations: The Case of the Prison. *Administrative Science Quarterly* 4: 1–10.

Currie, Elliot (1985). *Confronting Crime: An American Challenge*. New York: Pantheon Books.

Foucault, Michel (1979). *Discipline and Punish: The Birth of the Prison*. New York: Vintage Books.

Garland, David (1990). *Punishment and Modern Society: A Study in Social Theory*. Oxford: Clarendon Press.

Gendreau, Paul & Ross, Bob (1979). Effective Correctional Treatment: Bibliotherapy for Cynics. *Crime and Delinquency* 25(4): 463–489.

Grimes, Ruth-Ellen M. (1996). Walnut Street Jail, in McShane, Marilyn D. & Williams, Frank P. (eds.), *Encyclopedia of American Prisons*. New York & London: Garland Publishing, Inc.

Hollin, Clive R. (1992). *Criminal Behaviour: A Psychological Approach to Explanation and Prevention*. London & Washington, DC: The Falmer Press.

Lappi-Seppälä, Tapio (2003). Prisoner Rates: Global Trends and Local Exceptions, in *Annual Report for 2002 and Resource Material Series No. 61*. UNAFEI, Fuchu, Tokyo, Japan.

Logan, Charles H. & Gaes, Gerald G. (1993). Meta-Analysis and the Rehabilitation of Punishment. *Justice Quarterly* 10(2): 245–263.

MacKenzie, Doris Layton (2000). Evidence-Based Corrections: Identifying What Works. *Crime and Delinquency* 46(4): 457–471.

Martinson, Robert (1974). What Works?—Questions and Answers about Prison Reform. *The Public Interest* 35: 22–54.

Martinson, Robert (1978). Martinson Attacks His Own Earlier Work. *Criminal Justice Newsletter* 9.

Mathiesen, Thomas (2000). *Prison on Trial*, 2nd ed. Winchester: Waterside Press.

Pears, Edwin (ed.) (1872). *Prisons and Reformatories at Home and Abroad. The Transactions of the International Penitentiary Congress, London July 3–13, 1872*. London: Longmans, Green, and Co.

Pisciotta, Alexander W. (1983). Scientific Reform: The "New Penology" at Elmira, 1876–1900. *Crime & Delinquency* 29(4): 613–630.

Reppucci, N. D. (1973). Social Psychology of Institutional Change: General Principles of Intervention. *American Journal of Community Psychology* 1: 330–341.

Sellin, Thorsten (1944). *Pioneering in Penology: The Amsterdam Houses of Correction in the Sixteenth and Seventeenth Centuries*. Philadelphia: University of Pennsylvania Press.

Silver, Eric & Miller, Lisa L. (2002). A Cautionary Note on the Use of Actuarial Risk Assessment Tools for Social Control. *Crime and Delinquency* 48(1): 138–161.

Westermarck, Edvard (1906, 1908). *The Origin and Development of the Moral Ideas*, Vol. 1–2. London: Macmillan & Co.

26

Contemporary Juvenile Justice Issues in Japan*

Michael S. Vaughn & Frank F. Y. Huang

Introduction

Although most of the Japanese criminal justice and criminological literature reports low rates of crime, Japan is not without social problems. Rapid social transformation accompanied by modernization and socioeconomic development is radically changing the social order in Japan. Even the concept of filial piety, an anchor on which society depends, is not as strong today as it was a few years ago. For example, in 1963, 41 percent of Japanese respondents said that caring for elderly parents was their "natural duty"; by 1990 the number declined to only 30 percent (Ogawa & Retherford, 1993). Moreover, only 3 percent in 1963 said caring for elderly parents was "not a good custom," compared to 12 percent in 1990. These sentiments are disproportionally held by Japanese under age 30. Young women are also changing very rapidly in contemporary Japan. In a society that overtly discriminates against women, many young Japanese women are becoming more independent, waiting longer to get married, and delaying childbirth. For example, the median age of marriage for Japanese women rose from 22 in 1949 to 26 in 1993 (Greenfeld, 1994).

Young Japanese are exposed to Western ideas of democracy, individualism, and egalitarianism at an unprecedented rate, which competes with their traditional culture based on conformity and deference to authority. Among young Japanese, diversity, openness, and pleasure-seeking behaviors are ushering in an era in which the legitimacy on which authority is granted and respected is challenged. For example, Japanese youths are so enthralled with the English language that its use is considered a symbol of

Prepared especially for *Comparative and International Criminal Justice, 2/E*.
*Portions of this article were taken from: Vaughn, 1990; Vaughn & Huang, 1992; Huang & Vaughn, 1992; Vaughn & Tomita, 1990; Vaughn, Huang, & Ramirez, 1994.

individualism, freedom, and nonconformity. Research shows that many Japanese study the English language because it liberates them from the "rigid social obligations inherent in" Japanese culture (Applbaum, 1992, p. 18).

Despite rapid change in Japan, the country is not besieged by escalating violent crime. Hence, scholars who study Japanese society and crime must embrace the importance of cultural relativism when conducting cross-cultural criminal justice research (Beirne, 1983). Because of the relatively low levels of crime in Japan as compared to the United States, researchers may erroneously conclude that crime is not a serious social concern in Japan. Japanese juvenile crime, however, remains a high priority of criminal justice officials despite the small numbers of arrests.

This article examines a variety of issues that have been problematic for contemporary Japanese juvenile justice agencies. First we present Japanese crime and social control in a cultural context, arguing for cultural relativism in cross-cultural criminal justice and criminological research. Next, we briefly describe the legal structure of the Japanese juvenile justice system. We then focus on three areas: juvenile motorcycle gangs *(bosozoku)*, juvenile school violence, and juvenile drug use and abuse. We compare and contrast the historical, social, and cultural phenomena that lead to contemporary problems for the juvenile justice system. We conclude that the modernization and internationalization of Japanese society and culture will continue to present the juvenile justice system with unique challenges well into the twenty-first century.

Structure of the Juvenile Justice System in Japan

Juvenile justice in Japan is administered under a system similar to the parens patriae philosophy found in the United States. The system is grounded in the philosophy that minors are to be distinguished from adults so they may be protected and rehabilitated (Bayley, 1991; Westermann & Burfeind, 1991). In reality, however, many juveniles are funneled into the system for purposes of control (Steinhoff, 1993). One who enters into the system may be exposed to formal or informal agents of social control, because the Japanese focus on both formal sanctions from the criminal justice system and informal social control mechanisms in the community.

The juvenile justice system is administered under two special laws: the Juvenile Law and the Child Welfare Law. The Juvenile Law is designed "to carry out protective measures relating to the character correction, and environmental adjustment of delinquent juveniles" (Shikita & Tsuchiya, 1976, p. 55). The Child Welfare Law promotes the "welfare of all the children into healthy development in adulthood" (Shikita & Tsuchiya, 1976, p. 55). The Juvenile Law controls juveniles with sanctions from the formal criminal justice system, whereas the Child Welfare Law is designed to deter juveniles through informal social control.

Juveniles within this system are categorized into one of three areas: juvenile offenders, lawbreaking children, and preoffense juveniles (Berezin, 1982; Terrill, 1992). Youths between the ages of 14 and 19, juvenile offenders, violate the penal code or special laws. The second category, lawbreaking children, are youths who are under age 14 and who commit offenses in violation of the penal code or special law but are deemed per se incapable of criminal conduct. Table 1 reports cases cleared by the police for juvenile offenders and lawbreaking children. Data indicate that the number of cases has stabilized in recent years.

Preoffense juveniles are youths who have not broken any laws but who show a propensity toward inappropriate and unsociable behavior. The preoffense category generally includes four types of behavior: (1) showing disrespect and disobedience toward parents and teachers, (2) truancy from school, (3) associating with individuals who have criminal records, and (4) continually engaging in activities inconsistent with a good moral character.

Due to increasing juvenile crime in the 1960s, the police established the Police Activity Rule for juveniles, which specified a new juvenile category called *predelinquents* (Yokoyama, 1989). The Police Activity Rule gave the police more discretion and greater latitude when processing juvenile offenders, and it allowed the police to play a more active role in supervising juvenile miscreants. This resulted in more juveniles being funneled into the juvenile justice system. Figure 1 shows that total juvenile arrest rates have increased over the last four decades. Heightened police scrutiny increased the number of juvenile offenders who were processed through the system for minor offenses. This is especially true for young Japanese women, who are perceived by many to be out of control; hence, law enforcement officials increasingly are involved in policing juvenile females. For example, the police detained over 100 young girls who were charged with selling their used underwear to pornographic vendors in Tokyo (Vending Machines, 1993). Police officers also cracked down on young girls in female gangs involved in hot rodding, sniffing paint thinner, and intimidating the public (Sato, 1991). Figure 2 shows that while juvenile felony rates declined in the late 1980s, they increased once again in the late 1990s.

Taking their cue from journalists in the United States, the Japanese press frequently sensationalizes juvenile delinquency, leading many to regard Japan's juvenile crime problem as a serious threat to social cohesion and order. The public believes that many juveniles reject traditional Japanese values and are more concerned with rock music and pursuit of material wealth than with school success and filial piety (Vaughn & Huang, 1992). Juvenile involvement in three areas of delinquency—motorcycle gangs, drug abuse, and school crime—helps feed the perception of disorder and of wayward youths victimizing society.

Table 1   Juvenile Penal Code Offenders Cleared by the Police and Rate per Population, by Age Group (1988–2000)

Year	Total			Under 14 years		14–15 years old		16–17 years old		18–19 years old	
	N	Rate	%	N	Rate	N	Rate	N	Rate	N	Rate
1988	231,210	12.1	53.0	38,004	5.3	96,019	23.4	69,800	17.4	27,387	7.2
1989	199,644	10.6	57.4	34,591	5.0	83,572	21.1	59,453	14.5	22,028	5.7
1990	182,328	9.8	56.7	28,160	4.2	73,441	19.5	58,034	14.2	22,760	6.3
1991	177,097	9.8	54.7	27,434	4.2	67,118	18.6	56,785	14.3	25,760	6.3
1992	157,167	8.9	51.0	23,285	3.7	57,347	16.5	50,483	13.4	26,052	6.4
1993	158,300	9.3	49.0	25,168	4.1	57,802	17.2	49,764	13.8	25,566	6.5
1994	155,079	9.4	46.7	23,811	3.9	55,281	17.1	50,564	14.6	25,423	6.8
1995	149,137	9.3	47.2	22,888	3.8	53,449	17.1	50,075	14.9	22,725	6.3
1996	156,826	10.1	49.2	23,245	4.0	55,298	18.1	54,713	16.9	23,570	6.8
1997	178,950	11.8	52.7	26,125	4.6	64,013	21.2	61,747	19.7	27,065	8.1
1998	184,290	12.5	52.5	26,905	4.9	66,124	22.0	61,952	20.3	29,309	9.0
1999	164,224	11.4	48.6	22,503	4.2	59,252	20.2	55,629	18.4	26,840	8.6
2000	152,813	10.8	46.3	20,477	3.9	56,305	19.9	52,455	17.2	23,576	7.8

Source: Ministry of Justice (1993–2001). *Hanzai Hakusho* (White Paper on Crime). Tokyo: Research and Training Institute.

Figure 1   Total Arrest Rates of Japanese Juveniles, 1936–2000*

Figure 2   Felony Arrest Rates of Japanese Juveniles, 1936–2000*

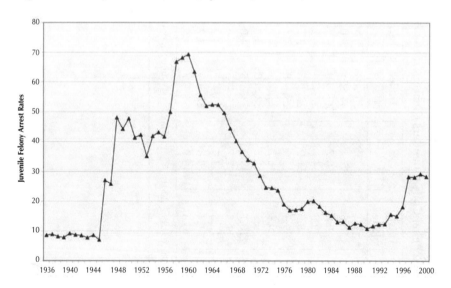

*Standardized per 100,000 population

Motorcycle Gangs

For the most part, delinquent motorcycle gangs are the product of affluent societies. After World War II, countries in Western Europe and North America experienced a proliferation of motorcycle gangs as the per capita incomes of citizens increased. Following a similar trend, as disposable incomes rose, Japan experienced a growth in motorcycle gang activity. Thus, Japanese motorcycle gangs are a reflection of the society from which they originate. Since 1954, the Japanese police have identified motorcycle gangs as a social problem (Huang, 1987), when "55 juvenile delinquents on motorcycles gathered at the Meiji Shrine in Tokyo" (Greenfeld, 1994, p. 38). From 1954 to 1964, juvenile groups used motorcycles to create noise and the illusion that community members were in jeopardy. The gangs of the so-called *kaminarizoku* period (1954–1964) were made up of youths who rode motorcycles primarily to make noise (Sato, 1991). *Kaminarizoku* gangs were not well-organized into clearly defined groups; their activities did not encompass serious criminal offenses. Since these gangs did not pose a serious threat to the social order, the public did not demand increased law enforcement to curb their activities.

During the *sakitozoku* period (1965–1973), the composition of motorcycle gangs shifted from school students to juvenile laborers. Modern motorcycles were more powerful, and as a result gang members committed more serious traffic violations and became involved in more accidents. One of the distinguishing features of this period was that gang members were increasingly involved in driving contests. These contests were held on weekends in densely populated areas, which attracted a large number of spectators. Because of the popularity of the events, the police experienced problems in crowd control. Deviance of motorcycle gangs during the *sakitozoku* period was primarily contained to fast and reckless driving and various traffic violations.

The National Police Agency of Japan first coined the term *bosozoku* in 1974 to represent motorcycle gangs (Kusakabe, 1981). During the *bosozoku* period (1974 to the present), more and more gang operations were linked to criminal activities. Motorcycle gang membership grew rapidly during this period. *Bosozoku* members increasingly were involved in erratic driving and gang fights. Citizens began to demand a harsh law enforcement response to deal with the escalating violence and disturbances to the social order. Driving events were now held on a year-round basis in both urban and rural areas.

In addition, the organizational structure of motorcycle gangs became more sophisticated, better organized, and more formal by establishing a ruling hierarchy of leadership. Many *bosozoku* gangs created symbols, which members wore proudly on shirts, jackets, and hats. These gang symbols also appeared on geographic territory in which *bosozoku* groups claimed ownership. During the *bosozoku* period, gangs began to receive much negative attention from the mass media, fueling public opinion that gang activities were criminally harmful and deleterious to society. Table 2 shows membership in *bosozoku* groups from 1975–1999.

According to Sato (1991), one salient characteristic of *bosozoku* activities is that membership in a *bosozoku* gang is considered a form of delinquency because of the alternative lifestyle embraced by the groups. However, although youths in *bosozoku* gangs disobey their parents, teachers, and elders, they are not generally involved in violent crime. Juveniles who engage in *bosozoku* events are said to engage in *asobigato hiko*, which means play-type delinquency. Most *bosozoku* members engage in gang activities and related delinquencies for the pursuit of excitement and thrills rather than for financial gain. Membership is most likely made up of frustrated youths attempting to escape from the pressures of family and

Table 2   Driving Events Involving Motorcycle Gang Members, 1975–1999

Year	Number of Driving Events	Individuals Participating in Events	Motorcycles at Driving Events
1975	2,328	170,300	92,300
1976	1,950	182,600	88,600
1977	1,984	230,000	116,900
1978	2,700	291,539	138,945
1979	2,004	134,006	66,391
1980	3,661	240,063	109,955
1981	3,272	160,999	72,364
1982	2,967	140,962	63,123
1983	2,251	113,738	50,034
1984	2,107	101,746	43,222
1985	2,723	120,715	54,108
1986	2,796	104,480	49,953
1987	3,249	127,867	60,051
1988	5,713	157,989	76,295
1989	5,875	150,349	70,430
1990	5,864	170,102	79,232
1991	7,073	154,147	76,436
1992	5,821	154,287	77,623
1993	5,203	105,527	54,957
1994	N/A	N/A	N/A
1995	5,825	107,486	49,852
1996	6,674	115,205	55,688
1997	6,357	112,056	54,623
1998	6,720	124,711	53,109
1999	6,542	139,402	34,692

Source: Ministry of Justice (1980–2000). *Keisatsu Hakusho* (White Paper on Police). Tokyo: National Police Agency.

school (Asgawa, 1980; Dojo, 1982). Moreover, members do not readily conform to traditional Japanese notions of appropriate behavior; they may not study for entrance examinations into high schools or universities.

Sato (1991) uses attraction theory to explain the formation of *bosozoku* gangs. Juveniles join motorcycle gangs to buffer the dullness and monotony of traditional Japanese society, which they accomplish by disrupting the social order—by riding motorcycles fast. Although *bosozoku* gangs intimidate adults, they serve as a mechanism of social play for youths by allowing them to drive fast, dress in unconventional clothing, and exhibit extravagant interpretations of their egos. Thus, membership in *bosozoku* groups allows juveniles to attain fellowship, camaraderie, and fraternity.

According to the Ministry of Justice (1993), *bosozoku* groups are primarily composed of juveniles (under age 20). Most *bosozoku* members are teenagers between the ages 16 and 19. During the 1980s, juvenile members represented 70 percent of total *bosozoku* membership. Most also are detached from the traditional teenage activities involved in pursuing an education. However, research also shows that most *bosozoku* members mature out of this delinquency and adopt conventional, noncriminal adult lifestyles. Most reintegrate into mainstream Japanese society. In short, association with a motorcycle gang is considered a youthful indiscretion, not an indication of a lifelong commitment to criminal activity. Recently, however, reports indicate that some *bosozoku* members join organized crime *(boryokudan)* gangs. Greenfeld (1994, p. 38) argues that *bosozoku* members "perm their hair, dress like wise guys, and drive flashy cars or motorcycles without mufflers, hoping to be noticed by the local" organized crime family.

Although table 2 shows that the number of motorcycles involved in *bosozoku* activities has decreased since the late 1980s, the number of driving events has increased. Moreover, the total membership in *bosozoku* groups is still large. In 1989, the police estimated that the *bosozoku* had 35,472 members, a decrease from 40,629 in 1981. Although the actual number of disturbances attributed to *bosozoku* gangs also decreased from 4,203 in 1977 to 582 in 1989, these conflicts and disturbances still result in a large number of injuries and property damage, which brings a great deal of media scrutiny (Mugishima & Tamura, 1976). In 1994 hundreds of gangs remained, "including Medusa, Fascist, Black Emperor, Imprisoned for Life, Kill Everybody, the Crazies, and the Midnight Angels, many loosely federated, some with dozens of chapters and hundreds of members" (Greenfeld, 1994, p. 38). In the late 1990s, *bosozoku* activity was still a concern of Japanese juvenile justice authorities.

Drug Abuse

The policies of the imperial government during World War II created the conditions for stimulant drug abuse to become a major problem in

Japan after the war. Until the war began, opium-derived substances were the primary drugs abused in Japan because production techniques remained primitive. During the war, however, techniques for producing stimulant drugs improved as the government accelerated its research on sleep deprivation and performance enhancement. The wartime imperial government produced stimulants for Japanese soldiers and factory workers in the war effort (Hughes, 1977; Kato, 1969; Yokoyama, 1992). As the war continued, and as more drugs were introduced into Japan, the number of Japanese addicts increased significantly.

Immediately after the war, there was an "epidemic of amphetamine psychosis with symptomatology strikingly similar to that of schizophrenia" (Utena & Niwa, 1992, p. 68). This epidemic occurred because the streets were inundated with surplus methamphetamine that was left over from the war. The potential financial rewards for manufacturers, distributors, and traffickers helped to spur significant postwar increases in stimulants (Kato, 1969).

By 1963, abuse of inhalants became a problem among juveniles (Suwanwela & Poshyachinda, 1986). The abuse of solvents reached epidemic proportions in 1967 and continues today in the form of sniffing glue, paint thinner, and gasoline (Suwaki, 1989; Tamura, 1989). The police reported 20,000 contacts with juvenile solvent abusers in 1968; the number increased to 50,000 in 1971. Solvent-induced deaths are also reported widely in the contemporary literature (Castberg, 1990; Clifford, 1976).

A record number of juveniles and females began to abuse stimulants in the 1970s. By the mid-1980s, they accounted for 25 percent of all persons arrested for possession of illegal stimulants (Ministry of Justice, 1993). Some scholars claim that an increase in juvenile and female drug use is related to the diminishing influence of informal social control within families (Ministry of Justice, 1983). Kokuchi (1971) contends that most juvenile and female drug abusers start their delinquent careers earlier than nonabusing delinquents. Research also shows that stimulant drug abusers possess unstable personality traits and are self-absorbed; their lack of self-control in early childhood is a predictor of drug abuse in adolescence and young adulthood. This research conforms to Gottfredson and Hirschi's (1990) idea that crime results from poor impulse control.

In today's Japan, market forces create a demand for "fatigue killers," which were advertised aggressively to young Japanese as therapeutic and beneficial. As a result, stimulants, both illegal and legal, are much in demand in contemporary Japan (Bailey & Segers, 1990). "Experts estimate that as many as 600,000 Japanese" routinely take stimulants (Schoenberger, 1987, p. 34). In fact, the distinction between legal and illicit stimulants is not clear-cut. In 1990, for example, a caffeine- and vitamin-based drink called Regain became a national sensation. Regain was advertised by the pharmaceutical colossus Sankyo as a health tonic that could provide instant strength or cure a hangover. A song produced by Sony

Records, promoting the beverage, sold more than 300,000 copies and rose to the top of the music charts. In 1991, the annual sale of stimulant products and hangover drugs reached 60 billion yen. The most recent legitimate stimulant on the Japanese market is the so-called "wake-up" gum. There is a thriving market for caffeine chewing gum or lozenges marketed under the names "Strong Man" and "Sting" (Hardy, 1993).

These marketing techniques have been successful at enticing Japanese youths to purchase and experiment with these remedies. Unfortunately, young persons who consume legal stimulants also are more likely to use illegal stimulants. Research shows that persons between the ages 16 and 30 appear to be most at risk of stimulant addiction (Suwaki, Toshida, & Ohara, 1985). Table 3 supports this claim; juveniles in later adolescence are more likely to use stimulant drugs than are younger juveniles. Juveniles between the ages of 18 and 19 are most likely to be referred for prosecution for stimulant abuse. The latest data also indicate that stimulant abuse has not declined and that stimulant drugs remain a serious problem.

Table 3   Juveniles Referred to Public Prosecutors for Violation of Stimulant Drug Laws, 1975, 1985, 1991–2000 (by percent)

Age Group	1975	1985	1991	1992	1993	1994
14–15	5.7	4.2	4.3	3.4	2.8	2.2
16–17	27.9	29.0	24.6	24.1	21.0	23.1
18–19	66.4	66.8	71.1	72.4	76.2	74.6
Totals	100 (N = 265)	100 (N = 2,214)	100 (N = 1,106)	100 (N = 1,205)	100 (N = 1,172)	100 (N = 990)
Age Group	1995	1996	1997	1998	1999	2000
14–15	3.5	3.1	4.4	5.6	3.7	7.1
16–17	23.9	31.0	28.4	27.4	29.2	29.7
18–19	72.6	65.9	67.2	67.0	67.1	63.3
Totals	100 (N = 1,332)	100 (N = 1,839)	100 (N = 1,954)	100 (N = 1,208)	100 (N = 1,210)	100 (N = 1,388)

Source: Ministry of Justice (1993–2001). *Hanzai Hakusho* (White Paper on Crime). Tokyo: Research and Training Institute.

School Crime

Many educational experts claim that the schools are not teaching Japanese values and etiquette, but instead are opting for rigid academic criteria suited to scholastic entrance examinations (Ogura, 1987; Tokuoka & Cohen, 1987). This environment creates anomie and strain in students who cannot receive an education from a prestigious university (Lee, 1991). The Japanese academic environment is geared toward preparation for *juken jigoku*, "examination hell" (Becker, 1988). Students who fail early entrance examinations are more likely to be stigmatized as failures, a situation leading to frustration and an increase in delinquency. This problem is compounded by the fact that in any given year about half the students taking university entrance examinations fail (Feiler, 1991). Likewise, students who are prevented from seeking a university education are more likely than others to turn to delinquency. These students are called *ronin*, a "name once given to samurai who were cut off from their masters and forced to roam the countryside" (Feiler, 1991, p. 183). Their delinquency usually takes the form of property crime.

Structural inequalities in Japan are due to an education system based on hierarchical levels of prestige (Lee, 1991). Attending the appropriate schools in Japan determines an individual's professional relationships, occupational opportunities, and eventually career placement (Kariya & Rosenbaum, 1987). The competition begins early in life; parents usually enroll their toddlers in supplementary schools (White, 1987). In junior high school, the fierce competition for college placement intensifies (Katoh, 1991). Achievement on examinations for admission to distinguished senior high schools determines a student's prospects of entering a prestigious university. Research shows that poor school performance is related to delinquency (Kitajima, 1982); the onset of delinquency is related to students' failure in junior high school (De Vos & Mizushima, 1962; Iwai, 1966).

The pressure of school entrance examinations may lead two types of students into juvenile delinquency. First, students uninterested in college, who do not benefit from the junior high school curriculum designed to prepare them for senior high school examinations, may turn to delinquency. This hypothesis appears to be supported by a recent study (Seishonen Hakusho, 1990). The researchers found that nondelinquents sought admission to the most prestigious schools, whereas delinquents did not seek admission to good schools.

Second, juveniles who place a high priority on senior high entrance examinations but who do not gain admission to an appropriate senior high school and thus cannot attend a prestigious university may turn to delinquency (Sakuta & Saito, 1982). Junior high school-aged youths (14–15) start delinquent careers as a result of school problems. It appears that senior high school students do not commit delinquent acts as frequently as junior high school students, perhaps because senior high schools are divided into two categories. One category is reserved for students striving for a university degree; the other, less stringent division serves students who are not on the university track. This two-track system in senior high school ameliorates pressures on the noncollege-track students (Kariya & Rosenbaum, 1987).

Three additional factors characterize the seriousness of educational problems and their impact on juvenile delinquency: a test-oriented educational system, weakened teacher-student relationships, and problematic mentoring. These factors are not mutually exclusive in creating school-induced delinquency: the sheer volume of information disseminated creates pressure that threatens meaningful learning and leads to alienation between teachers and students. Test-oriented education promulgates a single standard and judges students by a single criterion: the passing of stringent examinations. Problematic mentoring means that contemporary Japanese teachers primarily focus on school performance geared toward scholastic examinations instead of cultivating and shaping students' personalities. As a result, students who do poorly are labeled as failures, and this situation leads to potential problems. Most delinquents who commit violence toward teachers are school dropouts.

Campus violence may be the most accurate indicator of dysfunctional schools. There are three types of campus violence: violence toward students, violence toward teachers, and school vandalism. Castberg (1990) contends that violence toward teachers is a product and a reflection of weakened social bonds between students and teachers. Another form of violence in Japanese schools is bullying, or *ijime* (Castberg, 1990), the physical or psychological harassment of a weaker party by a stronger party or of a minority by a majority. The bullying problem was widespread in the mid-1980s. The Ministry of Education conducted a study and found that 52, 69, and 43 percent of school officials in elementary, middle, and high schools, respectively, reported bullying (Katoh, 1991). Critics claim, however, that there are many more cases of bullying not reported to the authorities.

Although bullying occurs most frequently in schools, the phenomenon itself is an indication of parents and teachers abdicating their responsibilities. As for parents, bullying may be a sign of decline in physical contact between parents and children; as a result children are raised without proper supervision to guide and structure their activities. As parents and children become less attached and interdependent, violence toward teachers and bullying of classmates will continue. School officials, including teachers and principals, also are criticized for allowing bullying to occur at school. Oka (1993) faults teachers for not aiding the victims of bullying; teachers conceal and deny the existence of bullying in fear of allegations that they cannot control their classrooms. This "hands-off" policy has led to Japanese courts recently recognizing the complicity of school officials in allowing bullying to occur. In 1994, the Tokyo High Court ordered Tokyo's Nakano Fujimi Junior High School to pay $110,500 to the parents of a 13-year-old boy who committed suicide because he was bullied by classmates. In holding that school officials have a duty to monitor student behavior and discipline wrongdoers, the court opined that the bullying forced the boy to

Part IV: Corrections, Punishment, and Juvenile Justice

experience psychological pain, humiliating treatment, and devastating personal attacks (Hirakawa, 1994). One study estimated that 25 to 33 percent of all youth suicides in Japan were caused by bullying (Thornton & Endo, 1992). Table 4 reports data on violent incidents committed at school.

Table 4 Violent Incidents at School Cleared by the Police, 1988–1995

Year	Number of cases	Number of victims	Victims per case	Persons arrested/counseled			
				Total	Persons per case	Junior high school	Senior high school
1988	943	1,490	1.6	2,581	2.7	2,409	172
1989	939	1,598	1.7	2,651	2.8	2,479	172
1990	780	1,410	1.8	2,260	2.9	2,130	130
1991	625	990	1.6	1,702	2.7	1,568	134
1992	567	923	1.6	1,600	2.8	1,430	170
1993	470	767	1.6	1,293	2.8	1,137	156
1994	494	741	1.5	1,166	2.4	1,092	74
1995	464	624	1.3	1,005	2.2	917	88

Source: Ministry of Justice (1993–1996). Hanzai Hakusho *(White Paper on Crime)*. Tokyo: Research and Training Institute.

Conclusion

Many have asked the question, "Why does Japan have relatively few violent juvenile delinquents in comparison to other industrialized democracies?" The answers are complex and multidimensional. From the law enforcement perspective, the police perform special services such as counseling juveniles. Because Japanese policing embodies some of the concepts of community policing, officers, while perhaps an intimidating force, are accepted by the citizenry (Fairchild, 1993). This accounts for a high degree of citizen-reported crime to the police and a high rate of total penal code offenses cleared by arrest (64 percent in 1987). Moreover, the Japanese are rewarded for taking personal responsibility for their actions; adults are rewarded for their involvement in crime prevention activities. On a structural level, streets are narrow and houses are small, but this proximity fosters an intimacy so that many Japanese know when juveniles are misbehaving. Such closeness also fosters community unity insofar as the Japanese believe that "we are all together, and what I do intimately affects others." This intimacy is lacking in many Western nations. In addition, within some Japanese communities, each house in each neighborhood is located on a billboard map, listing the occupants' names for each house.

Taken in their totality, these factors serve as an incalculable tool for social control because communities know neighbors and immediately recognize outsiders or potential troublemakers.

According to Quinney (1970), each society constructs a "social reality of crime," in which the codes of conduct and behaviors acceptable to mainstream culture are defined. Although comparisons across national boundaries are difficult to make, driving a motorcycle fast, taking stimulant drugs, or bullying school children are considered more serious in Japan than in the United States. In the United States, violent gangs, automatic weapons, crack houses, and drive-by shootings are of much more concern, whereas these problems are comparatively nonexistent in Japan. In this respect, placing juvenile delinquency in the proper cultural context allows for a fuller understanding of Japanese perceptions of juvenile delinquency. In Japan, where harmony, politeness, and delicate social relationships are nurtured and considered essential to social order, taking drugs, racing motorcycles, and engaging in school violence are viewed as social dislocation.

Japanese juvenile delinquency continues in the twenty-first century. The modernization and transformation of Japanese society is forcing Japan to become more interdependent on other nations and societies. Economic changes in Japan will continue to occur side by side with rapid social change: lifetime employment is no longer sacred; some question the legitimacy of the Emperor; others do not practice filial piety. Whenever rapid social change occurs, some juveniles are involved in self-expression and individualism whereas others engage in delinquency. As disposable income increases, Japanese youths have more money to spend on luxury motorcycles and on drugs. Experts also predict increasing school-related delinquency as more students respond negatively to the pressure-packed educational system. Although overall delinquency rates have leveled off and are even declining in Japan, problems with youth crime will continue in subtle yet definite ways.

References

Applbaum, K. (1992). I feel coke: Why the Japanese study English. *Asian Thought and Society, 17*(49), 18–30.

Asgawa, A. (1980). Bosozoku mondai no gensho to kadai. [The problem and situation of bosozoku]. *Keisatsugaku Ronshu [Journal of Police Science], 33*(6), 21–34.

Bailey, J., & Segers, F. (1990). Japanese set a double standard over drugs and rock 'n' roll. *Variety, 338*(7), 341–342.

Bayley, D. H. (1991). *Forces of order: Policing modern Japan* (2nd ed.). Berkeley: University of California Press.

Becker, C. B. (1988). Report from Japan: Causes and controls of crime in Japan. *Journal of Criminal Justice, 16*(5), 425–435.

Beirne, P. (1983). Cultural relativism and comparative criminology. *Contemporary Crisis, 7*(4), 371–391.

Berezin, E. P. (1982). A comparative analysis of the U.S. and Japanese juvenile justice systems. *Juvenile and Family Court Journal, 33*(4), 55–61.

Castberg, A. D. (1990). *Japanese criminal justice.* New York: Praeger.

Clifford, W. (1976). *Crime control in Japan.* Lexington, MA: Lexington Books.

De Vos, G. A., & Mizushima, K. (1962). The school and delinquency: Perspectives from Japan. *Teachers College Record, 63*(8), 626–638.

Dojo, T. (1982). *Dokyumento bosozoku [Document bosozoku].* Kobe: Kobe News Printing.

Fairchild, E. (1993). *Comparative criminal justice systems.* Belmont, CA: Wadsworth.

Feiler, B. S. (1991). *Learning to bow: Inside the heart of Japan.* New York: Ticknor and Fields.

Gottfredson, M. R., & Hirschi, T. (1990). *A general theory of crime.* Stanford: Stanford University Press.

Greenfeld, K. T. (1994, June 26). Generation. *The New York Times Magazine,* pp. 36–41.

Hardy, Q. (1993, March 16). Wake up and chew the coffee just doesn't sound quite right. *The Wall Street Journal,* p. 1-B.

Hirakawa, N. (1994, May 30–June 5). Bullying led to suicide, court rules. *The Japan Times Weekly International Edition,* pp. 1, 6.

Huang, F. F. Y. (1987). Facing the problems of outlaw motorcyclists [in Chinese]. *Teacher Chang Monthly, 117,* 9–10.

Huang, F. F. Y., & Vaughn, M. S. (1992). A descriptive assessment of Japanese organized crime: The Boryokudan from 1945 to 1988. *International Criminal Justice Review, 2,* 19–57.

Hughes, P. H. (1977). *Behind the wall of respect: Community experiments in heroin addiction and control.* Chicago: University of Chicago Press.

Iwai, H. (1966). Delinquent groups and organized crime. In *Sociological review: Monograph no: 10 Japanese sociological studies* (pp. 199–212). Keele, Straffordshire: University of Keele.

Kariya, T., & Rosenbaum, J. E. (1987). Self-selection in Japanese junior high school: A longitudinal study of students' educational plans. *Sociology of Education, 60*(3), 168–180.

Katoh, H. (1991). The development of delinquency and criminal justice in Japan. In H. G. Heiland, L. I. Shelley, & H. Katoh (Eds.), *Crime control in comparative perspectives* (pp. 69–81). New York: Walter de Gruyter.

Kato, M. (1969). An epidemiological analysis of the fluctuation of drug dependence in Japan. *The International Journal of the Addictions, 4*(4), 591–621.

Kitajima, T. (1982). The rise of juvenile delinquency. *Japan Echo, 9* (Special Issue), 84–92.

Kokuchi, K. (1971). Hiko shonen ni okeru yakubutsu ranyo no kenkyu [The study of juvenile drug abuse]. In S. Itamatsu et al. (Eds.), *Yakubutsu ranyo no rinsho igaku [Clinical epidemiology of drug abuse]* (pp. 50–61). Tokyo: Medical Dentistry Publications.

Kusakabe, N. (1981). Bosozoku mondai ni tsuite jakan no kosatsu [Some observations on the problem of bosozoku]. *Keisatsu Koron [Journal of Police Essays], 36*(8), 26–31.

Lee, W. O. (1991). *Social change and educational problems in Japan, Singapore, and Hong Kong.* New York: St. Martin's Press.

Ministry of Justice. (1980–2001). *Hanzai hakusho [White paper on crime].* Tokyo: Ministry of Justice.

Ministry of Justice. (1980–2000). *Keisatsu hakusho [White paper on the police]*. Tokyo: National Police Agency.

Mugishima, F., & Tamura, M. (1976). Bosozoku no jitai bunsagi II [An analytical study of bosozoku II]. *Keisatsugaku Ronshu [Journal of Police Science], 29*(4), 94–119.

Ogawa, N., & Retherford, R. D. (1993). Care of the elderly in Japan: Changing norms and expectations. *Journal of Marriage and the Family, 55*(3), 585–597.

Ogura, Y. (1987). Examination hell. *The College Board Review, 144* (Summer), 8–11.

Oka, M. (1993, April 5–11). Bring bullying into the light. *The Japan Times Weekly International Edition*, p. 9.

Quinney, R. (1970). *The social reality of crime*. Boston: Little & Brown.

Sakuta, T., & Saito, S. (1982). Current state of delinquent behavior among Japanese adolescents. *Hanzaigaku Zasshi, 48*(5–6), 35–41.

Sato, I. (1991). *Kamikaze biker: Parody and anomy in affluent Japan*. Chicago: University of Chicago Press.

Schoenberger, K. (1987, December 9). Japan faces widespread drug problems, takes harsh measures against abusers. *The Wall Street Journal*, p. 34.

Seishonen hakusho [White paper on juveniles]. (1990). Tokyo: Department of Juvenile Policy of the National General Affairs Agency.

Shikita, M., & Tsuchiya, S. (1976). The juvenile justice system in Japan. In *Juvenile justice: An international survey* (pp. 55–82). Rome: United Nations Social Defense Research Institute.

Statistics Bureau. (1949–2003). *Japan statistical yearbook*. Tokyo: Sorifu.

Steinhoff, P. G. (1993). Review essay: Pursuing the Japanese police. *Law and Society Review, 27*(4), 827–850.

Suwaki, H. (1989). Addictions: What's happening in Japan. *International Review of Psychiatry, 1*(1-2), 9–11.

Suwaki, H., Toshida, T., & Ohara, H. (1985). A survey of methamphetamine abusers in prison, on probation, and in mental hospitals in Kochi Prefecture. *Japanese Journal of Social Psychiatry, 8*, 144–150.

Suwanwela, C., & Poshyachinda, V. (1986). Drug abuse in Asia. *Bulletin on Narcotics, 38*(1-2), 41–53.

Tamura, M. (1989). Japan: Stimulant epidemics past and present. *Bulletin on Narcotics, 41*(1-2), 83–93.

Terrill, R. J. (1992). *World criminal justice systems* (2nd ed.). Cincinnati: Anderson.

Thornton, R. Y., & Endo, K. (1992). *Preventing crime in America and Japan: A comparative study*. Armonk, NY: M. E. Sharpe.

Tokuoka, H., & Cohen, A. K. (1987). Japanese society and delinquency. *International Journal of Comparative and Applied Criminal Justice, 11*(1), 13–22.

Utena, H., & Niwa, S. I. (1992). The history of schizophrenia research in Japan. *Schizophrenia Bulletin, 18*(1), 67–73.

Vaughn, M. S. (1990). Are Japanese police practices increasing teenage arrest rates? Long-term juvenile delinquency rates in Nippon from 1936 to 1987. *Police Studies, 13*(1), 33–44.

Vaughn, M. S., & Huang, F. F. Y. (1992). Delinquency in the land of the rising sun: An analysis of juvenile property crimes in Japan during the Showa era. *International Journal of Comparative and Applied Criminal Justice, 16*(2), 273–300.

Vaughn, M. S., Huang, F. F. Y., & Ramirez, C. R. (1995). Drug abuse and antidrug policy in Japan: Past history and future directions. *British Journal of Criminology, 35*, 491–524.

Vaughn, M. S., & Tomita, N. (1990). A longitudinal analysis of Japanese crime from 1926 to 1987: The prewar, war, and postwar eras. *International Journal of Comparative and Applied Criminal Justice, 15*(2), 149–165.

Vending machines offer used underwear. (1993, September 13–19). *The Japan Times Weekly International Edition*, p. 2.

Westermann, T. D., & Burfeind, J. W. (1991). *Crime and justice in two societies: Japan and the United States*. Pacific Grove, CA: Brooks/Cole.

White, M. (1987). *The Japanese educational challenge: A commitment to children*. Tokyo: Kodansha.

Yokoyama, M. (1989). Net-widening of the juvenile justice system in Japan. *Criminal Justice Review, 14*(1), 43–53.

Yokoyama, M. (1992). Japan: Changing drug laws: Keeping pace with the problem. *CJ International, 8*(5), 11–18.

27

Perspectives of Juvenile Crime Prevention
The Case of Finland

Ahti Laitinen

During the last three or four years many European countries, including Finland, have been living under conditions of economic recession. Social programs of the welfare state have been cut. At the beginning of 1990s, unemployment increased dramatically in Finland from 5 percent to 20 percent by 1993. In November 2003 the unemployment rate was reduced to "only" about 7 percent. Even in the face of such dramatic changes, much attention has been paid to juvenile delinquency. Many commentators have argued that it is one of the most serious social problems. Is this true? Does the problem deserve more attention than other concerns?

According to police and social workers, there has been an increase in the abuse of and trade in illegal drugs in Finland. The phenomenon is linked with the collapse of the Soviet Union. After the breakdown of the Soviet bloc, the mobility of criminals and the smuggling of drugs and other commodities have increased between Russia, Estonia, and Finland. In addition, much economic and other organizational crime has been revealed. Many important decision makers, including one at the ministerial level, were at least indirectly connected with illegalities of this kind. It might be argued that for some politicians and other decision makers it is advantageous to draw attention to juveniles instead of organizational crime, in which the decision makers themselves could be implicated. Young, poor people are a better target for the campaign against crime than powerful institutions and people in high social positions!

This is not to say that juvenile delinquency is not a social problem, although the debate over it is in danger of becoming bigger than the problem itself. There are no easy solutions for the prevention of the offenses of the young. It is important to realize that it is also possible to influence the level of criminality before the crime has been committed, by means of pre-

Prepared especially for *Comparative and International Criminal Justice, 2/E.*

ventive work. Finding out the different components of juvenile delinquency is therefore extremely important.

The Extent of Juvenile Crime

When we consider the total crime rate in Finland, the proportion committed by 15- to 20-year-old juveniles is lower than would be expected. In
1982, juvenile offenders made up 26 percent of the total, while in 1991 they
accounted for 20 percent and in 2001 only for 19 percent (Rikollisuustilanne, 1991; Yearbook of Justice Statistics, 2002). The figures in table 1 illustrate that the percentage of 18- to 20-year-old juveniles who have committed
property crimes and violent crimes has decreased since the late 1920s.

Table 1   Crimes Committed by 18- to 20-Year-Olds, Selected Years (percent)

Year	Property Offense	Violent Offense
1928	22	21
1937	15	14
1980	17	15
1990	17	11
2001	16	13

Source: *Yearbook of Justice Statistics*. Helsinki: Statistics Finland, Justice 2002:18.

The percentage of persons under the age of 21 suspected of certain
offenses in 2001 is presented in table 2. Most offenses committed by juveniles are related to how they spend their leisure time and the fact that certain
activities are offenses only because the offenders are underage. Auto theft is
a typical crime committed by juveniles. In addition, some property offenses—
especially thefts and petty thefts—and damage to property have been committed mostly by juveniles, whereas crimes requiring more systematic planning—such as fraud or embezzlement—are seldom committed by juveniles.

The number of suspects for offenses against the Penal Code increased
during the decade of the 1980s. Most of this increase in criminality, which
continued until 1990, can be attributed to persons over 20 years of age.
Similarly, the decrease in crimes in 1991 applies mostly to persons over age
20. The main reason for the decrease was a change in how certain offenses
were recorded, grouping several illegal acts into a single crime category
after 1991. Until 1990, the share of offenses committed by juveniles 15–20
years of age against the Penal Code decreased somewhat. It was 24 percent
of all suspected in 1993, but in 2002 the figure was 21 percent.

Changes in demographics affect the crime rate. According to police
statistics, the most "criminally active" stage of life is during the years
between 15 and 20. The criminality of juveniles aged 15–17 years slightly

increased in the 1980s, and the increase continued in the 1990s. The share was 12 percent in 1993, and in 2002 it was 15 percent. The main reason for the overall decrease in the percentage of juvenile suspects is the fact that the most criminally active age groups have become smaller (see Lappi-Seppala, 1991; Rikollisuustilanne, 2002).

Table 2   Persons Under the Age of 21 Suspected of Certain Crimes in 2001

Offense	Suspects for Solved Offense	Percent of Suspects
Illicit possession and transport of alcoholic substances	3,245	83
Violation of the law on public entertainments	293	58
Unauthorized use, petty unauthorized use, aggravated unauthorized use of motor vehicles	9,770	44
Damage to private property, aggravated damage to private property, petty damage to private property	16,313	37
Driving without a license	22,043	31
Giving false or misleading information to an official	1,645	31
Narcotics offenses	15,992	30
Theft, aggravated theft, petty theft	67,667	27
Assault, aggravated assault, petty assault	25,652	24
Assault of an official and impeding an official in the performance of his duties	3,372	21
Means of payment fraud	2,118	18
Drunken driving, aggravated drunken driving, driving while under the influence of intoxicants other than alcohol	23,088	17
Rape	324	17
Manslaughter, murder or attempted murder, infanticide	530	17
Criminal mischief and attempted criminal mischief	351	16
Endangerment of traffic, aggravated endangerment of traffic, hit and run, traffic infraction	260,368	16
Forgery, petty forgery, possession of forgery materials	6,653	16
Embezzlement, petty embezzlement, aggravated embezzlement	2,160	16
Fraud, petty fraud	10,551	10

Source: *Yearbook of Justice Statistics*. Helsinki: Statistics Finland, Justice 2002:18.

There has been a slight increase in theft—the largest offense type among 15- to 20-year-olds, whereas there is a notable decrease in theft offenses committed by juveniles under the age of 15 after 1988 until 1995. After that, the number of crimes has been quite steady. As far as assault crimes are concerned, there have not been any changes worth mentioning in either age group under examination. There was a sharp increase in the number of suspects for the unauthorized use of motor vehicles after 1987, especially in the 15–20 age group. It is not possible to estimate the situation after 1991 because of a change in the offense title. The number of thefts has remained relatively constant. A slight overall decrease can be found after 1993, although the thefts in the 18–20 year-old age group has increased a bit. The drunken driving offenses of juveniles under age 15 have remained at the same low level since 1984, while the number of drunken driving cases of young persons aged 15–20 have remained high after the jump of 1988. The change has been explained by an increased risk of being caught.

The crimes committed by persons under 15 are mainly petty theft offenses. Forty-four percent of the theft offenses have been classified as petty thefts. Together with damages to property and unauthorized use of motor vehicles, these three offense types cover 86 percent of all crimes against the Penal Code committed by this age group. Drunken driving and assaults appear only in the criminality of 15- to 17-year-olds. In addition to the above crimes, fraud offenses are common in the criminality of juveniles at the age of 18–20. Theft offenses, however, are definitely the most common offenses in all age groups. Theft, fraud, and drunken driving are the most common offenses against the Penal Code committed by the population group over 20 years of age.

Juveniles become subject to violence more often than other age groups. According to the victim studies conducted by the Central Statistical Office in 1980, 1988, and 1997, street violence had decreased by one-third, even though the number of cases reported has increased (Heiskanen et al., 2000). The reason for the increase in the number of cases known to the police is the increased tendency to report to the police. It is exactly the younger age groups in which there has been the most notable decrease in violence for both males and females.

The level of criminality also can be assessed using studies focusing on so-called self-reported crime. It has become evident in these studies that most juveniles commit offenses, but still most of the crimes have been caused by a small group. Only a small number of juveniles gets involved with the police because of crimes. In addition, criminal behavior usually recedes as a youth grows up.

The statistics suggest the problem of juvenile delinquency is not so serious as common perception and discussion would have us believe. Crime rates are higher than 20 years ago, but the proportion of juvenile offenders is no larger than before; on the contrary, it is declining.

The number of crimes per offender has increased. In other words, juveniles with a tendency toward criminal behavior are breaking the law more and more often. Does this mean a polarization of the young into the two categories of the irreproachable and the criminal?

The Finnish Juvenile Justice System

Legislation

According to Finnish legislation, juvenile delinquency usually refers to illegal acts committed by persons under 21 years of age. Important age limits are 15, 18, and 21 years. The lower age limit of criminal liability is 15 years. Offenses committed by persons younger than that remain unpunished. A person under 15 years of age, however, is liable to compensate for the damages caused by him- or herself. A young offender refers to a person who is older than 15 but younger than 21 at the time of committing a punishable act. Juveniles have been placed in a special position in the Finnish criminal legislation. There is a stipulation in the provisions concerning young offenders that a young offender sentenced to conditional imprisonment normally should be under supervision during probation. Additionally, there is a stipulation in the Penal Code, according to which a punishment for offenses committed by a person under 18 should be imposed using a lighter scale. Since the beginning of 1990 it has not been possible to sentence a person to unconditional imprisonment for offenses committed when younger than 18, unless it is required by weighty reasons. New stipulations concerning the waiving of charges and sentence entered into force at that time, and they extended the field of the application of wavering measures, especially in cases of offenses committed by juveniles under 18.

Under the Child Welfare Act, a person under 18 is regarded as a "child," and a person under 21 as a "juvenile." As a consequence of an offense committed by a child or a juvenile, there are obligations to social authorities. Social authorities must usually be represented at the preliminary investigation of an offense committed by a person under 18 and at the hearing of the case in court. An offense committed by a child or a juvenile may also give a reason to take measures based on the Child Welfare Act, primarily to support measures of open welfare.

Young offenders serve their sentences mainly in a juvenile prison. The law governing juvenile prisons was enacted in 1940 (262/1940), and the current stipulations regarding juvenile prisons are from 1974 (612/1974). The general principle is that young offenders are not placed in the same prisons with "old crooks." They are given an opportunity for useful work in the prison; education is organized, and they have a chance to complete the schooling they did not finish. This principle is based on therapeutic and socializing aims.

If a young offender serves his or her punishment in a youth prison, in accordance with § 9 of the decree on the enforcement of punishments (703/1991), ". . . the prisoner may be released from the youth prison after he or she has served . . . one-third of the sentence." The sanction system work group of the Penal Code project of the Ministry of Justice proposed early in 1994 that the above stipulation should be deleted from the law. Young offenders would then, like "common" prisoners, serve half or two-thirds of the sentenced punishment before release on parole. This amendment was justified to increase the credibility of punishments and to simplify and unify the stipulations concerning parole.

In Finland, as well as in other Scandinavian countries, there are no special juvenile courts. The cases of juveniles are addressed in ordinary courts. However, in 1997 the Juvenile Punishment Experiment Act became law, and it continues in force today. In the future, the law may be changed to cover the whole country and most probably will be permanent.

This act encompasses seven court districts: Helsinki, Espoo, Joensuu, Tampere, Turku, Vaasa, and Vantaa. Juvenile punishment can be imposed on a young person who has committed a crime at the age of 15 to 17 if a fine is considered to be too lenient and unconditional imprisonment too severe a sanction. In 2002 58 juvenile sentences were given altogether (Yearbook of Justice Statistics, 2002).

A preliminary enforcement plan for the court is created for a youth who, according to the assessment of social authorities and the Probation Service, can be sentenced to a juvenile punishment. The document is an appendix to the personal history report and is drawn up jointly by a child welfare worker, probation supervisor, the young offender, and possibly his or her parents.

Juvenile punishment consists of juvenile service (10–60 hours) and supervision (4–12 months). Juvenile service includes working programs (e.g., Young Persons and Crime, Young Persons and Intoxicants, and Young Persons and Society) and unpaid work. The assignments to these programs are scheduled in advance to meet the specific needs of young persons.

Supervision of Conditionally Sentenced Young Offenders

An offender who has committed his or her crime when under 21 years of age can be ordered to supervision in addition to the conditional sentence passed by the district court. Supervision is ordered if it is conducive to improving the offender's social reintegration and preventing recidivism. The Finnish Probation Service is in charge of organizing supervision throughout the whole country. At the beginning of the year 2003 there were some 1,600 conditionally sentenced young offenders under supervision.

A personal history report clarifies each youth's life situation and expresses an opinion concerning eventual supervision in connection with a conditional prison sentence. In addition, the impact of different sanction alternatives on the young person's situation are assessed. (As mentioned previously, a youth under 18 years of age is sentenced to unconditional imprisonment only for weighty reasons.)

When the supervision starts, the risks, needs, and resources of the offender are assessed. On the basis of the assessment, an individual supervision plan is drawn up, together with the person to be supervised, in which the targets and means of the supervision period are determined. During the supervision appointments, different themes are addressed according to the supervision plan, for instance by means of discussions, tasks, and exercises. Supervision supports the client in his own efforts to change, and may include collaboration with the family of the client and also various authorities.

Besides the officials of the Probation Service, there are also persons in the private sector who function as supervisors. Under the direction of the Probation Service, they take care of nearly half of the supervisions of conditionally sentenced young offenders.

Conciliation

The search for an alternative to the regular proceedings of offenses and civil cases began in Finland in the early 1980s. Conciliation was regarded at that time as a criticism of the clearly punitive nature of the juvenile sanction system. The purpose of conciliation is to seek alternatives to settle the conflict situations caused by disputes and offenses and to offer a simple way to settle them outside the official legal system. Assuming personal responsibility for the offenses and for the damage caused is emphasized in conciliation; the offender and the victim try to reach an agreement in a way satisfactory to both parties. Conciliation also aims at increasing joint responsibility and cooperation between the local inhabitants as well as reducing crime.

The first conciliation experiment was started in the Helsinki area in Vantaa in 1983. Several years later, experiments were begun in other municipalities, in the metropolitan area, and in larger towns all over Finland. During the last few years, this practice has spread to smaller municipalities. In 1999, conciliation of offenses was practiced in 412 of 452 municipalities, covering 91 percent of the country. Municipalities that purchase conciliation services from neighboring municipalities have been included in this figure. Conciliation is usually linked with municipal social authorities. Only in a few places is conciliation managed by an organization or an association (e.g., a registered "settlement" or "conciliation" association).

The actual conciliation (i.e., meeting between the victim and the offender) is made possible by voluntary mediators; they are trained laypersons who remain neutral in the conciliation situation. In 1999, there were about nine hundred conciliators in the whole of Finland, and about half of them were actively involved in the conciliation practice (Iivari, 2001).

Even though conciliation is a practice outside the official legal process and is not regulated by law, in case of offenses subject to public prosecution it may affect the prosecutor's consideration of charges and the court's ultimate decision. In case of complainant offenses, it is possible to avoid court proceedings totally if an agreement on compensation in work or money is reached and the victim abandons the claims for punishment. The decree on the enforcement of the Penal Code at the beginning of 1991 (15a §) increased the options of the prosecutor and the court to waive charges after the disputing parties have reached an agreement. For instance, half of the offenders who settled with their victims had their charges of assault waived on an equity basis during the second half of the same year. About 40 percent of these agreements were conciliation agreements (Sulin, 1992; Iivari, 2001). Most cases taken into conciliation were thefts, petty thefts, assaults, or damages to property. Only in special cases have offenses classified "aggravated" been included in conciliation, in these cases mainly assaults.

An essential precondition for conciliation is the consent of the parties involved. The complainant must be known, and the suspect for the offense must not deny the offense. In conciliation, the complainant may be either a private person, a public corporation, or a private corporation. The conciliation process is started on the initiative of either of the parties involved, the guardians of a child or a juvenile, or the authorities. In most cases, the disputing parties have been rather passive in initiating the conciliation process.

Many prosecutors seem to consider conciliation an appropriate method to compensate damages caused by offenses. The number of decisions to waive charges increases after there have been successful experiences of the conciliation practice in a locality. Recently, the role of the police in directing cases to conciliation has become more pronounced and while the proportion of offenses taken to conciliation from all offenses known to the police is still small, it has increased during the last three years (Järvinen, 1993; Iivari, 2001).

During the last few years there has been more and more discussion about child welfare, social work, and social policy in connection with conciliation. *The Conciliator's Handbook* (1991) sets social and educational aims as the main objectives of conciliation.

Community Service

Community service is quite a new penal sanction in Finland. Although it is not specifically a juvenile punishment, it has been considered particularly suitable for juveniles. It had not been tried in Finland until the 1990s, even though it has been used in its present form in several countries for over 30 years. An impetus for the development of alternative punishments in Finland was Resolution No. 10, presented by the Minister Committee of the European Council on March 9, 1976, where the governments of the member states were urged to seek new alternatives to imprisonment. There was a special request to consider the possibility of community service.

Practical support for community service was obtained from experiences in the United States and New Zealand. In 1966, persons sentenced for petty offenses in Alameda, California, were given a chance to expiate their offenses by participating in the work of voluntary organizations. This practice spread from Alameda to other counties. In New Zealand work has been combined with the weekend confinement of young offenders since 1963. Juveniles live in dormitory-like confinement centers from Friday evening until Sunday afternoon and do supervised community work on Saturdays.

Until the end of 1980s, the idea of community service received little attention in most Western European countries. The decisive factor behind the rising interest has been the increase in crime, which has led to both physical and financial overloading of prisons. These factors have forced the decision makers to look for new alternatives.

At the beginning of 1991, community service in Finland was introduced in some regions as an experiment. The population of the experimental regions, whose centers are Turku, Vaasa, Mikkeli, and Rovaniemi, is about one-tenth the population of the whole country. In an experimental region, the court may order a sentence of unconditional imprisonment with the maximum length of eight months to be replaced by the punishment of community service. According to Takala's (1992) report, the frequency of use varied by regions. In Rovaniemi, community service was used in 45 of 100 sentences of unconditional imprisonment, while in Turku the figure was below 10 and, in the regions of Vaasa and Mikkeli, 15–18 percent. In 1997 community service was enacted as a permanent form of sentence (Law 1055/1996).

Community service consists of a certain number of hours of regular unpaid work performed under supervision. It has a minimum of 20 and a maximum of 200 hours, and one hour corresponds roughly with one day of imprisonment. The service is usually done in periods of two to four hours, two or three days a week.

Community service was used 3,589 times in 2002. This represents approximately 35 percent of the number of those sentences that would have been eligible for community service. According to The Criminal Sanctions Agency (under the Ministry of Justice) the number in the twenty-first century has been steady but is about 300 cases lower than at the end of the 1990s. Of this number, the proportion of persons under the age of 21 years has, however, been quite low. For example, in 2002 it was only 13 percent of all community service sentences.

In 2002, less than half (43 percent) of the cases which requested assessment for suitability resulted in community service. About 25 percent received an actual unconditional sentence of imprisonment (2 percent were sentences longer than 8 months). The remaining 28 percent received a punishment more lenient than unconditional imprisonment. The average length of community service in the 1990s was about 80–90 hours, which corresponded with a (gross) imprisonment time of around three months.

The average age of the persons sentenced to community service was 34. During the suitability assessment, half of them were unemployed, but this share grew as unemployment figures increased. In general, the persons sentenced to community service were older (31–34 years old) than those who were imprisoned. Seventy-five percent of those guilty of drunken driving received community service, compared to 54 percent who were imprisoned. Theft was the main offense for 10 percent and assault for 5 percent of the persons sentenced to community service. A tentative finding from material compiled in the autumn of 1991 was that two-thirds of the persons sentenced to community service had previously been in prison. As the figures indicate, community service has not been applied to juveniles as often as had initially been projected.

By the end of 1991, 49 out of 92 community service sentences had been completed, while 12 sentences had been converted to imprisonment because of violation of the service conditions. At the end of 2002 the result was better: 2,931 out of 3,589 community service sentences (82 percent) had been completed successfully (Rikollisuustilanne, 1991:149–51; Takala, 1992; The Criminal Sanctions Agency: http://www. rikosseuraamus.fi).

Fines and Imprisonment

Sentences given to juveniles are somewhat more lenient than those given to adults over 20 years of age. Finnish criminal law is based on the idea that punishments given to juveniles should be more lenient than punishments in general. Severe punishments may be considered unreasonable, because it is thought that juveniles are more ignorant of the law than adults, and because the punishment may endanger the social development of a young person. Above all, the aim is to avoid sending a juvenile to prison, since it has been found to have a harmful influence on the development of young persons.

Table 3 contains information about fines and both conditional and unconditional imprisonment in 1980, 1991, and 2001. It seems that regardless of the principles of the criminal policy, there has been a slight increase in the share of unconditional sentences of imprisonment given to the youngest offenders.

There was a decrease in the share of imprisonment given to 15- to 17-year-olds of all punishments from the end of the 1970s until the middle of the 1980s, after which there was a slight increase. Imprisonment received by 18- to 20-year-olds remained relatively constant during the entire decade of the 1980s. There was a sharp decrease in unconditional sentences of imprisonment at the beginning of the 1980s in both age groups, but especially for 15- to 17-year-olds. The percentage of young convicts in the prison population on the first day of January in different years is presented in table 4.

Table 3   Sentences Given to Offenders of Different Ages in Legal Proceedings in 1980, 1991, and 2001 (percent)

Sentence	1980			1991			2001		
	15–17	18–20	20+	15–17	18–20	20+	15–17	18–20	20+
Fine	69.1	65.2	66.2	71.9	68.1	63.7	78.1	64.5	59.9
Conditional imprisonment	26.6	24.0	18.0	22.9	20.2	20.2	19.8	22.5	22.1
Unconditional imprisonment	4.3	12.8	15.8	5.2	11.7	16.1	2.1	13.1	18.0
Total	100.0	100.0	100.0	100.0	100.0	100.0	100.0	100.0	100.0
N	8,043	10,555	53,233	7,570	11,850	60,371	5,006	9,940	65,030

Source: *Rikollisuustilanne* (Criminality in Finland) 1992:97–98; *Yearbook of Justice Statistics*, 2002.

Compared with the 1980s, the present number of young prisoners has decreased. The majority of young offenders are male (less than one-tenth of the juvenile suspects for offenses solved by the police are female, and about 2 percent of the juveniles in prison are female). The traditional forms of juvenile delinquency, i.e., property and violence offenses, are activities more likely to be committed by males.

In Finland, sentences of imprisonment are not very lengthy. The median length of all sentences of imprisonment in 1999 was 4.6 months, and that of conditional sentences of imprisonment 2.4 months. The median size of fines for offenses against the Penal Code was 13 day-fines.[1] The sizes of both imprisonment and day-fines vary greatly by offense type. Examples of the median length of prison sentences include: assault (2.9 months), theft (2.0 months), aggravated assault (15.4 months) and robbery (10.3 months). Examples of the median amounts of day-fines include: assault (35 day-fines), aggravated drunken driving (65 day-fines), theft (34 day-fines), damage to property (22 day-fines) and fraud (37 day-fines). (Rikollisuustilanne, 1999).

Table 4   Number of Young Convicts in Penal Institutions (Remand Prisoners Not Included) on the First Day of January in Different Years

Year	Aged under 21	
	N	%*
1980	313	5.6
1985	408	7.7
1990	201	3.8
1995	169	4.3
2001	184	5.7

* Percent of total numbers (all ages) imprisoned.
Source: *Yearbook of Justice Statistics*, 2002:18.

Reactions to Juvenile Crime

Decision makers, social workers, citizens, and others involved in the understanding and treatment of juvenile delinquency have all presented their own solutions to the crime problem. Mostly these reactions have not been based on scientific information, and the debate has often been very emotional.

The concern for juvenile delinquency is not strictly a modern phenomenon in Finland. In 1792 the governor of a province wrote to the king that teachers:

> . . . complain about children . . . that inclination to strong liquors becomes rooted, and diligence and working hard diminishes, which is a consequence of luxury, and that innocent people are often bothered by drunken, unruly and unthinking juveniles who gather in big villages . . . because juveniles spend their time in inns in vain in games and futile tasks, and one incites the other to immorality and intemperate use of alcoholic beverages. . . . (quoted in Suolahti, 1991:137–38)

Strict control, rigid discipline, and order were considered the best means against this demoralization.

Similarly, in a 1939 government proposal (10/39) for legislation concerning young offenders, increased juvenile crime was considered a serious problem:

> Juvenile delinquency is a phenomenon to which very much attention is paid nowadays in all civilized countries. The reason for this is the fact that young offenders form a remarkable share—approximately one-third or one-fourth—of all offenders. This has been influenced partly by the fact that increased criminality among juveniles constitutes a danger to the future of the nation.

It is not only a Finnish phenomenon that, at any given time, juveniles are seen to be more criminal and violent than was previously thought. For example, according to an opinion survey conducted by *Time Magazine* (June 12, 1989), 88 percent of U.S. citizens thought teenage violence was a bigger problem than ever before. The prevailing belief in the seriousness of the juvenile problem has been strengthened by many newspaper articles and readers' letters. The view of crime policy adopted by some researchers supports the conclusions of public discussion.

Virén (1992), for example, concludes that the decrease in crime rates can be explained mainly by the increased risk of arrest, the toughening of sentences, and the increase in working hours. Based on arguments such as these, some decision makers have put forward "fresh" ideas for criminal policy. At the end of 1991 some members of Parliament proposed a change in the Criminal Law that would lower the age of criminal responsibility from 15 to 14 years.

Reasoning of this kind is, however, rather inadequate since it is based on incomplete information about juvenile delinquency. This defect appears as much in the field of criminal statistics as in the understanding of the different dimensions of criminality. Another reason for such proposals being presented in Parliament might be a wish to turn attention away from complicated social problems to "easier" ones. Juveniles are a visible enemy, a scapegoat against whom an easy attack can be made (cf. Christie and Bruun, 1986). Politicians can demonstrate their social activism to voters by "solving the problem of juvenile delinquency." Young, poor people do not constitute any political threat to political decision makers.

As a result of the debate described above, the Ministry of Justice established a committee called Working Party on Rascals (Vintiö-työryhman muistio, 1992), which recommended the following measures:

1. Measures must be directed more than hitherto toward 10- to 12-year-old children; among other things, leisure activities after school hours must be arranged;

2. Measures for preventing the absences in school-attendance must be made more effective;

3. Obstacles to cooperation between different officials must be eliminated;

4. Field groups for the aid of adolescents in trouble must be established in the area;

5. Measures for preventing the constant shuttling of a child from foster home/institutions to other foster home/institutions must be made more effective; and

6. Financial resources must be directed to measures that would prevent the asocial behavior of the child and on measures that would break the circle of criminalization in which the child can so easily become involved.

In principle these proposals are good ones. The committee did not, however, define the methods for carrying out these proposals. Many important questions remain unsolved in the report.

The Reform Committee of Finnish Criminal Law[2] suggested a special sentence for 15- to 17-year-old offenders. It would be a combination of effective supervision and juvenile service, which would be a form of community service. Certain means of enforcement linked with supervision should be possible as well. This juvenile sentence could be used as a punishment for an offense committed when younger than 18, when a fine is not sufficient because of the severity of the offense. The juvenile sentence is thus meant to be applied to offenses for which sentences of conditional imprisonment are presently given.

A juvenile sentence should always contain supervision. If mere supervision were not an adequate sanction because of the severity of the offense, juvenile service would be included in the juvenile sentence, which would be some sort of community service adapted for 15- to 17-year-olds. The Probation and After-Care Association (KHY) would take care of the enforcement of the sentence.[3] The Committee explained that it is important to avoid sentencing juveniles to prison because it has been found harmful to their development.

The number of hours proposed for juvenile service is low, a minimum of 10 and a maximum of 60 hours, whereas in community service it is a minimum of 20 hours and a maximum of 200 hours. The punishment for an offense committed by a person under 18 should be, in principle, more lenient than that for a person over 18. The final proposal does not directly address the problems of juvenile crime prevention, but during the last few years these have been almost the only proposals on the level of legislation concerning juvenile delinquency. The proposal, realized in 1997 as the Juvenile Punishment Experiment Act, is described in the previous section on the Finnish Juvenile Justice System.

In the following section some selected research findings are presented to illustrate the complexity of the field of juvenile crime prevention.

Research Findings on the Young Offender

In the prewar proposal (Nr. 10/1939) for the Law on Young Offenders, the Finnish government insisted on investigating "the conditions and social background of the young people in question as being of essential importance for the socialization of the person." For this purpose, a special investigation into the individual's circumstances was required in the law. The original idea was adopted from the Decree on Child Welfare (8.5.1936/203) and required that the result of the investigation be taken into account at trial.

The primary purpose of the individual investigation is the prevention of recidivism. The original idea was that if authorities were aware of the social conditions of the juveniles, they would be able to make the improvements needed for their resocialization. The procedure has remained unchanged so that today individual investigations are always required in the trial of a young offender.

The author obtained a sample of 21 cases of typical juvenile delinquents and examined documents relating to their individual investigations. The oldest cases are from the year 1966. This permits following the career of an offender over the years. Fifty-five documents were examined. The information obtained from these documents provides some ideas about the social circumstances of juvenile offenders. Put briefly, the family situation has mostly been poor. The parents typically have had alcohol problems, divorce has been common, the father has often been violent, unemployment of both parents is not unusual, the educational level of the parents has been low—in general, not a positive situation. Because of circumstances such as these, the child has often been put into a children's home or reform school. Children have had troubles at such schools, and their achievement there has been generally poor. Problems involving offenses have usually appeared soon after the child's tenth birthday.

Outside their own families, young people seek a reference group with which to identify. The solidarity within these groups is increased by shared experiences—including crime. Integration and solidarity with other problem youths expands the gap between organized society and members of these groups. Members of extreme and criminal groups reject the prevailing norms and values of society. They build a kind of counterculture with opposite views of morality from those of our society at large. In their model, wrong becomes right and bad becomes good; there is no need to feel guilt for crime. Membership in the group gives the power that makes a poor and weak person strong.

Drugs and alcohol have played some, but not very important, roles in the lives of the adolescents investigated. According to their own or their parents'/guardians' opinion, only four persons in the sample had never used alcohol or drugs. For the rest of the group, both alcohol and drugs were very familiar. In addition, some had sniffed paint thinners and glue and had taken pills. Yet, the behavior of this group is very similar to that of "ordinary" adolescents. According to another study in our research project (Aromaa and Laitinen, 1993), approximately 70 percent of 14- to 15-year-old schoolboys and schoolgirls without any criminal history had drunk beer, wine, and strong alcohol during the previous year. Furthermore, almost 10 percent had either used pills to get intoxicated or had sniffed paint thinners. The conclusion is that alcohol and drugs exclusively cannot explain the criminal behavior of juveniles.

Apart from a few exceptions, all the persons investigated were recidivists. The majority of the group has continued committing crimes regardless of sentences received. By 1992, the criminal history of these people made depressing reading. A curious detail appeared: more girls than boys have committed the offense of drunken driving.

It seems that the number of offenses per person in a case will increase in relation to the number of previous court appearances of that person. At the same time, the offenses are becoming more and more serious. Without any doubt, this pattern traces the development of a criminal career.

The results of our project confirm Oksanen's (1990:7–9, 74) findings that the attitudes of problem juveniles are unrealistic. They imagine that in the future their opportunities for educating themselves, getting a good job, and freeing themselves from lawbreaking are good. They have their own definitions of crime: essentially, an action is criminal only if the offender is arrested.

A common justification for committing theft is to say that it is more profitable to steal—for example, food and clothes—and risk few day-fines if caught than to pay for the purchases. Besides, juveniles are in the habit of saying, food is one of the basic needs of a human being, and therefore the theft of food cannot be a crime. Oksanen (1990) concludes that basically the youths he studied were timid and their self-awareness was weak. They were only trying to cover up these feelings of inadequacy by arrogant behavior and impudence.

The opinions of those investigated as to the causes of their offenses differ in some respects from the opinions of authorities. In three cases, the offender was unable to present any explanation for his or her crime. The rest of the group put forward many causes that can be classified as follows: (1) coincidence, sudden notion, or lack of consideration; (2) bad company and/or the bad influence of companions; (3) intoxication by alcohol or drugs; (4) home life; and (5) need to get something desired rapidly and easily.

Social workers making individual investigations put forth their own opinions about the causes of the offenses. In three cases the authorities were unable to explain the causes of the criminal behavior. In order of generality, the social workers attributed behavior to: (1) home life or institutionalization; (2) psychopathy; (3) timidity and involvement in bad company; (4) childishness; and (5) alcohol. Neither offenders nor investigators focused in their explanations on the level (macro) of society.

According to a Swedish study (Rakt på ungdoms brotten, 1990), a criminal's development follows a certain series of steps described in figure 1. From the last step it will be easy to start a professional criminal career and a vicious circle of constant crime and imprisonment.

With respect to crime prevention, it is essential to intervene in the problems of the individual concerned, even when he or she is on the first step. Then it will be important to consider alternative measures of cooperation between the police, the social worker, the families, and other parties to the problem.

Principles and Means of Juvenile Crime Prevention

Crime prevention based on the investigations of individual concerns is becoming more and more bureaucratic. The documents generally do a good job of describing the social situation and circumstances of the young delinquent. However, the original purpose of the investigations was to provide a means of resocializing the juvenile. Currently, the content of the documentation produced by these investigations seems formal and bureaucratic. It is often necessary to conduct another investigation one or two years later; sometimes the procedure has to be repeated many times. Yet the comparison of different investigations of the same person indicate that the newer documents are often merely copies of older ones. Indeed, the investigator has only changed the dates and added, for example, information about offenses committed after the previous investigation.

Figure 1   Steps in Criminal Development among Juveniles

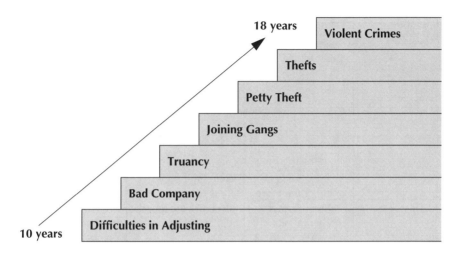

Furthermore, the prospects for the future of the juvenile described in the documents are often portrayed in a very positive light. A report might give the picture of a well-motivated, studious and promising youth who has only accidentally made some minor mistakes; this story is repeated in report after report. Ultimately, the person in question ends up in prison. Documents are written for the courts in the hope of gaining more lenient sentences for the delinquent, but they fall short of addressing what to do to prevent future problems. From the point of view of resocialization these documents are unrealistic and not very useful.

Generally speaking, crime prevention is a complex phenomenon that consists of different levels and targets of operations. If we only take into account one single piece of that complexity, we can do more harm than good. The different levels and operations are described in figure 2.

Juvenile Crime Prevention in Practice: An Example

Several projects have been carried out in the Nordic countries to help juvenile delinquents. Often these projects have been based on the voluntary work of civic organizations. One example of such a project in Finland is the LOKKI Project (LOKKI, 1993).

The LOKKI (seagull) development and research project in child welfare began in 1988. It targeted juveniles between the ages of 10 and 17 in need of the support measures of open child welfare. The parties responsible for carrying out the project were one civic organization, the city of Turku, the Ministry of Justice, and the University of Turku. The project ended in 1992. The hope was to expand this type of action based on the experiences gained from this project.

Figure 2   The Level of the Crime Problem/Operation

Target of the operation	Primary	Secondary	Tertiary
Offender	Responsible parenthood, legal education in the schools, the prevention of truancy, campaigns against violence, and the abuse of alcohol and drugs	Youth/gang work, youth clubs and houses, education, integration into working life, foster homes	Rehabilitation, supervision, education, integration into working life
Situation	Making the target of the crime more "difficult," environmental planning, replacement of traffic, lighting	Redesigning the areas of high crime level, private guarding, janitors	Specifying and locating the object of the problem, searching for more suitable places for the activities in question
Victim/Object	Educational campaigns, special stress on guidance for children	Special protection of threatened persons, private guarding of residential areas	System of compensation for the harms caused by the crime, support for the victims, shelters

Source: Aromaa, 1993:138.

The primary aim of the LOKKI project was to find new methods to prevent the start of criminal behavior by juveniles and thus to prevent an endless cycle of crime. An additional aim was to look for sanction alternatives better than the traditional ones for those juveniles already found guilty of offenses. An important aside was to help parents assist in the problematic situation of the juveniles. In essence LOKKI hoped to help juveniles develop control and coping skills for dealing with social problems—and to provide the preconditions for success.

LOKKI focused on the needs of youth as the starting point and sought extensive cooperation of authorities, exceeding the traditional boundaries. According to the parties responsible for carrying out the project, positive results were achieved by the cooperation of the social authorities, the police, the system of prosecution, the city court and the youth work, and the school system. It was entirely voluntary to join LOKKI, and the final selection was made by the juveniles themselves.

At the first stage, social workers completed interview forms with the juveniles. A group of seven persons was selected on the basis of the forms. At the second stage, a meeting was arranged between each juvenile, the parents, social workers and LOKKI worker—the purpose being to develop a positive contact with the juvenile and the parents. At that time, the goals and procedures of LOKKI were explained to the young person and his or her parents. After the juvenile and the family had announced they were willing to join the program, the cooperation between the parents, the social worker, and the LOKKI workers was finalized.

The core of the action was an intensive twelve-week program. Its purpose was to give concrete support for the positive development of the juvenile—to teach practical skills needed in interaction, human relationships, and in solving problems. The program consisted of an introduction camp, growth and leisure groups meeting twice a week, and the final camp. There were 25 group meetings and between 9 and 12 camp and excursion days. The purpose of the introduction camp was to provide a positive first experience to the juvenile and to give a positive impression of future LOKKI activities.

The primary purpose of the growth group was to strengthen the positive self-concept of the young person, to increase self-knowledge, and to teach new models for solving problems. The purpose of the leisure group was to strengthen the operation of the growth group. The five-day final camp was the culmination of the group action and a symbol of the achievement of the objectives set together. After that the juveniles could stay with LOKKI in a less formal manner, e.g., participating in camps and special-subject days.

The final aim was the return of the young person to society, better equipped to be a contributing member. This three-month period also included family work, where methods of family-oriented work were adapted to the LOKKI action. The parents' group met 6 to 8 times, and there were two social workers in the parents' group.

The program encountered difficulties pertaining to socialization and dealing with the conflicting roles of problem adolescents. It is not yet possible to estimate the lasting effects. The participants need to be interviewed again and efforts made to assess whether the program succeeded in preventing criminal behavior and associations.

The case of Petri.   The background of 16-year-old Petri is typical of persons participating in the LOKKI project: divorced parents, father moved abroad, single-parent mother who has alcohol problems and a new, occasionally violent male friend. Petri's relationship with LOKKI began with the cooperation of school and the child guidance center, and the child welfare authorities were contacted on this basis. The reasons for initial contact were Petri's difficulties in school attendance, petty thefts, and occasionally violent behavior. Additionally, the school and neighbors were concerned because of the mother's use of alcohol.

In defining Petri's problems, the conclusion was drawn that because of the difficult family environment he was defensive and more likely to react, which had led to uncontrolled situations. Petri himself wanted his life to change. He was lonely, and there was a definite longing for a group. He couldn't create lasting contacts with the social workers, who changed periodically.

Petri heard about LOKKI from a friend who had previously participated in a LOKKI group and had liked it. At first Petri was timid and his group role was merely that of a follower. Early in the introduction camp, however, one could notice that he had a sense of responsibility for himself and others. Later, Petri clearly became the most active participant in his group. In addition to the camps, he took part in almost all group events. Solid relationships with LOKKI workers developed, and he eventually discussed personal and family issues that he had never before talked about. This phase took place in the final camp. During the intensive work, Petri was able to separate himself from his family situation. He has been able to grow as an individual, even though contextual problems have remained mostly the same.

Several positive changes took place in Petri's life situation. In the spring of 1990, in a LOKKI camp in Lapland, he met his girlfriend Tiina, whom he steadily dated. In the summer of 1991, Petri was at work for the first time in his life. He also worked successfully as an assistant supervisor in a camp organized by the social welfare center. Despite this excellent progress, however, Petri took part in the theft of a car, which led to court proceedings and a conditional sentence of imprisonment.

Immediately after release from the police jail, however, Petri returned to LOKKI. This was interpreted as a positive sign that he had developed a capacity for solving problems and for consulting people who are important to him. It also was considered important that Petri had understood that failures are a part of development and had decided to continue in the program. Within the project, he was regarded a good example of positive progress.

Petri's mother participated in the parents' group component of the LOKKI project. She believes that it has been the only place where she found help. One example is the development of a close relationship with the family worker during the LOKKI action.

Leo Nyqvist (1993) analyzed the operation of the LOKKI project. His assessment found that the project itself may have been successful when in operation but that its long-term benefits often were virtually nonexistent. The reason for this is probably that all effective levels of LOKKI had not been operationalized. It is not enough to carry out the actual basic tasks (customer work) well. Various outside organizations and interest groups should have been in place to continue the work begun by LOKKI. In other words, such projects must seek legitimacy and cooperation with other outside resource organizations. The LOKKI project addressed current needs as a starting point; however, the skills fostered in the program needed to be reinforced by future outside associations. If such projects are treated merely as an administrative duties for one specific series of actions, they will fail as a preventive action against future problems.

According to Nyqvist, it is important to combine the methods of projects like LOKKI with municipal child and juvenile welfare programs. A relatively short-term program, detached from other services, cannot achieve change alone. LOKKI was intensive action with an expert organization that allowed innovations, creativity, and rapid decisions to achieve one basic goal. That initial success should have been linked with other organizations to ensure long-term success.

The strong approval among the customers, both juveniles and parents, was considered the most significant achievement of the LOKKI action. The aim of the project to include both young persons and their parents seemed to be very successful. In groups, the juveniles were given an opportunity to express themselves and to bring out their strong points. This enabled parents to see their children's progress, and their opinions about the young persons changed. LOKKI functioned as a channel of direct help for juveniles and their parents in situations where there was distress, fear, anguish, and helplessness in their lives. If LOKKI's creative methods could have been channeled into other organizations in an ongoing support system, it would have provided an excellent model for the prevention of juvenile delinquency. The important goal is this, as in all such projects, to seek alternative approaches to a problem for which traditional methods have failed.

Notes

[1] For all court cases the system of daily fine is the following: one daily fine was the monthly gross income of a person divided by 90. The minimum daily fine was 20 FIM (3.5 USD). Nowadays, one daily fine is the monthly net income divided by 60. The minimum daily fine is 40 FIM (7 USD). As of 2002, the currency of Finland has been a common European money Euro. In November 2003 one USD equated 0.86 Euros.

[2] Juvenile sentence. Proposal of the Criminal Law Project, *Criminal Law Project*, August 27, 1993. Law drafting department of the Ministry of Justice.

[3] Probation and After-Care Association (KHY) was a public association, founded by law in 1975 as an independent association controlled by the Ministry of Justice. KHY was granted government subsidy by the Ministry of Justice. The purpose of KHY was to carry out and develop probation and after-care work with the aim of improving the chances of persons who were subject to penal sanctions to manage in freedom. As of 2001 KHY was affiliated as a part of Criminal Sanctions Services (under the Ministry of Justice), and its name is now Probation Service.

Bibliography

Aromaa, Kauko (1993). "Poliisi ja rikoksia ennalta ehkäisevä toiminta" [The police and measures of crime prevention]. In Ahti Laitinen (ed.), *The Young, Criminality and Crime Prevention*. Helsinki: The Ministry of Interior, Police Department (Publication Nr. 8/1993).

Aromaa, Kauko, and Ahti Laitinen (1993). *Turun koululaiset "rikollisina"* [The pupils in Turku as "criminals"]. Helsinki: The Ministry of Interior, Police Department (Publication Nr. 2/93).

Christie, Nils (1993). *Crime Control as Industry*. London: Routledge.

Christie, Nils, and Kettil Bruun (1986). *Hyvä vihollinen* [A good enemy]. Espoo: Weilin & Goos.

Heiskanen, Markku, Kauko Aromaa, Hannu Niemi, and Reino Sirén (2000). *Tapaturmat ja väkivalta* [Accidents and violence]. *Oikeus* 2000:1, Helsinki: Statistics Finland.

Iivari, Juhani (2001). *Rikos- ja riita-asioiden sovittelun valtakunnallinen organiaointi* [The Country-wide Organisation of conciliation of crimes and disputes]. Publication Nr. 2000:27, Helsinki: Ministry of Social Affairs and Health.

Järvinen, Saija (1993). "Rikosten sovittelu Suomessa. Sovittelukäytännöt ja vaihtoehtoisuuden arviointi. Oikeuspoliittisen tutkimuslaitoksen julkaisuja 116." [Conciliation of offenses in Finland. Conciliation practices and the assessment of alternatives.] Publications of the National Research Institute of Legal Policy 116. STAKES, studies 21. Jyvaskyla.

Lappi-Seppälä, Tapio (1991). "Rikosoikeudellisista toimenpiteista luopumista koskeva uudistus" [A reform on the waiving of penal sanctions]. *I. Lakimies* 89: 902–28.

LOKKI-seminar, Turku (1993). Seminar paper: The child welfare association Mannerheimin lastensuojeluliitto, the district of Varsinais-Suomi (3/18).

Nuorisorangaistus. *Rikoslakiprojektin ehdotus, rikoslakiprojekti. Oikeusministerion lainvalmisteluosasto* [Juvenile Sentence. A proposal of the Criminal Law Project] (1993). The law drafting Department of the Ministry of Justice (8/27).

Nyqvist, Leo (1993). "Miten projekti säilyy hengissä? Organisaatio, asiakkaat ja yhteistyö" [How can a project survive? Organization, customers and cooperation]. LOKKI seminar, Turku. Seminar paper, the child welfare association Mannerheimin lasten-suojeluliitto, the district of Varsinais-Suomi (3/18).

Oksanen, Hannu (1990). *Steissi. Raportti nuorista Helsingin asemalla. Kansalaiskasvatuksen Keskuksen julkaisuja 89* [Steissi. A report on juveniles frequenting the Helsinki railway station. A publication of the Educational Center for Citizens, Nr. 89]. Helsinki: Educational Center for Citizens.

Rakt på ungdoms brotten (1990). Stockholm: Rikspolisstyrelsen.

Rikollisuustilanne 1991 [Criminality in Finland 1991] (1992). Helsinki: National Research Institute of Legal Policy.

Rikollisuustilanne 1992 [Criminality in Finland 1992] (1993). Helsinki: National Research Institute of Legal Policy.

Rikollisuustilanne 1999 [Criminality in Finland 1999] (2000). Helsinki: National Research Institute of Legal Policy.

Rikosoikeuskomitean mietintö. Komiteanmietinto [Committee report] (1976). Helsinki.

Sulin, Marja (1992). *Seuraamusluonteinen syyttämättä jättäminen* [Waiving of charges as a sanction]. Helsinki: University of Helsinki, the Faculty of Law, the Institute of Criminal Law and Judicial Procedure.

Suolahti, Gunnar [1909] (1991). *Elämää Suomessa 1700-luvulla* [Life in Finland in the 18th century]. Jyväskylä: SKS.

Takala, Jukka-Pekka (1992). "Yhdyskuntapalvelu ja siihen valikoituminen: uuden rangaistusmuodon kokedun alkuvaihe" [Community service and the selection for it: the early stages of experimenting with a new form of sanction]. Unpublished manuscript.

Vintiötyöryhmän muistio [The memorandum of the working party on rascals] (1992). Helsinki: The Ministry of Justice.

Virén, Matti (1992). *Omaisuusrikollisuus taloudellisena ongelmana* [Property crime as an economic problem]. Turku: University of Turku, Department of Economics (Research Report Nr. 18).

Yearbook of Justice Statistics. Statistics Finland, *Justice* 2002:18. Helsinki. http://www. rikosseuraamus.fi (accessed February 25, 2004).

28

Juvenile Delinquency in the Cross-Cultural Context
The Egyptian Experience

Sam S. Souryal

Egypt (officially The Arab Republic of Egypt) is a unique country with an exotic history and a perplexing present. Although its history has been chronicled in textbooks and periodicals worldwide, a closer look into its culture and society may puzzle the unfamiliar observer. The country combines the natural and the supernatural, the ancient and the modern, the sacred and the secular, the native and the adopted—all within an intriguing tautology. Nowhere has this paradigm been so manifest as in the Egyptian experience with children. For example, the temples of Egypt seldom display the image of Pharaoh without a child affectionately seated near his throne. Consider furthermore these paradoxes: Moses, the son of an enslaved Israelite, was brought to the pinnacle of Egyptian priesthood by the daughter of Pharaoh; young Joseph, who had been sold into slavery by his brothers, was elevated by Egyptians to a legendary historical figure; but more significantly, consider the pivotal case of Christianity which would have been born dead if the child Jesus was not offered refuge in Egypt during the peak of Roman persecution. These paradoxes serve as theodicean indicators, which may explain Egypt's special attachment to children.

While the Egyptian society today is predominantly Moslem, this ancestral attachment has not abated but indeed intensified. In Islamic theology, children are considered both *baraka* (gifts from God) and *zeena* (ornaments of life), and caring for their special needs is an article of worship. No wonder, when Moslem families are compared to Western families, they appear to be more possessive of their children, more committed to their needs, and more affectionate—attributes recognized by social control the-

Previously published in the *International Journal of Comparative and Applied Criminal Justice*, Vol. 16, No. 2 (fall, 1992):329–52. Reprinted by permission.

orists as conducive to social bonding (Hirschi, 1969; Elliot and Voss, 1974; Gottfredson and Hirschi, 1990; Souryal, 1988). Given the figures that will be presented later, it might well be argued that Egypt does not have a problem with juvenile delinquency, at least as defined in the West. Rather, it is more likely that Egypt's over-occupation with children is what gave impetus to this fashionable concern. On the other hand, given the perennial economic and political hardships of Egypt, it is particularly puzzling to the Western researcher why a full-blown juvenile delinquency problem has not developed. The answer to this puzzle may be found somewhere between two plausible hypotheses: (a) Egypt's Byzantine sociocultural paradigm (known as *satr min Allah*, or spiritual guidance), and (b) the unspoken presence of "hidden delinquency," especially since victimization surveys or self-reported studies are not used and available data are based solely on police statistics.

Egypt: Land, Education, and Economy

The Arab Republic of Egypt occupies the northeastern corner of Africa. Its land mass is estimated at 385,110 square miles (about the size of Texas and New Mexico combined) with an inhabited area of only 13,578 square miles, one and a half times the size of Vermont. According to the 1986 census, the population of Egypt is estimated at 48.3 million, the annual birth rate is 36.6 per 1,000, the overall growth rate is 2.8 percent, the death rate is around 10 per 1,000, and life expectancy is 62 years (*Statistical Year Book*, 1991:3). The risks associated with this rapid rate of population growth are further complicated by the obvious scarcity of cultivable land relative to population. As such, more than 97 percent of Egypt's population is crowded in approximately four percent of the total territory (*Statistical Year Book*, 1991:4). This pattern of population concentration gives Egypt an overall density rate of 72 persons per square mile albeit an overall 1,700 persons per square mile of inhabitable land.

Another factor that complicates (or ironically validates, as critics would say) the Egyptian sociological paradigm is the population's modest level of education. The illiteracy rate is 37.4 percent for males and 62 percent for females (an overall average of 50 percent). The rate of those who hold a primary certificate, the equivalent of an eighth-grade education in the United States, is 23 percent for males and 14.9 percent for females (an overall average of 19 percent). The rate of those who hold a high school education is 25.2 percent and 14.7 percent respectively, and the rate of college graduates is 4.7 percent and 1.4 percent respectively (*Statistical Year Book*, 1991:22).

The Egyptian economy has never been noted for its vibrancy. This is due basically to lack of natural resources, the absence of modern technology, and a long string of colonial periods. The economy further experienced a sharp nosedive after the 1952 revolution, which restricted land ownership and all but devastated the private sector. Further still, the economy suffered because of the wars with Israel in 1956, in Yemen in 1965, and again with Israel in 1967 and 1973. Despite vitriolic attempts by Presidents Sadat and Mubarek to turn the economy into a free-market economy, official policy has not changed. Subsequently, the Gross National Income of Egypt remains a meager LP 50,511 million ($16.293 billion U.S.), the unemployment rate is estimated at 15 percent, and per capita income is $336 annually (*Statistical Year Book*, 1986:237).

The Egyptian Society

In *Social Ethics of Islam*, Al-Sayed (1982) observes that Egyptians ideologically reject the Western doctrine of separation of church and state and have greater difficulty accepting the role of the state as a superstructure that transcends identification with religion and family (p. 259). The Egyptian society, therefore, remains essentially a conservative and religious society. It is conservative in terms of its close affinity with Durkheim's representation of a mechanical solidarity society (Durkheim, 1964) and religious in terms of its identification with Berger and Luckman's (1967) model of the sacred canopy. Islam continues to be the basis of social, intellectual, and political integration and provides the rational cohesive force that ties together groups and individuals into an *umma*, or a nation of believers. This view is based on the unshakable belief that divine law preceded society and that the role of the state is specifically to enforce *Shari'ah*, or God's law. Over the centuries, this perception has remained intact and Islam continues to be the most decisive factor in social and political cohesiveness (Al-Sayed, 1982:258).

Consistent with Al-Sayed's views, Moslems in Egypt (who constitute about 90 percent of the population, the remaining 10 percent being Coptic Christians) firmly believe that religious behavior and individual attitudes are inseparable, that *siyasa* (politics) and *din* (religion) are two sides of a coin, and that issues of delinquency and crime are unarguably caused by a deteriorated Islamic community. Perhaps because the Egyptian society has been traditionally poor and uneducated, social beliefs have mirrored the view of religion as a "unified system of belief and practices relative to sacred things set aside and forbidden" (Durkheim, 1964:61). In Islamic jurisprudence, the individual is considered naturally good although weak and subject to temptation. It is imperative, thereupon, that an Islamic society protect its members from succumbing to secular temptation and corrupt behavior. Social values are, subsequently, inseparable from religious values just as law and education are undetached from religious norms (Al-Sayed, 1982:13). The Egyptian society that boasts of having more than 46,000 public and private mosques—almost one for every 1,000 men, women, and children (Hammouda, 1987:214)—categorically distinguishes between the obligatory and the forbidden, the sacred and the profane, and commands worship as a group activity. The totality of such beliefs forms a determinate system that has a life of its own; one that Durkheim calls the collective or common conscience (Durkheim, 1964:79). This preoccupation with religiosity has naturally given Islamic institutions a moral stranglehold on the day-to-day behavior of the people, giving further credence to the belief of *satr min Allah*, or spiritual guidance (Al-Sayed, 1982:260).

Based on these observations, it should be safe to suppose that the Egyptian society is obsessed with sacredness that demonstratively influences how people feel, behave, appear, and judge. The predominant logic is not whether an issue is economically sound, politically correct, or even ethically sound, but whether it is condoned or condemned by God (Souryal, 1988). To maintain legitimacy, the political structure—as a matter of policy—must support, or appear to support, the legitimate Islamic institutions. As a result, the Ministry of Religious Affairs (which is always headed by a distinguished cleric) monitors and actively influences all mass media in terms of what is shown on television or appears in the newspapers; religious education is required at all levels, including college; Islamic banks have proliferated to replace foreign banks (which charge usury), and Islamic teachings have been promulgated as the *summum bonum* of all virtues.

On the other side of the sociological paradigm, there is the inexorable force of liberal intellectualism in Egyptian society. Largely due to French and British colonial influences (Napoleon invaded Egypt in 1798 and the British finally withdrew from Egypt in 1956) and the presence of a vibrant Coptic (Christian) minority, Western enlightenment and social thought have remained resourceful in the Egyptian mind. Even before the turn of the twentieth century, Egypt has had an influential group of intelligentsia, a large middle class, a fairly democratic society, and a relatively free press. Notwithstanding the military rule of President Nasser (1952–1970), subsequent governments under Presidents Sadat (1970–1981) and Mubarek (1981–) have been noticeably democratic, and a popularly elected parliament has been passing an array of liberal policies unmatched in any other Middle-Eastern country. For instance, drinking alcohol and disco-dancing is allowed in most urban hotels and casinos, gambling is permitted in exclusive clubs, Western music is played in public places and tapes (especially Elvis and Julio Iglesias tapes) are sold in city stores, Christian schools operate even in small rural areas, overseas travel is unrestricted, scantily-clad tourists leisurely walk past the most sacred shrines, and Christmas mass is annually celebrated on government-controlled television. Once again, one must ponder the paradox of the Egyptian sociological paradigm.

Family Structure in Egyptian Society

The family, perhaps more than any other social institution, has predominant influence on the lives of Egyptian youths. As mentioned, it is a closely-knit unit in which the behavior of children mirrors in large measure Hirschi's (1969) social control model. Youngsters grow up in a socially controlled environment that provides both strict discipline and deep affection reminiscent of Braithwaite's (1989) shame/reintegration model. During their adolescent years, children are usually subjected to a possessive and authoritative father, an ever-present *yiddische* mother, and a substantial hierarchy of siblings who impose a normative identity; one essentially characterized by submission to the will of God and deference to instructions by parents and elders.

In their growing-up years, Egyptian children typically identify with the tenets of social learning theory (Akers, 1977). They directly and indirectly learn Islamic values and internalize the virtues of Islamic modal behavior. Direct learning follows, by and large, the "operant conditioning" theory, which proposes that one is a product of his/her immediate environment. The call for prayer is the first sound Egyptian children hear at sunrise and the last before going to bed each day. In the meantime, they are made cognizant of religious symbols all around them: Quranic recitation at school, group prayer on television, and the display of religious literature in public places and store windows (Souryal, 1988:21).

Indirect learning, on the other hand, occurs through social interactions in which the behavior of other persons becomes either reinforcing or discriminating. As Akers explains, indirect learning is not necessarily the product of rewards one receives for his or her actions but is vicariously acquired by watching modal behaviors being rewarded (Akers, 1985). Children watch their father's routine trips to the mosque, their mother performing prayer at home and veiling her face on the street, abstaining from eating during the month of Ramadan, and segregation by gender—in a scramble—when guests drop by unannounced (Souryal, 1988:22).

As a matter of culture, Egyptian youths do reside at home until they are married (this is even more common today due to shortages in housing). This prolonged episode of at-home residence can be particularly critical to their social and moral development. It can reinforce one's participation by intensifying his/her conformity to conventional goals and belief in the moral validity of social norms, or it may cause deprivation and induce separation through rites of passage. Given the conservative nature of the Egyptian society, these core vectors of participation and separation may very well offer the most integral clue to explaining delinquency among Egyptian youths (see Shoham's psychological model of human development cited in Kelly and MacNamara, 1991; and Braithwaite's theory on interdependence and communitarianism, 1989).

In the Egyptian experience, prolonged episodes of at-home residence do indeed direct youths toward participation rather than separation. This judgment can be supported by two succinct observations: (a) considerable numbers of youths—even after they are married—choose to continue living at home with their brides; and (b) the rate of delinquency in rural areas—where the likelihood of living with parents is greater and the duration of at-home residence may be longer—is substantially lower than in urban areas (as will be shown later in table 1). Once again, when compared to Western culture, which values freedom, individuality, and independence at a young age, family bonding in the Egyptian society remains the nucleus of social life, and the idea of *parens patriae* seems nowhere more deeply ingrained than in the Egyptian family structure.

Juvenile Justice: Philosophy and System

Although Egypt is a third-world country by economic standards, its institutions of juvenile justice feature a level of social enlightenment traditionally restricted to more advanced nations. The Western researcher would be astounded by some of the distinguished features in the Egyptian juvenile law. Consider for instance these legal requirements: (a) parents or guardians must be formally informed in writing if the child is suspected of predelinquent behavior, (b) delinquent children who are suspected of mental or emotional disorders automatically undergo medical supervision, (c) delinquent children under the age of 15 are treated with social measures rather than criminal penalties—regardless of the number or seriousness of crimes committed, (d) delinquent juveniles under the age of 18 are categorically spared the penalties of capital punishment or a life sentence regardless of any accentuating factors that may exist. This feature is distinctively significant since the United States and only five other countries (Bangladesh, Pakistan, Barbados, Iran, and Iraq) continue to execute juvenile offenders under certain conditions (The National Coalition, 1992); and (e) juvenile courts are staffed by at least two certified social workers—one of whom *must* be a female. The Western observer would also be markedly thrilled to learn that the Minister of Social Affairs in charge of all national legislation in the field of juvenile delinquency is a female intellectual with a Ph.D. degree in social sciences and that the entire class of workers who operate juvenile institutions are college-educated professionals.

The leading philosophy of delinquency in Egypt is based on the belief that deviance is a product of emotional and intellectual immaturity caused by social imbalances in the juvenile's immediate environment or by "coincidences of unfavorable circumstances" surrounding the child's upbringing—i.e., involvement with the wrong crowd in the neighborhood, at school, or at the workplace (see in particular the study of Juvenile Delinquency in the USSR cited in Finckenaur, 1988). As such, delinquency is considered first and foremost a *social phenomenon* that can be remedied by *social measures* rather than the imposition of criminal penalties. Such measures must be nonpunitive in nature, rehabilitative in purpose, and sufficient in force to remedy without causing stigmatization and alienation. Otherwise, they may aggravate a fairly natural situation by turning delinquents into hard-core criminals (for further discussion of this philosophy see Braithwaite's views in *Crime, Shaming, and Reintegration*, cited earlier).

Toward institutionalizing this philosophy, the Egyptian government has chartered a twofold policy: (a) launching a preventive campaign directed at educating parents, guardians, schoolteachers, and clerics, and (b) putting into effect a "sympathetic" administrative system for governing the behavior of delinquent juveniles. The latter consists of specially-trained police squads, independent courts, independent prosecutors, a cadre of college-educated social workers who are mostly women, and a number of modern correctional facilities that vary both by the age of the juvenile and his/her rehabilitation needs. These facilities offer a wide range of programs directed at providing educational, social, religious, occupational, and recreational treatment for delinquent children.

One of the rather controversial characteristics of the juvenile justice system in Egypt is the way it is administered. The system is managed jointly by two ministries: the Department of Insurances and Social Affairs (equivalent to the Department of Health and Human Resources in the United States) and the Department of Interior, the national agency in charge of police. The former is responsible for handling all legislative and judicial aspects of delinquency, as well as administering juvenile courts and correctional facilities. The latter oversees the operational aspects of the juvenile system. Juveniles who are suspected of predelinquency, who are surrendered to police by their parents or guardians, or who are charged with criminal acts are processed by regional police centers and tried in juvenile court; and if found guilty, they are remanded to the appropriate correctional facility. Coordination between the two ministries is the responsibility of the National Child Council, a blue-ribbon panel consisting of executives from both ministries and representatives from private child-related organizations. While relations between the two ministries are usually cordial, decisions and/or actions are stymied at times by bureaucratic communication and differences in operational style; police officials complain of the slow responses by the Ministry of Social Affairs and ministry officials are concerned about the police tendency to overreact by locking up children with adult prisoners, by roughing them up for confessions, or otherwise causing them undue emotional strain.

Despite the previously cited features of the Egyptian juvenile system, it would be inaccurate to suggest that the system is as sophisticated as those in the United States or Western countries. The differences, however, are principally in the corporeal sense rather than the philosophical. This can be explained in terms of two main observations: (a) the lack of *imkaniaat* (resources), which has become a perennial household complaint indicating inadequacy of financial resources. System effectiveness, as a result, has in large measure suffered; it is impeded by shortages of note pads, incident report forms, fuel, inadequate detention facilities, lack of training tools, medical instruments, and recreational equipment, as well as by badly needed physical repairs and maintenance; and (b) the absence of stringent trial procedures as required by American case law (i.e., the *Kent* case, 1966, or the *Gault* case, 1967). The Egyptian juvenile trial system is still rather soft—it does not require rigorous or advanced rules of evidence, nor does it allow for as many appeals as in Western systems. With these qualifications in mind, one must also add that the Egyptian juvenile trial system, for all practical reasons, "somehow" manages to serve the best interest of the child, the victim, and the society. As if it is directed by an "invisible hand" or by a "sense of natural justice," the system appears to operate effectively, affectionately, and smoothly. As General Seddiq of the juvenile police administration aptly described, the system is endowed with a natural sense of justice—"one that operates two guardian eyes, one legal and the other social."

Highlights of Juvenile Delinquency Law in Egypt

Juvenile delinquency in the Arab Republic of Egypt is currently governed by Public Law 31, 1974. In Egyptian law, juveniles become involved in the justice system in three situations: (a) when suspected of *tasharud*, or predelinquency, (b) when surrendered to the authorities by a parent or a guardian who is no longer able to control him, or (c) when charged with a crime. The following section articulates the main characteristics of the law, which, because of their self-evidencing nature, will be presented here without any undue elaboration:

Chapter One, Article One defines a juvenile as one "who did not exceed eighteen years of age at the time of committing a crime or being involved in an act of predelinquency" (Public Law 31, 1974). Article Two identifies predelinquency in terms of eight kinds of socially unacceptable behaviors: (a) involvement in acts of vagrancy, which include selling trivial goods, offering insignificant services, or performing acrobatic exhibitions in public as a means of living; (b) involvement in collecting cigarette butts or rummaging through garbage or trash cans as a means of living; (c) involvement in acts of prostitution, gambling, or drug-related activities; (d) being without a permanent address and sleeping in the streets or in places not designed for human living; (e) being in the company of delinquent individuals who are known to be of ill repute; (f) being a habitual escapee from juvenile institutions; (g) being a wayward child (a runaway) who renounces parental authority; and (h) having no certified means of living.

Chapter Two, Article One enumerates the social measures to be applied to the juvenile charged with predelinquency provided he/she is under the age of fifteen. These are: judicial rebuke, return to parents or guardians, community service, vocational training, being committed to a detention institution for a period not to exceed three years, probation for a period not to exceed three years, or being committed to a mental institution (Public Law 31, 1974).

Chapter Two, Article 15 lists the penalties that can be applied if a juvenile is charged with a crime when older than fifteen but younger than eighteen years of age. The law states that if such a juvenile is convicted of a crime the stated penalty of which is death or a life sentence, he/she can only be punished by a prison term for no less than ten years; if the stated penalty is a prison term, he/she can only be punished by a jail sentence for no less than six months; and if the stated penalty is a jail sentence, he/she can only be punished by a jail sentence not to exceed two thirds of the stated penalty. Chapter Two, furthermore, states that in all juvenile cases no corporal punishment can be applied, the accused is exempt from paying any fees or court costs, and if the penalty is incarceration, imprisonment must be carried out in one of the detention institutions under the control of the Ministry of Insurances and Social Affairs (Public Law 31, 1974).

Of particular interest is a number of innovative social precautions required by Public Law 31 (1974). They include, for instance: (a) fining the parent or guardian if a delinquent child who had been entrusted to their stewardship returned to delinquency or was involved in another crime. In the latter contingency, the parent or guardian may be sentenced to a jail term; (b) requiring the presence of a lawyer to defend the accused juvenile during all stages of trial, and (c) requiring that the judge review and consider a pre-sentencing report to be prepared by a social worker prior to the sentencing phase (Public Law 31, 1974).

The Extent and Patterning of Delinquency in Egypt

Juvenile delinquents in Egypt are essentially boys (girls are invariably involved in low-level acts of prostitution) who are nonviolent, unarmed, unadventurous, and criminally unsophisticated. During visits by this researcher to the Al-Giza and Al-Azbekhia juvenile detention institutions, the vast majority of residents looked and behaved the same way as lower-class nondelinquents in the street-poor, undernourished, impassive, confused, submissive, and hapless. When compared to delinquents in the United States who are usually defiant, aggressive, and determined, one cannot help but characterize delinquency in Egypt as essentially benign rather than iniquitous, subtle rather than overt, perfunctory rather than systematic, and amateurish rather than organized.

As evidence of this characterization, consider, for example, these sociocultural differences between delinquent acts in Egypt and the United States: (1) drive-by shootings are unknown in light of the strict ban on firearms, the lack of access to a car, and the fact that most of the streets are too narrow to allow for a successful getaway even if such an act was contemplated, (2) motor-vehicle thefts are most infrequent since the vast majority of juveniles are unacquainted with auto mechanics, cannot drive, and lack the necessary skills to hot-wire a vehicle or pry open its doors; (3) forcible rape is almost nonexistent, since it is viewed as a cowardly act that brings about a "dirty" social stigma upon the accused and his family—forcing oneself on a female against her will is an affront to the image of the "macho man"; (4) organized crime activities (other than pimping) are elementary, at best, since they require sophisticated networks of adventurous individuals who are sworn to secrecy—a rare commodity in a culture that thrives upon story-telling, inquisitiveness, and braggadocio; (5) street gangs and activities associated with "mod" or "skinhead" subcultures do not exist, since society is invariably racially monolithic and ethnically homogeneous. Furthermore, demonstrating machismo by enhancing one's facial features or by wearing costumes and accessories is considered effeminate; (6) cult worship and satanic-related deviance are out of the question, since they are inherently sacrilegious and culturally scandalous; (7) murder is extremely rare, since it is viewed as a sorry misadventure and the potential of being accused of such an act shocks the conscience of the entire neighborhood; and (8) aggravated robbery is an infrequent incident that is associated with American action movies, while in reality it is a "real stupid" means of making a living (see table 2 in the section on statistical data).

Of even greater importance is the fact that most acts of delinquency in Egypt are neither committed under the influence of drugs or alcohol nor inspired by racism or sexual fantasies. Furthermore, firearms are strictly banned (therefore they are not expected to be found in burglarized residences), narcotics are scarce and expensive, and sexual attractions (i.e., X-rated movies, topless bars, and peep shows) are not only *rigs min al shitan* (wickedness from Satan) but are categorically prohibited. Once again, the Western researcher should be intrigued by such significant differences; elements that further reinforce the Egyptians' belief in the validity of their sociological paradigm.

On the other hand, these observations should not be simply taken at face value. Unofficial data seem to confirm the presence of two categories of "unpublicized delinquency," namely, "American style violence" and "Jihad crimes." The first category refers to acts of violence normally associated with adolescents from upper-middle-class families who are frustrated with the means for achieving success within the confines of a "reactionary" society. These are reportedly perfidious individuals who may have traveled extensively abroad and are fascinated by Western adventure; they may have access to firearms, and under the influence of drugs (usually pills) they may commit bank robberies, extortions, and forceful rapes. Those in this category are, however, a minority, and their crimes usually go unpublicized for fear of the "copycatting effect." Jihad crimes, on the other hand, are committed in the name of religion and involve violent acts to destabilize the secular government, to sabotage the national foreign policy, or to terrorize other religious groups. Given the global rise in Islamic fundamentalism in the Middle East, these activities are closely watched by police, and suspects are monitored and treated with extreme measures (this data was received from confidential interviews with government officials).

In the final analysis, it is imperative to reiterate that the vast majority of delinquent acts in Egypt remain basically low-level street deviance consisting of petty thievery, residential burglaries, pickpocketing, vandalism, fraud, assault, sexual offenses, as well as acts of truancy, and obstruction of traffic (see table 3 in the section on statistical data).

There are several theoretical explanations for this state of benign delinquency in the Egyptian society: (a) the formation of delinquent patterns is usually maximized by criminalistic environments where delinquent behavior is generated by a competitive materialistic society and takes the form of direct or indirect assaults on property (Gibbons and Krohn, 1991:347). By contrast, the Egyptian society, by virtue of its traditional economic structure, does not lend itself to such an environment; (b) violent delinquency patterns are viewed as consequences of social class variations that lead to situations where legitimate avenues to the attainment of goals are blocked (Merton, 1968; Cohen, 1955; Cloward and Ohlin, 1960). The Egyptian society, by contrast, continues to adhere to a socialistic ideology that inhibits, to a large measure, class stratification and the emergence of such situations. Indeed, it is much more common today to encounter young doctors, lawyers, teachers, army officers, police officers, and government officials who have bridged the social lines and assimilated themselves in the upper-middle-class professional echelons; (c) patterns of delinquency are widely believed to be products of strained familial situations such as parental rejection or deviant sexual socialization (Hirschi, 1969). The Egyptian family, as mentioned earlier, appears much more unified and strongly bonded by religious values and conservative social norms than the average Western family; (d) the popular perception of the Egyptian police as an omniscient institution (although in reality it is not) has led the young citizens to believe that they are continuously under intensive police surveillance. This factor, especially when combined with its corollary perception that having recourse to police brutality is practically nonattainable may contribute to dampening any adventurous inclination on the part of juveniles to be too criminally aggressive.

Statistical Data

In the following section, statistical data pertaining to incidents of predelinquency and kinds of crime committed by juveniles in the Arab Republic of Egypt (1984–1990) will be presented. Table 1 illustrates the frequency of predelinquent incidents by urban, rural, and desert provinces; table 2 represents felony acts of delinquency by category of crime; and table 3 represents misdemeanor acts of delinquency by category of crime.

Table 1 indicates a roughly normal distribution between urban and rural predelinquency in the Arab Republic of Egypt; a sharp increase in urban provinces and a slight decrease in rural provinces (predelinquent acts in desert provinces are too few to indicate a trend). The rate of increase in urban areas during the period of 1984–1990 is 117.3 percent while the rate of decrease in rural areas is 12.7 percent during the same period. This ratio may trigger one or more of the following hypotheses: (a) a gradual surge in urban predelinquency independent of the surrounding provinces, (b) a state of displaced predelinquency inspired by increasing urbanization and industrialization in urban areas bringing to cities large numbers of rural migrants in search of employment or in pursuit of the

Table 1   Number of Predelinquency Incidents Classified by Urban, Rural, and Desert Provinces (1984–1990)

Provinces	1984	1985	1986	1987	1988	1989	1990	Increase Decrease 1984–1990	Increase Decrease %
Urban									
Cairo	288	447	273	294	406	613	610	322	111.8
Alexandria	74	104	108	109	66	167	142	68	91.9
Port Said	219	319	313	333	316	403	371	152	69.4
Ismailia	63	35	14	27	13	20	24	−39	−61.9
Suez	5	5	60	256	247	326	263	258	5160.0
Subtotal	649	910	768	1019	1048	1529	1410	761	117.3
Rural									
Domiat	18	9	2	11	48	24	4	−14	−77.8
Qalubia	9	106	9	95	15	38	13	−4	44.4
Dekahlia	9	21	5	17	15	34	19	10	111.1
Sharquia	15	99	68	23	16	303	169	154	1026.7
Behira	7	113	14	2	8	24	21	14	200.0
Gharbia	22	19	25	13	51	263	123	101	459.1
Kafr-el-Sheik	62	5	8	0	8	2	5	−57	−91.9
Monufia	6	9	3	6	14	19	27	21	350.0
Giza	20	28	18	29	85	97	145	125	625.0
Beni Suef	276	237	17	54	18	68	132	−144	−52.2
Al Fayum	233	340	94	8	30	11	39	−194	−83.3
Al Minia	92	70	51	35	8	34	9	−83	−90.2
Asyut	5	8	28	37	33	42	39	34	680.0
Sohag	60	32	3	0	13	8	27	−33	−55.0
Qena	7	9	12	27	14	19	73	−66	942.9
Aswan	148	6	6	11	9	5	18	−130	−87.8
Subtotal	989	1111	363	368	385	991	863	−266	−12.7
Desert									
Red Sea	0	1	0	1	0	2	2	2	0.0
Matruh	3	0	0	0	1	4	1	−2	−66.7
New Valley	0	0	0	0	1	0	0	0	0.0
Northern Sinai	1	0	0	5	2	3	4	3	300.0
Southern Sinai	0	0	0	0	0	0	0	0	0.0
Subtotal	4	1	0	6	4	9	7	3	75.0
Total	1642	2022	1131	1393	1437	2529	2280	498	38.9

Source: Public Security Report (1991). Cairo: The Ministry of Interior.

"good life," or (c) an aggregate decline of predelinquency in rural areas for unclear reasons since neither birth rates nor the economic and social variables in rural areas have changed significantly.

If the first and/or second hypotheses are correct, then the Egyptian data are inconsistent with trends in the United States where the rate of arrest has been declining for more than a decade (Uniform Crime Reports, 1981–1990). In the United States, however, the decrease in rates has been primarily due to declining birth rates rather than the function of changes in the everyday behavior of American youths (Siegel and Senna, 1991:34). The Egyptian data, on the other hand, are consistent with cross-cultural trends. According to Baur's report (1964) on juvenile offenses in the Netherlands, court cases increased by 108 percent in the nation's capital between 1954 and 1961 and parallel increases occurred in the same period in Belgium, Norway, and Denmark. Baur also indicated that this rate of increase was consistent with most other nations (Baur, 1964:359–69). Similar data were reported by Cavan and Cavan (1968), who collected a mass of material bearing on juvenile delinquency in Mexico, India, Russia, England, and eight other European nations. According to their findings, juvenile lawbreaking is least frequent in Mexican villages and increases "as we move from villages to small towns to Mexico City" (Gibbons and Krohn, 1991:164). This finding is especially consistent with the Egyptian pattern of increase since the closest rural provinces to Cairo (Qalubia, Dekahlia, Sharquia, and Behira) have also experienced an increase rather than a decrease as is characteristic of other rural provinces. The researchers also found that delinquency in India is most common in the larger cities (although less often encountered than in Western societies). Cavan and Cavan concluded by stating that "city delinquency, like much of city life itself, is in a rudimentary stage of development. It grows out of poverty, dire need, and lack of social organization" (Cavan and Cavan, 1968:100–1).

In a comprehensive study of thirteen Arab nations by The International Arab Organization for Social Defense (1982) and based on a self-reporting methodology, the study found that among the most significant reasons for juvenile delinquency in Middle Eastern countries (Israel not included) was the migration of youths from *badia*, or rural areas, to *mudon*, or cities. The top three nations citing that variable as the most significant were Egypt, Morocco, and the Sudan. The study further noted that the sociocultural gulf between adolescents and adults tends to increase due to changes in the economic order as well as certain other factors. Among the "other factors," the study cited poverty, poor living conditions, unemployment, idleness, and high divorce rates. By the same token, the study indicated that the traditional agencies of socialization and social control that are designed to "contain" the behavior of juveniles within socially approved limits tend to break down under the influences of urbanization and modernization (The International Arab Organization for Social Defense Report:21–22).

In a related study of delinquency in Israel by Shlomo Shoham and Leon Shaskolsky (1969) the researchers contrasted 100 referrals to the juvenile court in Tel Aviv with an equal number of nondelinquents. The study showed that Israeli delinquents "did not differ from the nondelinquents on a variety of scales and measures dealing with personality characteristics, feelings of powerlessness or normlessness, family cohesiveness, and social background characteristics" (Gibbons and Krohn, 1991). Although the researchers were somewhat perplexed by their research instrument, their findings are specifically consistent with the observations previously mentioned regarding the lack of differences between delinquents and nondelinquents in Egyptian juvenile institutions. A logical explanation for the similarity between the Israeli pattern of delinquents and the Egyptian pattern may be found in the close sociocultural similarity between the role of family in the Moslem society and its counterpart in the Jewish society (for more detail on this observation, see Wegner, 1982; and Souryal, 1988).

According to table 2, the extent of juvenile delinquency in the Arab Republic of Egypt is negligible, by any stretch of the imagination. If official statistics are to be taken at face value (which in this case we must do because of the lack of any other form of data), then the total number of arrests for felony crimes (crimes against the person including murder, aggravated assault, kidnapping, and robbery) during the arbitrary year of 1990 are less than 75 incidents. Given the total number of juveniles in the

Table 2   Number of Felony Crimes Committed by Juveniles Classified by Kind of Crime and Year

Kind of Crime	1985	1986	1987	1988	1989	1990	Increase/ Decrease 1985–1990	Increase/ Decrease %
Murder	10	7	15	14	14	20	10	100.0
Aggravated assault	6	12	4	12	10	19	13	216.7
Kidnapping	—	—	16	2	2	1	1	
Sexual deviance	58	52	2	61	84	66	8	13.8
Robbery	11	12	21	18	35	32	21	190.9
Arson	—	4	2	6	2	7	7	
Animal poisoning	—	—	—	—	—	—	—	
Fraud	—	—	—	—	1	14	14	
Bribery	1	—	—	—	—	—	—	
Aggravated fraud	3	5	4	2	9	1	2	−66.7
Forgery	—	—	—	3	—	2	—	
Rioting	—	—	—	1	—	1	1	
Total	92	102	64	119	157	163	77	83.1

Source: Maguire and Flanigan, 1990

population-at-risk category (age 10–18, N = 5,333,059), the rate of these felony crimes is 1.41 per 100,000 (*Statistical Year Book*, 1991). When this rate is compared to the rate of arrest for Index Crimes in the United States (N = 450,557)—or a rate of 225.3 per 100,000—the Egyptian rate would be the equivalent of 0.0063 the American rate or a ratio of 1 to 159 (The American figures are derived from Maguire and Flanagan, *Sourcebook of Criminal Justice Statistics*, 1990: Table 4.6).

When the Egyptian data is examined in terms of direction of crime, they indicate that the largest number of arrests in 1990 is in the category of misdemeanor crimes (crimes against property including theft, fraud, and embezzlement). The total number of incidents is fewer than 4,760 or a rate of 89.25 per 100,000 of the population-at-risk category (*Statistical Year Book*, 1991). The second largest number of arrests is in the category of sexual offenses, both felonies and misdemeanors. The total number of incidents is 147 incidents or a rate of 2.76 per 100,000. By the same token, the smallest number of arrests is in the category of felonies (crimes against the person, which include murder, aggravated assaults, kidnapping, and robbery). The total number of incidents is 72 or a rate of 0.092 per 100,000. By comparing these rates, a trend clearly emerges: the most common category of delinquency in Egypt is property crimes, the least common is violent crimes, and sexual crimes rank high on the continuum between both categories. The ratio of crimes against property to sexual crimes is 63 to 1 and the ratio of sexual crimes to violent crimes against the person is slightly more than 2 to 1.

Table 3   Number of Misdemeanor Crimes Committed by Juveniles Classified by Kind of Crime and Year

Kind of Crime	1985	1986	1987	1988	1989	1990	Increase/ Decrease 1985–1990	Increase/ Decrease %
Theft	2485	2870	3271	3347	4373	4710	2225	89.5
Fraud	16	5	10	4	12	7	−9	−56.3
Sexual offense	75	58	68	57	71	81	24	8.0
Battery	5019	4323	4757	5181	5898	6390	1371	27.3
Accidental killing	309	321	320	285	293	292	−17	−5.5
Animal poisoning	—	—	—	—	—	—	—	
Criminal mischief	195	170	182	216	245	250	55	28.2
Embezzlement	55	54	65	49	51	40	−15	−27.3
Avoiding payment on public transit	477	532	812	1154	901	829	352	73.8
Total	8631	8333	9485	10293	11844	12599	3986	46.0

Source: Public Security Reports (1985–90). Cairo: The Ministry of Interior

Based on these mathematical relationships, one can safely conclude that juvenile delinquency in Egypt (while insignificant by American standards) has a special character consistent with the socioeconomic nature of third-world societies. It typifies the characterization of a conservative society with limited material resources, an effective level of communitarianism, and a "religious" abhorrence to violence. Unsurprisingly, the hierarchy of criminal activities in Egypt—property crimes-sexual offenses-crimes against the person—is also consistent with the regional trend of delinquency among Middle Eastern countries. The International Arab Social Defense Report (1982) indicates that theft is the most common act of delinquency in Jordan, Syria, Iraq, Morocco, Bahrain, Ras El-Khaima (The United Arab Emirates), and Egypt while murder and violent crimes against the person are the lowest (p. 12). Of special interest, however, is the perception of the extent of delinquency by the Egyptian officials and lay citizens with whom this researcher talked. Comments ranged from a "reprehensible surge in deviance," to a "juvenile crime wave," to a "total reversal of morality," to the "destruction of Islam." Again, the Western researcher may marvel at the "social lens" Egyptians use to gauge how they expect their children to behave.

Discussion of Causation

In attempting to understand the causes of crime, researchers usually discover a variety of contributing indicators, with a few usually proving to be more influential than others. In attempting to examine the phenomenon of "minimal delinquency" in Egypt (especially since we are essentially left with a preponderance in the category of property offenses) a number of theories from the literature can be cited. Prominent among these I propose: (a) social control theory, which may offer the best explanation for the relatively low level of delinquency in Egypt and answer the question of "why is it so low?"; and (b) strain and relative deprivation theory, which may explain the distribution of delinquency by category (as indicated by table 2) and may shed some light on the suspected hidden delinquency acts. Such acts are believed to be inspired by the religious fundamentalist movement, especially during the period of *infitah*, or economic opening. Each of these possible causal relationships will be discussed in greater detail in the following section.

Social Control Theory

The increased popularity of social control theory (Hirschi, 1969; Vold and Bernard, 1984; Traub and Little, 1985; Liska, 1987; Jeffery, 1990) can be attributed to two important factors. First, its popularity was fueled by the emphasis Hirschi placed on the role of family in the lives of youth at a time when American society and the family structure during the 1960s and early 1970s were threatened by turbulent social and political events (see Cullen and Gilbert, 1982). Therefore, the timing of social control theory was most appropriate. It helped rectify a striking anomaly in the study of criminology—the tendency to downgrade the importance of intrafamily relationships. Second, Hirschi suspected that the basic assumptions of strain and cultural deviance models' ability to explain juvenile delinquency were flawed. He, therefore, laid out several basic assumptions for his control theory, critiqued strain and cultural deviance theories, and tested both theories against social control theory (Burton, 1991).

The core of social control theory can be summed up in the thesis that delinquent acts result when one's bond with society is weak or broken (Hirschi, 1969). The theory's first assumption is that when one's bond to conventional social institutions is eroded or severed, one is more susceptible to get involved in delinquency. Therefore, "individuals who are tightly bonded to social groups such as the family, the school, and peers would be less likely to commit delinquent acts" (Vold and Bernard, 1984). The theory's second assumption is that the seduction of crime rests equally within everyone. Therefore, the primary question is not "why do they do it, but rather why don't they do it" (Hirschi, 1969:34). The elements of Hirschi's social control theory should be well known material to every criminological researcher by now: attachment, commitment, involvement, and belief. It would serve little value to elaborate on them especially since the main purpose here is to focus on the extent of their applicability to delinquency in Egypt.

According to Hirschi (1969), attachment plays the most crucial role in insulating youths from delinquency since the "essence of internalization of norms, conscience, or superego" lies in one's attachment to others (p. 19). Attachment becomes a powerful restraining mechanism that inhibits children from committing criminal acts. Lacking attachment, the youth becomes free from moral restraints. A high level of attachment to family (among other social institutions with varying degrees) would reduce delinquency. Hirschi, however, puts stronger emphasis on attachment to parents since he believed it is a "central value" (p. 86). If the bond to parents is weakened, the probability of delinquency increases, and if strengthened, the probability of delinquency decreases (p. 88).

Attachment to family, rather than the other elements of commitment, involvement, or belief appears to this researcher as the overriding factor behind the minimal deviance in the Egyptian society. Egyptian parents and children seem to spend more time at home (together) than their counterparts in Western cultures. This is not necessarily because parents and children want to or have to, but is more so because neither group can afford to do otherwise. There are four plausible explanations for this supposition: (a) From a religious standpoint, Moslem fathers and guardians are committed to coming home early and staying up late at night in order to make their regular prayers on time, especially the *maghreb* and *isha* (the evening and night prayers). This increases the opportunity for children to watch their parents perform prayers, to absorb the meaning of religious values, and to internalize the conventional norms of a "good" Moslem family. (b) From a socioecological standpoint, most public and private enterprises operate from 8 to 2 o'clock (six days a week) and the majority of mothers, especially in rural areas, do not work (Official Reports do not cite figures related to the number of working mothers). This allows both parents to be at home every day between the late afternoon and the morning. This further extends the children's opportunity to internalize family "routine activities" by interacting with both parents rather than with one or none, as is common in Western families. (c) From an economic standpoint, opportunities for recreational endeavors (for both parents and children) are far less available and costlier than in Western cultures. Most Egyptian youngsters do not own cars or bicycles, do not play music or engage in artistic endeavors, do not have access to recreational facilities, cannot consume liquor, and cannot afford to go to the movies more than once every two weeks or so. As a result, the most common pastime for youths is participating in family-style picnics by the riverside, visiting neighbors, watching television (mostly religious and uncreative programs), and (only for boys) playing soccer in the neighborhood streets. (d) From a cultural-logistical standpoint, the vast majority of youths live at home for longer periods of time, thus still furthering one's bond with the moral validity of family rules.

Because of these reasons, the chances are that most Egyptian youths have less opportunities for developing "outside fields of meanings" and end up being more conservatively disciplined than in Western societies.

As a result, they tend to remain: (a) more respectful of parents and adults, therefore more amenable to obeying conventional rules; (b) more committed to pursuing a line of legitimate (religiously condoned) activities, such as getting an education, building up the parents' business, or acquiring a reputation for virtue, thus further limiting the opportunity of being involved in delinquent acts; and (c) less susceptible to outside delinquency-producing influences, therefore moving more readily from childhood to adulthood with minimum snags of delinquency. In sum, as Hirschi states, "they owe a life of virtue to the lack of opportunity to do otherwise" (1969:21). To illustrate this point, this quotation from Hirschi's work seems certainly in order:

> . . . not that I would not, if I could, be both handsome and fat and well dressed, and a great athlete, and make a million a year, be a wit, a bon vivant, and a lady killer, as well as a philosopher, a statesman, [a] warrior, an African explorer, as well as a tone-poet, and saint. . . . The thing is simply impossible.

While social control theory obviously fails to explain the causes behind Egypt's rate of 0.092 per 100,000 violent crimes, the 2.76 rate of sexual crimes, and 89.25 rate of property crimes, it should be accepted—in the absence of more compelling theories or new research findings—as a sensible explanation of the "minimal state" of delinquency in Egypt.

Strain Theory and the Idea of Relative Deprivation

To the unfamiliar observer, President Sadat may have been the greatest Arab statesman since Salah-al-Din made peace with Richard the Lion-Hearted after the battle of Akka in 1191 (Hitti, 1967:650). Yet, history may well show that Sadat was the one person most responsible for contributing to the delinquency of Egyptian youths through his policy of *infitah*, or the opening. After the war with Israel in 1973, Sadat opened another front of much greater risk at the domestic theater; one which broadsidedly struck the heart of conventional values and ideals. He suddenly and brashly started to replace a mechanical solidarity society with an organic one. He endorsed unregulated capitalism, opened "free-trade zones," invited foreign banks and foreign investments, and encouraged the influx of consumer goods from the West (especially from the United States). The infitah enterprises involved private jet aircraft, luxury automobiles, exotic food stocks, Parisian fashion clothes, and stock market manipulation. Being unfamiliar with the restraints of responsible capitalism, infitah businessmen and businesswomen turned into a mob of profiteers alienating a generation of unsuspecting youths and turning them anomic. This shift, in a sense, declared that traditional values were no longer important—indeed, obsolete. The state of anomie that followed provided a fertile ground for deviance and antisocial acts to flourish.

Hammouda (1987) describes the infitah era by saying that "during the second half of the 1970s, the number of millionaires in Egypt jumped astronomically from 30, to 8,000, to 17,000, then to 250,000 while, at the same time, the number of homeless people who lived in cemeteries outside Cairo and made less than a dollar a day, increased to more than a million" (p. 260). With the infitah came the opportunity to make huge wages and to experience the good life. But along also came the onslaught on conventional values and principles. The good life was socially interpreted in terms of the Travolta phenomenon with all the trimmings of blue jeans, studded leather jackets, video equipment, and perhaps a car. Terms like "girl friend," "date," "disco," "rock and roll," as well as the TV shows *Dallas* and *Dynasty* became household terms among children who did not speak English and "JR"—rather than Sadat—became the true hero of infitah. To share in the profits of infitah one must naturally "possess a good appearance, speak a foreign language, own private transportation, and secure a *wasta*, or an influential referral" (p. 260). To succeed, moreover, one must master how to close a fast deal, to lie, to deceive, to manipulate, and be an expert in *fahlawa*—the art of outwitting each and everyone without regard to principle. By failing to get on the bandwagon of infitah, the youths realized they were destined "to remain forever jobless or to accept menial jobs which would not pay for a pair of shoes" (p. 260). In describing the social strain of infitah, Mansour (1988:293) wrote that "all of a sudden a whole generation found itself divided between a minority of those who have everything and a majority which has nothing—except utter disgust for society and the state it represents." Ghanem in Al Afial (1981:147) elaborated on the state of despair the youths experienced during that period:

> . . . the good old-fashioned youth who was natively looking for a spirit to worship, for a force to obey, or a compassion to relish, found madness . . . everything fell in front of him. . . . The family lost its mercifulness, the school lost its guidance, and his father, brother, and teachers lost their self-respect. . . . The elders only talked about theft, embezzlement, and bribery; accusations they assigned to anyone and everyone who turned his back to them. . . . He turns into a rebel . . . he feels trapped . . . he embarks on the destruction of everything in his world—at least in his wide imagination.

The reaction to infitah by the Egyptian youths can make a textbook case in support of strain theory and the concept of relative deprivation (Cohen, 1955; Cloward and Ohlin, 1960; Runciman, 1966; Box, 1981; Blau and Blau, 1982) In *Delinquency and Opportunity* (1960), Cloward and Ohlin attempted to deal with the "problem of adjustment" encountered in the face of strain and the absence of legitimate opportunities to achieve middle-class success goals. Like in the case of Egyptian delinquents, Cloward and Ohlin (1960)—differing from Cohen's thoughts (1955)—viewed young delinquents as "rational actors" who commit "utilitarian" offenses. To achieve success goals, they rationally choose to pursue illegitimate means (Burton, 1991:22).

According to strain-opportunity theory, Cloward and Ohlin suggested that the "problem of adjustment" occurs when lower-class youth (especially those with poor socialization) aspire for success goals that are denied when legitimate institutional means are lacking. Lower-class youths must also contend with structural barriers that place them at a disadvantage. Faced with infitah, the lower-class youths realize they have to overcome the obstacles of having to own decent clothes, to speak a foreign language in "their father's house," and to have to find an upper-class individual who is willing to offer him a wasta—a good referral. What further complicated dissonance among Egyptian youths were: (a) the realization that even with an adequate level of education, they were still deemed unfit since in infitah subculture underprivileged kids lack the "right stuff" for success; (b) the humiliation of having to "beg" someone for a wasta in a society that claims democracy, equality, and religious egalitarianism; (c) the appalling deprivation associated with the differential in compensation paid by infitah companies and regular employment opportunities—the former is approximately $800 per month while the latter is the equivalent of $50; and (d) the perception of "vulgarity" associated with the operation of infitah enterprises, which includes deception, manipulation, immorality, and the denial of conventional Islamic values.

Faced with enormous strain and deprivation, frustrated Egyptian youths who were unable (or unwilling) to conform to infitah society, reacted in one or another of these adaptation modes:

(a) Retreatism by renouncing society altogether and seeking employment in rich Arab states. Migration rates increased by 400 percent in the later half of the 1970s and Egyptian workers constituted more than 60 percent of the labor force in some Arab countries (Hammouda, 1987:261). This method of adaptation in itself led to further deterioration in family values at home since most of the parents who migrated left their wives behind leading to what became known as the "feminization of the family"; a single-parent family. The migration option may have also contributed to an increase in divorce rates and a higher rate of prostitution by wives who felt abandoned by their husbands (p. 263).

(b) Rebellion by seeking to bring into being a new and greatly modified social structure (Merton, 1968:209). Young Egyptians frustrated by infitah subculture staged acts of rebellion by joining underground Islamic fundamentalist organizations. Given their religious and conservative socialization, that choice appeared to be the most appealing to God, especially since Islam commands believers to confront corruption and eradicate its sources. Notorious among these organizations are *Altakfeer wa Alhigra* (the excommunicating and rejection of society), the *Ikhwan Almuslimeen* (Moslem Brotherhood), and the *Gamaat Islamia* (Islamic associations) with a membership in the hundreds of thousands. Most members, especially of the latter groups, are male and female students in college, which in the Egyptian educational system could be attended at the age of 15. Moreover, Hammouda cites, "about 30 percent of the membership were juveniles. . . a larger number of farmers and laborers also joined the movement . . . and cases of suicide increased dramatically" (Hammouda, 1987:91). He cites, for example, the case of a Shoukri Mustafa who joined one such organization at the age of eleven, became the supreme commander of *Gamaat Al Muslimeen* (Organization of Islam) and was executed by the Sadat government shortly before the president himself was assassinated by members of Mustafa's organization (p. 174). While each of these organizations has a slightly different revolutionary platform, they all, nevertheless, are devoted to "Jihad crimes"—to use violence to purify society, to install an Islamic government, and to terrorize apostates.

(c) Innovation by resorting to a full fledged life of delinquency. This mode of adaptation usually works when the individual has assimilated the cultural emphasis on success goals while rejecting the institutional ways and means for their attainment. As Merton (1968) argues, "here in the face of blocked or denied institutional means the sacrosanct (success) goals virtually consecrate the means" (p. 196). Through this mode of adaptation, Egyptian youths applied a "moral deviation mechanism" by which infitah goals of prosperity could be attained through illegitimate means. Through that mechanism, the conventional values of honesty, decency, and fear of God were ignored in favor of deviant behavior and criminal activity. Also, as Merton explains, "the greatest pressures toward deviation are exerted upon the lower classes specifically when any recourse to legitimate channels for 'getting in the money' is limited by a class structure which is not fully open at each level to men of good capacity" (p. 199). As a consequence, a substantial surge has been reported (especially in the mid-1970s) in sexual assaults, kidnapping, and bank robberies by middle-class youths—the category previously referred to as "American-style crimes" (Hammouda, 1987:182).

In sum, it should be safe to argue that the second and third modes of adaptation can best explain the patterns of delinquency among Egyptian youths. The former may satisfactorily explain the low rate of murders (table 2), the latter may explain the substantially higher rate of property crimes and sexual crimes among the Egyptian juvenile subculture.

Conclusions

From the previous investigation it appears that Egypt does not have a problem with juvenile delinquency, at least as defined in the West. Powerful influences inherent in the socioreligious structure have impeded any full-blown development of such a problem. Delinquent behavior has nevertheless been benign in nature and minimal in frequency primarily due to a social structure molded along the lines of a mechanical solidarity society—under the "canopy of religious values and ideals." Furthermore, there are the cultural forces of attachment to children and a mystical belief in satre min Allah, or spiritual guidance.

Juvenile delinquency in the Arab Republic of Egypt remains basically a phenomenon involving urban lower-middle-class males with low educational attainment and poor prospects for economic and social mobility. As is the case in other Middle Eastern countries and third-world nations, the most common form of youthful lawbreaking appears to be in the category of property offenses, and, to a smaller measure, sexual offenses.

Since 1977, however, a strategic variable was interjected in the equation of delinquency; the infitah subculture emerged, sharply redefining the lines between success goals and legitimate means. The infitah juveniles had to either adapt to exogenous socioeconomic values or reject such values that clashed with their religious socialization and sense of identity. Those who chose the latter option either resorted to "Jihad crimes" or channeled their deprivation into innovative forms of delinquency, living a life of crime. The Jihad converts go underground and are involved in political murders and acts of terrorism that mostly go unpublicized by the political authorities. The others engaged in a litany of petty thievery, vandalism, sexual offenses, fraud, embezzlement, truancy, and acts of rebelliousness. They became Egypt's habitual delinquents or its "usual suspects," so to speak, to quote a famous line from a famous movie.

Bibliography

Akers, R. (1985). *Deviant Behavior: A Social Learning Approach*, 3d ed. Belmont, CA: Wadsworth Publishers.

Al-Sayed, Abdul Malik (1982). *Social Ethics of Islam*. New York: Vantage Press.

Baur, E. Jackson (1964). "The Trend of Juvenile Delinquency in the Netherlands and the United States." *Journal of Criminal Law, Criminology, and Police Sciences* 55: 359–69.

Berger, Peter, and Thomas Luckman (1967). "The General Prevention Effects of Punishment." *University of Pennsylvania Law Review* 114: 949.

Blau, J., and P. Blau (1982). "The Cost of Inequality: Metropolitan Structure and Violent Crime." *American Sociological Review* 47: 114–29.

Box, S. (1981). *Deviance, Reality and Society*. New York: Holt, Rinehart and Winston.

Braithwaite, John (1989). *Crime, Shame, and Reintegration*. New York: Cambridge University Press.

Burton, V. (1991). Explaining Adult Criminology: Testing Strain, Differential Association, and Control Theory. Unpublished Ph.D. Dissertation, the University of Cincinnati.

Cavan, Ruth, and Jordan Cavan (1968). *Juvenile Delinquency and Crime: Crosscultural Perspective*. Philadelphia, PA: Lippincott Publishers.

Cloward, R., and L. Ohlin (1960). *Delinquency and Opportunity: A Theory of Delinquent Gangs*. New York: Free Press.

Cohen, A. (1955). *Delinquent Boys: The Culture of the Gang*. New York: Free Press.

Cullen, F., and K. Gilbert (1982). *Rearmed Rehabilitation*. Cincinnati, OH: Anderson.

Durkheim, Emile (1964). *The Division of Labor in Society*. New York: Free Press/Berger.

Elliot, D., and H. Voss (1974). *Delinquency and Dropout*. Lexington, MA: D. C. Heath.

Finckenaur, James (1988). "Juvenile Delinquency in the USSR: Social Structural Explanations." *International Journal of Comparative and Applied Criminal Justice* 12 (1).

Ghanem, Fathy (1981). *Al Afial* (The elephants). Cairo: Rose El Yusef publishers.

Gibbons, D., and Marvin Krohn (1991). *Delinquent Behavior*, 5th ed. Englewood Cliffs, NJ: Prentice Hall.

Gottfredson, M., and T. Hirschi (1990). *A General Theory of Crime*. Stanford, CA: Stanford University Press.

Hammouda, Adel (1987). *Al Higra Ila Al Unff* (The migration to violence). Cairo: Sina Press.

Hirschi, T. (1969). *Causes of Delinquency*. Berkeley: University of California Press.

Hitti, Philip (1967). *History of the Arabs*. New York: St. Martin's Press.

International Arab Organization for Social Defense (1982). Report. Riyadh: Arab Center for Police Studies and Training.

Jeffery, C. (1990). *Criminology: An Interdisciplinary Approach*. Englewood Cliffs, NJ: Prentice Hall.

Kelly, Robert J., and Donal MacNamara (1991). *Perspectives on Deviance: Deviance, Degradation, and Deviance*. Cincinnati, OH: Anderson.

Liska, A. (1987). *Perspectives on Deviance*. Englewood Cliffs, NJ: Prentice Hall.

Maguire, K., and T. Flanagan (1990). *Sourcebook of Criminal Justice Statistics*. Washington, DC: U.S. Government Printing Office.

Mansour, Anis (1988). *Gamal Abdel Nasser*. Cairo: Al Maktab Al Masri Al Hadieth.

Merton, R. (1968). *Social Theory and Social Structure*. New York: Free Press.

"The National Coalition Against the Death Penalty Report." (1992). *The Dallas Morning News* (March 8).

Public Law 31 (1974). Cairo: Government Printing Office.

Public Security Report (1985–91) (published annually). Cairo: Ministry of Interior.

Runciman, W. (1966). *Relative Deprivation and Social Justice*. Berkeley: University of California Press.

Shoham, Shlomo, and Leon Shaskolsky (1969). "An Analysis of Delinquents and Nondelinquents in Israel: A Cross-Cultural Perspective." *Sociology and Social Research* 53: 333–43.

Siegel, Larry J., and Joseph Senna (1991). *Juvenile Delinquency*. St. Paul, MN: West Publishing.

Souryal, Sam (1988). "The Role of Shari'ah Law in Deterring Criminality in Saudi Arabia." *International Journal of Comparative and Applied Criminal Justice* 12 (1): 1–25.

Statistical Year Book (1991). Cairo: Central Agency for Public Mobilization and Statistics.

——— (1986). Cairo: Central Agency for Public Mobilization and Statistics.

Toby, Jackson (1969). "Affluence and Adolescent Crime." The President's Commission on Law Enforcement and Administration of Justice. *Task Force Report: Juvenile Delinquency and Youth Crimes*. Washington, DC: U.S. Government Printing Office.

Traub, S., and C. Little (eds.) (1985). *Theories of Deviance*, 3d ed. Itasca, IL: Peacock Publishers.

U.S. Department of Justice, Federal Bureau of Investigation (1981–1990). *Crime in the United States*. Washington, DC: U.S. Government Printing Office.

Vold, G., and T. Bernard (1984). *Theoretical Criminology*, 3d ed. New York: Oxford University Press.

Wegner, Judith Romney (1982). "Islamic and Talmudic Jurisprudence: The Four Roots of Islamic Law and Their Talmudic Counterparts." *The American Journal of Legal History* XXVI: 25–71.

Whitaker's Almanac (1982). London: Heffers Books.

29

Kyogoin Home in Japan
Light and Shade of Tradition

Akira Hattori

Family is one of the most important social units in any country. However, it seems that culture shapes the concept and the significance of the family and the measures to take in case it does not work. What characterizes the family in Japan? How should the children be treated in a dysfunctional family? What is happening to the traditional system that was designed for caring for the children? This article examines these types of questions and examines some aspects of the social structure and changes in the system in relation to the Kyogoin Home.

Kyogoin Home means, if translated literally, "the facility to educate and protect the children" who are adjudicated as delinquent or predelinquent. This article, however, characterizes it as "a family-substituted treatment facility" in consideration of the roles and the functions that are occurring in the system. Traditionally, the most distinctive feature of the Kyogoin Home from other facilities is that members of the married-couple staff live with the client children in a cottage for months in place of their biological parents. The problems of the client children that take the form of delinquent behavior are usually attributed to the disruption, dysfunction, or poor conditions of their family. The Kyogoin Home gives these children a family that is indispensable for their development, as well as helping them become independent through the married-couple staff that live with them. The staff look after them with both fatherly and motherly interests. This has often been referred to as the "Parent-Cottage System." Except in two of the private Kyogoin Homes, the staff consist of predominantly public employees. The philosophy behind the treatment is "living together," and this idea has been the basis of the Kyogoin Homes for many years, at least traditionally.

In the summer of 1993, I entered into a participant observation in one of the Kyogoin Homes (Syutoku Gakuin) in Osaka to see how things were

Prepared especially for *Comparative Criminal Justice, 1/E.*

progressing. By examining the methods in which the children were treated, what efforts the children were making, and what difficulties they have experienced, the function of the Kyogoin Homes will be better understood. At the same time, references should be made to several related topics, such as the correlation between juvenile delinquency and the family structure, the meaning of child independence, and the reason why community-based care such as foster homes or group homes are lacking instead of the placement into Kyogoin Homes.

Overview of the Kyogoin Home Concept

History

The first Kankain Home, predecessor of the Kyogoin Home, started in Osaka in 1884. By the end of the nineteenth century, ten Kankain Homes were established, all of which were privately operated. Kateigakko (Home School), one of the Kankain Homes, was founded in 1899. Kateigakko started with the "Parent-Cottage System" and upholds the same principles as those in the present system. Kosuke Tomeoka, the founder, visited and learned from the Elmira Reformatory and other juvenile institutions in the United States. Tomeoka had the greatest influence on the further development of the concept in Japan.

With the enactment of the Kankain Home Law in 1890 and its revision in accordance with the Article of the Distracted Person (under 14 years of age) that was created by the new Criminal Code in 1908, the movement began spreading on a nationwide scale. In this period, 25 prefectures started Kankain Homes in their jurisdiction. In 1910, the first national Kankain Home was established, and by 1922 the first juvenile law was enacted. Following this, rules were established requiring that Kyogoin Homes serve those below the age of 14, and juvenile schools to serve those 14 years of age and above. In 1933, the Children Kyogo Law was adopted, renaming the Kankain Home as the Children Kyogoin Home, and by 1947 the Children Welfare Law was altered to its current name of Kyogoin Home.

A new juvenile law, enacted in 1949, prescribed that the family courts may order protective dispositions, including placement to a Kyogoin Home and in 1956, the reformed municipal corporation law required large cities with populations exceeding 500,000 to establish them within their jurisdiction. Today there are 57 Kyogoin Homes in Japan: national (2), private (2), municipal (4), and prefectural (49). They are primarily minimum security except for incidents of special confinement for those in the national Kyogoin Homes, for preventing runaways in cases where the family court decides a higher level of confinement is necessary. Most are located in the suburbs surrounded by a quiet environment. The Syutoku

Gakuin Home, containing 13 parent cottages (where many studies such as this were conducted), is located on a 35-acre piece of land.

Classification of the Kyogoin Homes

Kyogoin Homes can be categorized by the different types of cottages and staff in charge of the cottages. The cottages are classified according to their size (small, medium, or large), and the staff by whether they are married couples or a shift staff. The married-staff system usually is associated with the smaller cottages, while the shift system, although not always the case, is usually associated with the larger types of cottages. In Kyogoin Homes adopting the parent-cottage system, the married staff can be expected to take care of approximately ten client children in addition to their own children in the same cottage. In the shift system, many of the staff members commute from their own homes to the cottages where they care for the client children. Those with the parent-cottage system attempt to provide a "homey" atmosphere. The cottage in which I stayed, Syutoku Gakuin, is about 2,500 square feet in area and has the parent-cottage system. There is a kitchen and living room in the center area and three bedrooms for the client children; the living space for the parent staff is located in each wing.

Process of Independence

The usual definition of independent is "free from the influence, guidance or control of another or others," but this can differ from culture to culture. In Japan, the concept of an "individual" is not so clear compared with that in the United States or European countries. For Japan, a group like the family, school or a company to which one belongs is a more basic unit. We Japanese are apt to introduce ourselves by the group to which we belong, not by telling what we do. Family especially plays an important role for the development of children. Some Japanese psychoanalysts point out that independence is achieved through one's experiences of being accepted by the parents, and the mother-child relationship is regarded as very important. In other words, it is believed that each child becomes independent, not only as an "individual" who is distinguishable from others but also through the sense of being with someone close to him or her. In this sense, family is the most important element, and, for children, maternity and paternity is indispensable to their development. When the family is working, a child achieves life tasks at every stage; but when it is not, there is a fear that these tasks are not being accomplished, and a "crisis of independence" may take the form of some delinquent behavior. Commonly, we find that delinquent behavior is a symptom of a crisis of independence caused by a disrupted or dysfunctional family.

In Japan, statistics show that the number of juveniles arrested per year has decreased since 1983, but the family environment around juveniles is getting worse (e.g., the number of divorces is more than 150,000 a year); it is reported that about 20 percent of elementary school students in Tokyo have single parents, and the number of child abuse cases reported to the Child Guidance Center is increasing. These numbers suggest that we are moving toward an age of difficulties for children in Japan. Kyogoin Home is one of the places for relief, where the married staff look after the children who lack the necessary experiences in the family. It is obvious that community care is more desirable than placement in a facility, and we should assist with keeping them at home to the best of our ability. Even if we should separate the child from his or her home, foster care or a group home (which the United States and European countries have developed) is better than placement in a facility. But I am afraid that we should not expect the development of foster care in Japan. In 1993, the number of foster parents in Japan was only 2,207, and the number of children committed to foster care was only 2,737. In addition, there are few applicants who want to be a foster parent of the juveniles at the age of adolescence who have previous records. The main reason why we do not expect the development of foster care relates to the fact that we respect the blood relationship of the family. The bond among the members of a family is very strong in Japan, and it has great control on the members. On the other hand, it excludes others who are not members of the family and, therefore, does not function to help others. Thus, the group is dominant in Japan, and it is difficult to help each other among individuals. Once a child is abandoned by his or her parents, there are few social resources to help the child in the community. Eventually, such children reach the Kyogoin Home; there is no in-between. Here lies the significance of the Kyogoin Home in the system and the reason I characterize it as "family-substituted," although it may be second best in comparison to foster care.

Treatment in Kyogoin

In this section, I will provide further information on Syutoku Gakuin Home where I conducted my participant observation research. Founded in 1907 by the Osaka prefecture and moved to the present place in 1923, Syutoku Gakuin Home is one of the Kyogoin Homes with the parent-cottage system (thirteen parent cottages are on site). Twelve couple-staff are in charge of a cottage and thirteen staff members support them. Staff include:

- one principal
- three chief directors
- twenty-four couple-staff in charge of cottages
- thirteen support staff for the couple-staff in the cottages
- two staff exclusively in charge of the school curriculum
- one psychologist
- three full-time office clerks
- two part-time school doctors
- two part-time workers

The capacity of the Syutoku Gakuin Home is 155 children; as of March 1993, 140 were in residence. About 40 percent of them are female and about 90 percent are between the ages of 13 and 15 years. The people who have custody of them are as follows:

- father and mother (33 percent)
- father (18 percent)
- mother (27 percent)
- father and mother-in-law (5 percent)
- mother and father-in-law (10 percent)
- other or none (6 percent)

This means that 67 percent of their parents are divorced or unknown. In Japan, the number of divorced couples who have children is 122,196, and the annual divorce rate per 1,000 people was only 1.28 in 1992; the divorce rate of the parents of the children in Kyogoin Homes is extremely high.

There are two main processes for a child to be referred to a Kyogoin Home: one route is by the Child Guidance Center, where the child is placed (only with the parent's consent) according to Child Welfare Law; another is through family court, where a judge orders the placement to the Kyogoin Home as one of the protective measures in juvenile law including supervision or placement to juvenile training school. About 80 percent of the cases are from Child Guidance Center. The main reasons they were referred to Syutoku Gakuin are theft (42 percent), drug abuse (20 percent), runaway/loitering (16 percent), disorderly conduct (10 percent), sexual behavior (6 percent), robbery (4 percent), and truancy (1 percent). In fact, however, most of them have a variety of other problems besides theft, such as drug abuse, truancy, and being a runaway.

The child referred to Syutoku Gakuin should spend the first three to four weeks in the cottage for reception and classification. During this time, a psychologist and other staff members observe and give guidance to the child, and decide in which cottage he or she should be placed according to his or her problem and personality; e.g., the child who has emotional problems goes to the third cottage. Males and females are separated into different cottages, and each cottage has about ten client children.

It is said that the treatment in the Kyogoin Home aims to give children three types of skills: living skills, learning skills, and vocational skills. A typical weekday in Syutoku Gakuin is as follows: in the morning, the children go to the classroom in the main building. Most of them are dropouts at a stage of elementary or junior high school, so the focuses are on the very basic learning skills and attitude toward learning. At noon, they come back to their cottage for lunch. In the afternoon, they do some supervised work in the field inside the facility. Sometimes they go outside for community services, including weeding in the garden of a senior citizen's home. In the evening and at night, they stay in their cottages. Their cottage is the base for their daily lives, and its homey atmosphere sets them at ease. The female staff members play a very important role at the cottage; they stay with the children, prepare meals and care for their physical and mental conditions. Male staff members double as teaching staff. Both male and female staff members have a different role and cooperate in taking care of the client children. On Sunday they have some free time.

The average stay in Syutoku Gakuin is about one year, with 37 percent staying under one year, 29 percent from one to 1.5 years, 16 percent from 1.5 to two years, and 18 percent staying more than two years. The reason the stay extends over this long period is that many of the children cannot come back to their home because their parents have rejected them or there are little resources to care for them in the community. If a child comes to a Kyogoin Home at the age of 13, it is likely that he or she will stay there until the age of 15 (when primary schooling ends).

After leaving the Syutoku Gakuin Home, 4 percent of the children went back to junior high and 36 percent entered high school. This percentage is very small in comparison with the fact that 96 percent of junior high school students go on to high school in Japan. Thirty-nine percent were living independently after they left Syutoku Gakuin because of economic conditions or abandonment by their parents. The employment they received was as craftspersons, factory workers, and so forth. There are few surveys on the recidivism rate among those who leave the Kyogoin Home, but Musashino Gakuin Home, one of two national Kyogoin Homes, is doing research on this issue. The samples of this study are 113 children who successfully completed the course of Musashino Gakuin Home (they left at least two years before April of 1993). Follow-up was possible for about 86 of those 113 children by means of records at the Child Guidance Center and the supplementary information from the staff in Musashino Gakuin Home. According to the survey, the percentage of those who were placed in a juvenile training school for committing a crime was:

- 7 percent within three months
- 12 percent within six months
- 18 percent within one year
- 18 percent within 1.5 years

The percentage of those who were found in trouble was:

- 34 percent after three months
- 42 percent after six months
- 35 percent within one year
- 22 percent after 1.5 years

I must add, though, that they are dealing with the most serious cases in the Musashino Gakuin Home because the children who could not adapt themselves in other Kyogoin Homes are referred to this home. Therefore, the recidivism rate among the children who left common Kyogoin Homes should be estimated lower.

Kyogoin Home in Change

As I mentioned earlier, the most significant character of the Kyogoin Home is that the married-couple staff take care of the children in a cottage. The basic idea of treatment is to "live together," and I think that the parent-cottage system is essential to the Kyogoin Home. In recent years, however, Kyogoin Homes are experiencing great change.

Out of 57 existing Kyogoin Homes, 36 homes started with the parent-cottage system; but by 1983, 15 of them changed to the shift system or a combined system of these two, and thereafter (by 1993), 6 homes gave up the parent-cottage system in part or completely. There are a few Kyogoin Homes that may switch to the shift system in the future. In contrast, six Kyogoin Homes moved to the parent-cottage system that had been founded in a different form. Now, 23 (43 percent) of the Kyogoin Homes are administered by the parent-cottage system.

Why did some of these homes switch over to the shift system? What made it difficult to keep the parent-cottage system? The main reason is the restriction of working hours by Labor Law. Article 32 of Japanese Labor Standards Law prescribes that an employer shall not employ the worker for more than 8 hours a day excluding recess, or 48 hours a week. The working conditions in Kyogoin Homes with the parent-cottage system went against the standards because the staff spent too much time with the children at the cottage. The first request to reduce the working hours was not made by the staff in the Kyogoin Homes, but was part of the claims by the union of local government employees. On the contrary, the staff insisted that they did not "work" all day long but "lived" with the children. Actually, they did not want the formal application of Labor Standards Law to their field because it restricted their lives. However, with the five-day system prevailing, especially in the public services, the problem of working hours in the Kyogoin Homes became inevitable. This is the major reason that it was difficult to maintain the parent-cottage system.

Another reason was difficulty in finding successors to the married-couple staff. Male staff in charge of a cottage should have one of the following qualifications:

- completion of the training course of the institute in national Kyogoin Homes
- B.D. of psychology or education and at least one year of practical experience at a Kyogoin Home
- completion of a high school educational course or approval of the equivalency by the minister of education, and at least three years of practical experience at a Kyogoin Home

- license to teach at an elementary, junior high, or high school and at least one year of practical experience at a Kyogoin Home
- specialization in the field and the approval of the minister of health and welfare or the governor
- married or engaged status

Eligibility for female staff requires:

- certification as a nursery school teacher
- at least three years of practical experience at Kyogoin Home and the approval of the minister of health and welfare or the governor
- married or engaged status

The aforementioned conditions make it difficult to keep the parent-cottage system. Several Kyogoin Homes moved to the shift system when they rebuilt the old cottages. It is important to improve the working conditions of the staff, but we should remember the specialty of their job and guarantee that it is rewarding. I am afraid that the formal application of the labor standards deprives them of these values. It may not be easy to find the couple-staff, but we do not need tens of couple-staff a year for a Kyogoin Home. It is enough to find a pair of couple-staff with aptitude for several years. I think it is important to give the opportunity for potential staff to receive the information about Kyogoin Homes and decide if it is the right place for them. Until now, Kyogoin Homes were not known even to the university students who majored in social welfare, nor are there any internship programs for them to obtain practical experience in Kyogoin Homes. With these chances expanded, the number of potential staff will increase.

I am not opposed to the shift system within the Kyogoin Homes. It has assets that make possible a many-sided approach by the staff, and it avoids burdensome work for them. However, it must be pointed out that the shift system in Kyogoin has liabilities, such as lack of continuity in treatment, difficulty in adjusting differences of opinion among staff, and unfavorable reactions by clients to a changing staff. The most important thing in deciding on a system is thinking over questions such as: with what children Kyogoin Homes work, what lies behind these children's delinquent behavior, and what treatment is effective to them. Surprisingly enough, some staff confessed that they did not consider which system was better when they moved to the shift system. The only thing that they took into account was adjusting their working conditions to the standards. In addition, it happened that a person without any practical experience in Kyogoin Homes got posted as the member of the management through personnel changes, and this person was apt to pay more attention to prefectural government than to staff requests or the clients' needs. Thus, they switched over to the shift system without full consideration of the role of the Kyogoin Home or the clients' needs.

As I pointed out, the children referred to the Kyogoin Home are in a crisis of independence because of disruption, dysfunction, or poor conditions of their family. They are lacking in such fundamental experiences as trusting or being trusted by someone, accepting or being accepted by someone—experiences required for their development. The parent-cottage system has the consistent commitment and the homelike atmosphere under which children can adjust and flourish. I believe that the system is the right way to help them solve their problems. Unfortunately, there is little empirical evidence as to which system effectively prevents recidivism because there is insufficient follow-up data after the children leave Kyogoin Homes; however, some reports describe the instability in the Kyogoin Homes employing the shift system, which surfaced in the children's daily lives or in such behavior as running away from the facility. In such cases we should be reminded of the reason for being at the Kyogoin Home and analyze the effectiveness between the different systems.

Conclusion

I characterized the Kyogoin Home as "a family-substituted treatment facility" in this article because it offers a way of living for children from disrupted families. We regard the delinquent behavior of the children referred to the Kyogoin Home as the sign of a crisis of independence. Children need the experience of being accepted to nurture their positive development. The children referred to the Kyogoin Home are those who have not had such experiences in their own family. The Kyogoin Home is the place where staff couples are sharing children's lives and giving them the experiences that are required for their successful development. In this process, the Homes aim to help the children recover their self-esteem and independence.

In societies where the concept of the "individual" is subordinate to that of the group, one is still respected as an individual and may be assisted by other individuals within the group. In Japan, however, the concept of the "individual" is not as clear when compared to that of the United States or European countries. Intermediate groups such as the family, school, or company to which one belongs are very important. On one hand, these groups play a great role in social control, but on the other hand, once one is out of the group, one may find few resources for assistance in the community. In other words, the group works inwardly to control its own members, but does not work outwardly to help members from another group. In Japan, the blood relationship is respected and makes it difficult to develop foster care. Here is the significance in the system of the Kyogoin Home, which gives assistance to children who were abandoned by the family, school, and community.

Culture may shape the concept and process of independence, but it seems to me that independence is achieved with the sense of being accepted by and being with someone in childhood. In my opinion, independence means learning how to live with or work with others in a new existence based on the experiences of loving and being loved by a family. It does not mean merely standing alone. As I mentioned earlier, in Japan we have not nurtured children as individuals within the family group. We are not used to facing each other as "individuals," and I think that this is one of the reasons why the idea of counseling has not been rooted in Japan. Considering these cultural backgrounds, it is possible to describe the treatment in Kyogoin Homes as "modeling" a way of living by the staff. The staff and client are not facing each other as individuals, but sharing among the members of the same group. In such circumstances, the clients identify with the "model" that the staff is offering in everyday life.

Thus, Kyogoin Homes play a very important role in the system. However, several Kyogoin Homes have given up the parent-cottage system and moved to the shift system. Almost half the Kyogoin Homes are administered under the shift or combined system. The biggest reason for this is the restriction of staff working hours in Kyogoin Homes within the parent-cottage system. The conditions were thought to go against the Labor Standards Law. Even now a few Kyogoin Homes are in the process of moving to the shift system in the name of "modernization." However, the tendency is not based on the consideration of which system is better for the children, and I am afraid that such trends will detract from the positive features that Kyogoin Homes have traditionally developed. For now, Kyogoin Homes are at the crossroads.

The discussion in this article is based on a participation observation conducted by the author during the summer of 1993. Detailed information about the Kyogoin concept may be obtained from Akira Hattori, Associate Professor, Faculty of Law, Aichi Gakuin University, Iwasaki, Nisshin-cho, Aichi-gun, Aichi, Japan 470-01.

Appendices

Basic Principles for the Treatment of Prisoners
United Nations A/RES/45/111

General Assembly
Distr. GENERAL
14 December 1990
ORIGINAL: ENGLISH
A/RES/45/111
68th Plenary Meeting
14 December 1990

45/111. Basic Principles for the Treatment of Prisoners

The General Assembly,

Bearing in mind the long-standing concern of the United Nations for the humanization of criminal justice and the protection of human rights,

Bearing in mind also that sound policies of crime prevention and control are essential to viable planning for economic and social development,

Recognizing that the Standard Minimum Rules for the Treatment of Prisoners, adopted by the First United Nations Congress on the Prevention of Crime and the Treatment of Offenders, are of great value and influence in the development of penal policy and practice,

Considering the concern of previous United Nations congresses on the prevention of crime and the treatment of offenders, regarding the obstacles of various kinds that prevent the full implementation of the Standard Minimum Rules,

Believing that the full implementation of the Standard Minimum Rules would be facilitated by the articulation of the basic principles underlying them,

Recalling resolution 10 on the status of prisoners and resolution 17 on the human rights of prisoners, adopted by the Seventh United Nations Congress on the Prevention of Crime and the Treatment of Offenders,

Recalling also the statement submitted at the tenth session of the Committee on Crime Prevention and Control by Caritas Internationalis, the Commission of the Churches on International Affairs of the World Council of Churches, the International Association of Educators for World Peace, the International Council for Adult Education, the International Federation of Human Rights, the International Prisoners' Aid Association, the International Union of Students, the World Alliance of Young Men's Christian Associations and the World Council of Indigenous Peoples, which are non-governmental organizations in consultative status with the Economic and Social Council, category II,

Recalling further the relevant recommendations contained in the report of the Interregional Preparatory Meeting for the Eighth United Nations Congress on the Prevention of Crime and the Treatment of Offenders on topic II, "Criminal justice policies in relation to problems of imprisonment, other penal sanctions and alternative measures",

Aware that the Eighth Congress coincided with International Literacy Year, proclaimed by the General Assembly in its resolution 42/104 of 7 December 1987,

Desiring to reflect the perspective noted by the Seventh Congress, namely, that the function of the criminal justice system is to contribute to safeguarding the basic values and norms of society,

Recognizing the usefulness of drafting a declaration on the human rights of prisoners,

Affirms the Basic Principles for the Treatment of Prisoners, contained in the annex to the present resolution, and requests the Secretary-General to bring it to the attention of Member States.

Annex

Basic Principles for the Treatment of Prisoners

1. All prisoners shall be treated with the respect due to their inherent dignity and value as human beings.
2. There shall be no discrimination on the grounds of race, colour, sex, language, religion, political or other opinion, national or social origin, property, birth or other status.
3. It is, however, desirable to respect the religious beliefs and cultural precepts of the group to which prisoners belong, whenever local conditions so require.
4. The responsibility of prisons for the custody of prisoners and for the protection of society against crime shall be discharged in keeping with a State's other social objectives and its fundamental responsibilities for promoting the well-being and development of all members of society.
5. Except for those limitations that are demonstrably necessitated by the fact of incarceration, all prisoners shall retain the human rights and fundamental freedoms set out in the Universal Declaration of Human Rights, and, where the State concerned is a party, the International Covenant on Economic, Social and Cultural Rights, and the International Covenant on Civil and Political Rights and the Optional Protocol thereto, as well as such other rights as are set out in other United Nations covenants.
6. All prisoners shall have the right to take part in cultural activities and education aimed at the full development of the human personality.
7. Efforts addressed to the abolition of solitary confinement as a punishment, or to the restriction of its use, should be undertaken and encouraged.

8. Conditions shall be created enabling prisoners to undertake meaningful remunerated employment which will facilitate their reintegration into the country's labour market and permit them to contribute to their own financial support and to that of their families.

9. Prisoners shall have access to the health services available in the country without discrimination on the grounds of their legal situation.

10. With the participation and help of the community and social institution, and with due regard to the interests of victims, favourable conditions shall be created for the reintegration of the ex-prisoner into society under the best possible conditions.

11. The above Principles shall be applied impartially.

Economic and Social Council
United Nations Resolution 1997/36

36th Plenary Meeting
21 July 1997

1997/36. International Cooperation for the Improvement of Prison Conditions

The Economic and Social Council,

Gravely alarmed by the serious problem confronting many Member States as a result of prison overcrowding,

Convinced that conditions in overcrowded prisons may affect the human rights of prisoners,

Bearing in mind the Standard Minimum Rules for the Treatment of Prisoners,[1] adopted by the First United Nations Congress on the Prevention of Crime and the Treatment of Offenders and approved by the Economic and Social Council in its resolutions 663 C (XXIV) of 31 July 1957 and 2076 (LXII) of 13 May 1977,

Recalling General Assembly resolution 45/111 of 14 December 1990, adopted on the recommendation of the Eighth United Nations Congress on the Prevention of Crime and the Treatment of Offenders, in which the Assembly affirmed the Basic Principles for the Treatment of Prisoners, annexed to that resolution,

Recognizing that prison overcrowding requires the implementation of effective policies directed towards the rehabilitation of prisoners and their social reintegration, as well as the application of the Standard Minimum Rules for the Treatment of Offenders and the Basic Principles on the Treatment of Prisoners,

Mindful of the fact that the physical and social conditions associated with prison overcrowding may result in outbreaks of violence in prisons, a development that could pose a grave threat to law and order,

Recalling the United Nations Standard Minimum Rules for Non-custodial Measures (the Tokyo Rules),[2]

Recalling the resolutions on the conditions of prisoners adopted by United Nations congresses on the prevention of crime and the treatment of offenders, in particular resolution 16 on reduction of the prison population, alternatives to imprisonment and social integration of offenders and resolution 17 on the human rights of prisoners, adopted by the Seventh United Nations Congress on the Prevention of Crime and the Treatment of Offenders,[3]

Noting the resolution adopted at the seminar entitled "Criminal justice: the challenge of prison overcrowding", organized by the Latin American Institute for the Prevention of Crime and the Treatment of Offenders, with the support of the European Commission, and held at San José, Costa Rica, from 3 to 7 February 1997, in which it was recommended, inter alia, that the number of prisoners should not exceed the number that could be held in decent conditions,

Noting the Kampala Declaration on Prison Conditions in Africa, annexed to the present resolution,

Also noting the nomination of a special rapporteur on prisons in Africa by the African Commission on Human and Peoples' Rights, in accordance with recommendations contained in the Kampala Declaration,

Mindful that many Member States lack the necessary resources to resolve the problem of prison overcrowding,

1. Requests the Secretary-General to assist countries, at their request, and within existing resources or, where possible, funded by extrabudgetary resources if available, countries in the improvement of their prison conditions in the form of advisory services, needs assessment, capacity-building and training;

2. Invites other entities of the United Nations system, including the United Nations Development Programme and the United Nations Crime Prevention and Criminal Justice Programme network, as well as intergovernmental organizations, to assist the Secretary-General in implementing the request contained in paragraph 1 above;

3. Urges Member States, if they have not yet done so, to introduce appropriate alternatives to imprisonment in their criminal justice systems;[4]

4. Recommends that Member States, if they have not yet done so, adopt appropriate effective measures to reduce pre-trial detention;

5. Invites international and regional financial institutions such as the World Bank and the International Monetary Fund to incorporate in their technical assistance programmes measures to reduce prison overcrowding, including the construction of adequate infrastructure and the development of alternatives to imprisonment in their criminal justice systems;

6. Requests the Commission on Crime Prevention and Criminal Justice to discuss the issue of prison overcrowding in the context of technical cooperation at its eighth session, with a view to achieving greater international cooperation in that area;

7. Requests the Secretary-General to report to the Commission on Crime Prevention and Criminal Justice at its eighth session on the implementation of the present resolution.

Annex

Kampala Declaration on Prison Conditions in Africa

Prison Conditions

Considering that in many countries in Africa the level of overcrowding in prisons is inhuman, that there is a lack of hygiene, insufficient or poor food, difficult access to medical care, a lack of physical activities or education, as well as an inability to maintain family ties,

Bearing in mind that any person who is denied freedom has a right to human dignity,

Bearing in mind that the universal norms on human rights place an absolute prohibition on torture of any description,

Bearing in mind that some groups of prisoners, including juveniles, women, the old and the mentally and physically ill, are especially vulnerable and require particular attention,

Bearing in mind that juveniles must be separated from adult prisoners and that they must be treated in a manner appropriate to their age,

Remembering the importance of proper treatment for female detainees and the need to recognize their special needs,

The participants in the International Seminar on Prison Conditions in Africa, held at Kampala from 19 to 21 September 1996, recommend:

1. That the human rights of prisoners should be safeguarded at all times and that non-governmental agencies should have a special role in this respect,

2. That prisoners should retain all rights which are not expressly taken away by the fact of their detention,

3. That prisoners should have living conditions which are compatible with human dignity,

4. That conditions in which prisoners are held and the prison regulations should not aggravate the suffering already caused by the loss of liberty,

5. That the detrimental effects of imprisonment should be minimized so that prisoners do not lose their self-respect and sense of personal responsibility,

6. That prisoners should be given the opportunity to maintain and develop links with their families and the outside world,

7. That prisoners should be given access to education and skills training in order to make it easier for them to reintegrate into society after their release,

8. That special attention should be paid to vulnerable prisoners and that non-governmental organizations should be supported in their work with these prisoners,

9. That all the norms of the United Nations and the African Charter on Human and Peoples' Rights on the treatment of prisoners should be incorporated into national legislation in order to protect the human rights of prisoners,

10. That the Organization of African Unity and its member States should take steps to ensure that prisoners are detained in the minimum conditions of security necessary for public safety.

Remand Prisoners

Considering that in most prisons in Africa a great proportion of prisoners are awaiting trial, sometimes for several years,

Considering that for this reason the procedures and policies adopted by the police, the prosecuting authorities and the judiciary can significantly influence prison overcrowding,

The participants in the International Seminar on Prison Conditions in Africa, held at Kampala from 19 to 21 September 1996, recommend:

1. That the police, the prosecuting authorities and the judiciary should be aware of the problems caused by prison overcrowding and should join the prison administration in seeking solutions to reduce this,

2. That judicial investigations and proceedings should ensure that prisoners are kept in remand detention for the shortest possible period, avoiding, for example, continual remands in custody by the court,

3. That there should be a system for regular review of the time detainees spend on remand.

Prison Staff

Considering that any improvement in conditions for prisoners will be dependent on staff having pride in their work and a proper level of competence,

Bearing in mind that this will only happen if staff are properly trained,

The participants in the International Seminar on Prison Conditions in Africa, held at Kampala from 19 to 21 September 1996, recommend:

1. That there should be a proper career structure for prison staff,
2. That all prison personnel should be linked to one government ministry and that there should be a clear line of command between central prison administration and the staff in prisons,
3. That the State should provide sufficient material and financial resources for staff to carry out their work properly,
4. That in each country there should be an appropriate training programme for prison staff to which the United Nations African Institute for the Prevention of Crime and the Treatment of Offenders (UNAFRI) should be invited to contribute,
5. That there should be a national or subregional institution to deliver this training programme,
6. That the penitentiary administration should be directly involved in the recruitment of prison staff.

Alternative Sentencing

Noting that in an attempt to reduce prison overcrowding, some countries have been trying to find a solution through amnesties, pardons or by building new prisons,

Considering that overcrowding causes a variety of problems including difficulties for overworked staff,

Taking into account the limited effectiveness of imprisonment, especially for those serving short sentences, and the cost of imprisonment to the whole of society,

Considering the growing interest in African countries in measures which replace custodial sentences, especially in the light of human rights principles,

Considering that community service and other non-custodial measures are innovative alternatives to imprisonment and that there are promising developments in Africa in this regard,

Considering that compensation for damage done is an important element of non-custodial sentences,

Considering that legislation can be introduced to ensure that community service and other non-custodial measures will be imposed as an alternative to imprisonment,

The participants in the International Seminar on Prison Conditions in Africa, held at Kampala from 19 to 21 September 1996, recommend:

1. That petty offences should be dealt with according to customary practice, provided this meets human rights requirements and that those involved so agree,
2. That whenever possible petty offences should be dealt with by mediation and should be resolved between the parties involved without recourse to the criminal justice system,

3. That the principle of civil reparation or financial recompense should be applied, taking into account the financial capability of the offender or of his or her parents,

4. That the work done by the offender should if possible recompense the victim,

5. That the community service and other non-custodial measures should if possible be preferred to imprisonment,

6. That there should be a study of the feasibility of adapting successful African models of non-custodial measures and applying them in countries where they are not yet being used,

7. That the public should be educated about the objectives of these alternatives and how they work.

African Commission on Human and Peoples' Rights

Considering that the African Commission on Human and Peoples' Rights has the mandate to ensure the promotion and the protection of human and peoples' rights in Africa,

Considering that the Commission has shown on many occasions its special concern on the subject of poor prison conditions in Africa and that it has adopted special resolutions and decisions on this question previously,

The participants in the International Seminar on Prison Conditions in Africa, held at Kampala from 19 to 21 September 1996, recommend that the African Commission on Human and Peoples' Rights:

1. Should continue to attach priority to the improvement of prison conditions throughout Africa,

2. Should nominate a Special Rapporteur on Prisons in Africa as soon as possible,

3. Should make the Member States aware of the recommendations contained in this Declaration and publicize United Nations and African norms and standards on imprisonment,

4. Should cooperate with non-governmental organizations and other qualified institutions in order to ensure that the recommendations of this Declaration are implemented in all the Member States.

Notes

[1] First United Nations Congress on the Prevention of Crime and the Treatment of Offenders, Geneva, 22 August–3 September 1955: report prepared by the Secretariat (United Nations publication, Sales No. E.56.IV.4), annex I.A.

[2] General Assembly resolution 45/119, annex.

[3] Seventh United Nations Congress on the Prevention of Crime and the Treatment of Offenders, Milan, 26 August–6 September 1985: report prepared by the Secretariat (United Nations publication, Sales No. E.86.IV.1), chap. I, sect. E.

[4] See the United Nations Standard Minimum Rules for Non-custodial Measures (the Tokyo Rules) (General Assembly resolution 45/110, annex) and Human Rights Pre-trial Detention: A Handbook of International Standards relating to Pre-trial Detention (United Nations publication, Sales No. E.94.XIV.6).

Resolution Adopted by the General Assembly
[on the report of the Third Committee (A/57/556/Add.2 and Corr.1-3)]
United Nations A/RES/57/214

General Assembly
Distr.: General 25 February 2003
Fifty-seventh Session Agenda Item 109 (b)

57/214. Extrajudicial, Summary or Arbitrary Executions

The General Assembly,

Recalling the Universal Declaration of Human Rights,[1] which guarantees the right to life, liberty and security of person, and the relevant provisions of the International Covenant on Civil and Political Rights,[2]

Having regard to the legal framework of the mandate of the Special Rapporteur of the Commission on Human Rights on extrajudicial, summary or arbitrary executions, including the provisions contained in Commission on Human Rights resolution 1992/72 of 5 March 1992[3] and General Assembly resolution 47/136 of 18 December 1992,

Mindful of its resolutions on the subject of extrajudicial, summary or arbitrary executions, of which the most recent is resolution 55/111 of 4 December 2000, and resolutions of the Commission on Human Rights on the subject, and taking note of the most recent, resolution 2002/36 of 22 April 2002,[4]

Recalling Economic and Social Council resolution 1984/50 of 25 May 1984 and the safeguards guaranteeing protection of the rights of those facing the death penalty, annexed thereto, and Council resolution 1989/64 of 24 May 1989 on their implementation, as well as the Declaration of Basic Principles of Justice for Victims of Crime and Abuse of Power adopted by the General Assembly in its resolution 40/34 of 29 November 1985,

Recalling also Economic and Social Council resolution 1989/65 of 24 May 1989, in which the Council recommended the Principles on the Effective Prevention and Investigation of Extra-legal, Arbitrary and Summary Executions,

Dismayed that in a number of countries impunity, the negation of justice, continues to prevail and often remains the main cause of the continuing occurrence of extrajudicial, summary or arbitrary executions in those countries,

Acknowledging the entry into force on 1 July 2002 of the Rome Statute establishing the International Criminal Court,[5] thereby contributing to ensuring prosecution and the prevention of impunity concerning extrajudicial, summary or arbitrary executions,

Convinced of the need for effective action to combat and to eliminate the abhorrent practice of extrajudicial, summary or arbitrary executions, which represent a flagrant violation of the right to life,

1. *Strongly condemns once again* all the extrajudicial, summary or arbitrary executions that continue to take place throughout the world;

2. *Demands* that all Governments ensure that the practice of extrajudicial, summary or arbitrary executions is brought to an end and that they take effective action to combat and eliminate the phenomenon in all its forms;

3. *Acknowledges* the historic significance of the establishment of the International Criminal Court on 1 July 2002, and the fact that a significant number of States have already signed, ratified or acceded to the Rome Statute,[5] and calls upon all other States to consider becoming parties to the Statute;

4. *Notes with deep concern* that impunity continues to be a major cause of the perpetuation of violations of human rights, including extrajudicial, summary or arbitrary executions;

5. *Reiterates* the obligation of all Governments to conduct exhaustive and impartial investigations into all suspected cases of extrajudicial, summary or arbitrary executions, to identify and bring to justice those responsible, while ensuring the right of every person to a fair and public hearing by a competent, independent and impartial tribunal established by law, to grant adequate compensation within a reasonable time to the victims or their families and to adopt all necessary measures, including legal and judicial measures, in order to bring an end to impunity and to prevent the further occurrence of such executions;

6. *Reaffirms* the obligation of Governments to ensure the protection of the right to life of all persons under their jurisdiction, and calls upon Governments concerned to investigate promptly and thoroughly all cases of killings committed in the name of passion or in the name of honour, all killings committed for any discriminatory reason, including sexual orientation, racially motivated violence leading to the death of the victim, killings of persons for reasons related to their peaceful activities as human rights defenders or as journalists, as well as other cases where a person's right to life has been violated, and to bring those responsible to justice before a competent, independent and impartial judiciary and ensure that such killings, including killings committed by security forces, paramilitary groups or private forces, are neither condoned nor sanctioned by government officials or personnel;

7. *Urges* Governments to undertake all necessary and possible measures to prevent loss of life, in particular that of children, during public demonstrations, internal and communal violence, civil unrest and public emergencies or armed conflicts, and to ensure that the police and security forces receive thorough training in human rights matters, in particular with regard to restrictions on the use of force and firearms in the discharge of their functions, and that they act with restraint and respect international human rights standards when carrying out their duties;

8. *Stresses* the importance of States taking effective measures to end impunity with regard to extrajudicial, summary or arbitrary executions, inter

alia, through the adoption of preventive measures, and calls upon Governments to ensure that such measures are included in post-conflict peace-building measures;

9. *Encourages* Governments, intergovernmental and non-governmental organizations to organize training programmes and to support projects with a view to training or educating military forces, law enforcement officers and government officials in human rights and humanitarian law issues connected with their work, and appeals to the international community and requests the Office of the United Nations High Commissioner for Human Rights to support endeavours to that end;

10. *Reaffirms* Economic and Social Council decision 2001/266 of 24 July 2001, in which the Council endorsed the decision of the Commission on Human Rights, in its resolution 2001/45 of 23 April 2001,[6] to extend the mandate of the Special Rapporteur of the Commission on Human Rights on extrajudicial, summary or arbitrary executions for three years;

11. *Takes note* of the interim report of the Special Rapporteur to the General Assembly[7] and the recommendations contained therein;

12. *Recalls* that the Commission, in its resolution 2001/45, requested the Special Rapporteur, in carrying out her mandate:

(a) To continue to examine situations of extrajudicial, summary or arbitrary executions and to submit her findings on an annual basis, together with conclusions and recommendations, to the Commission, as well as such reports as the Special Rapporteur deems necessary in order to keep the Commission informed about serious situations of extrajudicial, summary or arbitrary executions that warrant its immediate attention;

(b) To respond effectively to information that comes before her, in particular when an extrajudicial, summary or arbitrary execution is imminent or seriously threatened or when such an execution has occurred;

(c) To enhance further her dialogue with Governments, as well as to follow up on recommendations made in reports after visits to particular countries;

(d) To continue to pay special attention to extrajudicial, summary or arbitrary executions of children and to allegations concerning violations of the right to life in the context of violence against participants in demonstrations and other peaceful public manifestations or against persons belonging to minorities;

(e) To continue to pay special attention to extrajudicial, summary or arbitrary executions where the victims are individuals carrying out peaceful activities in defence of human rights and fundamental freedoms;

(f) To continue monitoring the implementation of existing international standards on safeguards and restrictions relating to the imposition of capital punishment, bearing in mind the comments made by the Human Rights Committee in its interpretation of article 6 of the International Covenant on Civil and Political Rights,[2] as well as the Second Optional Protocol thereto;[8]

(g) To apply a gender perspective in her work;

13. *Recognizes* the importance of raising awareness for the elimination of extrajudicial, summary or arbitrary executions, for which impunity should be neither condoned nor tolerated, and of stressing that extrajudicial, summary or arbitrary executions are a flagrant violation of human rights, in particular the right to life, of which no one should be arbitrarily deprived, and in this regard encourages the Special Rapporteur to continue, within her mandate, to collect information from all concerned, to respond effectively to reliable information that comes before her, to follow up on communications and country visits and to seek the views and comments of Governments and to reflect them, as appropriate, in her reports;

14. *Urges* the Special Rapporteur to continue, within her mandate, to bring to the attention of the United Nations High Commissioner for Human Rights situations of extrajudicial, summary or arbitrary executions which are of particularly serious concern or where early action might prevent further deterioration;

15. *Welcomes* the cooperation established between the Special Rapporteur and other United Nations mechanisms and procedures relating to human rights, as well as with medical and forensic experts, and encourages the Special Rapporteur to continue efforts in that regard;

16. *Strongly urges* all Governments, in particular those who have not yet done so, to respond without undue delay to the communications and requests for information transmitted to them by the Special Rapporteur, and urges them and all others concerned to cooperate with and assist the Special Rapporteur so that she may carry out her mandate effectively, including, where appropriate, by issuing invitations to the Special Rapporteur when she so requests;

17. *Expresses its appreciation* to those Governments that have invited the Special Rapporteur to visit their countries, asks them to examine carefully the recommendations made by the Special Rapporteur, invites them to report to the Special Rapporteur on the actions taken on those recommendations, and requests other Governments to cooperate in a similar way;

18. *Calls upon* the Governments of all States in which the death penalty has not been abolished to comply with their obligations under relevant provisions of international human rights instruments, keeping in mind the safeguards and guarantees referred to in Economic and Social Council resolutions 1984/50 and 1989/64;

19. *Again requests* the Secretary-General to continue to use his best endeavours in cases where the minimum standards of legal safeguards provided for in articles 6, 9, 14 and 15 of the International Covenant on Civil and Political Rights appear not to have been respected;

20. *Requests* the Secretary-General to provide the Special Rapporteur with adequate human, financial and material resources to enable her to carry out her mandate effectively, including through country visits;

21. *Also requests* the Secretary-General to continue, in close collaboration with the High Commissioner, in conformity with the mandate of the High Commissioner established by the General Assembly in its resolution 48/141 of 20 December 1993, to ensure that personnel specialized in human

rights and humanitarian law issues form part of United Nations missions, where appropriate, in order to deal with serious violations of human rights, such as extrajudicial, summary or arbitrary executions;

22. *Requests* the Special Rapporteur to submit an interim report to the General Assembly at its fifty-ninth session on the situation worldwide in regard to extrajudicial, summary or arbitrary executions and her recommendations for more effective action to combat that phenomenon.

77th plenary meeting
18 December 2002

Notes

[1] Resolution 217 A (III).

[2] See resolution 2200 A (XXI), annex.

[3] See *Official Records of the Economic and Social Council, 1992, Supplement No. 2* (E/1992/22), chap. II, sect. A.

[4] Ibid., 2002, *Supplement No. 3* (E/2002/23), chap. II, sect. A.

[5] *Official Records of the United Nations Diplomatic Conference of Plenipotentiaries on the Establishment of an International Criminal Court, Rome, 15 June–17 July 1998, vol. I: Final documents* (United Nations publication, Sales No. E.02.I.5), sect. A.

[6] See *Official Records of the Economic and Social Council, 2001, Supplement No. 3* (E/2001/23), chap. II, sect. A.

[7] A/57/138.

[8] Resolution 44/128, annex.

Resolution Adopted by the General Assembly
[on the report of the Third Committee (A/58/508/Add.2)]
United Nations A/RES/58/183

General Assembly
Distr.: General
18 March 2004
Fifty-eighth Session
Agenda Item 117 (*b*)

58/183. Human Rights in the Administration of Justice

The General Assembly,

Bearing in mind the principles embodied in articles 3, 5, 8, 9 and 10 of the Universal Declaration of Human Rights[1] and the relevant provisions of the International Covenant on Civil and Political Rights and the Optional Protocols thereto,[2] in particular article 6 of the Covenant, which states, inter alia, that no one shall be arbitrarily deprived of his life and prohibits the imposition of the death penalty for crimes committed by persons below 18 years of age, and article 10, which provides that all persons deprived of their liberty shall be treated with humanity and with respect for the inherent dignity of the human person,

Bearing in mind also the relevant provisions of the Convention against Torture and Other Cruel, Inhuman or Degrading Treatment or Punishment,[3] the International Convention on the Elimination of All Forms of Racial Discrimination,[4] in particular the right to equal treatment before tribunals and all other organs administering justice, the Convention on the Rights of the Child,[5] in particular article 37, according to which every child deprived of liberty shall be treated in a manner that takes into account the needs of persons of his or her age, and the Convention on the Elimination of All Forms of Discrimination against Women,[6] in particular the obligation to treat men and women equally in all stages of procedures in courts and tribunals,

Calling attention to the numerous international standards in the field of the administration of justice,

Convinced that the independence and impartiality of the judiciary are essential prerequisites for the protection of human rights and for ensuring that there is no discrimination in the administration of justice and should therefore be respected in all circumstances,

Emphasizing that the right to access to justice, as contained in applicable international human rights instruments, forms an important basis for strengthening the rule of law through the administration of justice,

Mindful of the importance of ensuring respect for the rule of law and human rights in the administration of justice, in particular in post-conflict situations, as a crucial contribution to building peace and justice and ending impunity,

Recalling the Guidelines for Action on Children in the Criminal Justice System[7] and the establishment and subsequent meetings of the coordination panel on technical advice and assistance in juvenile justice,

Calling attention to the relevant provisions of the Vienna Declaration on Crime and Justice: Meeting the Challenges of the Twenty-first Century,[8] and of the plans of action for its implementation and follow-up,[9]

Recalling its resolution 56/161 of 19 December 2001, as well as Commission on Human Rights resolution 2002/47 of 23 April 2002[10] and Economic and Social Council resolution 2003/30 of 22 July 2003, entitled "United Nations standards and norms in crime prevention and criminal justice,"

1. *Reaffirms* the importance of the full and effective implementation of all United Nations standards on human rights in the administration of justice;

2. *Reiterates its call* to all Member States to spare no effort in providing for effective legislative and other mechanisms and procedures, as well as adequate resources, to ensure the full implementation of those standards;

3. *Affirms* that States must ensure that any measure taken to combat terrorism, including in the administration of justice, complies with their obligations under international law, in particular international human rights, refugee and humanitarian law;

4. *Invites* Governments to provide training, including anti-racist, multicultural and gender-sensitive training, in human rights in the administration of justice, including juvenile justice, to all judges, lawyers, prosecutors, social workers, immigration and police officers and other professionals concerned, including personnel deployed in international field presences;

5. *Invites* States to make use of technical assistance offered by the relevant United Nations programmes in order to strengthen national capacities and infrastructures in the field of the administration of justice;

6. *Appeals* to Governments to include in their national development plans the administration of justice as an integral part of the development process and to allocate adequate resources for the provision of legal-aid services with a view to promoting and protecting human rights, and invites the international community to respond favourably to requests for financial and technical assistance for the enhancement and strengthening of the administration of justice;

7. *Encourages* the regional commissions, the specialized agencies, United Nations institutes active in the areas of human rights and crime prevention and criminal justice, and other relevant parts of the United Nations system, as well as intergovernmental and non-governmental organizations, including national professional associations concerned with promoting United Nations standards in this field, and other segments of civil society, including the media, to continue to develop their activities in promoting human rights in the administration of justice;

8. *Takes note with interest* of the debates held in the Security Council on the agenda item entitled "Justice and the Rule of Law: the United Nations role";

9. *Invites* the Commission on Human Rights and the Commission on Crime Prevention and Criminal Justice, as well as the Office of the United Nations High Commissioner for Human Rights and the Crime Programme of the United Nations Office on Drugs and Crime, to closely coordinate their activities relating to the administration of justice;

10. *Calls upon* mechanisms of the Commission on Human Rights and its subsidiary bodies, including special rapporteurs, special representatives and working groups, to continue to give special attention to questions relating to the effective promotion and protection of human rights in the administration of justice, including juvenile justice, and to provide, where appropriate, specific recommendations in this regard, including proposals for advisory services and technical assistance measures;

11. *Calls upon* the United Nations High Commissioner for Human Rights to reinforce, within his mandate, his activities relating to national capacity-building in the field of the administration of justice, in particular in post-conflict situations;

12. *Encourages* the Office of the High Commissioner to continue organizing training courses and other relevant activities aimed at enhancing the promotion and protection of human rights in the field of the administration of justice, and welcomes the publication of the Manual on Human Rights for Judges, Prosecutors and Lawyers within the framework of the United Nations Decade for Human Rights Education, 1995–2004;

13. *Welcomes* the increased attention paid to the issue of juvenile justice by the High Commissioner and the United Nations Children's Fund, in particular through technical assistance activities, and, taking into account the fact that international cooperation to promote juvenile justice reform has become a priority within the United Nations system, encourages the further activities of the High Commissioner and the United Nations Children's Fund, within their mandates, in this regard;

14. *Calls upon* the coordination panel on technical advice and assistance in juvenile justice to further increase cooperation among the partners involved, to share information and to pool their capacities and interests in order to increase the effectiveness of programme implementation;

15. *Invites* Governments, relevant international and regional bodies, national human rights institutions and non-governmental organizations to devote increased attention to the issue of women in prison, including the children of women in prison, with a view to identifying the key problems and ways in which they can be addressed, and notes the proposal of the Subcommission on the Promotion and Protection of Human Rights to prepare a working paper on this question;[11]

16. *Underlines* the importance of rebuilding and strengthening structures for the administration of justice and respect for the rule of law and human rights in post-conflict situations, and requests the Secretary-General to ensure system-wide coordination and coherence of programmes and activities of the relevant parts of the United Nations system in the field of

the administration of justice in post-conflict situations, including assistance provided through United Nations field presences;

17. *Stresses* the special need for national capacity-building in the field of the administration of justice, in particular through reform of the judiciary, the police and the penal system, as well as juvenile justice reform, in order to establish and maintain stable societies and the rule of law in post-conflict situations, and in this context welcomes the role of the Office of the High Commissioner in supporting the establishment and functioning of transitional justice mechanisms in post-conflict situations;

18. *Decides* to consider the question of human rights in the administration of justice at its sixtieth session under the item entitled "Human rights questions".

77th plenary meeting
22 December 2003

Notes

[1] Resolution 217 A (III).
[2] See resolution 2200 A (XXI), annex, and resolution 44/128, annex.
[3] Resolution 39/46, annex.
[4] Resolution 2106 A (XX), annex.
[5] Resolution 44/25, annex.
[6] Resolution 34/180, annex.
[7] Economic and Social Council resolution 1997/30, annex.
[8] Resolution 55/59, annex.
[9] Resolution 56/261, annex.
[10] See *Official Records of the Economic and Social Council, 2002, Supplement No. 3* (E/2002/23), chap. II, sect. A.
[11] See E/CN.4/2004/2-E/CN.4/Sub.2/2003/43, chap. 11, sect. B, decision 2003/104.

Contributors

Jeffrey E. Arrigo is currently an officer with the Boulder, Colorado Police Department and a recent graduate of Eastern Kentucky University with a M.S. in criminal justice.

Abdullah I. Alobied is an instructor at King Faud College of Security Studies in Riyadh, Saudi Arabia. He received a Master's Degree from Sam Houston State University in 1990.

Timothy Austin is a professor of criminology at Indiana University of Pennsylvania. He has a Ph.D. in sociology from the University of Georgia (1972), and his primary research interests include informal control strategies in Asian cultures.

Jawad I. Barghothi is a professor emeritus of political science at Appalachian State University and holds a Ph.D. in government (1968) from Southern Illinois University.

Tom Barker is a professor of criminal justice and police studies at Eastern Kentucky University. He is the author of numerous articles and texts, and his current research focuses on outlaw motorcycle gangs.

Dorothy H. Bracey is a professor of anthropology at John Jay College of Criminal Justice, City University of New York and has been a visiting professor at Britain's Police Staff College at Bramshill, The American University, and the South Australia Institute of Technology, among others. She has written extensively on topics in comparative criminal justice, with particular emphasis on China.

Salih Hakan Can began his career in law enforcement in 1984 with the Turkish National Police (TNP) and earned a B.S. in criminal justice from the Police University in Ankara, Turkey and in political science from Ankara University. He holds a M.S. in criminal justice from University of North Texas and is currently a doctoral student at the College of Criminal Justice at Sam Houston State University.

Marina Caparini is a senior fellow at the Geneva Centre for the Democratic Control of Armed Forces (DCAF), where she coordinates DCAF's working groups on internal security (police, intelligence, border management) and civil society. She is a doctoral candidate in the Department of War Studies, King's College, University of London.

Dae H. Chang is a professor emeritus in the Department of Administration of Justice at Wichita State University. He received his Ph.D. from Michigan State in 1962 and is the founding editor of the *International Journal of Comparative and Applied Criminal Justice*.

David K. Chiabi is an associate professor of criminal justice at New Jersey City University, New Jersey. He holds an LL.M. from Columbia Law School and a Ph.D. in criminal justice from the City University of New York. His research interests and publications are in the areas of the Fourth Amendment, police civil liability, police public policy, crime in developing countries, and comparative judicial systems.

Edna Erez is a professor of justice studies at Kent State University. Her research areas include comparative justice, sociology of law, victims in the justice system, violence against women (including immigrant women), and victimization of immigrants.

Chris W. Eskridge is a professor of criminal justice at the University of Nebraska at Omaha. He served as a visiting professor at Canterbury Fellow at the University of Canterbury (NZ) and has served for a number of years as the executive director of the American Society of Criminology.

Gregory Ferrell is a visiting professor of criminal justice at Eastern Kentucky University and is currently ABD from Indiana University of Pennsylvania.

Charles B. Fields is a professor of criminal justice at Eastern Kentucky University. His research interests include drug policy, comparative and international justice systems, and the Terza Scuola. He is past president of the Southern Criminal Justice Association.

Marc Gertz is a professor of criminology and criminal justice at Florida State University, where he has been on the faculty since 1976. He has written extensively on European court systems, and his other research interests include courts and social policy as well as international justice systems.

Akira Hattori is a professor of juvenile law and criminology at Aichi Gakuin University (Japan) and has law degrees from Rikkyo University and Waseda University. Current research focuses on the comparative study of the administration of juvenile justice and treatment for juvenile offenders.

J. David Hirschel is a professor of criminal justice at the University of Massachusetts at Lowell. He has extensive experience in the juvenile justice systems of both England and the United States, and in addition to comparative criminal justice his publications include works on spouse abuse, victims and the justice system, search and seizure, and drugs and crime.

Matthew Holt is a doctoral student in criminal justice at the University of Cincinnati. He received his M.S. in criminal justice from Eastern Kentucky University in 2004.

Frank F. Y. Huang is chair of the Department of Crime Prevention and Corrections at the Central Police University in Taiwan. He has a Ph.D. (1993) from Sam Houston State University and has written in the areas of criminology and women's issues, as well as the psychological aspects of crime and justice.

Ronald G. Iacovetta is an associate professor of criminal justice at Wichita State University. His teaching areas include organized- and white-collar crime, and he has written in the areas of delinquency and juvenile corrections. He has a Ph.D. (1972) from the University of Connecticut.

Sanja Kutnjak Ivkovich is a faculty member of the School of Criminology and Criminal Justice at Florida State University. In spring of 2001 she was a Byse Fellow at the Harvard Law School and has taught at the University of Hartford and the University of Delaware.

Hannu Kiehelä is the director of the Prison Personnel Training Center in Vantaa, Finland. He has a Ph.D. in administrative sciences from the University of Tampere.

Hamid Kusha is an associate professor of criminal justice at Texas A&M International University and has held teaching positions at Minot State University, Maryville University, and Texas Christian University. He received a Ph.D. in sociology from the University of Kentucky in 1989.

Matti Laine is head lecturer at the Prison Personnel Training Center in Vantaa, Finland.

Ahti Laitinen is an associate professor of the sociology of law at the University of Turku and is docent of the sociology of law at the University of Helsinki.

Otwin Marenin is a professor of political science/criminal justice at Washington State University. He received a Ph.D. in political science at University of California, Los Angeles in 1973. Research interests include transnational policing and police reform in Central and Eastern Europe.

Monique Marks is currently a research fellow based at the Australian National University and is a faculty member at the University of Natal (South Africa) in the Department of Sociology. Her particular areas of research are police labor relations, police transformation, and public-order policing.

Zoran Milovanovich is a professor of sociology and anthropology at Lincoln University (PA). He received a LL.B. from the School of Law in Belgrade, Yugoslavia (1976), Master's degrees from George Washington University (forensic sciences–1981) and The School of Law, Belgrade (criminal law and criminal justice–1982), and a Ph.D. from the School of Law, Belgrade (1987).

Richter H. Moore, Jr. (deceased) was a professor and former chairperson in the department of political science/criminal justice at Appalachian State University. He was past president of the Academy of Criminal Justice Sciences and the Southern Criminal Justice Association, and his research focused on comparative legal systems (especially Islamic) and futurist criminal justice.

Travis Morris received his undergraduate degree in criminology from Northern Illinois University and his graduate degree in criminal justice from Eastern Kentucky University. He currently resides in the Middle East, studying languages and culture

Greg Newbold is a senior lecturer at the University of Canterbury (NZ) and a frequent advisor to the New Zealand Department of Justice on prison issues. A former prison inmate who served five and a half years for a drug offense, he has since published three books on crime and criminal justice in New Zealand.

Nonso Okereafoezeke is an associate professor in the Criminal Justice Graduate Program at Norfolk State University. He holds an LL.B. (Hons.), B.L. in law, an M.A. in criminal justice and a Ph.D. in criminology. He researches and writes on legal pluralism, particularly on the role of unofficial, nongovernmental parties, groups, organizations, institutions, and structures in social control in postcolonial societies.

Dennis W. Potts is a supervisor in the Court Services Division of the Harris County (TX) Pretrial Services Agency. He has previously worked in both municipal and state-level law enforcement, adult probation and parole and has a Ph.D. in criminal justice from Sam Houston State University.

Rudy Prine is a professor of sociology, anthropology and criminal justice at Valdosta State University. He has a Ph.D. (1994) from Florida State University, and his teaching and research interests include the courts, legal liability in criminal justice, sociology of unconventional crime, and issues in law.

Frederick P. Roth is an associate professor of sociology and anthropology at Marshall University. He has a Ph.D. in sociology from the University of Connecticut and an M.S. in criminal justice from Rutgers University, and he has worked as an educational administrator in correctional institutions for a number of years.

Sam Souryal is a professor of Criminal Justice at Sam Houston State University and has a Ph.D. (1971) in political science from the University of Utah. He has published extensively in the areas of police administration and ethics in criminal justice, among others.

R. Bankole Thompson is currently a judge with the United Nations Special Court for Sierra Leone and is on leave from his position as a professor of criminal justice/police studies at Eastern Kentucky University. His research interests include the victimization of women and children in Africa and the role of customary law in modern Africa.

Michael S. Vaughn is chairperson of the criminal justice department at Georgia State University. He received a B.S. (1984) and an M.S. (1988) in criminal justice, an Ed.S. (1990) in human services from Central Missouri State University, and has a Ph.D. (1993) in criminal justice from Sam Houston State University. He has written extensively on legal issues in criminal justice, cross-cultural crime, and social control.

Matti Vuorinen is an inspector general of the Provincial Police in Southern Finland. He has a law degree from the University of Helsinki. He began his career as a deputy police chief and has been police chief of three departments in Southern Finland.

William Wakefield is a professor of criminal justice at the University of Nebraska at Omaha. Prior to his appointment at UNO he held positions at South Dakota State University and Dana College. His primary teaching and research interests revolve around comparative criminology and criminal justice, corrections, juvenile justice, and theoretical criminology.

Kelly R. Webb is a graduate student in criminal justice at Eastern Kentucky University.